THE ULSTER ANTHOLOGY

THE
ULSTER
ANTHOLOGY

edited by

PATRICIA CRAIG

THE
BLACKSTAFF
PRESS

BELFAST

First published in 2006 by
Blackstaff Press
4c Heron Wharf, Sydenham Business Park
Belfast BT3 9LE

Supported by

 The National Lottery®
through the Arts Council of Northern Ireland arts council of Northern Ireland

The acknowledgements on pages 705–719 constitute
an extension of this copyright page

Typeset by CJWT Solutions, Newton-le-Willows, Merseyside

Printed in England by The Bath Press

A CIP catalogue record for this book is available from the British Library

ISBN 0-85640-792-5

www.blackstaffpress.com

Contents

Introduction

'Ulster always has been one of the salty, stinging, unexpected elements in the life and flavour of this planet,' Hugh Shearman wrote in 1949. He goes on: 'All down through the centuries Ulster has given sleepless nights to statesmen and generals, and kings and dictators have cursed the place and its ingenious and irrepressible inhabitants.' The north of Ireland, in other words, has always constituted a problem and a headache for those, particularly those from outside its boundaries, who try to govern it, or even to make sense of it.

But what are its boundaries? The first difficulty facing twentieth-century commentators is what to call the place, what term will cause least (or in some cases, most) annoyance to those of an opposing political persuasion. Since three counties were lopped off the province of Ulster in 1921 to create a political entity which is at the same time an incomplete geographical entity, dissenters and paradox-mongers have had a field day with what they see as the resulting anomaly. For instance, great glee surrounds the fact that Ireland's most northerly county, Donegal, is in the South – a circumstance confirming the view of the rest of the world that all parts of the country are fit to be lumped together under the epithet 'mad'.

It is, of course, perfectly simple, though it suits some people, playfully or otherwise, to emphasise the elasticity of any would-be hard-and-fast definition. (And we shouldn't forget that the problem of nomenclature merely underscores the deeper problem of intractable animosities.) Everyone knows that the part of 'Ulster' which chose to stick to the United Kingdom consists of six counties, and that 'Northern Ireland' and 'the North'* are equally valid terms for this region. If something other than the existing state of Northern Ireland is indicated, then the context should make it clear. For example, I should like to make it clear at once that this anthology will ignore political boundaries and take in material from all nine counties – and to add that I don't regard this as a political gesture, more a nod in the direction of inclusiveness.

Of course, it's been suggested from time to time that the present border

---

*Throughout this introduction, and indeed throughout the anthology, you will find these terms used interchangeably.

follows a prehistoric cut-off point for the province, 'an interesting old earthwork' known as the Black Pig's Dyke – the implication being that Ulster was always a place apart. But is the Black Pig's Dyke merely a resort of the pig-headed? The idea of separateness has a certain validity, if you take the bywords at face value: most Gaelic of all the provinces, most adulterated, most cultivated, go-ahead, remote, recalcitrant, uncouth or whatever. Today, indeed, for people living in the Republic of Ireland, Ulster is neither here nor there, neither properly attached to the rest of the country nor decisively detached from it. It's a non-entity, in other words. The people of the North know differently, however; for all of them, whatever their ancestry or affiliation, a strong sense of identity and local attachment prevails – and this remains true, by and large, even of those for whom the narrowness of their birthplace represents a nightmare. The pungency of Brian Moore's, or Derek Mahon's, or Louis MacNeice's case against the North (to take those examples) testifies to the impact, for good or ill, of a singular region.

Northern Ireland provides much to lament but also much to cherish, as the following pages will show. A place of battles and bigotry on the one hand, it offers a rich history and an inspiriting diversity on the other. Clashing allegiances, 'domestic hate' in William Drennan's phrase, which have kept it volatile throughout the centuries, divert attention from an essential civility coexisting with all the bad blood and squalid sectarianism. The last, indubitably, have earned the North an evil reputation and led to its constant depiction as a place of ill-judged policies and fixed mind-sets. But all the negative aspects of Ulster – its incorrigibility, deadliness, provincialism, its matching cults of violence and so forth – are somehow themselves negated by an unbiased contemplation of its scenic glories, for example, its special brands of humour, its vigorous approach to living, its literary heritage (confounding those for whom the province is inescapably tied up with philistinism) and other things provoking a sense of delight. It would, of course, be wrong to minimise the horrors or the savagery which overtake the North from time to time, erupting in episodes of slaughter and mayhem stretching all the way back to 1641 and beyond. And we still have a noisy minority bent on asserting what it sees as ancestral imperatives – underscoring, for the rest of us, the point that what's bred in the bone quite often needs to be overhauled in the head. Fortunately, the North has never been lacking in thoughtful commentators whose purpose is to interpose an egalitarian ethic between competing bigotries.

In the course of the twentieth century, Northern Ireland went from obscurity to notoriety in the eyes of the world, reducing itself to an archetypal embodiment of devastation and disaffection. Belfast in particular 'tore itself apart and patched things up again', in the words of Ciaran Carson; now, post-Troubles, a brave new city, complete with all kinds of gimcrack and standardised accoutrements, has largely replaced the ramshackle structures of the past. Belfast, along with the rest of the province, has never embraced the principle of conservation (or, at best, has embraced it only half-heartedly). What it doesn't seem to grasp, or care about, is the loss of character occasioned by each elimination of an historical landmark, whether explosives, blight, indifference or bureaucracy is at the root of it. (It's cheering to find something like the typical Ulster farmhouse, Sentry Hill in Newtownabbey, preserved in its original setting.) One thing the North now has in common with the rest of the United Kingdom, and the rest of Ireland, is the need to make a stand against the depredations of developers, and those government departments which encourage developers. There's hardly a town in Ulster in which the sight of some elegant eighteenth-century building left to rot doesn't cause consternation in the responsive beholder. Like Richard Hayward coming face to face with an instance of architectural decay in 1950s, Newry, we're provoked, again and again, to a heartfelt exclamation, 'sad beyond words'.

On the other hand — the outlook is not irreversibly bleak. Enough remains to distil that sense of order and continuity which is vital to the acquisition of stability in the present. In the course of the last thirty-odd years, many visitors arriving with a mental image of ravaged streetscapes, burning buses and riot shields, have had to adjust their attitudes in accordance with the province's unexpected saving graces — whether it's a breathtaking vista opening before them, strong sunlight on the Cave Hill, hospitality and apparent normality, or the ambience of some decorous suburb that scuppers their preconceptions. 'I expected bleachworks and burnt-out cars, not fuchsias', wrote the poet Carol Rumens, 'Not cedar and sky-tickling larch ...'. It's a part of the regenerative process to record such surprise, to slant the emphasis away from bloody disruption to indigenous attractiveness — for indeed, by the 1970s, the north of Ireland had taken on an existence in people's minds as a place that few, especially those of a nervous disposition, would choose to travel to.*

People watched in amazement, and then with exasperation and a measure of boredom, as things fell apart, as the bombs went off, endless lives were lost, whole areas were destroyed, and one 'initiative' after another came to nothing. Aware of all this, writing in 1999, the essayist Chris Arthur (a native of County Antrim) concluded: 'The astonishing beauty of the Province is one of the many victims of its long terrorist war, now hopefully abated.'

Of course, you could always find pockets of calm and brightness even in the midst of all the upheaval, if you knew where to look for them —

---

*Even before the Troubles, the province had not gone out of its way to present an enticing image to potential visitors. Barbara Pym's dry comment about Northern Ireland, in a letter to Philip Larkin, that it seemed 'a very original place for a holiday', is typical of an attitude of faint disparagement.

'unhaunted places, full of blessing', like John Hewitt's booleys. Gracehill, near Ballymena, for example, with its Moravian perfection of architecture and atmosphere; the modest Plantation house, Springhill, between the western shore of Lough Neagh and the Sperrin Mountains; the wonderful Temple of the Winds at Mount Stewart; Wellington Park Terrace in Belfast, hidden away, where the social commentator Denis Ireland had his home; Killard Point in County Down with its abundance of wild orchids. And more. 'Portrush, Portstewart, Portballintrae', Derek Mahon wrote, before going on to complete the couplet in a mood of despair: 'Un beau pays mal occupé'.

If the things that have happened in the North, its whole sorry range of enormities and uphill negotiations in the present, are enough to drive anyone to despair, it nevertheless remains a region which familiarity renders more and more beguiling. Its alluring out-of-the-way localities, its contributions to culture and progress in the world, all the contradictions and complexities in the Ulster psyche ... these are features that add to its mystique. To arrive at an appreciation of the latter, though, you need to be in possession of as much information as possible concerning the nature and traditions of the place, all the ways in which a specific identity and mode of existence evolved. One of the functions of an anthology such as this is to make such information available in condensed form, to assemble an abundance of comment, description, argument, appraisal or what-have-you, which taken together tends towards an ultimately illuminating effect.

Not that it needs to be, or should be, taken all at once. An anthology is made up of bits and pieces, voices of individual authors which sometimes endorse one another's perceptions, and sometimes strike sparks from, or tell against, one another. The arrangement of the material is important. Mostly, with the current undertaking, I've tried to avoid a too-abrupt change of mood or metre; but sometimes a change along these lines has seemed salutary rather than jarring. To obtain stimulation, and cut out blandness, is one of my aims.

Perhaps I should say a word about my own perception of this particular 'Ulster anthology'. In the first place, it's not a collection of writings by Northern Irish authors, but rather a gathering of extracts which, in my view, exemplify or clarify some facet of life in the North, at any moment from the seventeenth century on. Why draw the line there? Well, all anthologies reflect their editors' interests, and I'm not particularly interested in the distant past, whether pre-Christian, monastic or medieval. Ulster as we know it has its origins in the seventeenth-century Plantation and that, give or take an extract or two relating to an earlier time, is my starting-point. I've opted for quite a large amount of material from the nineteenth century and more from the twentieth; these eras (well, the first, and half of the second) are at a sufficient remove from the present to be intriguing but not impenetrable. Most readers, I imagine, will have lived through the second half of the twentieth century, or some of it, and will therefore have their own experience to act as a touchstone in terms of the anthology's relevant inclusions.

Like my earlier *Belfast Anthology*, this one is arranged by theme, not chronology, and for the same reason: to avoid ending up with something along the lines of a composite academic or social history. The thematic approach, I believe, allows more scope for obliquity, idiosyncrasy and humour. What I want to do, above all, is to present to the people of Northern Ireland a cumulative, and enlarging, picture of themselves and their surroundings; and to alert other readers to rarities of spirit or milieu, beyond the confusions and commotions, that might otherwise get overlooked. I also want to restore, for the length of time it takes to read about them, the ethos of vanished communities and ravaged landscapes (landscapes at present slashed by motorways, or recreated pell-mell as nondescript suburbs).

There is, of course, a personal element to all this. Growing up in Belfast in the 1950s and 60s, I relished the city's old 'Burke and Hare' atmosphere (noted by Sean O'Faolain if no one else), 'the damp Lagan fogs', cobbled alleyways, coalmen's carts, sedate department stores, raucous workingmen's pubs, late-Victorian terraces, the dripping shrubberies of Malone Road or Antrim Road villas, with mahogany seats on the lavatory and maids in the kitchen – all endangered at the time and now largely disappeared, or at least vitiated. I was also enchanted by the country towns of the north, both seaside and inland, each with its fine main street and distinctive background quality, and by the grandeur of the landscapes from Carlingford Lough to the Bloody Foreland in north Donegal. The strand at Helen's Bay or Ballycastle I knew as well as the pavements of streets off St James's Road. And Portrush – 'How charming, then, was the descent to the sands', to repeat the words of Robert Lynd, with bucket and spade to make enjoyment complete.

Buckets and spades, or equivalent bygone artefacts (sooty old kettles, Ulster gateposts, St Brigid's crosses) get a section to themselves, entitled 'Bright With Ancestral Delph'. These are things 'unshiftably planked / In the long ago, yet willable forward /Again and again and again', like Seamus Heaney's inherited settle bed. This section accommodates a spirit of nostalgia (sometimes tinged with irony) but more besides, including old-fashioned customs and spooky fireside entertainments, and not excluding 'the lore of the lone thorn bush', as Estyn Evans has it. Folk beliefs are a powerful ingredient of the rural past, along with the cultivation of flax and 'the Auld Meetin-Hoose Green' as a centre of social activity, and very decorative and fascinating they all are too. The backward look, indeed, can favour quaintness over historical accuracy – the word 'olden', for example, which has crept into the anthology in one or two places, causes one's bullshit-detecting hackles to rise – but a scholarly, documentary, ambivalent or matter-of-fact approach (which

I've sought out) can generally be relied on to keep the tone untainted in this respect. Not that quaintness is altogether absent – but neither, I hope, is it obtrusive. It merely resides in the odd burst of rapture over a soda farl, or over-the-top enthusiasm such as you find in Cathal O'Byrne's enumeration of the Nine Glens: all very fine and buoyant in its place.

An upbeat note, a celebratory approach to everything peculiar to the North, from the spirit of 'No Surrender' to the whitethorn hedges of Kells, from an eighteenth-century egalitarian consciousness to Victorian skaters on ice-bound Lough Neagh, or Aunt Laetitia's bluebell picnic at Ballyvoy: this is a dominant aspect of *The Ulster Anthology*. But some sections are grimmer than such a slant suggests. 'Darkest Ulster', for example, which posits a distorted moral universe; 'Poverty Mountain'; or the one towards the end reserved for comment (necessarily curtailed) on the just-past Troubles of an always troubled and generally troublesome province. The liberal impulse in the North has its emphatic opposite in the kind of zealotry that causes someone in the nineteenth century to inveigh against 'the rotten, sickening policy of conciliation', a policy which (in the eyes of the speaker) began with the decision to relax the Penal Laws. You could say that every attempt at conciliation, ever since, has met with some atavistic reaction such as this, to the extent that 'not-an-inch' obduracy has become an accepted part of the Northern character. Protestant or Catholic, it sometimes seems impossible to eradicate bigotry, or to temper an instinctive leaning towards one side or the other. Terence O'Neill, one-time prime minister of Northern Ireland and famous for encouraging a bit of conciliation himself in the 1960s, was nevertheless able to write approvingly in his autobiography of a typical Belfast Protestant working man, describing this character as 'strongly anti-Catholic, but decent'.

Of course, it's one thing, and a wrong thing, to be strongly anti-Catholic in the sense of finding something obnoxious about the whole breed, and another to take rational exception to the damage inflicted by the Catholic Church in the political, social or psychological sphere, damage attested to more than once in the following pages. It's generally those with first-hand experience of church manipulation who make the most cogent critics of that particular system, even if elements of the consequent recoil aren't wholly to be trusted. Ex-Catholics like William Carleton and M.J. McCarthy, for instance, are apt to bend over backwards in the effort to cry up Protestant industry, progressiveness and so forth, as though these attributes, and others, didn't occur throughout the North irrespective of sect.

And that brings me to another – crucial – purpose of this anthology, which is to note the stereotypes (nationalist integrity/unionist iniquity, Protestant diligence/Catholic fecklessness, and so on) and then to undermine them by showing another side to the argument – so that layers of complexity are constructed bit by bit. For example – a lot of interesting work has been done recently on the contribution of Presbyterians (and other non-Catholics) to the Irish language revival, with enthusiasts like Robert MacAdam and the essayist Robert Lynd being prominent among them; and although I haven't made this into a central feature of the anthology, I find it a heartening circumstance, and one rife with subversive potential; and it's touched on here and there. And through the entire text, you will pick up the lucid tones of an authentic Northernness, whether it comes via John O'Connor capturing the genuine voice of an Armagh mill town in the 1920s, Art McCooey's formal (Gaelic) lament for young Art O'Neill, or the exuberant Christina Reid's encapsulations of a mid-twentieth-century urban Protestant street-smartness.

The Ulster Anthology is a large book, heavy enough to knock some sense into the heads of bigots or belligerents, but you'd have to be a mad anthologist – given a subject this wide – to aim at anything approaching comprehensiveness. An anthology is by its nature selective. The most I can say is that I've tried to cover a good range of topics, and to seek out some unpredictable extracts. I want the book to be enjoyable, and so I haven't included too much in the way of statistical accounts or economic surveys; and I've had to exercise a stringent right of choice when faced with vast amounts of topographical, historical and political literature. Then, when it comes to the incomparable store of Ulster songs, songs collected and recorded by scholars and singers such as Len Graham and David Hammond – the words of these tend to fall outside my brief (with one or two exceptions): for, as the late Frank Harte, singer, from Dublin put it, 'a song is nothing unless it's sung'. I should just like to put it on record that I've kept the song tradition in mind, while amassing other kinds of indigenous riches. And while I'm on the subject of omissions, I should add that sports in Ulster are largely absent, for two reasons. The first is that sports coverage is already pretty well ubiquitous; and the second is a blind spot on my part. It's as well to have editors' quirks identified. (As far as quirks are concerned, among my own *bêtes noire* is the fearfully anti-feminist writer Anthony C. West; but I have tried to overcome this prejudice – if it is a prejudice – and be fair to this odd author by finding space for a passage from *The Ferret Fancier*.) You will find, of course, as well as quite a bit of overlap between sections, a few identifiable threads running through the whole anthology – and these, no doubt, are attributable to my own enthusiasms and obsessions.

Some things are left out deliberately, then, and others, I am sure, have been omitted by accident. You can trawl as much as you like, but you can never guarantee that some luminous passage hasn't slipped through the net (every anthologist's dread). But enough remains, I would claim, to add up to a kind of collective self-knowledge and provide much food for thought – as well as acting as a stimulus to the imagination.

The titles of most sections speak for themselves – 'Backroads', 'The Rebel Tradition', and so on – but one or two, perhaps, require a word of explanation. Childhood experiences and recollections of childhood, with a view of the world evolving in an Ulster setting, are mostly gathered together under the heading, 'Nuair a Bhí Mé Óg' ('When I Was Young'), after the title of Seamus Ó Grianna's charming account of a Gaedhaltacht boyhood. 'It Goes as Follies' is borrowed from Ciaran Carson's masterly book about Irish traditional music, *Last Night's Fun*, where it forms a chapter heading which is itself called after a fiddle tune. For my purposes, it seemed a suitable heading under which to group some anecdotes and incidents: set-pieces, in other words. And my final section, 'An Ulster Imagined' (Patrick Kavanagh's phrase), contains what seem to me to be among the most vivid, resonant, highly charged, densely freighted segments of poetry and prose I can lay my hand on, to make a fit summing up of the spirit of the whole undertaking. Some of these pieces are, like Stevie Smith's novels, foot-off-the-ground meditations that came by the left hand. But even where this is true, the other foot – whichever they dig with – is firmly planted on good Ulster ground, as solid and singular as a fat white gatepost, and as faithful as horses and ponies in the stable yard, uncomplainingly tethered 'till the second sermon was done'.

I should like to thank the Authors' Foundation, via the Society of Authors, for much appreciated financial assistance. I am also greatly indebted to the Arts Council of Northern Ireland, whose award of a Major Bursary in 2004 not only made the project possible in a practical sense, but provided a tremendous incentive to tackle it wholeheartedly. Particular thanks are due to Ciaran Carson, whose translation of the poem on p. 24 was written specially for *The Ulster Anthology*; and to John Gamble, Owen Dudley Edwards and Norman Vance. Others who have helped in various ways are Anne Tannahill, Polly Devlin, Michael Longley, Patricia Mallon, Brice Dickson, Naomi and Nigel May, Gerry Keenan, the late Archie Reid, Margaret Gatt, Sheila Stinson, Margaret Smyth, Margaret Campbell and Brian Walker. I am grateful, as well, to Patricia Horton, Janice Smith, Wendy Dunbar and everyone at Blackstaff; to John Killen and Gerry Healey of the Linen Hall Library; to Patricia Walker of Belfast Central Library for access to the Special Irish Collections including the Francis Joseph Bigger Archive; and to Alan McMillan of the Presbyterian Historical Society of Ireland. Jeffrey Morgan, as ever, supplied endless encouragement, practical advice and critical vigilance throughout the course of this project.

PATRICIA CRAIG
ANTRIM
AUGUST 2006

The Nature of
the Place

... by Ulster I mean not the mutilated area which Belfast
now calls by that name, but the old nine–county Ulster,
that politicians cannot expunge from the map. Being myself
a native of Down, I sympathise with the desire for a crisper
designation for the 'Six Counties' than 'Northern Ireland'.
That is an awkward term, and incorrect geographically; but
to use 'Ulster' for the area is even more misleading.

ROBERT LLOYD PRAEGER, *The Way That I Went*

No book that treats of Ulster would be complete without
... the three counties of Monaghan, Cavan, and Donegal.
While they are not included in the present Northern
Ireland, they are part of the province historically and
culturally, and by virtue of the fact that all come under the
influence of the Ulster Plantation; in fact, Monaghan was
the earliest of the counties to be planted.

DENIS O'D. HANNA, *The Face of Ulster*

WHAT A LOVELY NAME THAT COULD BE – The Six Counties. Like
Housman's 'the coloured counties'; or The Home Counties;
or The Shires. It isn't a lovely name. It falls numerically on the
ear, much as if one said, the six-cylinder. Why? Because there is no such
place. If I were an Ulsterman I should retort to the southern demand for
the return of the Six Counties to Eire by demanding the return to Ulster
of Donegal, Cavan, and Monaghan, the three counties formerly part of

Ulster. Ulster has a magnificent history, as old as Mayo, as colourful as Kerry, as Irish as Connemara. How can she pride in it with a digital name and a partitioned land. Sometimes she bears that worse name – Northern Ireland, which recalls (Was it?) Disraeli's taunt that *Ireland* is merely 'a geographical term'. The solution I foresee to the partition of Ireland is that Ulster will awaken to the cruelty of the partition of the north. The end to this minorities problem, so badly handled in this division of Ireland into Northern Ireland and Southern Ireland (as if Donegal by any manner of means could be called a part of Southern Ireland, or Monaghan or even Cavan!) should be that the men of the north will develop a raging sense of national pride; take over the whole of Ulster; call the rest of us *shoneens*, West British, and secret imperialists; and demand that we return to the true faith first declared in Belfast by the Republican Presbyterians and Protestants of the eighteenth century.

SEAN O'FAOLAIN, *An Irish Journey*, 1940

THE CHOICE OF NAMES FOR NORTHERN IRELAND is ... wide: British-occupied Ireland, the Six Counties, Ulster, the North and Northern Ireland. The first is used only by maniacs, the second by moderate anti-partitionists. 'Ulster' is the favourite term of most of the region's residents but is grossly misleading since three of Ulster's nine counties are within the Republic, and Northern Ireland is equally misleading since Donegal is further north than most of Northern Ireland. But at least 'Northern Ireland' has the merit of being the region's legal name, according to the Government of Ireland Act (1920), and throughout Ireland an acceptable abbreviation is 'the North'. (No wonder the English have given up trying to fathom either end of a country that keeps its most northerly county in the south ...).

DERVLA MURPHY, *A Place Apart*, 1978

WE WILL NEVER MAKE ANY SENSE of the whole business unless we place ourselves in the opening years of [the twentieth] century, realising clearly that Ulster then meant, and had for many years meant, an area divided into nine counties, covering the complete northern portion of Ireland. A large Protestant and Presbyterian element in those nine counties centred mostly in the north-eastern corner of the country around the city of Belfast. That element originated in the early seventeenth century under King James the First of England. Hugh O'Neill's great battle against the new state had ended in defeat for O'Neill. To displace O'Neill's broken and disordered followers the divine right of King James introduced a number of immigrants or 'planters', mostly men from

Scotland who followed the new faith of Knox and Calvin. They were a colony and they preserved the colonial outlook.

BENEDICT KIELY, *Counties of Contention*, 1945

IN 1607 TYRONE, WITH RORY O'DONNELL, Earl of Tyrconnel, fled in somewhat mysterious circumstances to the Continent. This 'flight of the earls', as it is called, made possible the Plantation of Ulster, for it left their large territories extending into four counties – Donegal, Londonderry, Tyrone, and Armagh – at the disposal of the Government. It was a time of discovery and settlement of new lands, and King James was easily persuaded to embark on a scheme of colonising Ulster, or rather six counties of it, namely, Fermanagh and Cavan in addition to the four already mentioned, with English and Scots. This course, it was thought, would so alter the national characteristics of the country that the spirit of independence would die out and no further rebellion need be feared. Possibly if, in the execution of the scheme, more attention had been paid to the rights of the native occupier of the soil, the project would have been successful. Ulster was then thinly inhabited and provided ample room for colonisation ...

The Plantation, however, was effective in its main object, for it introduced sufficient outside blood to affect the political feeling of the province. Ulster, which had once been more Irish than Leinster, became a mixed country, in which the strains recently introduced eventually became dominant...

D.A. CHART, *A History of Northern Ireland*, 1927

HISTORICAL INFLUENCES ARE VERY IMPORTANT. Foremost amongst these are the long term effects of the settlement of English and Scottish families of Protestant faith during the seventeenth century. These newcomers took over land from the native Irish, here the Maguires and their sub-septs. While a great part of this land in Fermanagh was probably not in effective use nevertheless in some cases this plantation resulted in the displacement of the native Irish. The effects of the plantation were twofold. First was the change from the Irish system of land ownership and chieftainship to a new class of absolute landlords on the English model. In so far as the same family retained possession of their farm the change was only from one landlord to another. Secondly, the new planter families came to the better lands and set up a community with a different outlook and inheritance, looking on the original inhabitants as English colonists in Kenya view the inhabitants there. This wide gulf in cultural values has never been bridged and the two communities, native and planter, exist side by side to this day with little intermixture. The distinctions between them are religious, cultural and economic. It is usual to assume that the various religious groups represent the different historical elements in the population: Roman Catholic for the Irish; Church of Ireland and possibly Methodists for the English and Presbyterian for the Scottish. This can be very misleading in individual cases but forms a rough guide for groups of people as a whole.

JOHN M. MOGEY, *Rural Life in Northern Ireland*, 1947

WHATEVER GOD OR DEMON may have led the first of them to these shores, the Anglo-Irish and Scottish Ulstermen have now far too old a title to be questioned: they were a hardy race and fought stoutly for the pleasant valleys they dwell in. And are not Derry and Enniskillen *Ireland's*, as well as Benburb and the Yellow Ford? – and have not those men and their fathers lived, and loved, and worshipped God, and died there? – are not their green graves heaped up there – more generations of them than they have genealogical skill to count? – a deep enough root those planters have struck into the soil of Ulster and it would now be ill striving to unplant them ...

JOHN MITCHEL, *The Life and Times of Aodh O'Neill*, 1845

AN ULSTERMAN

This is my country. If my people came
from England here four centuries ago,
the only trace that's left is in my name.
Kilmore, Armagh, no other sod can show
the weathered stone of our first burying.
Born in Belfast, which drew the landless in,
that river-straddling, hill-rimmed town, I cling
to the inflexions of my origin.

Though creed-crazed zealots and the ignorant crowd,
long-nurtured, never checked, in ways of hate,
have made our streets a byword of offence,
this is my country, never disavowed.
When it is fouled, shall I not remonstrate?
My heritage is not their violence.

JOHN HEWITT, *An Ulster Reckoning*, 1971

I N SEEKING THE REAL ULSTER, we shall find little of it merely through
the study of successive political frontiers, though all those frontiers have
had their meaning and their reality, particularly in their contemporary
form as the frontiers of Northern Ireland. The real Ulster is the land and
the people, a community living in certain surroundings and having a
continuous history and tradition and a developing and distinctive culture.
The real Ulster, in fact, is a natural, organic development. From time to
time, administrative and constitutional mechanisms have been made for it
which have had a very powerful influence upon it. But the real Ulster is
the organism rather than the mechanism, however much the latter may
affect the former.

HUGH SHEARMAN, *Ulster*, 1949

L OOK AT A MAP OF IRELAND and see how this Border weaves its crazy
way across our countryside. Through farmsteads and villages and lakes
it takes an erratic path, over hilltops and even through individual houses,
so that one family may actually sleep in Northern Ireland but sit around
its own fireside under the selfsame roof in the Republic. It does indeed
look as though the lurching Irish drunkard made the lurching Irish
Border. But sober history tells a different tale and it is astonishing to see
how closely that snakelike, apparently haphazard, line hugs territorial
limits, and townland and barony demarcations and mearings, of ancient
standing, many of which indeed go back far beyond the times of recorded
history. Through the ages men have not hesitated to lay down their lives
for the maintenance or destruction, according to their lights, of this
enduring line, nor, thank God, have other men failed to find some
humour in its grim reality. I shall never forget the occasion when I
approached a quiet part of the Border in my car and knocked at the door
of the Customs Hut to have my triptyque scrutinised and stamped. It was
nearly six o'clock of a fine summer's evening and there was no response.
But a farmer near the end of his labour in an adjoining field saw what I
was at and called out to me: 'You needn't knock there, mister. Sure
there's no Border at this time of the day: the man's away for his tay.'
Which to me was but another proof of the fact that Ireland is a highly
civilized country. There may be laws here, and plenty of them, but
humanity is always breaking through.

RICHARD HAYWARD, *Border Foray*, 1957

from EPILOGUE

I am Ulster, my people an abrupt people
Who like the spiky consonants in speech
And think the soft ones cissy; who dig
The *k* and *t* in orchestra, detect sin
In sinfonia, get a kick out of
Tin cans, fricatives, fornication, staccato talk,
Anything that gives or takes attack,
Like Micks, Tagues, tinkers' gets, Vatican.
An angular people, brusque and Protestant,
For whom the word is still a fighting word,
Who bristle into reticence at the sound
Of the round gift of the gab in Southern mouths.
Mine were not born with silver spoons in gob,
Nor would they thank you for the gift of tongues;
The dry riposte, the bitter repartee's
The Northman's bite and portion, his deep sup
Is silence; though, still within his shell,
He holds the old sea-roar and surge
Of rhetoric and Holy Writ.
Three hundred years ago our foundling fathers
With farthing fists and thistles in their eyes
Were planted on this foreshore,
Bibles for bibs and bloody pikes for rattles
And tombs for keeps. There was not time
To wade through wedding to a birth.
Calvin and culverin sang the cradle-song
And Cromwell made the bed.
Put to a frugal breast of swollen hopes
They did their levelling best and left it flat
As water. Winding-sheet and swaddling-band
Were one. Needle-flute and thimble-drum
Stitched the way to kingdom-come, to Derry,
Aughrim, Enniskillen, and the Boyne:
Rat-a-ta-ta, rat-a-ta-ta, rat-a-ta-ta,
Humdrummery of history.
And I, born to the purple passage,
Was heir to all that Adamnation
And hand-me-down of doom, the late comer
To the worn-out womb.

The apple blushed for me below Bellevue,
Lagan was my Jordan, Connswater
My washpot, and over Belfast
I cast out my shoe.

W.R. RODGERS, *The Character of Ireland*, 1963

THE SIX-COUNTY AREA WAS DEVISED, and its separate legislature erected, solely by outsiders. The design and the guilt of Partition are England's. No honourable excuse can be made for it. It is not historic Ulster that was given autonomy; for that would have included Donegal, Monaghan and Cavan, and would have been rational at least. It is not the *bloc* of Protestant territory; for that is restricted to an area less than half the size of the Six Counties. Of the autonomous area, all Tyrone and Fermanagh, the city of Derry, half of County Down, half of County Armagh, and a considerable part of County Antrim, to say nothing of a quarter of Belfast, are patriotic territory, passionately longing for their due place in national Ireland.

The Six-County Government was erected in June, 1921, and the truce in the Anglo-Irish war came in July.

AODH DE BLÁCAM, *The Black North*, 1938

ORIEL IS NOW AN UNDEFINED TERRITORY roughly stretching from north Meath to north Louth and south Down, west to Cavan, Monaghan and south Armagh. In relation to the song and literary tradition it is mainly concentrated on south Armagh, north County Monaghan and the coastal Omeath area of the Cooley peninsula in County Louth. Though parts of it belong physically to Leinster, the poets and scribes of the area, from the middle of the seventeenth century to the middle of the nineteenth century, regarded themselves as being from Ulster; they spoke the dialect of Ulster and cultivated Ulster literature. The collecting of folklore material in this region during the early twentieth century was not a unique or an isolated occurrence in the area but a continuation of a long manuscript and literary tradition in south-east Ulster which had existed for centuries. It is the region where much of the large corpus of heroic tales in Irish literature originates – the Ulster Cycle – which was the literature of greatest prestige in the early period. The central and basic story in the cycle is *Táin Bó Cuailgne* (The Cattle Raid of Cooley). Dating from the first millennia, this most famous of the early sagas, and other stories, were handed down orally and in manuscript in parts of Ulster to recent times. Since the beginning of the seventeenth century this region was the main centre of the cultivation of literature in *Leath Chuinn* – the northern half of Ireland.

PÁDRAIGÍN NÍ UALLACHÁIN, *A Hidden Ulster:*
People, Songs and Traditions of Oriel, 2003

ULSTER, CONSIDERED AS A REGION and not as the symbol of any particular creed, can, I believe, command the loyalty of every one of its inhabitants. For regional identity does not preclude, rather it requires, membership of a larger association. And, whether that association be, as I hope, of a federated British Isles, or a federal Ireland, out of that loyalty to our own place, rooted in honest history, in familiar folkways and knowledge, phrased in our own dialect, there should emerge a culture and an attitude individual and distinctive, a fine contribution to the European inheritance and no mere echo of the thought and imagination of another people or another land.

JOHN HEWITT, 'Regionalism: The Last Chance', *The Northman*, 1947

A STUDY OF THE MAP OF NORTHERN IRELAND, and a survey of the geographical features of this tough, rugged but most attractive province, bring to light two salient facts. First, the province forms, by its internal physical structure, a distinct unit and a natural home for a distinctive local economy and culture. Secondly, the area has strong external frontiers of rocky sea–coast, lakes, hills and rivers; and, in earlier historical times, these were made much more formidable on the land side by the forests and bogs of south Ulster, now long vanished. This external frontier has further tended to make Ulster a separate unit and to favour the development of its historical and political individuality.

HUGH SHEARMAN, *Northern Ireland*, 1948

I STEPT INTO THE DERRY MAIL, a place of purgatorial suffering: – a public coach, travelling by night and full withal, is my antipathy; – with bent body and contracted limbs, and every sense in a state of suffering, hearing, smelling, feeling, seeing; – at all times the undertaking is hateful, but with a nurse and young child beside you – Oh, it is horrible!

By morning's dawn we had got into the province of Ulster. The moment you enter it, you perceive its peculiar features, its formation quite distinct from every other portion of Ireland. There are hills, swells, plains and flat table lands in the other portions of the kingdom; but here it is all hill and valley, all acclivity and declivity. Driving along the new line of road that winds around these never-ending hills, you seldom see for a quarter of a mile before you. At first you are struck with the beauty of these eminences, so minutely subdivided, so diversified with patches of grass, oats, flax, and potatoes; the intervening valley, either a lake, bog, or meadow; – but soon you get tired; your eye becomes tantalized with having a constant barrier presented to its forward prospect; you are displeased that you cannot obtain any extended view of the country you are going through; you are in an eternal defile. As I am no courier bearing despatches; as I leave home to exercise my eye and my mind, I like the old straight forward road over the hills; I can then see and breathe more freely. But I am not intending to describe the province of Ulster; and shall only say that its natural features explain why the English found this portion of the island so difficult to conquer. It was easy for O'Neill, amidst the interminable fortresses of his hills, woods, bogs, and defiles, often to defy, and always to elude his invaders.

CAESAR OTWAY, *Sketches in Ireland*, 1827

THE BLACK PIG

Ballinagh, its flat, main street;
that sudden, sharp turn North.
Nearby, a ridge of the Dunchaladh,
the Black Pig's Dyke, or Race, –
the ancient frontier of Uladh.

Straying through a Breton forest
once, I heard a fierce scrabbling,
saw his blunt snout when,
with lowered tusks, a wild boar
ignored me, bustling past.

And can still believe in
some mythic bristled beast
flared nostrils, red in anger,
who first threw up, where North
crosses South, our bloody border.

(Or some burrowing Worm
slithering through the earth
from Ballinagh to Garrison,
a serpent's hiss between
old Uladh and Ireland.)

And now he races forever,
a lonely fearsome creature,
furrowing a trough we may
never fill, the ancient guardian
of these earthworks of anger.

JOHN MONTAGUE, *The Dead Kingdom*, 1984

THE TUDOR MAP OF THE COUNTY looks a bit like Australia kicked sideways. It was drawn up by Henry VIII's natural son, Sir John Perrot, in 1585. Tudor language is still common, with quirks of speech and pronunciation rarely heard elsewhere. 'I'll tell you the kind of fellow he is, you wouldn't know what kind he was!' The border mind, thinking two ways, looking ten ways, conspiratorial, contradictory and cautious. Sir John's map subdivided the county into five baronies: three hundred years later the Great Northern Railway bisected it from Clones to Inniskeen, Kavanagh's country. Some maintain there is a marked difference between people north and south of this line, and cite as example the difference between Clones and Carrickmacross lace. Clones lace is sturdy and chunky – you can wear it, wash it, boil it and it remains beautiful. Carrickmacross lace delights in fine detail – organdy appliquéd on tulle, purpose-made for billowing in summer windows ... northern practicality as against southern lyricism (a strained comparison maybe in a county some twenty miles by forty).

Certainly there was no north/south county thing when the baronies were mapped and named and no change since: Truagh, Dartry, Cremorne, Monaghan and Farney in the south, confiscated and granted by the first Elizabeth – all sixty-seven thousand acres of it! – to her dubious boyfriend the Earl of Essex.

EUGENE McCABE, *from* 'Co. Monaghan', *32 Counties*, 1989

ULSTER, THE MOST NORTHERN and third in size of the four provinces of Ireland, includes the counties of Antrim, Down, Londonderry, Tyrone, Armagh, Monaghan, Donegal, Fermanagh, and Cavan.

Its greatest width from Malinmore, County Donegal, to the Ards peninsula, County Down, is 140 miles, and from Lough Sheelin, County Cavan, to Malin Head, County Donegal, is 115 miles. Lough Neagh forms the most prominent natural feature both from its unusual extent and the fact of it forming the mutual boundary of the five counties of Londonderry, Antrim, Down, Armagh, and Tyrone.

Although the northern mountains are generally in groups and extend along the coast, yet the leading chains cross Ulster almost parallel to each other from east to west.

Towards the north the range penetrating the counties of Antrim, Londonderry, and Donegal is divided by two great valleys down which the Foyle and Bann flow into the Atlantic, whilst the southern heights continue through the counties of Down, Monaghan, Cavan, and Fermanagh.

The extensive central plateau comprises, with slight exceptions, the fertile lands of the Ulster Plantation, well watered by many pleasant streams and lakes, of which the beautiful Lough Erne is the best known. Other romantic lakes that attract both the angler and the lover of natural scenery are loughs Melvin and MacNean on the boundary of Connaught, the chain of lakes adjoining Leinster and the wilder lakes of Donegal.

As the great inland sea of Lough Neagh lies at the upper end of the limestone plain forming central Ireland, and its level is barely fifty feet above Belfast Lough, the scenery around its margin would be flat and monotonous were it not for the historic woods of the O'Neills at Shane's Castle and other demesnes extending along its pebbly shore ...

Perhaps the finest sea cliffs in Europe for majestic beauty of form occur on the long sea-board of Ulster. Nothing can surpass the savage jagged wall of Slieve League rising in its manifold colours to a height of almost two thousand feet, on the northern side of Donegal Bay. With it may well be contrasted the fantastic colonnaded walls of the Giant's Causeway and Fairhead, the latter cliff towering six hundred feet above the stormy Moyle.

In Down and Donegal the most picturesque mountain scenery is found. In the former, confined to the ancient kingdom of Mourne, where the huge granite bastion of Slieve Donard rises nearly three thousand feet, and from its summit a glorious panorama is disclosed, embracing the mountains of Wicklow, Armagh, Derry, and Antrim, with the Isle of Man and Scotland. Errigal's sunny summit of glittering quartz forms a landmark visible over most of Tir Connell.

Owing to the remarkable difference between the rocks, much delightful variety of scenery results.

ROBERT M. YOUNG, *Belfast and the Province of Ulster in the Twentieth Century*, 1909

ULSTER IS A TINY COUNTRY of 4,000 square miles. An afternoon's journey will take you to the farthest part of it. Yet within the small scope of its six counties there is a wide play of landscape; of wood and glen, lake, bog, cliff, and coast. Here are slow, fat lowlands with apple orchards: and there is bare mountainy country with stone walls and dripping fuchsia hedges. Geologically, Ulster is the most varied part of the British Isles. And always there is the soft wet air and the drifting curtains of Atlantic sea cloud that open and close endlessly over the land, making it evergreen, and giving a delicate range of colouring to the light that is unsurpassed anywhere. A Viennese friend once pointed out to me a certain subtle blueness in the Ulster sky which he called 'Irish blue' since he had seen it nowhere else.

W.R. RODGERS, The Ulstermen and Their Country, 1952

from VALEDICTION

Country of callous lava cooled to stone,
Of minute sodden haycocks, of ship-sirens' moan,
Of falling intonations – I would call you to book
I would say to you, Look;
I would say, This is what you have given me
Indifference and sentimentality
A metallic giggle, a fumbling hand,
A heart that leaps to a fife band:
Set these against your water-shafted air
Of amethyst and moonstone, the horses' feet like bells of hair
Shambling beneath the orange cart, the beer-brown spring
Guzzling between the heather, the green gush of Irish spring.
Cursèd be he that curses his mother. I cannot be
Anyone else than what this land engendered me:
In the back of my mind are snips of white, the sails
Of the Lough's fishing-boats, the bellropes lash their tails
When I would peal my thoughts, the bells pull free –
Memory in apostasy.
I would tot up my factors
But who can stand in the way of his soul's stream-tractors?
I can say Ireland is hooey, Ireland is
A gallery of fake tapestries
But I cannot deny my past to which my self is wed,
The woven figure cannot undo its thread.

LOUIS MacNEICE, Poems 1925–1948, 1949

O F [THE] GROUPS OF ULSTER HILLS, perhaps the best known is the Antrim Plateau, an area of about 600 square miles of wild and lonely mountainous country, through which a series of glens descends north-eastward to the North Channel, the famous Glens of Antrim. Another well-known Ulster mountain area of quite different character is the Mourne Mountains in South Down. Seen from the north, they form a long 'sierra' of conical granite mountains, the highest being Slieve Donard which rises from beside the sea to over 2,700 feet. When seen in clear weather, with long streaks of granite gleaming in the sunlight, or when covered with snow, they have an appearance strangely foreign to the visitor's expectation of Ulster or British scenery. A third group of Ulster hills, rarely visited by tourists, is the Sperrin Mountains in the counties of Londonderry and Tyrone.

In mentioning the hill scenery of Ulster, it is also proper to mention the Belfast hills. Although only a relatively small group of hills, between 1,000 and 1,600 feet in height, they have played a great part in influencing the plan of the city of Belfast; and together with the long inlet of the sea, called Belfast Lough, they have provided the city with one of the most handsome metropolitan sites in the world.

HUGH SHEARMAN, *Northern Ireland*, 1948

CAVAN JOINS MONAGHAN. It is not unlike it in that it possesses many small lakes, but it is a higher country and not so rich. It breaks into sudden bleak hills and uplands, which in their heather and rocks are nearly mountainous in character. Its roads are mostly byways. They twist and turn and writhe up and down among their hedges. Now and again a large estate gives a prosperous feeling to the country, but soon you get back to the rushy fields and the hard boglands.

At Virginia you find yourself among the intricate waterways of Upper Lough Erne. It has much charm and in places is pleasantly timbered, but it could be greatly enhanced by further forestation. The sheets of water are much narrower here than at Lower Lough Erne, and at times you get the impression that the country is flooded or that a river has run amuck on inundated pasture land, but at times, as in the case of the large reaches near Killashandra, Upper Lough Erne becomes a lake in the true sense of the word. It was at Virginia in this country that one of Ireland's finest Celtic brooches was found.

DENIS O'D. HANNA, *The Face of Ulster*, 1952

THE BEST WAY TO APPROACH Northern Ireland is by boat to Belfast. At eight o'clock in the morning the visitor can stand at the rails while the ship glides up the lough, showing all at once the countryside and the hills beyond and the city's spires and stately towers of steel gantries in the shipyards. Also to be seen from mid-channel is the striking difference between the lough's opposite shores.

County Down lies on the port bow, a soft, undulating landscape of blues melting into greens, a gentle landscape set with trees and studded with cloud-shadows as soft as wool. White cottages and farms and seaside villages nestle there. Gulls whirl in the brown velvet of newly ploughed uplands among straggling forests of beech and oak.

To starboard the forbidding escarpment of County Antrim rises from the sea, changing its colour and mood with every change of sunshaft and cloud. The Antrim coast alternates between ranges of black basalt cliff, as impregnable as the dark Norman walls of Carrickfergus Castle at its feet, and other stretches of cliff like blue-veined cheese. At nightfall, the Antrim side becomes a vaguely menacing mass of indeterminate indigo.

The lough's two shores have each their own beauty but County Antrim's black and white is more dramatic than County Down's green. The two extreme colours of black and white symbolize Antrim. Even the names of places around its coast echo the curious interplay of black and white, the counterchange between chalk cliff and black basalt. Blackhead stands close by Whitehead. Whitehouse lies before the Black Mountain which stands sentinel over Belfast. Charles Kingsley was so taken up with this black and white counterchange of the Antrim coast that in *Westward Ho!* he described its island of Rathlin as 'looking like a half-drowned magpie'.

ROBIN BRYANS, Ulster: A Journey Through the Six Counties, 1964

IN THE POPULAR SPEECH OF ULSTER 'Protestant' is an epithet which not only distinguishes differences of religion, but serves as a label to describe all kinds of excellence. So stereotyped is the use of the word in this sense that I have heard a Catholic farmer urge his labourers who were engaged on some special task to make 'a good Protestant job' of it. This tradition of efficiency, and the desire to maintain it, are far and away the most valuable products of the gospel of work which Belfast preaches so strenuously. As a matter of fact, in his utterances on this subject the Northerner unconsciously does himself a grave injustice. He pretends to think that work in itself is the be-all and end-all of existence, and speaks as if he measured its value solely in terms of hard cash. This attitude has misled his friends as well as his foes, but to anyone who has taken the pains to go deeper than surface appearances it is obvious that, as a rule, he is merely repeating a formula which does not express his real convictions. Those who know the Ulster worker well are aware that though he may flaunt his 'big money', as he calls it, as a final answer to his critics, it is not his sole, or even his greatest, compensation. He retains in a high degree the pride of craftsmanship, and this pride is based not only on his individual contribution to the finished product but on the finished product itself.

JAMES WINDER GOOD, Ulster and Ireland, 1919

IT MUST ALWAYS BE REMEMBERED that in the north of Ireland, indeed throughout the whole of Ireland, the word Protestant in those days meant strictly churchman. The prevalent religions were divided into Papists, Protestants and Presbyterians; the Presbyterians not being regarded as Protestants in our numeration of faiths. The Church of Ireland was the Protestant Church and alone had the right to use the word Protestant. On the one side of it were Papists and on the other side Presbyterians and Methodists. In the middle were what in England would be called Anglicans which we called, and still do call, simply Protestants, meaning by the word, members of the Anglican Communion. But our Protestantism was different in quality from anything of the kind which exists in England. We pronounced the word as if its third consonant was a D, thereby giving it an explosiveness and an obstinacy which no religion in England has possessed since the days of Cromwell's Ironsides.

GEORGE A. BIRMINGHAM, *Pleasant Places*, 1934

'THROUGH-OTHER', MEANING FECKLESS, is ... a transliteration of *tri n-a cheile*, confused, and if it cannot be called a translation because it is not English, at least no one is likely to be in doubt as to the meaning of a through-other way of doing things.

In the back streets of Belfast the dialect is as ugly as any in the British Isles, though even it has its virility; but the talk of the countryman in Londonderry, Tyrone, and Fermanagh has a general effect of strength without harshness, raciness without extravagance, the sweetness of fine old words that have become embedded in the soil. The English talk vaguely of an 'Irish brogue', but the language of Enniskillen differs as much from that of Dublin or Galway or Cork − which, incidentally, differ to an equal degree from each other − as Norfolk from Devonshire. They say that the broadcaster and the film actor are affecting the accent of the younger generation, but this is hardly noticeable as yet.

CYRIL FALLS, *The Birth of Ulster*, 1936

THE LIBERAL'S LAMENT
after 'Tit Willow' by Gilbert and Sullivan

On a stool in a bar-room an old Unionist
Sang, 'British, I'm British, I'm British.'
I said to him, 'Old man, why do you insist
You're British, you're British, you're British?

Does it come from an inferiority complex?
Or did you have problems in childhood with sex?'
He banged on the bar and he looked sorely vexed:
'I'm British, so British, so British.'

Just then another appeared on the scene,
Singing, 'Ulster, I'm Ulster, I'm Ulster.'
And a man at the back, who was dressed all in green,
Said, 'I'm Irish, and Celtic, and Gaelic.'
I cried, 'Stop! For this whole thing could soon come to blows!
We none of us know who we are, and it shows.'
All three of them punched me, once each, on the nose,
One for Britain, one Ulster, one Ireland.

As I left I called out, 'Sure our family tree
Is part Scottish, part Irish, part English.
I don't give a toss about identity,
Whether Ulster, or Irish, or British.
For each of your gods I have only a curse!'
At this, the three of them looked fit to burst,
And they all then agreed that agnostics were worst,
Whether Ulster, or Irish, or British.

ROBERT JOHNSTONE, *Eden to Edenderry*, 1989

IN SPEECH, IN TEMPER, IN OUTLOOK, the Ulsterman of all creeds contrasts more sharply with the natives of the other provinces than the Black Country does with the Home Counties; and Nationalists who refuse to admit that such a difference exists for them, are simply playing into the hands of their opponents, who insist that the cleavage between North and South is purely along the lines of race and religion. However race and religion may have accentuated divisions in the past, environment in the present is a more potent element than heredity. There may not be complete assimilation, but there has undoubtedly been widespread modification. If Ulster Protestants are, as some of them love to boast, Scots improved by three centuries of residence in Ireland, Ulster Catholics are Irishmen improved, or at least modified, by three centuries of contact with Scots.

JAMES WINDER GOOD, *Ulster and Ireland*, 1919

IT NEED ONLY BE SAID ... that Arthur Chichester was a savage and ruthless foe, a stern but just ruler, an able soldier, a still more able administrator, high-tempered but cool, resolute but given to self-questioning, a pessimist with a conscience and a sense of humour. No man, not Strafford, nor Cromwell, nor William III, has left his mark deeper on Ireland. He was the 'Planter of Ulster'; and the fruits of his Plantation, however they taste in the mouth, are there today to bear witness to him.

CYRIL FALLS, *The Birth of Ulster*, 1936

SWATRAGH AND DRAPERSTOWN; Magherafelt and Toome; Plumbridge and Castledawson: her family couldn't understand her interest in these places. She drove through pinched villages where the edges of the footpaths were painted red, white and blue, where there were Orange Lodges and locked churches; through more prosperous towns with their memorials from the Great War and their baskets of lobelia and fuchsia hanging from brackets from the street lamps, with their Tidy Town awards on burnished plaques and their proper shopfronts. She drove through villages where unemployed men stood on street corners and dragged on cigarettes, or ambled up and down between the chip shop and the bookie's, past walls which bore Republican graffiti or incongruously glamourous advertisements on huge hoardings. She saw Planter towns that had had the heart bombed out of them; 'Business as Usual' signs pasted on the chipboard nailed over the broken windows of the Northern Bank and Williamson's Hardware. Now and then she would see a Mission tent, or a temporary road sign indicating the way to a 'Scripture Summer Camp'. She drove along narrow roads between shaggy wet hedges of hawthorn and beech. Once, somewhere in South Derry, she saw a field where a few pale cattle stood up to their knees in nettles and scutchgrass before a ruined building with 'INLA rule' painted on it in crude white letters. The cattle stared at her mildly as she passed by.

She saw signposts for places which had once held no particular significance but whose names were now tainted by the memory of things which had been done there: Claudy, Enniskillen, Ballykelly. She drove and drove and drove under grey skies and soft clouds. The towns and fields slipped past her until she felt that she was watching a film, and then she realised that if she had been asked to pick a single word to sum up her feelings towards Northern Ireland she would be at a complete loss, so much so that she didn't even know whether a negative or a positive word would have been more apt.

DEIRDRE MADDEN, *One by One in the Darkness*, 1996

SUNSET OVER GLENAAN

As the vague sun that wrapped the mellow day
in a grey haze hangs red, about to drop
behind the western mountain rim, I stop
to name the peaks along their dark array,
for these are more than mountains shouldered clear
into the sharp star-pointed atmosphere,
into the sunset. They mark out and bound
the utmost limits of my chosen ground;
beyond them, and beyond the heather and moss
that only lonely roads and shepherds cross,
lie the fat valleys of another folk
who swarmed and settled when the clansmen broke
and limped defeated to the woody glens.

These inland Planter folk are skilled in toil,
their days, their holdings, so well husbanded,
economy has drilled the very soil
into a dulled prosperity that year
by reckoned year continues so; but here
the people have such history of wars,
that every hilltop wears its cairn of dead
and ancient memories of turbulence,
clan names persisting in each rocky stead.
They take life easier on their hillside farms,
with time to pause for talk, remembering
they'll be outlasted by the marching stars,
and, though there may be virtue still in charms,
no man dare be too sure of anything.

My breed is Planter also. I can shew
the grey and crooked headstones row on row
in a rich country mastered long ago
by stubborn farmers from across the sea,
whose minds and hands were rich in husbandry,
and who, when their slow blood was running thin,
crowded in towns for warmth, and bred me in
the clay-red city with the white horse on the wall,
the jangling steeples, and the green-domed hall.

Inheritor of these, I also share
the nature of this legendary air,
reaching a peace and speech I do not find
familiarly among my kin and kind.

Maybe, at some dark level, grown aware
of our old load of guilt, I shrink afraid,
and seek the false truce of a renegade;
or is it that the unchristened heart of man
still hankers for the little friendly clan
that lives as native as the lark or hare?

And though to keep my brain and body alive
I need the honey of the city hive,
I also need for nurture of the heart
the rowan berries and the painted cart,
the bell at noon, the scythesman in the corn,
the cross of rushes, and the fairy thorn.

JOHN HEWITT, *The Day of the Corncrake: Poems of the Nine Glens*, 1969

FIRST THERE WAS THE PRIMEVAL Ulster of many geological periods, bringing us finally to Ulster as the site of a great ice cap. Then we had Ulster as the gateway to Ireland for primitive man and the centre of a Stone Age industrialism. We had Ulster as the scene of a distinctive megalithic culture. We had the Ulster of the heroic myths and of Cuchulainn. Then we had the Ulster which was the cradle of Christianity and Christian civilization for Ireland, and for Scotland and northern England as well. We had the Ulster which withstood the successive invaders right to the end of the sixteenth century. Then we had plantation Ulster, the policy of plantation coming as a sort of rebound from what had gone before. Then we have the Ulster that was a decisive battlefield for the great European Powers at the close of the seventeenth century and was, in the following century, one of the main wellsprings of the American Revolution and the great American republic. Then came nineteenth-century Ulster, the Ulster of industrialism and Unionism, developing into the Ulster of the gun-running and of the Battle of the Somme. In our own time Ulster is represented mainly by Northern Ireland, a semi-autonomous province within the United Kingdom, the province which had such a vital strategic importance in the Battle of the Atlantic and in the defence of Britain's lifeline during the darkest period of the war of 1939–45.

We can trace out how all these things successively happened and all these different phases of Ulster life came to the surface. Yet may there not be a deeper and more mysterious factor in it all? Has the rock and soil of Ulster some age-long stimulating influence upon the strenuous peoples who have lived there? One can imagine a place inhabited at one time by a vigorous and stirring people and then perhaps later falling to other people who would be dull and inactive. For whatever reason, this has not yet happened to Ulster. Even the most unpromising people have come alive when they have been in Ulster for a little while.

It has always been the same. No matter what community has inhabited Ulster, it has always been a stirring community, and Ulster always has been one of the salty, stinging, unexpected elements in the life and flavour of this planet. All down through the centuries Ulster has given sleepless nights to statesmen and generals, and kings and dictators have cursed the place and its ingenious and irrepressible inhabitants. And the unremitting export of men and women of first-class talent from Ulster has influenced every continent in the modern world.

And now there is the future to be faced. Modern inhabited Ulster has existed for only about eight thousand years, and, as every healthy, right-thinking Ulster child well knows, we are only at the beginning of things. During the next eight thousand years Ulster may well be worth watching.

HUGH SHEARMAN, Ulster, 1949

IN THE LATE 1960S AND EARLY 1970S, what had once been a 'mixed' area, meaning a neighbourhood where Protestant and Catholic families had 'got on well', experienced the shock of having to face the truth about Belfast's sectarian divisions. Similarly, the traditional Protestant and Catholic areas which had previously been negotiable by bus or foot, when leaving a girl home after a dance, or meeting a pal, or going to a party, became increasingly more dangerous and ultimately amounted to a perilous risk upon which few would chance their lives. By the mid-1970s when assassination squads roamed what became known as 'twilight zones', or interfaces between the dominant working-class districts, Belfast had ceased to be a living city and had become, for a decade and more, a ghost town.

Districts played, and still play, a key role in defining the identity of Belfast. Even though there have been extraordinary population shifts within the city over the last twenty-five years, because of intimidation and violence, on the one hand, and redevelopment on the other, the sense of being from a particular area is strong and lasting. It is a pattern common to many industrial cities such as Belfast.

Put at its simplest, Belfast is physically indistinguishable from the industries which were established in the nineteenth and twentieth centuries: linen-mills, ropeworks, tobacco factories, shipbuilding, engineering works.

Erected literally within this formidable industrial landscape were the streets and houses of the workers. It is not physically possible to think about Belfast as if it were different from this industrial past. Consequently, Belfast is unique in Ireland and has much more in common with Liverpool or Glasgow since the pattern of its streets as much as the commercial nature of the city centred on the industrial heartland; little else.

Each district had its own factory and customs linked to the work-practices of the factory; its own destiny, and well-being, tied irrevocably to that factory. The Falls, a predominantly Catholic road, had its mills; York Street in the Protestant lower northside had the famous Gallaher's tobacco factory while the shipyards dominated the east of the city. It was a pattern replicated throughout the city, layer by layer, from the dockland upwards until the prosperous higher roads circle the outer city and wind into the nearby countryside.

GERALD DAWE, *The Rest is History*, 1998

M ANY IMAGES HAVE BEEN APPLIED to the politics and society of Northern Ireland. In my experience shoreline metaphors are the most popular, for these carry within them the idea of something beached, washed-up, stranded, which is probably the general perception of the situation in Northern Ireland, as seen from the rest of the British Isles.

In my salad days I might have subscribed to these metaphors, but now my chosen image would be two trees, old and vast, standing side by side. If we were to delve below the surface of the earth on which they stand, as in a section drawing from one of my childhood encyclopedias, passing through the top soil and the subsequent strata of clay and rock, we would discover that their white roots twist and intertwine to such an extent that it is impossible to sort out which roots belong to which tree.

Back above ground the trees stand apart. They have no ostensible connection, yet they draw nourishment from the same soil, and so bound up are their roots with one another that to pull one tree out would kill the other.

CARLO GEBLER, *The Glass Curtain*, 1991

THE ULSTER WAY

This is not about burns or hedges.
There will be no gorse. You will not
notice the ceaseless photosynthesis
or the dead tree's thousand fingers,
the trunk's inhumanity writhing with texture,
as you will not be passing into farmland.
Nor will you be set upon by cattle,

ingleberried, haunching, and haunting
with their eyes, their shocking opals,
graving you, hoovering and scooping you,
full of a whatness that sieves you through
the abattoir hillscape, the runnel's slabber
through darkgrass, sweating for the night
that will purple to a love-bitten bruise.

All this in your head. If you walk
don't walk away, in silence, under the stars'
ice-fires of violence, to the water's darkened strand.
For this is not about horizons, or their curving
limitations. This is not about the rhythm
of a songline. There are other paths to follow.
Everything is about you. Now listen.

ALAN GILLIS, *Somebody, Somewhere*, 2004

I Take My Stand
by the Ulster Names

The old placenames – Uladh (Ulster), Béal Feirsde (Belfast), Dún (Down), Ard Macha (Armagh), Doire (Derry), Inis Ceithleann (Enniskillen), Tír Eóghain (Tyrone), Latharna (Larne) – told, and continue to tell, the story of the Gaelic past.

FLANN CAMPBELL, *The Dissenting Voice*

Oh! 'tis pretty to be in Ballinderry,
'Tis pretty to be in Aghalee;
But prettier far in little Ram's Island
Sitting in under the ivy tree:
          Och anee! Och anee!

ANONYMOUS

TOWNLANDS

Aghnasillagh, Glenagarey, Donacloney, Annalong,
Like a rustle in the twilight, or the lilting of a song.

Knockaderry, Inishkeeragh, Aghendarragh, Drumaness,
Like a wind among the birches full of lyric loveliness.

Gortalassa, Inishargy, Corrymeela, Tullylusk,
Sweet as bells across the waters in the silences of dusk.

Limavady, Cloonnagashel, Donaghedy, Carrowdore,
Like the purling of a fountain, or the wave upon the shore.

Ballinderry, Shanagarry, Kilnamona, Assaroe,
Like the sound of fairy music, poets named them long ago.

JOHN IRVINE, *By Winding Roads*, 1950

IT IS IMPOSSIBLE HERE to give in detail the varieties of the Six Counties. Look at the map and you should find a stimulus in the place-names themselves; most of them are Gaelic, dating back to early Irish history. Of the more common Gaelic prefixes, Bally- means 'town', Dun- 'fort', and Kil- 'church'. The component names, you will notice – names like Ballymena, Ballynahinch, Ballygawley, Dromore, Drumquin, Cushendall, Cushendun, Donaghadee, Tandragee, Carrickfergus, Aughnacloy, Dungannon, Limavady – are quite unlike place-names in England. They should remind you at once that their historical background is also unlike. Downpatrick for example commemorates St Patrick; this is the part of Ireland from which Christian missionaries in the Dark Ages sailed *eastwards*. (It is also perhaps the part of Ireland which has most contributed to folksong.) Since then linen-mills have shot up their chimneys and spread out their smoke, gantries have arisen at the head of Belfast Lough, workers have congregated into drab streets of cement-covered houses, but the peat-bogs are still brown and the mountains are still blue and the present is inter-shot with the past. And for most of the population life is still full of colour; the cottagers coat their houses with a dazzling whitewash and against this white you may see a blaze of gorse plant known here as 'whin' or fuchsias planted in a hedge.

LOUIS MacNEICE (c.1941), *from* 'Northern Ireland and Her People', *Selected Prose*, 1990

THE LAMENT OF NUALA O'NEILL FOR DONEGAL IN THE REIGN OF JAMES I, KING OF BRITAIN

Is aoibhinn aoibhinn Tir Aodha na n-each,
Is aoibhinn a bladh is a conach;
Ní haoibhne liom nó ó sin amach
Ó Dhrom Thuama go Muirbheach.

I

Pleasant indeed is Tirhugh of the steeds,
And pleasant its climate and bounty;
No prospect there to please me more
Than from Dromhome down to Murvey.

24

II

A feast for your eyes and a feast for your soul
Are Inver of the fishes, and Donegal Bay,
Balleeghan stretched out in the sun
And the handsome monastery of Donegal town.

III

Pleasant indeed is Gweebarra's inlet
Rising from the morning mist;
No prospect there to please me more
Than from Ballyshannon down to Drumhome.

IV

Pleasant indeed is MacNeice's Isle
With heavy dew and scented flowers,
With slender foals, and cuckoos sweet
And speckled trout that crowd its shores.

V

In Donegal are the choicest gems,
Ballydonnell and Lisnaree;
My blessing once, my blessing twice
On Barnesmore Gap in the Land of Hugh.

VI

Pleasant the grass and the fruit that grow,
Pleasant the flowers and the tops of the trees,
Bright the sunshine, and heavy the dew
And pleasant are you, sweet Donegal.

VII

Many's the fruit on low ground and high,
Fine are the sheep and the rising sap,
The antlered stag and the free-running doe,
And the salmon abounding besides.

VIII

Yonder west lie the Rosses
And there tonight I might be yet,
Queenly Caitriona, shield of the clergy,
And the king's son in her train each day.

IX

Pleasant indeed the sight of the Ards,
And the two fine banks of the River Finn,

From the Blue Stacks to the land of Gorey,
From Mulroy Bay as far as Binnion.

X

Pleasant indeed is Lettermacaward,
The easy isle of Inniskeel,
Kiltoorish of the white sandbanks,
And the streams of the shore besides.

XI

Yonder's the way I'll go with them,
To O'Boyle of the gifts and victories,
Where gems are freely bestowed
On the barons and lions of Ireland.

XII

I am the fish that swims the wave,
I am the vessel whose sail is gone,
I am the apple the blossom has left,
And in spite of all I still live on.

XIII

I am Nuala, daughter of the O'Neill,
That once held sway in Donegal,
Like the blackbird that sings by itself in the bush,
I'm far from home and my song is slow.

translated by CIARAN CARSON, 2005

THERE IS A TOWNLAND IN CAVAN called Castleterra, which gives name to a parish; the proper pronunciation, as O'Donovan found by conversation with the people, is *Cussatirry*, representing the Irish *Cos-a'-tsiorraigh*, the foot of the colt, which has been so strangely corrupted; they accounted for the name by a legend, and they showed him a stone in the townland on which was the impression of a colt's foot.

In the parish of Kilmore, in the same county, the townland of Derrywinny was called by an intelligent old man, *Doire-bhainne*, and interpreted, both by him and O'Donovan, the oak-grove of the milk; so called, very probably, from a grove where cows used to be milked ...

We have a vast quantity of topographical and other literature, written from a very early period down to the seventeenth century, in the Irish language, by native writers. Much of this has been lately published and translated, but far the greater part remains still unpublished.

Generally speaking, the writers of these manuscripts were singularly careful to transmit the correct ancient forms of such names of places as they had occasion to mention; and accordingly it may be stated as a rule, subject to occasional exceptions, that the same names are always found spelled in the same way by all our ancient writers or with trifling differences depending on the period in which they were transcribed, and not affecting the etymology.

At those early times, the names which are now for the most part unmeaning sounds to the people using them, were quite intelligible, especially to skilled Irish scholars; and this accounts for the almost universal correctness with which they have been transmitted to us.

P.W. JOYCE, *The Origin and History of Irish Names of Places*, 1869

HARD DRIVE

With my back to the wall
and a foot in the door
and my shoulder to the wheel
I would drive through Seskinore.

With an ear to the ground
and my neck on the block
I would tend to my wound
in Belleek and Bellanaleck.

With a toe in the water
and a nose for trouble
and an eye to the future
I would drive through Derryfubble

and Dunnamanagh and Ballynascreen,
keeping that wound green.

PAUL MULDOON, *Moy Sand and Gravel*, 2002

BACK OF ALL THE LITTLE PORTS along the shore of Mourne one sees the yawls among the fields, waiting for their excursions into the water on harvest nights. In Carlingford Lough herring are caught in some seasons into February, but it seems that the movements of the shoals are uncertain. In former times the catches seem to have been heavy.

Nothing illustrates more clearly the intimate knowledge of Mourne and its mountains possessed by fishermen who were also farmers, the close association of land and water in this country where the mountains go down to the sea, than the landmarks which were used to guide the boats to and locate their fishing grounds. The names read like a poem. There are, for example, the Two Hills, the Blue Hills, the Three Tallies and the North Mountain Foot; the Small Pike, the Long Land and Marleys-on-the-Ditch; the Horsemen, the Bleachyards, McVeigh's-in-the-Glen, Rook's Chimney, Henry's Lumps, Nicky's Easens, and the Old Mill Stump. To illustrate their uses one of the marks – the mark of the Two Churches – meant getting Kilkeel Church Tower in line with the West Mountain Foot and Kilhorn (Annalong) Church in line with the North Mountain Foot.

Some of these numerous landmarks can readily be identified by the landsman for they are the hill-marks on Binnian and the other mountain tops. The Horsemen, for example, are the tors on Chimney Rock, with the General leading the others, his horse's back proudly curved against the clouds. Others have a delightful intimacy, based often on nicknames of long-vanished shore-dwellers, Nip-me-hip's and Kibby's Easens (probably referring to the eaves of his house). These, and marks such as the Rector's Bushes and Isaac's-on-the-Hill, were guides to the inshore fishermen who were never far from land and knew its every curve, tree and chimney.

E. ESTYN EVANS, *Mourne Country*, 1951

from LAMENT FOR ART ÓG Ó NÉILL

Tá Contae an Dúin faoi chumhaidh 'na dhiaidh sin,
Contae Thír Eoghain, dár ndoigh, 's ní hionadh;
Contae Ard Mhach' go cráite buartha;
Duthaigh an Fheadha dá easba gan oidhre,
Gruaim is tuirse ar a maireann de Ghaelaibh,
Ó thaobh Shliabh gCallánn go Cábhán Uí Raghallaigh ...

County Down is lonesome without him;
County Tyrone as well – no wonder;
County Armagh broken in sorrow;
The Fews abandoned, without an heir
Bleakness and sadness on the Gaels who live on
From the slopes of Slieve Gallen to O'Reilly's Cavan.

Glasdrumman is troubled and her branches drooping;
The shoals of fish in distress are dying;
The tall castle is fallen in pieces;
The wood overgrown and without blossom;
For the loss of each limb of royal blood:
The tribe of Féilimí Rua of the sharp tempered swords.

Crossmaglen is in sorrow, without Ó Néill's house,
Where the nobility frequently feasted:
Two from Louth, three from the Erne;
A great many from Meath and from Ireland's north,
Playing and drinking from shining goblets;
The youth would gather, as Ireland's poets.

If the bards who once were in state survived,
Séamus Mac Cuarta would account on you wisely;
Padraig Mac Giolla Fhiondáin would exact each line,
Randall Dall Mac Dónaill would give learned discourse,
But since all have died there is no one to keen you
But me – an isolated drop contending with the deluge.

To Art's court, alas, I will go no more,
Making music at bright delightful tables,
With Baachus where I'd spend months in bondage,
Drunk from each wine and all thirst quenched.
This generous man's death brings desolation to poets
And a burden like black coal lies beneath my breast.

ART MAC CUMHAIGH (1769), translated by PÁDRAIGÍN NÍ UALLACHÁIN,
A Hidden Ulster: People, Songs and Traditions of Oriel, 2003

A T THE FAR END OF THE BAY, under the railway lines, the waters spread out into the Strand Lough and bogs. The railway line is a steel and sleepered road snaking off in two directions, and the road at the pub leads off past the brickyards to Downpatrick and far places. At the end of Fisherman's Row a small road heads off for St John's Point and the lighthouse, while over the Quarter Hill is Rossglass, Minerstown, Tyrella and beyond. The existence of an even wider world is hinted at by the advancing and receding peaks of the Mournes, by the spires and castles and water tower of Ardglass on the other skyline, and by the sounds borne in on the wind: the angelus bells of Ardglass and Legamaddy and occasionally Downpatrick, the foghorn and the asylum horn and sometimes the foghorns of ships at sea. It was the seaward edge which carried the most magic, was more open and fluid and most subject to

change. Not only the tides and the weather, but the very sea itself. On
the horizon, the Isle of Man swam in and out of view. Most of the time
a light tracing of faded peaks in the background, it could disappear
altogether for days at a time, or loom so close as to be almost reachable,
solid, blue, with little specks of white and flashes of reflected light.

MAURICE HAYES, Sweet Killough, Let Go Your Anchor, 1994

THE SINGER'S HOUSE

When they said *Carrickfergus* I could hear
the frosty echo of saltminers' picks.
I imagined it, chambered and glinting,
a township built of light.

What do we say any more
to conjure the salt of our earth?
So much comes and is gone
that should be crystal and kept

and amicable weathers
that bring up the grain of things,
their tang of season and store,
are all the packing we'll get.

So I say to myself *Gweebarra*
and its music hits off the place
like water hitting off granite.
I see the glittering sound

framed in your window,
knives and forks set on oilcloth,
and the seals' heads, suddenly outlined,
scanning everything.

People here used to believe
that drowned souls lived in the seals.
At spring tides they might change shape.
They loved music and swam in for a singer

who might stand at the end of summer
in the mouth of a whitewashed turf-shed,
his shoulder to the jamb, his song
a rowboat far out in evening.

When I came here first you were always singing,
a hint of the clip of the pick
in your winnowing climb and attack.
Raise it again, man. We still believe what we hear.

SEAMUS HEANEY, Field Work, 1979

A TRAIN CARRIES US ALONG one side of Belfast Lough, in a light
cheerful mist, which gradually clears before the sunshine of a mild day.
We're going home for the summer holidays. Now the train circumvents
Larne Lough; passes the swans on the water at Glynn; and comes to the
untidy bay that sets its weedy sand close to the station platform.

At table in the rectory conversation is becoming more hilarious. My
father makes puns and has (at a time when James Joyce is yet unknown)
a knack of inventing strange words by combining or twisting classical,
biblical, French and German tags.

Off we go on our usual courses. With Lyle, we make expeditions across
the country, to Kilwaughter Castle, Shan's Hill, Knockdu, Glenarm; to
distant bays for bathing, including bays of the peninsula Islandmagee, to
which we're ferried from Larne Harbour; play cricket in the back field;
play extensive wandering games, taking in a neighbouring farm, where,
among the other children, a brown-eyed daughter is to appear beautiful
to us for a time.

GEORGE BUCHANAN, Green Seacoast, 1959

T O A BELFAST CHILD, Cecil Frances Alexander's familiar hymn, 'All
Things Bright and Beautiful', seemed to have been written specially
for her. This was Nature as we knew it: the heather-covered hills, the
small creatures, the skies, the clouds, the sunsets. We looked at the world
around and marvelled and sang:

> The purple-headed mountain,
> The river running by,
> The sunset and the morning
> That lightens up the sky.

The ring of hills was all around us: Cave Hill, Squire's Hill, Divis,
Knocklade, and Black Mountain. We watched the crimson rim of the sun
sinking behind them, the storm clouds gathering over them, the sun
shining out after rain, and the sparkle of rainbows behind them.

Weather was a matter of vital importance to us: a picnic could be ruined by rain, a summer holiday spoiled by icy winds and cold water. We watched the weather and Daddy taught us:

Dirty days hath September,
April, June, and November.
All the rest have thirty-one
Without a bloomin' blink of sun.
If any of them had two-and-thirty
They'd be just as wet and twice as dirty.

ALICE KANE, *Songs and Sayings of an Ulster Childhood*, 1983

THE WAY IN WHICH THE NOISE of departing trains thinned and vanished, gradually receding into silence as, diluted by space, they became lost in the inaudible background hum of things, offered in sound the same leitmotif of transience that the trains offered to the eye. The symmetry of the rails, the way they gleamed in the sun, like lines ruled on the ground with iridescent silver, the predictability of the signals, when the station would be bustling and crowded, when it would be deserted, the orchestration of the timetable, the neat flowers on the platform, all this suggested order, a lulling sense of regulation. Things orchestrated into human scale and priority. And the litany of stops between Lisburn and Belfast: Hilden, Lambeg, Derriaghy, Dunmurry, Finaghy, Balmoral, Adelaide – a route travelled scores of times by me, my friends and family – were little beads in some reassuring rosary. It's amazing how much can be summoned to the mind when I say them now. Travelling by train on winter evenings when it got dark early, it sometimes felt as if the line from Lisburn to Belfast was like an incision drawn into Ulster and that travelling it, looking through uncurtained windows at the lives briefly illuminated within, was like seeing into an ants' nest, like taking a cross-section through a living landscape.

CHRIS ARTHUR, *from* 'Train Sounds', *Irish Willow*, 2002

HAVE YOU HEARD THEIR NAMES, we mean the names of the Nine Green Glens? No! Well, here they are for you, and there is poetry and music in every one of them.

There is Glenaan, the hemmed-in Glen; Glenarm, the Glen of the Army; Glenariff, the Fertile Glen; Glencloy, the Glen of the Dykes; Glencorb, the Glen of the Coaches; Glenravel, the Glen of the Ravel

River; Glenshesk, the Sedgy Glen; Glentasie, the Glen of the Sorrel; and Glendun, the Glen of the Dun River.

And they are beautiful beyond all imagining ...

CATHAL O'BYRNE, As I Roved Out, 1946

THE WILD SKY OVER SAINT DABHEOC'S SEAT is typical of Donegal. One often gets the impression of standing under bellowing, flapping wet clothes pegged out on a clothes-line. The Donegal mountains make good theatre as they jostle together, the light playing on peaks that stand head and shoulders over the rest. The place-names are the stuff of poetry. Stevenson was excited by the lovely names he passed in his American coast-to-coast rail journey: Ohio, Delaware, Minnesota. 'Rich, poetic, humorous and picturesque,' he calls them in *Across the Plains*. As for Susquehanna, 'the beauty of the name seemed to be part and parcel of the land'. The same could be said of the Donegal places: Gweebarra, Falcarragh, Cloghaneely, Carrigart and Dunfanaghy (which is on the edge of the world).

STEPHEN RYNNE, All Ireland, 1956

THE OFFICES OF BUTLER, BAKER AND COOK were in some monasteries, chiefly of later date, of considerable importance. The smith (*gabha*) was probably in most cases also the brazier (*cherd*); the profession, which included all branches of metal working, was held in the highest esteem in early times and is preserved in hereditary surnames and place names in various forms today, such as in the surnames Gowan, Macgowan, Maccoun or Macoun, and in the place names Ballygowan, Lisnagowan, and Ballykennedy (*Baile 'ngabhan*).

H.C. LAWLOR, The Monastery of Saint Mochaoi of Nendrum, 1925

CLONFEACLE

It happened not far away
In this meadowland
That Patrick lost a tooth.
I translate the placename

As we walk along
The river where he washed,

33

That translates stone to silt.
The river would preach

As well as Patrick did.
A tongue of water passing
Between teeth of stones.
Making itself clear,

Living by what it says,
Converting meadowland to marsh.
You turn towards me,
Coming round to my way

Of thinking, holding
Your tongue between your teeth.
I turn my back on the river
And Patrick, their sermons

Ending in the air.

PAUL MULDOON, New Weather, 1973

THERE IS NO PLACE IN THIS WORLD for aspirations towards ancestry. In any case our ancestry and that of everyone around lives on in the foundations of our daily lives, and is enshrined in the names of the townlands, the landmarks, the small hillocks – the Moor Hill, Biddy's Brae, the Eglish Rising; in the corners and twists in the single road – Dan Daisy's Bend, the Kiln Corner, Grainne's Corner; in the names of the trees – Matty's Thorn, the Pig Tree, Treanor's Rookery, the Pin Tree. Every field too has its name, crop, characteristic and lore. The Fallow Field has never been ploughed; the Bush Hill has a fairy tree in the middle which is never lopped or disturbed; the Car Road Field lies alongside the old original road that once was the main traverse across the district; and Matty's Hill commemorates an old widower whose tiny cottage has long since gone to earth. Yet we have already begun to slip out of this world, or occupy a slightly ambivalent position within it – partly because of our parents' occupations in a district where everyone else's work is connected with the land or the water, and partly because of that long reach our male forebears made to bring in mates from outside the district and from a different class – the class that finds it demeaning, rather than descriptive, to be called peasants.

POLLY DEVLIN, All of Us There, 1983

Having said that Tyrone is two counties, East and West, I look at the map which I carry in my mind and see it shading itself off, still splendidly and varyingly coloured and in spite of the times it now suffers, into at least four counties, the Lough Shore, east on Lough Neagh, the Clogher Valley, the valleys of the Strule and the Mourne, and the great unifying centre which, like the boss on a shield, *is* the true heart of historic Ulster: the Sperrin Mountains.

If I were sending to Tyrone a friend who had never been there before, I would naturally send him first to my home town, Omagh, and to my friends therein, and after that, by Gortin and Plumbridge and Crannagh, into the Sperrins, along the Glenelly River, under the shadows of Sawel and Dart mountains to look in our legendary Glanconkyne where, after the fatal battle of Kinsale (1601), that great Hugh O'Neill, a fugitive on his native sod, thought his black thoughts. Then on to emerge, by Slieve Gallen Braes, renowned in a famous ballad, at Cookstown and on to the Lough Shore at the High Cross of Ardboe. My friend might be in great danger of being found trespassing in County Derry, or Londonderry, depending on your politics. But up in that chaste and lonely mountainland, county or other boundaries would not seem to be of much importance.

BENEDICT KIELY, from 'Co. Tyrone', 32 Counties, 1989

TRADE WINDS

I

Through Molly Ward's and Mickey Taylor's Locks,
Through Edenderry, Aghalee and Cranagh
To Lough Neagh and back again went *Perseverence*
And *Speedwell* carrying turf, coal and cinders.

II

Was it an Armagh man who loaded the boat
With the names of apples for his girlfriend:
Strawberry Cheeks, Lily Fingers, Angel Bites,
Winter Glories, Black Annetts, Widows' Whelps?

III

For smoking at wakes and breaking on graves
Carrick men christened clay pipes in Pipe Lane
Keel Baltic, Swinyard Cutty, Punch Quelp,
Plain Home Rule, Dutch Straws, Bent Unique.

Among the Portavogie prawn-fishermen
Which will be the ship of death: *Trade Winds,*
Guiding Starlight, Halcyon, Easter Morn,
Liberty, Faithful Promise, Sparkling Wave?

MICHAEL LONGLEY, *Gorse Fires,* 1991

T HE VARIETY OF BANNER SUBJECT IS ENDLESS – an exotic variety like
the names of the lodges and bands. These come from all over the
world to display their Protestant allegiance on the Twelfth of July 'walk'.
One follows another in a fabulous succession – Sir William Young's
Chosen Few, Israel's Truth Defenders, Pride of Motherwell, Purple Star
Ladies, Hearts of Oak, The Silent Valley Flute Band, The Saintfield
Amateur Silver, Bailliesmills Accordion, Britannia Temperance Reed,
and, of course, the Girls' Pipe Bands. Trades are also represented by such
bodies as the Transport True Blues complete with banner pictures of big
lorries similar to those which I saw grinding their way carefully beneath
Portadown's Twelfth arches.

ROBIN BRYANS, *Ulster: A Journey Through the Six Counties,* 1964

D URING THE THIRTEENTH CENTURY English settlers came to Antrim
and Down, the most noted names being Mandeville, Savage, Logan,
and Bisset. They lived for the most part on or close to the sea coast or
around the great castles and abbeys which de Courcy had erected. The
native tribes were driven inland to the fastnesses of mountain, forest, or
bog. The two eastern counties were, therefore, only half-conquered, and
very little impression had been made on the rest of the North. Armagh,
Derry and Tyrone had been raided rather than settled, and it is doubtful
whether the Normans ever penetrated to Fermanagh.

D.A. CHART, *A History of Northern Ireland,* 1927

S O WE CAME TO HAVE TEA AND SANDWICHES and lemonade in a
meadow by the crossroads in the exact centre of the wide saucer of
land where seven streams from the surrounding hills came down to meet.
The grass was polished with sunshine. The perfume of the meadowsweet
is with me still. That plain seemed to me then as vast as the prairies, or
Siberia. White cottages far away on the lower slopes of Dooish could
have been in another country. The chief stream came for a long way
through soft deep meadowland. It was slow, quiet, unobtrusive,

perturbed only by the movements of waterfowl or trout. Two streams met, wonder of wonders, under the arch of a bridge and you could go out under the bridge along a sandy promontory to paddle in clear water on a bottom as smooth as Bundoran strand. Three streams came together in a magic hazel wood where the tiny green unripe nuts were already clustered on the branches. Then the seven made into one, went away from us with a shout and a song towards Shaneragh, Blacksessiagh, Drumragh and Crevenagh, under the humpy crooked King's Bridge where James Stuart had passed on his way from Derry to the fatal brackish Boyne, and on through the town we came from.

– All the things we could see, said my father, if this spavined brute of a so-called automobile could only be persuaded to climb the high hills. The deep lakes of Claramore. The far view of Mount Errigal, the Cock of the North, by the Donegal sea. If you were up on the top of Errigal you could damn' near see, on a clear day, the skyscrapers of New York.

In his poetic imagination the towers of Atlantis rose glimmering from the deep.

– What matter, said my mother. The peace of heaven is here.

BENEDICT KIELY, *A Journey to the Seven Streams*, 1963

from THE WINDING BANKS OF ERNE

Farewell, Coolmore, – Bundoran! and your summer crowds that run
From inland homes to see with joy th' Atlantic-setting sun;
To breathe the buoyant salted air, and sport among the waves;
To gather shells on sandy beach, and tempt the gloomy caves;
To watch the flowing, ebbing tide, the boats, the crabs, the fish;
Young men and maids to meet and smile, and form a tender wish;
The sick and old in search of health, for all things have their turn –
And I must quit my native shore, and the winding banks of Erne!

Farewell to every white cascade from the Harbour to Belleek,
And every pool where fins may rest, and ivy-shaded creek;
The sloping fields, the lofty rocks, where ash and holly grow,
The one split yew-tree gazing on the curving flood below;
The Lough, that winds through islands under Turaw mountain green;
And Castle Caldwell's stretching woods, with tranquil bays between;
And Breesie Hill, and many a pond among the heath and fern, –
For I must say adieu – adieu to the winding banks of Erne!

The thrush will call through Camlin groves the live-long summer day;
The waters run by mossy cliff, and banks with wild flowers gay;
The girls will bring their work and sing beneath a twisted thorn,

Or stray with sweethearts down the path among the growing corn;
Along the river-side they go, where I have often been,
O, never shall I see again the days that I have seen!
A thousand chances are to one I never may return, –
Adieu to Belashanny, and the winding banks of Erne!

WILLIAM ALLINGHAM, Irish Songs and Poems, 1887

NORTH QUEEN STREET WAS ONCE CALLED Carrickfergus Road because it was the main road to that town. Crumlin Road was the only road out of town to the north, and the old coach road from Ardoyne through Legoniel was a rough and hilly way, indeed. The Antrim Road is of comparatively recent formation. A country lane used to run out from the old Poor House in Clifton Street to a farm and dwelling house known as Vicinage, on the site of which St Malachy's college is now built. Wolfhill is noted for being the place where the last Irish wolf was killed.

Ballymacarrett means the townland of the son of Art (O'Neill). It was densely covered with trees, and, from the old Long bridge to 'Con's water', there were only two houses. Castlereagh gets its name from the grey castle from which Con O'Neill once ruled all lower Clandeboy.

Mount Pottinger was once the residence of the Pottinger family, which gave its name to the entry off High Street. A Thomas Pottinger of this family paid twenty pounds a year for all Ballymacarrett!

There was no road through the Pottinger estate in the old days; the water of the lough extended up to what is now Strandtown, and was crossed by a ford.

Arthur was a favourite name in the Donegall family, who, by the way, spell the name with two *l*'s. Hence the recurrence of the name in the street nomenclature of the town – Arthur Street, Arthur Lane and Arthur Place. The origin of the name, Corn Market, is obvious, and the great weighbridge was kept under the colonnade of the old market house. Corn Market was, however, once called The Shambles, because of its many butchers' shops.

In the old days some well known localities had rather strange names, Clabber Loney, Blackstaff Loney and Buttermilk Loney; Tay Lane and Lovers' Lane; Cripple Row; the Gooseberry Corner and Pepper Hill steps. New Lodge Road was once Pinkerton's Row, and McClean's fields was later known as the Chapel fields; while Lombard Street was called Legg's Lane; Victoria Street was Cow Lane, the street through which cows were driven to graze in the Point fields at the foot of Corporation Street. North Street was Goose Lane and was named for a similar reason. Skipper Street was the residence of the skippers and captains of the vessels that lay at anchor in the old dock beside it. Bridge Street was so named because the principal bridge, a stone one, that covered the Farset river was situated in High Street at this point. Church Lane was named after the old corporation church, now St George's. Earlier it was known as Schoolhouse Lane, for the reason that the first schoolhouse founded in the town by the earl of Donegall was situated in it.

CATHAL O'BYRNE, *As I Roved Out*, 1946

THE OLDEST STRATUM OF GAELIC BELFAST survives in the palimpsest of its placenames. A small stream running into the river Lagan created a sandbank which at low tide provided its most easterly ford. The Irish for a sandbank which can also serve as a river-crossing is 'fertas', which through time became 'fersat', then 'fersaid', and the Farset river took its name from the sandbank. There is some debate as to the exact translation of the Irish form, Béal Feirste. Most scholars now reject the version 'the mouth of the Farset (river)', but are divided between 'the mouth of' and 'the approach to' the sandbank ford. Dozens of placenames in the area surrounding the ford have Gaelic roots – Divis, Malone, Cromac, Shankill, Falls, Knockbreda, Cregagh, Legoniel, Ballymurphy, Castlereagh, Benmadigan, Stranmillis. Some older townland names, such as Multyhogy and Ballydownfine, survive only on property deeds, and the splendidly named Ballyroculgalgalgie – the townland in which the castle stood – has disappeared. Many of these placenames are descriptive; Cromac, for instance, refers to a bend in the Lagan, and Legoniel means the hollow of the limestone, but others have historic resonances. Among these latter is Knockbreda, the hill of the Bréadach, a people of Cruithin origin whose annual tribute of a hundred cows, sheep and pigs to the Ulaidh is recorded in a Gaelic poem in the eleventh century Book of Rights. Skegoniel means 'the bush of the earl' and may refer to the Norman earl of Ulster. Baile na mBráthar, the original name for Friar's Bush, is likely to refer to an old monastery, and Shankill, the name of the parish in which Belfast was set, means 'old church'.

AODÁN MAC PÓILIN, *from* 'The Irish Language in Belfast until 1900',
The Cities of Belfast, 2003

A LOST TRADITION

All around, shards of a lost tradition:
From the Rough Field I went to school
In the Glens of the Hazels. Close by
Was the bishopric of the Golden Stone;
The cairn of Carleton's homesick poem.

Scattered over the hills, tribal
And placenames, uncultivated pearls.
No rock or ruin, dun or dolmen
But showed memory defying cruelty
Through an image-encrusted name.

The heathery gap where the Raparee,
Shane Barnagh, saw his brother die –
On a summer's day the dying sun
Stained its colours to crimson:
So breaks the heart, Brish-mo-Cree.

The whole landscape a manuscript
We had lost the skill to read.
A part of our past disinherited;
But fumbled, like a blind man,
Along the fingertips of instinct.

The last Gaelic speaker in the parish
When I stammered my school Irish
One Sunday after mass, crinkled
A rusty litany of praise:
Tá an Ghaedilg againn arís ... *

Tir Eoghain: Land of Owen,
Province of the O'Niall;
The ghostly tread of O'Hagan's
Barefoot gallowglasses marching
To merge forces in Dun Geanainn

Push southward to Kinsale!
Loudly the war-cry is swallowed
In swirls of black rain and fog
As Ulster's pride, Elizabeth's foemen,
Founder in a Munster bog.

* We have the Irish again

JOHN MONTAGUE, The Rough Field, 1972

INVISIBLY, BECAUSE THEY ARE UNMARKED on road signs or on small-scale maps and are virtually unknown to outsiders, the countryside of Northern Ireland is divided into a patchwork of small territories called townlands. It's hard to describe just what they are; my choice of 'divided' and 'territories' already sounds the wrong notes and suggests some sort of antagonistic separateness, making them seem like little fiefdoms, each clearly demarcated and defended by its inhabitants. In fact, their precise boundaries are hazy, one shading gradually into the next, and sometimes a whole handful of townlands will be known collectively by the name of only one, which, for reasons lost in history, has fixed in people's minds more securely than the rest. They have no intrinsic political or religious significance (though given Ulster's indelible sectarianism, Catholics and Protestants often tend to live apart in unmixed tribal clusters, whether in urban or rural areas).

Townlands are almost like the secret names given to individuals in some cultures and used only within the confines of a clan. The whole landscape is dotted with these intimate semi-secret namings, usually known only to the locals, or to those with a penchant for studying large-scale maps. Now, it's often only the most elderly residents of a place who remember the names at all and what they mean – another small indication of the way in which we have increasingly distanced ourselves from the land, forgotten the once familiar embrace of place, loosened the ties between language and geography. Driving for half an hour on the narrow country roads that criss-cross County Antrim, you might pass through ten or twenty townlands. There is nothing to show where one begins and another ends. It's rather like rowing across a reservoir, unaware of the old villages, long deserted and flooded to make way for it, which stretch out their ghostly submerged streets and houses below the accumulated weight of water, providing an invisible declension of its rippled, seamless surface.

Legatirrif, Aghanamoney, Tullyballydonell, Cluntirrif, Ballylacky, Drumanduff, Derrykillulltagh, Aghacarnan, Island Kelly, Drumankelly, Ballydolly, Ballyclogh – these are a few of the townlands [of Antrim] which cluster around the place I want to focus on, a catechism of lost meanings, an almost extinct tongue, names which hold within them echoes of original namings – 'place of the stones', 'hollow of the bog', 'Donal's hill homestead'. Now they encompass anonymous hawthorn-hedged fields, marshlands, farmhouses, cottages, barns, stone bridges. I used to cycle through them thirty years ago, the roads so quiet it was rare to meet a car. Things have changed.

CHRIS ARTHUR, *from* 'A Paper Star for Brookfield', *Irish Nocturnes*, 1999

HE COULD LOOK DOWN ON the hiving playground, the view like a map. He was level with the school-eaves and could see into the upper-classroom where Miss Gibson and Nan Connell sat on a desk and sipped their tea: the sun-bright yard, the children talking, playing, squabbling, eating their lunches, their voices muted, a million unseen insects humming round him in the tree, swallows slicing down the steep face of Drumbar Hill and sliding up over the school, the high swifts beating the bounds of the sky.

The children were like a family, the school knitting them together like brothers and sisters. He couldn't dislike any of them, he knew them all, their ages, homes, how they tried to live – the spit on the hard hand and the spade in the sod, their food rising yearly out of the ground ... their names and religions were built into British history: O'Rourke, Brady, Gallagher, Goggins, Mulligan, O'Neill, Carmichael, Sheridan, Connolly, McMahon, McConnell, Ferguson, Molyneaux, Fuegard, Hawe, Smith, Black, Thorne, White, West, North, Hewitt, Lowe, Lowry, Armstrong, Johnson, Montgomery, Gaunt, Grady, Gahan, Clarke, Burgess, Archer, O'Brien, Lindsay, Jones, Barrett, Talbot, Fitzpatrick, Fitzsimmons, Collins, Tirrel, Weir, Mee, Pratt, Price, MacCabe, McGrath, Igoe, Richardson, Moneypenny ... names English, Irish, Norman, Scots, French and all under the power of a man called Rainey [the teacher], a name like a cold wet day.

ANTHONY C. WEST, *The Ferret Fancier*, 1963

H IS FIRST FREE DAY WHEN THE BOARDERS were allowed out he made his way to the docks to see the ships. Their huge red funnels, white paintwork and varnished masts filled him with delight. At the other side of the harbour were the coal-boats, the crane buckets descending into their bowels and disgorging shining pyramids of coal on the quay. Over the Queen's Bridge lines of coal-carts rattled; trams mumbled; and once a donkey passed drawing a cart of steaming coal-brick. Colm stood on the bridge counting the big cross-channel boats, looking at the Lagan water swirling round the quoins of the bridge, holding captive in one corner orange peel, straw, and empty cigarette packets. From the opposite side of the bridge he saw coming down the river barges laden with turf-mould and going to dock under a black shed which had on the roof big white letters – PEAT, MOSS, LITTER. He wished with all his heart that Jamesy was with him.

On his way back to the College he wandered about the city learning the names of the streets: Oxford Street, Victoria Street, Cromac Street, Durham Street, Townshend Street, Carlisle Circus, and he thought of the island names – Lagavristeevore, Killaney, Crocnacreeva, Carnasheeran, Crocaharna – words full of music, and he said them aloud to himself as he went along.

MICHAEL McLAVERTY, *Call My Brother Back*, 1939

O NE OF MY CURRENT RECURRENT DREAMS of Belfast focuses on streets dominated by a church, St Peter's Pro-Cathedral in the Lower Falls. Looking at it on the Ordnance Survey plan of 1931 (a modern map would not show the demolished streets, or versions of them, in which the dream takes place), I note how the church is like the hub of a crooked wheel, with streets bounding it and radiating from it: Alexander, Derby, Milford, Ardmoulin, Irwin, Baker, Massarene, Scotch, Bow, English, Cinnamond. Completed in the neo-Gothic style in 1866, the church occupies what looks like medieval space, although the streets do not exist by virtue of its presence, as they would have done in medieval times; their *raison d'être* is to house the workers in the spinning mills and foundries that made Belfast a once-great city.

CIARAN CARSON, *The Star Factory*, 1997

M OVING OUT FROM WHERE THE City Hall sits inside Donegall Square, the roads and avenues form a compass of religious and cultural division. Rising up out of Donegall Place, Royal Avenue and York Street are the famous districts of the Falls, Shankill and Crumlin: what is now called West Belfast. Turning east towards the Lagan and crossing the river 'over the bridge' are the Newtownards, Albertbridge, Beersbridge and Woodstock districts. The land is densely housed, each neighbourhood a protectorate all on its own.

The predominantly protestant east of the city is like a triangular wedge, bordered by one of the longest roads in the city – the Newtownards Road – and by the Castlereagh and Knock roads. Within the triangle reside the neighbourhoods of Ballymacarret, Bloomfield, Strandtown, Ballyhackamore, Castlereagh, Cregagh and Orangefield.

GERALD DAWE, *The Rest is History*, 1998

J UST BESIDE LOUGH NEAGH the land is very flat, and has been used for military airfields. In this district is Nutt's Corner Airport, the principal airport of Northern Ireland and one of the most important in the British Isles. Who Nutt was I have never discovered, but the name Nutt's Corner is very characteristic of Ulster, where places are very frequently called after local characters. The greater part of the Lough is in County Antrim, though five counties share it. The Lough's one little island, Ram's Island, a little wooded place less than a mile long, with a round tower on it, is County Antrim territory and is celebrated in the well-known ballad which asserts that

'Tis pretty to be in Ballinderry,
'Tis pretty to be in Aghalee;
But prettier far on Little Ram's Island
Trysting under the ivy tree.

The fairly flat but slightly tilted country that lies between the Belfast hills
and Lough Neagh has for many years been the annual scene of a well-
known motorcycle race, one of quite a number held in Northern Ireland.
The course is rather long and has several very fast straights on it, including
the famous seven-mile straight ending in the hairpin turning at Clady
Corner. For a while this race held the position of being the fastest road
race on earth, and there was much excitement when a neighbour of ours
was the first man to do a complete lap round the course at an average
speed of over a hundred miles an hour. It was one of my schoolday thrills
to go and watch the race from along the seven-mile straight.

HUGH SHEARMAN, *Ulster*, 1949

'TIS PRETTY TAE BE IN BAILE-LIOSAN

'Tis pretty tae be in Baile-liosan,
'Tis pretty tae be in green Magh-luan;
'Tis prettier tae be in Newtownbreda,
Beeking under the eaves in June.
The cummers are out wi' their knitting and spinning,
The thrush sings frae his crib on the wa',
And o'er the white road the clachan caddies
Play at their marlies and goaling-ba'.

O, fair are the fields o' Baile-liosan,
And fair are the faes of green Magh-luan;
But fairer the flowers o' Newtownbreda,
Wet wi' dew in the eves o' June.

'Tis pleasant tae saunter the clachan thro'
When day sinks mellow o'er Dubhais hill,
And feel their fragrance sae softly breathing
Frae croft and causey and window-sill.

O, brave are the haughs o' Baile-liosan,
And brave are the halds o' green Magh-luan;
But braver the hames o' Newtownbreda,
Twined about wi' the pinks o' June.

And just as the face is sae kindly withouten,
The heart within is as guid as gold –
Wi' new fair ballants and merry music,
And cracks cam' down frae the days of old.

'Tis pretty tae be in Baile-liosan,
'Tis pretty tae be in green Magh-luan;
'Tis prettier tae be in Newtownbreda,
Beeking under the eaves in June.
The cummers are out wi' their knitting and spinning,
The thrush sings frae his crib on the wa',
And o'er the white road the clachan caddies
Play at their marlies and goaling-ba'.

JOSEPH CAMPBELL, *The Mountainy Singer*, 1909

I T WAS ON A SUMMER DAY, a day of brisk breezes with little sun, that
we took our way through Malone by the Lagan Valley, across Shaw's
Bridge, up the tree-lined hill-road to the village of Miltown, once famous
– or otherwise – for its 'Goat Inn', by Ballylesson, a little, sheltered
pleasant place of loud, swift streams, of green heights and wooded
hollows, by winding roads to the old graveyard of Drumbo.

By a steep road, arched over with spreading trees, we climbed the last
hill up to the 'Ridge of the Cow' (Drumbo), and saw above us the dark,
ivy-clad ruin of the old Round Tower standing fair on the hill-crest
against the blueness of the sky. Through the entrance gate of the
Presbyterian Meeting House, a square, bare, box-like place, we entered
the graveyard, and made our way, by grass-grown paths, to the Tower.
Cheek by jowl with it a vandal has built an out-house and a great ugly
barn with a corrugated iron roof, which, as if designed for the purpose,
completely shuts out, what would otherwise be, the matchless view of the
shelving hillsides, densely wooded, and, beyond the river, the high
ground rising into the Antrim hills, Colin, Divis, the Black Mountain,
and Mac Art's Fort.

CATHAL O'BYRNE, *As I Roved Out*, 1946

A T FIVE MINUTES AFTER THE ADVERTISED TIME the little green rail-bus
chugged, a trifle bumpily, out of Enniskillen's railway yards. I
noticed that a pane of glass in the side of the driver's cabin had been
mended by plugging it with a crumpled paper bag. It had been a big day
in Enniskillen, the day of the cattle fair; but already, one minute out on
our journey west, we were rattling along a sort of private green lane. At

the iron bridge over the Erne, I looked back and got a last glimpse of Enniskillen framed between tree trunks, rising like an Irish Venice from its lagoons, its skyline crowned by eighteenth-century cupolas and that north-western equivalent to Nelson's Pillar, the Lowry Cole monument.

Soon there were no cupolas or monuments. We were out in a wild dark stretch of Fermanagh, with enormous vistas of untidy sky and vast black plains that had once been forest. It's true there was a station called Florencecourt, calling up visions of a justly famous Georgian mansion. But nobody got on or off at Florencecourt, and there wasn't a pillared portico in sight – nothing but untidy sky and far-spreading black plain. This was western Ulster in the act of becoming western Ireland.

The transformation accelerated with every mile along the shore of Lough Macnean. The view across the lough was infinitely sad, infinitely subtle, a symphony in black and silver, with the black mass of Cuilcagh mountain (beyond which the Shannon rises) as back-drop across the water. We traversed a narrow neck of land between the upper and the lower loughs; halted at a solid-looking station of grey stone where the platform name-boards dramatically announced 'Belcoo and Black Lion'. Then, rattling and vibrating, we began to climb, leaving on the right a long blue arm of Upper Lough Macnean surrounded by fresh green belts of afforestation, and so on into the desolate upland emptiness of Glenfarne and the grey-stone station of the same name.

At Glenfarne a Customs man climbed into the rail-bus, took a good look at all three of us, then climbed out again. We chugged on deeper into the Irish Republic and the lonely heart of Leitrim.

DENIS IRELAND, *From the Jungle of Belfast*, 1973

I AM PRETTY SURE THAT THERE IS NOT in the Kingdom a city at once a great seaport and a great manufacturing centre, so favourably placed as regards natural scenery. The approach to it by sea on a summer morning is very lovely. The Lough is sufficiently narrow to allow of many interesting details of the heights on each side being seen in the sunlight. There are miles of dark cliffs on both coasts at the entrance, and an occasional stretch of beach, and, above all are irregular slopes of green, well wooded in places, and dotted with villas in the centre of their gardens. The little town of Bangor, which I recollect as a fishing village, has now spread itself all along the low cliffs to the west of its bay. Just beyond this point is another village of beautiful houses at the water's edge, called Helen's Bay ...

On the same coast one passes the districts of Craigavad, Craig Owen, Cultra and Marino – all tracts of villas and gardens – until Holywood is reached, and one sees a charming little town backed by timbered hills. This is where the channel of the estuary of the Lagan narrows, passing scores of villas at Strandtown on the one side and Greencastle on the other. Here the majestic scene of the Cave Hill asserts itself beyond the artificial banks where the shipbuilding yards of Messrs Workman and Clark and Harland and Wolff make themselves very audible. The Cave Hill dominates Belfast pretty much as Table Mountain dominates Cape Town.

F. FRANKFORT MOORE, The Truth About Ulster, 1914

THE LECTURER THEN TURNED ON ME and wanted to know the date of the Norman Conquest.

Wasn't I proud to be able to answer ten sixty-six and I saw how well Beth was pleased. Noble and Hugh slipped out of the room and I wondered dare I do that too, for you never knew what questions these strange lecturers would ask, maybe the capital of some heathen country at the other side of the world, or how many wives a certain King of England had – but I knew that one.

These English lecturers were too full of curiosity, and indeed they didn't know much themselves. Even Papa tried them with our nice easy names of places, Strughenaugher, Mullaghadonaghy, Ballyslagluttery, and as for 'The Moyntiaghs', our big Ulster bog, not one of them could say it at all.

LYDIA M. FOSTER, Manse Larks, 1936

from A SEVERED HEAD

Yet even English in these airts
Took a lawless turn, as who
Would not stroll by Bloody Brae
To Black Lough, or guddle trout
In a stream called the Routing Burn?

Or rest a while on Crooked Bridge
Up the path to Crow Hill;
Straight by Ania's Cove to Spur Royal,
Then round by Duck Island
To Green Mount and New Town Civil?

A last look over the dark ravine
Where that red-tufted rebel,
The Todd, out-leaped the pack;
Turning home by Favour Royal
And the forests of Dourless Black.

And what of stone-age Sess Kill Green
Tullycorker and Tullyglush?
Names twining braid Scots and Irish,
Like Fall Brae, springing native
As a whitethorn bush?

A high, stony place – bogstreams,
Not milk and honey – but our own:
From the Glen of the Hazels
To the Golden Stone may be
The longest journey
                    I have ever gone.

JOHN MONTAGUE, *The Rough Field*, 1972

OWEN:

Now. Where have we got to? Yes – the point where that stream enters the sea – that tiny little beach there. George!

YOLLAND:

Yes. I'm listening. What do you call it? Say the Irish name again?

OWEN:

Bun na hAbhann.

YOLLAND:

Again.

OWEN:

Bun na hAbhann.

YOLLAND:

Bun na hAbhann.

OWEN:

That's terrible, George.

YOLLAND:

I know. I'm sorry. Say it again.

OWEN:

Bun na hAbhann.

YOLLAND:

Bun na hAbhann.

OWEN:

That's better. Bun is the Irish word for bottom. And Abha means river. So it's literally the mouth of the river.

YOLLAND:

Let's leave it alone. There's no English equivalent for a sound like that.

OWEN:

What is it called in the church registry?

(*Only now does* YOLLAND *open his eyes.*)

YOLLAND:

Let's see ... Banowen.

OWEN:

That's wrong. (*Consults text.*) The list of freeholders calls it Owenmore – that's completely wrong: Owenmore's the big river at the west end of the parish. (*Another text.*) And in the grand jury lists it's called – God! – Binhone! – wherever they got that. I suppose we could Anglicize it to Bunowen; but somehow that's neither fish nor flesh.

(YOLLAND *closes his eyes again.*)

YOLLAND:

I give up.

OWEN:

(*At map*) Back to first principles. What are we trying to do?

YOLLAND:

Good question.

OWEN:

We are trying to denominate and at the same time describe that tiny area of soggy, rocky, sandy ground where that little stream enters the sea, an area known locally as Bun na hAbhann ... Burnfoot! What about Burnfoot?

YOLLAND:

(*Indifferently*) Good, Roland. Burnfoot's good.

BRIAN FRIEL, *Translations*, 1981

THERE ARE SOME VERY STRANGE NAMES on ordnance survey maps, and some of them are almost certainly incorrect, having arisen from a misapprehension as to what the natives called a place. There is one example near Belfast – or it may not be an example, but I rather like to think it is. There is a hill near Squire's Hill, called McIlwhan's. I never met anybody with such a name as McIlwhan, and, though I have been given a learned explanation of how a name could have been twisted into that form, I rather prefer to imagine a simple little scene, enacted a century ago, when the ordnance survey was being made. I imagine a courteous ordnance survey officer stopping one of the innocent natives of the district, pointing to the hill and saying: 'Now, my good man, could you tell me what that is up there?' And then I can imagine the native scratching his head and saying: 'I doubt there's just muckle whans up there, sir,' meaning that there was just a lot of whins there. And then I picture the ordnance survey officer ingeniously naming the hill

McIlwhan's Hill. How could he do otherwise, having received assurances
from a reliable native that that was what it was called? And in County
Down there are all those mysterious names on the map, So-and-So's
Loan Ends. Presumably they originated from So-and-So's Loaning.

HUGH SHEARMAN, *Ulster*, 1949

A NEW SONG

I met a girl from Derrygarve
And the name, a lost potent musk,
Recalled the river's long swerve,
A kingfisher's blue bolt at dusk

And stepping stones like black molars
Sunk in the ford, the shifty glaze
Of the whirlpool, the Moyola
Pleasuring beneath alder trees.

And Derrygarve, I thought, was just,
Vanished music, twilit water,
A smooth libation of the past
Poured by this chance vestal daughter.

But now our river tongues must rise
From licking deep in native haunts
To flood, with vowelling embrace,
Demesnes staked out in consonants.

And Castledawson we'll enlist
And Upperlands, each planted bawn –
Like bleaching-greens resumed by grass –
A vocable, as rath and bullaun.

SEAMUS HEANEY, *Wintering Out*, 1972

THE WATER HERE WAS IN FACT another arm of the sea, though longer
and more lonely than Belfast Lough. Norse invaders originally gave
this long stretch of water its name, Strang Fiord or the Violent Fjord.
Through the lough's extremely narrow neck, opening to the sea,
hundreds of millions of tons of ocean rush up and down with every tide.

Earlier when I had reached the upper end of Strangford Lough the tide
was out. And long before I could see, I could hear the cries of the

wildfowl delighting in the sloblands and rocks of the shallows. The lough is said to have three-hundred-and-sixty-five islands, great and small. Few of the islands were farmed and most were given over as haunts for Arctic tern and ringed plover, red-breasted merganser, shelduck and oyster catcher. Currents round the neck flow up to eight knots but this only adds to the sport of seals and porpoises.

It pleased me to know that at least one place in Northern Ireland had retained its original Norse name, for not many were left bearing traces of the Scandinavian invaders.

ROBIN BRYANS, Ulster: A Journey Through the Six Counties, 1964

A SURVEY OF THE SEE LANDS OF ARMAGH made in the year 1703 provides us with a detailed account of apple culture on farms held by the Archbishop's tenants. In Ballygowanoughtra, for instance (a townland in Drumcree Parish now known as Ballynagowan), there was, to the west of John Atkinson's farmstead, a good orchard of his own planting and east of the house and stable a very pretty young orchard of above one hundred trees planted by him since the late wars, and to the north of the house a very pretty young nursery of crab-trees. His brother, Edward, in the same townland, had two orchards, one old and the other young. The reference to the 'late wars' is somewhat puzzling as trees planted following the Civil War of 1641–42 could not be very well described as 'young' in 1703. We must, therefore, assume that the orchards in question arose after the Revolution of 1688–90. At that time and according to the same authority, there were orchards attached to farms in 'Cavan, Ballytrue, Ballyossone, Money, Ballywilly, Ballyhagan, Roghan, Killmakente,' etc. in O'Neiland Barony, and at various places around Armagh city such as 'Drumsallan, Ballyrath, Farmacaffley, Dromard, Ballyrea, Tyra, Cabragh, Tyross, Ballybroll, Drumbee, Balliteren, Knockacone, Ballyherclan,' etc.

T.G.F. PATERSON, Harvest Home: A Selection of the Writings of T.G.F.P., 1975

ULSTER NAMES

I take my stand by the Ulster names,
each clean hard name like a weathered stone;
Tyrella, Rostrevor, are flickering flames:
the names I mean are the Moy, Malone,
Strabane, Slieve Gullion and Portglenone.

Even suppose that each name were freed
from legend's ivy and history's moss,
there'd be music still in, say, Carrick-a-rede,
though men forget it's the rock across
the track of the salmon from Islay and Ross.

The names of a land show the heart of the race;
they move on the tongue like the lilt of a song.
You say the name and I see the place —
Drumbo, Dungannon, Annalong.
Barony, townland, we cannot go wrong.

You say Armagh, and I see the hill
with the two tall spires or the square low tower;
the faith of Patrick is with us still;
his blessing falls in a moonlit hour,
when the apple orchards are all in flower.

You whisper Derry. Beyond the walls
and the crashing boom and the coiling smoke,
I follow that freedom which beckons and calls
to Colmcille, tall in his grove of oak,
raising his voice for the rhyming folk.

County by county you number them over;
Tyrone, Fermanagh ... I stand by a lake,
and the bubbling curlew, the whistling plover
call over the whins in the chill daybreak
as the hills and the waters the first light take.

Let Down be famous for care-tilled earth,
for the little green hills and the harsh grey peaks,
the rocky bed of the Lagan's birth,
the white farm fat in the August weeks.
There's one more county my pride still seeks.

You give it the name and my quick thoughts run
through the narrow towns with their wheels of trade,
to Glenballyemon, Glenaan, Glendun,
from Trostan down to the braes of Layde,
for there is the place where the pact was made.

But you have as good a right as I
to praise the place where your face is known,
for over us all is the selfsame sky;
the limestone's locked in the strength of the bone,
and who shall mock at the steadfast stone?

So it's Ballinamallard, it's Crossmaglen,
it's Aughnacloy, it's Donaghadee,
it's Magherafelt breeds the best of men,
I'll not deny it. But look for me
on the moss between Orra and Slievenanee.

POSTSCRIPT, 1984

Those verses surfaced thirty years ago
when time seemed edging to a better time,
most public voices tamed, those loud untamed
as seasonal as tawdry pantomime,
and over my companionable land
placenames still lilted like a childhood rime.

The years deceived; our unforgiving hearts,
by myth and old antipathies betrayed,
flared into sudden acts of violence
in daily shocking bulletins relayed,
and through our dark dream-clotted consciousness
hosted like banners in some black parade.

Now with compulsive resonance they toll:
Banbridge, Ballykelly, Darkley, Crossmaglen,
summoning pity, anger and despair,
by grief of kin, by hate of murderous men
till the whole tarnished map is stained and torn,
not to be read as pastoral again.

JOHN HEWITT, *Freehold and Other Poems*, 1986

THE STEWARDESS CAME AND STACKED the empty meal trays, crowded them one on top of the other and pushed them into her trolley. Catherine thought of the geography of the places of death in her own country — it was a map which would not exist if women made the decisions — Cornmarket, Claudy, Teebane Crossroads, Six Mile Water, the Bogside, Greysteel, the Shankill Road, Long Kesh, Dublin, Darkley,

Enniskillen, Loughinisland, Armagh, Monaghan town. And of places of multiple deaths further to the east – Birmingham, Guildford, Warrington. It was like the Litany. Horse Guards' Parade. Pray for us. Tower of London. Pray for us. Alone or with others. For the dead it didn't matter how many companions they had or where it happened.

BERNARD MacLAVERTY, Grace Notes, 1997

I Give You Fuchsia Hedges
and Whitewashed Walls

... I give you fuchsia hedges and whitewashed walls.

I give you the smell of Norman stone, the squelch
Of bog beneath your boots, the red bog-grass,
The vivid chequer of the Antrim hills, the trough of dark
Golden water for the cart-horses, the brass
Belt of serene sun upon the lough ...

LOUIS MacNEICE, *from* 'Train to Dublin'

THERE IS MUCH THAT THE STRANGER will see different in Ulster. The smallness of the farms, for example, with their tiny fields that make the country look like a jigsaw, will remind him that this is a land of 'great passions and little room'. And the lovely careless growing hedges, so different from the clipped hedges of England, are not mere signs of men's neglect. They represent something of exuberance in the Ulsterman's character. Although he is a hard worker, he dislikes a way of life that is too tied and tidy. He likes life to have loose edges and elbow-room. More important to him than neat working-principles or schedules are his relations with people. You will find this 'personal' emphasis over and over again in Ulster. Even the railway trains will wait for you, and your fellow-travellers will want to know who you are and where you are going.

W.R. RODGERS, *The Ulstermen and Their Country*, 1952

IN NUPTIAL FLIGHT THE BIRDS SWEEP in a wide arc, alternately flapping and gliding with tail expanded and looking very fine. I have noticed that certain places are favoured for these posturings just as Birds of Paradise regularly resort to particular trees. One such spot is where the cliffs and steep screes of the mountain behind my home give place to those rounded slopes diversified into a patchwork of small fields which are so characteristic of Northern Ireland. A stony lane or 'loanin' rambles between tall thorn hedges towards the sea, passing a church which stands, backed by trees, on a little eminence, and looks out over the sunny lough to the green and purple hills of Down. The magpies can be heard in earnest conclave between the singing of the canticles. It is the most beautifully situated church I know. The churchyard, with its bees and birds and flowering shrubs is the kind of place to which good bird-watchers should be allowed to go when their end is near; there, while rapt in all the scents and sounds of a summery noon to be translated to the Celestial Meadows whose warden is Saint Francis.

EDWARD ALLWORTHY ARMSTRONG, *Birds of the Grey Wind*, 1940

MY JOY IN THESE TRIPS ON THE LAKE did not come from fishing, but from merely sailing in and out of the creeks and inlets. Fermanagh spread out before me in a jigsaw of islands. At sundown, the lakes became millponds of shining ormolu-varnish, enriched with sparkling inlaid patterns where the engine frothed the wake behind us. We touched at many of the islands, pulling our small boat just out of the water, while we went to explore the tangled forests, crammed with oak and aspen, spindle-tree and willow, blackthorn and guelder-rose. There was never an outing when the women did not alight first and make off in a group for the bushes. We knew what they went for, yet they brazenly returned declaring that they had been looking for wild flowers.

They had not to look far. Nobody inhabited these small humps of land, each flung on the water's surface like a brilliant arras woven with purple loosestrife and marigold-goldins, strings of sovereigns and the majestic standard-bearers of golden-rod. A sweet scent suffused from hemp agrimony, an irresistible lure to the gaudiest butterflies, who fluttered as though drawn by magnets to the raspberry-and-cream groves. There were reed labyrinths where the black scoter went to breed, and desert island shores turned by sandpipers into excited playgrounds. Birdsong sounded like the music of paradise and wings whirred on glissando flights from sunshine to shadow, in and out of the woods. From surrounding drumlins the wood-pigeon let fall his billing notes, and as we made for home, the throbbing of the nightjar filled the air with a mechanical, insistent purr.

ROBERT HARBINSON, *Song of Erne*, 1960

At DERRY I CHANGED TRAINS. The Guildhall clock boomed, disturbing the pigeons; the train slid out through leafy suburbs, following the banks of the Foyle. Towers and pinnacles withdrew suddenly behind a screen of fresh springing green; the darkness of the Sperrins reared itself against the evening sky; we roared and rattled between the cliffs and the sea, past Bellarena and its wooded mountain, the waterfalls of Downhill, and the long sandy tongue of Magilligan. Beyond the entrance waters of the Foyle lay the hills of Inishowen, the land where time stood still. Atlantic breakers crashed, apparently noiselessly, only a few yards from the carriage window. The thought of London depressed me. I watched ghostly breakers, their crests gleaming whiter in the gathering dusk. *Adieu to Bellashanny and the winding banks of Erne.* The light on Inishowen Head winked suddenly, reassuringly, against the blackness of the hills behind.

DENIS IRELAND, *Statues Round the City Hall*, 1939

THE HILL

In the heather–dips on either side
   The fallen winds persist;
The big grey bird with the long neb
   Wheels and cries in the mist;
The moorland river tumbles down
   With its black peaty load;
The moorfowl and the darting snipe
   Cry themselves over the road;
In the swirling mist the sheepfolds cling
   To the dark face of the hill;
The wild duck skreaks behind the rath
   And drops into a rill.

JOHN LYLE DONAGHY, *The Flute Over the Valley: Antrim Song*, 1931

Among THE BLAEBERRY BUSHES the Irish red grouse, now rare, has its haunts, feeding on the blue-black berries which also attract picnic parties and were once the object of special 'gatherings' on the first Sunday in August. At lower elevations the bracken likes well-drained slopes and soils of some depth, and it is more typical of the slates than the granites. In general ... the slates carry a more varied flora than the granites, and have been cultivated in the past to greater elevations. Bracken flourishes in fields that have gone out of cultivation, but it is nowhere so common in the Mournes as on hillsides in Scotland and Wales. It competes most successfully with the whins on lower slopes having some protection from the winds.

'Alien' shrubs which flourish around the mountains are the rhododendron, the laurel and the fuchsia. The rhododendron (popularly 'rosydandron') makes dense thickets in the Newcastle demesne and in the cleared woods at Kinnahalla. Luxuriant and fantastic growths of laurel may be seen in several old woods, notably at Burrenwood near Castlewellan. Here the 'cottage,' a small seventeenth-century planter's house, has recently lost its thatch, but it makes a brilliant picture in June, ringed around with bluebells and tangled trees. The fuchsia is a familiar roadside hedge-plant everywhere along the coast and is nowhere more abundant than at the Bloody Bridge, which might have been named from its spilled blossoms. Only on inaccessible cliff ledges where even the mountain sheep cannot nibble does one see a flora that is not affected in some way by man and his animals. There the ferns and mosses have their habitats, and the woodrush grows with surprising vigour on tiny ledges that seem from below to be almost bare granite. It is in such places, especially on north-facing slopes, that the venturesome explorer may hope to find rare plants.

E. ESTYN EVANS, *Mourne Country*, 1951

from MOURNE

Mourne country. Under
    Chimney Rock,
they cut the granite
    block by block.

Mourne country. When
    a neighbour dies
he chops the mountains
    down to size.

Mourne country. Half a
    parish sent
its contours for a
    monument.

Mourne country. On the
    broken bones
we pile the hills for
    symbol stones.

Mourne country. Daily,
　chink by chink,
the tombs rise and the
　mountains sink.

Mourne country. Will
　we soldier on
till all our Commedaghs
　are gone?

Mourne country. We
　have graves to make.
How many Binnians
　will it take?

KERRY CARSON, A Rage for Order, 1995

AFTER A DOWNPOUR, the scarps and inclines of the Silent Valley scintillate with water. Waterfalling veins pulse down the mountainsides, with cloudy wisps blown off them. Pebbles of smoky quartz shine rapidly in screes and cascades. Stones chatter and shiver; in the distance, you can almost hear the clink and tinkle of the ancient granite men about their work. Granite for setts, granite for gravestones; granite for dolmens, plinths and mass-rocks. Granite for the ubiquitous bullauns, thought to be basin-stones for grinding barley, but now venerated everywhere as holy wells, for the water they contained had many virtues, especially for healing warts. Embedded in overgrown haggards or churchyards, it seemed the bullauns had put roots back into the rock from whence they were hewn, and were metamorphosed into conduits for a subterranean realm of water.

CIARAN CARSON, Fishing for Amber, 1999

HERE I AM IN THIS UP-TO-DATE HOUSE [in County Monaghan], looking over the improved cattle and improved poultry that my friends are raising, and walking in the sunny fields. But autumn has come. The signs that its coming makes in this particular countryside are here, they suggest verses to me, and I write them down:
　　Black tassels, black tassels upon the green tree,
　　The high tree, the ash-tree that tops the round hill –
　　Black tassels, black tassels, and they are the crows.

Red streamers, red streamers along the hedgeways,   ·
Where roadways are claubered and stubbles are brown –
Red streamers, red streamers, and they are the haws.

A lone song, a high song that comes from the hedge,
That tries for a round and that falls on the turn –
A short song, the robin's, and Samhain's at hand.

PADRAIC COLUM, Cross Roads in Ireland, 1930

I WAS DELIGHTED WITH MY EVENING'S WALK. I met crowds of people returning homewards, their books on their shoulders, and women and children by their side. They all bade me good e'en as they passed. Several were smoking. I was not sorry to see this. Men will intoxicate themselves some way or other, and smoking is a better way than drinking. I do not think I met a single wheelcar between Lisburn and Belfast. The vehicles for the conveyance of goods were all waggons and carts. Every step, indeed, I advanced, I felt more forcibly I was in the neighbourhood of a great town. Had it not been for the lofty ridge of mountain on my left hand, which seemed to move along with and accompany me, I should have thought myself in the environs of London. The country was in the highest state of cultivation – it looked like one continued garden, shadowed with trees, interspersed with thickets, and neat white-washed houses, smiling in beauty, scented with fragrance, thrilling with harmony, delightful to the eye, ear, and smell.

JOHN GAMBLE, A View of Society and Manners in the North of Ireland, 1813

AUNT LAETITIA JOINED IN ONE OUTDOOR AMUSEMENT, indeed the only pleasure outing she organised in the year. In late Spring, she held her bluebell picnic. At the dawning of a sure-to-be-beautiful day, she was up preparing sandwiches to be packed in baskets along with mugs, tea, milk, sugar and the teapot. With the other children carrying the baskets and Frederick the tea kettle, they all set off as soon as the luncheon was over, to walk the four or five miles uphill to the Sheep Lair at Ballyvoy. There they knew they would see one of the magnificent sights of Spring, the massed blue carpet spreading, shadowy and scented, under the slim trees on the hillock, while behind them, beyond the richly-patterned Six-Mile-Valley, lay the azure crests of Ben Madigan's greater family of hills. The bluebells were incredibly beautiful, but while all this magnificence touched a responsive chord in the children's hearts, it was none-the-less but a short while until Frederick started sidling off to Mrs Walker's little whitewashed cottage by the holly tree with a request to 'boil the kettle, please'. And soon the clattering of mugs and the chattering of children had attracted every sheep and frightened every hare and bird for half a mile around.

FLORENCE MARY McDOWELL, *Other Days Around Me*, 1966

THE DIVISION BETWEEN THIS FIELD and the portion of the farm which ran down the other side of the hill was a clay bank upon which yellow-blossomed whins grew. Flinging his jacket across the fence he walked back a few steps and took a race to the fence to see if he could leap it. His second love had always been athletics and on summer mornings he was usually to be seen running in his stockinged feet round the home farm, over hedges and drains and palings.

He leaped on to the fence among the whins and found himself standing above the world of Drumnay and Miskin and looking far into the east where the dark fields of Cavan fanned out through a gap in the hills into the green fertile plains of Louth.

The rain had stopped and the sun was coming out and the bees and stinging clags were coming alive again.

PATRICK KAVANAGH, *Tarry Flynn*, 1948

THE BOOLEYS

Crackling on burnt whin, springing over moss,
stopping to search our memories for the names
of little unfamiliar flowers, we sought,
over the rough-grassed hillside in the warmth
of a June morning, for the twin earth-circles
the map shewed for this townland, Ballyvooley.

Once a brown mare led off her tall fawn foal,
and grazing cattle lurched across our path,
larks singing in the light, and sinister rooks
plotting in heather what to do in corn;
and in one place a pause to chart our steps
where cannavaun shook out its warning tufts.

Then suddenly we found our whin-bright mounds,
small neat earth-circles, each a lake of rushes,
where centuries ago the young folk came

to pasture their scragged cattle all the summer
on lush warm slopes above the growing corn
where the old people yawned for their return.

I thought, and surely you thought, somehow these
laboriously raised, forgotten rings
were richer than the lichened walls of castles,
held cleaner memories than those of kings
and their blood-sodden tapestries of guilt,
and were unhaunted places, full of blessing.

JOHN HEWITT, *The Day of the Corncrake: Poems of the Nine Glens*, 1969

ANOTHER SEASONAL SMELL OF DISTINCTION is the Smell of the Blooming Whin. For the enlightenment of the Englisher, be it said that the whin is his gorse. But the smell of the Antrim whin is not the smell of his gorse. In the fat lowlands one may find lazy, undemonstrative whin in the hedgerows, hanging out odd patches of pale, lemon-coloured bloom, and if one goes near enough and sniffs vigorously, a pale odour will enter the nostrils. But this anaemic scent is to the rich perfume of the proper whin, as water is to wine. Sweet are the uses of adversity to the whin. Fighting for life on poor, rocky hill-slopes near Cushendall, and breathing the sea air, it clothes itself in spring and early summer in rich deep gold, wraps every member round and round, and down to the ground. And here there is no need to bend over the plant and sniff for an odour – the delicious smell is cast, open-handedly, on the breeze, making the air of these rough scaurs as sweet as that on the box-covered slopes of the Pyrenees. It is a hot smell, a smell of sunlight, a tonic smell, heather and violets, dashed with burnt cinnamon, on a ground-odour of its own – incomparable, indescribable. The story of Linnaeus kneeling by the whin, and thanking God for its creation, may be apocryphal – the whin deserves that it should be true.

JOHN STEVENSON, *A Boy in the Country*, 1912

ARDGLASS TOWN

The sun is hid in Heaven,
  The fog floats thick and brown,
I walk the streets of London
  And think on Ardglass town.

About the point of Fennick
  The snowy breakers roll,
And green they shine in patterned squares,
  The fields above Ardtole.

Oh, there by many a loaning,
  Past farms that I could name.
Thro' Sheeplands to Gun Island,
  The whins are all aflame.

And my heart bleeds within me
  To think of times I had,
Walking with my sweetheart
  The green road to Ringfad.

RICHARD ROWLEY, Selected Poems, 1931

IN THE AFTERNOON WE DROVE through County Down. Ballynahinch,
Dundrum, Newcastle – drab rows of houses of dun-coloured or slate-
coloured stucco. To tea with two elderly ladies under the Mourne
Mountains. The spring had pampered their garden. All the trees were
blossoming six weeks early – syringa, rhododendron, cherry. Enormous
rooks exploded out of the tree-tops. Of six adults at tea three were deaf.
   We drove back with the sun sinking on our left. The country was
extravagant with gorse as if a child had got loose with the paints. Gorse
all over the fields and sprawling on the dykes. Rough stone walls dodged
their way up the mountain. A hillside under plough was deeply fluted
with shadows. The pairs of fat white gateposts with cone tops showed the
small fields of small farmers. Brown hens ran through a field, their combs
like moving poppies. Then Belfast again, swans on the Lagan, and home
towards the Black Mountain, now a battleship grey, by a road called
Chlorine Gardens.

LOUIS MacNEICE, Zoo, 1938

FROM THE MOUNTAIN OUR LAKE had the sinister look of a flood that
had submerged a forest region; very often, indeed, it was a true flood,
creeping up under everlasting rains to the foot of the hills, destroying
crops and fuel, making roads impassable, leaving a precious deposit on
meadowland that made the haycocks thicker when summer came again.
If, however, in more normal times, you climbed the Rock, standing
prominent and nearby on the south side, the lake had a kindlier aspect;
placid, irregular, the shores fringed with reeds and woods, rounded hills

and little farms, at intervals fine residences of the gentry, a church, a tower, dim mountains far north and the peat smoke of a town, yachts tacking about, a ferry-boat crossing, someone fishing in a cot near the bulrushes for bream or perch, and between the shores many green islands. It is said that these islands number three hundred and sixty-five in all; without doubt I counted last year more than twenty below the Rock, a few large enough for habitation, any one of them offering verdant hiding from the police to adventurers risking a poteen still.

SHAN BULLOCK, *After Sixty Years*, 1931

KATE WHISKEY

I kept the whiskey in the caves
Well up in the hills. It was never safe
To have it about the houses,
Always crawling with excise and police.

The people could still get the stuff
As often as they liked, and easily enough,
For those were still the days
When making whiskey broke nobody's laws.

Selling it, though, was as grave
An offence as teaching those people to love,
Fathers and husbands and boys.

Water rushed through my caves with a noise
To tell me how I should always live.
I sold the water, the whiskey I would give.

PAUL MULDOON, *New Weather*, 1973

THE BARONY OF ANTRIM ... contains the village of Kells, [celebrated] for its neatness, and fine white-thorn hedges, and the village of Connor which gives name to the see, a very poor place indeed. Broughshane to the north, on the river Braid, has about 100 houses, though few very good ones. Near it is Tullymore lodge, well situated above the town, on a branch of the same river. To the east lie the ruins of the ancient church of Skerries; this parish, in old accounts of the diocese of Connor, was called *Vera Deseria*.

Doagh lies to the north-east of Antrim, near the Six-mile water, and contains about 30 houses. In this village is a book-club, furnished with many valuable works, and with globes, &c.; and it is said that, since its establishment, the barbarous practice of cock-fighting has been entirely given up in the neighbourhood. Close to it is Fisherwick lodge, a hunting seat belonging to the Marquis of Donegall; the building itself which is very handsome, and the plantations have much improved and enlivened the look of this well placed hamlet, which has, in addition, a good inn.

THE REVEREND JOHN DUBOURDIEU, *Statistical Survey of the County of Antrim*, 1812

from THE THATCHER

He turned and watched the whole long glen
And I went with him watching.
Our eyes could strip the slates away
And I could see him thatching.

He'd lie up there the summer's day,
His wise hands working over
The homely bundled oaten straw
That made the golden cover.

His small fork tucked the handfuls in,
Like little oat sheaves sleeping.
He'd guard them sweetly, safely, with
The sallies he'd been steeping.

And winds might blow and rain might fall,
His roof was warm and tight,
A benediction in the day,
A blessing in the night.

'The slates,' he said, 'are useful things
But doleful to the view,
The glen without the thatch is not
The glen my boyhood knew.

I'd like to see the sunlight slant
Again on golden gables,
For the slates are cold as tombstones.
But the straw was warm as cradles ...'

SIOBHÁN NÍ LUAIN, *The Sally Patch*, 1971

THERE WERE BITS OF LEVEL ROAD which they walked sedately hand in hand, and steep little gusts of hill which they raced up for the fun of the thing. Sometimes they stood and looked back at the many coloured hills across the valley, and drank in great draughts of air which even on that June afternoon had the cold sweetness of the north country and the hills in it. On their left, Belfast lay at the foot of the mountains hidden in blue-grey smoke. They saw the spires of churches and mill chimneys rising through it, and the funnels of ships in the great shipyards, and they heard the low, musical hum of the city and the lark's song overhead.

Down below them in one of the loveliest valleys in Ulster were farmhouses set in orchards and lawns, and neat little cottages and wooded slopes; and green cornfields and grasslands, and meadows filled with ripening hay. A tiny line of chimneys down there meant Gape Row. Behind it on the hill – for the valley had little hills and dents of its own – they saw the square, dark grey tower of the church, and in the churchyard the dusky yews.

Half-way up the hill they looked back and saw Slieve Donard peer over the shoulder of the Castlereagh hills inquiringly, and at the summit, the long, blue range of the Mourne Mountains, huddled and linked together, came suddenly into view. They walked on until the road began to slip down suddenly in front of them. Then they turned into a field and sat down among heather and rocks, with Belfast Lough sparkling in the sunshine below them, and the mountains beyond it covered with delicious shadows and shadow-dimples. They could see the coastline stretch away to Blackhead. It was here the great ships came and went to the far ends of the earth. At their feet Holywood was tucked cosily under the hill.

'Do you see thon big house thonder among the trees?' said Johnny, 'that's where you and me will live when we get rich. We'll have a butler and a coachman and a motor car, and lashins and lavins of everything! And you'll have a woman to redd your hair every mornin' in life.'

'The dear forbid!' returned Ann fervently. 'I'd as lief redd it myself. If you're goin' to live in a house like that you'll have to marry somebody else.'

AGNES ROMILLY WHITE, *Gape Row*, 1934

ALONG THE HEADLANDS OF THE GLENS, skirted by the coast road, there are still traces of the cairns or beacons on which fires were kindled to bring aid to the McDonald from his Scottish clansmen across the fifteen-mile channel, when that clan was beset by English from the south. Garron Point is one of the most beautiful of the headlands. On its wooded slopes stands the mansion of Garron Tower, once the home of Lord Vane Tempest. For some time it was an hotel, and now, I gather, it is to become a Roman Catholic public school on English lines. Near this point is 'Madman's Window', a crevice where the rock forms a natural arch overlooking the sea. It got its name from a maniac who, more than a century ago, from this spot hurled himself to his death in the stormy waters below.

Glenariff is probably the most famous of the Antrim glens. Lurigedan, a flat-topped table mountain, forms its northern side. I never can rid myself of the idea that this mountain is the coffin lid of a giant lying in state. The black drapery of its basaltic cliffs falls in awesome solemnity, but in the patchwork of its lower slopes, with the song of the harvester and tossing of yellow hay on pitchforks, it is genial and human as most Ulster country is. Here the river Ariffe flows to the sea through a pretty wooded ravine with two waterfalls, the Ess-na-Crub and Ess-na-Largh. A third waterfall drops at the side of the road in a thin ice-cold ribbon of water. The glen opens out funnel-wise to Red Bay, with the town of Waterfoot on its shore. Beyond, across a narrow channel, stands the grey mass of Kintyre Peninsula in Scotland, its sides deeply furrowed with glistening watercourses, its white houses visible in Ireland on a clear day.

DENIS O'D. HANNA, *The Face of Ulster*, 1952

THOSE DAYS ... COME TO ME NOW faintly fragrant with what seems an old-world charm – they are like old letters one finds after long years hidden in a sachet.

I was conscious of that charm at the time: I was even trying to get it – with its lazy, unexacting familiarity and sociability – into my story; which was to contain, for that matter, everything I had ever loved.

There was to be room found for the little country churchyard near Ballinderry, which I had discovered hidden away among fields and lanes, the church itself a grey old ruin. It was a neglected spot, and nature had half reconquered the ground, making of it a wild tangle through which the battered gravestones peeped. Yet some of the inscriptions were still decipherable, though a dark lichen had covered most of them. I had chanced on this graveyard quite unexpectedly one morning when out for a walk. The season was spring, but a spell of summer seemed to have fallen on this place: the winds were hushed, the air mild and caressing. And as I sat on a sun-warmed, fallen headstone, I felt that I had wandered into the very heart of Peace. Thrushes and rooks and starlings flitted about the church tower, while directly in front of me was a mass of flaming crimson blossom, where a flowering currant had found a root-hold among the crumbling stones. I know not what there was about this place that so entranced me. It was a beauty that seemed mingled with innocence and simplicity; it had a definitely *moral* quality, which dropped deep down into my soul and made me feel good. I very seldom felt good.

I very seldom *was* good, though I loved goodness in other people. But as I sat in that churchyard all my restless thoughts and impulses sank away: I was like one of Wordsworth's little boys or little girls, and could have held a dialogue with the sage precisely in their manner had his mild old ghost come woolgathering by.

FORREST REID, *Apostate*, 1926

THE COUNTRY I GREW UP IN had everything to encourage a romantic bent, had indeed done so ever since I first looked at the unattainable Green Hills through the nursery window. For the reader who knows those parts it will be enough to say that my main haunt was the Holywood Hills – the irregular polygon you would have described if you drew a line from Stormont to Comber, from Comber to Newtownards, from Newtownards to Scrabo, from Scrabo to Craigantlet, from Craigantlet to Holywood, and thence through Knocknagonney back to Stormont. How to suggest it all to a foreigner I hardly know.

First of all, it is by southern English standards bleak. The woods, for we have a few, are of small trees, rowan and birch and small fir. The fields are small, divided by ditches with ragged sea-nipped hedges on top of them. There is a good deal of gorse and many outcroppings of rock. Small abandoned quarries, filled with cold-looking water, are surprisingly numerous. There is nearly always a wind whistling through the grass. Where you see a man ploughing there will be gulls following him and pecking at the furrow. There are no field-paths or rights of way, but that does not matter for everyone knows you – or if they do not know you, they know your kind and understand that you will shut gates and not walk over crops. Mushrooms are still felt to be common property, like the air. The soil has none of the rich chocolate or ochre you find in parts of England: it is pale – what Dyson calls 'the ancient, bitter earth'. But the grass is soft, rich, and sweet, and the cottages, always white-washed and single storeyed and roofed with blue slate, light up the whole landscape.

Although these hills are not very high, the expanse seen from them is huge and various. Stand at the north-eastern extremity where the slopes go steeply down to Holywood. Beneath you is the whole expanse of the Lough. The Antrim coast twists sharply to the north and out of sight; green, and humble in comparison, Down curves away southward. Between the two the Lough merges into the sea, and if you look carefully on a good day you can even see Scotland, phantom-like on the horizon.

C.S. LEWIS, *Surprised By Joy*, 1955

CASTLE McGEE WAS A VILLAGE of about six cottages and as many bigger houses, a damp mouldy place that always impressed the children with a feeling of hunger and death. They rarely saw anybody about but the sexton, and he seemed to be perpetually at work digging graves in the churchyard. Then, too, there was no shop, and they had no friends in the village, and after the long walk from home, all that could be hoped for was a turnip out of a field. The church, surrounded by yew trees, stood in the middle of the village. The whitewashed walls of the parsonage blinked through an avenue of the same trees. Lull said the church was a Presbyterian meeting house, and on Sundays people came from miles around and sang psalms without any tunes, and the minister preached a sermon two hours long, and then everybody ate sandwiches in their pews, and the minister preached another sermon two hours long.

The children had often climbed up and looked in at the window; the cold, bare inside and the square boxes for pews had added to their dreary impressions of the place. If it had not been for the snowdrops they would never have gone near Castle McGee, but at the right time of year the graveyard was a white drift of these flowers, and the sexton had given them leave to pick as many as they pleased.

KATHLEEN FITZPATRICK, *The Weans at Rowallan*, 1905

AT CASTLEREAGH CHURCH

The sun goes out in pink and purple
late on a late Easter Sunday,
while at the gates a courting couple
begin to take their winding way
from church down towards Gilnahirk,
through whin-blossom and blackcurrant
along the hedgerows where they walk:
primroses, docken and wild mint.

My father in his travelling clothes,
my mother in her summer coat:
they feel the chill, and walk in close
to each other on a dropping road
past fields and gardens, weeks before
the clematis will risk a flower.

PETER McDONALD, *Pastorals*, 2004

IN ANNISH [INNISHOWEN] WE LIVED in a world which we realised as a floating planet, and in a beauty which we had been taught to appreciate, as greatly as small children are capable of enjoying spectacle. I at least enjoyed it by deliberate vision, for its sunrises and sunsets remain with me as pictures as well as a sense of glory and magnificence. I remember very well the aspect of the lough from the Oldcross road into Dunvil, a road over which I must have passed hundreds of times, especially in the spring or summer evenings. From above, the great lough, lying among its ring of mountains, would seem in the evening light like a long, low hill of water, following a different curve from the Atlantic beyond. This was because the sun, setting behind us, would cast its last greenish light on this side of the lough and leave the far side in a shadow, except where, if the wind was westerly, a silver line marked the surf. At this time, just before sunset, the sky would be full of a green radiance, fading gradually over the Derry mountains towards Belfast, into a dark blue-green transparency. As the car twisted in the winding road, we would come round to see the clouds behind us, like jagged coals in a grate, each surrounded by fire. But their centres, of course, were grey instead of black, and their fiery edges were as cold and lively with little sparks as phosphorescence on water.

The air itself, which was so dark, seemed made of this dark light, limpid like that coloured water which chemists show in their windows, and through it we could clearly see, when the car brought us round again, the iron piles of the Redman light, sometimes even the chimneys of Crowcliff on one side and Dunamara, a mile away to the south, against the livid sheen of the water.

At that time our legs could not reach to the footboard of an outside car. When it dipped outwards on a steep corner, our feet swung out until they seemed to hang over the gulf, and keeping tight hold of each other and Anketel and the side rails, we could see Dunvil straight beneath them, like a map cut out of black paper and stuck down upon a globe of foil. Even the separate boats in the harbour, as small as water beetles, could be seen at their moorings, or clustered round the pier like new-hatched beetles caught in the bubbles round a willow leaf.

JOYCE CARY, *A House of Children*, 1941

JUST AS VIVID AS HIS WHITEWASHED FARMHOUSE or his orange-and-blue country cart is the speech of the Ulsterman. He talks in a leisurely way, and he speaks the English language, of course. But it is an English which is salted and flavoured by the poetical idiom of the Celt. Here you will find, still in common use, rich and rare words or phrases which belonged to the England of four hundred years ago. Ulster people have the gift of imagination, instantly seeing 'likeness' in the most different things, and putting it into startlingly apt metaphor. I remember, one summer day, walking with an Ulster countrywoman through a wood when suddenly we came upon a planting of rhododendron, or as we say in Ulster, 'rosydandron.' The lovely heads of blossom had fallen, and the ground was covered with spilled petals. 'Look!' said the woman, 'Isn't the *dandruff* lovely?'

Again, you will find that the Ulsterman is fond of making imaginative puns and twists upon words. I once asked an old man to show me the way in an Ulster town. 'Go down yon street,' said he, pointing it out to me, 'and as you go down it you'll see *laughin'* on the right-hand of you, and *cryin'* on the left-hand.' On inquiry I found he was referring to two shops with their owners' names on them – *Laffin* and *Crihan*.

W.R. RODGERS, The Ulstermen and Their Country, 1952

SHEEPDOG TRIALS

Sheila and Roy and Mick: at Waterfoot
(Remember) they obeyed each whistled call,
Alert to each small signal; the pursuit
And herding in of sheep was gentle, wise
And moving to us watching at the edge.
They won again today the paper says.
And, reading, I remember hill and hedge
Shaggy with rain, the tea and sandwiches
Sold in a corner of the barking field:
And, in the foreground, you embracing him,
The champion, who, tolerant, would yield
Neither to hand nor word, but sat erect
In solitary pride; no, pride is wrong:
In ancient loneliness; yes, gazing out
Across the sheep-pens and the fuchsia hedge,
To where the hills are blurred by thickening cloud.

ROY McFADDEN, The Garryowen, 1971

THE SUN WAS SETTING, spilling gold light on the low western hills of Rathlin Island. A small boy walked jauntily along a hoof-printed path that wriggled between the folds of these hills and opened out into a crater-like valley on the cliff-top. Presently he stopped as if remembering something, then suddenly he left the path, and began running up one of the hills. When he reached the top he was out of breath and stood watching streaks of light radiating from golden-edged clouds, the scene reminding him of a picture he had seen of the Transfiguration. A short distance below him was the cow standing at the edge of a reedy lake. Colm ran down to meet her waving his stick in the air, and the wind rumbling in his ears made him give an exultant whoop which splashed upon the hills in a shower of echoed sound. A flock of gulls lying on the short grass near the lake rose up languidly, drifting like blown snowflakes over the rim of the cliff.

The lake faced west and was fed by a stream, the drainings of the semi-circling hills. One side was open to the winds from the sea and in winter a little outlet trickled over the cliffs making a black vein in their grey sides. The boy lifted stones and began throwing them into the lake, weaving web after web on its calm surface. Then he skimmed the water with flat stones, some of them jumping the surface and coming to rest on the other side. He was delighted with himself and after listening to his echoing shouts of delight he ran to fetch his cow. Gently he tapped her on the side and reluctantly she went towards the brown-mudded path that led out of the valley. The boy was about to throw a final stone into the lake when a bird flew low over his head, its neck a-strain, and its orange-coloured legs clear in the soft light. It was a wild duck. It circled the lake twice, thrice, coming lower each time and then with a nervous flapping of wings it skidded along the surface, its legs breaking the water into a series of silvery arcs. Its wings closed, it lit silently, gave a slight shiver, and began pecking indifferently at the water.

MICHAEL McLAVERTY, *from* 'The Wild Duck's Nest',
The Game Cock and Other Stories, 1949

BEYOND DEVENISH THE LAKE CONTINUES to widen, with islands, often densely wooded, of whale-backed form – for they are mounds of Glacial drift – stretching away in a long vista, and you will need more than a row-boat if you wish to go further, especially as the lake gets more and more open. The islands are interesting – some of them, especially about Ely Lodge, have been planted, others have been cleared of timber and are grazed, but many are occupied by dense native wood which has never been interfered with; these harbour a purely indigenous flora and fauna, and are consequently of great attraction to the naturalist, as they tell us what the countryside was like before ever man began to cut or burn down trees or to graze herds of cows and sheep, or to break up the land for tillage. The largest native trees are Oak and Ash, of which Oak is much the commoner; then come Birch, Alder, Aspen, Holly, Mountain-ash, Crab-apple, Hazel, Hawthorn, with bushes of Spindle-tree, Buckthorn, Guelder-rose, Blackthorn, and several willows; there is also a remarkably fine bramble, of which I do not know the name, with pinkish flowers two and a half inches across. Underneath the tree canopy a dense vegetation occupies the ground, largely of showy wild-flowers such as Primroses, Wood Anemones, and Wild Hyacinths, mixed with abundance of ferns. The stony shores have a different vegetation: they are more exposed, are liable to floods, and are more limy. Here are groves of Purple Loosestrife, Mint, Hemp-agrimony, Hare-bell, Golden Rod, and carpets of Creeping Jenny. Some of the plants of the shore grow extraordinarily luxuriantly – imagine a tuft of Milkwort bearing a hundred stems a foot high, crowned with deep-blue flowers, or Golden Rod like a torch up to four feet in height. The most delightful time on Lough Erne is May or early June, for then the trees are at their freshest, the wild-flowers are in full blow, and the bird population of the lake at its busiest.

ROBERT LLOYD PRAEGER, *The Way that I Went*, 1937

from DONEGAL MACRONIC

A stone's brooch of lichen, and the low flash
of a yellowhammer through sedgy thickets

flushing *buíóg*, the Murlin gabbling, glistening –
bank growth littered with a slough of trash.

Tormentil too, foam of gorsebuds in windbreaks,
blackbird notes: bay a windy conch, a brazen disc

darkening the Glen. And Ó Searcaigh's flag-iris, dewiness
beading the lost silences of the Western corncrake.

CHRIS AGEE, *First Light*, 2003

DONEGAL IS NOT ONLY ULSTER'S most beautiful county but many people consider it the finest scenery in Ireland. I would place only one county before it, namely Kerry. The beauty of Donegal leaves no room for debate. It is rugged and hard like the Scottish Highlands at their most awe-inspiring, and yet this hardness is redeemed by valleys and creeks of the ocean, dense with woods and sheltered from every wind that blows.

At the back strand near Port-na-blagh, the dying swell licks the lowest branches of the trees as they overhang the water. Here and at Marble Hill, and again at Sheephaven, the strands are yellow as ripe corn, unmarred by boulder or even pebble, flawless as a heap of wheat. Doe Castle has such a setting in a landlocked arm of the ocean. It stands in complete loneliness, the strands coming up to its weatherworn walls. One wonders why such a stronghold was built in such a place, which in medieval times must have been scarce worth defending, for in those days before tourist agencies no one realised the potentialities of Donegal.

DENIS O'D. HANNA, *The Face of Ulster*, 1952

PORTAFERRY, COUNTY DOWN. Today I rode from Belfast to Portaferry on a push bicycle, a splendid method of progression in that one can dismount, sit by the roadside, and spend hours looking back the way one has come. With a motorcar there is no looking back, whereas half the fun of progressing through life or anything else consists in orienting one's self with what has gone before; to tear blindly ahead is to lead only half a life, to go to the devil with all the other road hogs. And what a view there is today to look back at! A full tide has set the lough brimming with deep blue water; the green hummocks of the islands on the farther shore, with white farmhouses gleaming here and there in the sunshine, appear to be floating on the brimming tide; beyond them again, and apparently changing position as the road leads on, rises the dim blue outline of the Mournes. Backwards the road leads towards Belfast, smoking somewhere beyond the hills to the north-west, past Greyabbey and Mount Stewart, following the lough shore, with heavy woods crowding close to the water's edge. An attractive country, full of variety, with water, woods, islands, distant mountains, ploughed land, pasture land, and, close inshore, the surface of the lough white with wild swans.

DENIS IRELAND, *From The Irish Shore*, 1936

ONE DAY IN AUGUST

One day in August, going by bus to Annalong,
Past fields brown-pimpled with haycocks,
And whitewashed rectangular houses,
I tried – expatriate now – to overhear
The homely rhythms that my people use
As running murmur to a simple way of life.
Through their world's wilderness of tangled hate
I tried to see the obverse of the coins
That tinkle brash in every little till
And echo that intolerance I know too well.
Then came the answer on that August day:
If you would find the virtue of this place
Then search it out in tidy village streets

And in the narrow, stone-walled fields,
For there they build and work in quietness,
Far from the bigots' drumming rant
That stills the mind, that twists the heart.

ROBERT GREACEN, Young Mr Gibbon, 1979

IT WAS AFTER THIS THAT MRS CALDWELL went to visit her relations in England, accompanied by two of the children. It was in the summer, and Jane took Beth to the Castle Hill that morning to see the steamer, with her mother on board, go by. The sea was iridescent, like molten silver, the sky was high and cloudless, and where sea and sky met and mingled on the horizon it was impossible to determine. Numbers of steamers passed far out. They looked quite small, and Beth did not think there was room in any of them for her mother and brother and sister. They did not, therefore, interest her much, nor did the policeman who came and talked to Jane. But the Castle Hill, and the little winding path up which she had come, the green of the grass, the brambles, ferns, the ruined masonry against which she leant, the union of sea and sky and shore, the light, the colour, absorbed her, and drew her out of herself.

SARAH GRAND, The Beth Book, 1897

SUNRUSH
for Valerie Lynch

Ó Mhín na Craoibhe go Gort a' Choirce
tá an gleann seo órnite
tar éis maidin de sciúradh gréine. …

From Mín na Craoibhe to Gort a' Choirce
The glen gleams in a wash of gold
Scoured by the sun since morning.

Now the struggling wheezers come –
Sunday conquistadores –
Staking their share of the sun!

CATHAL Ó SEARCAIGH, translated by GABRIEL ROSENSTOCK,
An Bealach 'na Bhaile/Homecoming: Selected Poems, 1993

THE HAY NEEDS TO BE TURNED, with long wooden rakes with wooden teeth, or by large horse-drawn tumblers or swathe-turners, great mobile combs with curved bright steel teeth that turn the hay over and leave it in long neat rows. Then the rushing, all hands to help, to get it piled up before the next shower.

The memory, though, is of endless, shining summer, with blue skies, a blazing sun and not a cloud to be seen. Why, then, were we always praying for fine weather, and why is there an underlying memory of impending doom, as the clouds bank down over the Mournes or the mist swirls in cold from the sea, a sense of urgency and bustle to get it in before the rain comes and all is lost, the sense of triumph as the first large drops splatter the faces as the last cock is capped, or the feeling of dejection and loss as the bedraggled army retreats from a sodden field, leaving the hay to soak and rot unless the weather changes quickly?

The rush to get the hay safe involves raking with pitchforks or graips or rakes, or, for the children pressed into service, using the hands to roll the hay into tight balls which can then be kicked down towards the cocks which begin to dot the field in a geometric pattern. The dried stalks prick bare arms, and bare legs are scratched by thistles, but the excitement of the effort persists until broken by the luxury of strong tea brought out in kettles and drunk out of crockery cups with milk and sugar, and great hunks of soda bread, farls split down the middle and liberally spread with salty, yellow country butter, and drunk lying on a cock of new hay, or in the shade of a tree beside the ditch, along with the men who take out their pipes, scrape them clean with penknives, unwrap a plug of tobacco, slice it carefully, shred it and roll it between the palms, fill the bowl of the clay pipe carefully, push the tobacco in with the little finger and firm it with the thumb, before lighting up with a redhead match struck on the sole of the boot or against the underside of the thigh of a well-filled, tight-stretched pair of corduroy trousers, and then the relaxation of the smoke and the talk.

MAURICE HAYES, *Sweet Killough, Let Go Your Anchor*, 1994

ONE WHO IS INTIMATELY ACQUAINTED with the Roman Catholic portion of Ireland cannot fail to be struck by what he sees in the country around Belfast. For instance, in Protestant Antrim, even if one goes no farther than the well-known route from Belfast to Larne, one may realise what all Ireland would be if it were emancipated from the priestly spells. The Northern Counties Railway is essentially a northern institution, being entirely confined to the counties of Antrim and Derry. Although one of the smallest lines in Ireland, it is as well managed as the largest, and pays the highest dividends. Its terminus at Belfast reminds one of an English railway station; well-designed, altogether bright, and built all through to meet the convenience of the public. When you emerge from Belfast, and, as you move along the shore of Belfast Lough, you cannot help being struck by the orderly and prosperous appearance of the country. The rolling-stock of the railway attracts you; long goods trains are moving about, conveying merchandise between the various Antrim and Derry towns. The stations are pretty, and on every platform there is evidence of local life, independence, character, and prosperity. The country houses that come within view are pleasant to look upon. After a while you can scarcely believe that you are in Ireland. When you have passed by Carrickfergus, and arrive at Whitehead, near the head of Larne Lough, the train runs along by the shore of the lough, and you get a good view of the peninsula, known as Island Magee, across the water, which looks like a mere cockspur on the maps, but which is in reality a fine stretch of land, cultivated with the greatest economy and energy. There is no waste, there is no poverty, on Island Magee. As you get close to Larne you remark that there are no convents, parochial houses, or even church spires to be seen. If you chance to meet a parson, he is not better off than his flock; he is not their master; he is their equal and their friend. The town of Larne, at which you arrive, is a thriving place, containing a population of 7,000 people. There is not a tumble-down house to be seen in it; and it is expanding.

MICHAEL J.F. McCARTHY, *Priests and People in Ireland*, 1902

THE DWELLING, WHEN WE REACHED IT, I found to be a fine comfortable sample of the respectable farmhouse, to which the compact and well-fitted offices were suitable in every sense. Wallace and his family were Presbyterians, and, indeed, the fact might almost be guessed from the cleanliness, neatness, taste, and comfort which were everywhere visible. The house itself was as white as snow, the little space before the door was covered with fine gravel, and the yards adjoining the offices were particularly clean. The offices themselves were just what might have been expected – dry, commodious, and roomy. A pump and an oblong stone trough were in the centre, and I observed another concave round trough near it, the purpose of which I did not understand. Mr Squander told me, however, that it was used for pounding barley into groats, which, in addition to a variety of vegetables, makes a very nutritious and savoury description of northern broth, being very nearly identical with a recipe for soup, which M. Soyer published while in Ireland. Mr Squander also told me that some of the remote families, descendants of those who came over in James's time, occasionally use the old-fashioned *quern*, or hand-mill, for grinding oats, even to the present day, but only for the purpose, as they term it, of 'trying the new meal'. In the beginning of the season, they will grind a peck or a bushel, in order to taste the flavour of the early crop; but beyond this they seldom use it.

Nothing could be more gratifying than to proceed through his farm, and observe the cleanliness and neatness and skill of the culture. No head-ridges nor foot-ridges, wasted or uncultivated; no weeds visible, no thorn-bushes or cars used for gates. The contents of the hag-yard were beautifully thatched and trimmed, and the form of the stacks quite symmetrical.

WILLIAM CARLETON, *The Squanders of Castle Squander*, 1852

MY FATHER'S A CLERGYMAN – small, with dark brown moustache; a voice unexpectedly rich. He lives at Kilwaughter, near the Antrim coast. His parish is wide. There are two churches nearly 10 miles apart. At breakfast on Sunday he's worried, every delay annoys him. He's afraid, with his slow pony-trap, of arriving late for the services. To any child who comes late for breakfast he complains 'How do you expect to get to church in time?' He breathes heavily, and offers breakfast to the offender.

Now he cuts a slice from the loaf. 'This bread,' he says 'is too stale for Communion.' Another loaf is fetched, from which he cuts a new slice; he divides this into tiny cubes, which he puts into a tin box, for the altar.

It is time to go, my mother runs upstairs and downstairs. 'Have you got your keys? Your glasses? Your sermon?' After each question has been repeated, my father says 'Yes.'

Outside on the gravel, white-bearded Finlay holds the pony ready in the trap. My father, plucking at the reins, says 'Go on, Simon.' The trap emerges from the avenue and goes five miles over small hills on a road between thorn hedges and rusty wire.

Already for ten years my father has worked in this soft damp place, with sunny, but never hot, summers, under bosomy clouds – where bramble, wild parsley, dandelions, celandine, primrose, congregate and flower in their seasons – here, at a corner of the sea. A couple of miles away over the fields, there is the blue North Channel. From this road you can't in fact see the shore; the sea appears, then, to have no sand or rocks skirting it but to be edged by the green country.

'It's going to rain,' my father predicts. 'You can see the coast of Scotland too clearly.' It's bad to see Scotland too clearly. Far off, in the distance, its promontories lie on the water like half-collapsed balloons.

GEORGE BUCHANAN, *Green Seacoast*, 1959

from THE NARROW GAUGE LINE

Looking up through the trees,
Leaning out from the door,
I shall never again
See the train from Parkmore
With its small shining engine
So sturdy and grand
And it winding its way
Through the length of the land.

Oh, there once was a time,
And a time there was then,
When the train, like the river,
Was part of the glen,
And the thread that connected us,
Silver and fine,
With the rest of the world
Was the narrow-gauge line.

You never knew what
That small train might be bringing
To the halt by the bushes
With all the birds singing;
With its soft trail of smoke
And its rumble of thunder;
And who would get out
Would be half a day's wonder.

There's no child will ever
Go running again
To stand on the bridge
And see the small train
Leap straight at the darkness
And thunder beneath
And out and away
To the wind and the heath.

SIOBHÁN NÍ LUAIN, *The Sally Patch*, 1971

THE STATION FOR THE LITTLE Narrow Gauge Railway was part of Doagh Village itself, unlike the Broad Gauge Railway Station (always called the Upper Station), which was two miles outside the village. The tiny trains from the Village Station were without corridors, and had varying numbers of carriages according to the time of day and of year, and the consequent rise and fall in the numbers of passengers to be expected. A carriage had separate compartments with two facing seats, each holding three people in comfort and four at a squeeze, while the netted racks overhead took the parcels, baskets, umbrellas, Gladstone bags, school satchels and other paraphernalia of the travellers.

Once under way, the little train would puff along proudly to Ballyclare, and eventually to Larne on the coast, but this straightforward journey can give no impression of the various detours, halts, and branch lines that operated most unexpectedly on the Narrow Gauge system. One could even arrive eventually at Ballymena, which lay in the opposite direction, if one remembered the correct halts and various changes required.

But the Narrow Gauge Railway, although so affectionately regarded and so constantly used, held none of the glamour of the Upper Station. Its red brick waiting room and ticket office, its goods- and passenger-trains going from one city to another, touched the imagination and generated such excitement that walking to the Upper Station was a very popular outing in itself. Little groups of people, the young and even the not-so-young, strolled the two miles (and often more) just to climb the steps to the station and see the train pull in, let down some passengers, take up others, and pull out again with a delicious smell of steam, a shriek, and a great puffing of smoke. One felt somehow that the busy world of lights and excitement lay just over the horizon, and that the Broad Gauge train was the key to it all. The little groups sauntered home again in the summer twilight that smelt of sweet-briar, feeling that part of the excitement of living was theirs too. It was a naive and inexpensive entertainment, that generated a great nostalgia.

FLORENCE MARY McDOWELL, *Other Days Around Me*, 1966

FIELD DAY

The old farmer, nearing death, asked
To be carried outside and set down
Where he could see a certain field
'And then I will cry my heart out,' he said.

It troubles me, thinking about that man;
What shape was the field of his crying
In Donegal?

I remember a small field in Down, a field
Within fields, shaped like a triangle.
I could have stood there and looked at it
All day long.

And I remember crossing the frontier between
France and Spain at a forbidden point,
and seeing
A small triangular field in Spain,
And stopping

Or walking in Ireland down any rutted by-road
To where it hit the highway, there was always
At this turning-point and abutment
A still centre, a V-shape of grass
Untouched by cornering traffic,
Where country lads larked at night.

I think I know what the shape of the field was
That made the old man weep.

W.R. RODGERS, Collected Poems, 1971

This Jewel that
Houses Our Hopes
and Our Fears

I sleep above a flagged resounding street,
and men from shops deliver all I eat.
I burn cart coals and breathe the gritty airs,
and rock in trams about my brisk affairs.

JOHN HEWITT, *from* 'Conacre'

Belfast was for many years happily deficient in sites for
statues; but recently the city has been deprived of its
advantages in this respect, and the result – will be awaited
with interest. Belfast is slow about placing anyone on a
pedestal.

F. FRANKFORT MOORE, *The Truth About Ulster*

AFTER SOME ... CHANGES OF FORTUNE in the wars of Elizabeth, the Castle and the surrounding land were finally granted to Sir Arthur Chichester. He was the first to plan the town of Belfast, as distinct from the castle. In 1611 the town is reported to be 'plotted out in a good form and to contain many families of English, Scotch, and some Manxmen. The artificers among the new settlers had built timber houses with chimneys after the fashion of the English Pale, and an inn with very good lodging which was a great comfort to travellers.' Chichester was rebuilding the castle, and had enclosed in the suburbs a park three miles round. He had prepared 1,200,000 bricks for the building.

In 1612 Chichester was raised to the peerage with the title of Baron Belfast, and in the following year his little town received a charter.

D.A. CHART, *A History of Northern Ireland*, 1927

A NUMBER OF SMALL TOWNS developed in Ulster, both inside and outside the six Plantation counties. Some of them were situated at the sites of fortified posts established or occupied during the war of conquest, this being the case at Enniskillen, Omagh, Derry, Dungiven, Coleraine, Dungannon and Armagh. Among the new towns was Belfast, a little place on a stream which flowed into the estuary of the River Lagan. There was nothing then in its condition or size to suggest that it would one day become one of the largest cities of the British Empire. Half a dozen squalid streets – that was all. There was no indication there of the wide-spreading city of the future, with its half million inhabitants. Only the hills were there as they are today, ready to surround the future city on the north and east with a broad embrace and to make it one of the most beautifully situated in the world.

HUGH SHEARMAN, *Northern Ireland*, 1948

IN 1660 BELFAST BOASTED of but five streets, viz., High Street, Bridge Street, North Street, Skipper Street, and Waring Street, and some narrow lanes leading between them, all of which lay on the north side of the castle; the mean thatched houses irregularly built, the streets narrow and ill kept, giving little indication of the greatness and importance it was destined to attain in our day. The little river Farset of ancient days flowed down in its open course through Castle Place and High Street, its green banks lending freshness and interest to the view. At a later date each householder was obliged to build a low wall opposite his place of residence, to prevent stragglers from dropping into the stream. The stream was afterwards covered in as far down as Skipper Street, and it now happily flows underground. A stone bridge existed at Bridge Street – hence the name.

The original creek or dock which formed the harbour at the foot of High Street, in which only a few ships of small tonnage could lie, extended up as far as Skipper Street. Beyond the importance given to the locality by the castle, the prospect must have been poor enough. Here on market days the scene would be enlivened by the advent of Scotch skippers with their commodities; the air filled with the loud jargon of traffic; the streets in front of the castle and the whole length of High Street crowded with cattle and produce, and merchandise of all kinds, booths for material refreshments and 'usquebagh' must have presented a striking spectacle.

ROBERT M. YOUNG, *Belfast and the Province of Ulster in the Twentieth Century*, 1909

SLATE STREET SCHOOL

Back again. Day one. Fingers blue with cold. I joined the
    lengthening queue.
Roll-call. Then inside: chalk-dust and iced milk, the smell of
    watered ink.
Roods, perches, acres, ounces, pounds, tons weighed
    imponderably in the darkening
Air. We had chanted the twelve-times table for the twelfth
    or thirteenth time
When it began to snow. Chalky numerals shimmered down;
    we crowded to the window –

These are the countless souls of purgatory, whose numbers
    constantly diminish
And increase; each flake as it brushes to the ground is yet another
    soul released.
And I am the avenging Archangel, stooping over mills and
    factories and barracks.
I will bury the dark city of Belfast forever under snow: inches,
    feet, yards, chains, miles.

CIARAN CARSON, *The Irish for No*, 1987

BELFAST THEN WAS ... A SMALL COUNTRY TOWN in comparison with its present greatness; and it is only among a community limited in point of numbers, and not spread over a very extended space, that the services of a bell-man could be suitable or effective. However, so it was – the bell-man was a reality. He wore a cocked hat and a long blue cloak with a yellow border. In this costume, which from some unaccountable cause soon lost its freshness, but with which he was perhaps furnished every year, he was accustomed to proclaim auctions; to announce that a boat of fresh herrings was on sale at Custom-House Quay; where cheap oaten meal was to be had; that a little girl had strayed away from home, giving, at the same time, a most minute account of the dress and appearance of the runaway; or that such an article had been lost, and offering a reward for its discovery; with the invariable addition 'that no questions would be asked.' ...

The time was, and not very distant either, when all the people in the town seemed in a manner to know one another; when the few magnates among us created quite a sensation on their appearance in the streets; but now the magnates are so numerous that they are quite indistinguishable in the crowd. There would also seem to be an entirely changed state of feeling, both on matters on which it is forbidden here to make any comment, and likewise on social questions. As an instance of the latter I have just time to remark that it is little more than forty years ago since two men were publicly executed on a scaffold erected in Castle Place, in the most public part of the town, for attempting to destroy the inmates of a house in Peter's Hill with an infernal machine. Half a century earlier perhaps the heads of culprits would have been exposed, as matters of course, on spikes above the town or castle gates.

GEORGE BENN, 'Reminiscence of Belfast', *Ulster Journal of Archaeology*, vol. 5, 1857

I WAS PERMITTED TO PAY a short visit to Belfast in 1820. I was then only fourteen years of age. Coming from a quiet country town [i.e. Ballymena], I was astonished to see the crowded streets, and to witness the activity which marked the movements of all around me. I had hitherto been accustomed only to peat fires, and as I entered the town by the way of York Street – then very partially built – I, for the first time, felt the smell of coal. When the peat is well dried it makes a very pleasant fire, and I did not much admire the new fad. The inhabitants of Belfast then amounted to little more than 30,000. Every night watchmen paced the streets and called the hours, so as to be heard by those who were not asleep – but this last arrangement has since been abandoned, as it was believed that it gave some encouragement to thieves and housebreakers. They could thus tell where the officials were employed at any one time, so that they could, in other quarters, without fear carry forward their depredations. The site of the markets – since then provided by the Corporation – was, at that time, a mere swamp. Cromac Street was almost unbuilt; and there were very few houses from the end of Church Lane to the bridge at Ormeau. The town scarcely extended beyond the back of the Linen Hall. There were two New Light meeting-houses in Rosemary Street, and two or three small places of Presbyterian worship in other localities; but the large building in Rosemary Street, where the Rev. Samuel Hanna officiated, accommodated the great mass of the orthodox Presbyterian community. About that time a small house, for the use of a section of the Seceders under the pastoral care of the Rev. John Edgar, was in contemplation. It was proposed to be built in what is now known as Alfred Street. On the day of opening it was at the very end of the town, and recent showers had converted the approaches into such a mass of mud that it was found necessary to lay a number of planks along the path, from the high road to the entrance, to enable the preacher and his congregation to find their way into it. The town was then illuminated with oil, and its feeble radiance was little better than darkness visible.

W.D. KILLEN, *Reminiscences of a Long Life*, 1901

MY EARLIEST IMPRESSION OF BELFAST was when I was about eight years old – that is, about 1808. I was sent to stay with my aunt and uncle Hyndman, in Waring Street, that I might attend a juvenile school along with my cousins, kept by Mrs Lamont, at the house yet standing in Donegall Street, corner of Commercial Court. This Mrs Lamont was a remarkably fine lady, and a great favourite with children. She wrote amusing books for the young, such as *Jack the Giant-killer*, etc., and was very entertaining. When going to and from this school, and at other times, we had many scampers round the town; and I entertain vivid impressions of its streets and houses.

I will first describe the outlet from Donegall Street towards Carrickfergus as it appeared to me at that time and during some years after. Walking from the house in Waring Street you came to Donegall Street, where the Exchange building and Assembly-rooms appeared to me a very large building ...

Passing up Donegall Street on the left hand, we come to the Brown Linen Hall, a square plot of enclosed ground, which yet exists unused, just as in these early times. It is, and was, furnished with many small, raised platforms, on which the buyers stood, while the sellers held up to them the webs of linen they wished to sell. After examination, the bargain was struck; or, if not, the seller took his articles to the next platform, and so on ...

We come to Academy Street, so named because the Belfast Academy occupied most of the west side of the street – a large plot of ground extending to what is now York Street, and fronting Donegall Street. At the west corner was a large house, the dwelling of the principal of the academy. At this time the Rev. William Bruce, D.D., resided there as principal, and the schools were well attended. Dr Bruce was also minister of the First Presbyterian (Unitarian) meeting-house in Rosemary Street, and we were members of his congregation. The site has now been sold, and the academy removed to new buildings at Cliftonville.

York Street comes next. It did not then exist as a street, but only as an opening to the rere of McCracken's cotton mill, in York Lane, and to the offices and stores of the Stevensons (linen merchants), who lived in the large house now known as the Queen's Hotel, extending from Donegall Street to York Lane. We now pass the house, then the residence of John McCracken, behind which was his cotton mill, extending back to York Lane, which is still standing, but not as a cotton mill. Opposite to this was

the Belfast Foundry, the property of Messrs Greg & Boyd, and managed
by an extraordinary clever man, Job Rider.

THOMAS McTEAR, 'Personal Recollections of the Beginning of the Century',
Ulster Journal of Archaeology, vol. 5, 1899

from PRO TANTO QUID RETRIBUAMUS

Turn back in thought to when a little town
at Long Bridge end, this city wore the name
of Northern Athens, with no irony
staining that title, for along its streets,
High Street, Ann Street, round the Linen Hall,
men walked, of many skills and sciences,
scholars, orators, philosophers,
physicians, poets of no meagre fame.

And now today remember that although
their names have withered from the common mind,
within these walls about us their bright hopes
have found their lasting home and covenant.

The common names of these uncommon men
should ring and sing like lilt of balladry:
Thompson, Tennent, Crozier, Patterson;
and yet there is no ballad of their names,
for we have lost the ear for public song.

Yet if a man should try, as I have tried,
to set the story in deliberate verse
as a preserving amber, not the chill
and acrid spirit of uncoloured prose,
how could he wake the fancy, overwrought
with tedious marvels of these latter days?

How could he stir the mind with chronicles
of artefacts and fossils, crumbling bones,
when all may crumble through our cleverness?

Let me be brief; speak quickly of the years
when that first ardour dwindled, and the dust
fell steadily of dancing mask and drum,
all, all grew stale and, as this city threw
its clay-red gables at the leafy lanes,
all seemed consumed by progress of that sort
the men who kept the ledgers reckoned with.

Yet of the few, one watched the gull's white wing
over the deepened channel, and one crammed
his swinging vasculum with moss and lichen;
another bribed the ploughman for the axe
his slow share jolted to the furrow's crest,
and kept and labelled till, his hoard complete,
he left the scarcely heeding town his heir,
though from Broughshane, among the
copper beeches.

And in another street, a clean, broad street,
where once was huddle of old crooked walls,
the Public Library, new built, gave roof
to painted canvas and to plaster Greek,
here space was yielded for such gifts as his.

O sandstone walls, I bless you as I pass,
for there, for me, for thousands, hope began
among your books, along your galleries,
reading the live words, seeing the bright shapes
that carry man's condition out of time.

JOHN HEWITT (1954), *The Collected Poems of John Hewitt*, 1991

SERENDIPITOUSLY, THE FARSET IS AN AXIS between the Catholic Falls and the Protestant Shankill, as its power source was responsible for a string of mills in which both denominations were employed, with separate entrances for Prods and Taigs from north and south of the divide, notwithstanding the same terrible conditions, producing linen which they could never afford to buy. Instead, the women who wrought in the mills made underwear for their children out of flour-bags.

The most satisfactory translation of Belfast … is 'approach to ford'. I register this meaning tentatively, remembering or peering at the Farset, though I didn't know its name then, between the rusted bars of the iron railing of the entry at the back of St Gall's Public Elementary School in Waterville Street, gazing down at its dark exhausted water, my cheeks pressed against the cold iron. I did not know its name then, but was mesmerized by its rubbish: a bottomless bucket, the undercarriage of a pram, and the rusted springs sticking out of the wreck of a sunk abandoned sofa.

CIARAN CARSON, *The Star Factory*, 1997

D ONEGALL PLACE, NOW FULL OF SHOPS, was, half a century ago, a quiet street of private houses. Some of them had gardens and trees in the rere, and there was quite a grove at the corner of the Square where Robinson & Cleaver now have their establishment. The residents were either merchants of the town, or country gentlemen who came to Belfast for society in winter, as fashionable people now go to London for the season. My father, Samuel Hyde Batt, has been a week in coming from England, and my uncle William, when in Trinity College, used to ride to Dublin with a groom behind carrying his luggage. There was good local society, and the people were hospitable. My mother was often taken in a sedan chair to spend the evening at some neighbour's ...

Though our premises behind reached to Callender Street, there was not much playground for me, so I used to take the air in the dull walk round the Linen Hall, or in Maclean's fields, then rural enough. The old paper mill, near the Gas Works in Cromac Street, with its dam and little waterfall, was a pleasant object for a walk; the Owen-na-Varra, or Blackstaff, being then comparatively unpolluted ...

Some of my early companions were unfortunate; three boys of good family, while yet young, destroyed themselves. I was too delicate for school, and only attended the academy in Donegall Street for a short time. It was a dingy edifice at the corner of Academy Street, but the masters were of the clever Bryce family. One of my tutors was James Rea (a brother of the famous attorney, John Rea), a most amiable man, who died young.

THE REVEREND NARCISSUS BATT, 'Belfast Sixty Years Ago: Recollections of a Septuagenarian', *Ulster Journal of Archaeology*, vol. 2, 1896

A T THE BEGINNING OF THE NINETEENTH CENTURY the people who flooded into Belfast from the surrounding counties in search of work brought their songs and folklore with them. In their new homes many lived for the first time in streets, with next-door neighbours only a wall's thickness away. Music and song was their touchstone in the unfamiliar surroundings of the town. Urban life was new to them, with its shops, streets, alleys, mills, factories, inns, taverns, theatres and public transport – experiences and sights far removed from the tranquil character of rural life.

As these surroundings became more familiar and Belfast became home, town life began to percolate into folk-song. The images of mountains, rivers and lakes were replaced by the features of an urban landscape:

'As walking up by Carrick Hill ...'
'Whilst walking down thru Castle Street ...'
'As walking down by York Street Mill ...'
'He works with me in Campbell's Mill ...'
'As I was walking up North Street ...'

Public transport was celebrated in the songs:

'There's a vehicle on wheels they call a Belfast Tram ...'
'I hope you all may give a call on the New Tramway ...'

Love songs abounded:

'It was beautiful Mary of sweet Belfast Town ...'

And the seedier side of town life was also described:

'Begone you dirty drunken sot where e'er you drank your brandy ...'
'A thousand lies to her I told all for to get her money ...'

The love songs that people had brought with them from their country birthplaces were easily adapted to the new urban landscape simply by changing placenames. Alternatively new love songs were composed using the predictable pattern of the genre and decorated with placenames local to Belfast. The songs now placed the singers in a new setting and demonstrated a new pride of place with their celebrations of 'my habitation in sweet Belfast Town' and 'Belfast Town of high renown'.

The urban folk-song tradition had been born and many songs in praise of Belfast appeared:

'I'm young McCance, I come from the Falls ...'
'And Mill Street is a bonny place ...'
'She is the darlin' of my heart and the pride of the Springfield Road ...'

A new Belfast song tradition grew with the development of the town to such an extent that the life-span of a song became intrinsically linked with the pulse of the town. In essence an urban folk cycle had evolved whereby songs came into being with new industries, were popular while the industries thrived, and disappeared when those industries went into decline. That is one of the reasons why so few Belfast songs survived: nobody wanted to sing mill songs when there was chronic unemployment, and nobody wanted to sing about horse trams when there were gleaming new electric trams that were faster and smoother. Another reason why Belfast songs disappeared was because they did not travel beyond the boundaries of the town, due to the parochial nature and content of the songs. Like the ballad sheets, a lot of songs were ephemeral, written to suit an occasion and forgotten when the occasion had passed.

MAURICE LEYDEN, Introduction to *Belfast: City of Song*, 1989

A T THE CLOSE OF THE EIGHTEENTH CENTURY Belfast was ... a small, dirty, crowded town on the west bank of the River Lagan. On its east side it was bounded by the river; towards the south it extended no farther than the present site of the City Hall; on the west it stretched as far as Smithfield; and on the north it nearly reached St Anne's Church, where the Cathedral now stands. Beyond these places lay the open country. The town was still connected with the County Down side of the river by the twenty-one arches of

> The old Long Bridge, some twenty feet wide,
> With numerous arches for spanning the tide;
> Holes made in the walls to drain off the wet,
> And niches for safety when vehicles met.

Within these limits lived a busy, rapidly growing population of about fifteen thousand people. John Wesley, who visited the town several times, wrote of his experiences in Belfast: 'I never saw so large a congregation there before, nor one so remarkably stupid and ill-mannered.'

HUGH SHEARMAN, *Ulster*, 1949

A N EARLY NINETEENTH-CENTURY PRINT shows a ship unloading in High Street, her masts and yards outlined against the rooftops and the sky. At the quayside a soldier in a green tunic and white pantaloons is talking to what looks like an old clothes dealer, in a top hat and carrying a sack over his shoulder. The inevitable black-and-white dog, tail and one forepaw daintily uplifted, is preparing in an early-nineteenth-century manner to cross the street. In the middle distance a man with a barrel on a cart is selling water; beyond him the long low lines of the houses on either side of High Street converge serenely against a sky only slightly darkened with coal smoke. It is all serene; the hook of the warehouse hoist on the right remains serenely half-way up and down; smoke rises serenely into a serene sky; two business men in top hats and coats with a multitude of capes carry on a serene conversation. Nothing moves; it is a piece of life frozen into the serenity of art, coldly and delicately coloured, like something worked on a firescreen ... Down by the harbour the area of slobland uncovered by the tide has still to resound to the activity of the shipyards; the squat-funnelled motor ships that will nightly reflect their floodlit upperworks in the water of the Lagan are still only a dream; the grandmothers of the mill girls who will one day foxtrot to the sound of saxophones and drums tramp through winter dawns to the mills, bare-footed and wearing shawls.

The Victorian procession has begun. In lamplit drawing-rooms in the suburbs crinolined matrons are already seated at silk-fronted upright pianos, tinkling out a succession of tunes that will resolve like a musical-box to 'Pale Hands I Loved Beside the Shalimar' and 'Less than the Dust Beneath thy Chariot Wheels', then with a sudden meshing of the cogs will slip to 'Alexander's Ragtime Band' and 'Oh You Beautiful Doll', with the tail-end of the Victorian procession vanishing amongst the leprous white monuments in the city cemeteries, leaving behind it a rearguard of discoloured statues round the City Hall to gaze with disapproval at red-and-green winking traffic lights and all the noisy, electric glitter of the post-war world.

DENIS IRELAND, *Statues Round the City Hall*, 1939

A LITTLE STATISTICAL STUDY of the birthplaces of illustrious Irishmen, written long ago by a journalist named D.J. O'Donnell, showed that County Antrim had been fecund in the gestation of scientists, 1798 revolutionaries, imperial administrators, generals, Belfast millionaires, and especially Presbyterian divines. But it had given birth to only the one poet, Sir Samuel Ferguson. That was in 1906. The very next year, though, a second Belfast poet-to-be did at last appear in the infant Louis MacNeice, so that we can calculate that one poet per century fills Belfast's quota.

MALCOLM BROWN, *Sir Samuel Ferguson*, 1973

I T IS IMPORTANT TO GET A PICTURE of the newly born Inst [Royal Belfast Academical Institution]. in its proper setting. Naturally the present-day setting requires enormous modification. In the first place, we think of Belfast itself as the great industrial city it is, bounded on the south by Finaghy, on the west by the vast factories stretching, it seems, to Divis, on the north by Glengormley, and on the east by Dundonald. And we see Inst. itself right in the heart of the busy hum of business and traffic, overshadowed by immense buildings that hem it in, its lawn a green oasis barely resisting the encroachment of red brick and blackening stone, yet adding dignity and a sense of spaciousness to the school building when caught in a glimpse from the top deck of one of the buses that pass ceaselessly along its front. We think of the endless queues waiting for buses and the unending stream of cars leaving the centre of the city at the end of a day's work, and of the hundreds of boys pouring out of the front gate of the school every afternoon, with their distinctive uniforms and black and yellow caps.

In all this picture the only thing that has undergone hardly any change is the school building itself; the rest bears not the slightest resemblance to anything that existed in 1814. Belfast was a town of about 28,000 inhabitants, and was bounded on the east by the river Lagan, on the north by Donegall Street, on the south by the open fields stretching from a point very little beyond the present Great Northern Railway station in Great Victoria Street, and on the west by the desolate wasteland reaching to the foot of Divis. The business part of the town was concentrated in an area enclosed between Carrick Hill, Donegall Street, the river, and High Street. Across the Long Bridge lay Ballymacarrett with its salt works and glass works, lying opposite the quays and budding shipyards. Donegall Place and the newly-to-be-named Wellington Place were quiet residential areas, while merchants and gentlemen were beginning to get the habit of acquiring country houses beyond Peter's Hill or out at Malone or over the river at Belvoir or near it in Cromac Wood. The well-to-do could get about the country by stagecoach at an average speed of about six miles an hour, and a journey to London or Glasgow was a high adventure occupying several days of slow sailing and laborious land travel. Commerce was the life-blood of the town, with its busy cotton and linen mills, its merchandise, and its bustling inhabitants who, according to a visitor in 1813, had little leisure for reading in the principal library housed in one of the rooms of the Linen Hall. On the whole, the streets were broad and straight, with the houses mainly brick-built. Outside the town were the bleaching greens, and fields in a high state of cultivation, especially those bordering the southern approach from Lisburn and Dunmurry.

JOHN JAMIESON, *The History of the Royal Belfast Academical Institution 1810–1960*, 1959

THE SUMMER OF 1877 saw the youth of seventeen leave Coleraine for Belfast, and exchange lodgings in a small town, where he had many relations and friends and was within easy reach of his family, for an abode in a large city, where new friends were yet to be made. So he settled down at 7 Park View Terrace (since renumbered), Ballynafeigh, then a wooded suburb on the south side of Belfast, where he was about half a mile from Marcus Ward's. Here he had his home throughout the six years of his stay.

Messrs Marcus Ward & Co. of the Royal Ulster Works were at that period at the head of the colour-printing business, in ordinary commercial work, in Christmas cards, and in colour printing as applied to book production. One of the children's books, printed and published by them in 1875, which lies before us has its colour pages as fresh and bright as when first produced. These were the days of colour reproduction by lithography, when photography (as adapted for such work) and three-colour processes were alike unknown. The Works was an extensive factory on the Dublin Road, on what was then the southern fringe of Belfast, for in front of the buildings were fields and hay-stacks – since which time the city has extended a further two miles up the valley of the Lagan. The hours during the time of Hugh's stay there – up to 1883 – were from 8.30 a.m. to 6.45 p.m., with a dinner-hour from 1 to 2, and a half-day on Saturdays: later on the time was modified to from 9 to 6.

M.H. SPIELMAN and WALTER JERROLD, Hugh Thomson, 1931

WHEN A BRANCH OF MY FAMILY first came to [Belfast] on a horse-drawn cart in 1909, one thing my mother remembered was how the white ribbon in her hair became so indelibly stained with fallout that she could never wear it again.

Grandfather, a displaced master painter in search of work, unloaded the family belongings into a tiny terrace house overshadowed by the tanks of the Victorian gas works (later to be eulogised by Sir John Betjeman) and awaited with trepidation the arrival of Grandmother, who was travelling by train. Mother recalled him sitting on a tea chest, playing 'Abide With Me' on his Salvation Army cornet. In the only extant photograph of him, dolefully walrussed, he looks like a kicked water spaniel.

Grandma, on the other hand, was a fox terrier. She appears to have hated it all from the word go. A small-farmer's daughter from the shores of Lough Neagh, she loathed the noise, the dirt, the stink and the proximity of people. She had good cause. The gas works scringed and wailed the night long, at times giving out a powerful stench, as if of one accord a million tomcats were pissing painfully on hot cinders. In the dewy mornings her boots crunched on a fine layer of black grinding paste, and the stench had but given way to a lower-keyed one, reminiscent of burning bones, from the mud flats of the River Lagan at low tide. People teemed, hammering in through paper-thin walls on either side – and all, in grandma's eyes, the wrong sort of people.

She belonged to the Episcopalian Church of Ireland, then still the church of the Ascendancy and the spiritual arm of the Empire in Ireland. Naturally, she hated Catholics ('Fenians') and could recite a blood-curdling list of their atrocities in her home barony stretching back to 1641. To a lesser degree, but not much, she abominated Presbyterians ('Blackmouths', so called for their habit in former times of eating wild berries when on the run from the tithe collectors of her established church). Here, in an ecumenical no-man's-land between the Catholic cattle drovers of the markets district and the true-blue tradesmen of Ballynafeigh, all lived cheek-by-jowl in the reasonable amity of unskilled poverty. But Grandma never compromised: not long before her death at the age of eighty-eight I heard her again use the term 'mixed marriage' to describe a union between Church of Ireland and 'Blackmouth'.

JOHN MORROW, Pruck, 1999

A S A LITERARY AND CULTURAL CENTRE, Belfast had laboured under considerable handicaps, for, in the past, nearly every advantage of a cultural nature that was conferred upon Ireland went to Dublin. This was the case with the two universities, the National Library, the museums and the art and portrait galleries. It was in Dublin, too, that the wealthy and leisured patrons of the arts were to be found. It was to Dublin that the eminent performers came. Almost anything that was achieved in Belfast in the direction of the arts had to be achieved by the unaided effort of the small business people and the professional class of that Cinderella city.

Looking back at comments which people made about Belfast at that period in the nineteenth century, one has the impression that many outsiders felt that Belfast people had really no business to do anything but work in factories and be dour. Belfast people themselves, however, felt differently. Several generations have been working now to change Belfast, and the foundations laid underground in the nineteenth century are now serving to support a visible edifice above ground in our own times. Some day somebody will perhaps write the epic of the humble people who struggled to break through the barriers and the handicaps in the last century. Their efforts have left many interesting literary relics, particularly in verse.

HUGH SHEARMAN, *Ulster*, 1949

from WILLIAM CONOR RHA, 1881–1968

... by your kindly skill,
the women gathered at some neighbour's door,
the shabby men against a windowsill –
the pity and the laughter of the poor –
stir the dull heart and prop the flagging will,
by mercy made more humble than before.

You, Conor, were the first of painting-men
whose art persuaded my young eyes to see
the shapes and colours which gave quiddity
to the strange bustling world about me then;
and if I would recall those days again,
yours are the shadows which companion me,
the shawled girls linked and stepping merrily,
the heavy-footed tread of Islandmen.

But now the years have blown that world away,
and drugged our days and dreams with violence,
your loaded canvasses may still provide,
in face of fear and hate, brave evidence
our people once knew how to pray and play,
and, laughing, take life's buffets side by side.

JOHN HEWITT, The Rain Dance: Poems New and Revised, 1978

THE CITY OF BELFAST HAS NOW become like the City of London in regard to its inhabitants. Few of them live within the mile and a half radius from the Post Office in Royal Avenue. Why should they, when villas by the row await them in every direction? The suburbs of Belfast are sufficiently various to suit all tastes. Such people as like the bold scenery of the northern mountain range can go to the Antrim Road or the Crumlin Road; those who prefer more pastoral slopes can live along the base of the Castlereagh Hills; and lovers of the woodland will have plenty of choice on the Malone Road or the Stranmillis Road, the latter affording a beautiful view of the River Lagan. In a southern direction the road to Lisburn is now almost covered with villas and gardens of the prosperous businessmen of this marvellous city.

F. FRANKFORT MOORE, The Truth About Ulster, 1914

CASTLE STREET WAS THE ROAD TO LISBURN, Dublin, etc., through Mill Street, Barrack Street, and Sandy Row, past Friar's Bush, Stranmillis, and on to the Malone Road at Beaumont. The present Malone Road was made to avoid the very bad hills on this old road. The approach to the banks of the Lagan and the canal was then, as now, from this old road. The new Lisburn Road, made in 1817, has been a great improvement on these, and enabled the mail coaches to attain greater speed. From Barrack Street the line of Mill Street diverged, at the old distillery, to the Belfast Flour Mills and the Falls, which were streams of water descending from the mountain, affording means for numerous bleach-greens and finishing works for linen. All outside Sandy Row, Durham Street, Boundary Street, and Carrick Hill, was open country, until we arrive back at the Belfast Charitable Society Poor-house.

THOMAS McTEAR, 'Personal Recollections of the Beginning of the Century',
Ulster Journal of Archaeology, vol. 5.3, 1899

MY FATHER USED TO TELL US that the second most beautiful sight in the world was Sydney Harbour at sunset. 'But what's the *most* beautiful, Daddy?' we would ask. 'Oh, Belfast Lough on a June morning,' he replied, as if everyone knew *that*.

It was the only city we had seen and while it was not very large or imposing, and inclined to be grey and wet, it was ringed around with hills and the sea came up to its doors, bringing ships from far away. Great ships were built there too at Harland and Wolff's on The Island. Our lives were touched everywhere by the sea.

ALICE KANE, *Songs and Sayings of an Ulster Childhood*, 1983

THE MOST ACCESSIBLE OF THE BELFAST HILLS is the Cave Hill, so called for the ingenious reason that there are several caves in it. It is the last of the range of hills which swings round the city from west to north. Standing at the north-eastern end of this range, the Cave Hill ends in a long front of steep precipice overlooking the city and the waters of Belfast Lough. The Antrim Road, the main road running north out of Belfast, to Glengormley and beyond that to the various towns of the counties of Antrim and Londonderry, passes below the cliffs of the Cave Hill, which rise out of steep slopes covered with fir trees to a height of nearly a thousand feet above the road. To the other side, as you go out along the Antrim Road, you have the waters of Belfast Lough. Across the Lough lie the Holywood Hills, and if the day is very clear you can see part of Scotland lying low on the horizon beyond the mouth of the Lough ...

A great part of the slopes of the Cave Hill which lie between the Antrim Road and the clifftops consists of three large municipal public parks. The first of these parks, as you go out from the city, is the grounds of Belfast Castle, containing many acres of wild woodland and some splendid forest trees, and running high up to the face of the cliffs, with magnificent views across the sea, the open country and part of the city. I am fond of going to places at times when other people are not there, and I can recommend the grounds of Belfast Castle as a place to visit in the early midwinter twilight, on an evening of hard frost, just when the stars are beginning to appear. Walk among the still trees then, and perhaps you will find that, as well as this solid physical world about us, there is also another world, not solid but more real.

The next of the three parks along the face of the Cave Hill is Hazelwood, with many little paths running up into the hillside; and next it is Bellevue, with a small zoological gardens, various mechanical amusements, and an intricate extension of little paths leading through shrubs, trees and bushes up the hill for a long distance towards the summit. In the lower parts of these parks you can get cafés, dance halls and certain special bus services; but, if these urban delights and sophistications are not congenial, you can easily get away from them.

The top of the Cave Hill provides one of the best views of Belfast and the countryside round it.

HUGH SHEARMAN, *Ulster*, 1949

DO YOU KNOW THE ARTIST QUARTER in Belfast? It comprises a streetful of attic-studios that catch the light which slips between the turrets of the City Hall and the lofty warehouses around Smithfield (Belfast's Whitechapel). In those airy lofts, the Muses' wings glitter amid the dust to the artist's inward eye. Such visions as flit through those bare chambers! And from the slanting skylights which are the only windows of those rooms, daily the fancy of these craftsmen pictures the New Jerusalem, or the sky-cracking towers of Tara, or flights of angels or of Gaelic fairy-hosts, athwart the sun-pierced Belfast smoke. For artists have an ambitious, if not a florid kind of imagination, and though this evil age condemns them to design advertisements and the like, they will dream their dreams. They are the most heroic of people, for no man becomes an artist save for love of his vocation, art being the least tempting of all professions in the matter of material assurances. In Belfast artists' quarter, therefore, there are the choicest spirits of that city. And it goes without saying that Belfast's accursed controversies are unknown here. No man could be an artist, or in other words, a hero and a man of intellect – and a bigot at the same time. O that Belfast were worthy of its artists! But the same prayer might be uttered for any of our cities.

AODH DE BLÁCAM, *From a Gaelic Outpost*, 1921

BABBERLY WAS NOT NERVOUS, and he has a very good voice. I imagine that at least half the audience heard what he said, and the other half knew he was saying the right things because the first half cheered him at frequent intervals.

He began, of course, by saying that our forefathers bled and died for the cause which we were determined to support. This, so far as my forefathers and Moyne's are concerned, is horribly untrue. The ancestors of both of us commanded regiments of the volunteers who achieved the only Home Rule Parliament which ever sat in Ireland. My own great grandfather afterwards exchanged his right to legislate in Dublin for the peerage which I now enjoy. But Moyne and I were no doubt in a minority in that assembly. Babberly's forefathers may possibly have bled and died for the Union; but I do not think he can be sure about this. His father lived in Leeds, and nobody, not even Babberly himself, knows anything about his grandfather.

When the audience had stopped cheering Babberly's forefathers, he went on to tell us that Belfast had the largest shipbuilding yard, the largest tobacco factory, the largest linen mill, and the second largest School of Art Needlework in the United Kingdom. These facts were treated by everybody as convincing reasons for the rejection of the Home Rule Bill, and a man, who was squeezed very tight against the platform just below me, cursed the Pope several times with singular vindictiveness.

GEORGE A. BIRMINGHAM, *The Red Hand of Ulster*, 1912

A S THE *BALTIC* SLID BOUNCILY OUT on to the Lagan ... the blast of ships' sirens resounded from the Cave Hill. At that moment, when the sirens shouted to the city and the river, I was heart and soul inside this cathedral of shipyard staging where the miracle had just taken place, this vast nave filled with shattering noise where small boys not much older than myself swung red-hot rivets on the end of tongs as if they were swinging censers. In the dusk of winter afternoons the red-hot rivets flew through the air like fireflies, so that the shadowy spaces under the gantries where the hulls of unfinished ships, surrounded by their mountains of staging, looked like giant foetuses in the womb, were always twinkling with light. The thunder of riveting was flung across the river, against the quayside sheds and the ranks of cross-Channel steamers with their white-painted upperworks and gaily-painted funnels; the gantries stood like towers against the sunset; red-hot rivets glowed like lamps in the interior of a cathedral where no sooner was one act of creation finished than another was shatteringly begun – creation only momentarily interrupted when, lifting her stern towards the stars, the *Titanic* slid down with a thunderous roar into the ice-cold Atlantic, abruptly extinguishing the plush-and-gilt Edwardian dream, confining my father firmly to his office – leaving Belfast to face the knavish tricks of the Fenians, and, favourite phantom of its tin-shanty gospel halls, the tortuous manoeuvres of the Pope in Rome.

DENIS IRELAND, *From the Jungle of Belfast*, 1973

U NTIL COMPARATIVELY RECENTLY it was no unusual thing in Belfast for a worker to come up to his employer and say 'So-and-so's an RC (Roman Catholic). I'm not going to work along with an RC'; and on occasions of special excitement the Catholic workers at the ship-building yards and elsewhere have had to stay away from their work till the heat of sectarian frenzy generated by some religious celebration or political crisis had died away, or at least diminished to a normal ill-humour. On such occasions there has been an almost medieval danger abroad – to limb, if not to life – but even on many occasion, it must be confessed, to life itself. Belfast, when maddened, is as capable of a Papist-hunt, as the French Revolutionaries were of a hunt for aristocrats. I have a friend, indeed, who, whenever he had been out looking on during a Belfast riot, used to go home and read Carlyle's *French Revolution*. He said that in movement and colour it read like a description of things in Belfast.

ROBERT LYND, *Home Life in Ireland*, 1909

THERE IS A FINE OPEN SPACE in front of the Custom House. Steps lead from this space or square up to the flagged esplanade, which is a few feet over the level of the pavement. Around the esplanade, separating it from the square, is a balustrade. The orators hold forth from the steps, or they lean over the balustrade.

It is an ideal place for open air meetings. The steps and the balustraded esplanade constitute a splendid platform. The space in front affords standing room for thousands of people. The speakers are in full view of their audience, and it is their own fault if they are not heard by a good many hundreds of the crowds who assemble to listen to them.

The Pope is dethroned, scalped, roasted and consigned to eternal perdition every Sunday afternoon during busy times from this platform. Popery with its works and pomps is denounced, menaced, and torn to pieces. Orange demagogues expatiate on the creed and politics of Papists and call forth thunders of applause. All things national and Catholic are thickly coated with mud, and the green flag is flittered into shreds.

WILLIAM BULFIN, *Rambles in Eirinn*, 1907

ANN STREET, IN THE OLD DAYS, was known as Back Street, the street at the back of High Street; then it became Bridge Street – Bridge Street was Broad Street – and later Ann Street. It was mainly residential, many – if not all – of Belfast's timber merchants lived in it. From Arthur Square to the Long Bridge it had one hundred and four dwelling houses, containing six hundred and twenty-six people.

Leading to the Long Bridge, it was a narrow, busy thoroughfare of which the sidepaths were cluttered up with the ware of its small shops – tinware, earthenware, delph and cast-metal goods.

Patterson's Portaferry coach started from Tom Campbell's hotel in Ann Street in the old days, and Belfast's first theatre, The Vaults, was situated in it.

Belfast's entrys, especially those off Ann Street, are the most picturesque, and certainly the most historic, bits of the old town that are left to us. As one goes through them from Ann Street to High Street, they suggest the little narrow ways that lie around the foot of Montmartre in Paris, the 'vias' of old Trastevere in Rome, the 'vieux Carre' (the old French quarter of New Orleans in Louisiana), and the maze of connecting alleys that radiates from St Paul's churchyard in London.

Pottinger's Entry – its name is carved in stone above the archway entrance in Ann Street – was named after the Pottingers of Mount Pottinger ... In the year 1822 it contained thirty-four dwelling-houses in which lived one hundred and ninety-one people.

CATHAL O'BYRNE, *As I Roved Out*, 1946

COURTS AND ENTRIES WERE STILL BEING CLEARED away in the 1890s. The new bye-law housing gave much of industrial Belfast its present-day character, for practically all the houses built after 1857 are still standing and occupied. West Belfast and Ballymacarrett now became endless rows of small identical houses, built to conform with the law and sturdy enough to serve several generations. Later in the century there were further bye-laws which sought the introduction of further improvements. One of the most important was the Act of 1878, which made the provision of a back-entry of 9 ft obligatory in all new houses; in addition each house was to have a water closet and an ash-pit; streets were to have intersections at 200 yards, and buildings on either side were not to exceed, in height, the width of the street. Again it should be stressed that the newer houses were set to a rigid pattern; and their appearance does not mean that the older houses were abandoned. In the late 1890s there were still 20,000 houses in Belfast, out of a total of 70,000, with no back access, and ... most of these streets still exist.

EMRYS JONES, *A Social Geography of Belfast*, 1960

THE HOUSE FROM WHICH grand-uncle looked out on the green of the yew hedge stood in a leafy suburb of Belfast, overlooking open country and the blue curve of Colin Mountain. From one bedroom there was a view at night of a string of streetlamps strung along the blackness of the Black Mountain; the Falls Road, that was; a place full of foreigners and Catholics, from which there sometimes came the sound of shots.

But down in the darkness of the garden there was peace, a single ash-tree standing sentinel between the tennis lawn and the lush meadows of the Lagan valley.

DENIS IRELAND, *Statues Round the City Hall*, 1939

DURING THE EARLY DECADES of the twentieth century, 'FJB's' spacious, ivy-clad home 'Ard Righ', on the shores of Belfast Lough and under the shadow of Cave Hill, was a power-house of learning, culture and conviviality. To his 'ceili' evenings around the cheery log fire in the vast library flocked the aspiring poets, writers and musicians of the day, among them Shane Leslie, the writer and cousin of Churchill; Alice Stopford Green, the passionate historian; Lord Ashbourne, the aristocratic Gaelic Leaguer; the talented Morrow brothers of the Ulster Literary Theatre; Joseph Campbell, the Belfast poet; Cathal O'Byrne, the writer and folklorist; Alice Milligan, the Nationalist poetess; Herbert Hughes, the arranger of Irish folk-songs; and Canon James Hannay, the Belfast-born novelist 'George A. Birmingham'. 'No searcher after historical truth or local "colour",' Dr Crone has written, 'appealed to him in vain.' His great knowledge was distributed as liberally as the contents of his purse to any truly deserving object. His house included a ''98 room' containing mementoes of the United Irishmen whom he admired so much.

EAMON PHOENIX, *from* 'Francis Joseph Bigger', *Feis na nGleann*, 2005

THERE WAS ONCE AN ARTIST who carried his easel through the Belfast streets, and was surprised to find himself followed by a large crowd. Not ragamuffins, but respectable businessmen; serious-looking women; surly, dour old fellows from the docks – these made up his following, which grew and grew as he wound through the maze of streets that puzzles the stranger who tries to find his way through the environs of Smithfield. As the artist was a stranger, he found himself coming back over the same corner again; but he was afraid to ask anyone the right road, for the mysterious crowd behind him was growing and growing, and his only wish was to get away from them.

The artist was a Dublin man and a 'Papish' – he recalled all the stories he had heard of Belfast intolerance, and wondered if his creed had leaked out to public knowledge. But the queer thing was that the crowd looked friendly! Were they mad, or was he? He would get on a tram and fly if only he could find the tram lines. He paused a second at another corner in indecision, and a leading figure of the crowd stepped forward and addressed him: 'This would be a good place for ya, mister,' said he. 'What do you mean?' asked the artist, nervously. 'Why the crowd's big enough the noo, an' this wud make a quaren good pitch for ya.' 'What the d——l do you mean?' asked the Dubliner, 'Do you want me to draw your blessed crowds?' 'Man, that's quaren strong language for a Meenister of the Gospel,' said the Belfastman. 'What!' shouted the Dubliner, 'What do you take me for?' 'Do you mean to say,' says the

Belfastman, 'that you're going round with yon lactern and collecting yon crowd and aren't goin' to preach the night?'

AODH DE BLÁCAM, *From a Gaelic Outpost*, 1921

L IVING AT THE LOWER END OF OUR STREET I was more familiar with the sordidness of Lord Street than with the respectability of Templemore Avenue. Rough families lived off Lord Street and the pubs were always the centre of brawls; sometimes the police from Mountpottinger barracks would appear on the scene, drawing their batons to restore law and order. The only prosperous family we knew in Lord Street owned the grocery shop opposite the Gut. Mother was on very friendly terms with Mrs McDowell and ran in and out of the shop three or four times a day. Father would sneer at her for buying 'a quarter of this and a quarter of that', wasting time on idle gossip, instead of giving the woman a decent weekly order on a Friday. He alleged that mother was the greatest gossip in our street and guilty of wasting not only her own time but everybody else's ...

Father continually warned me not to play near the Gut or in the 'wee field' but to stay in my own street and play games at the quiet Templemore Avenue end. To him, the Avenue with its tall terrace houses, each with a bow window, attic, bathroom, and indoor lavatory, epitomised the height of respectability. To me, the Avenue meant the public baths where I learnt to swim and dive, the public library, where I borrowed books once or twice a week, and the big cindery space near Madrid Street, where hobby-horses, swings, and side-shows miraculously appeared at Easter and Christmas and drew crowds from all over Ballymacarett.

One of Father's ambitions was to move from Chatsworth Street some day and rent a house in a quieter area.

JOHN BOYD, *Out of My Class*, 1985

from SONNET

Wet street and gantry, chimney, gaslit close,
   the piper in the alley pacing slow:
my native town a friendly kinship shews
   in heart and feature. When I heard last night
   that death had set its sober ways alight
I saw instead the flames in Sandy Row.

JOHN HEWITT (1941), *The Collected Poems of John Hewitt*, 1991

THERE WAS THE USUAL THRONG OF WOMEN in front of Norman's windows, their heads pecking back and forward as they stooped down to have a better look at the hats or frocks. To his right the door of Inglis's was open and he could see that the assistants were busy; the smell of the freshly baked pastries came to him and made him suddenly hungry. A carter's horse crossed his vision, plodding heavily over the square-sets and the iron wheels of the cart clattered so noisily that it set up a throbbing in his head.

He turned quickly away to the left, along the side of the Classic where a queue was beginning to form. There to his right he noticed a man coming out of the Bodega bar wiping his red moustache with his sleeve. As he passed the Abercorn the door opened and he had a snatched look at the white tablecloths and the burnished silverware – he felt envious of people who could afford to eat there. He walked on and his eyes raked up the side of the Royal cinema before halting in sensuous surprise at a lurid poster showing the big breasts of a half-naked woman.

He next passed Mooney's Irish House in Arthur Square, a strong, sour, portery pub-smell floating out from it. He curved round into Cornmarket. There was a queue for the Imperial picture house. The ice-cool smells from Rangecrofts swam towards him and he turned to stare at the lobsters and crabs, the shrimps and flatfish, the spraying candelabras of flowers ...

He crossed the street and went into Woolworth's, where there was the usual milling crowd, sweating and pushing. He had to carve a way through them by pushing his shoulder forward and he rather liked doing this; it made him feel that he possessed great strength. He went straight through the shop and out the far door into High Street. He glanced down at the Albert Memorial to see the time. It was half-five; too early yet for tea.

He strolled back as far as Leahy, Kelly and Leahy's and took a stand with his back to the window where he could sniff the aromatic scent of cigars. Well-sprung men with the expansive hands of citizens who can afford to buy well, passed him and went inside. Under the archway of Castle Arcade a newsboy was hoarsing out 'Secunderulster, teley, secunderulster'.

A long line of trams coughed its way up High Street and dropped a swarm of shipyard workers opposite Woolworth's. The Islandmen spread out in a tough, gluey crowd among the shoppers, their voices loud and harsh and full of strong talk.

Then he noticed that the lemon light was growing dull and looking up Castle Street to his left, he could see black clouds rising up behind the violet hills, now taller, growing purple, nearer than ever with the threat of coming rain. A whipping wind blew up suddenly and over the city the darkness grew, so that some offices and shops turned on their lights. Then the rain started in big, spattering drops suddenly giving way to a downpour.

M.F. CAULFIELD, *The Black City*, 1952

A DAMP NIGHT WIND, blowing along the Cavehill Road, almost took Mr Devine's hat with it as he entered the street where Tim Heron lived. It was a street of small, red-brick houses, their bay windows thrust out to repel the stranger; a street whose back-yard laundry lines offered an intimate census of the inhabitants. Children, now in bed, had fought all day long up and down its pavements, laying waste the tiny front gardens with the litter of their presence; chalked walls, overturned tricycles, sagging, abandoned prams. It was quiet now: the yells, the shouted refusals, the adult bicker done. Here, people went to bed early, rose early, and had a tiring day.

BRIAN MOORE, *The Feast of Lupercal*, 1958

I REPORT EVENTS, in the movement through time of a province – cities, towns, farms, of people struggling to be themselves. Yet my conscientious activity in all this doesn't amount to much. I exist in a kind of multiple fuss. Clearly it can't go on, however much it may be balanced by my standing in solitary reflection on a country road by moonlight, or other idle moments. About my rooms, now in Cliftonville, there's hardly a shop and plenty of trees. Five minutes in a tram take me into the country. I pass a crowd of houses that were built yesterday or the day before. They are of red brick and their gardens are black and empty. After that the road has green banks, with thorn trees and rusted barbed-wire fences. Beyond are mountains and, above, larks. While I stare over a bridge at a stream, a dog snuffles up to be stroked.

GEORGE BUCHANAN, *Morning Papers*, 1965

B ELFAST DOCKS, SUMMER MORNING. Pillars of smoke from the shipyards like pillars from war-time Troy. A dockside crane, its framework wrenched and twisted, lies overturned, its jib pointing derisively to the green, dawn-lit hills of Down. A ship, its upperworks pitted by bomb splinters, leans drunkenly against a quay, unnaturally embracing this outpost in the Atlantic, this island of saints and scholars.

No sound from red-brick factories under the Black Mountain; no ships' sirens re-echoing from the sullen Cave Hill; no squat red tramcars sliding over the Queen's Bridge festooned with shipyard workers – just the mockery of seagulls screaming round the shipyard gantries, wheeling over tell-tale oil patches in the ship channel – wheeling, screaming as they may still be wheeling and screaming long after the oil patches have cleared from the channel, green grass has smothered the launching-slips, and man accompanied by his mechanical monsters has vanished from the scene.

DENIS IRELAND, *From the Jungle of Belfast*, 1973

HMS *GLORY*

I was born on an Irish sea of eggs and porter,
I was born in Belfast, in the MacNeice country,
A child of Harland & Wolff in the iron forest,
My childbed a steel cradle slung from a gantry.

I remember the Queen's Road trams swarming with workers,
The lovely northern voices, the faces of the women,
The plane trees by the City Hall: an *Alexanderplatz*,
And the sailors coming off shore with silk stockings and linen.

I remember the jokes about sabotage and Dublin,
The noisy jungle of cranes and sheerlegs, the clangour,
The draft in February of a thousand matelots from Devonport,
Surveying anxiously my enormous flight-deck and hangar.

I remember the long vista of ships under the quiet mountain,
The signals from Belfast Castle, the usual panic and sea-fever
Before I slid superbly out on the green lough
Leaving the tiny cheering figures on the jetty for ever:

Turning my face from home to the Southern Cross,
A map of crackling stars, and the albatross.

CHARLES CAUSLEY, *Collected Poems*, 1992

'ONCE A 'YARDMAN ALWAYS A 'YARDMAN.' Once you've served your time in the shipyard only a tremendous effort, or more likely some unforeseen circumstance, will take you into another job. I risk overstating this point, for the Islandmen and their families are a distinct and highly individual community. Their work, their pastimes, their industrial history separate them in some way from their fellow citizens. At one time the streets in which they lived, some of them under the shadow of the tower cranes, were known as the 'shipyard districts'. Various factors have contributed to a wider dispersal throughout the city of the shipyard workers' homes. A boilermaker said: 'One good reason for the breaking-up of the old shipyard districts – although it was a bad one at the time – was the Nazi air-raids. They cleared out most of the homes, and now, in my opinion, the shipyard worker on the average is living out in a far better locality and has a far nicer home. One thing he needed very badly, and that modern houses have, is a bathroom; the shipyardman needs that when he comes home. And he has a bit of a garden now to do a bit of weeding in and grow some of his own food.'

SAM HANNA BELL, *Erin's Orange Lily*, 1956

APPROACH BELFAST ON A GREY MORNING by the Channel boat which steams slowly through miles of docks and shipyards, when the black bones of fleets a-building are all about you, and you will gain another impression of the sombre strength which is the mark of industrial Belfast. Every ton of metal must be imported for the building of the iron ships, and the lough was too shallow for them when the old wooden ships went out: the Belfastmen, determined to excel in this trade of human Vulcans, simply built the yards out into the deep water and made land where none had been.

Nearly the largest ship in the world has been built here, in the iron forest, to the rattle and ring of the riveting, the roaring of the blow-lamps and furnaces, the clangour of the engines at work and the strange, broken echo of human voices. At night, the flares on the tangle of girders, the glowing windows of workshops, the glare of industrial fires, make these Titanic yards mysterious and terrifying.

AODH DE BLÁCAM, *The Black North*, 1938

THE STREETSCAPES ARE FAMILIAR to anyone who has lived in a provincial industrial city. East Belfast in particular was defined by that industrial past since shipbuilding physically dominated the horizon. In a literal and imaginative sense the gantries, sirens, workers' houses and buses; the very sounds and sights of post-war Belfast were determined by the ups and downs of shipbuilding orders at the two great industrial sites of Harland & Wolff and Workman and Clark.

GERALD DAWE, *The Rest is History*, 1998

IT'S A PART OF IRELAND THAT LIVES entirely in the past. Down south, they have had to pay some attention to world affairs – they were in the League of Nations and are well respected for the work they have done since they got into the United Nations; and, of course, it was the South that was mainly responsible for the Statute of Westminster which gave complete independence to Canada, Australia and the other dominions. But the Northern Government has no part to play in the world – they have no power in foreign affairs or in defence or anything like that – it's a kind of superior municipal corporation. The result is that political discussion there is like parish pump politics and, having no power even in social welfare legislation, where they have to tag along after England, they can't look forward but only backwards. There's a good poem by the Belfast poet, Maurice Craig – who left his native city and wrote the best book ever written about Dublin. His poem is called *Ballad to a Traditional Refrain*:

> Red brick in the suburbs, white horse on the wall,
> Eyetalian marbles in the City Hall:
> O stranger from England, why stand so aghast?
> *May the Lord in His mercy be kind to Belfast.*

> This jewel that houses our hopes and our fears
> Was knocked up from the swamp in the last hundred years;
> But the last shall be first and the first shall be last:
> *May the Lord in His mercy be kind to Belfast.*

> We swore by King William there'd never be seen
> An All-Irish Parliament at College Green,
> So at Stormont we're nailing the flag to the mast:
> *May the Lord In His mercy be kind to Belfast.*

> O the bricks they will bleed and the rain it will weep,
> And the damp Lagan fog lull the city to sleep;
> It's to hell with the future and live on the past:
> *May the Lord In His mercy be kind to Belfast.*

The white horse on the wall refers to the paintings of King Billy on his dashing steed that you see on the side of houses all over the place, but particularly in the Sandy Row area which is a Protestant quarter. In the pubs here, you get the best pint of porter in Ireland, except for the Aran Islands, where it's even better, and the reason is that the Sandy Row men don't stand for any nonsense with their beer. They've actually shot publicans there for not having the booze in the best condition. The Battle of the Boyne that the paintings commemorate, is popularly regarded as a victory over the Pope but, in actual fact, the Pope had a Te Deum sung when he heard of William's victory. The reason was that King James had an alliance with the King of France and the Pope of the day wasn't talking to the King of France – nor to James either. If you tell an Orangeman this, he's likely to insist that the story is just another Fenian invention; but it happens to be the truth.

BRENDAN BEHAN, Brendan Behan's Island, 1962

M Y CONCERN IS NOT WITH THE SHIPS but with the men who build them. And the 'old hands' in the 'yard talk about the changes they have seen in the shipyard workers' homes, clothing and diet. 'There's been great changes in this dozen years,' a joiner remarked: 'but I've seen greater in my working life. When I went to serve my time, sixty years ago, the craftsmen at that time came to work dressed in a frock coat and a castor hat. At that time each journeyman had a tool chest about three feet long and nearly two feet wide with a recess at the back. In that recess he kept his long white apron and his white linen cap – just exactly like what chefs wear nowadays. When he arrived in the morning he took off his frock-coat and his castor hat, put on the apron and the cap, and laid the coat and hat in the recess until going-home time. Now that was the common dress sixty years ago of the old cabinet-makers and joiners and carpenters.'

I've seen one or two of these tool chests; lovely pieces of carpentry decorated with sailing vessels and steamships in mother-o'-pearl inlay. They were probably the last few in existence, for most of them were destroyed in the air-raids of 1941. Other trades were distinguished by some characteristic touch in dress. The riggers were originally sea-going men who occasionally took a month or so ashore and worked in the nearest shipyard. For generations afterwards their dry-land descendants wore the round woollen cap of the mariner. For the engineers or fitters it was the deep-sea glazed peak cap. The riveter dressed in moleskins tied below the knee with 'yorks', and in his leisure hours he wasn't counted a good riveter 'unless he had a black silk scarf and owned a whippet'.

SAM HANNA BELL, Erin's Orange Lily, 1956

I T IS THE WORKMEN, and especially those who regard themselves as an elite amongst the workmen – the shipbuilders – who give its character to Belfast, as it is the professional man – the lawyer, doctor, bureaucrat – who give its character to Dublin. The executives of the great businesses live outside, and hardly anything of their interests shows in the city. More than any other city I have ever been in, Belfast is a city of workmen. The wit and humour of Belfast – and there is much of both in it – is the wit and humour of men turning from a job they have actually in hand to deliver themselves of something as shrewd as a hammer-stroke. And because there is no other than the workman's mentality available, Belfast is a city ruled by very simplified conceptions – the loyalties the people hold to, the aversions they fight against, come out of these very simplified conceptions. The workman's helpfulness, kindliness, friendliness are also in Belfast, that city of hammering men.

PADRAIC COLUM, Cross Roads in Ireland, 1930

from THE LAGAN

Here is a richer beauty than you know
Among the willow-meadows, where you flow
Far from the town, altho' your waters there
Are bright and stainless as the sunny air
Which glows above them, or reflected lies
Within their innocent transparencies.
Here is a richer beauty, tho' the stain
Of labour dims you, and the salty main
Urges its grosser tides against your stream,
And the swift screws of ships disturb the dream
Wherein you mirror sun, and sky, and cloud.
Here is no sylvan silence; long and loud
The hooting sirens call; the rattling winch
Shrieks as it lifts its load slow inch by inch,
And in a rhythmic thunder hammers bang
Reverberant steel with harsh metallic clang.

RICHARD ROWLEY, Workers, 1923

NONO FOUND LIFE IN BELFAST crammed full with interests. There were not nearly enough nights in the week. There were Irish lessons, ceilidhte, concerts, meetings, lectures, and her seven-night week could not cover them all.

Although Daddy was living with them they saw very little of him. He was Secretary of the Transport Union, and that occupied almost all his time. He went out early in the morning and came back late at night, and he had two public meetings on Sunday and one in the middle of the week.

Nono grumbled at this, but stimulated by his interest in her activities, soon all her evenings, too, were occupied.

'I wish, Nono,' said Daddy one morning at breakfast, 'that you could spare time to come down to Corporation Street and see if you could give me a hand. The mill girls arrived in a body yesterday when they came out on strike.'

'But why? They're not in your Union, are they?'

'No, but most of their menfolk work on the docks. I suppose they think that since I was able to help the men to improve their conditions I can help them. They've great spirit. They are not in the Union; they've no funds. It's going to be difficult.'

'I'll finish the batch of work I'm on and then come down, but I don't see what good I'll be, or how I can help.'

'You must begin sometime, Nono.'

NORA CONNOLLY O'BRIEN, Portrait of a Rebel Father, 1935

THE STREAM THAT POWERED THE MILL was the same that gushed from a rocky orifice on Black Mountain and gurgled down the Mountain Loaney, a steep winding limestone path which was both river-bed and road, and in summer it was great to walk barefoot up it with your shoes tied around your neck, relishing the ache of your palpable soles against the pebbles, and the bracelets of cold water chilling around your ankles. When you'd made it to the spring, you'd put your mouth to its forceful gout and gulp it breathlessly and thankfully, as it spattered your face and hair and rinsed away, with a glacial shock to the brain, all thoughts of tiredness. Then it was time to turn around, and look back and down at the city you had come from.

Here and there, scattered throughout the maze of factories, mills, barracks, schools, the filing-systems of terraced houses, are glints and gleams of water: mill-dams, reservoirs, ponds, sinks, and sluices, all fed by the little rivers springing from the Antrim Hills: the Forth River, the Mile Water, the Clowney Water, the Falls Water. Without this water, there would be no Belfast as we know it, since its industries were impossible without it. Wandering at ground level within the dense urban fabric of brick walls, in the valleys of shadow cast by the tall factories with their blanked-out windows, it was beautiful to get, through the iron rails of a locked factory gate, a glimpse of a wind-rippled mill-dam on which drifted a flotilla of swans. All of Belfast murmurs with innumerable rills, subterranean and otherwise, like the Farset River that ran below the yard of St Gall's School in Waterville Street.

Without the Farset, the name of Belfast would not be.

CIARAN CARSON, The Star Factory, 1997

THE FALLS, WITH ITS OWN PUBS, its own shops, the library and the schools, generated a specific sense of community, and we rarely ventured into the centre of town except around Christmas. On each side of the Falls were two- or three-storey buildings, between which trolley buses trundled along slowly, almost silently on the overhead wire. There was a self-contained, enclosed feeling to the area, while from almost every street one could see the mountains, which always held a special attraction for me. Even in the midst of a tight, close-knit community you could glimpse the greenness of the place. As well as the mountains, there was the Falls Park, a walk of exactly one mile from the gate of St Finian's, and we went there once or twice a week with the school.

GERRY ADAMS, *Before the Dawn*, 1996

THE GLEN ROAD RAN FROM DIVIS DRIVE, beside the old tram depot, which is now Falls bus depot, and reached as far as the Colin Glen. It was a long country road with farming and grazing land on both sides and without the benefit of public transport. On entering from the Falls Road the first building to the left was Andersonstown police barracks with a neat little garden at the front. Farther up on the left were some large terrace houses, which are still there today, but beyond those it was all farmland. On the right side was McEnany's Off Licence close to Corrs' family grocer. Beyond this were some well built large houses as well as the small whitewashed Tramway Cottages situated at the bottom of Norfolk Parade. St Matthias' Church of Ireland church, commonly known then, as indeed it still is today as 'The Wee Tin Church', was situated at the corner of Turf Lonan. Turf Lonan ran from the Glen Road to the foot of the mountain and was famous for several things, not least of which was its popularity as a good walk. It was also renowned as the local 'lovers' lane'. Near the top of the lane was the ramshackle hut of the legendary Kate Bush and I remember often walking up the lonan keeping a wary eye out in case the 'Boul Kate' would come chasing after me with one of those big sticks she reputedly always carried to scare away nosey youngsters. St Matthias' Church was eventually bought for St Teresa's parish by Canon McNamara in 1971. St Teresa's was another outstanding building about half-way up the Glen Road.

Nearby was Air Field House, the home of the Caffrey family who at that time owned the brewery. Air Field House is now occupied by the Irish Christian Brothers and the Caffreys' New Mountain Brewery has become the Bass Ireland Brewery. The only other buildings on the Glen Road then were the Glen Road Cottages and they are still there today, looking as picturesque as ever.

JIMMY WEBB, *Raglan Street and Beyond*, c. 1980

FROM THE CITY ONE CAN PICK OUT a cottage high on the Black Mountain. That cottage used to be occupied by a parishioner of my grandfather's, and when he went to visit her he used to bring my father, then a small boy. This old woman was a centenarian and clearly remembered the soldiers coming in 1798. She was a shy lump of a girl at the time and she ran to hide from them. She continued living there, up on the Black Mountain until one day she was unfortunately inspired to wash her blankets, and, failing to dry them adequately before use, she caught a cold and had to be brought down to live with relatives in the Shankill district. The change from her mountain solitude was too much for her, and she died.

HUGH SHEARMAN, *Ulster*, 1949

THE FOLLOWING MORNING WHEN THE DAWN had crushed the darkness from the window and scattered the stars from the sky the old woman got up and announced to Mary that she was going to Mass. She went out by the back, and the astonished blackbirds flew up from amongst the vegetables in the garden and swayed on the fence. The dew lay like a heavy frost on the felt of the goat's shed and soaked the cabbage leaves. The silver wheel of a cobweb hung from the fence and drops clung to the bare clotheslines. The whole city was asleep and through the silence she could hear the snoring pump of the brick-yard draining water from the pit. She climbed to the thorn tree, her shoes wet, the grass sticking to them. She saw the sun rise, saddles of mist fall from the mountain, and smoke curl up from the houses. Over the roof-tops sounded the bells of the monastery, and she hurried down from the field, following her tracks in the dew.

MICHAEL McLAVERTY, *Lost Fields*, 1942

THE CLOCK IN CORNMARKET SAID FOUR. She walked down Ann Street with its jumble of cheap shops, its old shawled women and its loud crying fruit vendors. I wonder will the Technical School take me on for the embroidery class next term? Mr Heron said he hoped he would be able. But nobody does embroidery any more, that's the truth of it. They have to have enough to make a class. And you can't sell it. Ruin your eyes at piece rates.

She came out near the docks and turned hastily back towards the centre of the city. The docks were no place for a woman to be wandering about, in among all those rough pubs and the Salvation Army. At Castle Junction the clock said half-past four. Go home. She walked back towards Camden Street. It began to drizzle but she was thinking about money, so she paid it no heed ...

It was half-past five when she walked up Camden Street, wet with the rain in her shoes and her hair tossed by the blustery rainy wind. She let herself in as quietly as possible, hoping Mrs Henry Rice would think she had come home later, after having dinner out somewhere. She took her shoes off as she went up the creaky stairs.

The bed-sitting-room was cold and musty. She lit the gas fire and the lamps and drew the grey curtains across the bay window. Her wet raincoat she put over a chair with a part of the *Irish News* underneath to catch the drops. Then she took off her wet stockings and hung her dress up. In her old wool dressing-gown she felt warmer, more comfortable. She put her rings away in the jewel box and set a little kettle of water on the gas ring. It boiled quickly and she found only enough cocoa for one cup.

The rain began to patter again on the windows, growing heavier, soft persistent Irish rain, coming up Belfast Lough, caught in the shadow of Cave Hill. It settled on the city, a night blanket of wetness. Miss Hearne ate her biscuits, cheese and apple, found her spectacles and opened a library book by Mazo de la Roche. She toasted her bare toes at the gas fire and leaned back in the armchair, waiting like a prisoner for the long night hours.

BRIAN MOORE, The Lonely Passion of Judith Hearne, 1955

THE FLOWERSELLERS AT THE CITY HALL

Rainswept flagstones framed and mirrored back
Bouquets and sprays like a still life,
A pavement-artist's *oeuvre*;
While, shawled and buttoned from the rain,
Conor-like figures stood addressing life.

'She'd buy a rose', you said, 'a single rose' –
Recalling childhood's treats downtown –
'Caress her cheek with it,
Then lay it gently on my palm;
A kind of benediction it seems now'.

My grandmother as well, although estranged
From *my* childhood, mythologised
To a blurred image now

Of someone in a rainy street,
Holding a rose out to a laughing girl.

ROY McFADDEN, Last Poems, 2002

THE CREGAGH ROAD WAS ON ONE SIDE only a single row of houses above Bell's Bridge; stretching behind them on the west side to the Ormeau Road were faceless fields of tall grass, like the pampas. And farther yet to the west were the legendary Bog Meadows that were drained and built on only in the last couple of decades. It was there in the 19th century that you could hear the boom of the bittern, watch the staggering flight of the snipe, flush pheasant, and on one day in 1819 see a Glossy Ibis. The Meadows, part of the flood plain of the Lagan, were a paradise for those great Ulster naturalists: John Templeton, William Thompson, and Robert Patterson, men of British reputation. The book in my possession I prize most is Thompson's 1850's four-volume *Natural History of Ireland*, in which that country town Belfast that vanished with my own boyhood is richly and incidentally celebrated.

So the countryside lay all about us in our youth. Belfast more than thirty-five years ago was both rural and urban. It was, in humbler words both the town and the country. My father remembered the knackers working out of ordinary backyards in east Belfast where he grew up ...

I remember the skin-men, men and boys who came every week up the back alleys – entries we called them – with buckets, collecting potato skins and vegetable peelings for the pigs that lived not only outside of town but in the town. I still hear them calling, '*oi-raw*', a rough cry unlike the lonesome cry of the herring-man, a cry that arrived and dwindled like the song of Keats's nightingale, here and then gone, over the rooftops and past the next entry and up the sill-side of streets. Larkin in his poem 'The Importance of Elsewhere', written about his stay in Belfast in the early 1950s, commemorated the herring-hawker's cry.

Bread servers – bakers we called them – had ornate high vans, like stagecoaches, pulled by carthorses with feathered hooves as big as dinner plates. Milkmen, vegetable men, coalmen, skin-men, rag men, coal-brick men, roundabout men – all had carts pulled by horses or ponies. Horses were everywhere and their dung supported the subsidiary private enterprise of spade and bucket. We ran under the horses for devilment and bets, and we said that mongols were the way they were because they had unwittingly drunk horse piss or medicine prescribed for horses. Mongols or Down's Syndrome children seem to have dwindled in numbers, like children with buck teeth, harelips, humpbacks, club feet, or fearsome squints (scally-eyes we called them): those unfortunate to live at the wrong time in medical history. Gone too are the shellshock cases one saw after the war on slow and private promenades.

Horses everywhere. Every evening up the Woodstock Road that becomes the Cregagh Road at some indeterminate spot would come the unmistakable smart staccato of the *Belfast Telegraph* pony, high-stepping its trap with the early sixth edition on board.

JOHN WILSON FOSTER, 'A Country Boyhood in Belfast', *Irish Literary Supplement*, Autumn 1989

EVER SINCE I LEFT BELFAST as a boy-missionary of God-knows-what, my return visits home have been punctuated by points of awareness. One of these points of awareness was reached when the *Belfast Telegraph* took me on the hunt of my childhood haunts. Another had been when I wrote *No Surrender* and realised how fantastic my 1930s' childhood had been. In those days, I had known only one of Belfast's faces – Victorian Grisly.

Because I was born and reared in the city's meaner streets my interest in them is perhaps understandable. Although they are, architecturally at least, Victorian Grisly, they draw me each time I visit Belfast. In the years since I left them, these streets had changed little. The people were still as neighbourly. Much of the dire poverty, though not all, had gone. Children still swung on the lampposts outside the brightly painted houses with whitened doorsteps. They still sang skipping rhymes, though different from those my sisters knew:

> *Charlie Chaplin went to France*
> *To teach the cannibals how to dance*
> *With your heel and your toe and a birly-i-o*
> *Touch the rope and out you go.*

The most noticeable change was that cars now lined the streets, some of the bigger American models being longer than the width of the houses they were parked by. Windows and doors still had yellow brickwork, but the colour of flags and bunting and decoration in celebration of the great Twelfth of July had lost the wild enthusiasm they had. But the decline of the fiercer kind of loyalties has not taken away some of the older habits. In the backyards the elaborate paintings of King William III crossing the Boyne are missing, but today's youths still busy themselves in the elaborate wooden pigeon-lofts, and their fathers, scarves knotted round their necks, still take their muscled, nervous greyhounds out for exercise. But of the black peasant shawl I remembered so well, I saw nothing.

Like its industrial city counterparts elsewhere in Britain, Belfast had embarked on an ambitious re-housing programme. But such things come slowly in a democracy, and I saw that most of the city's people still lived in the rows of narrow, terrace houses. Many of the streets lie near the docks and the River Lagan which winds its way through the city. Originally this was marshland and the houses were built on screw-piles invented by Alexander Mitchell, a local engineer. Another Belfast resident was so inconvenienced by the alleyway cobbles he rode over on his bicycle that he invented the pneumatic tyre. This was John Boyd Dunlop, whose flowing, flying beard used to be a familiar sight in old Belfast.

ROBIN BRYANS, *Ulster: A Journey Through the Six Counties*, 1964

IN BELFAST

I

Here the seagulls stay in off the Lough all day.
Victoria Regina steering the ship of the City Hall
in this the first and last of her intense provinces,
a ballast of copper and gravitas.

The inhaling shop-fronts exhale the length
and breadth of Royal Avenue, pause,
inhale again. The city is making money
on a weather-mangled Tuesday.

While the house for the Transport Workers' Union
fights the weight of the sky and manages
to stay up, under the Albert Bridge the river
is simmering at low tide and sheeted with silt.

II

I have returned after ten years to a corner
and tell myself it is as real to sleep here
as the twenty other corners I have slept in.
More real, even, with this history's dent and fracture

splitting the atmosphere. And what I have been given
is a delicate unravelling of wishes
that leaves the future unspoken and the past
unencountered and unaccounted for.

This city weaves itself so intimately
it is hard to see, despite the tenacity of the river
and the iron sky; and in its downpour and its vapour I am
as much at home here as I will ever be.

SINÉAD MORRISSEY, *Between Here and There*, 2002

I WISH I COULD DESCRIBE FOR YOU Belfast as it was then, before it was
brought shaking, quaking and laying about it with batons and stones on
to the world's small screens, but I'm afraid I was not in the habit of
noticing it much myself. What reason was there to, after all? It was simply
The Town. I could give you the statistics you might find in any book –
population, industry, numbers of churches and bars – or I could tell you
that a week before the events I am describing I had woken in a room not
a quarter of a mile from the City Hall to the sound of chickens fussing in

the yard below. Only in recent years had the journey on foot from southern tip to northern fringe – from extreme east to far west – ceased to be a comfortable stroll, even now few people I knew missing their last bus home would have dreamed of taking a taxi. The BUM [Belfast Urban Motorway] was to change all that, of course. The BUM was to give us four-lane, six-lane carriageways in the sky, primary distributor routes, ring roads – inner, outer, and intermediate – with flats where there used to be ratty houses, growth centres where now there were small outlying towns. We were going to be modern tomorrow, but for today the city was little different from the city I had been born into. Ask me then did I like it and I don't know that I would have understood the question; you might as well have asked me did I like breathing. If I had seen other cities I would have understood that Belfast was in its way beautiful, as it was I reckoned there were probably better places to live and probably places a whole lot worse.

GLENN PATTERSON, The International, 1999

WHEN I CAME TO LIVE THERE IN 1926 I knew almost nothing of the geography of the city. I had heard of the Catholic Falls Road and the Protestant Shankill Road but I was surprised to discover that these two crowded segments of the city, inhabited by the militia of militant sectarianism, ran side by side almost from the city centre out to the foothills which rise above its western suburbs. The Catholics of the Falls and the Protestants of the Shankill literally look into one another's back yards. And seeing them from close range one wondered how the enmity which for so many generations has marked them as great nurseries of religious intolerance could have endured, for the occupants of those closely-packed, neighbouring streets have had so much in common. They have been equally touched by economic depression, by bad housing, by the dictates of autocratic employers, by participation in foreign wars, by emigrating sons and daughters, by social change, by the emergence of organised labour. There have been occasions when, under the stress of material deprivation, they looked like making common cause and turning their combined anger on the people or the institutions whom they saw as their oppressors, but any such moves were brief and unproductive. A prudently dropped hint from a more affluent area, a suggestion that 'the others' at the end of the street were plotting to take over, a whisper of 'Popery', invariably put the shutters up against collaboration. Inherited religious prejudices and fostered fears were too strong for the bonds created by immediate and very real grievances.

In that summer of 1926, with very little cash in my pocket, I spent many inexpensive evenings walking, finding out the sort of city to which I had come; the tightly packed streets, the surrounding hills, the riverside, the Victorian opulence of the Malone Road which the industrialists had reserved for themselves. On flat expanses of waste ground reclaimed from the marshes, men gathered to play 'House' (now called 'Bingo') or 'Pitch and Toss' and all over the city, in entries and small parks and muddy side streets, shabby, down-at-heel men played marbles until the evening light had gone. On Saturday afternoons the footpaths were busy with the footsteps of men hurrying to football matches. Those were the activities of people who were idle and poor in an undernourished city.

Belfast's saving grace is its setting. In its meanest street one is within sight of green, rising hills; the fields are never far away.

PATRICK SHEA, *Voices and the Sound of Drums*, 1981

BELLE:

Before I came here, I had two images of Belfast. A magical one conjured by my grandmother's songs and stories and recitations, and a disturbing one of the marches and banners and bands on the six o'clock news ... They are both true, but not the whole truth of this bizarre and beautiful city. Belfast is surrounded by soft green hills. All its inhabitants live within walking distance of the countryside, and like village people they are inquisitive, friendly, hospitable.

Belfast must be the best-kept social secret in the British Isles ... There was a bomb scare in Marks & Spencer's today. A voice from a loudspeaker asked the customers to evacuate the building. Nobody panicked. Nobody ran. The general feeling was one of annoyance that the shopping had been interrupted. One woman was very cross because the girl at the checkout wouldn't finish ringing through her purchases. 'It'll be another one of them hoax calls,' she said. And it was.

I wasn't frightened by the bomb scare, but I was frightened by their complacency, by their irritated acceptance that it's a normal part of everyday life, like being searched before entering the shops. The situation has existed for so long now that the people have come to accept the abnormal as normal. Armed soldiers in suburban streets. Armed police in armoured cars. An acceptable level of violence. There's a new generation of citizens who've never known it to be any other way.

I accepted Davy's offer to show me around but discovered that he has only ever been round here and the city centre. That's not peculiar to him. Belfast is not so much a city as a group of villages forming an uneasy alliance. My Aunt Vi has lived here all her life and has never set foot in West Belfast. Injun Country. The Badlands. Her images of the Falls Road are conjured by Nationalist songs and stories and recitations. And the news bulletins and the rhetoric of the Reverend Ian Paisley confirm everything she fears to be true. She votes for the Unionist Party to keep the Republican Party out.

DOLLY: *(sings)*

Will you come to our wee party will you come?
Bring your own bread and butter and a bun
You can bring a cup of tea
You can come along with me
Will you come to our wee party will you come?

Will you come to Abyssinia will you come?
Bring your own ammunition and a gun
Mussolini will be there firing bullets in the air
Will you come to Abyssinia will you come?

CHRISTINA REID, The Belle of Belfast City, 1989

'WE'LL GO THIS WAY, MOTHER,' Mary was saying as they crushed their way into the open-air variety market ...

There was no order amongst the crowds. The sun blazed from a blue sky, and the bundles of old clothes spread out on the counters exuded a warm, sour smell. Women with baskets jostled one another around the stalls, tramping on damaged fruit, lingering here to watch a man punching holes in a basin and mending them while-you-wait with liquid solder, or a little man standing on a high box, a hand thrust into a silk stocking, and with many flourishes of his wrist demonstrating the uses of his mend-the-ladder needle: 'Ladies, one moment. I'm not here to sell these needles, I'm here to advertise them! ... See, I pluck a ladder in this stocking. Now watch closely to see how this simply worked needle can mend it ... a baby in arms could use it ... See ... as good as new,' and he waves the stocking in front of the ladies' faces. 'Of course if there is any young lady in the audience would like one, I'll oblige her. Sixpence each! Though as I said before and I repeat again – I'm not here to sell these needles, I'm here to advertise them. I've only a few with me ... Sixpence ... Thank you, ladies. Money refunded if not satisfactory.' ...

Up between the aisles of stalls they pushed, grateful for the little breeze that eddied the thick heat or swayed the shadows of the hanging clothes. Shawled women sat on empty boxes, their wares spread out at their feet – old ornaments, brass fenders, portmanteaux with foreign labels and blue-moulded fastenings, boots in all stages of decomposition, and cups and bowls with straw and dust in them.

MICHAEL McLAVERTY, Lost Fields, 1942

I AM TAKING THE SHORT two-stop trip to Balmoral. Enclosed alone in a compartment that smells of tobacco and autumnal-coloured moiré cut-moquette upholstery, I try to anticipate the momentary dislocation which occurs when you think your train is moving off backwards, until you realise a parallel train has moved forward, and yours is stationary. Eventually, you do move off for real, accelerating slowly past marshalling yards, where goods trains have been shunted in linear alphabets of flat-bed trucks, closed wooden wagons and cabooses, cylindrical gas and chemical containers, cattle-carts, and brake-carts. The whole elaborate system of junctions, sidings and crossovers is corroborated by interlinks of rods and levers, wires plumbed into black tubings snaking parallel to the tracks, under intervallic staves of telegraph wires strung out between high poles, as the sleepers below exude oil and creosote, and the heraldic armatures of railway signals click their intermittent semaphores, trying to orchestrate the movements. There is a burned-out cindery feel to the landscape, and the air is full of grit and glitter. The skewed angles of the deep cuttings resemble those of an exhausted open-cast coal-mine, whose zig-zag downward gradients culminate in a black tarn. Derelict, scummed mill-ponds flash with brackish, desultory April light, as runnels and sluices sink into culverts under the water-towers and coal-depots and engine-sheds. High brick walls of overlooking factories advertise their wares of vitriol and linen in fading white-painted letters, and the gable end of a gospel hall commands us to prepare to meet our God.

Then, to the south-west, the rows of terraced houses, backyards teetering with crazy DIY pigeon-lofts of all shapes and sizes, weekly wash fluttering, back doors giving on to a cinder track behind the perimeter fence of wired-together railway sleepers. To the high north-west, clouds scud across Black Mountain; lower down, they are reflected in the meres and bayous of the Bog Meadows, a place abounding in waders, coots, dippers, grebes, swans, and other birds whose names I do not know. The broad acres of the Bog Meadows, where land and water are ambivalent, formed a natural buffer-zone between the Protestant Lisburn Road and the Catholic Falls: I knew that even then, at the age of eleven.

CIARAN CARSON, *The Star Factory*, 1997

THE DISADVANTAGE OF BEING BROUGHT UP in a working-class street in Belfast was that civilisation seemed far away and inaccessible and barbarism too close and dangerous. From the beginning of my childhood violence had always been round the corner. In Chatsworth Street we had lived too close to the rowdy pubs in Lord Street and the squalor of the Gut. I remember a drunk with close-cropped hair displaying for us children the baton scars on his skull and in a hoarse maudlin voice telling us how the police had kicked him unconscious before arresting him; and how he feared they'd arrest him again. We listened with wide eyes and open mouths to his drunken talk, for no one else paid attention to him as he lay sprawled on the pavement, until at last he cradled his head on his arm and fell asleep and we left him where he lay. At home there was always talk of the riots, but, much to my dismay, rioting nearly always broke out when I was in bed, and so I had to be satisfied with the cowboy pictures I sat watching, goggle-eyed, in the New Princess. Once there was a good riot in Templemore Avenue and a Catholic spirit grocer's shop was looted and set on fire, but when I was allowed out all I saw were the smouldering ruins.

> Fight for Billy!
> Fight for Billy!
> Fight for the Cock o' the North!

That was one of the best songs, and we used to shout it at the top of our voices as we paraded round the smelly back entries in defiance of the Catholics who were preparing to attack us. That none of us had ever seen a Catholic or knew anything about the 'Cock o' the North' didn't matter in the least. Somewhere near us there was a big fight on and we Protestants wanted to be on the winning side.

Such was the childish militancy of my early years of barbarism: the years before the civilising influence of books blew it away. I found intellectual liberation in Davy McLean's bookshop, the public libraries, the second-hand shops at Smithfield and in Uncle Willie's book shelves. I felt I belonged to the cultural vanguard of Belfast.

JOHN BOYD, *Out of My Class*, 1985

ULSTER HAS PRODUCED MORE SUCCESSFUL literary men and women in recent times than any other area of Ireland and probably more than nearly any other community of similar population in the British Isles, just as it has produced more famous generals, more scientists, more administrators and more painters than most other places. Belfast, in particular, is alive in a very interesting way, a city of great initiative, though initiative of an unassuming and unpretentious kind. It is a very quietly self-confident literary metropolis, a city of many bookshops, much thinking and much solid hard work at literary projects.

Being a Belfast boy, it was natural for me to think of writing books when I was quite young ... My generation in Belfast grew up to know that authors were just ordinary people who lived in houses, travelled in trams and looked like anybody else; and, living in such a literary capital, there was nothing to make us feel that it was a strange or ambitious idea to wish to become authors ourselves, with the natural result that some of us did become authors.

HUGH SHEARMAN, *Ulster*, 1949

OCCAM'S RIME

The philosophical effort to say matter in terms of spirit, or spirit in terms of matter, to make final unity.

ROBERT FROST

All Ireland under hoarfrost and blue skies
Swept in, as it seemed, on a djinn's carpet of Arctic air
Out of Iceland, or a birch-besom from Russia; ice-chandeliers

Of hoary gray riming a grand glitter of beeches
At Stranmillis, every spray and bough and bush
Is hung for a time

In crystalline dew, one morning's
Hour in aspic, a gnat's Jurassic spirit-speck
Outwith the amber fog of expanding light, vanishing matter.

CHRIS AGEE, *First Light*, 2003

THE TOW-PATH OF THE CANAL. A whitewashed mill, with attendant mill-race, stands on the bank, a relic of the time when fortunes were made in the linen trade in Ulster. Beyond the mill, glimpses of a blue wall of mountain, then the river enclosed by a nave of beech trees. Underneath the beech trees the earth, checkered now with sunlight and shadow, will soon be thick with bluebells. A horse plods slowly along the tow-path, towing an empty lighter in the direction of Lisburn; above the tree-tops a hawk cuts swiftly, like a scimitar, making for the Belvoir woods. Up here the red-brick city is still invisible, the sunlight still clear, untainted by coal smoke.

Then a mile or two down river the first tentacle of the suburbs comes in sight, laid along the crest of a hill, a wilderness of bow-windows, imitation timbered fronts, and atrocious stained glass. The city has begun. The soft green of the Castlereagh Hills closes in slightly beyond the woods to the right; a tiny whitewashed cottage stands islanded by a weir. Ahead begin the dark woods of Belvoir.

Only a few more turns of the tow-path now and the city will begin to reveal itself, its phallic red-brick chimneys belching smoke into the sky. I turn away from the river and begin to climb through the woods towards the rising ground on the left where in a corrugated-iron guarded enclosure the young men of the YMCA are supposed to cultivate *mens sana in corpore sano* on Wednesday and Saturday afternoons.

DENIS IRELAND, Statues Round the City Hall, 1939

from A BANGOR REQUIEM

Visible from your window the sixth-century
abbey church of Colum and Malachi,
'light of the world' once in the monastic ages,
home of antiphonary and the golden pages
of radiant scripture; though you had your own
idea of the beautiful, not unrelated to Tolstoy
but formed in a tough city of ships and linen,
Harland & Wolff, Mackie's, Gallaher's, Lyle & Kinahan
and your own York St Flax Spinning Co. Ltd;
daft musicals at the Curzon and the Savoy,
a bombing raid glimpsed from your bedroom window.
Beneath a Castilian sky, at a great mystic's rococo tomb,
I thought of the plain Protestant fatalism of home.
Remember 1690; prepare to meet thy God –
I grew up among washing-lines and grey skies,
pictures of Brookeborough on the gable-ends,
revolvers, RUC, 'B' Specials, law-'n'-order,
a hum of drums above the summer glens
shattering the twilight over lough water
in a violent post-industrial sunset blaze ...

DEREK MAHON, The Yellow Book, 1997

THE AREA OF KNOCK – *The* Knock, John Greer Ervine insisted, which we had settled in was locally known as Chinatown. It ran from the flashing trams on the Upper Newtownards Road to Ardgreenan Drive. Further away were Belmont, Sydenham, Strandtown, and beyond those not quite alien distances, foreign places on the other side of the hill.

Chinatown was an improvisation of living between the working and lower-middle classes. My father had a hard-hat for funerals. Davy Henderson next door always wore a duncher. Mrs Woods, a manager's wife, instructed my mother on her social standing as a middle-class wife. Commercial travellers, bank clerks, tram conductors, managers and civil servants all lived together in relative harmony in municipalised ground.

Chinatown was so called I suppose – and a lot is hearsay when you're a child – because of the intersection of Crescents (half loops), Places and Mounts (dead ends), and entries convenient for courting or evasion of authority. When someone said *Tecs* to my innocent ears, I thought the entry behind Belmont Church Road was littered with tacks to puncture bicycle tyres. Counter-revolution …

Stringer's Field wasn't a field at all. It was an enclosure around what estate agents call a Gentleman's Residence, which to my gaze, then, loomed like a mansion. It was an uncultivated acre or so of rough grass and a multitude of trees, glades, sunshaft and shadow. *Sunbeam* readers, we re-enacted Robin Hood and Will Scarlet; and Percy Clark was forced to be Friar Tuck because he was fat and couldn't catch a ball.

Later, there was McMaster's Field at Barnett's Road, a bike-ride away, because that was at Stormont, waste ground among the newly arrived red-faced houses. There we played cricket in the echoing dusk, and among the trees felt creeping undefined longings which were prompted perhaps by some big boys' boast of having perpetrated enormities on one of the local good things. But the trees, the dusk, and the plonk of ball off bat, were in themselves sufficient to create a mood of nostalgia and undefined desire. Dusk and the prompting of love, extension; a stirring of burgeoning wings.

The trams were very convenient to our house. *Dundonald, Knock Road, Belmont.* I remember the old trams with the upper deck open at the front and rear, so that when you sat there you felt the wind in your hair. The tickets were, individually, red, white and blue. Red 2d; white 1d; blue ½d. 2d got you anywhere. 1d was a wing, ½d was a make. The conductor's ticket-machine had a bell; it clipped holes in the tickets which you collected if they had a seven in the serial numbers. The black inspector emerged from time to time to make sure you had paid the fare. Every time the tram passed the Catholic church on the Newtownards Road, Hugh McFarland, who at 11 was a precocious orangeman, felt his head urgently itch, but withstood the compulsion to remove his schoolcap.

ROY McFADDEN, Threshold, vol. 26, 1975

IN NOVELS, PROVINCIAL-SUBURBAN SOCIETY is usually painted grey to black. I have not found it so. I think we Strandtown and Belmont people had among us as much kindness, wit, beauty, and taste as any circle of the same size that I have ever known.

C.S. LEWIS, Surprised By Joy, 1955

THE PEOPLE OF BELFAST ARE AS CIVIL, Orange or Green, as they were in 1690. The legend of the dour covenanting north-east of Ireland has remarkably little basis; and if there is evidence of ill-feeling, of organisation to protect oneself against the neighbour by tyrannising over him, the explanation must be looked for in events much nearer to the present day than the wars of William of Orange. It is not so easy to explain many things about Belfast. It is not easy to understand why a city, whose citizens are by nature civil, should have an unquestionably evil reputation for incivility.

BENEDICT KIELY, Counties of Contention, 1945

from THE OTHER VOICE

I make that crossing again
And catch the salt freshness
Of early light on Queen's Island.

I lay claim to those marshes,
The Lagan, the shipyards,
The Ormeau Road in winter.

TOM PAULIN, The Strange Museum, 1980

Nuair a Bhí
Mé Óg

I spent the early afternoon savouring the adventures of the Secret Three by the bay window. Bobby McConnell walked past and I flourished the books at him.

He pointed to himself and cocked an imaginary rifle to his shoulder and shot me. Then he took a run at the slide we'd made at the corner and whizzed out of sight.

MARJORY ALYN, *The Sound of Anthems*

Racing out of the houses and down the road, after the cessation of the rain, which had fallen, heavy and implacable all day, the boys had been unable to resist the sight of the swift-flowing sheugh water. All day they had been cooped up in their houses, but now the misery of those hours was forgotten. Their bare feet made wet, slapping sounds on the road, and the backs of their jerseys grew speckled with tiny pin points of water, cast up by their prancing feet. Now and then one of them yelled; a wild, unintelligible shout of joy, that pierced through the hum and clatter of the mill beyond.

JOHN O'CONNOR, *Come Day – Go Day*

WHEN I WAS A LITTLE GIRL

When I was a little girl,
In a garden playing,

A thing was often said
To chide us, delaying:

When after sunny hours,
At twilight's falling,
Down through the garden walks
Came our old nurse calling –

'Come in! for it's growing late,
And the grass will wet ye!
Come in! or when it's dark
The Fenians will get ye.'

Then, at this dreadful news,
All helter-skelter,
The panic-struck little flock
Ran home for shelter.

And round the nursery fire
Sat still to listen,
Fifty bare toes on the hearth,
Ten eyes a-glisten –

To hear of a night in March,
And loyal folk waiting
To see a great army of men
Come devastating –

An army of Papists grim,
With a green flag o'er them,
Red-coats and black police
Flying before them.

But God (Who our nurse declared
Guards British dominions)
Sent down a deep fall of snow
And scattered the Fenians.

'But somewhere they're lurking yet,
Maybe they're near us,'
Four little hearts pit-a-pat
Thought 'Can they hear us?'

Then the wind-shaken pane
Sounded like drumming;

'Oh!' they cried, 'tuck us in,
The Fenians are coming!'

Four little pairs of hands,
In the cots where she led those,
Over their frightened heads
Pulled up the bedclothes.

But one little rebel there,
Watching all with laughter,
Thought 'When the Fenians come
I'll rise and go after.'

Wished she had been a boy
And a good deal older –
Able to walk for miles
With a gun on her shoulder;

Able to lift aloft
That Green Flag o'er them
(Red-coats and black police
Flying before them);

And, as she dropped asleep,
Was wondering whether
God, if they prayed to Him,
Would give fine weather.

ALICE MILLIGAN, *Hero Lays*, 1908

JANE HATED GOING TO SCHOOL. She had begged to be allowed to go on doing lessons with Mr Rannigan, though he had said four children were too much for him. Then she had begged to be sent to a boys' school with Mick. But all her pleadings were in vain. Lull had arranged that she was to go to the select school for young ladies that Mr Rannigan's daughter had attended when she was a child. Lull secretly hoped that contact with the select young ladies would make Jane a little bit more genteel.

Every morning, driving into town on the car with Andy and Mick, Jane mourned for the good days that were gone. Mick annoyed her by liking the change. His school was quite pleasant.

'How would you like to be me,' she asked him, 'going to a school where whatever you do it's always wrong?'

She hid her unhappiness from Lull, partly because Lull had taken such pride in sending her to Miss Courtney's, partly because she could not have told Lull the offences for which she was reproved – offences nobody would have noticed at home. In spite of an eager desire to be good and polite, she was constantly accused of being wicked and rude. Mr Rannigan had never found fault with her manners, but Miss Courtney had sent her back three times one morning to re-enter the room because she had nodded her head and said, 'Morning!' when she came in. Jane in bewilderment repeated the offence and was punished.

'I wish I knew what it was she wanted,' she complained to Mick. 'If I had, I would have done it at once.'

She gathered that in school it was a sin to speak like the poor. Miss Courtney said a lady should have an English accent and a voice like a silvery wave. Jane trembled when she had to speak to her. In other things beside pronunciation she never knew when she was doing right or wrong. She was reproved for shaking hands with the housemaid, and sent into the corner to stand with her face to the wall because she had put her spelling book on the top of the Holy Bible. School was a strange world to her. To speak with an English accent, to have a mother who wore real lace and a father who did no work, these things made you a lady; and if you were not a lady you were despised. Jane could tell the girls nothing about her father and mother, her pronunciation was shocking, and the girls made fun of her magenta stockings and home-made clothes.

KATHLEEN FITZPATRICK, The Weans at Rowallan, 1905

FOR THE LINEN MILLS and bleachgreens, farms and village shops made up the industrial development of this little corner of the Six Mile Valley. But above all, perhaps, Cogry Mills, so imposing to the children's eyes, with the great chimney that seemed to turn with you as you walked past. It was ever malevolently ready to fall if you didn't keep watch, head turned, until a safe distance lay between you and the tall brick stack. On winter evenings, from the farmyard the children could see the serried rows of lights from the windows of its four-storey main block and the little odd twinkles of light here and there through its yards and sheds and stores. Electric light, too, unheard of anywhere else as far as the children knew.

All around the farm lay the soft South-East Antrim countryside, gently swelling to the hills that ringed it in the distance – Collin and Drumadarragh, Carnearney and Browndod, Lyle Hill and round the sweeping ridge by Divis to Ben Madigan. The children thought it a beautiful place in which to live. Had they not a river of their very own – or at least half their own, since it formed the division between their farm and Mr Gault's – and what can make a prettier playing-place than a shallow Irish river in summer? Were there not Shetland ponies for riding, and playmates within their own family circle?

FLORENCE MARY McDOWELL, *Other Days Around Me*, 1966

A SOFA IN THE FORTIES

All of us on the sofa in a line, kneeling
Behind each other, eldest down to youngest,
Elbows going like pistons, for this was a train

And between the jamb-wall and the bedroom door
Our speed and distance were inestimable.
First we shunted, then we whistled, then

Somebody collected the invisible
For tickets and very gravely punched it
As carriage after carriage under us

Moved faster, *chooka-chook*, the sofa legs
Went giddy and the unreachable ones
Far out on the kitchen floor began to wave.

Ghost-train? Death-gondola? The carved, curved ends,
Black leatherette and ornate gauntness of it
Made it seem the sofa had achieved

Flotation. Its castors on tip-toe,
Its braid and fluent backboard gave it airs
Of superannuated pageantry:

When visitors endured it, straight-backed,
When it stood off in its own remoteness,
When the insufficient toys appeared on it

On Christmas mornings, it held out as itself,
Potentially heavenbound, earthbound for sure,
Among things that might add up or let you down.

We entered history and ignorance
Under the wireless shelf. *Yippee-i-ay*,
Sang 'The Riders of the Range'. HERE IS THE NEWS,

Said the absolute speaker. Between him and us
A great gulf was fixed where pronunciation
Reigned tyrannically. The aerial wire

Swept from a treetop down in through a hole
Bored in the windowframe. When it moved in wind,
The sway of language and its furtherings

Swept and swayed in us like nets in water
Or the abstract, lonely curve of distant trains
As we entered history and ignorance.

We occupied our seats with all our might,
Fit for the uncomfortableness.
Constancy was its own reward already.

Out in front, on the big upholstered arm,
Somebody craned to the side, driver or
Fireman, wiping his dry brow with the air

Of one who had run the gauntlet. We were
The last thing on his mind, it seemed; we sensed
A tunnel coming up where we'd pour through

Like unlit carriages through fields at night,
Our only job to sit, eyes straight ahead,
And be transported and make engine noise.

SEAMUS HEANEY, *The Spirit Level*, 1996

OUR HOUSE [IN DONEGALL PLACE] was rather gloomy, but the front
windows commanded a good view of whatever was going on. An
old negro organ-grinder, with his dancing dogs, interested me.
Sometimes a party of Orangemen from Sandy Row encountered the
Hercules Street butchers, and stones flew about. Dr Tennent's mansion
was the only large house in Hercules Street. Lord Arthur Chichester and
Emerson Tennent, son-in-law of Dr Tennent, were once chaired
through Donegall Place, and I was sorry to see that the handsome chairs,

with their gilt canopies and rose-coloured silk hangings, were torn to pieces by the crowd after the procession.

Beards were uncommon sixty years ago, and the mob showed their disapproval of Lord Belfast venturing to wear one, calling him 'Beardie' when he was a candidate for Parliament in 1837.

The cholera cart in 1834 is a most dismal remembrance. It went through our street draped in black, with a bell to warn people to bring out their dead. There was a great panic, and people were afraid of being buried alive, as it was necessary to remove the infectious corpses speedily.

The cotton-spinning industry did not flourish in Ireland, nor did calico-printing, which my father attempted at Hyde Park (so called after my mother, Anne Hyde). The firm was Batt, Ewing & Co. The Ewings, after leaving their house at Cottonmount, resided in Donegall Street, where the Brookfield Linen Company now stands. Robert Ewing was married to a daughter of David Bigger, of The Trench, Mallusk, who had, in conjunction with Moses and Aaron Staunton, started the Carnmoney Cotton-Printing Works (now Mossley Mills). Robert Anderson, a poet, who contributed many pieces to the *Belfast News Letter*, was a designer in the firm, having been brought over from the north of England for this purpose. Some specimens of these printed calicoes are still in the possession of Mr F. J. Bigger, a grandson of the above.

The Belfast Bank was at the opposite corner of Donegall Street; where it now stands were the Assembly Rooms, where public balls were given and panoramas exhibited. I saw one of the Siege of Antwerp, at that time a recent exploit.

The Northern Bank was facing Castle Place, where the Bank Buildings now stand.

I was fond of seeing the machinery in the great factories on the Falls Road, but have a clearer recollection of a quaint garden there, where there were little ponds and islands, figures of Dr Syntax and other celebrities carved and painted, and a water-wheel, which, as it turned, made music on bells. In those days watchmen cried the hours at night.

Andrew Nichol, who drew many of the views in the *Dublin Penny Journal*, taught me drawing. He excelled in his water-colour drawings of the coast scenery of Ireland.

THE REVEREND NARCISSUS BATT, 'Belfast Sixty Years Ago:
Recollections of a Septuagenarian', Ulster Journal of Archaeology, vol. 2, 1896

A S FAR AS CAN BE DISCOVERED Belfast was not walled, but merely encompassed by an earthen rampart and deep ditch. The writer perfectly recollects the latter in at least two places. One of these places was between Hercules Street and Smithfield, in what was, at the time, to some extent waste ground. The other was somewhere near the line of Upper

Queen Street, then not much built upon; but both localities have been so entirely changed that it would be quite impossible to denote the situation of the ditch otherwise than by this general, perhaps vague description. The little boys of that day were accustomed to call these places 'the Ramparts'; they were very dangerous and ugly ditches; the depth was uncertain, as they were always full of stagnant and fetid water, but the breadth was probably not less than twenty feet. There were two town gates: one was called the Mill Gate, and is said to have stood at the junction of Chapel Lane with Mill Street, which is perfectly confirmed by finding the ditch in Queen Street not very far distant; the other gate was in North Street, near John Street, and was called the North Gate. These were the two great outlets from Belfast in ancient times, and they remained so till times not very ancient at all; as many persons will recollect when the way to Lisburn – by the County Antrim side, that is, – was by Castle Street, Mill Street, Barrack Street, Durham Street, and Sandy Row, and so on to the Old Malone Road: they will farther recollect when the Linen Hall was unenclosed at the back, and the broad roads, or now rather streets, which approach it in that direction, were not made. Indeed the writer has himself a sort of faint remembrance – or rather, he is drawing just now on the memory of another – to have heard, when a child, a person who came to visit his father from a distance complaining of the way he had ventured to come into town – by some new road they were making through the fields behind the Linen Hall. His horse, he said, was up to the saddle-girths for a long distance, and he thought he never would get extricated from the difficulties of that perilous way. This was the present Linen Hall Street. Now the other great outlet from the town, by the old North Gate, led not only to Antrim over the mountains by the Shankill Road, but also to Carrickfergus. The former route to Antrim and the interior of the country was the old Irish way, and was that used within memory; but there is no one now living who can recollect the way by North Street as that which was required to be taken in proceeding to Carrickfergus, and yet it really was so. The road to Antrim and other places led straight on; that to Carrickfergus turned to the right at the top of North Street, passing over Carrick Hill, so called from being the direct route to that town. The writer was once told, a great many years ago, by a very old lady, a native of Belfast, that when a girl she had seen the Judges of Assize proceeding down Waring Street to Carrickfergus. This was to avoid the circuitous route by North Street here described: for at the period in question, probably eighty or ninety years ago, not only was York Street not in existence, but the top of Donegall Street itself could not have been opened. Indeed York Street, he has been told, is not yet fifty years formed, and when it was being made there were trees, fields, and ditches in Donegall Street some distance below the Poor-house.

GEORGE BENN, 'Reminiscences of Belfast', *Ulster Journal of Archaeology*, vol. 3, 1855

GLIMPSES FROM THE EARLY YEARS come to mind, united round that surprised and curious feeling of a child looking at life. Even the objects in rooms are important. For example, the Red Box, a huge trough-like thing in the nursery, that held our toys.

I recall sensations – the pleasure of scribbling smoke from a house drawn in pencil, a blunt statement of door, windows and roof: THIS IS A HOUSE! Look, smoke from the chimneys! The scribbled energy of the smoke expressed the vitality of the unseen family inside. Once, perhaps in a wish similarly to vitalise our own home, I set fire to the nursery curtains. A fiery event, fortunately subdued. Was it a slight remembrance of this terror which – in a cinema (with piano obligato) – caused me so much alarm during a scene of a log hut being burned by villains with the good characters inside, a drawn-out scene, with photographs of the flames making headway at gable and roof?

I recall the many afternoons when we trundled hoops on our walks with different governesses. There was the attractive New Zealander (noticed one day by Sir Roger Casement) who later, on a visit to the seaside, thought Dick and me unmanageable, because we fought at 6 a.m. in our room.

We are taken in sailor suits to a children's dancing-class, in the glass-roofed ballroom of a Larne hotel. Once workmen, by accident, knock down part of the roof, and splinters of glass fly about our feet. During the Lancers the girls point their toes, as they bow to partners; and some appear so beautiful that I scarcely dare to ask them to dance.

GEORGE BUCHANAN, *Green Seacoast*, 1959

FOR MORE THAN THIRTY YEARS I have faced and addressed some fairly big audiences in different parts of the world; the greatest I had anything to do with was in our own city of Belfast. And I addressed it as a youngster from the shoulders of my father. It was the occasion of a protest against the Home Rule Bill, when political leaders from across the Channel were here to watch the march past of the people of Ulster. It was a general holiday, and Father had brought me to see the proceedings. Father and I were standing with our backs to the railings of the old Linen Hall that occupied the site on which now stands our City Hall. The crowds in Donegall Place and Wellington Place were so closely packed that I was in danger of being trampled. Father then took me up on his shoulders to save me from the crush. As the crowd still kept pressing I looked out over it and shouted: 'Keep back, there, you are crushing.' And they did. Not every speech I made met with such a good-humoured or instantaneous response.

THOMAS M. JOHNSTONE, *The Vintage of Memory*, 1942

THE MILE-LONG STREET

The long-mile street you trudge to school,
past factory walls and painted sills,
house doors, curtains, little shops,
that padlocked church with lettered board,
was staged and starred with asterisks.
First, harness-shop that flashed with brass,
bits, stirrups, bridles, whips and reins,
huge blinkers for shy animals,
round its door, the leather smells;
farther, under a large sign
which spelt that strange word Farrier,
an open gateway offered you
hammer on anvil, the sharp taste
of scorched horn hissing;
and, farther still, a narrow door,
with glint of straw, warm tang of hay;
scatter of grains fanned round the step
brought the flapping pigeons down.

If you were rich and had a mind
to buy yourself a little horse,
he could be saddled, shod and fed,
and never need to leave that street.

JOHN HEWITT, *Time Enough: Poems New and Revised*, 1976

THE CHIMNEY-SWEEPER AS WE KNOW HIM is not the chimney-sweeper of the past. No little boys go scrambling up the chimneys now with a hot poker at their latter end to accelerate their progress. Of course their services were not much in demand among the one-storey or two-storey thatched houses which formed the greater part of Belfast in those days; a bush and a rope did them. But they were needed in the great houses and mansions of the town and country. One of the bugbears of the infant years of my grandmother's grandfather was the fear that he might be stolen by or sold to the 'Chimney Doctor'. Hamilton Barr must have been an artist in his profession:

'Hamilton Barr, chimney doctor, performs curing of smoaky chimneys (no cure no pay) upon reasonable terms, and he performs his work in the neatest manner, and doubts not that he will give satisfaction to any that employs him, as he undertakes none but them that he is sure will cure; any gentlemen that wants their chimneys

cured may inquire at the New Inn, Belfast, and the sign of the Bear
in Lisburn.'

L.R. CRESCENT, *In Old Belfast (1740–1760)*, 1924

THE COALMAN AND THE SWEEP WERE KINSMEN, alter egos allied in a
carbon-burning life, whose aeons' residue was furred impalpably
within the chimney. Yet both were independent agents, and the sweep
was a solitary genius, teetering on his slow high bicycle down foggy gaslit side-streets, balancing the *fasces* of his trade on his right shoulder.
Arriving at the venue, he would unroll his equipment, and drape the
fireplace with a pall; operating in behind it like a blind man, he socketed
a length of cane into the brush-head, then another, feeling his way in
integers of telescopic stalk. Arriving at the end of it, he'd ask us children
to go out responsibly on to the street to check the apparition of the black
chrysanthemum: up periscope!

Now it is time for the lamplighter to make his rounds in the dusk. I
used to see him from my bedroom window, propping his short ladder
against the cold, cast-iron pole, opening the Aladdin glass door, applying
his taper. The gas lamp popped and flared, then steadied to a bright oasis.
Across the city, lights came on in ones and ones, linked by subterranean
realms of gas.

CIARAN CARSON, *The Star Factory*, 1997

I REMEMBER VIVIDLY MY FIRST VISIT as a small boy to Belfast. A faction
fight that lasted for weeks was flickering out, and my introduction was
sufficiently thrilling. Policemen with rifles and revolvers were massed at
every corner; in one of the danger zones which we skirted tired infantry
were dozing by companies on the pavements; and we passed a
detachment of Lancers escorting a mob of dishevelled prisoners, some of
whom were tied to the stirrup-leathers of the troopers. To me it was a
blend of the London of the Gordon Riots, of which I had read in
Barnaby Rudge, and of the Paris of *A Tale of Two Cities* – romance
brought up to date. The better I know Belfast the more I am convinced
that this idea of romance lurks in a muddled fashion in the minds of not
a few of those whose deeds have won it such an unsavoury reputation.
Clayhanger tells Hilda Lessways that in the Five Towns 'our poetry is
blood'. In Belfast it is blood that makes poetry, not symbolic but real
blood. Its faction fighters do not regard themselves as bad citizens or
wilful disturbers of the peace. To themselves they are rather moss-
troopers, whose debatable land is the tangle of frowsy streets that divide
the Protestant from the Nationalist quarter; and it does not affect the

parallel that bows and spears have been replaced by paving-stones and porter bottles and iron nuts.

JAMES WINDER GOOD, *Ulster and Ireland*, 1919

THE ANTI-CATHOLIC PASSION is almost the first passion that an Ulster non-Catholic child knows – or was until yesterday. Fanaticism among the working-classes is disappearing, but the badly educated middle-class Protestants, many of whom fear that the death of fanaticism will mean the birth of Socialism, have still an abundance of the old catchwords of distrust. When I was a child, the favourite wall-scribbling in Belfast was: 'NO POPE HERE'. The Catholic retort to this, which you would see chalked under it on many a red gable-end was:

> He who wrote this wrote well,
> For the same is writ on the gates of Hell.

– a couplet that, used in another connection, has been traced, I believe, to Dean Swift. The Protestants, on their side, are not without their rhymed statements of faith. It is an exceptional Protestant child who does not know the couplet:

> Up the long ladder and down the short rope,
> God save King William, to Hell with the Pope.

This cry of 'To Hell with the Pope', though in another generation it will be more silent, one hopes, than the harp on Tara's walls, has long been the shibboleth of true blue Protestantism in Ulster. Once when I was walking with a friend on the road near Lisburn, a man in a greasy cap, like an engineer's, came towards us on a bicycle and, just as he was passing us, he looked at our faces suddenly and, with a loud shout of 'To Hell with the Pope', pedalled off as fast as he could down the road. Evidently he had thought we looked like Catholics, and had felt it as a duty laid on him to challenge our faith.

ROBERT LYND, *Home Life in Ireland*, 1909

I HAD TRIED EVERYTHING WITH MISS McGRATH: extra pennies for the Black Babies box dropped in conspicuously; more than my share of flowers for the May altar – nothing worked. And there was no use complaining to Grandmother about this villain either. She considered Miss McGrath a Godsend to Catholics, a champion who turned out scholars to thwart the Orange Order's decree that Catholics were only fit for menial labour.

And it seemed the whole village agreed. I never saw any parent come to the door of that classroom decrying child abuse.

'There'll come a day, Jennifer, when you'll see Miss McGrath in a different light,' Grandmother said. 'Most of the wee girls in your class will be doffing in the mill the minute they hit fourteen – there'll be no secondary school for them.'

But Grandmother said the Labour Government had promised some important changes if they got elected and that Miss McGrath was seeing to it we were ready to take advantage of them. She even went as far as intimating some would make it all the way to University. The word 'socialise' studded her ramblings about the Labour Government, whatever that was. But it sounded friendly and if it helped me to get to University, where I knew they just read books, I supposed it was good. I didn't want to be a doffer. I knew how much Aunt Madge hated the mill and the cloying, sour smell of flax she brought home with her.

'Well, that's what is ahead of you if they have their way,' she said. 'You see that?' Grandmother poked her finger at the *Belfast Telegraph*. 'That's what you'll be up against – that's it in a nutshell!' Her fingernail stabbed up and down the black columns of newsprint at the repetitious 'Protestant Only Need Apply' that stood out boldly over the 'Help Wanted' appeals.

MARJORY ALYN, *The Sound of Anthems*, 1983

DEREK NOTICED THAT DA WASN'T LISTENING to him nor was he watching the TV. He went over and screwed the little knob at the bottom, and the MP that was talking started to get fatter and fatter, then his face slid past the screen faster and faster. Then Derek slipped back to his seat and Da was still sitting staring into the corner. All of a sudden he realised there was something wrong.

'Jesus – Derek – could we not get peace to watch something interesting for a change.'

Derek looks at me with a serious face. 'Did I touch it?'

'Not as far as I know,' I say.

'I know bloody well who messed it up. Who always does it.'

'I'll put it right,' I say. I tried and Ma came in. She nearly went mad because she said that I could get electrocuted. Ralph tried and Derek lay back killing himself laughing, because as soon as he touched it the picture split in half and still moved up. Then it started to crack and Ma held her hair and asked God to give her strength. Da and Ralph and me were all turning knobs when there was just a little crack and the screen went black.

'That's done it,' Da says.

'Try moving the plug,' Ralph says.

'Try shitting,' Da says.

'That's what you get for putting it on, on a Sunday,' Ma says. 'Now you know there's a man up above.'

'That's right Ma,' Derek says, making faces behind Ma's back. 'We might all have been struck dead.'

'I wish I seen Sunday over,' Ma says. 'I'll thank the Lord when this day's over.'

IAN COCHRANE, *A Streak of Madness*, 1973

B ELFAST IS CUT IN TWO BY THE RIVER LAGAN, and nearly all my earlier experience of the city was confined to the north side of the river, the older part of the city, the part which represents the direct development of Chichester's original little town and lies within the broad amphitheatre of the Belfast hills.

It was the hills ... which first called me on to wider explorations. I used to gaze up at them speculatively while I was wandering round the Cliftonville Waterworks ponds with my mother, a grave little boy, wearing little gaiters and a round hat fastened on with a piece of elastic under my chin. Growing up thus to look out to the hills nearly every day in life, it came as quite a strange discovery to me that many other cities were actually not provided with hills and that many people had to live in quite flat places where there was no upward tilt into heatherlands to mark the transition from city into country. When I learnt that there were such places, I thought them very badly planned; and Belfast people have told me that there is something rather upsetting in the experience of having to live in a city without hills after being accustomed to Belfast.

HUGH SHEARMAN, *Ulster*, 1949

C HAMP WAS A CHILD'S DELIGHT, potatoes lightly mashed (beetled) with hot milk, seasoned with salt and pepper and scallions, served in big soup plates, and eaten with a spoon, a spoon that pushed the potatoes in from the edge to the lovely melting butter in the middle. This was champ and it was served with a glass of buttermilk on the side. One summer I was down at Ballycarry for the haymaking and I was told that one allowed a quarter stone of potatoes for champ and a pint of buttermilk for each haymaker. Favourite of children and haymakers, this was also the theme of a nursery song:

> There was an old woman who lived in a lamp.
> She hadn't no room to beetle her champ

So she up with her beetle and broke the lamp
And then she had room to beetle her champ.

... In Ireland, potatoes were, of course, something else, something symbolic. Great-Aunt Minnie Whiteford, whose memory went back a long way, used to stop sometimes and look at the table and say, 'Thank God for the good potatoes.'

ALICE KANE, *Songs and Sayings of an Ulster Childhood*, 1983

from A CHILD'S SONG IN COUNTY DOWN

In County Down – where I live –
Are cornfields and heather,
Low hills and high hills
Sitting down together.
Rainbows and dewdrops,
And mosses everywhere –
Oh! County Down is beautiful,
And I live there.

In County Down – where I live –
The sea sweeps by.
Far above the ploughlands
The white gulls fly.
Bees in the clover,
Honey in the air –
Oh! County Down is beautiful,
And I live there.

S. ROSAMUND PRAEGER, *c.* 1897

ON THE WALK TO SCHOOL, there were many diversions for the children according to the season of the year. In spring, the nesting birds were watched for eagerly, and when each little hen had her clutch laid, the boys would steal one egg from each nest. The eggs, when pierced at both ends and blown, were placed carefully in a glass-topped wooden case in the drawing room, to be examined with constant wonder and delight at the delicate pastel colourings and tinted speckles. The young wild raspberry shoots forced their way up in spring too. The children gathered them and peeled off the outer covering. The juicy tender sterns were delightful to chew. The children called them 'Bread and Cheese'. They plucked the primrose blooms and sucked the nectar.

They loved the spring time with its energetic young life corresponding so closely to their own and blew a paean of joy on a grass blade held between the thumbs. As they danced along the road between Doagh Mills and the village school, they felt a surge of delight, as they looked up at the four tall, red-flowered hawthorn trees that glowed with almost exotic colour against the pale-blue spring sky. On the opposite side of the road was the 'Famine Wall' surrounding Fisherwick House, a former shooting-box of the Marquis of Donegall. In the interstices of the wall, they could hear the busy little tits jabbering and chattering in their nests, but the tiny openings in the wall were too small for even the children's hands to enter, so the Fisherwick tits raised their families in peace.

FLORENCE MARY McDOWELL, Other Days Around Me, 1966

THE LONG GARDEN

It was the garden of the golden apples,
A long garden between a railway and a road,
In the sow's rooting where the hen scratches
We dipped our fingers in the pockets of God.

In the thistly hedge old boots were flying sandals
By which we travelled through the childhood skies,
Old buckets rusty-holed with half-hung handles
Were drums to play when old men married wives.

The pole that lifted the clothes-line in the middle
Was the flag-pole on a prince's palace when
We looked at it though fingers crossed to riddle
In evening sunlight miracles for men.

It was the garden of the golden apples,
And when the Carrick train went by we knew
That we could never die till something happened
Like wishing for a fruit that never grew,

Or wanting to be up on Candle-Fort
Above the village with its shops and mill.
The racing cyclists' gasp-gapped reports
Hinted of pubs where life can drink his fill.

And when the sun went down into Drumcatton
And the New Moon by its little finger swung

From the telegraph wires, we knew how God had happened
And what the blackbird in the whitethorn sang.

It was the garden of the golden apples,
The half-way house where we had stopped a day
Before we took the west road to Drumcatton
Where the sun was always setting on the play.

PATRICK KAVANAGH, Collected Poems, 1964

I HAVE SOME WONDERFUL MEMORIES of the Glen Road, beginning when I was a boy [in the 1920s]. On nice summer days some boys from Raglan Street often went on walking trips to McCance's Glen. This was the only name we knew it by, but it is now known as Colin Glen. We also went on trips to the Black Mountain, going up Whiterock Road which led to the white stoned mountain loney. Hundreds of people would come and go, especially on Sundays as there was free access to the mountain for everyone. At the foot of the mountain there was a pipe always gushing with pure drinking water. Everyone drank from it by cupping their hands together. It was refreshing after the long climbing walk up the loney. We always did a tour around the famous Hatchet Field and an adventurous trip into the gully.

JIMMY WEBB, Raglan Street and Beyond, c. 1980

IN 1960 OR THEREABOUTS I transferred from St Finian's School, via St Gabriel's to St Mary's in Barrack Street. On our way home from school we walked along Divis Street and up the Falls, spending our bus fares in one of the many shops which littered our route. On brisk autumn evenings, with leaves carpeting the pavement and the road bustling with people, the great linen and flax mills made a formidable backdrop while, facing them, cheek to cheek, the rows of small shops served the miscellaneous needs of local customers. There were a couple of stretches of the road which I particularly favoured. From Northumberland Street up as far as the Baths, along the convent wall by St Dominic's or alongside Riddell's field.

Paddy Lavery's pawn shop at Panton Street did a roaring trade in those days, its windows coming down with family heirlooms, bric-à-brac, clocks, boots, even fishing rods, and inside, rows and rows of Sunday-morning-going-to-Mass-suits, pledged between Masses to feed the family or pay the rent. There was a horse trough at Alma Street and an old green Victorian lavatory facing it, beside the baths. In Dunville Park the fountain occasionally worked, cascading water around those who defied the wackey to paddle in the huge outer bowl.

In Divis Street a woman sold us hot homemade soda farls and pancakes plastered with jam. Brother Beausang packed us into the *Ard Scoil* for oral exams to win a place in the Donegal Gaeltacht; Ducky Mallon taught us our sevens; and lunch breaks were spent playing football beside the glass factory and afterwards seeing who could pee the highest in the school bog. Handball at gable walls in St Mary's, or cards and cigarettes for the big lads, were normal lunchtime diversions.

We were all part of a new generation of working-class Taigs, winning scholarships to grammar schools and 'getting chances' which, as our parents and grandparents frequently reminded us, they never had. We wore school uniforms – a fairly new and expensive luxury – and were slightly bemused to see our mirror reflections in Austin's, the school outfitters, just below Dover Street. I always noticed that the shop facing Austin's had its name sign painted in Irish. You could buy hurling sticks in another shop just below that, while almost opposite our school Wordie's kept their great shire horses in unique multi-storied stables.

GERRY ADAMS, *Falls Memories*, 1982

O N A TALLBOY, JUST INSIDE, he picked up a silver christening mug, given to Owen by Aunt Agnes. He stuck one of the candles in this mug and placed the mug on a Sheraton table near the window. Almost at once, a whistle blew in the street below. A voice called out. 'Hey, you. Put that light out.'

He looked through the broken window pane and saw a warden standing in the middle of the avenue, a stout elderly man, the same warden who had helped him with last night's casualties. 'What are you doing there?' the warden called. 'That house is condemned.'

Condemned. 'I live here,' he shouted down.

'Not any more, you don't. It's not safe. Put that light out and get out of there.'

He pulled down the blackout blinds and listened to the retreating sound of the warden's footsteps. The room was all shadows, half lit by the pale flickering light of the candles. This house is condemned.

He went toward the fireplace, holding a candle aloft and, in the round looking glass, saw himself, dirty and strange, his steel helmet askew. In that world, encircled by the looking glass, he had acted and reacted, had left his mark and had, in turn, been marked. His bare knees had helped wear down the old Turkey carpet, battleground of a thousand childhood games of Snap. From that gramophone, he had heard his first record. Over his mother's writing desk, the fierce stag still peered from a dark forest glade. But the picture which had hung beside it, a framed Raphael print, had fallen behind his father's bookcase. The looking-glass room, unchanged since his childhood, had changed at last. This house is condemned.

Condemned, the house was his. He could sleep in any bed he chose: he could break open the dining-room sideboard and drink his father's port. Yet, standing in the cowering light of the candles, he feared the house. It had died, its life had fled.

BRIAN MOORE, *The Emperor of Ice-Cream*, 1966

ONE DAY MOTHER SENT ME OFF to Newry to do some messages for her. It was a summer's morning, very early, when I went to the square and climbed on to Hughie Downey's long car. The driver tucked the rugs around the knees of the dozen or so travellers, six on each side facing outwards, settled himself in his high 'Dickey' seat, whipped up his horses and off we went down Newry Street and out into the country at an easy trot, perched over the tops of the hedges, waving back to people working in the fields, stopping to pick up or set down passengers, to collect or deliver parcels, to let the horses drink at wayside wells. For two hours we travelled on, pleasantly lulled by the rhythm of the horses' trotting hooves as the sun rose higher in the morning sky, and finally downhill into Newry where my aunt was waiting to supervise my shopping, then lunch at my grandmother's home and the drive back along the undulating, winding road lined with green hedges all the way to Rathfriland. I sat deep amongst the row of adult passengers, watching the passing countryside and listening to their talk about prices and absent friends and sick relations. At the foot of Newry Street the long car stopped and I got off with the men and walked with them up the hill to the Square where Mother was waiting for me. It had been a whole day of the sort of pure joy that can never be repeated.

PATRICK SHEA, *Voices and the Sound of Drums*, 1981

OF ALL THE FLOCK, NOW SCATTERED over the earth, not one I know fails at times to recall those happy evenings. Occasionally, during summer, we might stay from the second service and all go for a walk through the woods, Father and Mother pacing sedately in front and arm in arm, he wearing his silk hat and tailed coat, she in a beaded mantle and carrying a small parasol over her bonnet, the rest of us following in decorous order, not daring to shout or whistle or throw a stone at a rat, and inwardly thankful that six days in the week were not Sundays.

Then back to the parlour with its long table bountifully spread, plates of thick bread and butter, a raisin cake, a barmbrack, home-made jam, honey, Mother at one end beside the teapot and the high chair holding the latest born save one, Father facing her with his back to the old leather sofa. Our appetites would be huge. We might relax a little, ease a button, kick off a tight boot, might listen attentively and laugh our heartiest at Father's narration of some episode in the good old days when he wore petticoats till he was ten and every child carried to school a turf or two for the fire.

We would sit there maybe till evening fell, and about us, beyond the diamond-paned windows, the hill and its oaks and the big hawthorn tree, the woods and the lake and the long white bridge, all would soften down, dim, quiet, aloof a little as though leaving us to ourselves. Even in winter, when the lamp stood amidst us on the long table, I used sometimes to look at the curtainless panes, or cross and press my face against them, having that sense of the things without, trees asleep, a sprig of ivy tap-tapping on the casement, birds roosting in the laurels, rats and weasels on the prowl, they and all else outside in a world that had withdrawn to its secret unchanging self and was out there waiting. Dark out there, and ghosts, cold that struck, and queer creepy things. And, shrinking, I would turn to the warmth and light with a pleasant glow of comfort; would look at the room and all the faces and feel happy and put my face between my fists and bend again to my reading.

SHAN BULLOCK, *After Sixty Years*, 1931

BETWEEN MY SEVENTH AND FOURTEENTH BIRTHDAYS was the magic period of my youth ... I helped the fishermen on the lough, gathered scallops, willow sticks for thatching, ran errands, sold papers, played shinny, shot marbles, spun tops, went birdnesting, whistled from pillar to post with my hands in my pockets, with a tously head of red hair and scarcely enough clothing on me to dust a violin, a thing of 'shreds and patches', but dreaming – always dreaming.

In this period of dreaming I was unconsciously qualifying for usefulness. My first steady twelve-hour-a-day job involved no labour, so I had more time to dream. I was employed to guard a ten-acre field of potatoes and protect them from the crows. I was a scarecrow – and must have looked the part.

ALEXANDER IRVINE, *A Fighting Parson*, 1930

IT SEEMS IMPOSSIBLE NOW TO VISUALISE how even the children worked so hard and continuously. Before school, we carried the water from the spring well. Turf had to be brought in from the bog, cows brought from one place to another, and so on, and then run all the way to school. I learned to do most things at an early age. I milked the cows and made butter, made bread in the pot oven with hot coals on the lid. I made 'boxty' and potato cakes for the tea, while my mother was helping with the work in the fields.

I hear a lot about boxty these days, and it is a favourite with my grandchildren, made in the same way, as follows – well-washed unpeeled potatoes, raw and grated, with flour added to the consistency of pancakes, and also a little salt; baked by dropping onto a hot pan, and turned; kept hot and eaten with butter and sometimes with bacon.

To everyone's amusement I could attend to the butter when the men had finished churning. The churning was done by the men before they went out to work in the fields. The butter was salted. So much was kept for home use and the rest put into a box for the market. My mother was noted for her wonderful butter and it was always in demand, and in the market she was very proud when the buyers came to her specially. The making of butter required great cleanliness, all utensils being scoured, washed, and lastly scalded in boiling water. The crocks were placed on benches in that part of the barn kept so clean, and they were covered with wooden lids which were made by the cooper. He made the boxes too, and also the churns and the churn-dash. This dash was moved with the hands, up and down, until the butter was ready. The fresh buttermilk was lovely to drink. It was used for baking, and it helped to mix the feeding for the fowl, pigs and calves.

KATHLEEN SHEEHAN, 'Life in Glangevlin, County Cavan, 1900–1920',
Ulster Folklife, vol. 31, 1985

WHEN I WAS A BOY IN RAGLAN STREET [during the 1920s and 30s] the cry occasionally came down Peel Street, 'The cows are coming down the Falls'. We all ran up to the road as we knew this meant a large herd of cows would be coming down the Falls Road, normally accompanied by four drovers with sticks and two dogs. We watched with anticipation and excitement in the hope that a cow would run into Peel Street. When this did happen, a dog would head it off, holding it at bay and if the cow tried to use its horns on the dog the drover came to its rescue with his stick and forced the cow back to the herd. I never saw a cow going into a 'china shop' or any other shop, because the Falls Road shops took the precaution of closing their doors until the herds had passed. Afterwards the Falls Road would smell like a farmyard and corporation street sweepers would follow behind the herd to clean the road again. Sheep would usually be herded down the Falls Road in the same manner with drovers and dogs, but these were not as difficult to handle as cows.

JIMMY WEBB, *Raglan Street and Beyond*, c. 1980

IN THE WINTER THERE WERE OPEN FIRES, around which the classes stood in turn for their lessons at the blackboard while the others read or did sums. Children who had got wet walking in from the country were allowed to sit near the fire for a time to dry out. Myself and Carmel felt very deprived at not being let sit near the fire, and one rainy day we wet our shoes in puddles and wet our heads under Harry McSherry's broken downspout on Chapel Brae until we were thoroughly drenched. To no avail. Even on presenting ourselves in school wet and bedraggled we got no nearer the fire than usual, and sniffled and shivered through the rest of the day. Some of the children walked three miles each way, from Grangewalls on the Downpatrick Road, and from the lighthouse at St John's Point on the other side. There were no school meals, no tea or drinks, and there was little comfort. Some of the children were poorly dressed, and some ill-fed. A common excuse for absence was 'No boots, Miss. Our shoes were getting mended.' In the summer most of the country children came to school in their bare feet, and their natural freedom and ability to run about unhampered was a source of envy to those required to wear shoes or sandals.

MAURICE HAYES, *Sweet Killough, Let Go Your Anchor*, 1994

THE CHRISTMAS RHYMERS, BALLYNURE, 1941
an old woman remembers

The Christmas Rhymers came again last year,
wee boys with blackened faces at the door,
not like those strapping lads that would appear,
dressed for the mummers' parts in times before,
to act the old play on the kitchen floor;
at warwork now or fighting overseas,
my neighbours' sons; there's hardly one of these
that will be coming back here any more.

I gave them coppers, bid them turn and go;
and as I watched that rueful regiment
head for the road, I felt that with them went
those songs we sang, the rhymes we used to know,
heartsore imagining the years without
The Doctor, Darkie, and Wee Divil Doubt.

JOHN HEWITT, *Loose Ends*, 1983

I MIND WELL ONE NIGHT WE WERE MUMMING in Tullychurry. The winter floods had so swollen the streams and watercourses that those of us wearing boots or shoes had to be ferried across the fords on the shoulders of the wellingtoned brigade. My brother Joe, who was a lightly built short-trousered boy of twelve years at the time, was borne on the broad back of Packie Lawn for most of the way. You see he was our musician and rattled out rousing reels on the old fashioned melodeon with the three stoppers.

It was a delicate area for us to work as the inhabitants were entirely Protestant, and very strict in their observance of the proprieties. However, they did have an Orange Hall and a jaunty little fife and drum band and perhaps this preserved a tiny oasis of culture in somewhat arid surroundings. Maybe it was for that reason they gave us such a royal welcome and we in turn made sure that we visited every house and acted our play on every hearthstone in that townland.

The women in most of the houses there, both young and old, indulged in a little judicious levity when we entered. One never could decide whether it was our exotic costumes or the sudden invasion of their kitchen floors by so many virile young men that excited them. Whatever the reason for the strange behaviour, Oliver Cromwell and Turkish Knight were lucky to escape without their high and handsome headgear getting three or four belts of the brushy end of a broom wielded by one or other of these wild Tullychurry women.

However, it was the entry of Wee Divil Doubt, who sported the horns of the biggest buck-goat Paul McCabe ever kept in stud, that drove them out of their senses altogether. A female emerged from the shadows to grab a horn in every hand and when he chased her playfully round the house and dunted her in the hindquarters with his powerful antlers, she howled hilariously.

PADDY TUNNEY, *The Stone Fiddle*, 1979

THE FLAMES TWIRLED ROUND THE SODS OF TURF. The old woman patted her knee, but didn't speak. Johnny lifted the bucket from the corner of the dresser and went out.

He opened the wooden gate at the side of the house and crossed the field that sloped to the well. He noticed the tracks of her feet and her stick. 'She shouldn't come down here alone,' he said to himself, bending down over the black pool and brushing the floating leaves away with the bucket. He took a drink of the ice-cold water. The well was shadowed with quiet and a thin wind crisped through the overhanging hedges. He saw places where he used to do jumps as a boy, bushes where he had found nests, and above his head two poplar trees, cold as frost. He remembered making hay on warm days, lying on his back, and looking up at the poplar leaves flashing like many wings, and how his father had said: 'Johnny, Johnny, no wind can sneak by a poplar tree', and both had leaned back and listened to the rainy sound of their leaves.

He put down the bucket and crushed his way through the hedge into the neighbouring field. It sponged under his feet; it required stubbing; and he recalled how, when his father had worked it, it had yielded crops of corn and potatoes. But all that land had been mortgaged and nothing remained now, only the house and the small field with the well. The shape of the land had changed but little in the course of thirty years. Here and there a blown-down tree was honeycombed with holes, hedges had grown taller and wider at the legs, but the fields had not changed.

In his walk he had come to the top of a hill where he saw far away the River Bann scything through flat soggy country spreading itself out in Lough Beg where he saw the tree-covered island and the spire of a ruined church. He sighed and breathed in the fresh-cold air: 'It's no wonder the oul' wan wants to stay in it. It's a good country for them that can make a living in it.' Below him was the demesne, its walls tumbling, and rabbits running wild in its naked fields. Many's a wintry night he had poached for them when the air was coarse with frost, the hailstones clustered in the hoof-marks and the rabbits big as sheep against the moon.

He turned back to the well and where the bucket had laid there was a sharp circle in the mud and the marks of his mother's stick.

'Impatient as ever,' he said to himself as he walked up the field towards the white house.

'You're a nice one to send for a bucket of water. I thought you'd gone to the lough for it and the poor hens eating the lime-wash off the walls.'

MICHAEL McLAVERTY, *Lost Fields*, 1942

ABERCORN STREET NORTH WAS VERY NARROW, and all around it was a network of very busy little streets, with a secondary network of back entries, or alleys. At Getty Street, steps flanked by iron banisters or railings led down from the street into the entry. The pavements were high and were set off by large brown kerb stones. The whole Falls area, especially around Leeson Street, was riddled with yards, back entries and stables.

The gas-lamps which lit the streets weren't that high, so it was quite easy to 'speedy up' them. On the crossbar just below where the lamp itself was, we hung ropes for swings. We played handball at the huge gable at Harbison's corner and all sorts of games at the bottom of Abercorn Street, where it went into Sorella Street and Dunville Street, a small area at the bend adjacent to the Dunville Park where you weren't annoying anybody. There was a rag store and a small builder's yard, and we used the gates of the yard as goalposts. Apart from racing and football, we played hurling, or cricket or rounders using hurling sticks, and 'kick the tin'.

Amongst the sparse regular traffic were the carts of the coalman and the 'reg' men. We used to hop the horses and carts, and once I fell off, marking my head. Another frequent visitor to the street collected kitchen waste for the pigs. Of an evening a man used to go around lighting the gaslights. At my Granny Hannaway's house in Inkerman Street, there was a gas lamp attached to the wall, and I remember my mother telling me that it was by the light of this lamp that she had read at night.

The houses of Abercorn Street and its neighbourhood were old, and no one in the area had indoor toilets or bathrooms. To this day people ask, 'Are you going to the yard?' – meaning, 'Are you going to the toilet?' Tin baths, which were kept hung up in the yard, were placed in front of the fire on bath nights and filled with buckets of water. The small yards were invariably whitewashed and sometimes had a one-foot base of black tar. Some people had window boxes, in which geraniums were very popular, and some kept fowl. Everybody kept their coal in the yard, along with a big mangle and the bath.

GERRY ADAMS, *Before the Dawn*, 1996

IN THE RAIN-PIERCED GASLIGHT, Kitty watched the cart jolting and sloshing up the street, the four donkeys trailing behind.

It turned the corner, and the rattle of the wheels hardened and dimmed over the firmer, smoother surface of the road.

Kitty elbowed the boys down off the half-door.

'Come on, in you get, they're away.' The boys were dressed only in their shirts. 'Here! What do you think you're on, hanging over the door like that? You two'll get what's coming to you, if you're not very careful.'

The boys hopped down giggling, and ran back round to the fire.

Kitty came in, shrugging her shoulders and rubbing her elbows.

'Ah-oh! There's a stepmother's breath out there. That water's nearly up to the cribben, Malachey. I think it's time we started shifting a few things. You and your donkeys, Kelly,' she joked. 'Hell will never be full till you're in it. Here, you two, hurry up and get something on, and get off up the stairs out of this. It's always the same when there's anybody in. Give you an inch and you take a span.'

'Ah, Mammy,' Shemie wailed, 'it's too early for bed yet awhile. Look! The wee hand's at six and the big hand's at two. It's only two o'clock.'

'Ah, get away,' Neilly sneered. 'He can't even read the clock yet.'

'It's ten past six, Shemie,' Kelly instructed. 'You weren't far wrong.'

Shemie frowned up at the clock.

'Where does the ten come in?'

'Come on,' cried Kitty, 'plenty of time for arithmetic after. You needn't go to bed yet, though you won't be very long out of it. There is a fire in the front room and the gas is lit and all; take yourselves off now and let me get my head shired. I'll cut you a piece of bread for the time being. There's no use in making the tea yet a wee while, till we get everything upstairs and the other two studends are back. The flood'll be in on us in a minute.'

The boys took their cuts of bread and made for the stairs, their feet slapping on the bare tiles.

'And don't let me hear any pulling and hauling going on up there,' Kitty cried after them. 'I'll be up myself shortly.'

Malachey rose and, going to the door, opened it and peered out into the street. A flurry of rain swung in against his face, and he slapped the door again hurriedly.

JOHN O'CONNOR, Come Day – Go Day, 1948

THESE OLD SONGS AND RHYMING GAMES were sung through the streets of Belfast in the dim, forgotten nineties of the last century. They are now, alas, no longer heard in the streets, save for a few lingering echoes which still survive. It is for this reason that I have endeavoured to recapture the old tunes and songs: to take down, as it were, their last will and testament before their final departure to the land of silence, where so many of the singers have already gone. If I have unwittingly plagiarised in this collection of old folk songs and children's rhymes, from collections known only to the literary few, the fault is not mine. This is not a scissors-and-paste work, but a faithful account of all I have seen and heard in the days of my childhood, sixty years ago – when I went through the streets of Belfast, reciting the old rhymes and listening to the songs of the children, such as this skipping song. When a boy was teased by a girl, the only permissible reprisal on the boy's part was to steal the girl's comb and toss her hair. Without her comb, and with her hair in disorder, a young girl felt as helpless as a present-day miss without her cosmetics. You have to imagine the rhythmic thud of the skipping-rope.

THE SKIPPING SONG

I'll tell my ma when I go home
The boys won't let the girls alone.
They tossed my hair, they broke my comb,
So that's all right till I go home.
She is handsome; she is pretty;
She is the belle of Belfast City.
She is courting one, two, three.

Please can you tell me who is she?
Albert Mooney says he loves her,
All the boys are fighting for her.
They rap at the door and ring at the bell
And say, 'My true love, are you well?'
Out she comes, as white as snow,
With rings on her fingers, and bells on each toe.
Oh, Jenny Murray says she'll die
If she doesn't get a fellow with a rolling eye.
Let the wind and the rain and the wind blow high;
The snow comes falling from the sky;
Jenny Murray says she'll die
If she doesn't get a fellow with a rolling eye.
One young man is fighting for her,
All the rest, they swear they'll have her.
Let them all say as they will,
Albert Mooney loves her still.

You can imagine the 'salt, mustard, cayenne, pepper', as the song speeds up at the finish. But they were not all play-songs. Often the streets echoed to a different rhythm – plodding hooves on the square-setts, and the slap of leather on horses' flanks. The Trace Boys were familiar and envied figures in the streets of Belfast long ago. Belfast sits in a ring of hills: and the city streets climb up as they approach them. At certain points in the roads, therefore, it was necessary to have trace-boys with horses posted ready to assist the old horse trams up the steep gradient. The steepest hill was on the road leading to Ligoniel.

A TRACE-BOY ON LIGONIEL HILL

Do ye mind the old horse trams a long time ago
As they passed through the city at jog trot or slow?
On the level they cantered, but the pace it did kill
When they got to the bottom of Lig-o-niel Hill.

But the trace-boys were there with a heart and a hand
They let down the traces and buckled each band.
The passengers sat on contented and still
When they saw the bold trace-boys of Ligoniel Hill.

Away we did canter as fast as the wind,
And left the poor country carts plodding behind;
And that song of the wind in my ears I hear still
As when I was a trace-boy on Ligoniel Hill.

The youth of today hold their heads in the air,
And the young girls pass by with a golliwog stare,
Let them pity the crulge in my back if they will
But I once was a trace-boy on Ligoniel Hill.

My friends all departed, and work now so scarce,
The only thing left is a ride in a hearse,
For the sky is my roof and my bed a brick-kiln,
Yet I once was a trace-boy on Ligoniel Hill.

HUGH QUINN, 'Belfast Street Songs', Rann, 1952

SCHOOL. THE SCHOOL STOOD on a main thoroughfare in Belfast, with the statue of a famous Presbyterian divine overshadowing its railings. Outstanding memory, the heating system. Hot air was delivered into the classrooms through huge pipes, and a dart cleverly thrown at the vent-holes would turn and sail above the heads of the class, descending from the most unexpected quarters – even, on red-letter days, from behind the master's desk.

Item. The playground was extremely muddy and covered with brickbats.

DENIS IRELAND, From the Irish Shore, 1936

RETREAT, 1941

Early into the first term, a weekend retreat
To seal our barely stirring senses off.
(The Wehrmacht stalls before Stalingrad.)
Wartime rations already made a meagre diet,
Yet, skin pitted with boils, hands chilblained,
We still had to mortify our sinful appetites
With black sugarless tea, white butterless bread.

Silence as well as hunger was an obligation.
Around the Junior/Senior Rings we marched,
Monkish recruits, eyes lowered, or cowed
Heads bowed into edifying texts, after sermons
Where a Passionist preacher raged against temptation.
Daniel A. Lord on *Keeping Company with Women*
Before we had a chance to get around to them!

JOHN MONTAGUE, Time in Armagh, 1993

DURING MY BOYHOOD I VERY FREQUENTLY visited Glenwhirry. It was only seven Irish miles from Ballymena, and, as I grew up, I could readily walk the distance. Of the senior members of the family occupying the old residence, my grand-uncle, James Miller, alone remained. He died early in 1829 in the ninetieth year of his age. He retained his faculties to the last. He was born in 1739 – famous as the year of the Black Frost, and could tell what he had often heard of the awful severity of that visitation, and of the dearth which followed. He had also traditions of the fifty or sixty years preceding. He had once, in his youth, met with a very aged man who had, as he informed him, passed through 'the wars of Ireland', including the conflicts towards the close of the reign of James II and the battle of the Boyne. Thus, it would appear, there is only one link, that is my grand-uncle's, in the chain of tradition connecting me with those who were moving about in the days of William III.

W.D. KILLEN, *Reminiscences of a Long Life*, 1901

from A CHRISTMAS CHILDHOOD

An old man passing said:
'Can't he make it talk' –
The melodeon. I hid in the doorway
And tightened the belt of my box-pleated coat.

I nicked six nicks on the door-post
With my penknife's big blade –
There was a little one for cutting tobacco.
And I was six Christmases of age.

My father played the melodeon,
My mother milked the cows,
And I had a prayer like a white rose pinned
On the Virgin Mary's blouse.

PATRICK KAVANAGH, *Collected Poems*, 1964

THE SCHOOL WAS SMALL – a two-roomed ramshackle of a place that lay at the edge of the town beyond the last street lamp. We all loved it. Around it grew a few trees, their trunks hacked with boys' names and pierced with nibs and rusty drawing-pins. In summer when the windows were open we could hear the leaves rubbing together and in winter see the raindrops hanging on the bare twigs.

It was a draughty place and the master was always complaining of the cold, and even in the early autumn he would wear his overcoat in the classroom and rub his hands together: 'Boys, it's very cold today. Do you feel it cold?' And to please him we would answer: 'Yes, sir, 'tis very cold.' He would continue to rub his hands and he would look out at the old trees casting their leaves or at the broken spout that flung its tail of rain against the window. He always kept his hands clean and three times a day he would wash them in a basin and wipe them on a roller towel affixed to the inside of his press. He had a hanger for his coat and a brush to brush away the chalk that accumulated on the collar in the course of the day.

In the wet, windy month of November three buckets were placed on the top of the desks to catch the drips that plopped here and there from the ceiling, and those drops made different music according to the direction of the wind. When the buckets were filled the master always called me to empty them, and I would take them one at a time and swirl them into the drain at the street and stand for a minute gazing down at the wet roofs of the town or listen to the rain pecking at the lunch-papers scattered about on the cinders.

'What's it like outside?' he always asked when I came in with the empty buckets.

'Sir, 'tis very bad.'

He would write sums on the board and tell me to keep an eye on the class, and out to the porch he would go and stand in grim silence watching the rain nibbling at the puddles. Sometimes he would come in and I would see him sneak his hat from the press and disappear for five or ten minutes. We would fight then with rulers or paper darts till our noise would disturb the mistress next door and in she would come and stand with her lips compressed, her finger in her book. There was silence as she upbraided us: 'Mean, low, good-for-nothing corner boys. Wait'll Mister Craig comes back and I'll let him know the angels he has. And I'll give him special news about *you*!' – and she shakes her book at me: 'An altar boy on Sunday and a corner boy for the rest of the week!' We would let her barge away, the buckets plink-plonking as they filled up with rain and her own class beginning to hum, now that she was away from them.

MICHAEL McLAVERTY, *from* 'The Poteen Maker',
The Game Cock and Other Stories, 1949

BUT I BEGAN MY STORY ABOUT THE OLD SCHOOL. It was a three-windowed single-doored thatched house to the east on the edge of the cliffs overhanging the sea. The rafters and sidebeams were stained with soot and brown stains ran down the walls from leaks in the roof. A map of the world hung on the bottom gable. It was in the shape of two large wheels which were much larger than those on Muiris Mhéadhbha Ní Fhearaigh's cart, and two little circles about the size of the top of a bucket.

We always had a middling fire in wintertime. Every pupil had to bring two sods of turf to the school every day. I can still picture those same children coming in in the morning, and placing the two sods they were carrying under their oxters in the chimney corner. They all glanced from the side of their eyes to gauge what sort of humour the master was in.

The day's work would begin at ten o'clock. Most of the pupils would be assembled by half past nine, and they would spend that little while trying to put the finishing touches to the homework that had been set the night before. If you were in our old school at this time of the morning you would hear a few score who spoke nothing but Gaelic at home fervently murmuring:

'L-a-m-b, lamb, a young sheep. K-i-l-l-e-d, killed, put to death. W-a-g-g-o-n, a large cart.'

'Seven and one are eight, seven and two are nine, seven and three are ten.'

'Oh, say what is that thing called light
Which I must ne'er enjoy?'

'Derry, Londonderry, Newtownlimavaddy and Coleraine.'

'Charity, joy, peace, patience.'

'Grammar is the art of speaking a language correctly.'

'Queenstown is a port of call for American steamers.'

'Amplus, large, wide, full. Ample, amplify, amplification, amplitude.'

'Where Blake and mighty Nelson fell
Your manly hearts shall glow,
As you sweep through the deep
When the stormy winds do blow.'

This fervent whispering would persist until it was time to face judgement. And if anyone listened to us they might think that we had a reasonable command of English, but we had not, for half the time we did not know what we were saying.

SÉAMUS Ó GRIANNA (1942),
translated by A.J. HUGHES, *When I Was Young*, 2001

A S A SMALL CHILD HUGH was often a delighted visitor to his uncles at the farm at Ballygobbin – 'our ancestral hall', as he playfully described it in later years; and there, as well as at the old farmsteads at Dundooan, nearer to Coleraine, these old thatched farmhouses, wherein dwelt kindly, gentle kinsfolk, and the 'characters' in the way of farmhands, formed an important background to the early life of the artist. When school age came the boy was sent to the Coleraine Model School, where, under the headmastership of James Bresland, a man of high character and capacity, a sound elementary education was imparted; the subjects taught being the 'three Rs', geography, and singing, with geometry, elementary French, and science as 'extras'. The pupils being of mixed religious denominations, no history of any kind was taught. Hugh's exercise books and the fly leaves of all his lesson books, says his brother, were pencilled over with jottings of horses and dogs and men and ships. Certain 'humdrum lessons in perspective drawing' constituted the whole of his art education during boyhood.

M.H. SPIELMANN and WALTER JERROLD, Hugh Thomson, 1931

L IFE IN LOWER CRESCENT WAS WELL ORGANISED. Each morning Mrs Byers took assembly in the lecture hall, reading a portion of scripture with 'vim and vigour'. Prayers were at 9 a.m. after which the girls all walked round the hall to music and then bowed to the headmistress who sat on the dais at the far end of the hall. Every day she visited all of the classes and called the roll, for she knew the importance of regular public appearances among the girls. Lessons lasted from 9.30 a.m. until 2.30 p.m., with a break at 11 a.m. There were no school dinners in those days so pupils brought bread and jam to eat. Grace Moore remembered that when she was in Miss Miller's class there was an oven attached to the fire (for all the classrooms were heated by open coal fires), in which Miss Miller used to put a glass of milk with buttered bread on top. It came out all brown and sizzling and smelling most delicious to the hungry girls.

After school the boarders were taken for a walk up University Road past Queen's College, and, in crocodile, along the Stranmillis or Malone roads. Supper was served in the large dining room at 6 p.m. There were three tables in the room, with a teacher at each end of them. One table, where the older children sat, was supervised by a foreign assistant and they had to take turns at sitting next to the mademoiselle or fräulein to practise their conversation. There was prep. until 8.30 followed by recreation, often dancing in the lecture hall, until 9 p.m. when the younger girls went to bed. The senior classes of university pupils could study until 11 p.m.

Classes were even held on Saturday mornings when Miss Steele took geometrical drawing. In the afternoon pupils could visit friends approved by parents or guardians, while on Sunday morning all of them went to church, either Presbyterian or Church of Ireland, as their parents chose. A pew rent of 3s 6d per week was charged, for at that time people could select their own personal seat. Mrs Byers held a Bible class on Sunday afternoons, when the girls had to learn chapters of the Bible, two verses at a time. Usually this was not too arduous a task but occasionally she announced that she would hear the whole passage. This reduced delinquent pupils who had neglected their duty to such panic that some retired to bed or the sanatorium to avoid Nemesis.

Before the 1920s there was no school uniform, though girls were expected to wear sensible clothes, for example, a sailor dress with a blouse and collar and a pleated skirt. Grace Moore remembered wearing a scarlet jersey and navy skirt with a blue and white striped cotton blouse with long black stockings and laced or buttoned boots. In summer, strapped shoes could be worn with cotton frocks under short reefer coats with brass buttons. One former pupil remembered that some children had 'liberty bodices' with suspenders, while the older girls wore stays with a front attachment ... As the young ladies grew older, their skirts became longer, and they wore striped blouses with high, starched collars, ties and straw boaters. Some wore warm dresses with a frill and one rare memory of Mrs Byers in her later years was of a tirade she gave about the iniquity of wearing a frill until it was soiled.

ALISON JORDAN, *Margaret Byers: Pioneer of Women's Education and Founder of Victoria College, Belfast*, 2000

HILLSBOROUGH CHURCH WAS DESIGNED AND BUILT by one of the Hills, a beautiful eighteenth-century church, with a tall graceful spire. My favourite view of it was from the corner of the fort above and behind it. The tall spire rising among the tall old trees, and perhaps a rook or pigeon circling round, gave me an uncertainty about the extent and possibilities of space and the relative size of objects. Like the distant Belfast hills, which we could see twelve miles away, across the hollows and trees of the Lagan valley, from our doorstep on Hillsborough Square, the spire of the church and the tall trees created for my childish mind a beautiful mystery in three-dimensional geometry.

Another of Hillsborough's mysteries was the rectory, a big house standing well back from the main Dublin road in a very large garden. Looking at it on a still grey afternoon, with the trees of the park behind it, I used to feel that it had a life of its own in which its inhabitants played no part. Its rows of windows, its remoteness from other houses and its empty silence were not exactly menacing but certainly awe-inspiring. Indeed there were many mysteries in Hillsborough. There were, for example, the high walls over which I could not see. I did not imagine that there was anything very exciting behind them, not gunmen or machinery or anything like that, but I used to imagine that they concealed delicious places of deep cool greenery and perhaps running water and other pleasant things. There was a mystery, too, about the high whitewashed backs of some of the old houses. Even the routine things, the things that happened regularly, and as a matter of course, had behind them all the mystery of the big, complex world about which I, at that tender age, had still everything to learn. At that time of life everything that I encountered was new and therefore I gave everything my earnest and concentrated attention. I gazed solemnly at the big traction engine that hauled logs through the village and invented my first philological theory, to the effect that an engineer must be so called because he is always to be found 'neer' the engine. I went often to stare into a wonderful shop window full of hardware, pots, pans and all kinds of tools. I watched the July processions passing, men with sashes and bowler hats and blue serge suits and brown boots and bands and banners. I sat and meditated on a rug in the garden and maintained a polite but slightly reserved friendship with Togo, the cat, who was considerably my senior and had been called after the Japanese admiral in the war of 1905. And there were interesting sounds, too, which attracted my attention and have had a peculiar significance for me ever since. One of these sounds was the curious bumping sloppy sound of the whitewash brushes at work on the outside wall of the house. Another was the sound of a little engine at the bottom of the village echoing among the trees.

HUGH SHEARMAN, *Ulster,* 1949

WHEN NOBLE SAW 10 PLEASANT TERRACE, he said it should be 10 Unpleasant Terrace. And the door never opened till we had knocked – these town ways *were* queer. When we expected visitors at the Manse everybody went to the station to meet them except Mamma who was preparing for them at home, and she would be outside the gate watching, and go down the road to meet them when she saw them coming.

A servant nearly as old as Aunt Bethiah opened the door ...

Aunt Bethiah came into the hall when she heard us ... Inside the house looked as dismal as without. The blinds were half way down and I stumbled going up the dark stairs. My bedroom was to the front and the boys' to the back, looking out on a dreary strip of yard – our pig at home had a better view from his sty ...

After dinner Papa left and we felt desolate indeed. Aunt Bethiah seemed to guess something of what we were suffering, for she put on her bonnet and dolman and took us out for a walk.

The first thing that revived our spirits or made us think that there was any fun at all in Belfast was watching an amusing performance that we fortunately happened to see.

Passing a side street we saw a man beating a little drum and saw children gathering round something that looked a little to us like a pulpit, and we wondered what it meant.

Aunt Bethiah said it was a 'Punch and Judy show'. We forgot our unhappiness as we watched it. Punch had a great hooked nose and carried a stick that he used on everyone. He killed his wife Judy, and he killed the baby, and at the very end, when the policeman came to hang him for all his wicked acts, he hanged the policeman. He was a match for them all! There was a quaint little live dog called Toby with a frill round its neck that also took part in the play. Hugh thought Punch and Judy were living beings, but Noble and I knew right well that they were not. Aunt Bethiah said it was a very old show, and was introduced into this country from Italy in the reign of Queen Anne. She said Punch and Judy were dolls and were worked and made to move by a man who was low down, inside the box.

LYDIA M. FOSTER, *Manse Larks*, 1936

HOW GOOD IT WAS AS A SCHOOLBOY to leave the house to meet the friend who was waiting under a lamp-post, and to set off through the streets as though they were enchanted! We did not then think them dull. The gloomiest street of shut warehouses was good enough to walk and talk in. There was no avenue of villas too unsightly to be the setting of an argument. There was no back street of evil fame that did not stir the imagination like foreign travel. All places were alike to us if there was room for boys to walk in them. We could go down to the docks and watch the lights of the departing ships. We could walk up and down North Street, with its innumerable twopenny shows – sword-swallowers, dwarfs, mermaids, marionettes – lit up with invitation. We could go out beyond the trams and the lamps into the darkness of the country. But, wherever we went, it was not the scene that mattered to us. It was walking and talking and being alive.

ROBERT LYND, *from* 'The Promenade', *The Goldfish*, 1927

FOLLOWING MRS DUNWOODY'S SHOP came the four parlour-houses, all of which were dull to look at, and, except the third, dully occupied. The exceptional parlour-house was inhabited by the Cairnduffs. Mrs Cairnduff's father had been a Presbyterian minister in Derry, and she was considered to have married beneath her when she espoused the master of a small sailing-ship which tramped about the oceans of the world; but Mrs Cairnduff did not share this opinion, nor could anyone make her realise how she had fallen in society, so, after a while, no one tried. 'Anyway, the woman's happy' was the conclusion to which people came when they talked about her marriage. She had one daughter, Brenda, who frequently wore a white dress on Sundays and was the first girl in the Terrace to be seen wearing brown stockings. She was strictly forbidden to play with the rough children in Modesty Row. Her playmates, among whom Alec and Robert Dunwoody were included, were carefully chosen by her mother so that there might be no chance of roughness coming into her conduct or her conversation. She always said, 'I did so', when commoner children would have said, 'I did'. This was considered to be a great piece of refinement. She never said 'Aye': she always said 'Yes'. She called her mother 'Mamma' and her father 'Papa'. She wore a white petticoat every day.

Alec was very fond of Brenda, but Robert liked to play with her only when her father was home from one of his long voyages.

'Do you think your da would tell us about his trips?' he would say to Brenda, who would reply first, 'I wish you wouldn't say "Da", Darkie!' and then, 'I dare say!' Everybody called Robert 'Darkie Dunwoody' because he was the only member of his family who had not got very fair hair.

'Och, sure, what's wrong with "da"?' Darkie once demanded.

'It's common,' said Brenda.

ST JOHN ERVINE, *The Wayward Man*, 1927

IN SUMMER WE WENT TO A WHITEWASHED MEETING-HOUSE on Sundays. The meeting-house stood amongst the rocks on the seashore, so close to high-water mark that at full tide the thud and backwash of the waves mingled with the singing of the Psalms.

> O God, our help in ages past,
>   Our hope for years to come,
> Our shelter from the stormy blast,
>   And our eternal home

we sang. Sometimes the head of a seal appeared as a black dot in the channel between the big rocks, and from the gallery on particularly fine Sunday mornings you could look out through the small-paned windows clear across the Irish Sea to the tiny white farmhouses and the green squares of the fields on the Mull of Galloway.

The village shop had glass jars of sweets in the windows. At night it was lit by a single oil lamp that hung from the ceiling. Round the lamp clustered a conglomeration of boots, hams, tin cans, and brushes, all hanging together in confusion. The door had a bell that rang with a faint *ping*. You then made out in the background, beyond the zinc-covered counter, a pile of small dark-wood drawers with glass knobs. These drawers contained, as we knew from experience, everything that a normal man could require, from fish-hooks to pills and plug tobacco.

Saturday night was the big night in the village. On Saturday nights the shop was crowded with women, all patiently waiting with their tin cans concealed under their shawls and their pennies clutched in their hands. Then at midnight the bell would go *ping, ping, ping* and the women would file out into the darkness to wait for their men outside the public-house ... Across the street in M'Gimpsey's the barman would fling out the last customer, remove the corks from the automatic bottle-opener, and swab up the bar with a damp cloth.

Then he would come and stand in the doorway in his shirt-sleeves, outlined against the brilliant interior, survey the crowd, spit once, with emphasis, into the street, and shut the door.

Then more and more lights would go out throughout the village, and more and more plainly the sound of the waves would come up the steep, narrow side-street that led down to the sea.

DENIS IRELAND, *From the Irish Shore*, 1936

THE RIGHT ARM

I was three-ish
when I plunged my arm into the sweet-jar
for the last bit of clove-rock.

We kept a shop in Eglish
that sold bread, milk, butter, cheese,
bacon and eggs,
Andrews Liver Salts,
and, until now, clove-rock.

I would give my right arm to have known then
how Eglish was itself wedged between
ecclesia and *église*.

The Eglish sky was its own stained-glass vault
and my right arm was sleeved in glass
that has yet to shatter.

PAUL MULDOON, *Quoof*, 1983

MAY WAS AT ITS HEIGHT. All the apple trees were in blossom, and the red-thorn trees on the lawn. Through the open windows a soft wind brought the smell of hawthorn and lush green grass into the nursery. Bright patches of sunlight spotted the bare floor and Jane's red-and-white quilt. It was early morning and the children were still in bed, but they were wide awake – the sun had waked them an hour ago – and already they had planned how they would spend the day. It was Saturday, a whole holiday. Nobody had to do lessons today: the long rich sunny hours lay before them full of happiness. They had agreed that the rocks was the place for today's picnic; no other place would be so beautiful. This was the weather for the sea.

As they lay in bed they were thinking of the pleasures in store. First, there would be the walk across the soft spongy grass – past the whins for the sake of the hot sunny smell of their blossoms. They would be tempted to stop and picnic there, but they would go on towards the sea. The sheep would move off when they came near, and rakish black crows would rise slowly and sail away. Then the sea would come in sight, blue this weather, looking very deep and full. It would be washing against the grey rock with a soft splash, and it would slap your naked body as you slipped in for one dip after another.

KATHLEEN FITZPATRICK, *The Weans at Rowallan*, 1905

IT BEING SUMMER, THE WINDOW WAS OPEN, but it was rather out of her reach. She managed, however, with the help of her stool, to climb on to the sill, and there, in front of her, was the sea, and down below was the street – a goodish drop below if she had stopped to think of it; but Beth dropped first and thought afterwards, only realising the height when she had come down plump, and looked up again to see what had happened to her, surprised at the thud which had jarred her stomach and made her feet sting. She picked herself up at once, however, and limped away, not heeding the hurt much, so delightful was it to be out alone without her hat. By the time she got to Mary Lynch's she was Jane Nettles going on an errand, an assumption which enabled her to enter the shop at her ease.

'Good-day,' she began. 'Give me a ha'porth of pear-drops, and a ha'porth of raspberry-drops, Mary Lynch, please. I'll pay you on Saturday.'

'What are you doing out alone without your hat?' Mary Lynch rejoined, beaming upon her. 'I'm afraid you're a naughty little body.'

'No, I'm not,' Beth answered. 'It's my own money.' Mary Lynch laughed, and helped her liberally, adding some cherries to the sweets; and, to Beth's credit be it stated, the money was duly paid, and without regret, she being her mother at the moment, looking much relieved to be able to settle the debt, which shows that, even by this time, Beth had somehow become aware of money-troubles, and also that she learned to read a countenance long before she learned to read a book.

She straggled home with the sweets in her hand, but did not eat them, for now she was a lady going to give a party, and must await the arrival of her guests. She did not go in by the front door for obvious reasons, but up the entry down which the open wooden gutter-spout ran, at a convenient height, from the house into the street. The wash-house was covered with delicious white roses, which scented the summer afternoon.

Beth concealed her sweets in the rose-tree, and then leant against the wall and buried her nose in one of the flowers, loving it. The maids were in the wash-house; she heard them talking; it was all about what he said and she said. Presently a torrent of dirty water came pouring down the spout, mingling its disagreeable soapy smell with that of the flowers. Beth plucked some petals from the rose she was smelling, set them on the soapy water, and ran down the passage beside them, until they disappeared in the drain in the street. This delight over, she wandered into the garden. She was always on excellent terms with all animals, and was treated by them with singular confidence. Towie, the cat, had been missing for some time, but now, to Beth's great joy, she suddenly appeared from Beth could not tell where, purring loudly, and rubbing herself against Beth's bare legs. The sun poured down upon them, and the sensation of the cat's warm fur above her socks was delicious. Beth tried to lift her up in her arms, but she wriggled herself out of them, and began to run backwards and forwards between her and a gap in the hedge, until Beth understood that she wished her to follow her through it into the next garden. Beth did so, and the cat led her to a little warm nest where, to Beth's wild delight, she showed her a tiny black kitten.

SARAH GRAND, *The Beth Book*, 1897

M Y CHILDHOOD AND BOYHOOD in Belfast were very happy. I was the eldest of a family considered small in those days, for there were only four of us.

But if we were few we had as our constant companions a large family of cousins, the children of my father's sister, Marion Hannay, who married Frederick Kinahan. As children we were always together, sharing every kind of fun. In summer we picnicked at Crawfordsburn, bathed at Clandeboye and built ourselves forts high up among the branches of trees. In winter we gathered round Christmas trees, played riotously at blind man's buff and, fearfully, snapped burning raisins from the dish in front of an awful dragon. We even acted fairy plays, though this was an odd concession, for we were not allowed to go to the theatre. I still remember trying to make something of the heavy father part in *Beauty and the Beast* and greatly disliking having to kiss my cousin Emily several times during the performance. As we grew older we put away these childish things and took to dancing and tennis, playing in most of the tournaments though none of us ever excelled at the game. The fellowship and affection survived the inevitable separation which came with our going our own ways in life. Among those of that merry party who have weathered the passing years, the affection still survives.

GEORGE A. BIRMINGHAM, *Pleasant Places*, 1934

DICK AND I MAKE FOR THE RIVER beside the narrow-gauge railway, and wander through the valley. The river chatters over brown stones.

Dick is nine; wears a high white collar. I'm seven; with a fringe of straight hair over my forehead.

In a pine-wood each tree is poised with spread-out greenery. A mill with a black gable looks sombre. Overgrown with thorn trees, a waterfall drops gently from stone to stone, each covered with spongy moss. While we pause, Dick imagines a canopy and pediment on thin pillars which, he says, he would like to build at this spot, in which people might sit and hear the sound of the water.

He also says: 'We ought to form a secret society with a password, and look for gold under the cairns further up the river.'

A train, panting steam, goes past on the railway. The driver, unaware of our secret or beneficent imaginings, smiles and waves his hand.

We prowl about the rectory outbuildings, making trivial, but enjoyable, discoveries. In the harness-room, among cobwebbed tools, hammers, saws, bradawls, and gimlets, we find a rusted rat-trap; set it; and poke it with a rod to make it snap. Dick examines the dents in the rod. 'I wouldn't like to be the rat,' he considers. In the stick-house I swing an axe, splitting a waiting log among the chopped-up fuel. Dick turns to the wheel-pump; or peeps at his reflection in a rain-butt. But why not climb a tree? We climb a tree, scorch up a sycamore; which leads to a discussion, slightly protracted, on the business of nest-building as carried on by birds.

Up an exterior flight of stone steps we go to the red door of the barn, which, inside, by contrast with the sunshine, is dusky. From a circular window a mottled column of sunlight slants to a heap of straw, selecting it alone to brighten in the shadowy interior. We come upon a surplus book-case, laden with books no longer wanted. The books, when opened, smell of damp yellowing paper.

GEORGE BUCHANAN, *Green Seacoast*, 1959

EARLY WARNING

My father brought out his donkey-jacket,
Tipped a bucket
Of blue-stone into the knapsack sprayer,
A wing and a prayer
Against apple-scab disease,
And mizzled the lone crab-apple tree
In our back garden,
That was bowed down more by children
Than by any crop.

We would swing there on a fraying rope,
Lay siege to the tree-house,
Draw up our treaties
In its modest lee.

We would depend on more than we could see.

Our Protestant neighbour, Billy Wetherall,
Though he knew by the wireless
Of apple-scab in the air,
Would sling his hammock
Between two sturdy Grenadiers
And work through the latest *Marvel* comic.

PAUL MULDOON, *Why Brownlee Left*, 1980

HALLOWEEN CAME, AND THEIR DADDY took them over to Brian's house, for them to celebrate it with their cousins, as they did every year. He laughed when he got into the car and looked over his shoulder to see three small witches sitting in the back seat. They were all wearing pointed paper hats with moons and stars printed on them: he'd bought them for the children himself, in McGovern's. All three were wearing the masks they'd made in art class at school. 'You'd put the heart across a body,' he said to them, as he started the engine.

They ran screaming around the bonfire Uncle Peter had built for them, and Helen felt both frightened and excited as she watched the firelight on the blackened faces of her sisters and cousins. They had fireworks too: Roman candles and Catherine wheels, sparklers and rockets. The coloured lights flowed briefly like magical liquids when Uncle Peter set the fireworks off, and the children covered their ears at the loud noise. Afterwards, you couldn't remember the fireworks exactly as they had been: there was something about the nature of them that made it impossible, until another one was lit. Later, they moved into the back scullery, where Aunt Lucy filled a zinc bath with water, and floated yellow apples in it for them to try to catch and pull out with their teeth. She put piles of flour on dinner plates, and a wrapped toffee on the top, again for them to pick up and claim, without using their fingers. 'Make as much mess as you want,' she said indulgently: and they did.

DEIRDRE MADDEN, *One By One in The Darkness*, 1996

AND AS SOUNDS AND WORDS AFFECTED ME, so, too, certain things in life would suddenly sweep through me in a flood of beauty, that seemed to fill my whole being, and reduce me to a state of paralysed immobility. I remember one such happening which took place during a holiday at the seaside. An arrangement had been made among us to meet at night on the beach and bathe in the moonlight. But on the night fixed for the adventure a white mist had rolled up out of the water, and the whole bay was shrouded by a thick veil, through which the splashing of the invisible waves sounded mysteriously. There was only a faint wash of palest gilt where the moon should have been. It was as if the entire earth had suddenly fallen under an enchantment, and coming out of the warm lighted house into this totally unexpected and unrecognisable world, I stood spellbound and solitary on the verge of it. I could hear voices and laughter. I could see the ghostly naked forms of the bathers appearing and disappearing as they passed in and out of the mist and splashed through the shallows; but I did not, could not, join them. It was unearthly, fantastic. Five yards from the shore nothing was visible; and out of this milky void a disembodied voice would float, or a small dream-like figure for a moment emerge. Presently the voices of uneasy mothers were added to these spirit voices, urging the more adventurous to return. Half laughing, yet fussy and anxious as hens, they hovered where the shore dipped down to the water's edge, counting their broods. One or two boys were missing, and eager cries called them to come back. It was a picture such as A.E. might have imagined and painted, but no painting could give the peculiar glamour of the reality. What had been designed as a mere frolic, had by some strange alchemy been transformed into a scene of radiant loveliness, a kind of spiritual blessing, like Wordsworth's field of daffodils.

FORREST REID, *Apostate*, 1926

I STILL DREAM ABOUT THE HALF-ACRE BEHIND Mooreland, and its various stages of field, leftover landscape, vacant ground, plot, building-site, half-built houses, and completed semi-detacheds. Here, there is a network of small paths between the privet and convolvulus demarcations of back gardens, where it sometimes rains cherry-blossom, or the overpowering odour of sweet-pea stains the air with tinctures of pale lilac, purple, yellow-pepper-yellow, ruby, celadon, and dazzling apple-white. Starch-white sheets billow on clothes lines, washed in Surf or Tide. Little picket gates and hedgy archways provide interesting access points to the gardens and their crazy paving winding among small lawns, rose arrays and vegetable patches. One such creaking gate leads to the stepping-stones of the stream. There is a small beach of gravel here, where I can hunker for unknown hours and watch the current burl and bump across the pebbles.

Stepping across to the other side, I plunge into the era of the building-site: an aura of raftered pine and brick, wood-shavings and cement-dust.

It was a world of half-finished structures, whose exo-skeletons of scaffolding were connected, Babel-wise, in gangways, hoists, ladders, platforms, ropes and planks. It had the presence of a great interminable siege, as we stalked its storeyed parapets and battlements and gazed down across its blasted landscape of earth-works and ziggurats of brick, and churned mud where cement mixers were embedded like mortars. Discarded hods and buckets lay scattered everywhere, like details in a documentary of Breughel building techniques.

Before the building-site proper existed, deep trenches were dug in the back field. Roofed with corrugated iron and floored with bits of cast-off carpet, they made admirable suburban HQs, where our wish to be invisible could be realised, as it was in wardrobes, hedges, under stairs or attic roofs, in peek-a-boo routines of out-of-sight and out-of-mind.

CIARAN CARSON, *The Star Factory*, 1997

A Shared
Heritage

Ulster in the time of our great-grandfathers must have been architecturally beautiful. I say 'must have been', for today our heritage is much spoiled and in greater danger probably than that of any part of the British Isles. It is threatened now by prosperity and so-called improvement.

DENIS O'D. HANNA, 'Architecture in Ulster'

When one looks at the Plantation towns of Ulster, pleasantly sited and well designed as many of them are, with their central squares and wide streets which adequately fulfil the needs of present day traffic, one is amazed at the ability and far sightedness of the planners of the early seventeenth century to whom a great part of the credit for the siting and layout of these towns is due ... the street layout of the central portions of such towns as Derry, Coleraine, and even of Belfast, was carried out at the time of the Plantation and little change has since been made in these street layouts.

GILBERT CAMBLIN, *The Town in Ulster*

THE PROVINCE POSSESSES A VIRILE Vernacular Georgian architecture. It stems upon the home of the yeoman farmer.

The formula for this is simple yet always alive and original – a fanlighted door or window detail or some whimsical arrangement of fenestration. One would expect regional development in a country that for generations must have felt very remote from the capital, for in Georgian times Ulster was three days from Dublin, and it was not until the year 1788 that a stagecoach was first established between Dublin and Belfast, which reduced the journey to twelve hours. In spite of these difficulties, Ulster abounds in large Palladian mansions, some scarcely less ambitious than those of Leinster itself. Florencecourt (1764), by John Cole, and Castlecoole (1788), the work of James Wyatt, senior, are among the most important, and in or round Belfast many fine Georgian homes are located, notably Hillsborough Castle, Mount Stewart, Greyabbey House, Castleward, Castle Dobbs.

DENIS O'D. HANNA, *from* 'Architecture in Ulster', *The Arts in Ulster*, 1951

ULSTER POSSESSES MANY COUNTRY MANSIONS some of which are known to have been designed by well-known English and Irish architects of the front rank. Of the English architects, James Wyatt's Castle Coole, County Fermanagh (1788), for which large quantities of Portland Stone were imported through Ballyshannon; Sir John Soane's designs at Baronscourt, Tyrone, and the Royal Belfast Academical Institution (1810); and John Nash's rectory at Lissan, on the Derry-Tyrone border, and his Loggias at Caledon, are outstanding. Thomas Cooley (who came from England, in spite of his Irish-sounding name) designed the central core of Caledon House (built in 1779), and the Primate's Palace at Armagh (built *c.* 1770). Buildings which can be definitely attributed to well-known Irish architects are rare in Ulster, but the work of Francis Johnston merits particular mention for his creation of much of the attractive late Georgian character of Armagh. The most important of these buildings are the Observatory (1789–90) and the Court House (1809). Much of his work at Armagh, and of the work strongly influenced by him, was carried out in beautiful limestone from Armagh quarries, which resembles Portland stone in its whiteness but gives a more varied finish. These buildings, and others like Hillsborough Court House of the later eighteenth century ... and many in Newry, of fine grey or pinkish Mourne granites, show how much opportunity has been missed in Ulster when other than local materials have been used for mansions and important buildings.

E.M. JOPE, *Ancient Monuments in Northern Ireland*, 1952

SINCE 1956 I HAVE BEEN A COMMITTED and devoted conservationist. My interest has been in the artefacts of man, the modest but delightful buildings with which previous generations have endowed the towns, villages, and countryside of Ireland, rather than with the countryside itself or with its wildlife. I have devoted more hours than I care to think of to recording, praising, and caring about such buildings – whose merit has been far too little appreciated both by the Irish, and by the rest of the world. But I have watched, in two short decades, while half the heritage of Ulster has been lost. Was ever a conservationist more unfortunate in the time and place of his birth?

Yet I have not yet, quite, despaired. There has been a welcome and belated swing in public opinion, across all party and religious divisions, within the past ten years. The bureaucrats, the engineers, the developers, even the councillors, are beginning to respond – here and there. Curiously enough, a shared concern to keep what little is left of a shared heritage may yet serve to bring together aggressively loyalist Ulstermen and aggressively nationalist Irishmen. Is it too much to hope that even the paramilitaries, the gunmen who are the spiritual heirs of those who destroyed the Four Courts, and with them a great part of the history of Ireland, will yet learn to stay their hand? Probably it is; in the past, the destructive element in the Irish character has too often outweighed the constructive element. There are said to be some ten thousand medieval parish churches in England still roofed and used for worship. The corresponding number in Ireland is said to be less than ten. But I am not utterly without hope: and it remains true, as it has been for centuries, that the less there is to save, the more important remains its saving.

C.E.B. BRETT, Long Shadows Cast Before, 1978

IN 1783, ON A PLOT OF GROUND presented to the town by Lord Donegall, the White Linen Hall was built. This harmonious building, set in the midst of what became Donegall Square, served cultural as well as commercial ends, very much in the manner of the lovely Cloth Halls of Europe, and within its walls was formed the Belfast Reading Society, later to become the Belfast Library and Society for Promoting Knowledge, more familiarly known as the Linen Hall Library.

The frantic pursuit of money had not at that time swamped every other consideration, and Donegall Square was in fact allowed to become a square, which it is to this day. But the White Linen Hall is no more, for in 1890 the Corporation acquired the building and soon set their hands to its demolition. In its place we have the present ornate City Hall, which, whatever else it may do, marks a decline in taste from the graceful eighteenth-century building which it displaced, and the passing of which every person of sensibility cannot but deplore. The old White Linen Hall, surrounded by well-designed wrought-iron railings of the period, was something which Belfast could not afford to lose, symbol of that great eighteenth century when the town stood high in renown, gracious memorial to the pioneer merchants who laid the foundations of one of our major industries, and constant reminder of the inner grace and strength of the founders of our community. It was a building full of character and tradition, a building of the kind in which Belfast is so lamentably poor, and its demolition was at once significant and disastrous. In an English town, a continental town, or a town of New England or the southern states of America, it would have been preserved as an everlasting treasure and unending comfort.

RICHARD HAYWARD, *Belfast Through the Ages*, 1952

WHEN THE ANGLO-NORMANS INVADED Ireland in 1172, Ulster was not subjugated in the same manner as Leinster. The invaders came from South Wales to South Leinster, and so northward to Dublin. To them the North was a wild remote region, and its conquest was left to private adventure. John de Courcy, who had received from Henry II, perhaps in jest, a gift of Ulster, which he might make good with his sword if he were able, gathered together a small but well-armed and disciplined force, and in 1177 set out northwards. Marching with all speed, so as to take the Irish by surprise, he reached Downpatrick from Dublin in four days, took the city, and defeated MacDunlevy, King of the Ulidians, in a pitched battle.

But this dazzling initial success was followed by years of hard, and often unsuccessful, fighting. Still, in the end, de Courcy had made himself, if not complete master, certainly the strongest power in Antrim and Down. He had studded the country with his castles, and in the true Norman manner had built, in addition to his strong military works, large and splendid churches and abbeys, the ruins of some of which still survive.

D.A. CHART, *A History of Northern Ireland*, 1927

AT ONE TIME, THERE WERE FORTY-EIGHT religious establishments in County Antrim alone, and an immense number of ancient fortresses and raths. Interesting remains are still to be seen of the old castles at Greencastle, Olderfleet, Castle Chichester, Red Bay, Castle of Court Martin, Glenville, Dunluce, Dunseverick, Kenbane, Doonaninny, Castle Cary, Bruce's Castle, Castle Upton, Lissanoure, Castle Robin and Portmore. It is impossible to even name them all, but we cannot conclude without mentioning the ruins beside the old church at Kilroot, where Dean Swift was incumbent for two years. The graveyard is in a disgraceful condition, and the baptismal font is lying in the long grass, totally uncared for. The rectory where he lived in the year 1695 is beside Kilroot station and is still inhabited.

MARY LOWRY, *The Story of Belfast and Its Surroundings*, 1912

T HE VILLAGE OF KILLOUGH has a healthy smell of fish. When the tide
is out there is a slimy green carpet where the sea should be. Ardglass
is famous for herrings and castles. One of the latter, Shane's Castle as it is
known today, was restored by that interesting and patriotic man, Francis
Joseph Bigger. He was a Gaelic Leaguer and a Sinn Feiner (or at least a
neo-Sinn Feiner) and he served his country in the unusual way of
restoring castles and churches and re-erecting crosses and gravestones. In
a now rare book of caricatures and humorous commentary, Bigger is
depicted wearing kilts and carrying a banner with a Gaelic legend. The
caption reads: 'Occupation: Fellow of the Royal Society of Antiquaries.
Recreation: law. Favourite pastime: fishing in Lough Neagh,
accompanied on the war pipes. Pet aversion: Board of Works and brass
instruments.' The Belfast-born patriot died in 1926.

STEPHEN RYNNE, *All Ireland*, 1956

N EWTOWNARDS, WITH ITS HANDSOME TOWN hall and market cross,
betokens Scottish influence in its solid stonework and slate. The
town had its origin in the fifth-century schools of St Finian, where
Columbkille was educated. It passed into Norman hands and its centre
was moved from Movilla down to where the abbey now stands. Behind
this building may be seen to this day some medieval walls and corner
defence towers, as well as a monks' fishpond. The 'Black Abbey', as it is
called, is now in ruins and possesses one or two details of fifteenth-
century carving which are typically Irish in style, as well as a few grave
slabs of the tenth to fourteenth centuries. To Montgomery, Laird of
Braidstane, who headed the Scottish Plantation in Ards in 1606, must be
attributed the interesting Jacobean entrance to the abbey. The Jacobean
town of the Scottish Planters centred round the town cross, with its
ancient hostels and taverns, and the building which still incorporates the
lower storey of Montgomery's castle in which he lived when he first
came over. In the summers of 1605 and 1607 the harvests were good, and
we read that Sir Hugh Montgomery's lady 'built watermills in all parishes
to prevent the necessity of bringing meal from Scotland and grinding
with quairn stones as the Irish did to make their gradden'.

In the eighteenth century a handsome plan for the town was evolved
and the market house and square became the focal point of
Newtownards. It was here that the Ards Door, a Georgian type of
entrance, was introduced, possibly from England, although the Ards was
a Scots-planted area, just as Holywood, in County Down, adopted a
peculiar coach entrance, with the front door opening off it instead of
being placed on the facade of the building.

DENIS O'D. HANNA, *from* 'Architecture in Ulster', *The Arts in Ulster*, 1951

TOWN PLANS, EVEN AS FAR BACK as the early seventeenth century, have a late eighteenth-century deliberation about them, an element no doubt of the Plantation, as may be seen at Londonderry, Coleraine and Killyleagh, County Down. Town Halls and Court Houses were developed during the eighteenth century in a simple, well-proportioned classical style, as may be seen in many Ulster townships. The tradition, like that of classical façades on Meeting Houses, persisted late, well into the nineteenth century, the Court House at Newry having been built as late as 1843. The Court House at Hillsborough of the late eighteenth century ... (the designer of which is unknown although the original plan survives) is a pleasing combination of the textures of local materials, with its lower courses of beautifully textured granite from the Mournes, twenty-five miles away, its middle courses of Scrabo sandstone and its harled and colour-washed tower. It is an excellent example of a style of Civic Architecture which, with its classical frontages and pleasing cupolas, is to be found in many Ulster townships, emphasising in a most refreshing manner the individual character of the Province.

E.M. JOPE, *Ancient Monuments in Northern Ireland*, 1952

FROM [BELFAST] WE GO BY THE SEASIDE to Carrickfergus, which is a sorry old town. Here is the capital seat of the earls of Donegall built by Sir Arthur Chichester, the first and great earl of Donegall. It was a noble house, the architect of which is said to be Inigo Jones, but I don't think it his style of building. It was habitable fifteen or twenty years ago, and might have been kept up at a small expense but it has been so neglected that the roof is fell in and it is now in so ruinous a condition that I hardly think it can be repaired. In the church here is a fine monument of the first earl; there are statues of him and his countess; better care is taken for the reception of the family when dead than when alive.

EDWARD WILLES, 'Letters to the Earl of Warwick', *c.* 1759

THE CHILDREN THOUGHT HER STORIES about their own home were more exciting than the saints. There was a time, she said, when the dilapidated old house had been one of the finest in Ireland. When she came to Rowallan, a slip of a girl, more than fifty years ago, there had been no fewer than seven gardeners about the place. Auld Davy who worked in the kitchen garden now was all that was left of them. Now the house was falling to pieces; big patches of damp discoloured the walls, and most of the rooms were shut up. But Lull had seen the day when all was light and colour, when the rooms were filled with guests, and the children who slept in the nursery then had heard the rustle of silk dresses

– not the scamper of rats – on the stairs at night.

Her listeners knew that her stories were true; they could see for themselves when they opened the shutters of the big disused drawing-room how beautiful everything must have been, though the yellow damask curtains and the satin on the chairs were faded and moth-eaten, and the sconces on the wall tarnished.

KATHLEEEN FITZPATRICK, *The Weans at Rowallan*, 1905

L ONDONDERRY DID NOT LIVE TO SEE the completion of the house [i.e. Mount Stewart] as he had planned it, although by 1817 it only wanted the chapel and some additional bedrooms. The plain but imposing design in which the whole structure was carried out lent peculiar force to the Ionic columns with which it was finished, and showed that the Georgians even in Ireland still paid some attention to classic form and lines.

Bricks and mortar could also make some pleasing additions to the demesne. Elegant and suitably draped statuary were distributed at decent intervals throughout the grounds, and as no country residence was considered complete without a miniature Greek temple, one of these delightful buildings was erected in the Corinthian order. The Temple of the Winds (so it was called to commemorate a dramatic incident in Castlereagh's boyhood) soon became a landmark, for it could be seen from far out in the Lough peeping over the beech trees, and it served another practical purpose. By day members of the family and their guests would repair to it for rest and contemplation (the brothers Adam had made the interior most presentable), and by night for dessert and post-prandial conversation. 'I could have stayed,' confessed Dr Haliday when he was once called away from one of these latter gatherings to visit a patient (he dearly loved a symposium). 'An honest wine-glass is the well at the bottom of which squats truth.'

H. MONTGOMERY HYDE, *The Rise of Castlereagh*, 1933

F EW OF THE VILLAGES OF COUNTY ANTRIM are built on hills, but are usually located on level ground and are often in the form of one long street, as at Broughshane, the houses having been built on either side of a highway. The roadside village is not, of course, peculiar to Antrim, but is found in all parts of the Province. Such villages often lack the character of the hillside villages; at times, however, they possess considerable interest and charm, as when the buildings are of pleasing appearance and when trees have been planted in the village street. Moira, for instance, which has a row of fine trees in the centre of its wide street and mid–Georgian houses of rubble masonry, is a roadside village of very pleasing appearance. So, too, is Waringstown, with its simple thatched cottages, their unfenced lawns shaded by trees.

Very different from the straggling roadside village of Waringstown, with its thatched, whitewashed cottages, is the Moravian village of Gracehill, near Ballymena. Gracehill, indeed, is unlike any other village in Ulster, either in its layout or in the appearance of its buildings. It was planned and built by settlers who came from central Europe about the middle of the eighteenth century and it was laid out with two parallel streets, each a quarter of a mile in length; these being connected by two short streets, one on either side of a central square. The square was laid out as a garden and planted with trees and it was overlooked by the church, which was built in the centre of one of the long streets, the other buildings of importance being on either side of this edifice. The houses at Gracehill were constructed with large squared blocks of dark–coloured stone, and these dwellings must have aroused considerable interest amongst the inhabitants of the surrounding district when they were first built, for ... the farmhouses and cottages of Antrim were practically all whitewashed at this time.

GILBERT CAMBLIN, *The Town in Ulster*, 1951

from GRACEHILL
The Moravian Settlement, near Ballymena

Come to Gracehill, walk up along with me,
    A walk so sweet will cheer your gloomy mind;
Will your cold heart not glow with joy to see
    The little paradise that there you'll find?

Walk round the sylvan scene and fondly view
    The fragrant fruit-tree, and the blossom'd pea;
Herbs of all tastes, and flow'rs of every hue
    Pure as yon Vestal — and as fair as she.

How green these meads! How rich these fields of corn!
    The bean-field blooms, the flax bends to the breeze:
Prolific plenty fills her copious horn,
    And Nature smiles, where Vice and Folly cease.

Compact and clean the mansions that we've pass'd;
    And smooth these lawns, that milk-white hedges screen:
Tho' not long since, 'twas one wide lonely waste;
    No dome was beauteous, and no lawn was green.

But Culture spoke the word, His friends obey'd;
   The rock they raz'd, th' irriguous marsh they dried
The Genius of the Main uprais'd his head,
   And wonder'd at the changes on his side.

Nor stopp'd he here; the Pow'r who tam'd the waste,
   Went on to regulate the moral frame;
He taught his vot'ries Science, Truth, and Taste,
   And bade 'em pomp and pageantry disclaim.

JAMES ORR, Poems on Various Subjects, 1804

AMONG THE EARLIER DOMESTIC STRUCTURES which still remain, the yeomen's two-storied thatched houses are of great interest. Such houses are common enough in townships in most parts of Ireland, but isolated yeomen's houses in the countryside are generally found in regions which were colonised predominantly by the English settlers, such as north-west Down and adjacent parts of Antrim, and Armagh. They are not to be seen in areas settled by the Scots, such as east Down and Antrim. Some, like the yeoman's house at Waringstown, or Berwick Hall near Moira ... may be dated to the later years of the seventeenth century. The same type was still being built in the later eighteenth and early nineteenth centuries as at Ballinderry and Aghalee, County Antrim.

Derrymore House, near Bessbrook, County Armagh ... shows an unusual combination of a group of low thatched-roofed buildings with a more ambitiously conceived entrance. It has a patterned oval fanlight over the door which is so universal and striking a feature of Irish houses of the later eighteenth and early nineteenth centuries. It was built about 1780, and is where, reputedly, the Act of Union was drawn up in 1799. The Steeple House, beside Antrim Round Tower, is an example of a larger house, with its low pitched roof, expansive overhanging eaves, broad bow windows and corner pilasters, epitomising the Ulster country house of the early Victorian period. The Regency style persisted late in Ulster, where the Gothic Revival was only lightly felt, and Steeple House might be as late as 1840. Such good houses of the eighteenth and earlier nineteenth centuries, both small and large, are abundant in the Ulster countryside. They often lie unobtrusively away from the main roads, but are well worth seeking out.

E.M. JOPE, Ancient Monuments in Northern Ireland, 1952

IN ONE OF THE NORTHERN COUNTIES there is a high hill, its sides clothed with woods which are visible from most of the surrounding country. And on the summit of that hill stands the ancient house amid its purple beeches, yews and oaks, which must have been planted to shelter an exposed position from the stormy blasts of Winter. A straight avenue leads to the long whitewashed building that faces the newcomer, spreading its wings like arms stretched out in welcome. There are few Jacobean houses in Ireland, and at first sight the building gives the impression of having more resemblance to a French chateau than the square Georgian pile which is so common in the Emerald Isle.

The house is built round three sides of a wide, open courtyard, though the side buildings – with graceful curved gables surmounted by stone urns – are not joined to the main part of the dwelling. To the left, beyond an arched doorway, the old brew-house, turf-shed, slaughter-house and laundry surround a square grass plot, beyond which a walled alley leads up hill to the ancient and once fortified barn and onwards to the kitchen-garden. If a door in the wall to the left of this alley is opened, you have the surprise of finding yourself in a sequestered and old-world Dutch garden, ivy-walled and gay with box-edged flowerbeds sloping to the south west. Bygone hands have planted sweetbriar, honeysuckle, jessamine and old-fashioned roses in this garden ... [on] the far side of the house, where the side walls are slated from roof to ground and where formerly a second court – or 'bawn' – existed, we find an avenue of gigantic beeches leading up to a ruined watch tower. On turning to face the back of the house, it can be seen that its irregular pile has not the symmetry of the front, each successive generation having added a bit here and there at their own sweet will.

But Spring is here, and her enchantment bids us stay outside yet awhile. She has transformed this haunt into a veritable fairyland, for the lawns which slope away from the 'beech walk' to the lower woods are shimmering with bluebells which scent the air with sweetness, while a hundred birds warble in the pale green of woven branches. If the fabled dryads still inhabit these trees, they could tell many a tale of the nine generations of the family who have walked beneath their shade and have talked together of interests and projects, fears and misgivings for the dear old home, whose spell must have twined itself around their hearts. In Cromwell's day it may have been the two Williams – father and son – planning a place for the new 'bog-orchard', or, in James II's reign, 'Good Will' (the younger) pacing to and fro while scanning the fateful anonymous letter which told of coming massacre. Or later it may have been old George hastening to find Captain Ashe robbing his armoury, or his daughter, Mistress Anne, clinging to the arm of her gallant young brother who was about to sail with his regiment to take part in the Seven Years' War.

MINA LENOX-CONYNGHAM, *An Old Ulster House*, 1946

WE RETURN FROM CHURCH. The pony goes up the avenue, at the end of which the rectory, as it seems, rides steadily at anchor in a sea of meadowgrass, facing across a low valley where runs a narrow-gauge railway. It's a century-old grey house of no particular architecture, with walled garden, stables, outhouses, lost among shrubberies and trees – trees that vary in tone from light beech to sombre yewtree, from copper beech to milk-green ash. Upon the walls, ivy has drawn dark curious maps.

GEORGE BUCHANAN, *Green Seacoast*, 1959

THIS ROAD ALONG THE NORTH-EAST COAST is one of Ireland's chief beauties. For forty miles, it runs at very sea's edge, so that you could cast a biscuit into the waves, while on your other hand huge cliffs soar to the sunset sky. As we swing out beyond Larne, we see headland after headland northward, under storm-clouds, with the sea foaming at their feet. It is terrifying in its splendour. Sometimes the cliff thrusts out across the road into the sea, and we go through the living rock. Sometimes, lumps of chalk-stone as big as a house lie tumbled at the sheer cliff's edge, and you'd wonder if another might rush down on you, under the groaning storm.

Hardly another soul is on this wild and glorious coast road on this bright, wild evening. I would that we had time to halt and admire the black basalt that contrasts with the shining chalk; but it is darkening apace, and now the white cliffs are like snow heaps, or ghosts as tall as a mountain. A castle turned into an hotel we pass at Ballygalley, and I wish we had time to stay here; for this is the most beautiful hotel that I know: beautiful in its old, turretted tower, its oak panelling, its sconces and napery, its doo'cotes and sunken garden, its walled lawns, where it is pleasant to linger in the spring sunlight, while the sea that thunders from Scotland sends its wrack-scented, bracing air inland to the mountain wall.

AODH DE BLÁCAM, *The Black North*, 1938

THERE WAS NO SHORTAGE OF STONE in Ulster, and so inevitably masonry became the building material of the Province, though brick was introduced where English influence was strong. Many of the native houses in Ulster before Plantation times were oval and thatched with bracken, having stone walls, the chinks closed with mud, as in the style of the Scottish crofts. Turf-and-mud wall was common. Various forms of rubble masonry were in use, but there was always the tendency to use land stones, which in their smooth state weakened walls and caused buildings to fall into disrepair more easily than in the case of dressed stones. This practice accounts for some of the impermanence in Irish building. Thatch was almost the universal roof covering, both for native Irish and English settlers, but the Scots showed a preference for slates, probably on account of the hardness and dampness of their climate, and because in their own country they possessed a fine slate tradition. Corbie steps on the gable may be taken as a sign of Scottish influence. Mud-walled houses are common in Northern Ireland, and in some English districts the cruck roof may be seen. After the 1641 Rebellion the English rebuilt the settlement towns by more or less Irish methods, for it was in this rebellion that the Province suffered the irreparable loss of all her half-timber English houses, black oak beams, and white panels. These were burned down and pillaged to such an extent that not one example today remains in the whole settlement. This beautiful style of English yeoman building had been established in County Londonderry and in the Lagan Valley, many examples at one time existing in Lurgan, Lisburn, and the Guild towns of Derry.

DENIS O'D. HANNA, *from* 'Architecture in Ulster', *The Arts in Ulster*, 1951

As IN MOST OF THESE little plantation towns, there is a certain air of antiquity about Cavan, mingled with much that is ill-planned and out of place. And there are some pleasant Georgian houses about parts of the countryside, but often these old houses are spoilt by incongruous modern additions. In some cases it would seem that the style of architecture that clashes least with houses in the Irish rural Georgian style is the milder kind of modern functional architecture with simple, straight and unbroken lines.

HUGH SHEARMAN, *Ulster*, 1949

THE SUBSEQUENT DEVELOPMENT of the two planned sectors was very different. North of the town the straight streets were only occasionally graced by fine Georgian houses, for there development was closely linked with shipping, the timber yards and the quays along the Lagan side. This northern rim of the town was already becoming a poor district, and in the early nineteenth century there was a considerable expansion of small terrace housing in the area, alternating with factories and warehouses.

In the south the most important of the new streets had been Linen Hall Street (now Donegall Place), linking Castle Place with the new Linen Hall ... Here, and in other streets around the Linen Hall, the newly rich industrialists vied with one another and with the older moneyed class in building grand terrace houses. These were usually well designed and on a magnificent scale. Late survivals hint at a dignity comparable with good residential terraces in other larger cities. For example, one of these houses had two large parlours, hall, kitchen, scullery, larder, dairy, butler's pantry, eight bedrooms, five closets, garrets for servants, coach house and stables for five horses. Most of the houses were three or four storeys high. Their interior decoration must have been on a lavish scale if we can believe the statement of one lady that it took £1,000 to furnish a parlour in this part of town. The air of aristocracy which had once invested Castle Place was now transferred to this new sector. In 1803 Sir Stephen May took a plot of land in Donegall Square, and the Marquis of Donegall built his town house on the corner of Linen Hall Street and the Square. A year later the town's sovereign and four magistrates were among the residents of Linen Hall Street, which was entirely residential with the exception of a bank and a club. Building continued apace, but the demand was always higher than the supply, even at rents of between £50 and £110 a year. With the building of these handsome terraces, conditions in the streets also improved. In 1793 they were reported to be 'dirty beyond enduring', but five years later 'a horseman and trumpeter ordered the inhabitants to sweep the streets twice a week before a certain hour on pain of military punishment'. Another five years and our informant reports that 'our streets are well-lighted, paved, and perfectly clean'. A hint of the dignified architecture of these streets still remains in College Square North and in Chichester Street. Handsome though they were as dwellings, they are very ill-adapted to their present use as offices.

EMRYS JONES, *A Social Geography of Belfast*, 1960

THE LEISURELY DEVELOPMENT OF THE Georgian terrace house can be studied instructively in the area around Joy Street, Hamilton Street, and the district known as 'the Markets', most of which was built in the 1830s and 40s on land reclaimed either from the tide or from the former dam of the Cromac paper-mill. There are plain brick terraces of great character at 2–32 Joy Street and 4–18 Sussex Place; again at 7–19, 35–41 and 36–46 Hamilton Street (7 has an odd but pleasing massive Norman-Regency pointed doorway); and a fine stucco terrace at 20–30 Hamilton Street, set back a few feet from the street line, with hooded doorways, light pilasters, an ornamental frieze, acroteria, and a rusticated ground floor. This district more than any other gives a vivid impression of Belfast as it was before the full gale-force of Victorian industrial expansion struck. Most of the houses are in fair order, respectable, and cared for by their tenants, if not always by their landlords. It would be well worth preserving at least a selection of them when the time for redevelopment comes.

In this same district may also be observed the gentle transition from Georgian Gothic to Early Victorian Tudor. 118–124 Joy Street, brick terrace houses like their neighbours, have doorways and windows in the

Tudor taste, complete with label dripstones and appropriate fanlights in the upper parts of the ground-floor windows. Still more charming are the delightful terrace houses 130–38 Donegall Pass, likewise built about 1837, with their pointed doorcases and windows, roundel doors, and pretty balconies and fanlights. Originally, these houses stood amongst fruit gardens on the outskirts of the town. (There is a similar terrace, with ornaments from the same moulds but now irredeemably mutilated, at the opposite outskirt of the then town, at 85–91 Antrim Road.)

C.E.B. BRETT, *Buildings of Belfast*, 1967

THE HAPPY SITING OF THE MARKET HOUSE on the outside of the curve and at the corner of Shambles Street (Corn Market) provided a focal point to contain the view in both directions. The dignified, yet pleasant, brick houses, some with parapets to hide the roofs, some with dormer windows and many with signs hanging from a beam, give a street picture of great colour and warmth. The seventeenth-century market house, which was probably the only building of stone in the street, was very different from the public buildings erected during the eighteenth century, but it fitted beautifully into the street picture and took its place as one of the buildings in the group, although obviously the most important.

The design and the informal grouping of the buildings in High Street must have presented a great contrast with the character of those in Donegall Place in the early years of the nineteenth century. The buildings in the latter street ... were to follow a regular building plan so that the new street should be perfectly uniform. The houses were, of course, in the Georgian style, but they were much more formal than those in High Street and, as they were all the private dwellings of the wealthy citizens, there were no signs or shop windows to add to the gaiety of the street scene. This difference in the character of the two most important streets in the city shows how clearly the builders and planners of the day understood the basic principles of town design. Donegall Place was the avenue leading to the Linen Hall, and the buildings in the street had to serve as a foil to that great edifice; it was essential that they should be formal and dignified, but that they should not detract attention from the main building. The curve in High Street, on the other hand, made each building in the street of greater individual importance; the view was constantly changing as one travelled along the street, which, of course, was the marketing centre of the town, and consequently incapable of being treated with the same degree of formality as Donegall Place.

It is true that Belfast, like so many towns of the period, had a number of thatched houses on the outskirts – a cabin suburb of the type referred to by Thackeray – and it is one of the differences between the towns of the eighteenth century and those of today that the slums of the former period were on the outskirts, whereas today they are within the central area. The notes on the map of 1757 state that: 'The houses named the Plantation, them betwixt it and the N.E. end of the lane leading from the head of N. (North) Street towards Carrickfergus, likewise of that lane, are only low thatched dwellings of a mean appearance. So are the houses of Mill Street, Peter's Hill, the avenue N.N.W. out of Peter's Hill (Old Lodge Road), the lane betwixt the foot of Peter's Hill and Mill Street (Millfield), the alleys extending N'eastward out of North Street and the alley betwixt the Linen Hall and the lane running up N.W. from the Plantation.'

This cabin suburb gave a bad impression to travellers entering the town, and a writer in 1780 stated: ' ... in my entrance into Belfast I was vastly surprised and hurt to see a long string of falling cabins and tattered houses all tumbling down with a horrid aspect'. In the year 1751 an Act of Parliament was passed which gave powers to the Earl of Donegall and his trustees to grant leases for long terms to enable Belfast, which was 'old and ruinous', to be rebuilt. It is obvious that the attention of Parliament was drawn to the condition of the buildings in the cabin suburb in order to secure the passing of this measure, but the powers thus conferred were used to promote the development of fresh lands, rather than the rebuilding of the old and ruinous parts of the town. Indeed the slums of 1757 continue to be the black spots of the city at the present day and, although thatched houses are no longer seen, many of the streets mentioned still contain strings of 'tattered houses with a horrid aspect'.

Belfast at the end of the period must have had a fine appearance in spite of the unpleasant area described above. The terraces of Georgian houses around the White Linen Hall, in College Square and in the adjoining avenues were often in the very best tradition. So, too, were the buildings, such as those in Lower Crescent ... which were erected in the area around the university and which still give to that district a character of dignity and charm.

GILBERT CAMBLIN, *The Town in Ulster*, 1951

COMBER WAS SO RURALLY PEACEFUL that not even a bus threatened its seclusion so I started walking again, in the direction of Killyleagh where I wanted to spend the night. The countryside now seemed to be heavily wooded, though this was an illusion created by fine ash and sycamore and beech left in the hedges by the farmers. The gardens beyond Comber were loaded like flower shows, and wild sweet-pea vied with honeysuckle for supremacy of the hedges where for miles herb Robert was truly jack-of-the-hedgerows. Herds of Herefords seemed also to be competing with red Devons for the heavyweight contest as they went from one lush meadow to the next.

A grocer stopped his van and gave me a lift as far as Killinchy where I stayed long enough to admire the Non-Subscribing Presbyterian Church of 1845, a plain but dignified, pedimented building. Some of Northern Ireland's most interesting architecture of the Presbyterians belongs to the Non-Subscribing Church. Many of these simple, graceful buildings appear unexpectedly all over Ulster's countryside. They show how the Presbyterians hated the shams of the romantic revivals of bygone styles – an architectural activity associated strongly in their minds with the Church of Ireland. The qualities of these fine Georgian churches also clearly demonstrate the social differences, as well as ecclesiastical ones, between the two denominations at that time.

ROBIN BRYANS, *Ulster: A Journey Through the Six Counties*, 1964

FERMANAGH IS A COUNTY of fine mansions, many of Jacobean foundation, but today mostly in Georgian form: Florencecourt, built in 1764 by the Baron Mt. Florence; Castlecoole, a handsome mansion, the work of James Wyatt, senr; and Colebrooke, home of Sir Basil Brooke and his ancestors.

There are many remains of the Plantation, including a bawn of Scottish type of very unusual plan at Castle Monea. A fragment of Castle Balfour remains, once a typical Scoto-Irish building with corbie-stepped gables and turrets. All round the Lough you come suddenly on demesnes round the water's edge with lush green lawns and charming Georgian houses nestling among the trees.

DENIS O'D. HANNA, *The Face of Ulster*, 1952

THE FAMINE OF 1846 MARKS a turning point in the history of the towns and villages of the Province; thereafter there was a great movement of population from the rural areas, a turning from tillage to pasture and the introduction of the factory system into the linen industry. In addition, the first of a series of enactments dealing with land reform was passed a few years after the famine, and during the whole of the second half of the century there was a gradual breaking up of the large estates. The elimination of the large landowner and the lowering of the standards of taste, which was a marked feature of the industrial revolution, brought to an end the movement which had been manifested in the towns and countryside for more than a century. And so the famine may be said to mark the end of the great period of town and country planning in Ulster.

It is not difficult to understand why the countryside came to be neglected; the depression in the agricultural industry which followed the repeal of the corn laws and the absence of any person or body to carry out large improvement schemes in the rural areas is a sufficient explanation. In the urban areas, however, the growth of population and the establishment of new factories gave a great opportunity for the building of fine towns, a much greater opportunity indeed than had arisen in any previous period in the history of the Province. But the opportunity was lost, and instead of the fine streets and squares which might have been built, only muddle and ugliness resulted.

GILBERT CAMBLIN, *The Town in Ulster*, 1951

SOBER AS ST PATRICK I WENT into the busy Saturday streets of this biggish market town, which my guide book called an 'industrial town' and which St Patrick, or somebody thereabouts in time called Newry or Place of the Yews after the trees which St Patrick planted there.

I saw neither the yews nor the industry. There *were* some factories on the outskirts and some warehouses in the town, but not enough to ruin the place as industry inevitably does. Newry, in fact, had escaped comparatively unscathed from the nineteenth century, and looked very much as it must have done from the seventeenth century onwards. In character, the town shared much of the regularity and the idea of straight streets common to most Ulster towns. But Newry also had an alien and pleasing quality, approximating to the Dutch flavour found in Fenland towns in England. Newry had a canal lined by merchants' warehouses and this alone was sufficient to suggest an element of the Netherlands, an influence not altogether out of place since King William III himself came from the Lowlands and there are a few Dutch gable houses in the town dating from his reign.

Newry grew up at the important point at the head of Carlingford Lough, a thin finger of sea inserted deeply into County Down's southern coastline. The town was also a halt on the road to Armagh, and was the scene of many battles, standing as it does in the 'Gap of the North' where expeditions from Dublin met and fought the Northmen.

ROBIN BRYANS, *Ulster: A Journey Through the Six Counties*, 1964

WE COME TO THE END OF OUR WANDERING in this fine old frontier town somewhere in the region where Bagenal built his castle, in Castle Street, which leads into Abbey Yard. Hereabouts too the Cistercian Abbey stood. Not a stone remains of either of these historic buildings and by now that sad fact will not surprise us. Just across the way, in a disgraceful condition, stand two of the very few William and Mary houses still extant in Ulster. These are known as the 'Dutch houses' and their gables denote the influence of the House of Orange in Ireland following William's victory at the Battle of the Boyne. The date of erection is unknown but it is likely to be between 1690 and 1700. One of these houses was vacant during my last visit and unless something is done quickly by way of preservation both will disappear completely before long. Surely these memorials to a great and stirring epoch in the history of Ireland deserve something better than utter neglect. The little that is left of Newry's ancient architectural heritage will be wiped from the sight of man if the more aware of the townspeople do not quickly bestir themselves.

RICHARD HAYWARD, *Border Foray*, 1957

IRELAND IS NOT A RICH COUNTRY in architectural terms, and Ulster is poorer than many other parts of Ireland in this respect. County Londonderry acquired most of its towns and villages as a result of the involvement of the City of London ... Understanding and knowledge dispel ignorance: the two cultures (indeed two peoples) of Ulster desperately need to understand each other's backgrounds, histories, and achievements. Often achievements can be found in buildings, in the cultivation of land for agriculture and forests, in the development of towns and villages, and in the making of an infrastructure that makes civilised life and communication possible. Ulster can ill afford to lose any more of her built heritage, yet there is very little aesthetic appreciation of architecture apparent in the way many old buildings are treated in the Province.

JAMES STEPHENS CURL, *The Londonderry Plantation 1604–1914*, 1986

JUST AS ULSTER'S GEOLOGY INFLUENCED the design of its buildings, so its history has had a marked effect both on their character and their rate of survival. Repeated incursions from outside brought strong foreign strains into the local building style. Repeated destruction and internal strife resulted in widespread damage, while rebuilding produced some curiously mixed styles ... Such varied origins and ragged development [naturally] affected the external appearance of Ulster architecture. Waringstown House in County Down, begun in 1667, provides a fine demonstration of the merging of different traditions. The impressive symmetrical front, though simple in conception, has both the assurance of the classical tradition and the self-conscious character of designed architecture. By contrast, the side elevations have an agreeable jumble of Dutch and Scottish gables, with windows and chimneys varied in size and style. Here it is the natural growth of vernacular architecture which predominates, for though the original thatching has been replaced by Welsh slates, the rendered walls of rubble and earth, bound with lime mortar, are perhaps the most typical feature of Ulster's native building style.

HUGH DIXON, *An Introduction to Ulster Architecture*, 1975

NOT FAR FROM THE [BLACK PIG'S] DYKE at the end of a long, long drive, stands Bellamont Forest, which ranks with Mereworth and Chiswick as one of the purest examples of the Palladian villa in the British Isles. Rising clear out of the parkland, it surmounts an eminence, defying the dense regiments of fir trees which threaten to engulf it. Below the house an immense natural lake stretches out towards the neighbouring demesne of Dartrey.

Wide stone steps lead up beneath the handsome portico, decorated with a classical frieze of rams' heads, to the hall with its black-and-white squared floor. Busts of the Coote family, disguised as Roman emperors, gaze at one another across this plain but noble room. The drawing-room and dining-room are elaborate by comparison, richly decorated with bold and ornate stucco-work. Like the hall, they take up a storey and a half in height, creating little mezzanine rooms halfway up the stairs ...

It seems strange in a building of such open serenity and quiet dignity that defence should have been a consideration; [that it was,] was due partly to its remoteness and partly to the political situation of the time. The front door is the only means of access on the ground floor. There still exists at Bellamont an iron hall-door with a spy-hole covered by a metal flap. At the basement level, a broad paved passage runs around the house like a dry moat, and a tunnel 600 feet long connects the house with the stables. Paving around the house has been removed; it has always been understood that this was done for defensive purposes, rather than for giving more light to the basement.

The demesne of Bellamont Forest was originally named Coote Hill by its founder, Colonel Thomas Coote, who married a Miss Hill and came to County Cavan in the 1660s.

DESMOND GUINNESS and WILLIAM RYAN, *Irish Houses and Castles*, 1971

A NUMBER OF [MINOR] eighteenth-century buildings are still standing, most of them altered very largely from their original state. There are at any rate two pubs. Kelly's Cellars, 30–32 Bank Street, built about 1780, has a pleasant whitewashed outside; the downstairs rooms, with knee-height bar, low archways, and blackened snugs, are highly interesting and atmospheric if now somewhat self-conscious; the upstairs bar is, however, aesthetically deplorable. If local legend is to be believed, the United Irishmen when plotting divided their time between these cellars and a secret room in the roof-space of the second Presbyterian Church in Rosemary Street; true or not, this nicely symbolises the alliance upon which their plots were founded.

White's Tavern, 1–9 Winecellar Entry, was rebuilt in 1790 as a spirit warehouse by the Valentine Jones, wine merchant, who, at the age of ninety, danced a celebrated contre-danse in the Assembly Rooms with his son, grandson, and great-grandson, all Valentine Joneses. Until quite recently, it combined the picturesque and the practical to perfection, with its heavy timbered bays, barred windows and roof hoist. Unfortunately it has recently been disastrously restored in the 'Ye Olde' style; the outside boasts a poker-work inn-sign, the interior is replete with arty brass and electric bulbs in bogus lanterns.

Du Barry's pub, 6 Prince's Street, a haunt of sailors nowadays, boasts more-than-eighteenth-century-bottle-bottomed panes between the glazing bars amidst the pebbledash.

College Court, a pokey alley running from Castle Street to College Street, conceals a mysteriously unnumbered large whitewashed Georgian dwelling-house of the better sort, with a nice (though later) porch, and tubbed trees; this seems to be where the policemen of Queen Street house their families.

C.E.B. BRETT, *Buildings of Belfast*, 1967

NORTH BELFAST WAS A DISTINCTIVE HUMAN LANDSCAPE before it became a city suburb, and that landscape had an effect both on the nature of subsequent development and on the details of the urban landscape which replaced it.

The transformation of this land of fine parks and houses was not uniform, for it did not become entirely an upper-class suburb. The land between the first half-mile of the Antrim Road and North Queen Street shared considerably in the development of the Dock area of Belfast. As early as the 1830s, in the quadrangle formed by North Queen Street, Cliftonville Road, Antrim Road and Old Lodge Road, 'Casino', the house lying in the centre of the quadrangle, was already overshadowed by the infantry and artillery barracks, and by a cotton factory around which were growing terraces of industrial housing: and North Queen Street between the barracks and Old Lodge Road was already taking on the character of the industrial Dock sector. The building of terrace houses was restricted, however, even as late as 1880, when Fortfield, Mervue, Duncairn, Spamount, Greenfield and Casino were still intact, though now shut in by terraces built on the Limestone Road. Thorndale, west of the Antrim Road, was similarly a large open space. And so in the 1880s the Antrim Road and its increasing number of small villas for the most part still passed between demesnes.

EMRYS JONES, *A Social Geography of Belfast*, 1960

THEY WERE SEARCHING FOR A HOUSE that would be embedded in this landscape. There had been a discussion one Sunday, and the four had agreed on a course: they would take an old large house, share the cost and the space. 'These old mansions are a white elephant,' said Rose, 'in the ordinary way, but if several families combined ... !' ...

They found a house ... an old ivied house on the road to the Point, close to the sea, built by a prosperous Mr Linsy, who had driven to and fro in a coach with liveried servants; specially situated, with a few semi-tropical trees, for the admiration over the waves of the sunset: Victorian symbol of descending greatness and farewell. Perhaps in a room stained momentarily pink by the sinking orb, Mr Linsy had closed his eyes for the last time. Here would come – more herded, less well attended – men and women from families Mr Linsy would not have 'known'.

Luke's party stood on the gravel, seeing the stiff, silent front where martins and wagtails flipped about carelessly. Now children would dig in the flowerbeds, dance and scream on the weedy tennis lawn. In summer under an awning meals would be taken. Indoors, the old decorum would vanish. Men in jerseys and perhaps sandals would argue, where once a frock-coated gentleman had made his slow, usually courteous, periphrasis.

The house would not be available for some weeks. Meanwhile in the evenings they often went to gaze at it. 'When you look at a calm house beside water,' Rose said, 'you begin to think there's a sort of happiness growing out of the earth like an invisible vegetation, growing through, not so much the masonry, as the minds in this spot.'

GEORGE BUCHANAN, *Rose Forbes*, 1950

THE LAGAN VALLEY, HERE THICKLY WOODED. I pull the boat in below a rath crowned with a grove of ancient beeches. Silence except for the sound of a wood pigeon crashing its way through the upper branches, or the plunge of a water rat. The roar of the city, only a mile or two downriver, scarcely penetrates here. I land, climb the rath, and through a thick screen of green catch glimpses of an old red-brick Georgian mansion sunning itself in a clearing. The windows stare back blankly. No one has lived here for years, and the old house teems with memories. Nothing remembers like an old house.

DENIS IRELAND, *From the Irish Shore*, 1936

IN THE LAGAN VALLEY IN AND ROUND LISBURN one can almost feel the English influence. Stand in the park of the town and see that charming row of red Georgian houses through the trees; the cathedral spire (one of the best examples of Planters' Gothic in the country); an old town-gate; some walls; a bastion; a fine Georgian cupola on the town hall; and it is not difficult to reconstruct the early setting of the Planters of Lisnagarvey, as the town was then named.

DENIS O'D. HANNA, *from* 'Architecture in Ulster', *The Arts in Ulster*, 1951

THE CHURCH HAD BEEN REBUILT somewhere in the 1830s, but the tower dated from the days of the Ulster Plantation, and showed 1620 on the keystone of the low doorway. And behind the church were tombstones resting against the walls, stones 200 to 250 years old, which had been displaced in the rebuilding of the church; stones carved in high relief – all of a pattern – the centre occupied by armorial bearings or kneeling figures, the border being an inscription in quaint contractions of word and letter which, to be read, required the reader to describe a parallelogram with his eyes. For an eleven-year-old boy it was a find of hoary antiquity, and I pressed my fingers round the high letters and into the deep hollows of the stones to get near to the old Plantation carver and his heroic times.

JOHN STEVENSON, *A Boy in The Country*, 1912

I HAD THE PLEASURE during the time of my curacy [at Banbridge] of seeing [the parish church] largely rebuilt and entirely remodelled under the auspices of the eminent architect, Sir Thomas Drew, whose valued acquaintance I made at this time, so that it is now one of the finest modern churches in the United Diocese. During the time of its reconstruction services were held in the Temperance Hall and I well remember the shock we all received while unrobing after morning service there on the 7th May, 1882, when the news came in that on the previous evening Lord Frederick Cavendish, the newly-arrived Chief Secretary, and Mr Burke, the Under-Secretary, had been brutally murdered in the Phoenix Park, Dublin, within full sight of the Viceregal Lodge.

E.D. ATKINSON, *Recollections of an Ulster Archdeacon*, 1934

THE ABBEY [I.E. GREYABBEY] is a truly beautiful ruin of pinkish sandstone set off by the green of immense trees and the velvet sward of a vast park. The refectory is fairly well preserved. The remains of a rostrum is stuck, swallow's-nest-wise, to one of the walls. The west door of the church has a softness about it that tempts one to stroke it. The whole building has weathered in a most attractive fashion: some of the stones are so erased by time, frost and rain that their texture is like dozed wood. The eye goes seeking and finding whorls and spirals carved by the chisel of the elements in the hand of Time.

STEPHEN RYNNE, *All Ireland*, 1956

IT IS NOT SO LONG AGO SINCE old St Anne's, the Presbyterian church in Fisherwick Place and the Linen Hall were the most impressive buildings in the city; since the stretch of land between the Botanic Gardens and the Ormeau Road was 'the Plains', a barren, uninhabited tract; since the Blackstaff flowed visible and evil-smelling under bridges; since the wayfarer passed straight into the country when he left the Queen's College behind him, and St John's, Malone, a tiny church, stood among fields where cattle grazed. In less than the passing of a single generation the old buildings have disappeared. A cathedral rises where St Anne's stood. The sordid slums behind it have become orderly rows of warehouses. A great municipal building has taken the place of the modestly respectable Linen Hall. The Plains are thickly populated streets. The houses of prosperous businessmen stand one beside the other, in the middle of trim grounds, out to Shaw's Bridge. Living men have seen the foundation stones laid, have watched the walls grow, the streets widen, the tentacles of traffic routes stretch and extend their grasp. A sense of restlessness exists when rapid change challenges the attention, and restlessness is readily transmutable into energy.

GEORGE A. BIRMINGHAM, *An Irishman Looks at His World*, 1919

BEYOND THE RIVER was Ballymacarrett, already a small but flourishing industrial suburb where vitriol, iron and glass were manufactured, and where almost every cottage housed a weaver. But beyond the village the rolling glacial sands of Knock were still good farmland, and here and there – usually on a sandy outcrop – were the residences of the rich. The greatest of these, of course, was Ormeau House, the home of the Donegall family. Beyond that, in a southerly direction, was Belvoir House, and east of it, Orangefield, Connisbrook, Richmond Lodge, Belmont, Bloomfield and Cabin Hill, all within the Knock valley. Several large houses also graced the slopes of the Holywood Hills, facing the lough in a comparable position to those on the Antrim side. Within a hundred years, Belfast was to engulf all these, but the character of these districts was to make an impression on much of the development of the future city.

EMRYS JONES, *A Social Geography of Belfast*, 1960

GEORGIAN TERRACES CONTINUED to be built right up to, and indeed for a considerable time after, Queen Victoria's accession to the throne. A large number of these are still standing, though few will stand much longer. Many good examples are to be found in the area of Great George's Street, the finest being numbers 10 to 18, which, uncared-for and half-ruinous as they are, have still an opulent dignity. It is very evident, however, from their low-slung proportions that they were built as merchants' houses and not for the gentry. Each of these three-storey brick houses has a wide doorway with shallow fluting in the coved arches; the end ones have Doric pillars and fine fanlights: 12 has elaborate half-fluted Ionic pillars, with a floral stucco ornament on the lintel, and the old – perhaps the original? – roundel door. All have built-in bootscrapers beside the doorcases, and date from about 1825, though stylistically so late a date is barely credible. In the same street, 36 and 38 are rather earlier, built in 1819, an unusual pair sharing a single roof, one three-storeyed, the other with an extra storey crammed in under the eaves, resulting in some very eccentric window-spacing; numbers 6, 8, 61, 63, and 86 to 94 are less imposing but still good. Other terrace houses nearby of the same period are to be found in Great and Little Patrick Streets; Lancaster Street; Little York Street; Caroline Street; Tomb Street, and Gamble Street.

C.E.B. BRETT, *Buildings of Belfast*, 1967

NO. 1 TREVOR HILL IS PERHAPS the best preserved of all the fine eighteenth-century houses of Newry. Undoubtedly it owes its good condition to the fact that it serves as business offices and a well-maintained dwelling, for most of the older buildings of the town are in a sad state of dilapidation due to poor occupancy. This house was built in 1770 and is a very characteristic piece of Ulster Georgian. The door and the windows above it are especially typical and delightful, and it is heart-warming to see the whole place so well cared for amidst such shocking neglect. In my books about Ireland I have constantly referred to an ingrained disregard of the Irish people for all their buildings of quality and interest, domestic and ecclesiastical alike, and it is a real joy to be confronted with so charming an exception. This house displays that delightful blend of rugged texture with classical elegance that gives our Georgian its very special flavour.

The contrast between the condition of this fine house and another of earlier age and equal quality, which stands, but only just stands, at 21 Upper North Street, in a continuation of our line southwards, is sad to contemplate. This is surely an object lesson and a clarion call to the people of Newry to band themselves into that Old Newry Society which I have already conjured them to establish. In the room to the left on the first floor of this ill-used house some fine original panelling still endures, and I use the word advisedly, and the three-light window on this landing is a lovely example of its period. Some of the well-wrought door cases are in a state of fair preservation but the all-pervading sense of neglect and dilapidation is sad beyond words.

RICHARD HAYWARD, *Border Foray*, 1957

THERE MAY BE OTHER CITIES which present as weird a jumble of architectural styles, but in none known to me is the proportion of good to bad so reminiscent of the proportion of bread to sack in Falstaff's tavern bill. This craze for variety is always typified to my mind by the fate of a row of houses built by an earlier generation of Belfast merchants on the Georgian model so admirably preserved in Dublin. The houses were never masterpieces in any sense of the word; but when I knew them first the mellowness of the brick and a certain comeliness in their proportions made a gracious appeal to the eye. In their uniformity and sober dignity lay their charm, but these qualities were defects in the eyes of later proprietors. One innovator, speedily followed by others, relieved the monotony, as he felt it, by building out a bow-window; a second was inspired to cover the walls with pebble-dashed stucco; a third, not to be outdone, painted his bricks in a chequerboard of red and white; and residents, who could not rise to these sublime heights, experimented in fancy doors and fanlights filled with atrocious stained glass.

The curious thing is that Belfast achieves its worst outrages when it is, as it fondly believes, making concessions to beauty ... Where, however, a strictly utilitarian aim has been pursued, as in the city's cliff-like mills and factories, one gets an impression of naked power, that if not pleasant, is markedly impressive. Only those for whom aesthetics ended with Ruskin will deny beauty to Belfast Harbour and to the miles of shipyards that line the banks of the Lagan. The intricate steel tracery of the gantries that straddle over enormous liners makes an appeal to the imagination stronger than that of crumbling medieval castles, and the exquisite proportions and harmonious rhythm of the whole fabric would have delighted a Greek, even if it is despised by some who rave over the fretted stonework of Gothic cathedrals.

JAMES WINDER GOOD, *Ulster and Ireland*, 1919

A HOUSE DEMOLISHED
spring 1981

They might have waited had they been aware
that I still lived, before they knocked it down.
Bricked-up and blind, our terrace still stood there
as in so many streets in this sick town.
Sealed off from sight, rooms hugged bright memories,
the kitchen with its range, the dining room,
its coal fire lit for small festivities,

the room upstairs where singing friends would come.
And in the top front bedroom I was born;
familiar with each vivid place I grew
to manhood; every window, stair and door
led to the widening scene my senses drew.
Walls, woodwork shattered, textures shredded, torn,
those haunted corners hoard my dreams no more.

JOHN HEWITT, *Mosaic*, 1981

THE COUNTY HAS SUFFERED CONSIDERABLY from the Troubles of the years since 1969. The historic heart of Lisburn, in particular, has been smashed by successive bombs. Ballycastle and Cushendall lost their principal hotels, both buildings of architectural significance, by fire-bombs. Some other counties have suffered worse, but the damage has been pretty widespread, rivalled only by the redevelopment of the centres of Antrim and Ballymena, and the continuing exploitation of the former green fields around Carrickfergus and Newtownabbey. Large areas of the countryside have been infiltrated by inappropriate new houses and bungalows in a great variety of non-traditional styles, though fortunately, so far, most of the Glens and most of the coastline remain relatively – I emphasise the word relatively – unspoiled.

C.E.B. BRETT, *Buildings of County Antrim*, 1996

THE INNOCENT EYE

The cottages at Ballyhackamore,
For instance, or
Houses with names, before the builders came –
Demolished, vanished now –
Stage properties in an eternity

Of childhood rubbing shoulders with the scene,
Seem rather, in recall,
Actors, directors, sentient presences,
As time and place, in retrospect, stand still.

Vanished; usurped by structures no one loves,
No exile mourns.
But wait; for here and there about the town –
Behind veneers, façades,
On gable-walls at corners, or unmasked
By bulldozer or bomb – you may discern
Pale skeletons
Of family names, antique advertisements,
Obscured or elbowed-out before your time.

So, somewhere in the suburbs of the mind,
Landmarks remain;
And, if you're constant, the familiar
Timeless fraternity
Will hold your gaze against unaltered skies,
That shepherded the living and the dead,
When you were told
That the departed never travelled far
Beyond belief, or doubted their recall.

ROY MCFADDEN, *After Seymour's Funeral*, 1990

IF YOU WENT THERE NOW, it would strike you as unremarkable – just another busy street in another busy town. In recent years, the flow of cars has become so heavy that pedestrians need traffic lights to negotiate safe crossings, but you might guess that once, in quieter times, people lived in the terraced houses which line both sides of the street. A very few still do, but mostly the houses have been taken over by offices and shops. The handful of residents who remain must sometimes feel as if they inhabit a ghost town, regularly emptied of its inhabitants every night, until they return again, as if bewitched, the following morning. On the north side, where the original terrace line is best preserved, there used to be narrow gardens, separated by railings, distancing the front doors from the road. One garden still survives, intact and incongruous. It is beautifully maintained, a jewel of ordered vegetation set precariously amidst the encroaching pressure of its ever-more-urban surroundings. Several are in a state of dereliction, rough tussocks of grass threaded with litter, dandelions growing through the remnants of shrubs, bedraggled flowerbeds still just suggestive of the way things used to be. But most of what used to be gardens have been rooted up and concreted over to make room for parking. Shiny vehicles sit like gross wingless flies outside these houses-turned-to-offices. It is as if a swarm of alien insects had descended and, instead of supping nectar, moulted concrete to support the squat weights now resting so heavily upon the gardens they've entombed. On the south side, where the front doors open directly onto the pavement without any intervening patch of green, many of the old buildings have been demolished to make way for other premises – a garage, a takeaway, a hairdresser, an electrician – so that the original uniformity of nineteenth-century red brick is now a symmetry-assaulting mix of materials and styles, an awkward jumble that sits crookedly upon the eye, fitting into neither the pattern of the old or the new.

This is Bachelors' Walk in Lisburn, County Antrim, an Irish town (a city since 2002) eight miles south west of Belfast. It has no claim to renown. Unless you live thereabouts, you're unlikely to have heard of it.

CHRIS ARTHUR, *Irish Haiku*, 2005

WHAT REMAINS OF BELFAST'S INDUSTRIAL ARCHITECTURE has a strange marooned look to it. Similarly, the redbrick Gothic of insurance houses and banks, stores and churches, hotels and theatres which was once the city's Victorian legacy has all but vanished. Belfast underwent the fate of many cities in Britain and Ireland caught and mauled by the hectic redevelopment boom of the 1980s. What has taken over, inside out as it were, is the shopping mall, the steel-framed centre and the masked façade. These changes belie another truth, however, of the profound, irrevocable change Belfast experienced as the site of sectarian violence which took possession of the city from the late 1960s – bombing campaigns in the name of Irish national liberation vied with bombing campaigns in the name of preserving the British way of life. Peace-lines of metal girders divided communities against themselves, security barriers defaced the cityscape and turned the centre into a police zone.

GERALD DAWE, *The Rest is History*, 1998

THE FORCE OF CUSTOM is exceptionally strong in all that touches hearth and home, yet the endless boilings of potatoes over an open fire have driven the modern generation to rebellion. Unfortunately the farmer who is rebuilding his house, wishing to improve on the old, erects a tall brick villa or a flimsy bungalow, and the gain in convenience is offset by the loss of character and fitness to environment. It is the raw new house by the roadside that takes the eye, not the low whitewashed homestead sheltering under a ring of wind-blown trees. There is a crying need for a sympathetic architect to devise a Mourne farmhouse which should combine the solid virtues of the old style with the resources and opportunities of the modern age.

E. ESTYN EVANS, *Mourne Country*, 1951

RUIN OF HOUSE IN MIN NA CRAOIBHE
for Noel Ó Gallchóir

Tá creatlach an tseantí
ag baint ceoil as an ghaoth;
gan doras gan fuinneog gan sclátaí dín
gach foscailt ina feadóg fhiáin
ag gabháil fhoinn ...

The old house, with skeletal grace,
is making music of the wind.
Without door or window
or the shelter of slates,
every wound is a tin-whistle
making wild music.

From gable to gable
the exhausted house rises
into a storm-melody.
Such music, old house!
The likes of your lilting
has never been heard
on any windy day
in a comfortable, domestic place.

CATHAL Ó SEARCAIGH, translated by THOMAS McCARTHY,
An Bealach 'na Bhaile/Homecoming: Selected Poems, 1993

The Linen Industry

Linen is a thread of Belfast life, the web of its existence, the reason for its sudden dramatic growth in the nineteenth century when country people swarmed into the mills and factories around the Falls, the Shankill, the Crumlin. Conditions were grim and there was little elbow room in the redbrick streets but it was home, and a community, where the linen trades established their own hierarchies and their names tripped off the tongue like legends – doffers, weavers, winders, tenters, rovers, band tiers, spinners, drawers, peelers, flax-roughers and scutchers.

DAVID HAMMOND, *Songs of Belfast*

Pulling up flax after the blue flowers have fallen
And laying our handfuls in the peaty water
To rot those grasses to the bone, or building stooks
That recall the skirts of an invisible dancer,

We become a part of the linen industry
And follow its processes to the grubby town
Where fields are compacted into window-boxes
And there is little room among the big machines.

MICHAEL LONGLEY, *from* 'The Linen Industry'

from YOUNG McCANCE

At the foot of Divis mountain
My dwelling is to be seen
Where there runs a purling stream

Beside my father's green,
Well covered o'er with linen cloth
Which was wrought round Tandragee
And purchased by young McCance,
And a boy called Darby Gray.

ANONYMOUS

THE FORTH RIVER, TOGETHER WITH ITS TRIBUTARIES, is one focus of the linen industry. There is a group of mills at Legoniel, where spinning and bleaching had given rise to a mill village long before it became part of suburban Belfast: and extending from the Shankill Road to the Crumlin Road and beyond is a compact cluster of both spinning and weaving mills, well within the sector of closely packed industrial housing.

Associated with the Farset river, and extending along the Falls Road, is a group which approaches nearest to the centre of the city. Earlier factories and mills here represented the first growth of industry outwards from Belfast, as opposed to the inclusion in the growing town of mills which were formerly in the countryside. The Falls Road mills have a long tradition for the very first corn mills of Belfast were turned by the Farset. Today there are foundries and spinning and weaving mills here, in addition to flour mills.

EMRYS JONES, *A Social Geography of Belfast*, 1960

LINEN

From the photographs of bleach–greens
Mill–hands stare across the snowy acres.
In a frieze white as marble
Their lives are ravelled and unravelled –
Golden straw, bright thread, the iron looms
Are cast in tangled cordage.

The shapes of wheels and spindles shine
In darkness. When the weave is finished,
Light will fall on linen simply, as it would
On glass, or silverware, or water,
Things needed for a wedding or a funeral;
We will be reconciled to those cold sheets.

CIARAN CARSON, *The New Estate*, 1976

THE INTIMATE CONNECTION that always existed between spinning and weaving, and the number of subsidiary operations required by the latter, led frequently to domestic incidents in which the affections were concerned. The operation of spinning, as well as that of winding, was often performed in the same apartment with the weaving; and thus conversation and personal intercourse were uninterrupted. An Ulster ballad notices the rough system of wooing and gives us an idea of the very small number of necessaries incident to rural matrimony:

> A'll fix yer wheel behine my loom,
>   An' rowl ye on the bed,
> An' my dearest dear A'll marry ye
>   Whin I get out my web.

In another Ulster ballad, called 'The County Tyrone', a young man named Magennis is represented as a weaver, on his adventures; and he succeeds in bringing back a wife from the town of Newry:

> I am a bowld waver,
>   I've done my endayvour,
> In courtin' pretty fair maids abroad and at home,
>   An' bein' of sich mettle,
>   I nivver could settle,
> Till I seen some place else nor the County Tyrone.
>   My father he toul' me
>   He'd nivver controul me,
> But wud make me a draper if I'd stay at home,
>   But I tuk a notion
>   Of higher promotion,
> For to try farther parts nor the County Tyrone.

There is an incidental allusion to the fact that the hand-loom operative not unfrequently took advantage of his skill to become a 'draper' or master and employer; and changes of this kind have been more than usually frequent in Ulster within the last ten years.

A. HUME, from 'Spinning and Weaving: Their Influence on
Popular Language and Literature', Ulster Journal of Archaeology, vol. 5, 1857

AS FOR THE WEAVERS THEMSELVES, except for the occasional flare up and some personal dislikes, a spirit of comradeship existed among women who, for the most part, enjoyed their work, difficult as it might be. The closest bonds formed between those working in close proximity to one another, for the din in the shed made intimate communication at a distance impossible, and the necessity of watching one's looms intently kept one bound to a limited area. Good friends watched one another's looms when it was necessary for one of them to make a trip to the office for weft or to visit the lavatory, and they supported one another's efforts to make their pay: 'Hurry back. You're on the push. You've got to make the mark.'

Repeatedly, the women I interviewed spoke about their work in terms similar to the following, which appeared in a linen trade journal:

> My happiest hours were passed in the factory, so they were. I loved my work and my looms. I always got a thrill when I saw the pattern forming; often it would be flowers that took me back to my childhood's days. Some say it's slavery, but I always liked it; and cannot tell of my feelings of satisfaction as I carried my web to the Cloth Office, and knew I had little to fear from its inspection.

Liking her work was no guarantee that a woman would remain satisfied with one place of employment, however, and there was a fair amount of mobility. Young weavers might move, within a limited area of Belfast, with their friends until they found a factory and looms to their liking; among the others, 'some just couldn't settle down'. It was not unusual for a tenter to find several weavers waiting on him when he arrived in the morning with the usual request, 'Give us a pair of looms, Mister', and from among them he selected those he felt could work harmoniously with the other workers. These weavers, moving about restlessly, helped to pass along the lore of their co-workers from factory to factory.

BETTY MESSENGER, *Picking Up the Linen Threads*, 1975

The contribution of working women to the strength of Ireland's textile industry was most pronounced in the huge linen mills of Belfast. By 1912 the northern city, with its complement of over fifty such centres of mass employment and output, had become the world's most prolific maker and exporter of linen cloth. The labour force that guaranteed the leading global position of the new Linenopolis, as the city then was popularly called, was overwhelmingly female, with hundreds of thousands of women and girls involved in the myriad aspects of industrial linen production, from combing tow to spinning yarn, to winding bobbins and weaving cloth, to laundering, checking, packing and distribution.

However, women's participation in textile work was confined neither to factories nor to linen. The rural background to this industry remained particularly strong – the cultivation of flax, the foundation of Irish linen, was essentially an agricultural process, by nature highly labour intensive – while home-based activities, such as sprigging, flowering and other forms of embroidery and embellishment, provided a vital source of cash income in many country households. At the end of the nineteenth century, the Congested Districts Board actively promoted local ventures, such as lace-making and the production of woollen yarn and finished woollen commodities of tweed, carpets and knitwear, as a vehicle for the regeneration of marginal regions, particularly in the north and west of Ireland. Again, women played a key role in the success of these initiatives.

MYRTLE HILL and VIVIENNE POLLOCK,
Image and Experience: Photographs of Irish Women c. 1880–1920, 1993

THERE WAS [AN] INTERESTING COTTAGE INDUSTRY in these places when I was a boy. It was of that form of linen embroidery, locally known as 'sprigging' or 'cut work'. The process was practically the same as that of the great embroideries of Italy and Spain in the seventeenth century, only that the material demanded a more rigid treatment than was possible with the old silks and velvets. The latter were fastened to a frame with stretchers, but the Ulster linen work was stretched by being laid over one hoop of perhaps six or seven inches in diameter, while a second hoop, a shade larger, was pressed down outside the band of the first; thus the area of linen exposed became as tight as the skin of a drum. The design was outlined upon the fabric and worked in fine, hard stitches, and when completed, the point of a scissors was inserted, and the blank space within the outline was deftly cut away. It was beautiful and artistic work, but it had one fault in the eyes of the retailers – namely, its durability. It was almost impossible to – wear it out. This may have been the cause of the decay of the industry, though I am rather inclined to believe that the conventionality of the designs had a good deal to do with it. I have bought quantities of the Swiss embroidered lawn at Lucerne and Lausanne, and also of the Madeira work at Funchal and Las Palmas; but I do not think that I saw any at the islands that surpassed some that I remember in County Down.

On the doorstep of almost every small house in Bangor, Donaghadee, and the other towns, the girls used to sit in the long summer evenings, bending over their little hoops and stitching away as fast as a machine could go. Some of them earned enough money to make the industry a profitable one to themselves, but, of course, there was a middleman, and equally as a matter of course, he had the lion's share of the profit.

F. FRANKFORT MOORE, *The Truth About Ulster*, 1914

THROUGH THE WHOLE OF THIS DISTRICT – the Barony of Ards, and that of Castlereagh – a large proportion of the peasantry are employed in what is technically termed 'flowering' – embroidering muslin, chiefly for the Glasgow manufacturers, who supply the unwrought material, and pay fixed sums for the workmanship. The workers earn generally about three shillings a week – a small sum; but as the majority of the inmates of a cottage are similarly employed, sufficient is obtained to procure the necessaries of life, and, indeed, some of its luxuries, for the interiors of many of the cabins presented an aspect of cheerfulness and comfort. We found upon inquiry from the sources best informed upon the subject, that the number of girls occupied in this branch of industry may be thus stated: Between 2,000 and 3,000 girls, from five to twelve years of age, employed at veining, at weekly wages averaging from 1s. 6d. to 2s. 6d.; sewers employed at needlework for Belfast houses, between 2,000 and 3,000, at weekly wages averaging 3s.; about 10,000 employed as needleworkers for Glasgow houses, at weekly wages averaging 4s. Thus upwards of £3,000 are paid weekly, in the north of Ireland, for the manufacture of needlework.

MR and MRS S.C. HALL, *Ireland, Its Scenery, Character, etc.*, 1842

THE LINEN INDUSTRY DEVELOPED side by side with agriculture in the eighteenth century. It was encouraged by Government regulation from the time of William III. Huguenot settlers, brought to the Lagan valley as early as 1690, introduced new techniques in fine linen weaving and helped to found the modern industry. Elsewhere the manufacture of linen probably owes as much to good relations between landlord and tenant and to the opportunities for amassing capital as to the Huguenots. The woollen industry was almost entirely superseded by linen. The small woollen mills which are found in our survey areas are nineteenth century revivals of this old industry. Amongst the cottagers of the countryside linen working was the main occupation. The women spun the thread and the menfolk did the weaving. Flax was grown by the cottager on rented land.

JOHN M. MOGEY, *Rural Life in Northern Ireland*, 1947

AN IMPROVEMENT IN MODERN MACHINERY is a 'spinning jenny'; a fool 'weaves cobwebs'; an insect that crawls over our tables is known as a 'spinner'; and a person who is wanting in vivacity and acuteness is said to be 'slack spun'. An intricate piece of business is called in England 'a tangled skein'; the Scotch say it is 'a difficult pirn to wind'; and the Ulster Irish speak of it as 'a ravelled hank'. When the order of anything is completely lost, the people of Ulster say they have 'lost the lees of it', or that it is 'all through other', viz., confused. And as artisans of almost every kind adopt figurative expressions from the operations in their respective trades, so a physical beating is sometimes called a 'scutching', and a thorough intellectual discomfiture a 'heckling'. It was remarked of a late professor, who was not only highly intellectual, but especially amiable and irritable, that he 'soaped' his students when out of his class, and 'beetled' them in it ...

[T]he 'almond tree' or hoary head is 'as white as a streek o' flax'; and the expression 'flaxen' is applied in certain cases to the hair of ladies of a fair complexion. Shakespeare has the three cognate expressions 'as pale as a clout', 'as pale as a shirt', and 'linen cheeks'; and popularly, a silly fellow is 'not length and count', or 'has only eleven cuts to the hank', which is equivalent to 'wanting a penny of the shilling'. The firmament is not only spoken of as a tent or pavilion, but it is sometimes called a 'warp' or 'woof' of cloth; when people are too crowded they are said to be 'throng in the reed'; and an unusual intimacy is expressed by the term 'as thick [or great] as inkle-weavers'. A person who unites provincial and vulgar expressions with an affectation of pure English is said to 'speak drugget'; and when he carries a correct analogy too far, he is said to 'put in the weft too fine'. Shakespeare has 'speaking linsey-woolsey', in the case of uttering nonsense. A hand or foot unusually large is 'as broad as a crig'; a dried herring is 'a slay hook', from its resemblance in form to the instrument by which the threads are drawn through the reed; and a farm servant, in an argument, describes unsubstantial flummery as 'warped with water and wefted with the wind of the door'. The characteristics of a good weaver of the more substantial fabrics are 'a hawk's eye, a bear's foot, and a lady's hand'; and as the term 'remlit' (remnant), is often restricted to a residuary cutting of cloth, a peculiar meaning is sometimes given to the controversial proverb, 'there's a remnant of all to be saved'.

A. HUME, from 'Spinning and Weaving: Their Influence on
Popular Language and Literature', Ulster Journal of Archaeology, vol. 5, 1857

from ON MY COMING TO DROMORE

My fav'rite walk was where the floods divide,
And wash the flowery path on every side.
Here the mill-race pursued its usual course,
And there old Legan roll'd with rapid force.
The lofty fir, and ash of lively green,
With sloping hills, adorn'd the rural scene.

High o'er the rest, expos'd to many a storm,
The conic mount display'd its antique form,
Survey'd the river in its winding way,
Its verdant banks with splendid linens gay.

THE REVEREND SAMUEL BURDY, 1802

IN OUR ROAD WE PASSED THROUGH LURGAN, a little town about the size of Southam. It happened to be market day. I was quite surprised to see such a concourse of people and such a quantity of yarn and linen cloth, but more so when I was told that every market day there is from £3,000 to £5,000 worth of yarn and cloth sold there. At Lisburn, a pretty town about the size of Stratford, we lay. This town belongs entirely to Lord Hertford; he has a house here in a very charming situation with a fine river and meadows and large plantations and improvements. I was told he could enclose within a wall £9,000 a year without an acre belonging to anybody else. I could wish that among his other improvements his lordship would build a good inn for that which we laid at, although the best there, was a very bad one. But indeed the gentlemen of Ireland are satisfied with much worse lodging, be the claret but good, than we English choose to do.

EDWARD WILLES, *from* 'Letters to the Earl of Warwick', *c.* 1759

THE EARLY HISTORY OF BALLYDRAIN involves the Stewart family of Scottish origin, the first house being built there by William Stewart in 1608 as a fortified farmhouse. This estate is situated on the Upper Malone Road opposite Wilmont, which is now known as the Sir Thomas and Lady Dixon Park. However the Stewart family lived at Ballydrain for over two centuries and in the mid-eighteenth century the house was an L-shaped building situated directly at the head of an avenue of lime trees and on a site which today is a car park. During the eighteenth and the early nineteenth centuries the Stewarts were involved in farming and linen in common with many other landowners in the Lagan Valley, with a number of bleach greens being situated at Ballydrain, Wilmont, Edenderry, Newforge, Dunmurry and Lambeg.

KATHLEEN RANKIN, *The Linen Houses of the Lagan Valley*, 2002 *from* ARCHITECTURE

THE HOUSE ON THE BLEACH GREEN

This stump of a tree without any leaves
Can be occupied but never lived in
When snow is lying on the bleach green
And the smallest house you have ever seen
Lets someone inside to watch the linen
From tiny windows with a view of thieves.

MICHAEL LONGLEY, *The Echo Gate*, 1979

THE LINEN INDUSTRY, AS PRACTISED in the eighteenth century, was still domestic in its methods. The flax was grown by the farmer as part of his ordinary crop and prepared for spinning as part of the farm routine. It was then spun into yarn by the peasant women, and woven into cloth on handlooms by the weavers, who were not, as now, concentrated in towns, but lived in country cottages, scattered here and there through the flax–producing districts. When a good length of cloth had been woven, the weaver took it on his back to the nearest town and sold it to the merchant, who had the cloth bleached and finished and conducted to the subsequent exporter.

Arthur Young, a well–known English traveller, has left an account of a linen market which he saw in progress at Lurgan:

> This being market day at Lurgan, Mr Brownlow walked to it with me, that I might see the way in which the linens were sold … When the clock strikes eleven, the drapers (i.e., the cloth merchants) jump upon stone standings, and the weavers instantly flock about them with their pieces; the bargains are not struck at a word, but there is a little altercation whether the price shall be one half-penny or a penny a yard more or less.

Probably the stone standings referred to may still be found in Ulster towns. Until a few years ago they could be seen in a disused brown linen market in Donegall Street, Belfast. The methods of sale closely resembled those pursued with other agricultural products, such as butter. The whole industry was closely bound up with agriculture, and even the most skilled workman, the weaver, was not unconnected with farming, for he usually had a field or two attached to his cottage, and was able to resort to tillage when the linen trade became depressed.

D.A. CHART, *A History of Northern Ireland*, 1927

M ANY WEAVERS HAVE SMALL FARMS, and only employ themselves in
this way during the intervals of their farming occupations. Many of
them are the sons of farmers, who assist in the work of the land, and then
return to the loom; and most of those, who follow this trade, and live in
the country, have gardens and ground allowed for setting potatoes; so that
few are without some addition to their ostensible calling. These people,
thus living dispersed in the country, are, in general, of a better description
than those who live in towns; they are more out of the way of temptation
and of bad example.

REVEREND JOHN DUBOURDIEU, *Statistical Survey of the County of Antrim*, 1812

from THE AULD WIFE'S ADDRESS TO HER SPINNING WHEEL

Now fare thee weel, my cantie wee wheel,
In age an' youth my staff an' my stay,
How gladly at gloamin, my kind auld chiel
Has reeled our pirn, sae bonnie an' blae.
But men o' cunning an' pelf, an' pride,
Hae made thee a useless thing to me;
For they carena what puir bodies betide,
Or whether they live on the yirth or die.
Now the feck o' my fare is a heart fu' o' wae
An' the fourth o' a groat is the wage o' a day.

The mountain lass, at her wee bit wheel,
How blythe was her e'e, an' how rosy her cheek!
Her bosom was white, an' her heart was leal, –
Her mien it was modest, her manner was meek;
But now the pert maidens, wha ply in the mill,
How wan is their visage, – how dim is their e'e
For the ban they maun bide is enough to chill
The spring o' the heart an' to deaden their glee:
To toil for men that are hard to please,
In a hot-bed rank wi' vice an' disease.

An' when they speak, it maun be wi a squeal;
They maun rise an' rin at the toll o' the bell,
An' brook the insult o' a tyrant an' de'il,
An' the jargon they hear is the language o' hell.
To breed a bit lassie in sic a vile place,
Instead o' her ain father's cot on the green,
It puts the puir thing in a pitifu case –
Ah! black was the day when they made the machine.

It has added mair pelf to the hoards o' the great
And left those that were low in a far lower state ...

An' when I was rade, an' hale, an' young,
  My thread cam' level, an' fine as a hair,
An' the kitten purred, an' the cricket sung,
  An' the care o' my heart, was a lightsome care.
Now men ha'e erected a new ingine,
  An' left but little for us to earn,
An' little for me but to pinch au' to pine;
  I wish I had died when I was a bairn, –
For my guid auld man he has breathed his last,
An' I on the cauldrife warld am cast.

THOMAS BEGGS, The Poetical Works of Thomas Beggs, 1867

THE TARDINESS OF MECHANICAL DEVELOPMENT in the linen industry is shown by the late appearance of power weaving. Not until 1850 was the first extensive factory using power looms set up. This presaged the end of the system by which the country weaver worked in his cottage and sold his cloth to the travelling merchant or received from a merchant linen yarn which he undertook to convert into cloth. The cottage yielded to the great mill whose innumerable windows and tall chimneys are a feature of so many northern towns. The weaver became an urban dweller tending a power-driven loom and living in a side street instead of by a country road. He lost his good air and the produce of his cottage plots, but, on the other hand, he received a wage which lifted him above a mere subsistence, and was less subject to distress due to variations of demand.

D.A. CHART, A History of Northern Ireland, 1927

COTTON SPINNING WAS THE MAIN FACTORY PROCESS. Weaving was still done in the workers' homes to a large extent because power looms had not yet been introduced and cheap labour was plentiful. But cotton very soon suffered periods of depression. The Napoleonic wars and the American war of 1812 had already had an effect on supplies, and although these setbacks were only temporary, in 1825 there was a panic and the trade suffered a depression from which it never really recovered. The number of cotton mills had fallen to five by 1838. Perhaps the action of Mulholland was a prophecy of the future, when, after the burning down of his cotton mill in 1838, he rebuilt it as a linen mill, the first industrial linen mill in Belfast. Later in the century the American civil war dealt another blow at cotton manufacturing, but by that time cotton had long served its purpose: the industrialisation which it had introduced had by then been taken over by linen. By 1835 there were ten flax mills in Belfast, two of them having been converted from cotton; in 1852 there were twenty-eight. Linen had reached its dominating position in the town's economy.

The new mills were concentrated in the west, partly because of the usefulness of the streams even in steam mills, partly because they replaced cotton manufacturing which had already made the west industrial. Thirteen of the thirty flax mills existing in 1860 were in Shankill ward.

EMRYS JONES, *A Social Geography of Belfast*, 1960

INTERIOR WITH WEAVER

All we can see of him
are his arms, his shoulders,
and his head
hunched away from the door:

see how light
from the door and windows
has edged the tautness
of his face,

the clenched fingers
of the hand
where he holds the cords,
and light

lies along the loom
shaping it out of the darkness,
till the wooden beams
seem to fill the room

and the cross-frame
is repeated
in the bars of the window.
To see him seated

there, you'd think
his endless repetitions
were those of the loneliness
of human passion,

the pain that must
in the end give meaning
to the grass and trees
that blur outside the door.

CIARAN CARSON, *The New Estate*, 1976

WE SET OUT IN THE MIDDLE OF AUTUMN; and although the potato fields were generally dark and discoloured with blight, yet it was impossible not to feel at a glance, even through the railway windows, the warm, comfortable and industrial aspect of the country through which we passed. The trim hedges, the neat and clean culture, the superior dress, the sober and thoughtful demeanour, and the calm air of self-respect and independence which marked the inhabitants of the north, were such as could not for a moment be mistaken. Every object on which the eye rested was agreeable; for although the country is hilly, and presents not those graceful and undulating lines of beauty which are to be found in other countries, still there was before us every mark and symptom of industry and care. The fields waving with yellow grain; and, wherever the harvest had been got in, the neat hag-yards, the white farm-houses, begemming the warm landscape like stars – the quiet air of earnest attention to business among the people – and that most beautiful feature in a northern landscape, the white bleach-greens, with their snowy lines of linen shining in the distance – all this made me feel and understand the full value of northern character and industry.

WILLIAM CARLETON, *The Squanders of Castle Squander*, 1852

LARGE QUARRIES OF AN EXCELLENT blueish granite were opened upon the property and the mills [at Bessbrook] were erected from this material. The quarries were worked for many years in connection with the flax industry, and a considerable export trade was set up by means of a tramway running from the works into Newry, and afterwards electrified. It has been said that this was the first railway in the world to carry both passengers and goods. The generating station is worked by a waterfall at Millvale, about half-way. In 1894, the annual tonnage was 1,600–1,700 tons, the people carried 90–100,000 ...

At the time of building, much labour had been entailed by the distance from a railway, Bessbrook station not having been made and Goragh Wood being four miles away. The excellent main road from Newry passes under the main Dublin–to–Belfast line of railway by means of an imposing arch, which has always been called the Egyptian arch; it owes its massive classical lines, which follow those of the pylon of an Egyptian temple, to the direction and taste of the man who planned for beauty in everyday things.

The large clump of evergreen rhododendrons on the rising ground immediately inside the great gate of the works provides a wealth of colour in spring and greenery in winter. The long mill (said to be the length of a big American liner) with its two tall chimneys well masked by the surrounding hills, is set amid natural beauty which few great factories can boast. Its dazzling white stone and the intense greenness of the fields surrounding it, contrast with the distant blue mountains to make a picture entirely Irish ...

At one time as many as 4,500 hands were employed in the various departments, but with the introduction of more elaborate machinery the number has been reduced to rather less than half.

CHARLOTTE FELL SMITH, *James Nicholson Richardson of Bessbrook*, 1925

IN MY YOUNG DAYS THERE WERE COTTAGE INDUSTRIES in almost every town and village along the coast as well as in inland places. I remember that at Bangor in County Down there was a long row of cottages, in the front room of which there was rigged up to the rafters the simple apparatus of two looms for hand-weaving. When I was ten years of age I made the acquaintance of one of these weavers, and I used to watch him daily at his work. Our intimacy was so great that he allowed me more than once to wield the handle that threw the sliding shuttle from side to side, while he worked the cumbersome treadles, to which my feet did not nearly reach. In one corner of the same apartment, which I begin to think must have been somewhat congested, the mother of the family sat spinning the flax with a soft, purring sound. There was a curious and rather overpowering odour of damp flax that pervaded every room in the cottage. It was scarcely the kind of perfume that one would associate with Bendemeer's Stream; but it was certainly a refined version of that which greeted us in the old days when taking a stroll on a summer evening by the waters of Bangor where the newly pulled flax was under the process of rotting. The whole air was polluted for miles around, and at one time there was a likelihood of every fish being poisoned in the rivers of flax-growing Ulster.

F. FRANKFORT MOORE, *The Truth About Ulster*, 1914

A COUNTRY SMELL, TO BE CONSIDERED as of the first magnitude, is the Smell of the Flax Water. The dripping carts, carrying the wet bundles of retted flax from the pits of black, bubbling, gassy water, to the spreading-fields, leave on their tracks solid banks of this insistent, impudent odour. It is rightly called impudent, for on clothes and boots it has been known to effect entrance into a church, and, before it could be ejected, to have damaged most seriously the smell proper to the building. Slowly, but surely, it will take entire possession of whole townlands, so that people complain that they have to eat it with their meals.

JOHN STEVENSON, A Boy in the Country, 1912

A LESS ODIFEROUS METHOD was dew-retting. The flax, spread out in the fields rather than immersed in water, had then to be dried in a kiln before scutching. Farmers who did this hand scutched their own flax by beating it with a club over a flat boulder known as a melling stone. Kiln-dried flax was easier to hand scutch.

Kiln drying was done with a peat fire; the heat carried up an arched horizontal tunnel or 'logic hole'. 'A couple o' beats o' flax put on the rack at a time to dry. Then ye scutched it warm; it was much easier. Ye daren't let the fire near the flax, or a spark might get on it.'

'Aye, many's the year I planted lint. Good land here for it', I was told in 1980 by centenarian John Mullan of Belleron. 'Lint was a quick shillin', but a lot a' work wi' it. I got it scutched at McCollums, Macosquin and sold it in Coleraine. A feed a' praties and broghan at night and the same heated up in the morning, and praties and salt for your dinner with buttermilk. No tay in those days.'

WALLACE CLARK, Linen on the Green, 1982

THE POTATO AND FLAX FIELDS were particularly dramatic. In the spring the potato fields were a mass of green foliage and white flowers, rich and dense, which became a rich speckled blue, the colour of thrushes' eggs, after the plants had been sprayed with the blue stone and soda mix to protect them from the blight, the cause of the famine that is as much a watershed in Irish history as the Great War is in English history. In the late autumn, when the potatoes had been gathered and schools were closed so that we could help with the picking, the bare brown fields were studded with storage pits which looked like burial mounds.

Flax was a beautiful crop and its feathery growth had, from any distance, a limpid greenness that moved fluently in the slightest wind and became the background to a marvellous blueness when it flowered. There were few flowers to be seen in our district of tiny farms and no gardens, where all vegetation was green sprinkled with white or pink blossom on the bramble and thorn and wild fruit trees; and these sudden rich bluenesses seemed extraordinary in that landscape, exotic and unnatural. The flax had to be pulled out by hand, since it grew mingled with thistle and weed, so harvesting it was a painful and backbreaking business. After it was pulled, it was put to soak in the flaxholes that lay festering and stagnant in the corners of low-lying fields, surrounded by the heavy stones which held it under water. When the flax had rotted – or retted – in the holes for a month or more it was lifted out, slimy and fetid, and was spread on smooth pasture to dry, and its strange, sour stench hung across the countryside. You could almost see that smell, vaporising and shimmering acidly over the fields.

The word flaxen has lost – or has never had – its scorch and meaning for anyone who has not seen that lovely metamorphosis from a green plant to a glimmering strand, a silky blondeness, so shimmering with light that it seemed on the point of igniting into incandescence. It did ignite often, because of its extreme dryness, and the flax mill in Upper Ardboe went up in flames with defeating regularity and all the work and crop went with it, lost. 'You could be sure,' my father said, 'if you saw a pall of smoke over by Oiney's Michael's in Mullinahoe that the flax mill was on fire again.'

He said it with great restraint, considering that when it burnt down he had generally lost his crop. Every part of the process of making linen out of flax was tedious and fraught, and even, in the system of scutching – the crushing of the fibres by rolling and beating – dangerous, since they had to be held in the hand against spindles rotating at high speed; many a man lost more than a crop. When the linen was woven it was pale brown, or greyish-brown, not white at all, and it was stretched out on smooth pasture to be bleached by the sun and the weather.

POLLY DEVLIN, *All of Us There*, 1983

THE FLAX PULLING

First twilight glints in narrow leaves
  The ripe lint-seed's revealed,
The gate stands open by the lane
  And hard along the field
The men roll up their sleeves in line
  To pull the heavy yield.

The evening light slips in between
  The beats leaned eight and eight
Together on the rifled ground,
  Small-weedy, desolate;
The men take up their coats to go,
  The last man shuts the gate.

They go their way by threes and twos,
    These up, those down the lane,
With talk of years when flax was good
    And sowing it was gain;
But pulling, retting, scutching, now,
    Are little worth the pain.

The agent in the market place
    Last year, they say, bought bales
Were worth three times the price he gave
    But for the foreign sales –
Those two have made the turn of the road,
    Ahead, the last voice fails;

But one will come again tonight
    Here by the moon-streamed beats,
And paused by the gate think back until
    The first green growth repeats,
And under a Spring moon once more
    The silky flax-wave fleets.

JOHN LYLE DONAGHY, *The Flute Over the Valley: Antrim Song*, 1931

A S FOR LINEN, THAT IS ULSTER'S OWN incomparable fabric. The fine damasks, with 400 threads to an inch, the delicate fabric still made on handlooms as when Jemmy Hope worked at Downpatrick, these are the pride of the trade; but there are the great sheets of snowy napery, or the gold-tinted cloths that delight housewives, and the white, white linen that is made for God's altar. You cannot enter Belfast without seeing its noble linen in some form, for shop after shop exhibits the white folds and ornamented pieces; while you cannot but note the smart, starched collars that Belfastmen wear when the rest of the world has grown slovenly. So much linen is displayed that you know yourself instantly in the Linen World, and you think of old-world cleanliness and austerity. The day will come, let us hope, when every Irish woman in all Ireland and the Irish world overseas will have dresses for herself and playing-clothes for her children in this excellent washable fabric. Yet even the world-scattered Irish race could not use all the linen that Belfast makes. In the World War, the city made ninety-three million yards of the fabric for the use of aeroplanes, and the airmen of the allies flew on Belfast wings. Every year, linen enough to cover the city's area twenty-five times is made.

AODH DE BLÁCAM, *The Black North*, 1938

TOWARDS THE END OF THE WAR, many mills were producing very little else but aeroplane cloth. In 1917 the whole flax crop was commandeered by the Government and its use only allowed for such purposes as were approved in the general emergency.

However, the results justified these measures. Ulster supplied not only to Britain, but to all the allies, the wings on which the war in the air was won. Her total output of aeroplane cloth was ninety-three million yards. This amount of cloth would be sufficient to lay a belt a mile wide across the County Down from Belfast to the sea at Newcastle.

D.A. CHART, *A History of Northern Ireland*, 1927

from MARY'S SPINNING WHEEL

'Sé tuirne Mháire an tuirne sásta,
   shiúil sé lán d'Éirinn,
Chan fheil lios nó ráth ó mhá go trá
   nár caitheadh lá gá ghléasadh;
Chaith sé tráth ar Iúr Chinn Trá
   is ar mhullach gach ardán sléibhe,
Is gurb í an síogaí mná ar Chnoc na nGrá
   a shníomh le hábhar léine.

Soin-neamh soin-neadh 'sa bamh a liom bamh,
Soin-neamh soin-neadh sa bhaile,
Soin-neamh soin-neadh 'sa bamh a-liom bamh,
Soin-fhidil a bhamh bhamh Mholaí ...

Mary's wheel is a grand fine wheel,
   it travelled most of Ireland,
There's no fort or rath, from plain to beach,
   that a day wasn't spent to rig it;
It was a while in Newry town
   and on top of every high hill,
It was the fairy woman from the hill of lovers
   who wove yarn of shirt-linen.

Soin-neamh soin-neadh 'sa bamh a liom bamh,
Soin-neamh soin-neadh sa bhaile,
Soin-neamh soin-neadh 'sa bamh a-liom bamh,
Soin-fhidil a bhamh bhamh Mholaí

Mary's wheel is the grand fine wheel,
  she has vowed, there is no doubting,
The scattering of frost and the charge of a goat,
  caused the bobbin to hop up;
A hurricane came in under the wing,
  which would upturn the finest spinner,
The wing was split, the pedal and spindle,
  and the wheel itself took a leap.

Here was the wheel that couldn't last
  with the uproar and the marching,
Of fairy horsemen coming to awake us,
  in narrow cabins on hillocks;
A kindhearted housewife got up to spin,
  to serve the three who were carding,
And my new spindle was buckled and bent
  and me not able to rescue it ...

With a hack from Limerick, a screw from China,
  standards from lovely Quilly,
A measure of the finest silk in the land,
  to go with your spinning wheel, Mary;
A wing from London, a bobbin from Lurgan,
  a spit from O'Malley country,
A string of the very finest combed wool
  and of course that will please you.

According to the folklore of Omeath, Mary in this song was an old woman of poor eyesight on whom the neighbours played a trick by putting her spinning wheel out of order. She blamed the fairies who, apparently, had the wheel before she got it, and never ceased lamenting her trouble. There are references in the song to the fairies, which is not surprising as spinning is associated with legends about the fairy world. One story from Omeath tells of the horned hags who come, one by one, with their spinning wheels from a fairy fort to help a woman with her spinning. When they have all gathered, they sing this song, 'Tuirne Mhaire'. Eventually in order to rid them from her home the woman calls out that their fairy 'liss' or fort is on fire. On racing out to the hill, their horns break off. Then, failing to re-enter the woman's house by magical means, they leave screeching until the cock crows in the morning.

PÁDRAIGÍN NÍ UALLACHÁIN, *A Hidden Ulster:
People, Songs and Traditions of Oriel,* 2003

WE CUT ACROSS DIVISMORE PARK, through an entry between the houses, and down beyond the back gardens through the river. It wasn't a big river. It flowed off the mountain, meandered its way down through the back of Ballymurphy, on down and across the Whiterock Road, through the city cemetery and, as we discovered much later, through the Falls Park and then to the bog meadows. But it was our river. We could jump it. We could put up a swing, a rope, and, Tarzan-like, launch ourselves from bank to bank. We could go up towards a large bridge where it flowed below the Springfield Road, and paddle our way into the darkness, sending echoes of our passage reverberating below the road. Once we followed the river up as far as the rock dam on the lower slopes of the mountain. There were two dams, relics of a linen industry, the smaller one presumably where the flax was retted. Some people said the bigger one was bottomless, but once we went swimming there. The dams and the yellow house had been built by a mill owner from Barnsley in Yorkshire, who called his estate New Barnsley, and when houses were built up there they inherited that name.

GERRY ADAMS, *Before the Dawn*, 1996

IT WAS MID-AFTERNOON WHEN NONO ARRIVED at the Union offices. Daddy was listening to some very old women who were sitting crouched near the fire, their heads half hidden in the shadows of their black shawls. Daddy nodded to her, but said nothing to interrupt the speaker.

'Yes,' the woman near the fire was saying, her husky voice fierce and bitter, 'it's over forty-five years since I started working in the mills. I was just turned eight when I began. When you were eight you were old enough to work. Worked in steam, making your rags all wet, and sometimes up to your ankles in water. The older you got the more work you got. If you got married you kept on working. Your man didn't get enough for a family. You worked till your baby came, and went back as soon as you could; and then, God forgive you! You counted the years till your child could be a half-timer and started the same hell of a life over again.'

Then the other women took up the tale in the same fierce, bitter and husky voice till Nono was numb from the hopelessness and misery.

NORA CONNOLLY O'BRIEN, *Portrait of a Rebel Father*, 1935

WHEN THE TOW ARRIVED at the Cogry Mills for spinning it went through many processes before it was ready to go to the weavers to complete its translation into that most beautiful of all fabrics, Irish linen.

It had to be combed and hackled to straighten out the fibres; prepared and carded so that it coiled into the rove-cans in flattened, narrow widths; roved on large rollers on to big bobbins of sliver ready for spinning. In the spinning-room the great frames spun the sliver out finer and finer, twisted and strong, and coiling on to the small bobbins with incredible speed, while the doffers – an inferior breed, both boys and girls – changed the bobbins, cut the ends and did multitudinous odd jobs.

When the spun bobbins of yarn left the spinners, they were carried in 'cages' to the reelers, the Elite of the mill, and reeled into hanks. Ping! went the little bell on each machine as a hank was completed. The hanks were carried to the drying-loft to have whatever unnecessary moisture the spinning and reeling had left in them dried off. Then the bundlers, all men, made the dried and weighed hanks into ticketed, graded bundles ready for despatch to the weavers.

In theory and on paper the process was excellent, and certainly the work was well done. But on her one and only visit-by-favour to the Cogry mill, Mary cared little for the processes that turned her father's flax into yarn for weaving. She looked at the people.

She was aghast at the great troughs of cold water from which the spinners had to lift the armfuls of big bobbins of dripping rove, pressed to thigh and breast; and the bare feet, red and blue with cold, that pattered up and down the length of the spinning-frame. The black or yellow glazed aprons, which the workers had to purchase from the mill owners, afforded by no means complete protection against the icy, sopping bobbins of rove, and clothes were often soaked through. Those who could afford boots kept them as near to the steam pipe as they could, to put on when going home. A few even brought black knitted stockings as well.

Near the steam pipe too sat the row of cup-lidded cans of once-hot tea. There was a half-hour lunch break, when the dwellers in Cogry mill village ran home for a hurried meal, while those less fortunate who lived at a distance, unwrapped their soda-bread pieces from the ever-present 'Telegraph' and washed them down with tepid tea. In fine weather these workers sat in the shade of the wall opposite to the mill gate, under the ominous-looking chimneystack.

There was no break during morning or afternoon, but hungry workers who had left home between five and six o'clock in the morning could snatch a piece and a drink of still-warm tea while friends minded their machines. Then the like favour would be returned. Or they could eat and work at the same time.

During her tour of inspection Mary felt weary, for the mill was a big place. But to her dismay she found that it was impossible to sit down and rest for a few minutes. There was nowhere to sit. The workers were forbidden to sit down at any time so there was no necessity to provide seats. Any worker found resting for a moment on a bobbin-box or a rove-can was sacked on the spot as an example to the others, for workers were plentiful and any vacancy in the mill could be filled immediately.

FLORENCE MARY McDOWELL, *Other Days Around Me*, 1966

AT SMITHFIELD COLM HELPED THE MAN to lift the furniture on to the empty coal-van: a yellow armchair, a black sofa with a spring bulging out of the bottom, a little bamboo table, a chest of drawers, and a deal table. When it was all safely on top, the man sat on the armchair in front of the van, reins in hand and a cigarette in his mouth. Colm sat at the back, one hand holding the bamboo table. They set off along King Street and turned on to the Falls Road. Boys at street corners laughed and joked at the man driving from the armchair. At Hughes and Dickson's Flour Mill Colm saw, through an open door, steel hand-rails and a man naked to the waist feeding a furnace, but when he raised his eyes to the top of the high building his head got dizzy, and he turned his head away until the cart had passed. All the narrow cobbled streets were filled with playing children. A man was writing on a shop window: EGGS DOWN AGAIN. In a doorway a woman with a shawl over her head blew her nose in the tail of her skirt. A tram passed with a little boy clinging on to the lamp.

When the mill horns screeched loudly girls in their bare feet and black slips with scissors dangling from a strap came flowing out of the doors. They were pale-faced and there was a smell of tow and oil off them. The driver winked at them and they shouted back. Then four girls passed linked together, swinging their tea-cans and laughing.

'Aw, Lizzie, luck at Lord Alphonsus!'

'Hello, daughters,' answered the driver. 'Do you want a lift?'

The driver slowed down and Colm blushed when he saw the four mill-doffers running towards the back of the van. They hopped up, two to each side of him, their faces smeared with dirt and pouse in their hair.

'All aboard, ladies ... Gee up, Suzina!' the driver shouts at the horse, cocking his cap to the side of his head, and holding the whip as straight as a flagpole.

'That's a quare nice wee fella!' says one of the girls.

'Are you the Duke's son?' says another, and snuffled loudly.

Colm didn't answer and the cart rattled and bumped over the hard road. 'Is that yer da?' says another.

'Ah, Mary, lave him alone; he's my boy. Aren't you, dearie?'

At that moment one of the wheels came off and girls, furniture, and all slid off in a bundle on to the road. Fellows cheered. But when the trams came up and clanged their bells for the cart to move off, and it on its three wheels, Colm was so ashamed that he stood afar off pretending that he didn't belong to the annoyance.

He was glad when he was back in his own street again. They were waiting for Alec to come with the key when a young boy offered to get his mother's key to open the door. He called himself John Burns. He helped to carry in the furniture and later brought Colm up to his house where his mother gave him a mug of tea and a bap.

MICHAEL McLAVERTY, Call My Brother Back, 1939

THERE IS NO DOUBT THAT involvement in the many aspects of the textile industry bought security for a great number of women and their families. In many cases, money earned from textiles helped to stem the flow of emigration from the countryside, and from Ireland itself, which characterised Irish society after the Famine of the 1840s. For some women, however, it bought the means of escape, ransoming them from a life of spinsterhood and sad subservience which was so often the lot of the female poor and dispossessed. Thus, financial opportunity secured personal emancipation, giving women freedom to marry, to choose to stay or go, to disobey. The much-reported fierce independence of the mill girls, with their bold dress and behaviour, so disturbing to 'respectable' minds, is vivid testimony to the strength of women-power expressed in and engendered by the Irish textile industry.

MYRTLE HILL and VIVIENNE POLLOCK,
Image and Experience: Photographs of Irish Women c. 1880–1920, 1993

AUGUST 1969

As the huge façade of Greeves's Mill is washed in a Niagara
    of flame
The riot fizzles out. Still smouldering as the troops march in,
    this welcome,
Singing, dancing on the streets. Confetti drifts across the city:
Charred receipts and bills-of-lading, contracts, dockets, pay-slips.
The weave is set: a melt of bobbins, spindles, shuttles.

Happy days, my mother claims, the mill-girls chattering,
    linking arms.
But then, it all changed when I met your father. The flicker of a smile,
It lights again on this creased photograph, a weekend honeymoon.
She is crossing the Liffey, the indelible ink of *Dublin September 1944.*

CIARAN CARSON, The Irish for No, 1987

WE HAD A LITTLE TROUBLE about 1920–1921 in our damask weaving shed, when some of the militant 'prods' tried to get the 'mickeys' expelled, the Protestants being the majority. I knew the ringleader of this effort to get the looms stopped until the Catholics were put out. The foreman acted diplomatically. When he entered the weaving shed after starting time, no looms were working, and when he asked the reason, was told. As he went around, he stopped at a pair of looms. The weaver he knew as a sensible girl and asked why she had not started work. She told him Mr So-and-so had warned her not to start the looms until the Catholics were put out. The foreman used words to this effect … 'be a sensible girl, Lizzie, and start your looms'. She did so and the others followed. The foreman contacted the ringleader and told her he expected to see her looms working when he came back and said the Catholics had to live as well as the Protestants. So ended a situation which might have developed and become serious.

WILLIAM TOPPING, *A Life in Linenopolis: The Memoirs of William Topping, Belfast Damask Weaver 1903–56*, 1992

LYLE AND I WALK FREELY OVER THE LAND. Today we walk by Kilwaughter Castle, which John Nash, architect of Buckingham Palace, designed in 1806. A main, battlemented tower sits squat and round on a long slope, with woods and hills sticking up behind.

We talk about poetry …

The valley itself, the enjoyment of nature, doesn't fail. Today, as we wander, touching the trees, our mood has a kind of precarious satisfaction. In these hours by the river; by the mill-lead in the plantation; by the lake of the castle, what do we expect?

Sunlight twinkles in freshly sprouting trees. We feel the coolness of the lake with our wrists. We listen to the chat of birds. (Birds seldom sound as if they are singing; they're arguing or fussing or asking questions.) Grass tickles our bare knees. Unlike the pasty-faced town boys, we aren't in a hurry to wear long trousers. 'Put your hands over your eyes and look at the sun!' Between the fingers one has an impression of a soft red brilliance.

All this is plant-like; a communion of earth and blood. It's a happiness which has found expression in writers, such as Wordsworth, although we know little about that literary aspect designated 'romantic' which spoke in opposition to an industrial age. Our happiness exists in its own right, not as a cure to a disease of which we know next to nothing. Industry has crept only slightly into our neighbourhood, in the form of linen mills run by Yorkshire manufacturers in Millbrook, a village a quarter of a mile from the rectory.

Returning, our walk takes us through it: two factories and a couple of rows of whitewashed cottages, set among small green knolls. Half the workers are driven daily from Larne; the rest, unhealthy for country-dwellers, reside on the spot. On Saturday nights you can hear their roistering and singing a chorus:

> *Here come the Millbrook weavers*
> *Walking down the Fagin Row . . .*

Lyle and I pause to watch two swans on the bleach-green pond. Someone from the factory greets us: 'How's the boys? Are ye rightly?'

I've been in and out of these rows of cottages with my father or mother. In this field beside the redbrick elementary school, I've played in round games at Sunday school fêtes. Formerly factory youths would invade the rectory grounds on Sundays while my father was at church: which early discouraged him from seeking much result from his fruit trees; they would flirt with the maids; and I remember their playing with our swing, on which, when I went over to them, they gave me an exciting swing. We've often been at concerts and services in the old schoolhouse, later destroyed by fire. I remember seeing from my bedroom window the height of the flames. It was in this hall that I made my first public appearance, aged five, at a Band of Hope concert, reciting something about a pedlar. Now all such concerts end with a tableau, in the centre of which sits a local girl as Britannia, with cardboard helmet and shield, while others dressed as Tommies, and ourselves as Boy Scouts, salute to patriotic music.

GEORGE BUCHANAN, *Green Seacoast*, 1959

IN 1886 UPPERLANDS AS A BLEACHING CONCERN was 150 years old. No celebration was made but it is interesting to speculate as to what impression the works at that time would have made on a visitor.

A traveller might have come to Upperlands on the train and walked up the muddy road carrying his sample case, or if he was on a regular round of calls arrived in his own pony and trap. Let us accompany him. Crossing the stone bridge over the Claudy river he heard on his right the distant rumble of the beetling engines at the Mill and the Lower House, and close up the loud thump of the road engines, and the roar of the water falling over the by-wash in the lade. He then turned left up the rear approach to old Mr Clark's house which served as the works entrance. (It still looks more like the way to a private residence than a factory and is called the Back Avenue to this day). Going up a slow incline he had on his left the Plumb Brae, a bank falling some 50 feet to the river. It was an early autumn afternoon, a 'saft' day when the air was still, moist and warm, and Ireland at her most evocative. In the background cloud shadows chased each other slowly across the grapesoft flank of

Carntogher Mountain. Rooks cawed in the big trees arching over the avenue. At the top of the ascent three hundred yards from the road he eyed the Middle House tucked into the slope, the ridge of its roof level with his feet, with golden beech leaves dusted over the grey thatch; the creaky splash of its water wheel was just audible over the low thunder of the seven beetling engines inside. On a small flat area to the left of the road he saw beetle beams being prepared in the open. The trunk of a great sycamore tree was being marked and rough hewn on the ground by a man swinging an adze between his legs. Another fourteen-foot section held in a crude lathe was being rotated by one man spinning a cartwheel attached to its end, while his mate held a chisel against it.

On our visitor's right through a screen of beech trees, the Hall Field, with a rise in the middle like a slow ocean swell, lay left of the flower beds in front of old Ampertaine House. The short grass was spread with strips of wet wrinkled linen, making the whole atmosphere smell of washing soda. Approaching the long, low, whitewashed Green building he passed on his right three turf stacks, each a hundred feet long, fuel for the boiler which was only occasionally hotted up with a little coal. On the other side of the road was a great refuse pit for surplus lime mango and vitriol from the bleach house.

WALLACE CLARK, *Linen on the Green*, 1982

THE OLD TEAM

Dusk. Scope of air. A railed pavilion
Formal and blurring in the sepia
Of (always) summery Edwardian
Ulster. Which could be India
Or England. Or any old parade ground
Where a moustachioed tenantry togged out
To pose with folded arms, all musclebound
And staunch and forever up against it.

Moyola Park FC! Sons of Castledawson!
Stokers and scutchers! Grandfather McCann!
Team spirit, walled parkland, the linen mill
Have, in your absence, grown historical
As those lightly clapped, dull-thumping games of football.
The steady coffins sail past at eye-level.

SEAMUS HEANEY, *The Haw Lantern*, 1987

S TANDING ON THE FRONT LAWN of a great-aunt's farm, I know that this used to be a bleaching green for a long defunct linen mill. I can picture the enormous sheets of cloth laid out, brilliant against the springtime green of hawthorn hedges. Two centuries ago a fourteen-year-old boy who stole two tablecloths from here was hanged in the village square, still protesting his innocence against accusers certain that they had caught him in the act. The discovery of such bleak cruelty shakes the comfortable familiarity of this known place as surely as a bomb. (And who can guess how much the recent bombings and killings have wounded our sense of home?) It is as if its accustomed reality were suddenly to dim and wobble, like a faulty picture on the television, its identity no longer sure. And if, following the threads of history which we have woven into fabric as deliberately as the linen makers turned flax to cloth, if we go further back in time, the image of this place (any place) grows more complex, ever stranger.

Before 'Ireland' was a word, before any human language feathered our nest with habitable meanings, the land was stalked by creatures whose remains we name and gaze at in museums, their miraculous strangeness momentarily obscured by the sober cataloguing of display. And before them? Vague images of lava, lightning, elemental happenings fill the mind. And beyond that still? Home connects with the numbing mystery of being with alarming rapidity. The stark facts of mystery seem to reach their tendrils into the very heart of the everyday world which we think we know and understand and belong in. Or, if we follow the threads of history in the other direction, tentatively feeling ahead on time's strange cambric, the same thing happens. What will be here a hundred years, a thousand years, from now? For whom will it be home? What creature will stand here as I am standing now?

CHRIS ARTHUR, *from* 'Going Home', *Irish Nocturnes*, 1999

SPINDLE AND SHUTTLE

Last night I darned a damask tablecloth.

Back and forth
Warp and woof:

The cloth was old: a hundred years and more
Had come and gone since, master of his loom,
Some skilful weaver set the hare and hounds
Careering through the woodland of its edge
In incandescent pattern, white on white.
It was my mother's cloth, her mother's too

(Some things wear better than their owners do)
And linen lasts: a stuff for shirts and shrouds
Since Egypt's kings first built their gorgeous tombs
And wrapped their dead in linen, it may be
They held it symbol of a latent hope
Of immortality.

> Back and forth
> Warp and woof:
> Wing of angel,
> Devil's hoof.

The glinting needle with its fitful spark,
My Jack o' Lantern on the marsh's dark,
Would pause and shine, would flash and flit along
Divining scene and symbol for a song.

A field of blossomed flax in North Tyrone
Its lean and sheen and shine, its small blue flower
As shy and secret as an Ulster maid
Who saves her smiles like shillings, unaware
Life pays no dividends on thrifty love.

> Darning, learning
> Yarning, yearning,
> Spinning, weaving,
> Joying, grieving:

A black flax dam, a field of linen snow,
Linked opposites: the scar upon the soul
Of every Ulsterman. (The spindle turns
And turning winds a thread where clumsy splice
Or stubborn knot will lie upon the spool
To mar the damask's smoothness when the web
Is woven fast.)

> Back and forth
> Warp and woof:
> Wing of angel,
> Devil's hoof.

All times make time and all are good and ill;
Twin fibres twist to make the coiling rope
We label time.

And good was twined with ill
When, spinning yarn and weaving linen were
Still country crafts. The old blind woman with
Her spinning-wheel beside the open door
Would spin and spin with finger-tips for eyes
Matching the spindle's hunger to her own
Till each was satisfied; but she could feel
The warm sun on her face, the kindly wind
Lay gentle hands upon her faded hair.
The cottage weaver cramped and stiff from toil
That made a convict's treadmill of his loom
Could run a mile around his one green field
To flex his muscles; and could pause a while
To hear the blackbird's song, or sing his own.

Back and forth
Warp and woof:
Wing of angel,
Devil's hoof:

The hand-loom turns to lumber and the wheel
Becomes a thing to win a tourist's glance
When far from field and bird the factories rise,
A myriad spindles and a maze of looms
Cradled within four walls. On every side
Thin streets of small brick houses spawn and sprawl
Though none could give its neighbour elbow-room.
Sleep flies each morning at the siren's shout
And women hurry, shapeless in their shawls,
In multitudes made nameless, to the mill,
Some young, some old, and many great with child:
All wage slaves of the new industrial age,
All temple vestals of the linen god.
Some will put off their shoes from off their feet
And barefoot serve the spindles all day long,
Some will keep constant vigil where the looms
Like giant nightmare spiders pounce and crawl
With spider skill across the tethered web
While captive shuttles darting to and fro
Will weave, not hare and hounds, but shamrock sprays
To tempt nostalgic exiles. None may rest
Till day ends and the siren sets them free.
Even the children, sad as wilting flowers
Plucked in the bud, must give their days to toil,
Their nights to weariness and never know

How morning comes with laughter to a child.
But linen prospers and the linen lords
Build fine town mansions for their families
And plan a city hall whose splendid dome
Will soar above the long lean streets and look
Beyond them to the green encircling hills.

Back and forth
Warp and woof:
Wing of angel,
Devil's hoof:

Young men see visions and old men dream dreams:
Their beacons lit on summits far away,
Their faith entangled in the baffling rope,
Good twined with evil, evil twined with good.
Strand upon strand with whiter strands for some;
The spinner and the weaver in the mill
Now earn a living and have time to live,
Children whose mothers were half-timers once
Untouchables in factory and school

May learn to play and even play to learn
And think of spindle as a word to spell.
Mill-girls have shed their shawl-cocoons and shine
Brighter than butterflies. With gleaming hair
And ankles neat in nylon each can look
Into her mirror with a practised smile
And see herself the reigning linen queen.
The great domed hall four-square in stubborn stone
With polished marble floors magnificent
As any Rajah's palace has stood now
For nearly half a century. Strange how
The little laurel hedge that hems its lawns
Reveals we still are country-folk at heart
Deep-rooted in the fields our fathers tilled.

Back and forth
Warp and woof:
Wing of angel,
Devil's hoof:

The white strands catch the moment's light, and show
A pattern in the fabric, damask smooth.
We spin and weave, with yarns and years and tears

Our webs of linen and of destiny:
A people's life is netted in the loom
Their story echoes in the spindle's song.
Through slump to boom, through war to peace – this peace
The frightened hare with hounds upon her track
Running to meet the terror that she flees.

    Darning, dreaming,
    Thinking long,
Flax and flux and wheel and song;
    Good and evil,
        Right and wrong.

Spend and lend and buy and borrow,
Yesterday, today, tomorrow:
    Weaving linen,
    Spinning thread,
Weaving guns and spinning bread;
    Sheets and shrouds
    And shirts and collars
Earning dollars, dollars, dollars!

See how fast the wheels are turning:
Rome is burning, burning, burning!
Hear the crying of the fiddle:
Hands across and up the middle
Choose your partners for the dance
Weave your webs or take your chance!

    Hear the clatter of the loom:
    Atom bomb and day of doom!
    Will the clatter never cease?
    Work for war and hope for peace.
    Hear the spindle's gentler hum:
    Work for peace and peace may come.

In fields of North Tyrone the bright flax grows,
The blackbird sings
And past the farm a quiet river flows.

MAY MORTON, *Sung to the Spinning Wheel*, 1951

Plantation, Siege
and 'No Surrender'

We may note the principal milestones on [Ulster's] long
and chequered path. They are the Rebellion of 1641; the
Revolution of 1688; the Volunteer Movement of the last
quarter of the eighteenth century; the Rebellion of 1798
and its natural consequence, the Act of Union; the Home
Rule campaigns of the nineteenth century and the first few
years of the twentieth; the Rebellion of Easter Week,
1916; and the Partition of 1921.

CYRIL FALLS, *The Birth of Ulster*

But Derry had a surer guard
    Than all that art could lend her:
Her 'prentice hearts the gate who barred,
    And sung out 'No Surrender!'

COLONEL BLACKER

[C ERTAIN] MEMORIES REINVOKE a number of apparently disparate
events which are linked together and retold in the service of a
collective identity. Thus we have vivid reminders of such
seventeenth-century events as the massacre of Protestants in 1641, the
Siege of Derry in 1689 and the Battle of the Boyne in 1690. To these we
may add events in the second decade of the twentieth century: the
signing of the Ulster Solemn League and Covenant in 1912, say, and the
losses incurred by the 36th Ulster Division at the Battle of the Somme in

1916. Or, to bring matters up to date, we may include the successful Ulster Workers' Council strike in 1974, along with remembrances of the deaths suffered by ordinary British citizens and members of the security forces at the hands of the IRA since 1969. The point is that these memories and more interweave in a sort of grand cultural unionist narrative which emphasises three themes: the precariousness of Protestant experience in Ireland, the right of Protestants to belong in the North as a distinctive British presence, and the ongoing willingness of Protestants to make ultimate sacrifices for the sake of Britain in general and the Ulster unionist way of life in particular.

NORMAN PORTER, *Rethinking Unionism*, 1996

ONE CAN PICTURE THE WAGONS stuck in fords, or defiles, till, with doubled teams, they had been hauled out one by one. One can imagine the wayside camp in the rain and mud, watched over by a weary sentinel; for that woodland on the hillside might well hold a swordsman or two; and if there were no swordsmen in it there were surely wolves. Welcome at evening must have been the lights of fort or little town such as Monaghan or Omagh.

Then, upon the new holding, pleasant country at worst – it were hard to find any in Ulster not good to look upon – and for a few, as those whose lot was cast in Fermanagh or southern Donegal, a fairyland of beauty, even in winter; cattle, sheep, swine, and flour to be had cheap; perhaps some clumsy labour to be hired; but naught else. Contemplating the virgin fields, the settler might say: 'Here I will build my house; my garden and stables and cow-sheds will be there; over there, I hope, by my son's time if not in mine, there will be a village.'

The materials for house and village were not lacking, but they were in the uncut trunk and the unopened quarry. First, then, there must be built 'Irish houses' for the shelter of master and man, and an enclosure into which to drive the livestock at night. This was the most important work of all in the early stages. True, there was now in all Ulster hardly a single rebel of note 'standing upon his keeping', and not a robber band of any size. Yet in little nests of about half a dozen the shaggy, trousered outlaws still haunted the woodlands, and woe betide the colonist who let his cattle stray after dark. Sir Toby Caulfeild at Charlemont was one of the most powerful, experienced, and popular Englishmen in Ulster, yet within caliver-shot of his fortress the wood-kerne often shared with the wolf the spoils of his pastures. If such was the fate of a formidable servitor, with a fort behind him and soldiers at his bidding to avenge robbery or arson, what must have been that of the undertaker, set down in the open and almost as defenceless as a hermit-crab outside its shell? When he had protected himself, cut and shaped his timber, quarried and squared his stone, there was ahead of him the long drudgery of building houses, barns, stables, byres and flour-mills, while simultaneously the land had to be prepared for harvest. According to tradition, almost the only one of the Plantation period still alive in Ulster, the caliver, snapchaunce, pike or sword lay always in the furrow last turned, while the ploughman and his team turned the next.

CYRIL FALLS, *The Birth of Ulster*, 1936

THE IDEA OF ULSTER as 'a place apart' long pre-dated the introduction of Protestantism. Gaelic institutions survived there long after they had disappeared from the rest of the island and Ulster was the source of repeated attacks on the English settlement in Ireland until the province was finally subdued by the defeat of the great O'Neill rebellion in 1603, the flight of the remaining chieftains in 1607 and the Ulster Plantation which followed. The Ulster Plantation was quite unlike the earlier plantations in Ireland. It involved the positive importation of English and Scottish settlers rather than a simple change of ownership at the top. This led to the economic subjugation of the native Irish who were confined to less productive land and forced to pay higher rents and accept shorter leases than the imported settlers. Lower-class Protestant settlers and native Irish consequently lived in a proximity unknown elsewhere in Ireland. But the Penal Laws preserved the economic superiority of the former until the 1778 Catholic Relief Act brought the two communities into serious economic competition for the first time. In a province where sectarian awareness was already much more acute than elsewhere, the outcome was the development of protestant revenge gangs which aimed at restoring a privileged position thought to be under threat. The culmination of the campaign was the institutionalisation of that special cross-class Protestant identity with the formation of the Orange Order in 1795.

MARIANNE ELLIOTT, *Watchmen in Sion*, 1985

ULSTER WAS A SPECIAL CASE with its own peculiar virulence. Like all English monarchs, James I longed to find relief from the nagging headache of Irish disaffection, and in 1608 he undertook a radical experiment in pacification. Between the Lagan and the Bann lay a fertile lowland inhabited by a comfortable Catholic peasantry. These ancient inhabitants James dispossessed, driving them up into the worthless hill farms nearby ... The fertile land he then settled with imported Scots colonists. Cromwell brought in still more Scots settlers, so that at last Protestants made up a unique and purely local three-to-two majority in northeast Ulster.

The Scots were not Anglicans, but Calvinists, Presbyterian dissenters, heretics scarcely more respectable than the Catholics whom they had displaced. Fresh from their own religious wars against England, they feared and hated their Anglican betters no less than the Catholics under their feet. The religious polarity of Ulster thus became triple, adding a further dimension of conflict and confusion to the underlying colonial unrest.

MALCOLM BROWN, *Sir Samuel Ferguson*, 1973

WHEN THE DEBACLE OF KINSALE had been decided, and O'Neill, O'Donnell and ninety other followers found English squiredom intolerable and quit the country for the continent, an army of twenty thousand wood-kernes, now landless and destitute, was loosed upon a desolate Ulster. Hunted from their keeps by the Undertakers, these swordsmen banded together and sought refuge in the inaccessible forest tracts of the Sperrins of Tyrone and the Slieve Gullion range of south Armagh, from which they struck out against their evictors with savage fury. They were the guerrilla patriots, shielded from the *Sassanach* minions by the peasants, and the violence of their attacks was a response to the savagery by which the Protestant 'gentry' had established themselves. Sir Arthur Chichester, the Lord Deputy, records his part in the planting: 'I burned all along the lough (Neagh) within four miles of Dungannon, and killed 100 people, sparing none, of what quality, age, or sex soever, besides many burned to death. We killed man, woman and child, horse, beast and whatever we could find.' In the first thirty years there were sporadic flare-ups – a rebellion led by Cahir O'Doherty of Innishowen over land rights and an abortive popular rising planned by outraged tenants in 1615. But systematic confiscation, expulsion, rackrenting and legal subversion of the traditional way of life were the consequences of colonization. Popular resistance to land-grabbers by the roving bands of pursued wood-kernes (soon to be called 'tories') was met with the direst of penalties.

In 1641, when Phelim O'Neill sparked insurrections in Charlemont and Dungannon, the kernes hastened to his ranks. They would reclaim their holdings and redress a thousand wrongs. Though O'Neill hoisted the royal banner and marched in Charles's name on Drogheda, and though he allied himself to the Old English, forming the 'Catholic Army', his principal ambition was to restore Ulster to the Irish and to square accounts with the Protestant Undertakers. In a war begun as armed reclamation, the Irish must have perpetrated numerous atrocities, but their barbarity was matched and outmatched by English and Scots counterparts. Six months after Charlemont and Dungannon, O'Neill's forces had been pushed back over the Ulster border, and by 1643, the Rising blended into the War of the Three Kingdoms. When Cromwell finally beached his troops in Ireland in 1649, he had two objectives – to wreak bloody vengeance for the martyred Protestants and to carve the country into bounties for soldiers and adventurers.

DANIEL J. CASEY, 'Carleton and the Count', *Seanchas Ard Mhacha*, vol. 8.1, 1975–76

THE SECRET OF THE INTENDED RISING [i.e. of 1641] was well kept, the settlers were almost universally taken by surprise, and Ulster, save for a few towns and castles, was, within a week, in the hands of the rebels. For a short while restraint was observed by the victors, but before long private vengeance and national and religious animosity found vent in outrage and massacre. The settlers of both sexes and all ages were in many cases stripped and turned out in the winter weather to find their way to the coast or the nearest garrison held by their friends. Many died of hunger or cold on the way. In some places mobs gathered which seized upon persons held as prisoners and put them to death.

D.A. CHART, *A History of Northern Ireland*, 1927

THE RISING WHICH COMMENCED so suddenly spread over the greater part of Ulster and fortunate indeed were the citizens of a town which escaped destruction. Newry, Downpatrick, Dromore, Tandragee and Armagh were destroyed by the Irish, while a few years later the Scottish Army under Monroe burnt Dungannon, Lisburn and Antrim; in addition many of the villages and isolated dwellings of the planters suffered a similar fate at the hands of one or other of the rival forces. In County Antrim the towns of Carrickfergus and Belfast escaped the fate of the majority of the towns of Ulster and they formed places of refuge for many Protestant settlers. Derry and Coleraine likewise escaped, although Derry was besieged for a time, while the Ards, fortunate as ever, was the only part of County Down which was free from pillage and plunder.

GILBERT CAMBLIN, *The Town in Ulster*, 1951

from THE COLONY

We planted little towns to garrison
the heaving country, heaping walls of earth
and keeping all our cattle close at hand;
then, thrusting north and west, we felled the trees,

making quick profits, smoking out the nests
of the barbarian tribesmen, clan by clan,
who hunkered in their blankets, biding chance,
till, unobserved, they slither down and run
with torch and blade among the frontier huts
when guards were nodding, or when shining corn
bade sword-hand grip the sickle. There was once
a terrible year when, huddled in our towns,
my people trembled as the beacons ran
from hill to hill across the countryside,
calling the dispossessed to lift their standards.
There was great slaughter then, man, woman, child,
with fire and pillage of our timbered houses;
we had to build in stone for ever after.

That terror dogs us; back of all our thought
the threat behind the dream, those beacons flare,
and we run headlong, screaming in our fear;
fear quickened by the memory of guilt
for we began the plunder – naked men
still have their household gods and holy places,
and what a people loves it will defend.
We took their temples from them and forbade them,
for many years, to worship their strange idols.
They gathered secret, deep in the dripping glens,
chanting their prayers before a lichened rock.

JOHN HEWITT, *Collected Poems 1932–1967*, 1968

IN IRELAND OUR ANCESTORS suffered in the fiendish Romish
massacre of 1641, and we who are the victors of 1688 are not likely
to render tame submission to the offspring of the vanquished, for the
Protestants of Ireland are compelled to resist by every means in their
power this hated system of Popery, which is slavery and the taking
away the freedom of a people. Our forefathers were encouraged to
leave England and Scotland to colonise and hold Ireland for Great
Britain. They have more than fulfilled that duty; their blood has been
spilt for freedom, faith, and empire, and in the most trying and perilous
times their loyalty to their country and Protestantism has stood the test.
They have experienced a massacre more barbarous, and inhuman
cruelty, than any that characterised the most sanguinary period of the
French Revolution ...

Sir Phelin O'Neal and the rest of the infernal gang were barbarously
punctual to the villainies they had promised to perform. The persons,

houses, cattle, and goods of the English and Scotch were seized, and a universal massacre ensued.

PASTOR S. BOAL, *c.* 1907

I ASPIRED TO BE A MAN AS SOON AS I COULD; and therefore had a picke, and a muskett made to my size: and on ye 23rd of October, 1641, was in ye Garden performing ye postures of my Arms with my grandfather Sir William Stewarts foot company; himself viewing his soldiers and their Arms, and exercising them; when about fower houres afternoon (to our amazement) a man half-stript, came with a Letter, signifying ye Insurrections, Murthers, and burnings, on all sides, committed by ye Irish. The messengers one after another came (sweating and out of breath) from divers quarters; with Like consternation and haste (as Jobs escaped servants did, to tell him of his Losses), and they related the crewell Massacres of divers persons, also ere night many men and women fled into towns, and Sir William ordered his company and ye refugees in best manner for defence.

And that very night ye whole country (round about us) was in flames: and Mr James Montgomery of Ashra (a worthy gentl'm) was murdered after he had fought and gott quarters.

Sir William leaving a guard in his sd house, went next morning with his Lady and family to Strabane (where was a town full of British Inhabitants, as also at Lifford, on ye other side of ye river) and thence to Londonderry, ten miles further.

WILLIAM MONTGOMERY (1702), *The Montgomery Manuscripts*

I N PASSING LURGAN THERE WERE several fine bleaching greens glist-ening in the morning sun. 'This town,' said my clerical companion, 'was all but destroyed in the rebellion of 1641. That was a frightful time. It showed what Popery can do.'

'But,' I ventured to state, 'Edmund Burke always maintained that the rebellion of 1641 had been provoked by almost unbearable tyranny.'

'Oh, did he?' replied my reverend friend: 'Well, he knew nothing at all on the subject.' Then after a pause he added, 'I am sorry to say that the present Lord Lurgan is a Liberal. So is Lord Dufferin, who ought to know better. It is a pity.' We left Moira behind and soon afterwards approached Lisburn.

'This town too,' said my fellow passenger, 'was destroyed in the rebellion of 1641. The Huguenots who were driven out of France when the Edict of Nantes was revoked did much for the linen trade of Lisburn. You can yet see the tombstones of these Huguenots who were obliged to leave their native country. This will show you what the Roman Catholics are.'

'It seems to me that in Ireland you have good memories.'

'Yes, sir, we have. We forget nothing.'

'Would it not be better sometimes to forget?'

'Not at all under such circumstances. Macaulay says: "A people which takes no pride in the achievements of remote ancestors will never achieve anything worthy to be remembered by remote descendants." I have often quoted the sentence at our Twelfth of July meetings.'

'But Macaulay was a Liberal, and I think he added some qualifying words.'

'Such qualifications are of little consequence, but here we are in Belfast.'

THOMAS MacKNIGHT, *Ulster As It Is*, 1896

A YE, BUT DERRY WALLS – Derry walls. What have we to say about that siege of Derry in 1689 which is commemorated every year with processions, drums and angry speeches?

It was in the defence of Derry against the Jacobites that the slogan 'No surrender' first was uttered. King James II had come from France to Ireland with an ill-equipped army, hoping to win back one of his three kingdoms easily, since the great bulk of the Irish people then favoured the Stuart cause. Derry was the strong place of the North (for Belfast still was of little consequence) – the sea-gate through which Dutch William might come. To Derry, James marched. The civic chiefs were asked to surrender, and agreed; but a blundering display of force alarmed those townspeople who had been inflamed by fanatics, and the gates were closed, the King defied. It was April 18th – the siege was begun.

AODH DE BLÁCAM, *The Black North*, 1938

T HE SIEGE OF DERRY LASTED one hundred and five days, making it one of the longest sieges in European history. It is an event that still has huge symbolic importance for Ulster's Protestant community, encapsulating in their eyes something of the spirit of self-reliance, principled resistance, toughness and tenacity, independence of mind and freedom in religion, which are such integral features of their self-image. The closing of Derry's gates by thirteen Protestant apprentice boys in the face of the Catholic army of King James, is still celebrated by loyalist organisations today, over three centuries later. A recent statement from one of them tries to explain the significance of these commemorated events, not in terms of sectarian supremacy, but rather as a heroic struggle for civic and religious freedom. (An explanation most Catholics would reject, arguing that the contemporary parades are merely about loyalist triumphalism.) ...

There are always different ways of reading history. Just as, today, even the city's name is contested, some opting for Derry, the original name, some for Londonderry, the seventeenth-century re-naming done to mark the contribution of London's guilds in funding and facilitating Derry's reconstruction and development, so there are rival understandings of its past, each community favouring its own particular namings of what happened.

CHRIS ARTHUR, *from* 'Under Siege', *Irish Nocturnes*, 1999

THE JACOBITE ARMY DID NOT, upon the whole, behave in a very cruel or discreditable manner, considering the power in their hands and the amount of provocation which they received. For four months, from March till August 1689, all Ulster, except Derry and the district around Enniskillen, was completely at their mercy. They had garrisons stationed in Newry, Carrickfergus, Coleraine, Omagh, and all the principal towns. If they had possessed the wish, they certainly for a time possessed the power, to act in union with the Roman Catholic population and to murder all the Protestant people, of which there were great numbers who had failed in the attempt to reach Derry or to flee across the Channel. Most of the poorer Protestants were in this helpless position, and, had the Irish peasantry pleased, they might, under protection of the King's soldiery, have repeated on a larger scale the scenes of 1641; and under pretence of helping the King to put down his enemies, have exterminated their Protestant neighbours. This is what the citizens of Derry feared, when, on the 7th of December, 1688, they shut their gates in face of the Redshanks.

THOMAS WITHEROW, *Derry and Enniskillen in the Year 1689*, 1875

THE INHABITANTS [OF DERRY] were Protestants, but yet not all of one country, or of one Church; for we find Englishmen and Scotchmen, Episcopalians and Presbyterians, standing shoulder to shoulder to fight for Home and Fatherland, and all that was dear to them. Rumours from various quarters agreed in naming the 9th of December, 1688, as the day fixed for the exterpation of the strangers. While the minds of the citizens were agitated, news came that a regiment of one thousand two hundred Papists, commanded by a Papist, Alexander Macdounald, Earl of Antrim, had received orders from the Lord-Deputy, to occupy Londonderry for James II; this was on the march from Coleraine, a town built on the banks of the Bann, and which has ever been loyal to the cause of Protestantism, and there are in it today the descendants of the men of 'Derry. When the

Earl of Antrim came within sight of the city, some were for closing the gates and resisting; some for submitting; the Bishop, Ezekiel Hopkins, adhered to the doctrine of non-resistance and exhorted his flock to give in to the Lord's anointed, James II, and not be guilty of disobeying. But one of the young sons of 'Derry said to his Lordship: 'A very good sermon, my Lord; but we have not time to hear it just now.' Meanwhile Antrim was drawing nearer and nearer. At length the citizens saw from the walls his troops on the opposite side of the Foyle. There was no bridge in those days, but a ferry which ran between the two banks of the river, which Antrim used to bring his regiment across. He and his officers presented themselves at the gate, produced a warrant addressed to the Mayor, and demanded admittance and quarters for His Majesty James II's soldiers.

> Then loudly their war-cry o'er Ulster resounded,
>   And called forth the Protestant chiefs of the land;
> Who with zeal patriotic, and courage unbounded,
>   On the Foyle, for their freedom, determined to stand.
> George Walker and Murray rode here in a hurry,
>   Bold Mitchelburn, Baker, and Mackay unbending,
> Held out through all danger our rights to maintain,
>   Resolving to die for their freedom contending,
> Before the vile tyrant should over them reign.

But the men of 'Derry were not to be caught napping, for it was a fight with them for Home and Fatherland. Just at this moment, thirteen young Apprentice Boys – and from their names many have thought that they were of Scottish birth – rushed to the guardroom and armed themselves, seized the keys of the city, and rushed to the ferry-gate, closed it in the face of the King's Officers, and cried out: 'No Surrender!'

ANONYMOUS, *c.* 1907

from THE CATALOGUE

> What could the maiden city do
>   By all these troops invested?
> She raised her standard of true blue,
>   By freedom's foes detested;
> The goodly sign, like bow divine,
>   O'er Ulster brightly beaming,
> Brought quickly forth the sons of the North,
>   The post of honour claiming.

First to the town Squire Forward came,
  His bands from Burt proceeding;
And Stewart and Grove to the field of fame
  Lough Swilly's heroes leading;
In a meadow great, near Ballindreat,
  Brave Rawdon joined Lord Blaney,
While war's wild sound re-echoed round
  From the Foyle to the Southern Slaney.

Macnaghtan next came here a boy,
  From fair Benvarden blooming,
And Moore, with troops from Aughnacloy,
  A high command assuming;
To aid our town from warlike Down
  Hill came and cross'd our ferry,
The Hillsborough men were welcome then
  To the troubled men of Derry.

Here, too, was brave Lord Massareen
  In William's army serving;
From Port Glenone was Stafford seen,
  From Omagh Audley Mervyn;
Cairnes in our darkest day
  The tyrant's power slighted,
For gallant deeds in many a fray
  Was young George Maxwell knighted ...

Hillhouse and Boyd were both employ'd
  Our sacred walls defending;
Dobbin came far to the scene of war,
  With fortitude unbending;
Tracy, Fullerton, and Hume,
  With Manson, Smith, and Hilson,
Stood here against the slaves of Rome,
  With Wilkins, Keys, and Wilson.

Early in the opening spring
  Came Grigson, Black, and Bailly,
M'Causland, Fleming, Hare, and King,
  Were all in action daily;
Galtworth, Cathcart, and Adair,
  Oft weak from want of dinner,
Depress'd with care did oft repair
  To the walls with Robert Skinner.

Sir Tristram Beresford's array
   Coleraine some days defended,
And here at last they made their way
   In martial line extended;
Sir John Magill was ready still,
   Both night and day for action;
And Gary sought, and nobly fought,
   To crush King James's faction.

Cromie swimming in with Roche,
   Both in the water wounded,
Announced that Kirk would soon approach,
   Which Rosen's hope confounded;
Bennett, Christie, Pearse, and Bell
   Were to our cause devoted;
Count Schomberg stood for Derry well,
   And highly was promoted ...

With hearts like these, what blood could freeze
   Tho' dangers gathered round us?
From morn till night we stood the fight,
   The foe could ne'er confound us.
Not famine pale could ought avail,
   No feeling keen or tender
Make us relent, or once consent
   To say the word surrender.

At last, by all our sufferings moved,
   Kind Heaven its aid extended,
The Tyrant's arts abortive proved
   And Derry's woe was ended;
In one dark night the foe took flight,
   The country round them burning,
And ere 'twas day all far away –
   They thought not of returning.

THE REVEREND JOHN GRAHAM, *Lays of Ancient Derry*, c. 1880

T HE WALLS WERE BUILT IN 1617–18, at a cost of £8,500, a sum which represented a great deal more in those days than it does in ours. They were found to be impregnable by the Royalists, who besieged the Cromwellian garrison for four months in 1648. But the most memorable siege took place in 1688, when for 105 days it held out against the army of James II. The beleagured city endured the most terrible privations, and behaved with a heroism which Catholic as well as Protestant cannot but admire. The brunt of the fight fell on the 'prentice boys, and they won. King James was obliged to raise the siege. His generals may or may not have been incompetent, and the elements of attack inadequate. Be that as it may, James was worsted. Derry held her own against him, and he was obliged to leave her in peace:

In short, the fact is known, boys, she chased him from the hill,
For the maiden on her throne, boys, would be a maiden still.

The hero of the defence was the Rev. Mr Walker. Derry raised a great monument to his memory on the walls that he made famous. There it stands yet, overlooking the city. The sword which the right hand of the statue held aloft fell with a mighty crash on the night that Catholic emancipation for Ireland became law. The prominence given to this circumstance in Irish history of the nineteenth century shows that in neither religious camp was it regarded as a mere coincidence at the time.

WILLIAM BULFIN, *Rambles in Eirinn*, 1907

O N THE BRIDGE OF SIGHS AND FAREWELLS we found Tummus mending the woodwork. His mouth was full of nails.

'What an interesting looking old man!' said madame. 'Do you know him?'

'Oh yes,' I said. 'I know him.'

'Good evening,' she minced out in a way that was not the least like her former alert manner. She had adopted the peculiar tone which some people assume when they speak to children and poor people, and which has not a soothing effect on either.

'The same to you, ma'am,' said Tummus, removing the nails, and gazing fixedly at the masked ladies the while.

'We are strangers here,' she went on in her usual formula.

'Ye's are that.'

'And we are very much interested in the historical associations of the place.'

'The which?' said Tummus stupidly.

'Why, St Patrick and St Brigit and Lupita, and all the other saints you know.'

'I doubt they were no Protestants, them saints?'

'Well, you see, in the days of the Saints, the great Protestant movement – ... however ... Of course you are very proud to think that Brian Boru is buried here?'

'I am that,' said Tummus. 'Is it long since?'

'Oh, many, many years ago.'

'Before you and me was born?' he inquired, with dangerous sweetness.

She hesitated a moment, but soon continued. 'He was, you know, a really great and good king – a statesman and a general – the greatest king that Ireland ever had.'

'I'd sooner have William o' Ornge,' put in Tummus; but I don't think she heard him.

ELEANOR ALEXANDER, *Lady Anne's Walk*, 1903

I

T IS INCONCEIVABLE HOW FRESH the events of [bygone] days are in the minds of the people of Ireland. The wars of William and James are as little talked of in England as the war of Troy, and an immeasurable distance seems between the period in which they happened and the present one – but in Ireland, where accounts of them have been handed down from father to son, and the ideas been frequently revolved, they are as fresh as if the events had only occurred yesterday, and the siege of Londonderry is talked of with much less reference to distance of time than the siege of Boston is in England. One evil of this is the injury it does the character of the country. The country people, accosted by a stranger, will tell him of robberies and murders and assassinations, that make him tremble – he fears to walk a mile alone, and thinks himself in a country inhabited by demons – but were he to take pains to ascertain facts, he would find that the greater part of the events recorded in these terrific tales, occurred upwards of a century ago. There is not in the universe a country more free from violence or robbery than the north of Ireland. Highway robbery is almost unknown. House-breaking certainly does occur, but not often. The great thefts are horse-stealing and bleach-green robbing. In several counties not a man has been executed for many years.

JOHN GAMBLE, *A View of Society and Manners in the North of Ireland*, 1813

R

ELIGION ... HAS AN IMPORTANCE for Ulster people that it has for few modern peoples. You will find, for example, that the historic conflict of Protestant with Catholic which split Europe three centuries ago is still a living one in Ulster, and that everything is seen in terms of it. And you will be surprised by this fact, unless you remember that the peasant's memory is astonishingly long and vivid. The past is not 'mere history' to him, and he cannot be neutral about it. He 'puts himself into it', and it lives. Often I have listened to him talking about people and happenings of 150 years ago with as intimate a knowledge and as cunning a detail as if they had been his neighbours and contemporaries. So you will not long have arrived in Ulster before you learn of this opposition which exists between Catholic and Protestant. For it runs through the whole fabric of Ulster life, and it separates the people politically and socially into two groups. It operates from life to death. Each group segregates itself. In many Ulster towns one finds a Catholic quarter and a Protestant quarter ...

These characters, Protestant and Catholic, are complementary. They make the two halves of life. One takes a long view of life, the other a short and roundabout one. One is thoughtful and individual, the other is emotional and communal. One tends to a democratic and progressive way of life, the other to a hieratic and static way. It is this diversity and interplay of opposites that makes Ulster life such a rich and fascinating spectacle.

W.R. RODGERS, *The Ulstermen and Their Country*, 1952

HISTORY – OR WHAT PASSES FOR HISTORY – for the Irish has a reality that can be frightening and which can perpetuate ancient feuds. As a boy, from my aunts and mother I heard many a story of the suffering endured by the defiant Protestant citizenry, and in language no less eloquent than that of Trevelyan. I heard of the so-called traitor Lundy who had the same significance for us as Quisling for Norwegians during the Second World War. These tales of heroism and stoic endurance were, it was true, told me in Belfast to which my family had moved. Derry indeed was in decline. The Protestants were moving east as the city became more and more populated by Catholics. But even in true-blue, loyalist Belfast, the hearts of my mother and her sisters were still in the Maiden City of their youth when their lives had centred round the Presbyterian Church in Carlisle Road.

Derry for them – they said 'Derry' in conversation but used 'Londonderry' officially – meant Protestant Derry. History meant Protestant history. Suffering and heroism meant that undergone by Protestants. There was never a whisper of the sixth century Derry that had become a great centre of missionary zeal, long before we Scots-Irish had settled there – along with some English – sword in one hand and Bible in the other.

Nobody told me of Colmcille who founded a monastery on the hill overlooking the wide tidal river. Nobody spoke of how, in 563, now named St Columba, he created a great Christian settlement in Iona, so spreading the Gospel through pagan Scotland and northern England. Nor did I know of how Irish monks brought Christianity to western Europe after the fall of Rome and of how the saint wrote of his beloved place:

> Were all the tributes of Scotia mine,
> From the midland to its borders,

I would give all for one little cell
In my beautiful Derry.

No, not a syllable of all that history was uttered, for the very good reason that my mother and aunts knew nothing of it. Theirs, I repeat, was the Protestant version of history – the near-disaster of the 105-day siege before the boom was broken and ships sailed up the Foyle with food for the gallant Protestants. And of course they were gallant and determined, but no more exclusively in the right than their opponents. The past in Ireland, especially in the north, hangs round people's necks like a gigantic albatross.

ROBERT GREACEN, *The Sash My Father Wore*, 1997

THE VOLUNTEERS WERE A NORTHERN phenomenon. Originating in Belfast in 1778, they were the product of Ulster's impatient independence, distrust for politicians, and glorification of the right of every citizen to arm in his own defence. Though they originated as Ulster's solution to the defenceless state of Ireland during Britain's war with America, they nevertheless embodied the central tenets of protestant libertarianism, and with their conventions of 1782–93 and their advanced programme for parliamentary reform, the Volunteers became the most effective extra-parliamentary pressure-group of the age. Tom Paine regarded them as the only truly revolutionary body in the country, and it was the Volunteers which produced the most radical of the reform groups to emerge in Britain in the dramatic decade of the 1790s – the United Irishmen. It is a reflection of the 'loyalist' and 'nationalist' mis-representation of Irish history that the United Irishmen are traditionally considered part of catholic nationalist heritage. In reality they were a further manifestation of Protestant – largely Presbyterian – libertarianism, and non-Presbyterian United Irishmen fully recognised their debt to that tradition.

MARIANNE ELLIOTT, *Watchmen in Sion*, 1985

AS THE PRESBYTERIAN PEASANTRY began to emigrate from Ulster, the Catholics of the neighbouring counties came to take their place – introduced in many cases by the landlord, who wished to arouse a spirit of competition. Hence began a struggle for the land between the Presbyterians and Catholics, and this soon engendered a religious war. The Peep of Day Boys and the Wreckers massacred the Catholics; the Defenders retaliated and one evening in September, 1795, the Presbyterians, after their victory at the 'Diamond', near Armagh, founded the celebrated 'Orange' Society, with the avowed aim of driving the Papists from the province, and with the secret support of Government,

245

which has always sought to divide Irishmen. 'They call themselves Orangemen and Protestant Boys,' said the Protestant Grattan, 'They are a banditti of murderers committing massacres in the name of God, and exercising despotic powers in the name of liberty.' So the Catholics were exiled by force from Ulster, but one Papist house being left standing in the County of Armagh. Simultaneously the movement for a United Ireland collapsed, and the revolutionary movement, provoked by Ulster in 1792 and disowned by her in 1798, received its death blow. From these origins arose the two characteristic traits of Presbyterian Ulster: radicalism, which inclines her towards Irish nationalism; fanaticism, which separates her from it. These two traits appear again and again in Ulster history. Every time that radicalism would seem likely to unite Presbyterians and Nationalists, fanaticism stands in the way and makes enemies of those who the day before had worked in alliance.

L. PAUL-DUBOIS, *Contemporary Ireland*, 1908

I AM NOT A FRIEND TO ANY of these secret societies, because they were nothing but curses to the country. The Orange system is a curse to the country, and will be so as long as it exists. It is now comparatively harmless, but at the period of which I write it was in the very height of its ascendancy, and seemed to live only as if its great object were to trample upon 'Popery'. The truth, however, is, if there can be an apology for Ribbonism, that it was nothing more nor less than a reactive principle against Orangeism, of whose outrages it was the result. In my works I have depicted both systems to the marrow, without either favour or affection, as the phrase has it. I never entertained any ill feelings against the people on either side; it is their accursed systems which I detest.

WILLIAM CARLETON (1867), *Autobiography*, 1896

THE REAL TRUE-BLUE ORANGEMAN ... makes no claim of having ever been a reformer. His sentiments are summed up in the words of one of leaders, now safely ensconced on the Judicial bench, whose contribution to the political thought of his time was a fierce protest in Parliament against 'the rotten, sickening policy of conciliation'. This policy, the Orangeman holds, is not a thing of today or yesterday. It began as far back as the decision to relax the Penal Laws, and has continued with increased force ever since. England's fatal crime in Ireland has not been the denial of freedom, but the overthrow of Protestant Ascendancy, which the remonstrance of the Dublin Corporation defined as 'a Protestant King of Ireland, a Protestant Parliament, Protestant electors and Government, Protestant benches of Justice, a Protestant hierarchy, the army and revenue, through all their branches and details, Protestant, and this system supported by a connection with the Protestant realm of Britain'. Any whittling down of this is part of the 'rotten, sickening, policy of conciliation'; and whether it takes the shape of an Act of Union, Catholic Emancipation, or university reform, Orangemen can be relied on to oppose it tooth and nail.

JAMES WINDER GOOD, *Ulster and Ireland*, 1919

WITH THE MENACE OF HOME RULE, which was regarded in Ulster as equivalent to Rome Rule as well as to Home Ruin, people awoke to the fact that the Orange Institution would bear to be accepted as a force instead of a farce, since it had its feet resting on the very foundations of the Colony in Ulster – since the note that had come from every Orange fife at every celebration sounded the key to which Protestant Ulster was to be attuned, if it meant to hold its own against its enemies; and so for the past twenty-five years I fancy that the Orange Institution has been more highly respected than it was since the first glow of its inauguration was upon it. There is no more mystery about its founding and its objects than there is about the Good Templars or the Rechabites ...

Orangeism began with the crossing of the Boyne by the Prince of Orange in 1688 and – *longo intervallo* – we find as its legitimate descendant the Orange Institution. I am afraid that I cannot give the exact date of its birth; but I believe that it took place toward the end of the eighteenth century, when the need of such a movement was made apparent in many parts of the province.

It was founded as an organisation to resist the pretensions of the Church of Rome and its seditious following to a place of power in the province. This was the original object of its creation, and it remains the *raison d'être* of its existence today. This being so, it is not surprising that its popularity should have increased amazingly since all the Protestants of the province are actuated by the same motives and thus are Orange in principle, if not in name.

Loyalty had ever been the watchword of the Orange Institution; but its exponents must always be ready to define Loyalty as a readiness to uphold and to obey such laws as they approve of.

F. FRANKFORT MOORE, *The Truth About Ulster*, 1914

THE PROPOSAL TO GIVE HOME RULE to Ireland drew the Ulster community together in vehement protest. The main reasons for the Ulster opposition to successive Home Rule proposals may be summarised as follows. First, there were reasons of tradition and sentiment. The connection of Ulster with Britain was one of real kinship and affection. Ulster people felt that British institutions and traditions and ways of life were their own, in a way in which those of the majority in other parts of Ireland were not. Secondly, there were economic reasons. Free trade with Britain and equal participation in British overseas trade were essential to the industries and commerce of Ulster; and, while the early Home Rule proposals did not directly threaten Ulster's economic interests, it was believed – correctly, as events have shown – that a moderate measure of Home Rule would not be the end and that certain political tendencies in other parts of Ireland pointed towards a progressive expansion of the principle of self-government, perhaps to the point of the complete separation of Ireland from Britain. In the event of such developments, the breach between Ireland and Britain might well become economic; and it was felt in Ulster that the economic needs of the province would not be sympathetically cared for by a Dublin government representing predominantly agricultural interests. Among the Protestant workers in Ulster there was fear, based on certain experiences, that Home Rule would intensify the menace of undercutting by Roman Catholic workers and would cause standards for social and working conditions to fall far behind those prevailing in Britain. Thirdly, there were religious reasons. The prospect of being placed under the rule of a predominantly Roman Catholic government aroused acute anxiety in Ulster, both on account of antagonisms still lingering in Ireland from the less happy past and on account of several discouraging examples of reactionary rule provided in other countries at that time by governments which were predominantly Roman Catholic. Fourthly, in none of the proposals put forward was there evidence of a practical and constructive effort to recognise and meet these problems arising from the needs and feelings of the Ulster community.

HUGH SHEARMAN, *Northern Ireland*, 1948

IN 1912 THE COMPACT AND WELL-DISCIPLINED Irish Nationalist Party, which held the balance of power in the House of Commons, forced the Liberal Government to bring in the third Home Rule Bill. The reply of the colonists was the Covenant, similar in character to that of the seventeenth century – to which many of their forefathers had subscribed – pledging themselves to resist Home Rule by every means in their power and never to recognise an Irish Parliament in Dublin. Two hundred thousand signatures followed that of Sir Edward Carson, their new leader, on 'Ulster Day', 28th September. They then proceeded to arm themselves in order to resist force by force.

CYRIL FALLS, *The Birth of Ulster*, 1936

T HE PROTESTANTS' SELF-RELIANCE and assertiveness were hardened in the years before the Great War, when by signing the Ulster Covenant they pledged themselves to resist Home Rule, and by creating the Ulster Volunteer Force and running guns from Germany and elsewhere they prepared themselves to carry out the threat. Ironically and tragically, the Covenant was sealed with bloodshed not against British or rival Irish armies, but when the UVF, four years later, was cut to pieces by German machine-guns on the Somme.

Though many Catholics fought in the war, their folk-heroes were not those of the Somme, but the men who gave their lives for Irish liberty in the Easter Rising of 1916. Fifty years later, both sacrifices are still being celebrated, and they have added a new dimension to the division in Ulster life.

JOHN COLE, *Ulster at the Crossroads*, 1969

B Y NOON THE CROWDS OF PEOPLE had crushed into Donegall Square, around the building, the great City Hall, that is the centre of Belfast. The sky was grey over the city, huddled gloomily between the straight wall of Cave Hill and the wide waters of Belfast Lough. Specially appointed marshals wearing badges of red, white and blue kept the crowds in order, manoeuvred them into the places they would hold in the procession, kept them waiting in docile patience while a passing cloud emptied itself over the streets. It was harvest rain. The day was 25th September, 1911. When the march began, up the three miles of streets to the sloping fields south of the lough, the rain had ceased and the sky was clearing. In the head of the procession went the visiting County Grand Orange Lodges led by the men from Larne and Antrim and Ballymena; a journalist described them as an 'army of determined and earnest loyalists marching four deep and preserving splendid formation'.

On the heels of the sashed men from the visiting Lodges went the Unionist Clubs; then the Orangemen of Belfast, who had politely taken the lowest place, walked in the rear. They crossed Queen's Bridge, over the muddy Lagan, went by way of the Newtownards Road and the Holywood Road to Craigavon. The brethren of the Portadown district arrived late, lost their place in the line of visiting Grand Lodges, followed the polite Belfastmen over Queen's Bridge, through streets with crowded, waving windows. Some sense of the special dignity of the occasion dispensed with the genuine giant Orange drums; they drank in the elation and rhythm of marching from shrill fifes, kettledrums, bagpipes. They filled the sloping fields around Craigavon. Below them was the lough, the city, the factories, the skeleton steel arms over shipyards and dockyards; and across the water, Cave Hill and the Antrim shore. Over the house at Craigavon flapped the flag that had been used at the Ulster Unionist Convention in 1892. For the men there it was a link with the almost legendary visit of Randolph Churchill, with a sentence written somewhere that Ulster would fight and Ulster would be right. For men who had seen through Randolph Churchill that flag might have recalled the greatest English statesman of the nineteenth century and his heroic, vain efforts to uproot *the Upas tree*. But the vast majority of the men at that meeting revered the memory of Randolph Churchill. Every step they took on that parade to Craigavon was hammered out to the jingle of Randolph Churchill's rhyming sentence: Ulster would fight and Ulster would be right. Neither they nor the visitor from the English Conservative Party bothered defining what they meant by Ulster. That neglect of the Aristotelian business of definition still causes confusion.

BENEDICT KIELY, *Counties of Contention*, 1945

A S I WALKED THROUGH PORTADOWN on an autumn day in 1929, I had a memory of another autumn day on these streets – 25th September, 1912. The occasion was an historic one, and I was glad I had been present and had some souvenirs of the proceedings. It was 'Ulster Day', and I had come to Portadown to be an onlooker while a covenant was being signed that committed the Protestants of Ulster – of the whole of Ulster – to a violent resistance to a Home Rule Bill which Mr Asquith's government was putting through the Westminster Parliament. In those mild pre-bellic days the granting of a measure of self-government to Ireland was considered to be an event of major political importance: the Tory party in England patronised the idea of an insurrectionary movement in Ireland against a constitution that a Liberal government might bring into effect, and the Protestants of Ulster were encouraged to make revolutionary and warlike movements with the object of showing the people of the British Empire that they would enter upon civil war rather than pay taxes to and accept the laws of an Irish parliament. The first movement was to be the signing of the Ulster Covenant.

I was present at the covenant signing in Portadown. The proceedings began with a service in the First Presbyterian Church ... I expected, I remember, a flow of impassioned eloquence from the preacher, but got from him instead a carefully written statement. Some people pretended to think that clergymen in the north of Ireland were introducing politics into their churches, he told us. But their opposition to Home Rule was not political – it was a question of life and death. What would be their situation if a Home Rule Bill was passed? A prosperous community would be taxed for the upkeep of monasteries and convents, and a tolerant people would be put under the heel of an intolerant Church. Because they wanted to protect their birthright of free citizenship they

were going to sign the covenant. They would sign it with the name of
Jesus Christ upon their lips, and if they failed to abide by it they would
be branded as liars and cowards. He went on to remind the congregation
of the signing of the Scottish Covenant, and he told how some men
wrote 'Till Death' after their signatures, and others drew blood to sign
their names.

PADRAIC COLUM, Cross Roads in Ireland, 1930

MEMORIES OF THE OLD PARISH of Donaghcloney and its fine, old
parish church at Waringstown crowd in upon my mind, and I have
not yet recorded any of my recollections of my work and experiences as
Archdeacon! Before, however, I turn from the parish to the Diocese I
cannot refrain from recalling some of the incidents of the memorable
years of 1913 and 1914. Once more Home Rule for Ireland was brought
forward, and this time it seemed inevitable that it would pass through
both Houses of the Imperial Parliament. Ulster was in a ferment: 'The
Bill may pass Westminster,' it was said, 'but it will never pass Portadown!'
– the great junction on the main line from Dublin to the North and a
stronghold of Unionism. It was decided by the Unionist Council sitting
in Belfast that a Covenant should be drawn up binding those who signed
it to stand by one another and firmly resist the imposition upon Ulster of
Home Rule under a Dublin Parliament as proposed. It was further
arranged that the Covenant should be offered for signature by those in
agreement with it in every parish throughout Ulster.

E.D. ATKINSON, Recollections of an Ulster Archdeacon, 1934

IT'S THE PERIOD OF THE BRITISH CONSTITUTIONAL CRISIS. Ireland is
about to be granted Home Rule by a Liberal Parliament; but, at the
instigation of English Conservatives, armed opposition to this has been
organised in Ulster, through the Orange Order, composed of Protestant
workers. With these rebels, my father tends to side. The Orange workers
are docile towards the English industries that use them; and industry
brings advantages. 'It is better to build a new factory than an alms-house,'
my father says, with a picture in mind of impoverished, pre-industrial
parts in the south of the island.

Moreover, he's a Protestant. Protestants are people who have taken a
few steps away from old dogma towards liberty of thought. (They don't
necessarily wish to advance further.) They hate and fear their former 'bad'
selves, the serfs of strictness. A self-governing Ireland would so carry them
back, they think – a fear carefully played upon by interested politicians.

In the rectory my mother says: 'We have found leaders to take up our cause.' She's referring to Sir Edward Carson whose eloquence sways the crowd. She shows us a pen. 'With this,' she says, 'I signed the Covenant (a pledge to oppose Home Rule). You will show it to your grand-children with pride.' Evidently life has become noble and heroic. 'We live in stirring times, when a small province has the courage to face a large empire.'

We look at the pen. We repeat the slogans, such as *No surrender!* which are being repeated around us.

GEORGE BUCHANAN, *Green Seacoast*, 1959

CARSON'S CAT

Sir Edward Carson has a cat,
It sits upon the fender
And every time a mouse it gets,
It shouts out 'No Surrender!'

He left it by the fireside,
Whene'er he went away
On his return he always found
It singing 'Dolly's Brae'.

The traitors grew indignant,
At hearing such a noise
But Carson made the cat sit up,
And sing the 'Protestant Boys'.

The traitors then decided
To hang it with a rope
But every time they tried the rope,
It yelled 'Hell roast the Pope!

The people came from far and near,
To hear the pussy sing
Good old 'Britannia Rules the Waves'
And may 'God Save the King!'

A few said 'What a pity,
The cat is such a fool',
But Carson's cat yelled out the more,
'WE WILL NOT HAVE HOME RULE!'

ANONYMOUS

B UT AN ARISTOCRACY IS NOWADAYS a feeble thing, and a chamber of commerce, though stronger, is not very strong. Not even the union of the territorial aristocracy with the captains of industry would be able to resist the rest of Ireland if there were not a third member of the alliance, the northern Protestant working man. He, for his own peculiar reason, hates the idea of Home Rule so much that he is content to follow the leadership, and in matters purely political to do the bidding, of those whom working men elsewhere regard as the enemies of their class. His obedience is no evidence of a servile spirit. There is not anywhere to be found a working man more aggressively independent, more radical, than the Belfast artisan. He follows leaders and submits to discipline because he is mastered by a fear which is stronger than his class consciousness. He is not, any more than any other working man, passionately enamoured of the imperial idea. He cannot be supposed to be ready to fight in order to save his masters, the merchants and manufacturers, from having to pay an excessive income tax. He dreads the dissolution of the Union because he believes that the Pope would govern a Home-ruled Ireland. The root of his Unionism is religion, not so much attachment to one faith as fear of the domination of another.

GEORGE A. BIRMINGHAM, *An Irishman Looks at His World*, 1919

I T MUST INDEED BE DIFFICULT for our younger generation to conceive of the passions aroused before August, 1914, by the Irish question. My own childhood and youth were perplexed at the thunder of these controversies, by which I was (and am) profoundly bored. Yet even in my infancy I was aware that the red hand of Ulster held my mother in its unyielding grip and that at the mention of Mr Gladstone her eyes (so shyly gentle in all their movements) would become as fierce and fixed as those of Joan of Arc confronting the Duke of Burgundy at Compiègne. This marked distaste for Mr Gladstone was shared, I afterwards discovered, by Tom Moore, the house carpenter at Clandeboye. I would spend hours in his shop, planing little pieces of wood, fashioning clumsy picture-frames and talking happily until the evening sun crept round to those dusted lattices and I would return to tea in the schoolroom leaving bloodstains among the shavings but taking much sawdust with me, much paint upon my knees, much glue in the tangle of my hair. Tom Moore would tell me how he had wished to kill Mr Gladstone and how, if need be, he would 'fight for the right'. I can see him now with his long sandy beard, his bleared blue eyes, and the check cap he never discarded, raising his adze aloft in imprecations against the Catholics, and the traitors of Westminster. In the yard outside stood the gasometer which my uncle had installed to provide him with the acetylene gas that popped and blinked along the passages of Clandeboye. Accompanying me one evening into the outer sunlight Tom Moore had struck this vast drum with his adze in illustration of the kind of assault that he had wished to make upon the Liberal leader. It echoed with a horrible reverberation like the gong of doom. And in truth, before twelve years had passed, there was my Hamilton uncle drilling rebels in the great courtyard of Killyleagh.

HAROLD NICOLSON, *Helen's Tower*, 1937

IN THE WHITE-PAPERED DRAWING-ROOM at home, under the glare of the chandelier, I felt like Odysseus returned from his wanderings. Nothing was changed except that my mother's memory was weaker, my father given to longer periods of abstracted silence when he sat with his thick mop of curly white hair in his hands. The bank, it seemed, was pressing him again; at the moment the family business was running an overdraft that involved alarming rows of noughts. He did not reproach me for my wanderings, merely looked at me out of benign blue eyes behind gold-rimmed spectacles very much as he would have looked at a frisky horse. What I had been doing mooning about in Donegal for over a year, I'm sure he hadn't the foggiest idea; probably he suspected it had something to do with what he would have called Home Rule. People who were entirely sound on the Irish question rarely stayed more than a chaste fortnight in that outlandish region, if they went at all.

DENIS IRELAND, *Statues Round the City Hall*, 1939

TO AN ULSTER BOY BROUGHT UP in a district where the two parties, Nationalist and Orange, were almost equal in numbers, and political feeling consequently strong, the name of a Home Ruler had necessarily a sinister sound. Home Rulers to my childish mind were a dark, subtle, and dangerous race, outwardly genial and friendly, but inwardly meditating fearful things. I knew that when the signal was given, and one never could tell the moment, they were ready to rise, murder my uncle, possess themselves of his farm, and drive out my aunt and myself to perish on the mountains. It was some miles from our farm to the mountains. I used to wonder dimly how we should be able to make our way thither at such a time. But in my aunt's stories it was on the mountains we always died, and I felt that we were bound to get there somehow.

Looking back, it seems strange to me that both my aunt and myself should have tacitly exempted from our ban those Roman Catholics – for in my youth Roman Catholic and Home Ruler were synonymous terms – with whom we came into close personal relations. To me Paddy Haggarty, our second ploughman, was simply Paddy Haggarty. I took it as a matter of course that he should go to Mass on Sunday mornings, and eat fish on a

Friday; and attributed no particular turpitude to him on account of these things. As for my aunt, I know that in matters demanding honesty and fidelity she would have trusted Tom Brogan, her thirty years' retainer, sooner than the Worshipful Master of an Orange Lodge.

Nevertheless, the unknown Home Ruler remained to me an object of fear and suspicion, hateful as an individual, but in association an incubus. The United Irish League was at that time the body through which Celtic Ireland sought political regeneration, and the League Rooms were as abominable to me as the Temple of Dagon to a devout Israelite of old. Even in the daytime its green shutters had a sinister look. I would not willingly have gone past the building after nightfall.

LYNN DOYLE, *An Ulster Childhood*, 1921

HOME RULE BILLS FAILED TO PASS into law in 1886 and 1893. When, in 1910, it became probable that the Liberal government of Mr Asquith could and ultimately would succeed in passing such a measure, the feelings of all parties had been worked up by a whole generation of bitter controversy. There followed several years of acute tension, particularly in the period from the spring of 1912 to the spring of 1914. By the summer of 1914, the vigorous display in Ulster of a strong communal feeling, hostile to the proposed scheme for Irish self-government so far as it concerned Ulster, had resulted in the principle being virtually established that some form of special and separate treatment for Ulster should be embodied in the government's plan for Ireland. The principal leaders of the Ulster movement were Sir Edward Carson and Captain James Craig.

HUGH SHEARMAN, *Northern Ireland*, 1948

THE WORD 'RESIST! RESIST!' was on the lips not merely of Orange-men, but of Liberals, of those who by their profession were men of peace, merchants, manufacturers, bankers, medical men, and even clergymen ... That preparations for resistance were being made in some of the Ulster counties, most certainly in one, though I did not know it at the time, I have since been very circumstantially informed by persons whose good faith I have never had any reason for doubting, and who themselves took no part in the proceedings. Those preparations were not made by the humbler classes of Ulster Protestants, by the poorer Orangemen, who might be thought to run little risk except that of losing their lives. They were made by country gentlemen, by magistrates, by deputy-lieutenants, and by members of the aristocracy. Mr Haslett, afterwards Sir James, and then member for the West Division of Belfast, said to a correspondent of the *Birmingham Gazette*, 'There can be no doubt that the Loyalists are arming.' ...

Advertisements for the supply of twenty thousand Snider rifles and for the services of competent drill instructors appeared in the Ulster papers. These, however, were not then regarded as serious. When Mr Morley's attention to them was called by that anxious guardian of law and order, Mr W. O'Brien, the Irish Chief Secretary said truly enough that people who wished to arm the Ulster Protestants would scarcely advertise for twenty thousand Snider rifles. In Belfast, though there as elsewhere in Ulster resistance was undoubtedly contemplated, there were no manufacturers of arms. It was not only among the Orangemen of the country, but also among those who had always been Liberals, that according to subsequent information there was at the time the greatest danger.

The Irish Nationalist members, while the debate on the Home Rule Bill dragged its slow length along, were only too ready to maintain that Ulster was in a state little short of rebellion. On the second reading of the Arms Act Continuance Bill, Mr Morley allowed it to be understood that it was especially directed against armed assemblies of Orangemen. Mr Parnell declared that there had been tumultuous and riotous gatherings of Orangemen wishing to murder the Irish Catholics.

THOMAS MACKNIGHT, *Ulster As It Is*, 1896

THE NIGHT WAS SO STILL that I could hear distinctly the rattle of oars in rowlocks. Boats were plying between the *Finola* and the shore.

'Can they be landing anything from the yacht?' said Marion.

'I don't think so,' I said. 'Yachts do not carry cargoes, and if they did they wouldn't land them in the middle of the night.'

I looked at my watch. It was almost twelve o'clock. Then another noise was added to the rattling of oars. A cart, unmistakably a cart, lumbered across the stones at the end of the pier. After a while this cart emerged from the black shadows of the houses and we could see it toiling up the hill which leads out of the town. A very slight southerly breeze was setting across the bay from the town to us. We could hear the driver shouting encouragement to his horse as he breasted the hill. The cart was evidently heavily loaded.

'The boats haven't been out,' said Marion. 'There cannot have been a catch of mackerel.'

When there is a catch of mackerel the fish are packed in boxes on the pier, and carts, laden like the one we watched, climb the hill. There is a regularly organised service of those carts under the control of Crossan.

'It can't be fish,' I said, 'unless the *Finola* has been making a catch and has come in here to land them.'

Another cart bumped its way off the pier, and in a minute or two we saw it climbing the hill. Then the lights on the *Finola's* deck went out one by one. The boats ceased plying between the yacht and the shore.

'I don't see why they should land fish in the middle of the night,' said Marion.

The activity of the people on the pier increased. More lights appeared there and moved very rapidly to and fro.

'Unless they're landing what they're ashamed of,' said Marion, 'I don't see why they're doing it at night.' ...

I stood at the window and watched until the last cart had mounted the hill. The lights on the pier went out. A solitary boat rowed back to the *Finola*. The town and the bay were still again.

GEORGE A. BIRMINGHAM, *The Red Hand of Ulster*, 1912

SINCE THE EARLY AFTERNOON cars had been converging on Larne without the drivers being aware of the reason, or that other drivers were involved. A huge concentration of cars and other transport had secretly assembled during the day at Castle Upton, Lord Templetown's estate at Templepatrick, including a large contingent of the County Tyrone Motor Car Corps under Captain A. St Q. Ricardo, the Adjutant of the Tyrone Regiment. Towards evening this weirdly assorted convoy issued on to the roads leading north. In those days when the motor car still had a certain novelty, the sudden increase in traffic alarmed the country folk, and at Ballyclare many sought their neighbours' houses 'believing that war had broken out'.

About thirty cars from the North Antrim Regiment were under orders to reach Larne at 1 a.m. Another large squadron of cars and lorries had been organised from Ballymena and its surrounding district. But, as Adair had written a few days earlier to Captain O'Neill, 'We are lamentable (*sic*) short in County Antrim and have not half the transport we want.' For this reason the Belfast Motor Car Corps undertook to distribute the rifles to pre-arranged dumps and hiding places in County Antrim, and almost every available car in Belfast was pressed into service.

Few of the drivers suspected that they were involved in an operation on so massive a scale. One young volunteer, for example, was instructed to drive his father's 12 h.p. Rover with certain passengers to Larne that evening and to await orders there. He was allowed to know that 'something' was coming in by boat and guessed what it might be. In Larne, however, the town was quiet and when he looked across the empty harbour, he was sure that the operation would be a failure. Then, just as darkness fell, he 'saw a snake of bright lights appear on the hills – a great cavalcade of motor cars with brilliant headlights'. As it came nearer all the electric lights in the harbour flashed on, teams of men emerged from the shadows, and Larne suddenly came awake.

'The heel of an April evening was merging into night', wrote a more insouciant young man, 'when I met a friend who knew a friend who had a fast motor – a fast Ford of twenty horse power – and he casually, as he stepped aboard, suggested that I should come along. I did so with a light heart and not too heavy overcoat.' As they sped northwards along the Shore Road and on through Carrickfergus he saw UVF signallers on every eminence, men in semi-military uniform at every crossroads, while dispatch riders passed and re-passed in the loom of their acetylene headlamps.

At the village of Glynn they were halted by a line of men across the road, and again on the outskirts of Larne. Then, to their astonishment, as they turned to the right for the Curran Road and across the railway track, they found themselves obliged to get into a line of cars waiting, with engines throbbing, to move towards the harbour.

A.T.Q. STEWART, The Ulster Crisis, 1967

NONO WAS PLEASED THAT DADDY was at home these days. There was so much that needed explaining, expanding, and analysing. More than ever she was glad that he never just gave answers, but helped her puzzle her way out; and showed his disappointment if she ever accepted a statement without a torrent of 'whys' and 'buts' and 'ifs'.

One Sunday morning in April she came back from Mass bubbling with excitement.

'Daddy,' she cried, bursting into the sitting-room, 'everybody is talking about gun-running. The Ulster Volunteers ran in guns at Bangor and Larne last night.'

'What!' exclaimed daddy, and she saw he shared her excitement.

'Thousands upon thousands of rifles,' she said, 'and millions of ammunition. They say the coastguards never interfered; that motors and dispatches were rushing through Ulster all last night and the police and military never tried to stop them.'

Daddy was striding about the room.

'Is it true, do you think?' he asked.

'Oh, it must be. Everybody says that it is only because it is Sunday there isn't any "extras" out. We've no Sunday papers, you know. Daddy, how will it affect us?'

'Aha! You arrived at that very quickly.'

'It's bound to have an effect, isn't it? The National Volunteers are spreading all through the country. They are pledged to "train and equip". Now that the Ulster Volunteers have got arms they'll have to get busy to carry out that part of their programme. Can they do it? Where will they get the money? How will they do it? And will the police and military be as blind when the National Volunteers are running in guns as they were when the Ulster Volunteers did? And if they're not, what will it mean?'

NORA CONNOLLY O'BRIEN, *Portrait of a Rebel Father*, 1935

COMING OUT FROM AN AMATEUR theatrical performance in Larne, my mother finds the main street lined with members of the volunteer force. She recognises and questions a pedlar who has often called at the rectory. Heavy with pride in his duties, he says slowly: 'Go you home to bed, and ask no questions.' She continues to ask him and he concedes: 'All you need to know is that the Ulster Volunteers are doing their duty. We're out all over the country tonight.'

On her way home she passes a stream of cars and lorries, with full headlights, that are racing in the direction of the harbour.

And all through the night, on the road beside the rectory, we can hear the cars and we can see the trees constantly illumined by their headlamps.

In the morning it is understood that an extraordinary event has occurred. A ship from Germany landed a cargo of arms at Larne Harbour. The police barracks were surrounded and the telephone wires cut. Already the arms have been distributed to points through the province, some being concealed under chancel floors in Protestant churches.

From this night the rebellion passes beyond the stage of play-acting.

GEORGE BUCHANAN, *Green Seacoast*, 1959

SETTLERS

They cross from Glasgow to a black city
   Of gantries, mills and steeples. They begin to belong.
He manages the Iceworks, is an elder of the Kirk;
   She becomes, briefly, a cook in Carson's Army.
Some mornings, walking through the company gate,
   He touches the bonnet of a brown lorry.
It is warm. The men watch and say nothing.
   'Queer, how it runs off in the night,'
He says to McCullough, then climbs to his office.
   He stores a warm knowledge on his palm.
     Nightlandings on the Antrim coast, the movement of guns
Now snug in their oiled paper below the floors
   Of sundry kirks and tabernacles in that county.

TOM PAULIN, *A State of Justice*, 1977

A SHIP SAILS INTO LARNE HARBOUR one fine Friday evening, and immediately the Ulster Volunteers take possession of that town and seaport, the Royal Irish Constabulary are imprisoned in their barracks, the roads are held up by armed guards, the railway stations of Park Road, Belfast, of Larne, Bangor and Donaghadee are seized by the Ulster Volunteers and thousands of stands of rifles are landed together with a million rounds of ammunition. Along with the landing at Larne vessels are used to tranship arms and ammunition from the original gun-running steamer and land the cargo so transhipped at Bangor and Donaghadee. Some hundreds of motor cars were used to convey the arms and ammunition to safe places, that night, and the same motor cars worked all day on Saturday conveying them from temporary resting places to more secure and handy depots throughout Ulster.

JAMES CONNOLLY, *Forward*, 1914

A TRAMP STEAMER, the *Mountjoy*, steamed into Larne harbour with a cargo of 340 tonnes of rifles and ammunition. The police barracks and coastguard station were surrounded by UVF men. Not a man was allowed to pass through the cordon. Hundreds of volunteers were unloading the shipment of arms. Heavy and light motors were loaded up and disappeared into the darkness. A couple of steamers drew alongside the *Mountjoy*, transhipped part of the cargo, and glided away towards Bangor and Donaghadee. The police and custom men in these ports were also sealed off.

Six hundred motor vehicles were speeding in every direction along the roads of counties Down and Antrim, loaded with arms and ammunition. Arriving at their destination, a crowd of silent, grim-faced men would suddenly appear out of the darkness, unload the material, and fade as silently into the darkness again. The lorry would swing round and speed off on another errand.

The following day was Saturday. By the time the operation had concluded, those of us who were manual workers found it impossible to check in on our jobs. I was a plater's helper in the shipyard, so forfeited a day's pay. So did the majority of my comrades. On dismissal, I proceeded home to catch a few hours sleep ...

The news of the gun-running spread like wildfire through Ulster. Every town and village was celebrating the event. What the government intended to do about the affair didn't worry us much. The dummy rifles were pitched into the furnaces. In every hall, hut and arms dump, we were slapping the magazines of the rifles with affection. A new spirit was abroad. We felt pretty sure of ourselves now.

Sentries were posted at every arms dump in the province. In case of sudden raids on the arsenals, we had dispatch riders ready to spread the alarm that would bring thousands of volunteers to the spot in less than an hour. We were elated and ready for any emergency. Our women were neither alarmed nor enthusiastic. I don't believe they were terribly worried on our account either. The girls in the warerooms enjoyed the excitement and added extra pastry to their morning cup of tea just to celebrate.

Some five hundred thousand Ulster men and women had signed a Solemn League and Covenant on the 12th September 1912, declaring they would stand together in defence of Ulster against Home Rule. Previous to that date, we were against Home Rule for any part of Ireland. How or why our leaders had changed their attitude to a stand for Ulster alone, we neither questioned nor understood. Possibly, it was a safer and more logical defence.

Now we had sufficient guns and equipment to make a fight, there was no turning back. The men were too determined to carry the issue through for our leaders to even think of a future retrenchment. The organisation was nigh perfect in training and morale was high. In fact, many of us were eager to prove our ability to face the British government forces, or the Irish National Volunteers who were now recruiting in the south ...

Then came the rumours of war. Europe was tense with expectancy. The British people's minds went off the Ulster question and concentrated on, to them, more important matters. We, on the other hand, were still self-interested on our own affairs. Then the Germans invaded Belgium and set Europe aflame. Local issues became unimportant in the welter of world politics.

Although the Home Rule crisis passed off without the clash between the Crown Forces and the UVF as expected, you may take my word for it, if such a catastrophe had occurred, the rank and file of the movement would have fought it out. They were ready and willing to shed blood for the cause, their own or that of anyone else, so long as Ulster remained in the United Kingdom.

There was nothing comic regarding their determination to resist. They would have martyred themselves wilfully and recklessly. One shot fired would certainly have set Ulster ablaze. They allowed Carson to lead them, but he could not have held them back. Even to this day, I look upon the outbreak of the 1914 struggle as a coincidence which saved the country from a bloody civil war.

THOMAS CARNDUFF (1954), Life and Writings, 1994

HOWEVER ANXIOUS WE ARE for the insurrection to be reduced, we can't fail to perceive excitement in that handful being shelled in Dublin Post Office, of whom Pearse speaks in a manifesto:

If they do not win this fight, they will at least have deserved to win it. But win it they will, although they win it in death. Already they have won a great thing. They have redeemed Dublin from many shames, and made her name splendid among the names of cities.

This is Easter 1916.

The rebels are defeated; and several leaders, including Sir Roger Casement, put to death.

This is a year of death, indeed, for the Irish. In July those men whom we saw marching through Belfast are obliterated in France. At the command of English generals, the Ulster Division hurls itself to be mown down, across impossible terrain at Thiépval.

So end, for the most part, those kindly, obstinate, easily deceived neighbours of ours. The houses are full of mourning; and thousands of women walk in black dresses.

GEORGE BUCHANAN, *Green Seacoast*, 1959

PYPER:

God in heaven, if you hear the words of man, I speak to you this day. I do it now to ask we be spared. I do it to ask for strength. Strength for these men around me, strength for myself. If you are a just and merciful God, show your mercy this day. Save us. Save our country. Destroy our enemies at home and on this field of battle. Let this day at the Somme be as glorious in the memory of Ulster as that day at the Boyne, when you scattered our enemies. Lead us back from this exile. To Derry, to the Foyle. To Belfast and the Lagan. To Armagh. To Tyrone. To the Bann and its banks. To Erne and its islands. Protect them. Protect us. Protect me. Let us fight bravely. Let us win gloriously. Lord, look down on us. Spare us. I love –. Observe the sons of Ulster marching towards the Somme. I love their lives. I love my own life. I love my home. I love my Ulster. Ulster. Ulster. Ulster. Ulster. Ulster. Ulster. Ulster. Ulster. *(As the chant of 'Ulster' commences rifles and bayonets are raised. The chant turns into a battle cry, reaching frenzy ...)*

FRANK McGUINNESS, *Observe the Sons of Ulster Marching Towards the Somme*, 1986

IN HIS AUTOBIOGRAPHY, *Father and Son*, Mr Edmund Gosse describes the shuddering horror with which his parents taught him to regard the Papacy ... [so that when] in after life he met 'gallant "Down–with–the–Pope" men from County Antrim', in contrast with his own youthful fervour, [he] found 'their denunciations err on the side of the anodyne'. I suspect he met them elsewhere than on their native heath. A Sunday afternoon at the Belfast Custom House steps, with Protestant oratory in full blast, or the sort of speeches that invariably conclude an Orange meeting would cause him to revise his views. I remember an Orange sheet in Belfast in which an enterprising shoemaker advertised his wares in one glorious sentence: 'Wear Kelly's boots to trample the Papists'. I remember, also, a lecture on Rome by a clergyman who described a visit to St Peter's with much the same air as Daniel might have recounted his experiences in the den of lions. 'As I crossed the threshold,' he said impressively, 'my good Presbyterian boots creaked in protest.' These people lack the consolation which Mr Gosse enjoyed, of thinking that because the Church of Rome is old it is soon to die. Rather, in their eyes, it goes marching on from victory to victory, and they can never remember the time when the trumpet was not sounding 'To your tents, O Ulster!'

JAMES WINDER GOOD, *Ulster and Ireland*, 1919

ALTHOUGH THE STATE OF NORTHERN IRELAND, with the old fears of encirclement inbuilt, has more often than not presented the more conservative side of the Protestant ethos, the libertarian tradition is still active in the anti-authoritarian tendency which cases Protestants to band together in assertion of their own brand of direct democracy against feared 'sell-outs' by politicians who take no account of their special status within the governing process. To dig one's heels in and rest one's case on antiquity may appear reactionary; in Presbyterian terms it is a continuation of that radical tradition of resisting an authority which has betrayed its trust. Protestant thinking is a complicated phenomenon, combining so many contradictions as to defy any straightforward application of modern standards. But it is not as irrational as commonly supposed; and its strange seventeenth-century antiquarianism disguises genuine and deeply laid points of principle. An understanding of its roots shows the problems posed by it to be less intractable than imagined. The libertarian tradition behind much of Irish Protestant thinking can, and has, produced dramatic intercommunal alliances and radical solutions in the past and a better understanding of those attitudes might help the quite appreciable merits of that libertarian tradition to rise again in an atmosphere which accepts that the Protestants also need to be conciliated.

MARIANNE ELLIOTT, *Watchmen in Sion*, 1985

THE DILEMMA

Born in this island, maimed by history
and creed-infected, by my father taught
the stubborn habit of unfettered thought,
I dreamed, like him, all people should be free.
So, while my logic steered me well outside
that ailing church which claims dominion
over the questing spirit, I denied
all credence to the state by rebels won
from a torn nation, rigged to guard their gain,
though they assert their love of liberty,
which craft has narrowed to a fear of Rome.
So, since this ruptured country is my home,
it long has been my bitter luck to be
caught in the crossfire of their false campaign.

JOHN HEWITT, *An Ulster Reckoning*, 1971

The Rebel
Tradition

The town ... was much perturbed in the last half of the eighteenth century. It started both the Volunteering movement and the United Irish Society. Angry generals spoke of Belfast as a 'sink of rebellion'. The town, before and during the 1798 outbreak, was strongly held by armed force. Battles took place to the north and south of it, and six rebel leaders were executed in its streets, the most notable being Henry Joy McCracken, who had led the insurgents in the battle of Antrim.

D.A. CHART, *A History of Northern Ireland*

THE TROUBLES ARE ALMOST AS OLD as Irish history itself. They wax and wane with different historical epochs but they have never ceased in eight hundred years. In Tudor times the Catholic Gaelic *tadagh* (natives) resisted the Anglo-Norman conqueror. In the seventeenth century the Protestant Planters fought the dispossessed Catholic kernes (rebels). In the eighteenth century the Protestant Peep O'Day Boys attacked at dawn, murdering the enemy in their beds, whilst the Catholic Defenders came upon the enemy on the road and smashed their heads into the dust. It was colonialist Protestant Planter against Catholic Irish native. It was Prod against Papist. It was Protestant Royal Ulster Constabulary policeman against Catholic Irish Republican Army guerrilla. It was the British Crown versus the Irish. It was a creeping war of submerged hatreds that ran back into history and was explosively fuelled by contemporary political events. The objective was always the same – to remove the British Crown presence from Irish soil.

The key protagonists of the Troubles were the rebels, for without their unflagging commitment to fight on against overwhelming odds the conflict would have withered.

KEVIN TOOLIS, Rebel Hearts, 1995

CAHAL MacGEE WAS A HIGHWAYMAN, tory, or Rapparee. Many of these were the descendants of men, if not the actual men themselves, who owned extensive possessions of lands of which they were robbed through the operations of the penal laws, and the confiscations. Becoming desperate they took to the hills – 'went out on their keeping', as English legal phraseology has it, and began

> To spoil the spoiler,
> And from the robber rend his prey.

Cahal denies the charge of being a robber, and boldly affirms that in taking his wants from 'the bodachs of the English speech', he is doing nothing morally wrong. He claims relationship with the O'Neills and Maguires, the O'Reillys, O'Rourkes, MacMahons, and Burkes, but it may not be blood relationship that is meant, but relationship of misfortune …

A chuisle. In the opening verses Cahal addresses himself in a kind of soliloquy, and gives a detached description of himself in the third person. In verse III, he begins to speak in the first person.

A chos dheas i mbróig, O person of the right foot in the boot. An outlaw when surprised from sleep would not have time to dress, and would needs fly with his right boot on, and his other boot in his hand.

ÉNRÍ Ó MUIRGHEASA, Art Mac Cubhthaigh's and Other Songs, 1926

THROUGHOUT THE MIDDLE AGES the Mournes were a borderland between the thin coastal strip held by the Anglo-Normans and the Irish-held interior. Placenames are eloquent of their struggles: Greencastle and Dundrum Castle, Newcastle and Castlewellan. In church organisation, too, it became an exempt jurisdiction, an ecclesiastical no-man's-land. As befitted a borderland, the Mournes gave refuge to lawless elements and adventurers, among whom is numbered the famous Irish Tory, Redmond O'Hanlon – the Irish Robin Hood – who was killed near Hilltown in 1681. At the end of the eighteenth century and at intervals down to quite recent times, when land troubles or sectarian strife broke out in neighbouring areas, Roman Catholic refugees found a welcome here and carved out little farms among the hills. These refugees, clinging to their kin and their memories — all that was left to them — reinforced the natural tendency of the hill folk to cherish the past and resist change. The Gaelic language could still be heard in Hilltown in the late nineteenth century, and the last native speakers, as distinct from those who have learnt Gaelic in the schools, have only recently died out. For centuries the hill-margins kept their inner life, locked away in the secret of the native tongue and little affected by feudal order. The Mournes are a rich gathering ground for folklore and folk culture, and the kingdom is the only part of Northern Ireland where the wooden plough and the long-handled spade are commonly used. This richness in folk ways reflects material poverty, yet many things survive among the hills because they are best suited to the environment. I have taken a car up rocky lanes and have been glad to retreat and transfer my load to a sturdy cart and even, on occasion, to a slipe.

E. ESTYN EVANS, *Mourne Country*, 1951

THE BALLAD OF DOUGLAS BRIDGE

On Douglas Bridge I met a man
Who lived adjacent to Strabane,
Before the English hung him high
For riding with O'Hanlon.

The eyes of him were just as fresh
As when they burned within the flesh;
And his boot legs were wide apart
From riding with O'Hanlon.

'God save you, Sir,' I said with fear,
'You seem to be a stranger here.'
'Not I,' said he, 'nor any man
Who rides with Count O'Hanlon.'

'I know each glen from North Tyrone
To Monaghan, and I've been known
By every clan and parish, since
I rode with Count O'Hanlon.

'Before that time,' said he to me,
'My fathers owned the land you see;
But they are now among the moors
A-riding with O'Hanlon.

'Before that time,' said he with pride,
My fathers rode where now they ride
As Rapparees before the time
Of trouble and O'Hanlon.

'Goodnight to you, and God be with
The tellers of the tale and myth,
For they are of the spirit stuff
That rides with Count O'Hanlon.'

'Goodnight to you,' said I, 'and God
Be with the chargers, fairy-shod,
That bear the Ulster heroes forth
To ride with Count O'Hanlon.'

On Douglas Bridge we parted, but
The Gap o' Dreams is never shut
To one whose saddled soul tonight
Rides out with Count O'Hanlon.

FRANCIS CARLIN, *My Ireland*, 1918

THE RELIGIOUS AND OCCUPATIONAL geography of late eighteenth-century Armagh was quite distinctive. A flat northern part was the centre of the most lucrative end of the linen industry. Here the dominant group was Anglican, with only a sprinkling of Catholics. In the middle, south of Armagh city, and where the gentle rise of the land created that pleasant vista so admired by many travel writers, Protestants were still in the majority, but here Presbyterians and Catholics were more numerous – even though the combined total put Protestants marginally in the ascendancy. Moving towards the south of the county, the landscape changed dramatically, with a band of mountains, stretching south-west from Keady's 600 feet (200 metres) to Slieve Gullion's imposing 1,894 feet (630 metres). This was in every respect a cultural barrier, with Catholics increasing dramatically, until, as the mountains dropped, the parishes of Creggan, Forkhill and Jonesborough, at the other side of the barrier, were almost exclusively Catholic and largely Irish-speaking ...

The troubles, which by 1785 had produced the Catholic Defenders and Protestant Peep O'Day Boys, had built on localised faction fights and party parades over the past two decades. Parading to Anglican or Presbyterian church services, in full military regalia, had been a particular feature of Volunteering, as had its public celebration of William of Orange. The map of the spread of the troubles reveals incidents radiating out from areas of mixed settlement ... Outsiders were then attracted to the scene. By all accounts lower-class Protestants were the original aggressors. But very soon the Catholics returned like for like. Boycotts of traders of the opposing religion (by both Defenders and Peep O' Day Boys) extended the circle of malcontents. Parades and social events became factionalised. Fights at fairs increased. New regiments of Volunteers were raised on a purely Protestant basis. Neighbours began to withdraw goodwill from those of the opposite religion. Converts and those in mixed marriages became particular targets of Protestant rancour, and swaggering youths were to the fore in deliberately provocative actions. On Sunday 21 November 1788, one of the new, more lower-class Volunteer companies from Benburb marched to church at Armagh along the Eglish road. They planned to return by another road. However, their anti-papist comments and provocative drum-beating drew insults from Catholic countrywomen along the outward route. To avenge the insults of the morning, the Volunteers stocked up on arms and additional drums in Armagh and returned by the same route, 'playing tunes ['The Protestant Boys' and 'The Boyne Water'] which were an insult to Catholics'. Moderate negotiators failed to calm the young hotheads. At Drumbee stones were thrown, the Volunteers fired and two Catholics, one a Defender, were killed. Their funerals then became occasions for major shows of Defender strength and the following Sunday the Volunteers (reinforced by ex-soldiers from the American war) marched along the same road and cheered at the spot where the Catholics were killed. And so the situation rippled out of control, gathering pace as it spread farther afield.

MARIANNE ELLIOTT, *The Catholics of Ulster*, 2000

PEACEFUL, INDUSTRIOUS AND LAW-ABIDING as the dwellers in North Street invariably were, yet in the times of the Volunteers and the United Irishmen excitement often ran high in the neighbourhood. In October, 1796, a cotton spinner named McBride, said to have been a spy in the pay of the government, was shot dead in North Street at an early hour in the evening; and between twenty and thirty persons were arrested in the house of an inn-keeper named Alexander, at Peter's Hill, on the charge of being assembled for treasonable purposes. Dr Crawford of Lisburn, an eminent physician, and the Rev. Sinclair Kelburn, minister of the third Presbyterian congregation in Rosemary Street, were arrested at the same time and on the same charge. These arrests were made upon the information of a notorious informer named Newell – he lived in Mill Street – who afterwards left it on record that his representations were for the most part false.

CATHAL O'BYRNE, *As I Roved Out*, 1946

THE FIRST EDITION OF THE *Northern Star* appeared on 1 January 1792. Well printed and produced, it was an instant success, thanks largely to an excellent system of distribution. It had agents in every part of Ulster, and also in Dublin, London, Liverpool and Edinburgh. At a time when the columns of the *Belfast News Letter* and most contemporary newspapers were filled up with dispatches from Great Britain and abroad, the *Northern Star* was able to provide a larger content of local news and political comment, making it as critical and close to the bone as it dared. Political satire came to be its stock in trade, attracting the talents of able polemicists like the rising lawyer William Sampson who was Episcopalian, and a clutch of Presbyterian ministers, notably the Rev. James Porter of Greyabbey, the Rev. Sinclair Kelburn of Third Congregation, Belfast, and the Rev. William Steel Dickson, then minister of Ballyhalbert in the Ards Peninsula.

The moving spirit in the enterprise was Samuel Neilson. Born at Ballyroney near Rathfriland in County Down in 1761, he was the third son of the Presbyterian minister there. He became a very prosperous wholesale woollen merchant in Belfast and an active man in local politics. An ardent Volunteer and patriot, he took a leading part in the last of the Volunteer reform conventions, which was largely inspired by the United Irishmen, at Dungannon, County Tyrone, in 1793. He was the editor, and eventually the sole proprietor, of the *Northern Star*, which swallowed up his fortune.

A.T.Q. STEWART, *The Summer Soldiers*, 1995

THE LONDONDERRY AIR

Snow falls eternally within my souvenir
Of him, who wore the suit of Lincoln corduroy.
He was my noble pikeman, and my pioneer;
Snow falls eternally upon my Danny Boy.

I used to see him at the rising of the moon
With other fellows, exercising in the field,
For they'd refused to take the Saxon gold doubloon –
Indomitable hearts of steel, who'd never yield!

One Sunday, coming home from Mass, from him I stole
A kiss; he left on Monday for to join the war;
I never saw him more, yet he resides within my soul

Like some strange seedling of the plant of Liberty,
That breeds eternally beneath the Northern Star,
Returning as the blossom on the whitethorn tree.

CIARAN CARSON, *The Twelfth of Never*, 1998

THE NEW LORD [I.E. CASTLEREAGH] made an extensive tour of Ulster on horseback, and his worst fears were confirmed. He found the loyal generally depressed and in many cases wavering in their allegiance. Crown witnesses were being frequently murdered, trade was almost at a standstill, and the banks were only discounting short bills. Lord Hertford's tenants in Antrim were deeply involved in the treason, and it was gradually spreading to his father's estates in Down. 'I can have no doubt that there does exist a very serious affiliated conspiracy in the northern counties,' he reported ... 'Belfast is its centre, it is very general towards Lisburn, the county of Antrim has been largely infected and the county of Down is by no means exempt. There is sufficient information to ascertain that the societies gain ground rapidly, and that they have formed very sanguine and extensive hopes in consequence of the fatal turn affairs have taken on the Continent.' In Lisburn he obtained 'the depositions of one man whose information appears sufficient to convict six persons, two of whom are leaders.' The leaders were Samuel Neilson and Thomas Russell, principal proprietor of and contributor to the United Irish newspaper the *Northern Star*. Castlereagh now hastened to acquaint the authorities in Dublin of his discovery.

H. MONTGOMERY HYDE, *The Rise of Castlereagh*, 1933

MY OWN ANCESTORS, ON BOTH SIDES, so far as can be traced, that is for many generations, have been of the Ulster farming Presbyterian stock. Originally, of course, they came from Scotland – one branch, Father's, settling on the Killinchy side of Strangford Lough, in County Down, the other, Mother's, on the Greyabbey side.

I suppose it would not be far wrong to say that people, even the most individualistic, are made in part by their environment and experiences. It is worth noting that this John Patterson, my great-grandfather, was born in Greyabbey about the year 1773. Greyabbey had been for long a liberal stronghold. There was an old ballad to the effect that:

In Greyabbey town there lived men of renown,
Who ne'er were afraid to wear green.

The ballad is often only a reflection of the times, and the times were full of evil portent.

When my ancestor was about fourteen, namely, in 1789, there was set apart to the ministry of his church, in Greyabbey, the Rev. James Porter, a man of distinguished gifts, one greatly beloved by all, especially the young. It was a time of great unrest; landlord tyranny had driven the people almost to distraction. In most Presbyterian hearts surged the desire for reform, and among these agitators for justice was the Rev. James Porter. He paid dearly for his temerity. He was hanged on 2nd July, 1798, ostensibly for his supposed partnership with the United Irishmen; really, it was thought, for the fact that he was the author of a number of letters in which he satirically poked fun at the Marquis of Londonderry, Castlereagh's father, under the title of Lord Mountmumble.

THOMAS M. JOHNSTONE, *The Vintage of Memory*, 1942

BESIDE THE ABBEY [i.e. Greyabbey] there is a graveyard where the headstones stand as thick as men at a fair. Somewhere here lie the remains of the Rev. James Porter, Presbyterian pastor and Irish rebel. His chief contribution to the 1798 insurrection was the writing of sarcastic letters to the *Northern Star* under the pen-name of Billy Bluff. Poor Billy made the mistake of being particularly saucy about the local great man, Lord Londonderry. When the day of reckoning came, the insurrection having been good and properly squelched throughout the whole of Ireland, the minister was tried on what appears to have been largely a trumped-up charge of intercepting the mail. He was condemned to death. His wife, mother of seven children, hastened to Mountstewart, Londonderry's residence, and pleaded with the ladies of the family. They were kind and full of sympathy. One of them withdrew to confer with his lordship; the answer came back that the law must take its course, but Mrs Porter was allowed to see her husband in prison. While they were together, the order for his execution arrived, with a concession attached: his body might be returned to his family after the sentence had been carried out. 'Then, my dear,' said Porter, 'I shall lie at home tonight.' As he spoke, a wry, brave smile must have flitted across his lips. Poor satirical Bill Bluff was hanged in Greyabbey in full view of his home and his meeting-house. His wife was at the place of execution.

STEHPHEN RYNNE, *All Ireland*, 1956

THE WOMEN AT THEIR DOORS

The babes were asleep in their cradles,
And the day's drudge was done,
And the women brought their suppers out
To eat them in the sun.

'Tonight I will set my needles, Áine,
And Eoghan will have stockings to wear:
I spun the wool of the horny ewe
He bought at the Hiring Fair ...

'But what is the sound I hear, Nabla? –
It is like the cheering of men.
God keep our kind from the Devil's snare!'
And the women answered, 'Amen!'

Then the moon rose over the valley,
And the cheering died away,
And the women went within their doors
At the heel of the summer day.

And no men came in at midnight,
And no men came in at the dawn,
And the women keened by their ashy fires
Till their faces were haggard and wan.

For they knew they had gone to the trysting,
With pike and musketoon,
To fight for their hearths and altars
At the rising of the moon!

JOSEPH CAMPBELL, *The Rushlight*, 1906

THE BELFAST RADICALS WERE ALL PRESBYTERIAN. Two at least were sons of the manse, and so was their ideologue, Dr William Drennan, who was the son of a former minister of the First Belfast congregation. The elder Drennan had been a close friend of the philosopher Francis Hutcheson. Dr Drennan had practised medicine in Dublin since 1790, but his sister Martha was married to Samuel McTier, a veteran Belfast radical who was one of the society's founders, and who died in 1795. The Drennans were outstanding examples of that independent Nonconformist spirit in politics which characterised much of the thought behind the revolt of the American colonies, and which initially greeted the French Revolution as yet another giant step for mankind.

A.T.Q. STEWART, *The Summer Soldiers*, 1995

T HEY DESCENDED THE GRASSY SIDES of the old fort [i.e. Donegore], walked down the steep lane from Moylin's house, and joined the road again. Turning to the right, they went under the shade of fine trees which reached their branches over the road from the demesne in which they grew.

'The big house in there,' said Hope, 'belongs to one of the landlord families of this county. It has been theirs for generations. On the lawn in front of that house a company of Volunteers used to meet for drill. The owner of the house, the lord of the soil, was their captain. In those days we had all Ireland united – the landlords, the merchants, and the farming people. Now it is not so. Our landlords won then what they wanted – freedom and power. They have ruled Ireland since 1782. The merchants and manufacturers also won what they chiefly wanted – the opportunity of fair and free trade. They have grown rich, and are every year growing richer. They bid fair to make Ireland a great commercial nation – what she ought to be, the link between the Old World and the New. But both the landlords and the traders have been selfish. Having gained the object of their desires, they are unwilling to share either power or riches with the people. They have refused to consider reasonable measures of reform. They have goaded and harried us until –'

He ceased speaking and sighed.

'But,' he went on, 'they will not be able to keep either their power or their riches. In refusing to trust the people they are ensuring their own doom. They forget that there is a power greater than theirs – that England is continually on the watch to win back again her sovereignty over Ireland. Our upper-class and our middle-class are too jealous of their privileges to share them with us. They will give England the opportunity she wants. Then Ireland will be brought into the old subjection, and her advance towards prosperity will be checked again as it was checked before. She will become a country of haughty squireens – the most contemptible class of all, men of blackened honour and broken faith, men proud, but with nothing to be proud of – and of ruined traders; a land of ill-cultivated fields and ruined mills; a nation crushed by her conqueror.'

Neal listened attentively. It was curious that the fear to which James Hope gave expression was the very same which he had heard from Lord Dunseveric. Each dreaded England. Each saw that out of the turmoil of contemporary politics would come the restoration of the English power over Ireland. But Lord Dunseveric blamed the schemes of the United Irishmen. James Hope blamed the selfishness of the middle-classes.

GEORGE A. BIRMINGHAM, *The Northern Iron*, 1907

PRESBYTERIAN STUDY

A lantern-ceiling and quiet.
I climb here often and stare
At the scoured desk by the window,
The journal open
At a date and conscience.

It is a room without song
That believes in flint, salt,
And new bread rising
Like a people who share
A dream of grace and reason.

A bit starchy perhaps.
A shade chill, like a draper's shop.
But choosing the free way,
Not the formal,
And warming the walls with its knowing.

Memory is a moist seed
And a praise here, for they live,
Those linen saints, lithe radicals,
In the bottled light
Of this limewashed shrine.

Hardly a schoolroom remembers
Their obstinate rebellion;
Provincial historians
Scratch circles on the sand,
And still, with dingy smiles,

We wait on nature,
Our jackets a dungy pattern
Of mud and snapped leaves,
Our state a jacked corpse
Committed to the deep.

TOM PAULIN, *Liberty Tree*, 1983

SOMETIMES IN THE NORTH OF IRELAND, between the chill of spring and the oppressive days of midsummer, there comes a spell of remarkably fine weather, lasting perhaps a week or ten days. At dawn there is a white mist in the hollows, the air is warm and still, and as the sun climbs higher, a blue haze settles on the hills of Antrim and Down, that is the remembered bliss of childhood and a perpetual ache in the heart of the exile. 'Clay of the pit whence we were wrought yearns to its fellow clay.'

Just such a spell of warm dry weather began on 6 June 1798, and lasted until 19 June, when the temperature fell and there was some rain. The register of weather observations kept at the Library of the Belfast Society for Promoting Knowledge (now better known as the Linen Hall Library) recorded that on Wednesday 6 June the temperature was already 64 degrees Fahrenheit before noon, and the barometric pressure 30.44 inches of mercury. Over the next four days the temperature fell back a point, but the barometer rose. Then for three days there are no entries, and in the blank space an anonymous hand has written: 'The town shut up and no liberty to pass to and fro.'

A.T.Q. STEWART, The Summer Soldiers, 1995

PREVIOUS TO OUR MARCH for Antrim I was not appointed to any command; I had refused to accept of any. In the front rank there were eighteen men, most of them personal friends and acquaintances of my own, led by a man named John McGladdery. I was in that front rank; and it was allowed by our opponents the men belonging to it marched up the main street, and met the enemies' troops in good order, and did the duty assigned to them in a becoming manner. The first position taken was the churchyard, which commands the main street. There our green banner was unfurled, and McCracken was stationed with his principal officers about him.

When the street firing on us commenced, a girl came up to us, in the churchyard, and told our leader there was a loop-hole in the wall where he had better go. She had come there in the midst of the firing to point it out to him. When the panic occurred, and the party in reserve mistook the flight of some dragoons for a charge on their companions, McCracken on quitting the churchyard to check the disorder, left me in command of that place, and I maintained it as long as there was a hope of keeping possession of the town ...

Mr Macartney, and the yeomen he commanded, after the burning of some houses in the town, had taken refuge behind the wall of the park of Lord Massereene, in front of the high street, and occasionally rose up and fired some shots down the street. Close to the market-house, near the castle gate, some yeomen and horse soldiers kept their ground, the yeomen had two pieces of cannon there, which were soon silenced. We were about to attack the horsemen when a body of Ballyclare men entered the town by the west end street, and by Bow Lane. This caused some confusion, and the troops at the market-house profited by it to renew their fire, and took off some of our leaders. The people began to give way, and in attempting to stop the fugitives, McCracken, who proceeding with a party of men, by the rear of the houses, to dislodge the yeomen stationed in Lord Massereene's park, was borne down, disobeyed, and deserted by the panic-struck multitude. He then made his way to Donegore Hill, along with Robert Wilson, where he expected to find a body of men in reserve, but all his plans had been frustrated by the defection of the military chiefs.

JAMES HOPE, *from* 'Memoir', *Antrim and Down in 1798, c.* 1860

DONEGORE HILL

Ephie's base bairntime, trail-pike brood,
Were arm'd as weel as tribes that stood;
Yet on the battle ilka cauf
Turn'd his backside, an'scamper'd off.
                    PSALM 78, v. 9

The dew-draps wat the fiels o' braird,
That soon the war-horse thortur'd;
An falds were op'd by monie a herd
Wha lang ere night lay tortur'd;
Whan chiels wha grudg'd to be sae tax'd
An tyth'd by rack-rent blauth'ry,
Turn'd out *en masse*, as soon as ax'd –
An unco throuither squath'ry
                    Were we, that day.

While close-leagu'd crappies rais'd the hoards
O' pikes, pike-shafts, forks, firelocks,
Some melted lead – some saw'd deal-boards –
Some hade, like hens in byre-neuks:
Wives baket bonnocks for their men,
Wi' tears instead o' water;
An' lasses made cockades o' green
For chaps wha us'd to flatter
                    Their pride ilk day.

A brave man firmly leain' hame
I ay was proud to think on;
The wife-obeyin' son o' shame
Wi' kindlin e'e I blink on:

'Peace, peace be wi' ye! – ah! return
Ere lang and lea the daft anes' –
'Please guid,' quo he, 'before the morn
In spite o' a' our chieftains,
                          An' guards, this day.'

But when the pokes o' provender
Were slung on ilka shou'der,
Hags, wha to henpeck didna spare,
Loot out the yells the louder –
Had they, whan blood about their heart
Cauld fear made cake, an' crudle,
Ta'en twa rash gills frae Herdman's quart,
'Twad rous'd the calm, slow puddle
                          I' their veins that day.

Now *Leaders*, laith to lea the rigs
Whase leash they fear'd was broken
An' *Privates*, cursin' purse-proud prigs,
Wha brought 'em balls to sloken;
Repentant Painites at their pray'rs,
An' dastards crousely craikin',
Move on, heroic, to the wars
They meant na to partake in,
                          By night, or day.

Some fastin' yet, now strave to eat
The piece, that butter yellow'd;
An' some, in flocks, drank out cream crocks,
That wives but little valu'd:
Some lettin' on their burn to mak',
The rear-guard, goadin', hasten'd;
Some hunk'rin' at a lee dyke back,
Boost houghel on, ere fasten'd
                          Their breeks, that day.

The truly brave, as journeyin' on
They pass by *weans* an' *mithers*,
Think on red fiel's, whare soon may groan,
The *husbands*, an' the *fathers*:
They think how soon thae bonie things
May lose the youths they're true to;
An' see the rabble, strife ay brings,
Ravage their mansions, new to
                          Sic scenes, that day.

When to the tap o' DONEGORE
Braid-islan' corps cam' postin',
The red-wud, warpin, wild uproar,
Was like a bee scap castin';
For ★★★★★★★ ★★★★★ took ragweed farms,
(Fears e'e has ay the jaundice)
For *Nugent's* red-coats, bright in arms,
An' rush! the pale-fac'd randies
                Took leg, that day.

The *camp's* brak up. Owe braes, an' bogs,
The *patriots* seek their *sections*,
Arms, ammunition, bread-bags, brogues,
Lye skail'd in a' directions:
Ane half, alas! wad fear'd to face
Auld Fogies, faps, or women;
Tho' strong, untried, they swore in pride,
'Moilie wad dunch the yeomen,'
                Some wiss'd-for day.

Come back, ye dastards! – Can ye ought
Expect at your returnin',
But wives an' weans stript, cattle hought,
An' cots, an' claughin's burnin'?
Na, haste ye hame; ye ken ye'll 'scape,
'Cause *martial worth* ye're clear o';
The nine-tail'd cat, or choakin' rape,
Is maistly for some hero,
                On sic a day.

Saunt Paul (auld Knacksie!) counsels weel –
Pope, somewhere, does the samen,
That, 'first o' a', folk sud themsel's
Impartially examine';
Gif that's na done, whate'er ilk loun
May swear to, never swith'rin',
In ev'ry pinch, he'll basely flinch –
'Guidbye to ye, my brethren.'
                He'll cry, that day.

The leuks o' wheens wha stay'd behin',
Were mark'd by monie a passion;
By dread to staun, by shame to rin,
By scorn an' consternation:
Wi' spite they curse, wi' grief they pray,

Now move, now pause a bit ay;
'Tis mad to gang, 'tis death to stay',
An unco dolefu' ditty,
> On sic a day.

What joy at hame our entrance gave!
'Guid God! is't you? fair fa' ye! –
'Twas wise, tho' fools may ca't no' brave,
To rin or e'er they saw ye.' –
'Aye wife, that's true without dispute,
But lest saunts fail in Zion,
I'll hae to swear ✱✱✱ forc'd me out;
Better he swing than I, on
> Some hangin' day.'

My story's done, an' to be free,
Owre sair, I doubt, they smarted,
Wha wad hae bell'd the cat awee,
Had they no been deserted:
Thae warks pat skill, tho' in my min'
That ne'er was in't before, mon,
In tryin' times, maist folk, you'll fin',
Will act like Donegore men
> On onie day.

JAMES ORR, Poems on Various Subjects, 1804

AFTER THE BATTLE OF ANTRIM, the dead were brought down from the town in blockwheel carts and buried on the shore close to where the Sixmilewater flows into Lough Neagh. The ground there was sandy and easily trenched. Ezekiel Vance saw the carts leaving the town and assumed at first that they were laden with pig carcasses on their way from Derry to Belfast. On closer inspection he was horrified to see that the carts were piled high with human bodies, all of them naked ...

From the window of his cottage on the edge of the demesne, Lord Massereene's agent, Samuel Skelton, watched the yeomanry burying parties, digging in the hot sun. The bodies were shot in, a cartload at a time. 'Where the devil did these rascals come from?' the officer asked the driver of one cart. A poor wretch raised a blood-streaked face from the cart and feebly answered: 'I come frae Ballyboley.' He was buried along with the rest.

A.T.Q. STEWART, The Summer Soldiers, 1995

RODY M'CORLEY

Ho! see the fleet-foot hosts of men
Who speed with faces wan,
From farmstead and from fisher's cot
Upon the banks of Bann!
They come with vengeance in their eyes —
Too late, too late are they —
For Rody M'Corley goes to die
On the Bridge of Toome today.

Oh Ireland, Mother Ireland,
You love them still the best,
The fearless brave who fighting fall
Upon your hapless breast;
But never a one of all your dead
More bravely fell in fray,
Than he who marches to his fate
On the Bridge of Toome today.

Up the narrow street he stepped,
Smiling and proud and young;
About the hemp-rope on his neck
The golden ringlets clung.
There's never a tear in the blue, blue eyes,
Both glad and bright are they —
As Rody M'Corley goes to die
On the Bridge of Toome today.

Ah! when he last stepped up that street,
His shining pike in hand,
Behind him marched in grim array
A stalwart earnest band !
For Antrim town! for Antrim town!
He led them to the fray —
And Rody M'Corley goes to die
On the Bridge of Toome today.

The grey coat and its sash of green
Were brave and stainless then;
A banner flashed beneath the sun
Over the marching men —

The coat hath many a rent this noon,
The sash is torn away,
And Rody M'Corley goes to die
On the Bridge of Toome today.

Oh, how his pike flashed to the sun!
Then found a foeman's heart!
Through furious fight, and heavy odds,
He bore a true man's part;
And many a red-coat bit the dust
Before his keen pike-play –
But Rody M'Corley goes to die
On the Bridge of Toome today.

Because he loved the Motherland,
Because he loved the Green,
He goes to meet the martyr's fate
With proud and joyous mien.
True to the last, true to the last,
He treads the upward way –
Young Rody M'Corley goes to die
On the Bridge of Toome today.

ETHNA CARBERY, *The Four Winds of Erin*, 1902

IN THE END ONLY TWO COUNTIES STIRRED, and the pikemen, though gallantly led by Henry Joy McCracken and Henry Munro, were easily cut down and scattered over the flax fields of Antrim and Down. Their plans had been communicated to Castlereagh through an informer in plenty of time for General Nugent, who commanded the regular troops in Ulster, to make adequate preparations for meeting them.

For a short time, however, they were in possession of Newtownards and the surrounding district, and six of Londonderry's children who were at Mount Stewart barely succeeded in making good their escape before the insurgents reached the house. This success was shortlived, for the estate was evacuated a few days later in order to launch a concerted attack upon the loyalist stronghold of Ballynahinch. The consequent engagement on June 13 put a period to the rebellion in County Down. 'The rebels fought at Ballynahinch, as in Wexford, with determined bravery,' wrote Castlereagh, 'but without the fanaticism of the southerns. They made the attack and used some wretched ship guns mounted on cars with considerable address. The body there assembled was entirely dispersed. In their ranks were found two of my father's servants, a footman and a postillion.' Nugent and his second-in-command,

Clavering, now issued amnesties to all rebels, except their leaders, who would lay down their arms and return to their allegiance. The people took the hint, and with the capture and execution of McCracken and Munro shortly afterwards the rising in Ulster was over.

H. MONTGOMERY HYDE, *The Rise of Castlereagh*, 1933

IT WAS A FEARFUL SCENE. Three weeks previously James Dickey the attorney from Crumlin had been hanged, and his head cut off and placed on a spike on the Market House. Four days later the same sentence had been passed on John Storey the Belfast printer, who had been a fellow prisoner with Harry at Kilmainham. Both these men had fought at Antrim. In the beginning of July Hugh Grimes and Henry Byres, leaders at Ballynahinch had suffered likewise. There they were – four heads with their sightless eyeballs staring down on the little procession making its way to yet another hanging. In the glare and heat of that exceptionally warm summer flies buzzed around the festering flesh, and the town authorities issued a warning against the consumption of uncooked fruit.

When Mary Ann left him, Harry stood, tall and majestic, looking after her till she was out of sight. Later she heard from others of the calmness and composure with which he faced death and of the last minute intervention by Major Fox to save his life, moved this time perhaps more by admiration for his heroism than by the desire for information. Why, his uncomprehending mind may have wondered, must such incredible fortitude, such poise, such self-control, be so uselessly squandered, the fellow must be given one more chance to get away. Harry answered him with a smile.

MARY MCNEILL, *Life and Times of Mary Ann McCracken*, 1960

HENRY JOY McCRACKEN

It was on the Belfast mountains I heard a maid complain,
And she vexed the sweet June evening with her heart-broken strain
Saying: 'Woe is me, life's anguish is more than I can dree,
Since Henry Joy McCracken died on the gallows tree.

At Donegore he proudly rode and he wore a suit of green
And brave though vain at Antrim his sword flashed lightning keen
And when by spies surrounded his band to Slemish fled
He came unto the Cave Hill to rest his weary head.

I watched for him each night long as in our cot he slept;
At daybreak through the heather to MacArt's fort we crept,
When news came from Greencastle of a good ship anchored nigh,
And twas down by yon wee fountain we met to say goodbye.

He says: "My love be cheerful, for tears and fears are vain."
He says: "My love be hopeful, this land will rise again."
He kissed me ever fondly, he kissed me three times o'er,
Saying: "Death shall never part us, my love for evermore."

That night I climbed the Cavehill and watched till morning blazed,
And when its fires had kindled across the loch I gazed;
I saw an English tender at anchor off Garmoyle,
But alas! no good ship bore him away to France's soil.

And twice that night a tramping came from the old shore road;
Twas Ellis and his yeomen, false Niblock with them strode;
My father home returning the doleful story told,
"Alas", he says, "young Harry Joy for fifty pounds is sold."'

'And is it true?' I asked her. 'Yes it is true,' she said,
'For to this heart that loved him I pressed his gory head,
And every night, pale, bleeding, his ghost comes to my side,
My Harry, my dead Harry, comes for his promised bride.'

Now on the Belfast mountains this fair maid's voice is still,
For in a grave they laid her on high Carnmoney Hill,
And the sad waves beneath her chant a requiem for the dead:
But the rebel wind shrieks freedom above her weary head.

attributed to WILLIAM DRENNAN

MCCRACKEN:
  Three days to forge a nation in. With a couple of thousand men
  with pikes. One field piece, that fell apart the third time it was fired.
MARY:
  Hush, love.
MCCRACKEN:
  We actually had the town sewn up, even so. The cavalry were
  penned in. Then the men from Randalstown arrived, and met the
  cavalry clattering down towards them in a fast retreat. Except that
  they mistook it for an attack and ran like the hammers. The panic
  spread to my men. They ran too. So that was it. We were defeated
  by the enemy's retreat. It's not often you hear that said.

MARY:

Come and lie with me, Harry. There's still time enough. Please.

[She leads him to the bottom of the stairs. He stops, looks out front.]

McCRACKEN:

There's a streak of grey in the sky. Over the town. Look.

MARY:

The sun won't be fully up for a good half hour yet.

McCRACKEN:

You go on up, Mary, I'll follow you in a minute, I promise.

[She goes slowly up the stairs, lies down on the bed. He continues staring out front.]

McCRACKEN:

Why would one place break your heart, more than another? A place the like of that? Brain-damaged and dangerous, continuously violating itself, a place of perpetual breakdown, incompatible voices, screeching obscenely away through the smoky dark wet. Burnt out and still burning. Nerve-damaged, pitiable. Frightening. As maddening and tiresome as any other pain-obsessed cripple. And yet what would this poor fool not give to be able to walk freely again from Stranmillis down to Ann Street ... cut through Pottinger's Entry and across the road for a drink in Peggy's ... to dander on down Waring Street and examine the shipping along the river, and back on up to our old house ... we can't love it for what it is, only for what it might have been, if we'd got it right, if we'd made it whole. If. It's a ghost town now and always will be, angry and implacable ghosts. Me condemned to be one of their number. We never made a nation. Our brainchild. Stillborn. Our own fault. We botched the birth. So what if the English do bequeath us to one another some day? What then? When there's nobody else to blame except ourselves?

[He turns and proceeds slowly up the stairs. MARY begins to croon, quietly, 'My Singing Bird'.]

[Dawn is breaking]

McCRACKEN:

[By the rope at the top of the stairs] There is of course another walk through the town still to be taken. From Castle Place to Cornmarket, and down to the Artillery Barracks in Ann Street. And from thence back up Cornmarket to the scaffold. So what am I to say to the swarm of faces?

[He places the noose round his neck]

Citizens of Belfast ...

[The lambeg is loudly beaten, drowning out any further words: along with the singing of MARY and the blackbird.]

[Fade lights to black]

[End]

STEWART PARKER, *Northern Star*, 1984

NORTHERN STAR
(i.m. Stewart Parker, 1941–1988)

Ancestral voices bicker; ghosts
wrestle and dance; indignant hosts
of all persuasions dander down
to throng the lanes of Antrim, Down,
burnished pikes unsheathed from thatch,
sabre and flintlock quick to catch;
still the inspired conspirators
make history in Kelly's Cellars

or at Mac Airt's fort on Cave Hill,
their music above politics still
as starlight shines above a bog
– weaver and printer, ideologue,
children of nature, natural sons
and daughters, trenchant resolutions
echoing in that whin-scented air,
adrift like thistledown elsewhere.

Red dawn, white tide and starry night
dissolve to chaos, heartbreak, 'shite
and lunacy', the severed head,
townlands put to torch and sword,
leaving our souls still incomplete
and white noise of sectarian hate
echoing down the continuous past
in the loved entries of Belfast.

Wee corner shops we used to know,
'close-knit communities', the flow
of generational energy, streams
of consciousness, rain-traffic dreams,
the summer bus from glen to glen –
a common enough existence then,
or nearly, till the story broke
and the whole place went up in smoke.

White noise of gulls at rubbish dumps,
killers and victims both at once,
each blow a self-inflicted wound;
and always the holistic sound
of blackbirds on a summer night

in a world transfigured by starlight
– till all fade oblivionwards
'drowning out any further words'.

DEREK MAHON, *Collected Poems*, 1999

THE IRISH REBELLION OF 1798 left Ulster, outside Antrim and Down, practically untouched. In the month of June the Presbyterian rebels were soundly beaten at Antrim and Ballinahinch, and that was virtually the end of the revolt in Ulster. From that time forward the Presbyterians of the north showed no sign of disaffection, and from the first day to the last not a single Presbyterian yeoman violated his oath. Ulster's feet, after a moment's wavering, were set upon the path they have steadfastly followed ever since.

CYRIL FALLS, *The Birth of Ulster*, 1936

THE MAN FROM GOD-KNOWS-WHERE
a County Down telling of the winter time of 1795 and the autumn of 1803

Into our townlan', on a night of snow,
Rode a man from God-knows-where;
None of us bade him stay or go,
Nor deemed him friend, nor damned him foe,
But we stabled his big roan mare:
For in our townlan' we're a decent folk,
And if he didn't speak, why none of us spoke,
And we sat till the fire burned low.

We're a civil sort in our wee place,
So we made the circle wide
Round Andy Lemon's cheerful blaze,
And wished the man his lenth o' days,
And a good end to his ride.
He smiled in under his slouchy hat –
Says he, 'There's a bit of a joke in that,
For we ride different ways.'

The whiles we smoked we watched him stare,
From his seat fornenst the glow.
I nudged Joe Moore, 'You wouldn't dare
To ask him, who he's for meetin' there,
And how far he has got to go.'

But Joe wouldn't dare, nor Wully Scott,
And he took no drink – neither cold nor hot –
This man from God-knows-where.

It was closin' time, an' late forbye,
When us ones braved the air –
I never saw worse (may I live or die)
Than the sleet that night, an' I says, says I,
'You'll find he's for stoppin' there.'
But at screek o' day, through the gable pane,
I watched him spur in the peltin' rain,
And I juked from his rovin' eye.

Two winters more, then the Trouble Year
When the best that a man could feel
Was the pike he kept in hidlin's near,
Till the blood o' hate an' the blood o' fear
Would be redder nor rust on the steel.
Us ones quet from mindin' the farms,
Let them take what we gave wi' the weight o' our arms,
From Saintfield to Kilkeel.

In the time o' the Hurry we had no lead –
We all of us fought with the rest –
An' if e'er a one shook like a tremblin' reed,
None of us gave neither hint nor heed,
Nor ever even'd we'd guessed.
We men of the North had a word to say,
An' we said it then in our own dour way,
An' we spoke as we thought was best.

All Ulster over, the weemen cried
For the stan'in' crops on the lan' –
Many's the sweetheart an' many's the bride
Would liefer ha' gone till where *he* died,
And ha' murned her lone by her man.
But us ones weathered the thick of it,
And we used to dander along, and sit
In Andy's side by side.

What with discoorse goin' to and fro,
The night would be wearin' thin,
Yet never so late when we rose to go
But someone would say: 'Do ye min' thon snow,
An' the man what came wanderin' in?'

And we be to fall to the talk again,
If by any chance he was *one o' them* –
The man who went like the win'.

Well 'twas gettin' on past the heat o' the year
When I rode to Newtown fair:
I sold as I could (the dealers were near –
Only three-pound-eight for the Innish steer,
An' nothin' at all for the mare!)
I met M'Kee in the throng o' the street,
Says he, 'The grass has grown under our feet
Since they hanged young Warwick here.'

And he told that Boney had promised help
To a man in Dublin town.
Says he, 'If ye've laid the pike on the shelf,
Ye'd better go home hot-fut by yerself,
An' polish the old girl down.'
So by Comber road I trotted the gray,
And never cut corn until Killyleagh
Stood plain on the risin' groun'.

For a wheen o' days we sat waitin' the word
To rise and go at it like men.
But no French ships sailed into Cloughey Bay,
And we heard the black news on a harvest day
That the cause was lost again;
And Joey and me, and Wully Boy Scott,
We agreed to ourselves we'd as lief as not
Ha' been found in the thick o' the slain.

By Downpatrick gaol I was bound to fare
On a day I'll remember, feth;
For when I came to the prison square
The people were waitin' in hundreds there,
An' you wouldn't hear stir nor breath!
For the sodgers were standing, grim an' tall,
Round a scaffold built there fornent the wall,
An' a man stepped out for death !

I was brave an' near to the edge of the throng,
Yet I knowed the face again,
An' I knowed the set, an' I knowed the walk,
An' the sound of his strange up-country talk,
For he spoke out right an' plain.

Then he bowed his head to the swinging rope,
Whiles I said, 'Please God' to his dying hope,
And 'Amen' to his dying prayer,
That the Wrong would cease, and the Right prevail,
For the man that they hanged at Downpatrick jail
Was the MAN FROM GOD-KNOWS-WHERE!

NOTE: The 'man' of this ballad was Thomas Russell, who organised County Down, but was in prison and unable to lead in '98. He returned in 1803 to try and rally the North simultaneously with Emmet's Dublin rising, failed in his effort, and died on the scaffold at Downpatrick. At the opening of the poem, where he visits the inn, in the depth of winter, '95, we will suppose he does not make his name or mission known in mixed company, or maybe does not suspect the possibilities underlying the dour reticence of the group of countrymen, though they afterwards gave a good account of themselves. 'Warwick', alluded to by M'Kee was a young Presbyterian minister hanged at Newtownards as was the Rev. James Porter, at Grey Abbey, some miles away.

FLORENCE M. WILSON, *The Coming of the Earls*, 1918

1795

Lodgings for the night! Threw down his sword. Snow
   swirled in.
We made the circle wider round the blazing fire,
And dared not say aloud, *Look what the wind blew in*,
For he was someone; we could tell by his attire.

He opened up his jacket of the Arden green
To show two pistols hanging from a bandoleer,
His gorgeous waistcoat fit for any queen,
All in the highest fashion of a Volunteer.

A year or three went by, but still we minded him
Who'd staggered in that night, and every word he spoke,
For rebel armies rose up in the interim.

And now I'm standing in Downpatrick Jail, I stare
At him they're going to dangle from their tree of oak,
And know him from his dying words, the Man-from-
   god-knows-where.

CIARAN CARSON, *The Twelfth of Never*, 1998

W E CALCULATED TIME FROM ONE or other of three notable events –
'the year the meal was so dear', 'the year o' the big wun' (wind), or
'the flood', the latter having no reference to the Deluge, but to a memorable
three-days rain which occurred sometime in the forties, when the villagers
stood up to the waist in the river, fishing for corn-stacks and hay-ricks with
pitchforks, before they got through under the arches of the Brig.

We talked much of the Rebellion or 'turn-oot', taking pride in the part
which some of our forefathers had played in it. Nothing could have made
us so angry as hearing our ancestors jeered at and called 'pike men', or to be
reminded that the gallant patriots had gone to battle provided with
grindstones for the occasional sharpening of their spears. It was a base
calumny and unworthy of credence – almost as insulting as to be told that
the brave men had fired on the soldiers from the insides of houses and shops.

ARCHIBALD McILROY, *When Lint was in the Bell*, 1897

I T WAS WOLFE TONE'S ANNIVERSARY, and the Belfast Fianna were
celebrating it by a march to MacArt's Fort on Cave Hill. There was to
be an address and a picnic afterwards, and a Seanchas in the evening at
the huts.

On their way they passed the street where Henry Joy McCracken was
hanged in '98, and other streets and houses which had some particular
association with the United Irishmen in the days when Belfast was the
stronghold of Republicanism. Cave Hill itself was associated with those
days, for it was there that Wolfe Tone had sworn in Henry Joy
McCracken to the United Irishmen; and it was in its caves that some of
those men had hidden after the revolt of '98. And it was up its steep hills
that Mary McCracken, Henry's sister, had courageously brought food
and news to the hunted men.

Ernest Blythe delivered the address. As the Fianna stood on MacArt's
Fort he reminded them of all those associations; he told them of the aims
of the United Irishmen; of the struggle they were facing today because
they held the same aims and ideals; that today all over Ireland similar
celebrations were being held to demonstrate our loyalty and adhesion to
the principles of Wolfe Tone; and at the end, asked them to hold up their
right hands and here on this spot of sacred association to pledge
themselves to fight for the independence of Ireland, and never to cease
from their efforts till Ireland was free.

The Fianna raised their hands and repeated after him the words of the
pledge.

NORA CONNOLLY O'BRIEN, *Portrait of a Rebel Father*, 1935

THEY GOT UP AND WALKED ALONG the mountain's ridge into wild bare country. A cool breeze rushed at them.

'Fill your lungs with that!' said Alec. 'That's as good as the Rathlin air any day. It has come over Lough Neagh as clean and fresh as a spring well.'

Colm thought of the wind coming over Rathlin, shaking the grass on the top of the empty house, bounding over black Knocklayde, bumping through villages, ruffling Lough Neagh, and sweeping up to the mountain where they were now.

Alec stood with outstretched arms and inhaled loudly, the buttons almost bursting on his waistcoat, his face red, and the wind tossing his fair hair. Across a black stream he lifted Colm and Jamesy, one in each arm. Then they began to run and trip each other in the wiry grass – Rover barking at them and sniffing at fern tufts for rabbits,

Once they stopped to look back at the city which would soon disappear from view, and Alec held Colm and Jamesy tightly and pointed to Cave Hill with sun shining on it.

'Do you see that hill?' he said to them. 'Over a hundred years ago great patriots stood on it and looked down at Belfast; they were Wolfe Tone, Henry Joy McCracken, Neilson and some others whose names I forget – anyway they were all Protestants. And do you know what they swore? They took an oath that they'd never rest quietly in their graves till the authority of England over this country was overthrown and our independence achieved ... But that spirit has gone from amongst all of them except a few, scattered to nothingness within a hundred years.' He swept his hand towards the city: 'There they are below us now, a race of people living in a land that they do not serve!'

'And will they ever come to love Ireland again?' Colm asked.

'That's a poser,' smiled Alec. 'It's like asking us to march at the Twelfth of July. It will come, but not in our time ... Till then we must thole all; to give in would be as cowardly as suicide!'

MICHAEL McLAVERTY, *Call My Brother Back*, 1939

HUNGER WAS THE MAIN DRIVING FORCE behind the revolutions which convulsed much of Europe in 1848. The first barricades were thrown up in Palermo and in the weeks that followed the fire of revolt flared out from Sicily up the Italian peninsula; on 22 February King Louis Philippe was overthrown in Paris; in March Vienna, Budapest and Berlin were paralysed by insurrection; and by the early summer in central Europe there was not a city with a population of one hundred thousand or more which had not experienced revolution. 'Ireland's opportunity, thank God and France, has come at last!' Charles Gavan Duffy announced on 4 March: 'We must die rather than let this providential hour pass over us unliberated.'

Duffy, son of a Catholic bleacher in Monaghan, had edited the *Vindicator* for northern repealers but, impatient with O'Connell's parliamentary approach, had helped to found Young Ireland in 1842 to promote the new racial and romantic nationalism sweeping much of continental Europe. As editor of the *Nation*, Duffy employed the Banbridge solicitor, John Mitchel, as a leading contributor. Born in County Londonderry the son of a Presbyterian minister, Mitchel published the *United Irishman* in 1848, appealing to the spirit of '98 and calling for an immediate mass uprising. A starving people, however, had no interest in insurrection. The lord lieutenant sent his children home to England and troops poured into Ireland as the Whig administration watched the fall of government after government on the European mainland. But there was no need for alarm: Mitchel was arrested without difficulty and sentenced to fourteen years' transportation, and Ireland's sole contribution to the 'Year of Revolutions' was the 'Battle of Widow McCormack's Cabbage Patch', in which a small force of police, firing their carbines from a farmhouse in County Tipperary, dispersed some fifty insurgents at the end of July.

JONATHAN BARDON, *A History of Ulster*, 1992

I am a true-born Irishman, John Mitchel is my name:
When first I joined my comrades from Newry town I came;
I laboured hard both day and night to free my native land
For which I was transported unto Van Dieman's Land ...

I was placed on board a convict ship without the least delay;
For Bermuda's Isle our course was steered: I'll ne'er forget the day,
As I stood upon the deck to take a farewell view
I shed a tear, but not for fear; my native land, for you.

Adieu! Adieu! to sweet Belfast, and likewise Dublin too,
And to my young and tender babes; alas, what will they do?
But there's one request I ask of you, when your liberty you gain
Remember John Mitchel far away, though a convict bound in chains.

ANONYMOUS

THE CHARACTER OF THE AGITATION which resurfaced after 1870 was profoundly influenced by the upheavals of the 1840s. Above all, the land question came to the forefront of Irish politics, and stayed there until the end of the century. The assault on the Union was renewed on two fronts. In 1858 a number of men who had been involved in the abortive

Young Ireland uprising of 1848 founded the Irish Republican Brotherhood in Dublin. While accepting Thomas Davies's non-sectarian definition of nationality, they believed that Britain would never concede Irish independence unless forced to do so by violent revolution. They also realised that the Irish emigrant communities which had developed in the United States since the Famine provided an opportunity to widen the assault on Britain; consequently the Fenian Brotherhood was also founded in New York at this time. So began a recurrent theme of modern Irish history: the United States as a reservoir of money, men and grievance against Britain which could be tapped in the cause of Irish nationalism.

Today we see the Fenians as the men who passed on the torch of republicanism from the United Irishmen to the insurgents of 1916, and passed it on without examining the flame too closely. Ignoring all other issues, including to a large extent land reform, they concentrated on the theme of physical force. When finally they attempted their coup in 1867, the government knew all it needed to know about them, and most of the leaders were already in prison. The Fenians, like the Young Irelanders, were never more than a minority in nationalist politics, but once again their ideas, and perhaps more their actions, profoundly affected the shape of Irish history.

A.T.Q. STEWART, *The Shape of Irish History*, 2001

JAMES STEPHENS, [A] VETERAN OF 1848, had returned from Paris, where he had been perfecting his conspiratorial prowess, to found a revolutionary organisation in Dublin in 1858 dedicated to the establishment of an Irish republic by force of arms. Early the following year Stephens galvanised militant exiles in New York and set up the Fenian Brotherhood. The movement in Ireland, now officially called the Irish Republican Brotherhood but better known as the Fenians, spread rapidly amongst labourers, shopkeepers and others hard hit by the successive harvest failures of the early 1860s. It is difficult to assess the support for a secret oath-bound organisation, but it seems that Fenianism was at its weakest in Ulster, where it had trouble supplanting the more traditional sectarian Ribbonism. Constabulary reports failed to confirm Conservative claims that Ulster Catholics were joining the brotherhood in droves, but none the less, 'Fenian' joined 'Taig' at the top of the list of hostile epithets Protestants used for their Catholic neighbours.

When the American Civil War ended in the summer of 1865 a quarter of a million dollars was raised to finance the long-planned Fenian rising in Ireland but arrangements for insurrection were disrupted by fatal indecision, internal disputes, informers, arrests and the petulance of Stephens. Excitement was intense, however, when news came through of a Fenian raid on Canada and that the 'wolves' (mostly Union ex-servicemen) had set sail for Ireland in January 1867. In the same month nine Fenian suspects were arrested in Belfast, in possession of lead, bullets and bullet moulds, and more were held after twenty rifles were seized by police in the Pound.

JONATHAN BARDON, *A History of Ulster*, 1992

from THE BOLD FENIAN MEN

As down by the glenside I met an old woman,
A-plucking young nettles she n'er saw me coming,
I listened a while to the song she was humming,
Glory O! Glory O! To the Bold Fenian Men.

'Tis fifty long years since I saw the moon beaming,
On proud manly forms and on eyes that were gleaming,
I see them again sure through all my day-dreaming,
Glory O! Glory O! To the Bold Fenian Men ...

Some died by the wayside, some died with the stranger,
And wise men have judged that their cause was a failure.
They fought for their freedom and never feared danger,
Glory O! Glory O! To the Bold Fenian Men.

ANONYMOUS

THE RISING OF THE MOON

As down by the glenside I met an old colleen,
She stung me with the gaze of her nettle-green eyes.
She urged me to go out and revolutionise
Hibernia, and not to fear the guillotine.

She spread the madder red skirts of her liberty
About my head so I was disembodied.
I fell among the People of No Property,
Who gave me bread and salt, and pipes of fragrant weed.

The pale moon was rising above the green mountain,
The red sun declining beneath the blue sea,
When I saw her again by yon clear crystal fountain,

Where poppies, not potatoes, grew in contraband.
She said, *You might have loved me for eternity*.
I kissed her grass-green lips, and shook her bloodless hand.

CIARAN CARSON, The Twelfth of Never, 1998

THE FIRST TIME THE WORDS 'HOME RULE' came under my notice, I was a small girl in the County Tyrone, riding on a shaggy pony along a country road. A hired boy who rejoiced in the name of 'Roddy' held the rein. He was the first native Irishman I remember to have conversed with, and he was a veritable Rory of the Hills. As we went along he discoursed treason in fascinating style, and when we came to a quiet and suitable corner, he danced jig-steps to his own whistling. It was he who interpreted for me the words 'Home Rule for Ireland', which appeared in white painted letters on a grey stone wall, and why the harp rudely shaped was there without a crown. I went to the newspapers to learn more about these things, and found the names of Isaac Butt and Parnell, which were henceforth as interesting to me as those of the little Princes in the Tower, and Margaret of Anjou and Walter Raleigh, and other famous personages in the history book. I grasped the fact that history was a-making even in my own lifetime. I kept my eyes open. But the wall inscriptions were not allowed to remain unchallenged.

From time to time we found the harp obliterated, the legend altered to 'No Home Rule', and very rude remarks were added about His Holiness the Pope.

History really began to be made even in the sleepy town of Omagh in a couple of years when Parnell himself came there and aroused the people. I, alas, did not witness this, having been taken away to live in Belfast, where I was submerged amid an Orange population. Nearly ten years passed before again I had a chance of talking politics to a Home Ruler. Intermediate examinations and the glories of English and foreign literature absorbed my attention. I learned nothing of Ireland.

ALICE MILLIGAN, Dublin Evening Telegraph, c. 1887

I HAD READ ALL THE IRISH HISTORY within my reach and it was not encouraging. Defeat had followed defeat in an unending sequence. Armed revolt was beyond our means, and, if we had the means, would inevitably lead to another defeat. Constitutional agitation was only another name for surrender. How to break out of this circle of impossible alternatives was the question to which there seemed to be no answer.

Then in the autumn of 1901 I found the answer ...

In 1900 I had started in Belfast the first organisation with which I was connected. It was a club for boys, called the Ulster Debating Club. It held both private and public meetings and lectures, but its principal value to me was that it brought me in touch with a number of like-minded people. One of these, William McDonald, helped me to start another club called the Protestant National Society, the object of which was to try and convert young Ulster Protestants and to recruit them into a national movement.

I was greatly influenced by Ethna Carbery (Anna Johnston) and met at her house the local leaders of the Gaelic League, as well as many well-known people, like Douglas Hyde, Maud Gonne and John O'Leary.

In 1901, too, I joined the Tir na nOg branch of the Gaelic League in Belfast, which, at that time, consisted of a lot of young people working very enthusiastically together.

We asked Michael Cusack, the founder of the Gaelic Athletic Association, to come to Belfast to start the association in Ulster, and, representing the Tir na nOg Hurling Club, I became a member and, shortly afterwards, secretary of the first Antrim County Board of the Gaelic Athletic Association. I resigned this position because the board refused to do anything for the junior hurling clubs, a refusal which led me to leave them and start Na Fianna Eireann. Also as a representative of the Tir na nOg branch, I became a member of the Coisde Ceanntair of the Gaelic League in Belfast, and after some time I took on the secretaryship of that as well.

At this time, between 1901 and 1903, I was employed in a Belfast printing house from 8.30 a.m. until 6.30 p.m. and so had only the evenings, and sometimes a good part of the night, to attend to these various activities.

The Protestant National Association had a brief and unimportant life, but brought together a group which subsequently formed the Ulster Literary Theatre, a body which exercised some influence on the cultural development of the north of Ireland. It was started by David Parkhill and myself, with the intention of writing and producing distinctively Ulster plays, which would be a commentary on the political and social conditions in the north of Ireland.

In the meantime I had also joined Cumann na nGaedheal in Belfast. This body was founded by Arthur Griffith and William Rooney in 1901 in Dublin and became largely an open propagandist cover for the secret Irish Republican Brotherhood. For some years Griffith was a member of the IRB, but resigned from the organisation over some point of difference with which I am not acquainted. That all happened before I came to Dublin. Representing Belfast clubs, I came to Dublin to annual conventions of Cumann na nGaedheal, and became a member of the executive committee of that body.

From 1904 onwards a series of annual feiseanna was held in various parts of the Glens of Antrim. At the first of these I met Roger Casement and formed an intimate friendship with him, which lasted until his death. He was not a member of any of these bodies, although he supported the Gaelic League generously with funds.

BULMER HOBSON, Ireland Yesterday and Tomorrow, 1968

'WELL, NONO,' SAID DADDY, 'give an account of yourself. What have you been doing while I've been away?'

'What have I been doing? I've been awfully busy. I've got the Cumann na mBan started since you were here. Listen. Monday and Friday nights for Irish, and Saturday and Sunday afternoons, too. Sunday morning and night for the Fianna; then the nights for the Cumann na mBan and the Young Republican Party. Wouldn't it be lovely, Daddy, if we could tack on a couple of extra nights to the week? I need them badly.'

'Extra nights —' began Daddy.

'No, Mr Connolly. Stop twinkling. I don't want extra working days. I want extra free nights.'

'I don't see how we can manage that for you,' said Daddy. 'What do you do at the Cumann na mBan?'

'We have occasional lectures, and first aid classes and rifle drill.'

'Who teaches you rifle drill, and where do you practise?'

'Cathal McDowell, of the Volunteers, teaches us, and we practise in the Fianna Hut. What a use these huts are being put to these days!' Nono said smilingly. 'Built to house English soldiers during Belfast riots, and then passing into the hands of the Fianna, where boys and girls are taught and pledged to fight for the independence of Ireland. And now, lent by them to the Volunteers and Cumann na mBan, who are learning to fight for an Irish Republic. What a change!'

'A change, indeed,' said Daddy.

NORA CONNOLLY O'BRIEN, Portrait of a Rebel Father, 1935

SHE KNEW THAT IF ONE DAY, by some chance, men with guns did come and say 'Let there be no Mass', it would make no difference to Father Lavery or old Mrs Magill or Mrs Duffy. Nothing would stop *them*. And that was the way she felt about the IRA — they talked about changing a government. As if a bunch like Seamus Sullivan or Danny Canavan or even Hugh himself, could possibly overthrow the wigged judges, the courts of law, the policemen; a government which possessed enough millions to build a great white Parliament House like Stormont; how could you defeat a thing like that?

'All that'll happen is that you and the rest of you'll find yourselves up in Crumlin Jail.'

'D'ye think jail'd stop us?' he demanded. 'We're not afraid of jail. Nor death either.' His eyes quickly shot away from her, embarrassed at such a dramatic statement. Then he went on quickly to justify himself.

'There weren't many of them in 1916 and they managed all right,' he said. 'They set the country alight, all right.'

'*They* were great men,' she said, knowing that she never had nor never would meet a great person.

'They were just fellas like ourselves,' he said angrily. 'Fellas like Pearse and Connolly. Patrick Pearse was a schoolmaster and James Connolly was only a working man. We've got plenty of fellas like them in the IRA even now ...'

M.F. CAULFIELD, The Black City, 1952

CYCLING WAS HARD IN AMONGST the mountains; the roads were boggy and rutty, running through waste heather. A wind from the north-east cut across the country, often I had to lie down and put my back to the wind; its full force in my teeth stifled me. The coast was bare, with hardly a tree. Trees did not grow well in the sodden salt air; inland they were bent by the wind. Mountain valleys running north-west broke up the chains; in them were long, narrow, deep lakes. To cross Donegal from east to west one had to switch in angular zig-zags from north-west to south-west. The mountains were fine; Errigal towering high like a pyramid, a flame when it caught the evening sun on its slanting crags and Muckish, Pig's Back, always sheer. The grained red granite of the long Barnesmore Pass opened its thin bright gullet in the distance.

At Bloody Foreland, the sunset ruddied and drew blood from the cliffs, the white dome of Slieve Sneacht became rose. I met a man on horseback: he talked.

'Do you know why the bishops are against Sinn Féin?' he asked. 'Because themselves and the priests have all their money in the war bonds.' The people seemed open and friendly. I had known the Brigadier, Joe Sweeney, in the University; a student at Pearse's school he had fought with the St Enda's Company in Easter Week. The brigade was poor, there had been little supervision. I followed the companies along the ins and outs of the coast to the cliffs of Glen Columcille and Slieve League, along the pleasant bays between Killybegs Harbour and Donegal town. The brigade ran through Ballyshannon with its precipitous streets to the long sea rollers of Bundoran.

ERNIE O'MALLEY, On Another Man's Wound, 1936

THEN CAME JULY AND THE SUMMER HOLIDAYS, but there was no peace. Houses were raided by police and auxiliaries during curfew; and in the poorer Catholic districts the people were organised to raise the cry of 'Murder! Murder!' if anyone entered their streets at night.

One night a lorry load of police and specials was ambushed by the Republicans in Raglan Street. One policeman was shot dead and some wounded.

Sitting up in their beds the MacNeills heard the volleys of shots crackling like breaking sticks. Colm was the only one who knew that Alec was out with the Republicans, for that evening he had told him as he gave him his pocket-book and asked him to pray. Now as he listened with cold fear to the air alive with shots he couldn't pray; he thought of Alec with a light rifle at his shoulder firing from the cover of an entry or from behind a lamppost.

His mother had her beads in one hand and with the other was keeping the bed-clothes over Clare's head. But the ferocious din would have wakened the dead, and the whole night long it continued and even into the growing day.

MICHAEL McLAVERTY, *Call My Brother Back*, 1939

THE DRILLING WAS CARRIED THROUGH RELENTLESSLY. Sullivan was enthusiastic and barked command after command. Kelly found it difficult to keep his feet on the morass that was soon churned up. In a while his thoughts began to drift away and he began to think of the face of Pearse again and how it must have looked at the supreme moment. That, he thought, was how things ought to be. Not just walking with stiff legs, trying to keep your feet in the sucking ground, prickles of heat rising all over your body, making you want to scratch.

Canavan was shouting. Kelly looked round with the rest at the spindly figure on the edge of the plateau, which was at a higher level. Canavan was waving his arms like antennae. He began to point down the hill.

'What the bloody hell is it?' shouted Sullivan.

'Peelers!' Canavan's voice came muffled, blown into the air by the wind. It was as though he were trying to make himself heard from behind thick plate glass. He started to run towards them.

Kelly turned to watch the lazy, easy workings of Sullivan's thick body, the confident turn of his broad body.

'All right, fellas, you'd better run for it. But spread out a bit. Don't all bunch together!'

Kelly was about to run with the rest when Sullivan shouted: 'Come with me, Hughie. But wait for Canavan.'

'Ay, all right,' said Kelly ...

Canavan reached them, spluttering flecks of spittle from his excited mouth. 'They're on the Sheep's Path now. I don't think they know we're here. They look to me as if they're just patrolling.'

'Frig patrolling,' said Sullivan. 'They know we'll be up here somewhere at Easter. There'll be plenty of them around.'

'What about having a go at them?' said Canavan knowing that this was nonsense even as he said it.

'Be your age,' said Sullivan. 'Come on.'

He turned and led the way towards the nearest clump of gorse ...

They reached the trees, threaded their way through them and came out into tended grounds with cut lawns, flower borders and spaced, evergreen bushes. Sullivan slowed.

'Where are we?' asked Kelly.

'Ach, we're all right,' said Sullivan. 'It's the Castle grounds. I've been up here before. It's a great place to court a girl.'

They went forward in silence, each with relief in his heart that they had got away so easily. Kelly walked with quick, thin strides to keep up with the burly, forceful steps of Sullivan. Canavan gangled along beside them, pale and sweaty.

They reached the Antrim Road. They waited for a few minutes until a tram came along. Then they boarded it and went home.

M.F. CAULFIELD, *The Black City*, 1952

I WANDERED FOR MONTHS through the small lakes and little hills of Monaghan. I saw sieges of heron in the reeds and waited for bat-tailed otters near Carrickmacross where they are said to pass through when going from one lake to another. I was able to disprove the lines:

From Carrickmacross to Crossmaglen
You meet more rogues than honest men.

I was at the taking of Ballytrain barracks – the first barracks taken north of the Boyne – with Eoin O'Duffy, the Brigadier; a policeman who had been praying during the attack was blown by the explosion of our gelignite through a partition wall without injury. There were, I think, nine police and that meant nine bright carbines, bayonets, revolvers, hand grenades, Verey lights and ammunition.

ERNIE O'MALLEY, *On Another Man's Wound*, 1936

A S HE TOOK HIS BREAKFAST he told them about fellows that were arrested last night. 'When I was coming up the street,' he said, 'I met the postman and he was telling me that six were arrested in the Kashmir Road.'

He had the same story to tell every morning, and when Colm was going to school he would see lorry loads of prisoners, brought in from the country, and singing rebel songs as they were conveyed to Crumlin Road Jail. People would shake their fists at them and sometimes groups of women at street comers would jeer and wave Union Jacks. Colm would rejoice secretly when he would hear the Crumlin Road echoing with the 'Soldier's Song'.

MICHAEL McLAVERTY, *Call My Brother Back*, 1939

FROM THE GREEN LOWLANDS round Lough Neagh the road corkscrews up into the darkness of the Sperrin Mountains. In a lonely pass where it makes a last desperate effort to break through the opposition of the mountain wall ahead, the tattered remnants of a green, white and orange flag flutter from a telegraph pole. A ruined cottage stands by the roadside, its turf-browned rafters stark against the sky. Beyond it begins a brown waste of bogland from which in autumn come the muffled reports of sporting guns.

Up here in wind-swept passes the tricolour of the Irish Republic has a mysterious habit of appearing on telegraph poles when the police are not looking; broken road bridges and culverts remain – evidence of the days when Crossley tenders packed with dark-uniformed police patrolled the mountain roads and shots rang out from lonely wastes of mountain bog or green hillsides dotted now with the white, slug-like forms of sheep. Today the crack of rifles has been replaced by the report of sporting guns, but the rebel tradition goes on.

The car crests the rise, bursts with a last effort over the summit. Far below lies the silver-shining surface of Lough Foyle, with beyond it the black, many-folded outline of the Donegal hills. To the left beyond the green pasture land of the Roe Valley a patch of smoke above tree-tops shows where the Maiden City lies hidden in the windings of its historic river. We switch off the engine and coast downwards towards the wooded windings of the Foyle. No surrender. But behind us at the summit of the mountain, still signalling to the ruined cottage and the brown wastes of bogland, the remnants of the tricolour still flutter in the wind-swept pass.

DENIS IRELAND, *Statues Round the City Hall*, 1939

A NUMBER OF AREAS ARE REGARDED as heartland communities of the republican movement. There are characteristic differences between them, which can be interpreted as suggesting an internal homogeneity. There is west Belfast, which itself divides into parts of different character; there is north Belfast; there is Derry's Bogside and Creggan, and there are the rural areas of south Armagh and mid-Tyrone.

Alex Maskey, who comes from the New Lodge, has said that the people of the Falls did not really understand sectarianism the way the people of the New Lodge did, who lived close to a Protestant area. Father Denis Faul, describing his mid–Tyrone area for me, said, 'Here it is about land. People still talk about the Protestants having taken their field, even though it happened three hundred years ago. They still feel a sense of belonging to that bit of land and of being entitled to have it back.'

In south Armagh, people feel simply that they are Irish people invaded by British forces. Talking to the Carragher family, noted republicans in the area, I often heard the remark, 'There are no Protestants here. Why do we need the army in to keep people apart. There is no peace for them to keep that's better than the peace there would be if they left.' Crossmaglen has no easy affinity with the rest of the North. It is a southern town that suffered the misfortune of the border being laid down on the wrong side of it. It was always a centre of rebellion though. In the 1850s, this area was home to the Ribbonmen, whose secret trials and organisational framework were similar to those of the Provisionals today. It would not be at all surprising if the very grandparents of local republicans had been Fenians and their grandparents had been Ribbonmen.

Derry had the deepest grievance at the start of the civil rights campaign and suffered the greatest aggravation of it in the massacre of Bloody Sunday, but it settled down under direct rule into a Catholic city that doesn't agonise about its identity. The low level of violence in Derry in the 1980s and 1990s suggests that even though the most senior members of the IRA lived there, they could not mould a local annoyance into sympathy for frequent acts of murder. Republicans blamed their failings on informers. Many local people said simply that the nationalists of Derry loved their town and would not tolerate further attacks on it.

MALACHI O'DOHERTY, *The Trouble With Guns*, 1998

THREE MORE BANDS FOLLOWED, two pipe and one melodeon. The crowd cheered and clapped, their heads growing light with the music and the colour, and the great splendid flowing banners, on which were portrayed some of the more glorious and soul–stirring episodes from the history of Ireland. St Patrick banishing the snakes, pointing sternly downwards. Mass in the Penal Days! The priest crouching before the altar in the little dark cave; behind him the white, exalted faces of the worshippers, and then far, far out over the hills, two evil priest hunters, one pointing and grimacing with Satanic joy, the other aiming his rifle – the Battle of the Yellow Ford; the Siege of Limerick; the Battle of the Boyne; Brian Boru at Clontarf. The vivid wondrous banners, with their long golden tassels, cast a spell over Neilly and his friends. Their eyes devoured the front picture, as each band came up, and then, as it passed, they jumped up wildly to see what was on the other side.

JOHN O'CONNOR, *Come Day – Go Day*, 1948

IT [LISBURN] ROSE ... TO CONSIDERABLE PROSPERITY through the establishment of the linen industry here by Louis Crommelin at the very close of the seventeenth century. It was burned down by accident in 1707. And I remember as a very small child going quickly through the empty streets of the town in a car on the occasion of other disturbances there. That was the day after the murder of Inspector Swanzy and the day before a great part of Bow Street was burned down. But you will find it a quiet enough toxv.n at the present time.

HUGH SHEARMAN, *Ulster*, 1949

A FEW CATHOLICS TOOK THE OCCASION of Easter Monday to celebrate the Easter Rising, but there was never a procession or parade: the memorial was an individual matter, its only sign the wearing of a paper lily in colours of green, white, and gold. To wear an Easter lily on Easter Monday was regarded by the authorities as a gesture extremely hostile to the state of Northern Ireland and therefore flagrantly offensive. It was also illegal, since, by virtue of the Flags and Emblems Act, it is illegal to fly the flag of any nation in Northern Ireland except that of the British Empire, the Union Jack. Since the South has never had diplomatic relations with Northern Ireland, the question of flying a tricolour, the green-white-and-gold of Ireland, in Belfast or elsewhere has not arisen. But anyone who wore the Easter lily knew that he was making a provocative statement. I am sure that my father, as sergeant, took the names of those he saw wearing the lily, but I don't think he prosecuted any of those dissidents. Equally, it was illegal to sing the national anthem of a foreign country in Northern Ireland, except upon an officially recognised occasion. If a Catholic, passing a Protestant, started singing or whistling 'The Soldier's Song', it would be taken as an offensive act. But these provocations were rare. Most people in Warrenpoint were content to keep to themselves and to their own kind, letting the other crowd do the same.

DENIS DONOGHUE, *Warrenpoint*, 1991

THE STATE OF NORTHERN IRELAND came into being in 1921 amid confusion and violence. The continuing IRA campaign provoked similar paramilitarism on the 'loyalist' side, largely in the form of the hastily recruited Ulster Special Constabulary (USC or 'Specials'). But most of the confusion was on the nationalists' side. They remained as split after 1920 as before, and had no contingency plans to deal with the new situation, short of recurrent appeals for help to Dublin. 'Surely this cannot be happening' just about sums up their reaction to partition, and all hopes were centred on the Boundary Commission to rescue them. In the meantime they embarked on a policy of passive non-recognition of the Northern Ireland state. Because of the continuing hostilities in much of Ireland (first with the brutal Anglo-Irish war 1919–21, then with the civil war in the Irish Free State, 1922–3) and the delay in the report of the Boundary Commission, a sense of insecurity and impermanence prevailed. Although the boundary imposed by the Government of Ireland Act of 1920 put some 90,000 Protestants in the largely Catholic southern state, the size of the Catholic minority left in Northern Ireland was far more problematic (430,000 against a Protestant majority of 820,000). In June 1920 local government elections were held under new proportional representation (PR) regulations. As a result Fermanagh, Tyrone, south Down, south Armagh and Derry City returned local councils with Catholic majorities, and they promptly voted their allegiance to the Dáil and the republican government in Dublin.

MARIANNE ELLIOTT, *The Catholics of Ulster*, 2000

WITH THE COMING OF JUNE, riots broke out once more. A special police force was recruited from the Orange Order, and on his way to school Colm would see them in their cage-cars or standing at street corners with their rifles, canvas bandoliers, and rough black-green uniforms.

'Them's our Black-and-Tans,' he heard a shawled woman shout at them. 'It's a poor show and little sleep we'll get on the Falls Road now!'

Not a day passed in peace, and as Colm played on the waste ground he could hear the shots shattering the summer air, and was thankful that his street was sheltered and away from it all. It was strange to be living in a city where night after night shots rang out and to know nothing of what happened until they read the morning's paper. It was strange, too, to be leaving their game of football when it was still bright and to retire to their houses because of curfew.

But the hours of curfew were not peaceful. From early morning the snipers were at their posts and they did not cease with the coming of curfew and the bare streets ...

There came more nights of terror, but towards the end of that month of June a lull came as the King and Queen of England opened the Belfast Parliament and Ireland was partitioned.

MICHAEL McLAVERTY, Call My Brother Back, 1939

PEOPLE SUCH AS MY MOTHER'S Catholic ancestors and their Protestant neighbours would have carried pitchforks, peat spades, scythes, reaping hooks and sharpened harrow-pins fixed on poles, in their successful breaching of the bridge of Toome, their capture of Randalstown and subdual of Ballymena. But with the United Irishmen forced to fall back, the bridge was used as a scaffold for the rebels, one of whom featured in a rousing song I learned at my primary school ('They come with vengeance in their eyes/ Too late, too late are they./ For Roddy McCorley goes to die/ On the bridge of Toome today'). The failed rebellion and the hangings that followed were, I know, in the minds of the civil rights marchers when their procession crossed the bridge of Toome in 1969 on its way from Belfast to Derry. Further along the route, at Burntullet Bridge, the civil rights group was attacked by screaming loyalists, wielding bricks, bottles, iron bars and cudgels studded with nails. In Northern Ireland bridges do not always join communities; they often merely serve to split them.

CAL McCRYSTAL, Reflections on a Quiet Rebel, 1997

AT TOOMEBRIDGE

Where the flat water
Came pouring over the weir out of Lough Neagh
As if it had reached an edge of the flat earth
And fallen shining to the continuous
Present of the Bann.
      Where the checkpoint used to be.
Where the rebel boy was hanged in '98.
Where negative ions in the open air
Are poetry to me. As once before
The slime and silver of the fattened eel.

SEAMUS HEANEY, Electric Light, 2001

Confederations, Complications
and Contradictions

Kelt, Briton, Roman, Saxon, Dane, and Scot,
time and this island tied a crazy knot.

JOHN HEWITT, *from* 'Ulsterman'

T HE SENSE OF TRADITION CONTINUES to wield its ancient power to
dramatize and moralize Irish history and experience. As long as
the gable-ends of Belfast shriek 'Remember 1690' and patriots
remember Easter 1916 no Irishman will forget his traditions. The positing
of romantic continuities establishes hallowed identities, imparts
righteousness and assuages the pangs of insecurity and disruption. If the
great St Patrick had not existed it would have been necessary for
Catholics and Protestants, separately, to invent him. In a sense they have,
since there are rival hagiographical traditions. Yeats and an anonymous
medieval scribe both imagine dancing in the Holy Land of Ireland.
Cuchulain seemed to join Patrick Pearse in the Dublin Post Office. In
popular consciousness the 'boys behind the wire' imprisoned in
contemporary Ulster shake hands with the eighteenth-century United
Irishmen; nineteenth-century Irish folk-memory lined up Brian Boru and
Lord Edward Fitzgerald against Oliver Cromwell and King William III.
Chronology, critical historiography and common sense are powerless
against the emotional and imaginative force of such associations.

NORMAN VANCE, *Irish Literature: A Social History*, 1999

I N A CULTURE WHERE THE PAST is so much part of the present, a
Protestant who opposes perceived threats to his freedom and his

religion is acting radically, in the same tradition as the Covenanters, the Commonwealthmen and the 'real Whigs' of the seventeenth and eighteenth centuries, who made 1688 and the Protestant succession fundamental to the British tradition of liberty. Behind the seemingly antiquated bigotry, there is a dynamic libertarianism, at times a millenarianism, which still finds its inspiration in Old Testament imagery of the Israelites fighting their way to possess the promised land. It is, however, a brand of libertarianism ill-attuned to modern secular thinking which accepts nationality, rather than religion, as a badge of identity.

There is a tendency to see the problem of Northern Ireland simplistically in terms of a Protestant/Catholic conflict. But Protestantism is not a monolith, and it is the failure to recognise the libertarian tradition, particularly in Presbyterianism, which causes many commentators to dismiss such appeals to freedom as either rhetoric or pure hypocrisy. Yet the Presbyterians' heightened sense of persecution is as old as that of the Irish Catholics and the Irish problem is as much one of conflicting ideas of liberty as anything else. Because of the episcopalian character of Protestant political ascendancy in Ireland for most of the modern period, and more particularly because Presbyterians believed their faith to have preserved the original purity of the Reformation from the dangers of 'prelacy' and 'popery', any study of the Protestant idea of liberty must concern itself largely with Presbyterianism and with the area of its main concentration, Ulster.

MARIANNE ELLIOTT, *Watchmen in Sion*, 1985

TWO THOUSAND ... SCOTTISH STORM TROOPERS were drowned in the Moy, over in Connaught, while fighting on the side of the rebelly Burkes. They stiffened the great Ulster rising. They fell at Kinsale, when all Ireland fell, by the hundred. There they were witnesses of the exodus of the old Gaelic state. They profited by it too, for although the subsequent plantation of the north, where the history of the modern Six Counties begins, did not at first include Antrim (it did not include, either, Monaghan or Down), Sir Randall MacDonnell – a Highlander and a Catholic – was granted the greater part of Antrim by James and later made the first Earl.

Here I must interrupt [myself] to say farewell to the O'Neills of Ulster. Little trace of them remains: that is – of the Gaelic stock. The O'Neill of the present Shane's Castle at Randalstown, for example, was originally a Chichester. I do not know if I am wrong in saying that when Sean the Proud was murdered, and his head spiked in Dublin, he was buried in Glenarm. I did not find his grave.

SEAN O'FAOLAIN, *An Irish Journey*, 1940

B Y THE MID-CENTURY those who called themselves the 'Patriot party' in the Irish House of Commons were the champions of Ireland's rights, and began a process which led ultimately to the recovery of legislative independence in 1782. It was achieved by forcing Britain's hand during the crisis of the revolt of the American colonies. The war had denuded Ireland of troops, and a citizen army of Volunteers was raised to guard the country against invasion and internal unrest. The government agreed to it with reluctance, and this wariness proved to be well founded. Officered largely by the Patriot landlords, it very rapidly became politicised, providing in the end a more representative alternative to parliament itself. Though the movement was in the main Protestant Episcopalian, the Presbyterians of Ulster flocked eagerly to the Volunteer banners and became the backbone of the northern regiments. They deeply resented their exclusion from political influence, and were no friends to the Church of Ireland, obliged as they were by law to pay tithes to that Church, and suffering irritations such as not having marriages performed by their ministers legally recognised. They sympathised with the Americans, but also with the Irish Catholics, whose situation they saw as similar to their own, if undoubtedly worse. The politics of the Catholic and Presbyterian mercantile classes began for the first time to converge, and from the activities of the more extreme and radical elements of both, the Society of United Irishmen was born in 1791. Yet neither side in this alliance fully admitted how different were the sources of their political activism, or how far apart were their essential aims. As in Northern Ireland today, there was much confusion between ends and means.

A.T.Q. STEWART, *The Shape of Irish History*, 2001

I RELAND HAS HARDLY TAKEN one of its most enlightened sons to its bosom. In the year of the three-hundredth anniversary of his birth, we are still awaiting a full-length study from an Irish scholar of this astonishing figure. Francis Hutcheson, founder of the most fertile current of intellectual enquiry in eighteenth-century Scotland, taught David Hume much of what he knew and deeply affected the pre-critical writings of Immanuel Kant. His economic doctrine descended to his student Adam Smith, thus laying one of the intellectual foundations of the modern world. His philosophy was a major influence on Thomas Jefferson, helping to shape the American struggle for independence, and boomeranged back to Ireland in the shape of the revolutionary United Irish movement. Edmund Burke, author of the only other Irish aesthetic treatise of the eighteenth century, may have absorbed Hutcheson's doctrine of the native and patriotic affections, which would then make Hutcheson a remote precursor of Romantic nationalism. Hutcheson's ideas belong to the eighteenth-century ferment of Irish Whiggery and

Dissent: in the *Short Introduction to Moral Philosophy* he argues, *contra* Hobbes, that the state of nature was one of liberty rather than anarchy, and in his *System of Moral Philosophy* champions the rights of women, children, servants, slaves and animals in the course of an argument for the natural equality of human beings. He speaks up for marriage as an equal partnership, and comments that 'the powers vested in husbands by the civil laws of many nations are monstrous'. He also takes a radical Whig line on the right of the governed to throw off an unjust sovereignty, and emerges as a full-blooded Harringtonian republican. The moral sense, he stresses in the *System*, is a democratic faculty common to adults and children, the unlettered and the refined.

Hutcheson stands at the fountainhead of the Ulster Enlightenment: the richest radical culture which Ireland has ever known. Other oppositional currents in the country – O'Connell, Sinn Féin – may have proved more politically effective; but none can remotely rival the philosophical ambitiousness and intellectual fertility of this extraordinary period, with its complex blending of Lockeian rationalism, classical republicanism, radical Presbyterianism and political libertarianism. Its preoccupations range from the soul to the state, from sentiment to the nature of civil society, from the springs of consciousness to the sources of political authority. Contemporary Ireland, both north and south of the border, stands under the judgement of this precious heritage, and has yet to catch up with its past.

TERRY EAGLETON, *from* 'Homage to Francis Hutcheson',
Heathcliff and the Great Hunger, 1995

IRELAND IN THOSE DAYS was intellectually and spiritually alive. Men were quick to feel the influence of worldwide ideas, and in Ireland the love of liberty glowed brightly; nowhere more brightly than among the farmers and lower middle-classes of the north-eastern counties. The position was a strange one. The landed gentry, who themselves, a few years before, claimed and won from England the independence of their Parliament, grew frightened and drew back from the path of reform on which alone lay security for what they had got. The wealthier merchants and manufacturers, satisfied with the trade freedom which brought them prosperity, were averse to further change. The Presbyterians and the lower-classes generally were eager to press forward. They had conceived the idea of a real Irish nation, of Gael and Gall united, of Churchman, Roman Catholic and Dissenter working together for their country's good under a free constitution. But it soon became apparent that the reforms they demanded would not be won by peaceful means. The natural terror of the classes whose ascendancy or prosperity seemed to be threatened, the bribes and cajoleries of British statesmen, turned the hearts of those who ought to have been leaders from Ireland to England. The relentless logic, the clear-sighted grasp of the inevitable trend of events, and the restless energy of men like Wolfe Tone, changed a party of constitutional reformers into a society of determined revolutionaries. Threats of repression were answered by the formation of secret societies. Acts of tyranny, condoned or approved by terror-stricken magistrates, were silently endured by men filled with a grim hope that the day of reckoning was near at hand. Far-seeing English statesmen hoped to fish out of the troubled waters an act of national surrender from the Irish Parliament, and were not ill-pleased to see the sky grow darker. Everyone else, every Irishman, looked with dread at the gathering storm. One thing only was clear to them. There was coming a period of horror, of outrage and burning, of fighting and hanging, the sowing of an evil crop of fratricidal hatred whose gathering would last for many years.

GEORGE A. BIRMINGHAM, The Northern Iron, 1907

McCRACKEN:

You've no notion of what it was all about, have you?

MARY:

I'm a gamekeeper's daughter, with a bastard child to rear, I've no head on me for all your dreams of glory.

McCRACKEN:

There was a new idea, Mary. We thought we were its midwives. What did it mean to be Irish? When you distilled it right down to the raw spirit? It meant to be dispossessed, to live on ground that isn't ours, Protestant, Catholic, Dissenter, the whole motley crew of us, planted together in this soil to which we've no proper title ...

MARY:

I've got no wit for this, Harry.

McCRACKEN:

Listen to me! Please. Just this night. Look at me. My great-grandfather Joy was a French Huguenot, my great-grandfather McCracken was a Scottish Covenanter, persecuted, the pair of them, driven here from the shores of home, their home but not my home, because I'm Henry Joy McCracken and here to stay, a natural son of Belfast, as Irish a bastard as all the other incomers, blown into this port by the storm of history. Gaelic or Danish or Anglo-Norman, without distinction, it makes no odds, every mother's son of us children of nature on this sodden glorious patch of earth, unpossessed of deed or inheritance, without distinction, for the only distinction that matters is between the power and the wealth on the one hand and the bent knee on the other, and we

all of us suffer the bent knee, every one, and for why? Because the
power isn't ours and the wealth isn't ours, they ebb and they flow
from another source, always and only the one source, the island of
hope and glory across the water ...

STEWART PARKER, Northern Star, 1984

1789 MADE FERMENT THROUGH ALL EUROPE, and Belfast's reaction was
at first strongly for the French Revolution. In 1791 their Whig Club
drank toasts to Franklin, Tom Paine, and 'the destroyers of the Bastille'.
There were spirits, however, who wanted to go farther than toast-
drinking, and in October 1791 Theobald Wolfe Tone, the son of a
Dublin coachmaker, came down to Belfast and founded the first branch
of the United Irishmen.

The United Irishmen stood for the abolition of all privilege based on
religion; and since the Non-conformists of every kind were not much less
handicapped than the Catholics, Presbyterians as a whole sympathized
with the movement. But from 1795 onward matters turned to the worse.
The United Irishmen, denied redress by constitutional means, became a
society for rebellion. Wolfe Tone with three young northern symp-
athizers, Samuel Neilson, Thomas Russell, and Henry Joy McCracken,
climbed Cave Hill, the mountain which overlooks Belfast from the north,
and there, in the old rath called MacArt's Fort, swore 'never to desist
from their efforts until they had subverted the authority of England, saved
their country, and asserted her independence'.

All four paid for it with their lives, in 1798 or 1803; the first result of
the rebellion was the abolition of the Irish Parliament by the Act of
Union; and before that, out of the strife and turmoil, the Orange Order
had come into being.

Yet there are today in Belfast men high in trust and office, Orangemen
and Unionists, who pride themselves more than a little on descent from
some rebel of 1798.

STEPHEN GWYNN, The Charm of Ireland, 1927

FEW THINGS IN HISTORY ARE SO REMARKABLE as the complete and
rapid extinction of the rebellious spirit amongst the Northern
Protestants after 1798. The union of the parliaments of Great Britain and
Ireland in 1801 was accepted by them at first under protest, but
eventually with almost entire acquiescence, and the province as a whole
continued contentedly on [a] career of economic progress ... It was
otherwise with the rest of Ireland, where an agitation of great
vehemence, more than once rising to armed outbreak, was conducted

against the English connection. Whenever this movement seemed likely to succeed, determined and vigorous opposition arose in Ulster.

D.A. CHART, A History of Northern Ireland, 1927

BY THE END OF THE EIGHTEENTH CENTURY the Northern Presbyterians were Ireland's leading radicals, men under the influence of the American and French revolutions. They joined with Catholics in the Society of United Irishmen and in the rising of 1798. These efforts to unite Protestant and Catholic died in the nineteenth century, first as the Presbyterians achieved civil rights for themselves, then as Catholic Emancipation began to make all the Protestants uncomfortably aware that Ireland had a Catholic majority.

JOHN COLE, Introduction to Ulster at the Crossroads, 1969

TWO OPPOSING CAMPS WITHIN nineteenth–century Irish politics – the Presbyterian liberal unionists, and the Catholic republican nationalists ... both ... claim [Dr William] Drennan as their type of Irish patriot-poet. From the argument outlined there are clearly two ways, at least, of looking at what constitutes an Irish patriot-poet. Robert Johnston and the Parnellites seem to suggest that unless Drennan was, in fact, the poet of the '98 Rebellion, then his claim to Irish patriot-poet status is nullified. On the other hand, J.S. Drennan and the Duffin family clearly believe that there is no contradiction in anyone's being an Irish patriot-poet despite not being the poet of the '98 Rebellion. One side sees Drennan as a revolutionist and insurrectionist: the other views him as an anti-revolutionist, though an 'ardent patriot', and 'a sincere lover of his country'. Which side is correct? As with many political arguments the fact is that each side has elements of both truth and error woven into its opinions.

Although it is rather bemusing to think of an Irish nationalist poet quickly becoming a 'staunch Unionist', it must be said that it is not so highly improbable at all, given the unique political circumstances in the late-eighteenth and early to mid-nineteenth centuries in Ireland. The whole argument needs to be seen primarily against the background of the history of the Ulster Presbyterians in this period. They appear to go full circle, from being fervent Irish nationalists and separatists, to being staunchly patriotic servants of the Crown.

ADRIAN RICE, 'The Lonely Rebellion of William Drennan', The Poet's Place, 1991

THE ARIANS, AS THEY WERE TERMED, though many of them were in no sense Arians but Presbyterians who held that subscription to a creed was contrary to the tenets of their faith ... found in Henry Montgomery, the pastor of Dunmurry, a leader who equalled Cooke in his genius for debate, and surpassed him as a master of stately eloquence. The rivals, who for three years fought battle after battle in the church courts, had in their teens been fellow students at Glasgow University, but even then a wide gap divided them. Cooke's political creed, according to himself, was fixed by the sight of the soldiers burning a neighbour's house in 1798, and fixed in opposition to what he loved to call the 'pernicious principles' of the French Revolution. 'Atheism and infidelity,' his biographer states, 'were boldly avowed by the leaders of the United Irishmen, while the loyalists were in general orthodox.' Montgomery, on the other hand, always declared that 'the Rebellion was in its origin, and almost to its end, an Ulster Rebellion and a Presbyterian Rebellion.' House-burning had also its effect on Montgomery's principles, though, unlike Cooke, he did not learn at the expense of a neighbour. After the battle of Antrim his father's house was first looted and then fired by Orange yeomen, and the whole Montgomery family was left with nothing but the clothes they stood in as a punishment for 'merely asserting', as Montgomery wrote half a century afterwards, 'those ordinary human rights and self-evident principles of government, whose advocacy has since commanded the applause of senates, and secured the respect of the world.'

While Cooke was never weary of sounding a call to arms against what he described as 'fierce democracy on the one hand and more terrible Popery on the other', Montgomery was an avowed democrat, and so strenuous a supporter of the Catholic claims that at a meeting in favour of emancipation held in Donegall Street Chapel, Belfast, in 1829, he addressed the gathering from the altar with the Catholic Bishop standing by his side. In returning thanks for the welcome accorded to him, Montgomery expressed a sentiment which, had it been made a rule of action by those in authority, might have changed the whole history of Ireland. 'When even the expression of common sympathy,' he said, 'produces such a demonstration of grateful and kindly feelings, it ought to be a lesson to our legislators, and prove to them what they might expect from the Irish people if they treated them as justice and sound policy would dictate.'

JAMES WINDER GOOD, *Ulster and Ireland*, 1919

EXTREMES OF PARTY FEELING were particularly distasteful to him, for his generous large-heartedness cared for everyone's welfare, whatever their creed or class. His children were taught to look on exhibitions of party bigotry, on either side, with impartial disapproval. To heal the wounds of Ireland and repair her waste places was his dearest wish.

The scheme of National Education warmly supported by John Bright and other friends of Ireland pleased him much. Children of Protestants and Catholics, mingling together in school and playground from earliest years, would not, it seemed, continue the bitter animosities which divided their fathers. He was delighted to see among the first commissioners the name of Dr Whately, Archbishop of Dublin, united with that of Dr Murray, Roman Catholic Archbishop and Primate. During the time that this act was in force an unmistakeable increase of reciprocity and friendliness was, in his opinion, to be seen.

The removal of political disabilities from Catholics had brought him lively satisfaction, and the Land Acts of 1871 and 1881 he also regarded as beneficial, although he as landlord suffered thereby. The friendly feeling that seemed everywhere to develop in the years between 1846 and 1886 was very encouraging and gratifying to his intense love of Ireland.

CHARLOTTE FELL SMITH, *James Nicholson Richardson of Bessbrook*, 1925

IRISH PRIMARY EDUCATION became an affair of strictly denominational schools. The clergy, as managers, appointed teachers whom they could trust, chose books that they regarded as safe, and created the atmosphere they wanted. The last point gained was the right to teach history. For a long time the commissioners held out, refusing to allow history of any sort to be taught in Irish schools. Now history is taught; but it is the managers, that is to say the clergy, who decide what the history is to be. The result is a *reductio ad absurdum* of the position of the commissioners. An inspector, highly qualified and appointed to keep the commissioners informed of the progress of education, visits a school in the course of the morning. He discovers that the children know all about King William's battle at the Boyne and thoroughly understand that the victory won there was the foundation of the civil and religious liberty of Ireland. He reports that the teaching of history in this school is very good. In the afternoon he visits another school and discovers that the children there know all about the battle of the Boyne, thoroughly understanding that the unfortunate defeat of King James riveted the chains of the oppressor on the limbs of Ireland and commenced an era of savage persecution. He reports that the teaching of history in this school is very good. The commissioners read the reports with gratification and pay the salaries of both the teachers.

For a long time everybody in Ireland was entirely satisfied with this system.

GEORGE A. BIRMINGHAM, *An Irishman Looks at His World*, 1919

T HE TRUTH OF THE MATTER is ... that Ulster Protestants and Ulster Catholics are, to use an expressive phrase, very much of a muchness. There are broad-minded Protestants and broad-minded Catholics, bigoted Protestants and bigoted Catholics. There are cruel Protestants and cruel Catholics, gentle Protestants and gentle Catholics. There are Protestants who would like to see all the Catholics swept out of the country, and Catholics who would like to see Protestants swept out of the country; but, to match them, there are Protestants who want to live in peace and friendship with their Catholic neighbours, and Catholics who want to live in peace and friendship with their Protestant neighbours. For every bigot or black sheep you find on one side, you will, as an English commentator on Ireland would say, find two on the other. Protestant and Catholic have been looking at each other more closely and honestly of late, and have each been amazed to discover how human the other is. There may never have been a more bitter sort of bigotry in Ulster than at the present moment, but, on the other hand, never was so fine and general a spirit of broad-mindedness to be found. Middle-aged – or rather century-old – bigotry is uttering its last cry, and it is a loud and strident cry, so loud indeed that many people are unable to hear beyond it the more pleasant and gathering voices of the peace-bringers.

ROBERT LYND, *Home Life in Ireland*, 1909

O N THE MORNING OF 4 FEBRUARY 1896, during the demolition of the old White Linen Hall, there was discovered at the north-east corner by a Mr Robert Girvan, overseer of the work, the foundation stone of the old building, who had it removed to the Town Hall.

Under a plate concealing a cavity in the stone was found a bottle or glass tube containing a copy of resolutions passed at a meeting of the representatives of 143 corps of Volunteers of the province of Ulster, held at Dungannon on Friday, 15 February 1782, Colonel William Irvine in the chair; also the copy of the resolutions passed by a largely attended meeting of the inhabitants of Belfast in the Town Square on 7 March 1782, Thomas Sinclair, esq., in the chair, approving of those adopted at the meeting in Dungannon, and a copy of the bill relating to Ireland, which had received the royal assent on Thursday, 24 April 1783.

A large sheet of notepaper on which was written the following, was also discovered in the bottle:

Belfast. 28 April, 1783. These papers were deposited underneath this building by John McClean and Robert Bradshaw, with an intent that if they should hereafter be found, they may be authentic information to posterity by the firmness and unanimity of the Irish

Volunteers, this kingdom – long oppressed – was fully and completely emancipated.

If in future times there should be an attempt made to encroach upon the liberties of this country, let our posterity with admiration look up to the glorious example of their forefathers, who at this time formed an army independent of government, unpaid and self-appointed, of eighty thousand men, the discipline, order, and regularity of which army was looked upon by Europe with wonder and astonishment.

We took this method of enclosing these papers in a glass tube, hermetically sealed, as (in our opinion) the most durable that could be desired.

And exactly one hundred and ten years after that paper was written, in the year 1893, Mr A. J. Balfour stood outside the old Linen Hall to watch the march past of the eighty thousand Ulstermen of that day who 'would not have Home Rule'.

CATHAL O'BYRNE, *As I Roved Out*, 1946

'THE COUNTRY'S IN A QUEER STATE,' said Moyne. 'I don't understand what's going on.'

'If the people have got rifles,' I said, 'they're not likely to give them up because you and Babberly tell them to.'

'Babberly says there's nothing in it,' said Moyne, doubtfully, 'and her ladyship agrees with him. She thinks it's simply a dodge of the Government to spike our guns.'

It is curious that Moyne cannot help talking about guns, even when he's afraid that somebody or other may really have one. He might, under the circumstances, have been expected to use some other metaphor. 'Cook our goose', for instance, would have expressed his meaning quite well, and there would have been no suggestion of gunpowder about the words.

'I don't see,' I said, 'how you can very well do anything when both Lady Moyne and Babberly are against you.'

'I can't – I can't, of course. And yet, don't you know, Kilmore, I don't know –'

I quite appreciated Moyne's condition of mind. I myself did not know. I felt nearly certain that Bob Power had been importing arms in the *Finola*. I suspected that Crossan and others had been distributing them. And yet it seemed impossible to suppose that ordinary people, the men I lunched with in the club, like Malcolmson, the men who touched their hats to me on the road, like Rose's freckly faced lover, the quiet-looking people whom I saw at railway stations, that those people actually meant to shoot off bullets out of guns with the intention of killing other people. Of course, long ago, this sort of killing was done, but then, long ago, men believed things which we do not believe now. Perhaps I ought to say which I do not believe now. Malcolmson may still believe in what he calls 'civil and religious liberty'. Crossan certainly applies his favourite epithet to the 'Papishes'. He may conceivably think that they would put him on a rack if they got the chance. If he believed that he might fight. And yet the absurdity of the thing prevents serous consideration.

GEORGE A. BIRMINGHAM, *The Red Hand of Ulster*, 1912

OVER THE FLAT HEDGE-BOUNDED FIELDS of north County Dublin they rushed, along the sandy coast of grassy Meath, and into the historic town of Drogheda.

'The river Boyne,' said McGurk to Willoughby.

Willoughby rushed eagerly to look out of the carriage window, but he seemed disappointed somehow.

'I'd an idea from the newspapers,' he said, 'that all Ireland was camped on opposite sides of the river.'

'The Boyne is a Leinster river,' Bernard explained. 'We're nowhere near Carsonland yet.'

'Oh? I thought it was the frontier,' said Willoughby.

At Portadown they had to change trains, and Willoughby was told he was now genuinely in the 'North-East Corner'. He looked around eagerly for signs of Ulster Volunteers, but none were forthcoming.

'This is very disappointing,' he said, 'I thought the country was on the verge of civil war and I haven't seen as much as a bayonet.'

'Our military activities are carried on at night,' said Bernard. 'During the day we have our work to do. If you want to see what Ulster Volunteers are like, just look round you. That porter there is probably one.'

Willoughby became round-eyed with interest.

'Yes. He has a decidedly fanatical look,' he said. (The porter was as commonplace a porter as could be found.)

'Say, Bernard,' whispered McGurk, 'this English friend of yours is an awful eejit.'

The next change was at Strabane, where they took advantage of an hour's wait to have lunch, and Willoughby had his first experience of an Irish country hotel.

'Do you long for the inn at Deeping? ' said Bernard, as Willoughby picked a hair out of the butter.

'Oh, no,' replied Willoughby politely. 'Everything's very charming.'

On the light railway they leaped the Bann and plunged into the wildness of the Western World. The green pastures of Leinster and south-east Ulster were far behind them and they rattled through a land of bog and rocks. On and on they clattered and jolted, winding along in a serpentine track, now shrieking through rocky cuttings, now puffing peacefully over the open bog. Station after station fled past them, mere platforms of wood standing out of the heathery waste. To their left Errigal, grim and menacing, towered over his brother mountains. To their right stretched the flat surface of the bog, weird and lifeless in the gloaming.

'By the way, Jack,' said Bernard, 'you must remember that you're entering a democratic country. The people don't touch their hats to squire here. They reserve that for the priest. You must shake hands with them naturally and as a matter of course: not in a patronising way like a lord of the manor visiting a faithful retainer, or like a parliamentary candidate at an election, but as one gentleman with another. If you go into a shop to buy a threepenny packet of cigarettes, you must shake hands first and talk about the news or the weather, and if they give you sixpence worth of chocolate along with your cigarettes, remember it's a present and take it as such.'

'How delightfully Irish!' said Willoughby.

A few minutes later they alighted on the wind-blown platform of Cashelnagore, and, having deposited their baggage in a donkey-cart, cycled the three or four miles to the little village of Gortahork, at the principal hotel of which they had engaged rooms.

EIMAR O'DUFFY, *The Wasted Island*, 1923

T HE ULSTER CRISIS WAS UNDOUBTEDLY an influence, though not the only one, on the events leading to insurrection in Dublin in 1916. When, in later years, Eoin MacNeill was asked what the decisive factor was in bringing about the Easter Rising, he replied with one word: 'Carson'. Yet to suggest, as is so frequently done, that the Ulster unionists by their determination to stay British, in some way unleashed the violence that was to ravage Ireland between 1916 and 1923 is to misread the varied and complex factors which brought that conflict about, and to suggest that the history of Ireland since 1800 was other than it was.

The blood sacrifice of 1916, rejected at the time by the vast majority of the Irish population, is now seen as one of the birth-pangs of modern Ireland. It brought forward the last revolution of the period, the astonishingly swift transfer of sympathy from John Redmond and the Irish Parliamentary Party to Sinn Féin, which took place between the military executions of 1916 and the general election of 1918.

A.T.Q. STEWART, *The Shape of Irish History*, 2001

COMMENTATORS ON THE ULSTER QUESTION have for the most part failed to emphasise – what seems to me to be a fact of vital importance – that during the progress of the Home Rule controversy the Unionist case has been twisted right round. In its early stages Sir Edward Carson was making the sort of speeches that Fitzgibbon and Castlereagh would have applauded to the echo; before the end his denial of the right of British statesmen to intervene in Ulster was uncompromising and passionate enough to have satisfied Wolfe Tone himself. The change of attitude was, I admit, largely unconscious, but this so far from minimising its significance accentuates it by its revelation of a woeful lack of coherent logic and clear thinking about fundamental issues. The Ulsterman sees himself, and insists vehemently on others seeing him, as a plain blunt man who likes fair-dealing and hates manoeuvres, and who may be trusted, whether he is right or wrong, to drive straight forward through all obstacles to his goal. In politics, however, his weakness is to assume that because he is convinced his ends are right, he is at liberty to justify them by arguments that are mutually destructive, and secure them by every means legal or illegal.

JAMES WINDER GOOD, *Ulster and Ireland*, 1919

from AUTUMN JOURNAL

And I remember, when I was little, the fear
   Bandied among the servants
That Casement would land at the pier
   With a sword and a horde of rebels;
And how we used to expect, at a later date,
   When the wind blew from the west, the noise of shooting
Starting in the evening at eight
   In Belfast in the York Street district;
And the voodoo of the Orange bands
   Drawing an iron net through darkest Ulster,
Flailing the limbo lands –
   The linen mills, the long wet grass, the ragged hawthorn.
And one read black where the other read white, his hope
   The other man's damnation:
Up the Rebels, To Hell with the Pope,
   And God Save – as you prefer – the King or Ireland. ...

LOUIS MacNEICE, *Poems 1925–1948*, 1949

'I'VE NEVER BEEN IN BELFAST,' said Bernard, 'but from all I hear of them the people there must be a hard bigoted lot.'

'No,' said McCall. 'They're mad and ignorant on politics and religion, but otherwise they're just the same as the rest of the Irish – a decent, kind-hearted, hospitable people. Of course their politics are absurd. I had to leave Belfast on that account. I was never more than six months in a job before they found out I was a Nationalist and gave me the sack. And the whole thing's just sheer downright ignorance. In their schools they never learn a word about their own country. They know they're Irish and not English just as they know they're male and not female, or vice versa, but it's a matter of no importance. The only history they learn is English history and they think King William founded the Orange Order.'

'Didn't he?' asked Bernard.

'Not he. It was founded in 1795 as a political expedient. I once told an Orangeman that and he wouldn't believe me. I showed it to him in a book and he wouldn't believe the book; and it was written by an Orangeman. That's the Ulsterman all over. He knows what's so and nothing will ever convince him he's wrong ... But don't think the Ulsterman is loyal to England. He supports the Union because he's under the delusion that it makes Ulster prosperous. If he ever finds out his mistake – and some day he will – he'll cut the cable quicker than any of you. He's a businessman you know and sentiment counts for nothing with him.'

'The Ulster Volunteer movement shows how little he cares for parliament,' put in Bernard.

'Quite so ... Lord, what a mess the Irish party have made of things. Why on earth didn't they set out to convert Ulster instead of the English? The goodwill of the English doesn't matter a damn, whereas a united Ireland could bully the British government into anything. Instead of that they went abusing their possible friends, and conciliating their historic enemy. It'll serve them right if they get a kick up the backside for their trouble.'

EIMAR O'DUFFY, *The Wasted Island*, 1923

SOME DAY A [DEMOCRATIC] SPIRIT will come up North and the workers of the north-east corner will get tired of being led by the nose by a party captained by landlords and place-hunting lawyers. Here, in north-east Ulster, the ascendancy party does not even need to pretend to be favourable to the aspirations of Labour; it is openly hostile and the inculcation of slavish sentiments is a business it never neglects. In that is the main difference between the parties – the growth of a rebellious spirit amongst the Nationalist democracy has compelled the Home Rule politicians to pay court to Labour, to assume a virtue even when they have it not, but the lack of such a spirit in this section has enabled the Orange leaders to openly flout and antagonise the Labour movement.

But times change and we change with them. North-east Ulster democracy is awakening also, and we long for and will see in Belfast movements of Labour as great as, if not greater than any of which Dublin can boast.

In that glorious day Ulster will fight, and Ulster will be right, but all those leaders who now trumpet forth that battle cry will then be found arrayed against the Ulster democracy.

> JAMES CONNOLLY (1913), *Socialism and Nationalism:*
> *A Selection from the Writing of James Connolly*, 1948

ALL THAT HAS HAPPENED since August 1914 has not opened the eyes of the champions of Unionist Ulster to the truth about their position. To many of them the declaration of war came as a positive anti-climax; and it was with something like disgust they realised that, having set the stage for Armageddon on the Lagan and the Foyle, the real Armageddon was to be decided on the banks of the Marne and the Somme. Not a few of them indeed still cherish the hope that Sir Edward Carson will once again establish his headquarters at Craigavon ringed about by the bayonets of his faithful Volunteers; and that the remnant of the Ulster Division will joyfully apply at home the lessons they learned in France by constructing a Siegfried Line across the Gap of the North. As one of their poets has sung:

> Ulster will strike for England,
> And England will not forget

and what England must not forget is that Ulster's price for helping 'to make the world safe for democracy' is the perpetuation of a system which, even its defenders are constrained to admit, is the antithesis of democratic rule.

> JAMES WINDER GOOD, *Ulster and Ireland*, 1919

DURING THE AUTUMN [OF 1921] the Nationalists of the six-county area sent deputation after deputation to Dail Eireann to explain how terrible would be their future if their fellow countrymen accepted terms which would leave them at the mercy of the northern government. A deputation from Belfast, received by the President and cabinet on September 28th, declared: 'We will refuse to co-operate with any Partition Parliament or any Government other than the Government of the whole Irish nation.'

Tyrone and Fermanagh, with their Nationalist majorities, had, in every election since Partition became an issue, voted against separation from the rest of Ireland. The people of Fermanagh, their delegates declared, 'would never consent to be bartered and sold' but would do everything in their power to assert their right to self-determination.

The result of the London negotiations was nowhere awaited with more intense hopes and fears than in the six counties of the north-east.

DOROTHY MACARDLE, *The Irish Republic*, 1937

WHEN THE NEWS CAME THROUGH that Michael Collins had been shot dead at Beal na mBlath, she was filled with mixed emotions. The family at first had supported Home Rule, but latterly they had become very much involved in the War of Independence. Her views coincided with those of her brothers and sisters – but the fact that she was a widow with five young daughters, meant that she could only take a limited part in any political activity.

She read a lot and followed the reports of the peace negotiations taking place in London. When the Treaty was signed it seemed to her that a victory had been won, and in celebration she hung a large tricolour from her bedroom window. Her brothers sent word to her: 'Get that flag in to hell's gates, we've been sold down the river.'

That was December 1921 and history records the events that took place in the following nine months, leading up to that fatal day at Beal na mBlath.

Sarah's mind returned again and again to the September of 1921, when she and her brothers and sister had attended an open-air rally at Armagh, at which Michael Collins was the principal speaker. It wasn't often that she managed to enjoy a day out, and this was an occasion she'd really looked forward to. She was not disappointed. Her brothers had been appointed to act as Collins's bodyguards, and as a consequence she and her sister got quite close to him. So close in fact that her sister was able to take a photograph with the box camera she had brought along.

She was immensely struck by his appearance. Not only was he handsomer than she'd expected, but he looked far too young for all the responsibility placed on him. His bravery and his clever exploits were known to her, and had been keenly followed by her and her family throughout the war.

She was transfixed when he spoke, especially when he mentioned events in the North and pledged his loyalty to the beleaguered northern people.

Just to have seen him was a wonderful experience, she had often said: but how had it all gone so terribly wrong? How did he find himself in that situation, putting his signature to a Treaty that had, as her brothers said, 'sold us down the river'? She had felt so let down – but now that he was dead, shot by his former comrades as was assumed, she was distraught.

When the northern state came into existence she was utterly opposed to it, and supported her brothers who had joined the anti-Treaty forces – even though she knew that the exclusion of the six northern counties was not considered an important issue in the dispute between the pro- and anti-Treaty factions that led ultimately to the Civil War. She also believed that Michael Collins had not broken the pledge he made at Armagh, to stand by the people of the North.

Over the next few years, all her brothers were taken into custody by the forces of the new northern state. Four of them ended up on the prison ship *Argenta*, which was moored in Belfast Lough just off the coast of Larne. One brother, Gerry, never recovered from the tuberculosis he contracted on board that ship.

The photograph taken in Armagh on that memorable day in September 1921 was eventually presented to the National Gallery of Ireland in Dublin where it hangs to this day.

MARGARET GATT, 'Recollections of her Grandmother Sarah Brady', 2004

A S THE CITY WHERE THE HEROIC FORM of *Titanic* was raised, Belfast repays a closer look. Belfast, after all, is where the international cultural complex that *Titanic* composes – as well as the physical vessel – takes its rise. Moreover, that complex has its local version in Ulster and that local version is a huge but neglected component of Irish culture.

There are internal Irish reasons for this neglect, having to do with the kind of culture that is regarded as authentically Irish: up to now, the applied science culture of the Ulster-Scots has seemed to disqualify itself. There are also reasons indigenous to both Britain and Ireland, having to do with the kind of activity that is regarded as authentically cultural: up to now, industrialism (even when it has produced impressive collective artifacts) has seemed to disqualify itself. Besides, once the heroic days of steamships were over, Belfast declined into an unremarkable and unremarked provincialism wearing only (to adapt James Joyce) the mask of a capital.

The political situation, too – the constitutional status of the region of Ireland (Northern Ireland) of which Belfast became capital in 1921 – prevented Belfast from keeping or asserting the cultural potency of Liverpool and Glasgow. For complicated political reasons, Northern Ireland was complicit in its own low profile. Meanwhile, who – including its builders – wished to draw too much attention to *Titanic*, by the 1920s a notorious ship that elicited ambiguous pride and embarrassment in the city that built her? The decades' long official reticence about the ship began at least as early as March 4th, 1913 when the White Star Line wrote to Father Browne when they learned that he was presenting an illustrated lecture to appreciative audiences. They requested him to desist 'as we do not wish the memory of this calamity to be perpetuated'.

After the civil unrest in Ulster began around a quarter century ago, *Titanic* sank deeper not just in the Ulster mind but also in the minds of those abroad fascinated by *Titanic* yet disinclined to show interest in a city by then associated solely and cruelly with low-intensity civil war. Only recently has Belfast surfaced as a city worth celebrating as the home of *Titanic* and − I am at pains to add ... − of other vast products of modernity. Indeed, it seems that the ship's builders, Harland & Wolff, were for some time loath to associate themselves with research or commemoration, for understandable reasons. But perhaps the decline of shipbuilding in Belfast, the historical nature of the *Titanic* event, its inescapable popularity and current assumption into commemorative culture, have all dissipated corporate fear that association with tragedy is bad for business. Today *Titanic* is good for anybody's business.

Yet all along, *Titanic* worked its passage in Ulster culture and the Ulster psyche, sometimes in plain sight, at other times clandestinely.

JOHN WILSON FOSTER, *The Titanic Complex*, 1997

VI:

I've never been strong on religion, I'm all for people worshippin' as they please. But I've never had to pretend to agree with Jack's politics. I'm with him all the way on that.

ROSE:

No you're not, Vi.

VI:

We need somebody strong to speak up for us. To tell the British government that we won't be handed over to a foreign country without a fight. That we won't be patted on the head and complimented on our loyalty and patriotism through two world wars, but now it's all over, thank you very much, and your loyalty and your patriotism are an embarrassment to us and our American and European allies. We are bein' sold down the river because England doesn't need us no more. An' what we need now is somebody to shout our cause an' our rights from the rooftops. We are as much a part of Great Britain as Liverpool or Manchester or Birmingham. How would they feel if they were suddenly told that the Dublin government was to have a say in the runnin' of their country?

ROSE:

A third of the population of Northern Ireland were denied a say in how their country should be run.

VI:

> I've never been opposed to the Catholics havin' their say. Doin' their part. As long as they are prepared to do it with us and not against us. But they've made their position very clear. They don't want to share power. They want to take it.

ROSE:

> And the Unionists want to hold on to it. Absolutely. They have to. They will never agree to power sharing because they can't. Northern Ireland was created as a Protestant State for a Protestant People, and if they agree to power sharing, they'll have agreed to do away with the very reason for the state's existence. Don't you see that?

VI:

> And isn't the South a Catholic State for a Catholic People! You only see what suits you, Rose. And don't try to tell me it would suit you to live in a country where priests make the laws and tell you how to vote from the altar. Where things like contraception and divorce are a legal and a mortal sin. It's written into their Catholic Constitution. You're a great one for women's rights. We wouldn't have many rights in a United Ireland!

ROSE:

> We won't have many rights here either, if Jack and his gang get the Independent Ulster they want. Their right-wing Protestant Church is in total agreement with the right-wing Catholic Church on issues like divorce and abortion, on a woman's right to be anything other than a mother or a daughter or a sister or a wife. Any woman outside that set of rules is the Great Whore of Babylon. One of the first things they'll do if they get their Independent State of Ulster is vote that into their Protestant Constitution.

VI:

> So, the choice is the devil or the deep blue sea, is that what you're sayin'? Well, in that case I'll stay with the devil I know ... I don't see why we have to change anything. We were all gettin' on all right before the Civil Rights started the violence. We never had no quarrel with our Catholic neighbours.

ROSE:

> There was one Catholic family in this street, and they were intimidated out in 1972.

CHRISTINA REID, *The Belle of Belfast City*, 1989

IT IS ALL VERY WEARISOME and very perplexing: this parade of riots and speeches and speeches and riots going back beyond the making of the

Border, beyond the long three-tiered debate on the question of Home Rule, back to the agrarian disturbances of the eighteenth century and the gangs running in the night to burn houses and evict or murder the people who lived in the houses. No country could be proud of that chapter in its history. No movement should be proud of that black undercurrent to its aspirations and ideals. No citizens could congratulate themselves on the uncouth, vicious thing that comes to life at intervals to burn and kill and destroy. The remedy is in the power of the young people of Belfast; and there are signs that a minority of those young people, Catholic and Protestant, are realising their responsibility and their power. If you know the people of those noisy, humpy streets, between the high cloud-covered mountains and the flat arm of the sea, you will feel among them the movement of ideas, new ideas, generous ideas, constructive ideas; as energetic as the inspiration that built the factories, deepened the river, marked the black water with the shadows of tall cranes and leaning gantries. But these new ideas are more humane, more interested in the things of the spirit that the big men of Belfast never seem to have appreciated very well. Somewhere among them may be the inspiration that will end forever the bitter legend. Maybe, too, the last five years of cosmopolitanism may make the air of Belfast a little more lenient to democratic lungs that can settle differences by reasonable argument and without the assistance of the Islandmen. For the whole world has suffered and the whole world needs peace; and the spirit in the hearts of the young, and the spirit that is above and around the souls of men, cries out for peace, for the burying and forgetting of ancient differences.

BENEDICT KIELY, *Counties of Contention*, 1945

TRIAL RUNS

WELCOME HOME YE LADS OF THE EIGHTH ARMY
There must be some defiance in it because it was
painted along the demesne wall, a banner headline over
the old news of REMEMBER 1690 and NO SURRENDER, a great
wingspan of lettering I hurried under with the messages.

In a khaki shirt and brass-buckled belt, a demobbed
neighbour leaned against our jamb. My father jingled silver
deep in both pockets and laughed when the big clicking
rosary beads were produced.

'Did they make a papish of you over there?'

'O damn the fear! I stole them for you, Paddy, off
the pope's dresser when his back was turned.'

'You could harness a donkey with them.'

Their laughter sailed above my head, a hoarse clamour,
two big nervous birds dipping and lifting, making trial runs
over a territory.

SEAMUS HEANEY, Stations, 1975

THE ROAD FROM NEWRY down 'the legend-lighted vale' brings us soon to Warrenpoint, a town which is half a large-squared Ulster seaport and half a holiday resort. Hither come train loads of trippers from the industrial North, and you will see the Protestant factory workers buying rosaries and holy pictures at Calvary to take home as souvenirs to their Catholic fellow-workers: see that and rejoice, if you have believed hitherto that Protestant and Catholic cannot do a civil deed to one another.

AODH DE BLÁCAM, The Black North, 1938

IT IS PROBABLY INEVITABLE THAT ANY GROUP or class which has controlled government continuously for more than fifty years, which has had a specially privileged position in the country for centuries, should feel endowed with a divine right to govern and should resent any suggestion that the power and the privileges which have been at their exclusive disposal for so long should be shared with those who have been outside and often resentful of their special position.

It would however be wrong to leave the impression that over the past sixty years one-third of the people of Northern Ireland have spent their time brooding on these matters. Many, many people on either side of the 'religious divide' have, without any inhibitions or reservations, established the most cordial (what in other places would be called 'normal') relationships with their neighbours. If divisive issues impinged on their thinking, they managed to shut their minds to allegations of past wrongs and to discard inherited prejudices.

Unhappily recent events have revived mistrust and hostility. Now, when solutions are being sought, it is as well to understand that the roots of the evils that beset us lie deep in history.

PATRICK SHEA, Voices and the Sound of Drums, 1981

IN PRACTICE WHAT DEVELOPED in Northern Ireland, from 1921 to 1969, was an institutionalised caste system, with the superior caste – Protestants – in permanent and complete control of government, and systematically ensuring special privileges for its members in relation to local franchise, police, jobs and housing. This was most flagrant in the case of Northern Ireland's second city, Derry. The population of Derry was two-thirds Catholic, but the City Council, through gerrymandering, was two-thirds Protestant, and used its powers predictably. All this developed without significant interference from Britain, up to 1969. A convention even grew up that Northern Ireland internal affairs should not be discussed at Westminster. In general, the relation of Northern Ireland to Westminster came to resemble that of an American Southern State to Washington between the end of Reconstruction and 1957.

How could the very specific prohibition of religious discrimination in the Government of Ireland Act, be reconciled with Northern Ireland practice?

The official answer – until the Cameron Commission *Disturbances in Northern Ireland* … in 1969 officially acknowledged facts that had long been notorious – was that there was no religious discrimination. This seemed like a plain lie, but it was not as simple as that. Defenders of the status quo would acknowledge, in private, that there was discrimination, but would deny sincerely enough that it was religious discrimination. No one it was argued, was imposing any 'disability or disadvantage, on account of religious belief etc.' The *religious* beliefs of Catholics were their own affair. Their *political* allegiance and intentions were another matter. Politically their allegiance went to neither of the lawfully constituted parliaments, in Stormont and in Westminster, but to 'a foreign country': the Free State (Eire, the Republic). As a community, the Catholics aimed at the destruction of Northern Ireland, and the further disruption of the United Kingdom. Some of them were trying to accomplish this by force and violence, and the rest of them were either sympathetic to this endeavour, or – at best – unwilling to co-operate with the authorities in bringing it to an end. In these circumstances, the Northern Ireland government could not trust the Catholic community – as a social and political grouping, not on theological grounds – and was fully justified in taking such precautions, in relation to that community, as the security of the State might require. And the Northern Ireland government, with its intimate knowledge of the local scene, was in a better position than the British Government to say what these precautions should be.

CONOR CRUISE O'BRIEN, *States of Ireland*, 1972

IN NORTHERN IRELAND CATHOLICS are blacks who happen to have white skins. This is not a truth. It is an oversimplification and too facile an analogy. But it is a better oversimplification than that which sees the struggle and conflict in Northern Ireland in terms of religion. Catholics and Protestants are not quarrelling with one another (most of them) because of matters of theology or faith. There is no burning urge on either side to convert the other to the one true faith, nor does a member of one side strike a member of the other on the head with a club in the hope that he will thereby be purged of his theological errors and become a better candidate for heaven.

The Northern Ireland problem is a colonial problem, and the 'racial' distinction (and it is actually imagined as racial) between the colonists and the natives is expressed in terms of religion. It goes perhaps somewhat deeper than that; for it is necessary to maintain the distinction in order to maintain the colony as a colony. It is true that the colonizing of Northern Ireland took place a long time ago; it is true too that there was a time when it seemed that distinctions might be merged in a happy integration of the descendants of settlers with the descendants of natives, but for historical reasons this tendency was reversed almost two centuries ago, and it has always since seemed to be to the advantage of somebody to keep Ulster divided.

LIAM DE PAOR, *Divided Ulster*, 1970

IT IS A TRUISM THAT NORTHERN IRELAND has long had a divided community. The reasons for this division are rooted in the long sequence of historical events connecting the destinies of Ireland and Great Britain. However those events may be interpreted, they do demonstrate with absolute clarity the fact that Irish problems are deep-seated and not amenable to facile external solutions, however well intentioned. When, by an irony of history, the one area of Ireland which had consistently resisted home rule was the only part left to operate a home rule parliament, it was unfortunate but perhaps inevitable that opinion polarized on a religious basis. This polarization tended to push both sides into extreme attitudes.

TERENCE O'NEILL, *The Times*, 28 April 1967

BE THE EN' OF A YEAR in which a tried out twenty or more dead-en' jobs, a was fast becomin' the most spectacularly unsuccessful person in the whole of Belfast (that is, if ye don't count the wile shockin' big important high-up man be the name of the Reverent Ian Paisley that a nearly had the pleasure of meetin' on the day a done me Protestant day's work).

Paisley was bein' more unsuccessful than me on account of the fact that he was tryin' te stap some students outa Queen's University from goin' aroun' way placards demandin' that Catholics be given basic civil rights. Ivery time he tried te stap them he only made things worse for himsel' because the newspapers started te come along, an' the TV way their cameras, te take pictures of the students peacefully marchin', an' the wile shockin' big important high-up man shoutin' things at them about the scarlet harlot of Rome, which was wan of the nicer names he had for the Pope.

In no time at all the newspaper headlines were fulla nothin' but the protestin' students, an' iverybody in Northern Ireland was talkin' about them, an' dependin' on whichiver foot they happened te dig way (Catholics believe that Protestants dig way the wrong foot), sayin' that the students were the divil himsel' or god's only answer te all the problems in the land.

For a wheen of months te begin way the only people that went out marchin' were the students themsel's an' a wheen of the lecturers outa Queen's University, but as people listened more te the things that they were sayin', ordinary people started te join in too, for the students were callin' for the en' of discrimination, sayin' that iverybody should have a right te a house an' a vote an' a dasent job regardless of what their religion happened te be. They said that Stormont was a Protestant parliament for a Protestant people, an' that for fifty years, Catholics had been treated as second-class citizens.

Well, when this news broke, a lot of ordinary people were surprised te learn that they had been citizens all their lives, an' not only citizens, but second-class citizens too at that. My god, they were sayin' te wan another, te think that all this time we have been only wan step down from the tap an' didn't know it. They were delighted so they took te the streets in their droves, an' a went way them.

FRANCES MOLLOY, *No Mate for the Magpie*, 1985

AMONG THE YOUNGER PEOPLE, sectarian feeling in the North is tending to die out. A new generation is growing up which, in the middle and upper classes, could be said to be a sort of *New Statesman-Spectator*-reading youth (though I don't think the upper classes read anything other than *Home Fixtures* and recipes for Irish coffee) and among these people it's beginning to be not quite respectable to be anti-Catholic. At the last election, an Independent Labour man would have been elected in West Belfast, where there is heavy unemployment, if it hadn't been for the intervention of a third, Sinn Fein, candidate. And Queen's University last year elected a young lady barrister who stood in the Liberal interest and roundly beat the official Unionist candidate. So there's a wind of change up there too that Mr Macmillan might take note of also.

The Protestant worker, when he's unemployed – which he is frequently – has the British Health Service and other social welfare benefits to fall back on. He can't be blamed for not caring that the Conservative Party opposed all these measures in the British House of

Commons, and that it was only against their will that the Unionists at Stormont had to enact them also. He's got the benefits and that's all he gives a damn about just now.

BRENDAN BEHAN, Brendan Behan's Island, 1962

THE POSTSCRIPT TO MY BRIEF INTEREST in the professional theatre was a play in which I sought to recreate the Orange and Green conflict which had for generations periodically disfigured our community. My story was set in Belfast, in a district where, after years of peaceful co-existence, sectarian prejudices, inflamed by political agitators, had once more resulted in violence. My play had Catholic gunmen, Protestant assassins, a fanatical Republican orator, a spell-binding hot-gospeller, riots, intimidation and death. I finished a first draft and was well satisfied with its shape and its dramatic value. But it was 1958. Sectarian violence was a thing of the past; we had learned sense. A Belfast audience would not come to the theatre to be reminded of the sins of their forefathers, sins of which, thank God, our community was no longer capable. There was no point in wasting further time on what was clearly a non-starter.

I must have put my unfinished script in the waste-paper basket; over the past eight or nine years I have more than once searched eagerly for it but in vain.

PATRICK SHEA, Voices and the Sound of Drums, 1981

Those Glorious Twelfths

A minute or two later Lady Moyne turned to me with one of her brightest smiles.

'We want you to be with us on the Twelfth,' she said.

In England or Scotland a countess who gives an invitation for 'the Twelfth' is understood to mean the 12th of August, and her guest must be ready to shoot grouse. In north-eastern Ulster 'the Twelfth' meant the 12th of July, and the party, in this case at all events, was likely to end in the shooting of policemen.

GEORGE A. BIRMINGHAM, *The Red Hand of Ulster*

True Orangemen were Blunderbore and Duff,
Each spoke his mind, and each made noise enough ...

WILLIAM ALLINGHAM, from *Laurence Bloomfield in Ireland*

from DOLLY'S BRAE

The Castlewellan Orangemen they were the bravest
   fighters,
And fastest drove the rebels home, a squealing pack of
   blighters;
So now applaud, with one accord, the heroes of the day
Who knocked ten hundred Paypishes right over Dolly's
   Brae.

ANONYMOUS

LAST JULY, THE 'GOVERNMENT' got up a very horrid massacre in the County Down. There was a great Orange procession of armed men: they marched with banners displayed, through a district chiefly inhabited by Catholics; and there, at Dolly's Brae, between Castlewellan and Banbridge, a collision took place, of course: a large force of police and military was present, and they took part, also, of course, with the Orangemen: five or six Catholics were killed, five or six of their houses burned; only one Orangeman or two seriously hurt – and the procession went on its way in triumph. Lord Roden, it appears, had feasted the Orangemen at Bryansford, and excited them with 'loyal' toasts; and afterwards, when informations were sought against the Orange rioters at the hands of the said Lord Roden, presiding at a bench of magistrates, he very properly refused. Very properly, for there is no law in Ireland now. I know no reason why Orangemen should *not* burn Papists' houses now.

JOHN MITCHEL, *Jail Journal*, 1854

I MUST CONFESS THAT FOR THE greater part of the time I lived in Ulster, I was as much prejudiced against Orangeism as were most persons with whom I was acquainted. I had great hopes from an attitude of general toleration, for a cure of most of Ireland's social ills, and I had a feeling that the Orangemen were intolerant. I detested their incessant drumming, and I thought that their mixing of colours in their sashes and banners was absolutely atrocious. (It is from such immaterialities that some people come to conclusions on large questions.) But, in addition, I had noticed a certain element known as 'bumptiousness' on the part of several members of the Order with whom I had come in contact – a certain presumption that all the world would recognise the importance of a person who had risen from the humblest rank to the proud position of Deputy Master of an Orange Lodge in an Ulster village. But now I think that I can estimate such mental and temperamental weakness at their proper value, and to look at the Ulster Orangeman with his resolute face and aggressive drumsticks and feel that he is an important factor in the solution of every question that concerns the future of Ulster. I cannot say that I like him, but he is the last man in the world with whom I should like to be at loggerheads on any matter in which my future might be bound up.

F. FRANKFORT MOORE, *The Truth About Ulster*, 1914

I CAME IN SIGHT OF TANDERAGEE about two o'clock. As it is situated on a hill, I saw it at a considerable distance. The planting of the late General Sparrow's extensive demesne, which seemed to overshadow it, gave it a gay and picturesque appearance. Nor was the spectacle of the interior less riant. Only that the bright green of nature was displaced by the deep orange of party. Tanderagee was a perfect orange grove. The doors and windows were decorated with garlands of the orange lily. The bosoms and heads of the women, and hats and breasts of the men, were equally adorned with this venerated flower. There were likewise a number of orange banners and colours, more remarkable for loyalty than taste or variety, for King William on horseback, as grim as a Saracen on a signpost, was painted or wrought on all of them.

There was much of fancy, however, in the decoration of a lofty arch, which was thrown across the entire street. The orange was gracefully blended with oak leaves, laurels, and roses. Bits of gilded paper, suited to the solemnity, were interwoven with the flowers. I passed, as well as I could, through the crowd assembled under this glittering rainbow, and proceeded to the house of an acquaintance at the upper end of the street. I had purposed spending a day with him, but he was from home. I, therefore, sat half an hour with his lady, and after having taken some refreshment, descended the hill. The people were now dancing. The music was not indifferent. The tune, however, would better have suited a minuet than a country dance. It was the (once in England) popular tune of Lillybullero, better known, in this country, by the affectionate and cheering name, of the Protestant boys.

I stopped an instant, a man came up and presented me a nosegay of orange lilies and roses, bound together – I held it in my hand, but did not put it in my hat, as he expected.

'I am no party man,' I said, 'nor do I ever wear party colours.'

'Well, God bless you, Sir,' he replied, 'whether you do or not.'

JOHN GAMBLE, *A View of Society and Manners in the North of Ireland*, 1813

THE AUGHALEE HEROES
County Down

Ye Protestant heroes of Ireland,
  Give ear to these words I write down,
Concerning those Aughalee heroes
  That marched through the sweet Portydown.

It being the twelfth day of Jú-lie
  Our music of course it did play,
And the Protestant Boys and Boyne Watter
  Were the tunes we played marching away.

Like the sons of King William we marched then,
  Till at length Lurgan Town we did view,
Where the Church it was there decorated
  With Orange and Purple and Blue.

Round its spires our colours were flying,
  Small guns like big cannons did roar;
Long life to those Aughalee Heroes
  For they are the boys we adore.

Captain Black, like a bould Orange hero,
  Came riding down on his grey steed,
And he asked us what number we carried
  And where we meant for to proceed.

We told him the County of Antrim,
  Our number was six thirty-two,
We are the bould Aughalee Heroes
  That the rebels full soon did subdue.

We took off our hats to salute him
  As boldly he bade us march on,
And he rode like a hero before us
  Till we came to the banks of the Bann.

When in Aughalee we arrived safely,
  The whisky did flow like the Rhine;
So long life to those Aughalee Heroes
  For they are the Boys crossed the Boyne.

ANONYMOUS

THERE WAS THEN [I.E. DURING THE 1870S] undoubtedly a better feeling between the two extreme sections than there had been for a long time. Conservative country gentlemen at their convivial entertainments as grand jurors did not rail at their Catholic fellow-subjects as they had been accustomed to do thirty or even twenty years previously. The Charter toast had nearly ceased to be given at such dinners. That celebrated toast was now being regarded as an anachronism. As showing, however, the spirit which animated a large number of Protestant grand jurors against their Catholic fellow-countrymen, this toast may be here given:

To the glorious, pious, and immortal memory of the great and good King William III (not forgetting Oliver Cromwell), who saved us all from popes and Popery, knaves and knavery, slaves and slavery, brass money, and wooden shoes.

And all that refuse to drink this toast, may they be rammed, stammed, crammed, and damned into the great gun of Athlone, to be blown over the hills of damnation. May their teeth be converted into paving stones, to pave the way of the Croppies into hell, and their blood into train oil to light their souls to damnation. May I be at the end of the gun with a fiery flambeau to send them burring round the earth, the moon, the stars, and the sea, like flies round a sugar cask on a hot summer afternoon; may they be blown against the rock of blastation and come down in a shower of innumerable pieces, and may those pieces be picked up and made into sparables to mend the soles of Orangemen's boots to walk on the Twelfth of July.

Such was the Charter toast. From the convivial point of view, it can only be regarded as an elaborate joke. It is certain that the Catholics did not regard it as a joke, but thought it, as it was, offensive and insulting. Though at the time now referred to it still lingered in the memories of many thousands of people, during a later period, notwithstanding that the Home Rule question became very serious, it has not generally been drunk by grand jurors, and by the younger generation of the better classes of Orangemen themselves it has even been considered a mere fabrication, a thing devised by the enemy. But eight-and-twenty years ago the toast was regarded as undoubtedly genuine.

THOMAS MACKNIGHT, *Ulster As It Is*, 1896

SHEEP ON THE HILL OF SLEMISH and swine in the woods were his care. To reach this famous hill, which was called Slieve Mis and is now contracted to Slemish, one goes to Ballymena. I went on July 12th, because I wished to get as near as possible to the mentality of the fifth century. I was in the country of the Picts or Cruithne. Now, these were the people who colonised West Scotland and gave trouble to the garrisons of the Great Wall, for they were terrific fighters ...

They were sent back to Dalaradia from Scotland when Ulster was being planted in the reign of Charles and under the Republic of Cromwell and during the plantation of James. Illiberal notions, and perhaps a change of climate, have made it no longer fashionable to go nakedly depicted, so they wear their colours now outside their clothes; and very beautiful, and striking, if somewhat unvaried, I found them: sashes shaped like the stole of a bishop, but coloured a deep yellow, not exactly of the tone (of that yellow which Friar John acclaimed as 'By St Patrick, the true Irish saffron!' to the discomfiture of Panurge; but an orange dye. Purple stoles or 'sashes', as they are called in Dalaradia, provide a sacerdotal note and relieve any monotony which might otherwise arise from the sameness of the more primitive hue.

The Picts were in full war panoply on July 12th, to commemorate a royal legate who, like St Patrick before him, was confirmed in his mission by the Pope. I saw eighty thousand of them in Belfast, including twelve thousand who had come from the lowlands of Scotland, walking interminably, four deep, behind waggonettes in which sat silver-fringed chieftains with bowler hats. These were the Druids. At intervals of sixty yards or so large pictures were borne aloft on poles fitted to a yard-arm, to which the picture was attached. These were pictures of departed chieftains, some who died in their youth or early middle age. However, all looked mature. Here and there banners depicted a warrior with immense greaves or boots of a dark colour, who sat on a white or unpainted horse which was represented as if in motion. But motion was imparted, even to the picture of the gravest and most ancient of these chieftains painted on the banners, by the standard-bearers, who at intervals indulged in a kind of dance or rhythmic motion which invested what might otherwise have been taken for a grave ceremonial procession with a Bacchanalian character in keeping with that of the musicians, who played on fifes, tin whistles and other wind instruments; some, too short in the breath, used a wind instrument of a different kind – a concertina. All these instruments accompanied the drums, which seemed to be the chief musical factor of the festival: large drums beaten by drumsticks with a ball-like head covered in chamois hide. One or two of the marchers who had not the good fortune to possess a drum twirled drumsticks with amazing dexterity.

OLIVER ST JOHN GOGARTY, *I Follow Saint Patrick*, 1938

THE GREATEST SPECTACULAR EVENT of the Ulster year took place on the Twelfth of July. How wise of William to win his battle at the height of summer, so that festivities in its honour through the centuries after could be held in sunshine and fine weather! How we children waited for that day, and for the day preceding, when the riot of decorations received finishing touches in the streets. A Union Jack hung from every house, and masses of bunting criss-crossed the street from upper windows; crowns and mystical triangles; crescent moons each with seven stars, and flaming suns with faces; the burning bush and David's sling and five stones; streamers; red, white and blue rosettes bloomed in a profuse garden of paper and linen.

Each street vied with the next in the splendour of the main piece, its triumphal arch. Spanning between two houses, bedizened with orange and purple streamers, the arch was studded with pictures of British royalty. The climax of these preliminaries to the Twelfth was the lighting of bonfires. In the manner of the English November Fifth, we had effigies of Catholic leaders, that had sat for weeks on street corners collecting

pennies, and which were solemnly consigned to the flames like Guy
Fawkes.

Before the ashes had lost their red hearts, the drums of Lambeg rolled
like thunder through the summer night and ushered in our Glorious
Twelfth. Day dawned; everyone was up early, ready to go out and see
the sights and watch the traditional 'walk to the field'. It was a public
holiday, as important to us as the Fourth of July in the USA.

ROBERT HARBINSON, *No Surrender*, 1960

from JULY

But evening comes; and dewy hours invite
Stocks and sweet briars to exhale delight.
The cows are milked, pigs fed. Tea crowns the day.
Farls are consumed: the dishes cleared away.
Out to the glistening fields the children go,
To steal a last protracted hour or so;
And William John, the coming Twelfth in mind,
Whitens his gate posts till they'd strike you blind;
Or paints his cart in blue and tangerine;
Or goes, with neighbour men, to view the scene
On which they've planned to raise, they'll all be bound,
The finest arch in twenty townlands round.
The while his Maggie, with beseeming care,
Lifts the regalia from its tissued lair,
Shakes out the fringe, cons every symbol o'er,
And blithely hums 'The Sash my Father Wore'.
Then, as the West with lingering glory fills,
Bats flitter out, and on the chequered hills
The gradual, soft-coloured dusk descends,
You'll hear, from somewhere round the five-road ends
The vehement and all unequal strife
Of three big drums and one tendentious fife
Echo her song, till late-born darkness steep
Village and farm and pasture land in sleep.

NESCA ROBB, *Ards Eclogues*, c. 1974

THE GREAT DRUMS WERE SHALLOW – about a foot in depth – but in
diameter they exceeded three feet. These were the drums from
Lambeg. Lambeg came to mean these great drums or ' Lambegs'. They
were lashed with a cane or headless wand by men in shirt-sleeves, who

were seemingly of a lower caste than the other processionists, for they wore no bowler hats. Yet they were the envy of the onlookers, for theirs, as it were, was the King drum. They held sway over the circular dun of their drums, and they beat the imprisoned wind until it roared and retched in thunder and bellowed back in rage like Typhon under Aetna, or as if the old demons of the land had been caught up, impounded, and battered in the great circular cell. Whack! The Flagellants scourged the drums and they punished themselves in their frenzy. Blood flowed and splashed from bleeding wrists and stained a hand's breadth of the drum where the tendons of the adept came in contact with the rim. Boom! And the jailed giants roared and erupted sound like a volcano. Outside, the careless notes of the fifes and flutes led on. But the Typhonic thunder of the drums drowned all. The fifes wailed like panic-stricken furies from all this Congo of the drums. Boom! Boom! Blood. Boom! The crowd cheers. The waggonettes respond with Druidical dignity. No hats are raised. A halt. Time marked. A whistle. Silence. The kilted pipers come into view, cheeks distended, eyes bulging. Boom! On it moves. For two hours the procession passes. 'No surrender.' It is written on the drum. 'The Ballymena Boys' Brigade.' Boom! 'The Protestants of Portadown', a particular stronghold. Boom! Portadown! Doon! Boom!

OLIVER ST JOHN GOGARTY, *I Follow Saint Patrick*, 1938

TODAY THE TWELFTH BANDS content themselves with march tunes, hymns and innocuous Irish airs. But every now and again the melodious procession is punctuated by the tyrannical thunder of the Lambeg drums. They usually travel in pairs, beaten or *chapped* by shirt-sleeved men, and as they trot past, for the drummers have to take two paces to the bandsman's one, their reverberations drown every other sound, set windows chattering in their frames and print a stunned smile on the face of the onlooker ...

The Lambeg drums are beaten to the rhythm of a hornpipe, reel or jig. If you're inclined to doubt this you might try bawling a hornpipe at the top of your voice the next time you hear them. I can recommend 'The Ha'penny Gate', or better still, 'Willie John's Breakdown'. At one time the drummers were always led and controlled by a fifer. Even if the onlookers never heard him the drummers picked up enough of the shrill notes to help keep them in time. If necessary the fifer danced round and round in front of the drums or walked backwards on the line of march.

SAM HANNA BELL, *Erin's Orange Lily*, 1956

JULY

The drumming started in the cool of the evening, as if the
dome of air were lightly hailed on. But no. The drumming
murmured from beneath that drum.

The drumming didn't murmur, rather hammered. Soundsmiths
found a rhythm gradually. On the far bench of the hills tuns
and ingots were being beaten thin.

The hills were a bellied sound-box resonating, a low
dyke against diurnal roar, a tidal wave that stayed, that
still might open.

Through red seas of July the Orange drummers led a chosen
people through their dream. Dilations and engorgings, contra-
puntal; slashers in shirt-sleeves, collared in the sunset,
policemen flanking them, like anthracite.

The air grew dark, cloud-barred, a butcher's apron. The
night hushed like a white-mothed reach of water, miles down-
stream from the battle, skeins of blood still lazing in the
channel.

And so my ear was winnowed annually.

SEAMUS HEANEY, *Stations*, 1975

PORTADOWN IS WHERE THE ORANGE ORDER was founded in the late
eighteenth century, and it has remained a bastion of Orange bigotry
to this day. When Sir John Lavery wished to paint the strange tribal rite
known as 'The Twelfth', when the Orangemen parade on July 12 with
their drums, bands, sashes, and banners through the streets in celebration
of their domination over the sullen Papists, he chose – appositely – to site
his picture on Portadown's main street. I could have been one of the
small boys on Lavery's canvas, standing back on the edge of a Catholic
street to watch the parade from a safe, discreet distance. Catholic adults
stayed indoors, but even Catholic boys found it hard to resist the appeal
of the bands – accordion, flute, and best of all, the pipes in the 'kilty'
bands. And watching those parades as a very small boy was where I first
encountered a sense of England. The Orange phenomenon might have
been a purely indigenous ingrowth, but its iconography asserted the
might of England. The Union Jack was everywhere; the huge Lambeg
drums which thundered ceaselessly the warning 'Catholics lie down'
proclaimed 'God Save the King' on their gross swollen bellies; the
banners portrayed the crown; on them King William of Orange urged his
white charger across the Boyne to smash King James on them; Queen
Victoria, in full regalia on her throne, held out a Bible to a kneeling black
African who kissed it, over the legend 'The Secret of England's Greatness'

– a message easily translated and understood by Northern Ireland's negro population. The *Royal* Ulster Constabulary were out in force to prevent riot, revolvers in their shiny holsters and their oak-pale batons prominent. On their caps the insignia which emblematized our status – English crown above Irish harp. The Orangemen – and the whole state as well – were 'Loyalist'. Loyal to England. And the Orangemen hated us. So presumably England hated us too? I would never go to England: if it could be like this on its fringes what must it be like at the centre?

GEORGE J. WATSON, Yale Review, 1986

FROM TIME IMMEMORIAL – that is to say within the memory of the oldest inhabitant of the Falls Road area – there has always been a Twelfth of July procession in Belfast ...

When I look back on those old Twelfth days, no day of all the year was more peaceful. Not a sinner was to be seen in the side streets before eleven or twelve o'clock in the day. A bare feminine arm would protrude through a half-opened door and lift from a window sill a jug of milk covered with a saucer (there were no bottles in those days). The door would then close gently, as though the hand was afraid to disturb the slumber of those who were tired out after the orgy of singing and dancing at the street corners on the previous Eleventh night.

Of course as boys we had been up long before our elders, slipping out of bed to join the clan under the improvised arch (as fenians we had to have our own arch) to see that nothing untoward had happened to our beloved heroes of Ninety-Eight. Unharmed they gazed down on us – coloured supplements taken from the old Dublin papers, the *Irish Emerald* and the *Shamrock*. The grime and 'collie' from the burning chimneys of the night before had smudged their faces and settled in their eyes, giving them bored, wearied looks. As the sun rose higher in the cloudless sky and warmed the streets, the doors were opened one by one and people came out to enjoy the sunshine. They stood at the doors in leisured attitudes, yawning with delicious contentment. There was no work today and they had enjoyed a blissful slumber undisturbed by the groanings of mill and factory horn. Working men came out in their stockinged soles, dressed only in shirt and trousers, with not even the braces in position. They sat on huge stones outside their doors, puffing away with grunting contentment at their old clay pipes. We had seen them, as boys, go through this languid ritual last Twelfth and Thirteenth and would not see them do the like, alas! for another twelve-month. The rat-a-pan of the drums in the distance, theoretically provocative, acted merely as a sedative to their thoughts. The monotonous sounds were in keepng with the dreaming silence of the sunny street and the slow, creeping shadows of the houses.

Sometimes with the vagaries of the shimmering, heated atmosphere, the drums would flare up in a sudden crescendo, and as suddenly subside.

'That was an angry brattle,' one woman would comment to another standing at the opposite door.

'Aye, his heart's in his work,' was the laconic answer.

Surely the millennium, so inly desired and long dreamt of by the harassed and oppressed, had at last descended for a brief period at least, on those mean streets and humble houses, bringing fugitive gleams of a life nearer to the heart's desire to tired, toil-worn workers. Gradually the rat-a-pan of the drums grew fainter and fainter and at last died away. The Orangemen were in the Field making speeches!

'The Pope's ears are warm by now,' commented again the first woman.

'I'm sure he is in a sweat about them,' came the ironical rejoinder from the woman opposite.

There were at least two politicians – usually women, by the way – in every street, and they spent the time making running comments on the progress of the procession to the Field, and its likely repercussions on future events. Like the necromancers of old, they could tell what was happening in distant parts, but did not claim undue knowledge about events around them. Verb. Sap., as the late Horatio Bottomley used to say in John Bull.

From two o'clock to five in the evening was zero hour in the streets. The brethren were away in the field. The drums were silent. All tangible connection with the Twelfth had been cut off. People, growing tired of the oppressive heat, had retired to the coolness of their houses. Even the two women policiticans had disappeared, lacking with silence of drums, the microscopic pedestal of fact on which to build the airy edifice of conjecture. They could work wonders, but could not perform miracles.

But the boys of the clan, faithful to the death, still stood, or rather lay and sprawled under the arch, lazily enjoying the burning sun. Sometimes the halcyon calm would be disturbed by a woman bursting into the street with the startling news that 'they were gutting one another round Carrick Hill and North Street'.

But, alas, it was only another link in the chain of predestined events without which no Twelfth was complete, and in which rumour had an honoured place. The woman was known to be a notorious fibber and sensation monger, and nobody believed her.

Let us, however, delve deep in the matter, and try to find out what history has recorded in the pages of the rival newspapers of that day, of that famous battle ground.

Here are imaginative extracts (but not so imaginative as you might think) from the Unionist and Nationalist papers of the period.

As recorded by a Unionist paper.

As a section of the procession was proceeding home in a quiet and orderly fashion, after commemorating the inauguration of civil and religious liberty to all classes and creeds, it was set upon by a cowardly gang of hooligans when passing Carrick Hill – that notorious plague spot of our city. Stones and bottles were thrown at the processionists, who showed wonderful restraint under such provocation. Party expressions were used of such a filthy nature that we dare not stain the pages of our paper with them.

When reinforcements of police arrived, the cowardly miscreants took to their heels, and the procession was able to pass on its way. This deplorable state of affairs happens year after year. It is time that the authorities woke up to the fact that the only way to stop these disgraceful scenes is to cordon off Carrick Hill completely when the procession is passing.

The Nationalist version.

Yesterday the peaceful and quiet neighbourhood of Carrick Hill was subjected to another of these cowardly attacks which have made our fair city a byword among civilised peoples. As the people of the district were going about as usual, pursuing their lawful avocations, a gang of miscreants – so-called disciples of civil and religious liberty – made a sudden onslaught on the quiet, law-abiding neighbourhood. Stones and other missiles were thrown accompanied by the vilest imprecations. We will not tingle the ears, or bring the blush of shame to the faces of our readers by repeating the filthy phrases. The blood of those orange 'braves' had been roused, of course, by the inflammatory speeches delivered at the Field. The people of Carrick Hill showed wonderful restraint and wisely left these cowardly miscreants to the care of the police who scattered them right and left with their batons. This is now a yearly occurence. When will the authorities realise that it is time to make arrangements to deflect the procession from this danger spot, that law-abiding citizens may walk the streets in peace?

And Truth, that elusive jade, dwelt then, as she still dwells, in her ancient obscure abode at the bottom of a well.

HUGH QUINN, *from* 'Old Time "Twelfth" in Belfast', *Lagan*, no. 3, 1945

I WAS TWELVE YEARS OF AGE when I saw my first Twelfth of July demonstration. The Orangemen had come to Rathfriland from all over the south of County Down and for several hours they moved in procession past our door, walking four abreast, all of them dressed in navy blue suits, with bowler hats and ornate sashes of orange decorated with metal trinkets representing five-cornered stars and Jacob's ladders and Masonic symbols. At the head of each lodge the principal officers, highly ornamented with sashes and large matching cuffs and tasselated aprons and carrying Bibles or gavels or ceremonial swords as symbols of their distinguished positions, bore themselves with solemn dignity, There were bands by the dozen and large painted banners, held aloft by waltzing men, depicting in a hundred different themes the benefits which Protestantism and Britain had brought to mankind. Over the caption 'The Secret of England's Greatness' one banner showed a portly Queen Victoria handing a Bible to a black man; another showed the burning of Latimer and Laud at the stake; we saw Martin Luther nailing a wad of papers to an iron-studded door. Jacob's vision, Britannia holding her trident proudly in front of a Union Jack, Queen Victoria sitting on a Union Jack, a Bible sitting on a Union Jack; John Bull, Bible in hand, out with his bulldog; unsophisticated paintings of local squires, of aged clergymen, of Joseph Chamberlain, of Sir Edward Carson and other heroes of the Orange movement. Each lodge had a number and a fanciful title emblazoned on its banner. There were 'True Blues', 'Chosen Few', 'Loyal Sons', 'Boyne Defenders' and 'Purple Stars'. Nearly every lodge had its drumming party made up of six or more sweating shirt-sleeved men lashing big drums with canes, making an ear-shattering noise with a sort of primitive rhythm. Each party of drummers was led by a man blowing a yellow cane flute from which an occasional squeal could be heard over the thunder of the drums.

The procession went through the streets in the morning to the place of assembly, a field outside the town, and came back by the same route in the late afternoon by which time the surfaces of the drums flowed with blood from the chafed knuckles of the drummers. The marchers were still solemn and unsmiling, there was nothing lighthearted about this gathering of men in their Sunday suits.

My brothers and I watched all through the day. We had taken part in religious processions, had seen political celebrities marched through Athlone with bands playing and torchlights blazing but this had neither the devotional fervour of one or the immediate enthusiasm of the other. This was secular Protestantism soberly commemorating the Battle of the Boyne which was fought in 1690 and demonstrating with all those fantastic trimmings its support for the Protestant succession to the English throne which did not seem to me to be in any danger. My first impression, at that early age, was that whatever was to be said about the need to show an attitude to the Reformation and the Throne, this was a very primitive way of doing it. But the whole Protestant community was involved. Amazed, I had seen them all, merchants and farmers, shop-assistants and labourers, masters and men, marching four abreast with grim faces behind the bands and the thundering drums and the painted images of their 'betters'.

We were probably the only Catholics in the town to show any interest in the events of the day. Our co-religionists, to whom the procession was no novelty, were withdrawn and sullen. They pointed out to us that most of the music of the bands had been the airs of songs which were very offensive to Catholics. Later, when we learned the words of some of the Orange songs, we saw that this was not an unreasonable complaint.

PATRICK SHEA, *Voices and the Sound of Drums*, 1981

A S HE CAME DOWN THE FALLS ROAD towards Castle Junction, the
crowds began to thicken. Children were running wild, darting
through the small spaces between the knots of grown-ups, annoying
them by bumping against their thighs. There were girls in summer
frocks and groups of young men in open-necked shirts, sports coats and
flannels. There were older women, sharp, determined matrons, who
had already grabbed the best positions along the route; it would be from
these that would arise the loudest cheers when the procession finally
appeared.

Nolan could not watch these faces without resenting them. He did not
like their sanctimonious Presbyterian eyes. He did not like them because
they hated him. He did not like them because he was conscious of being
inferior to them.

From down the street came music and Nolan saw the brass spikes on
top of the banner poles flash in the sun. There was the high sound of
flutes.

'Man, that's a sight to do your heart good,' said the man beside him.
'Can you see if that's the Oldpark district coming up?'

Nolan did not answer.

'We're not in a very good position,' said the man.

Nolan remained silent.

'Can't see a thing hardly,' said the man.

Still Nolan said nothing.

'Do you like the flutes?' asked the man.

A spark of resentment flared up in Nolan. 'Frig the flutes,' he said softly.

M.F. CAULFIELD, *The Black City*, 1952

A ROMAN CATHOLIC BISHOP ISSUED a kind of pastoral to his flock
urging them to remain at home on the Twelfth of July, and above
all things not to attempt a counter demonstration in Belfast. It was a nice
pastoral, very Christian in tone, but quite unnecessary. No sane Roman
Catholic, unless he wanted a martyr's crown, would have dreamed of
demonstrating anywhere north of the Boyne on that particular day. The
newspapers were very interesting at this time, and I took in so many of
them that I had not time to do anything except read them. I had not even
time to read them all, but Marion used to go through the ones I could
not read. With a view to writing an essay – to be published in calmer
times – on 'Different Points of View', we cut out and pasted into a book
some of the finer phrases. We put them in parallel columns. 'Truculent
corner boys', for instance, faced 'Grim, silent warriors'. 'Men in whom
the spirit of the martial psalms still survives' stood over against 'Ruffians
whose sole idea of religion is to curse the Pope'. 'Sons of unconquerable
colonists, men of our own race and blood', was balanced by 'hooligans

with a taste for rioting so long as rioting can be indulged in with no danger to their own skins'.

GEORGE A. BIRMINGHAM, *The Red Hand of Ulster*, 1912

WE HEADED UP THE TOWN an' there was a wile shockin' lot of noise allthegether. First there were the ban's way their big drums beatin', then there were people cheerin' an' clappin' in the crowd behine the ban's, an' drunk men singin' Orange songs outa tune. There were some people in their houses that opened their upstairs windows. Some of them were sayin' the rosary wile loud, others were singin' 'Faith of Our Father's' or 'Full in the Pantin' Heart of Rome', some were dippin' holy palms that had come especially from the holy lan' for palm Sunday, inte big basin fulls of holy water an' shakin' them at the Orangemen. Others were swearin' an' cursin', an' wan of the weemen outa 'Korea' that had attacked the breadman way me godmother, was standin' on the steps of hir mother-in-law's cafe pullin' up hir skirts te show hir bare arse te the Orangemen an' the holy statues standin' lookin' out.

A walked wile close te June's ma because a was wile feared an' she put hir arm aroun' me an' give me a whole lot of biscuits an' chocolates an' sweets. Wheniver the march was over a went home, wile shockin' proud a mesel' allthegether, thinkin' that a had put a stap te all the squabblin' that went on aroun' the Twelfth between Protestants an' Catholics but a hadn't. It didn't do no good atall. Even me ma laughed when a toul hir. She said it musta been the Orange blood that a got from me Protestant granny that made me go out in answer te the call of the Lambeg drums.

FRANCES MOLLOY, *No Mate for the Magpie*, 1985

IF YOU ARE LIVING IN ANY OF THE SIX north-eastern counties of Ireland, if your religion is Catholicism, if your politics are Nationalist, then the outward display of Orangeism makes a certain impression on your mind. The opening years of the second European war did temporarily disperse the sashed processions and silence the drums; but six or seven years ago the Orangemen marched and fluted and piped and battered to the complete content of their simple souls. As the Nationalists or the Catholics regarded them, those processions were as regular as the sequence of seasons, and, outside Belfast, were, in themselves, quite harmless. They flaunted the banner with Dutch William on his white horse fording the River Boyne, they recalled the walls of Derry and the battle of Aughrim, the scuffle at the Diamond, the affair of Dolly's Brae. The pipes piped and the flutes fluted tunes that associated the whole proceedings with these same events, implied that King William was responsible for the whole business and that the details were possibly to be found in the chapters of 'Revelations'. The marching men had a very sociable day, marched to some big field and listened to speeches abusing the Church of Rome, consumed quite an amount of spirituous liquor, went home infused with enough loyalty to last them round the twelve months of the year. That was the twelfth day of July and that was the Orange mind as it chose to reveal itself to the neighbours and to the world. Quite harmless or almost harmless except in Belfast where the marching men did not always display a notable inclination to go home quietly, where what began as a procession could end in appalling civil disorder.

BENEDICT KIELY, *Counties of Contention*, 1945

O N THE BUS HOME SHE WATCHED the familiar landmarks she used as a child pass one by one. Toomebridge, her convent school, the drop into low gear to take the hill out of Magherafelt.

The bus stopped at a crossroads on the outskirts of her home town and a woman got off. Before she walked away, the driver and she had a conversation, shouted over the engine noise. This was the crossroads where the Orangemen held their drumming matches. It was part of her childhood to look up from the kitchen table on still Saturday evenings and hear the rumble of the drums. Her mother would roll her eyes, 'They're at it again.'

It was a scary sound – like thunder. Like the town was under a canopy of dark noise.

BERNARD MacLAVERTY, *Grace Notes*, 1997

THE OULD ORANGE FLUTE

In the County Tyrone, near the town of Dungannon,
Where many's the ruction myself had a han' in,
Bob Williamson lived, a weaver by trade
And all of us thought him a stout Orange blade.
On the Twelfth of July as it yearly did come
Bob played on his flute to the sound of the drum;
You may talk of your harp, your piano or lute,
But there's nothing compared to the ould Orange flute.

But Bob the deceiver he look us all in,
For he married a Papish called Brigid McGinn,
Turned Papish himself, and forsook the ould cause
That gave us our freedom, religion and laws.

Now the boys of the place made some comment upon it
And Bob had to flee to the province of Connaught.
He fled with his wife and his fixings to boot
And along with the rest went the ould Orange flute.

At the chapel on Sundays to atone for past deeds
He said *Paters* and *Aves* and counted his beads,
Till after some time, at the priest's own desire
He went with his flute for to play in the choir.
He went with his ould flute to play in the Mass,
But the instrument shivered, and sighed, O alas!
And blow as he would, though it made a great noise,
The flute would play only 'The Protestant Boys'.

Bob jumped, and he started, and got in a flutter,
And threw his ould flute in the blest Holy Water;
He thought that this charm would bring some other sound;
When he blew it again, it played 'Croppies Lie Down'.
And for all he could finger and whistle and blow,
To play Papish music he found it no go.
'Kick the Pope', 'The Boyne Water', it freely would sound,
But one Papish squeak in it couldn't be found.

At a council of priests that was held the next day,
They decided to banish the ould flute away.
For they couldn't knock heresy out of its head
So they bought Bob a new one to play in its stead.
Well, the ould flute was doomed and its fate was pathetic,
'Twas fastened and burned at the stake as heretic.
As the flames roared around it they heard a strange noise,
'Twas the ould flute still playing 'The Protestant Boys'.

ANONYMOUS

THE LILY RALLY

The Papists stole me then and tried to make me play
Their Fenian music, but my loyal embouchure
Resisted them, and all the Melodies of Moore.
I threw their Roman legions into disarray.

My cardinal inquisitors were robed in red.
They touched their foxglove fingers to my breathless holes.

They murmured prayers for the saving of their souls.
They read their Riot Act at me from A to Z.

So then they built a bonefire for to burn me in,
Of broom, and brush, and willow, and potato flowers.
They bore me towards it on a purple palanquin.

As the flames roared around me, they heard a strange noise
Through all – their chanting from their scarlet Book of Hours
'Twas my ould self still whistlin' 'The Protestant Boys'.

CIARAN CARSON, *The Twelfth of Never*, 1998

ON THE 13TH JULY THEY WENT TOGETHER to Scarva. There in a field
so big that it was like a hillside, edged with giant oaks, she saw
thousands of people in gruff good humour who had come to watch a
sham fight representing the Battle of the Boyne between King William
and King James in 1690.

Beforehand there was a procession of Black Preceptories. On the steps
of the big house an old woman took the salute. On the banners, as they
marched past, were the titles of the preceptories. Here were King
Solomon's Golden Knights (wearing bowler hats), Abraham's Chosen
Few, Erin's First Royal Blues. Some banners showed biblical scenes:
David choosing smooth stones from the brook for his fight with Goliath;
or Adam and Eve expelled from the Garden of Eden, with a sympathetic
elephant watching them. A band might consist of four drummers and a
flautist. The drummers, in their shirt-sleeves, had perched their bowler
hats on the drums.

The battle was simple. Into the sunlight, from under the shadow of the
trees, marched two small groups of men, both in long white trousers.
Excited children ran beside them; and the crowd closed in. Rose, seeing
over the people two tattered flags drawing closer to one another, knew
that the battle had begun. Muskets were fired.

Elbowing through she and Patrick saw, leaping forward from either
army, which comprised a dozen or so country boys, two swordsmen who
danced sideways, each holding his free hand carefully up. In perfect time
sword was struck against sword, on alternate sides in succession, with
exemplary noise. The other men blazed away with their muskets, aiming
blank ammunition at the opponents' flag.

Then they ceased.

Both parties merged backwards through the crowd, made a detour,
and held another encounter like the first in a different part of the field.
This manoeuvre was repeated several times, always with the crowd
pushing after the combatants. King James, a tall thin man with a red

moustache, was heard shouting: 'Up the hill! Up the hill!'; but he was not exhorting his soldiers, he was directing the crush of spectators to give room for the fight.

It was allowed that King James should win the earlier engagements, but tradition demanded his final reverse. Tradition, to support her, had a spokesman among the crowd, who shouted to King James: 'See and get bate this time!' Amid cheering and banter James and his men were defeated, and were led away, arm-in-arm with their captors.

GEORGE BUCHANAN, *Rose Forbes*, 1950

'AS I WAS SAYIN'', HE RESUMED, 'Did ever ye hear tell o' the battle o' Scarva?'

Of course I had heard of it. Who has not heard of that Oberammergau of the North? There, in a gentleman's prettily wooded park, on a large open meadow sloping down to a clear running brook, is yearly enacted a veritable passion play of the Battle of the Boyne.

'I suppose you have often seen it, Thomas.'

'I have that; many and many's a time. But there was wan battle that bate all – do ye know what I'm goin' te tell ye? I would give a hunderd pounds te see thon agin – so I wud. Boys, oh! it was gran' ...

"Come on ye thirsty tyrant ye," says William.

"Come on ye low, mane usurper," says James.

"Come on ye heedious enemy to ceevil and releegious liberty ye," says William.

"Come on ye glorious, pious, and immortal humbug ye," says James.

"Come on ye Gladstone ye, and Parnell, and Judas, and Koran – and Dathan – and Abiram," says William.

"Come on ye onnatural parasite ye, and Crumwell, and Shadrach – and Mesech – and Abednego," says James.

"Come on ye auld Puseyite, and no more about it," says William. With that he joined to go forrard, and James he should have come forrard fornenst him, but Andy's mare, she jest planted the fore feet o' her and stud there the same as she was growed in the ground ... William says, says he:

"Come on till I pull the neck out o' ye ... Come on, me brave boy ... Fetch her a clip on the lug. Hit her a skelp behint. Jab her with yer knee, man alive. Och, come on, ye bap ye."

'Well the skin o' a pig couldn't stand that, and Andy he was always middlin' smart at a repartee, so "Bap yersel'," says he, and with that he let a gowl out o' him ye might have heared te Portadown. Ye never heared the like, nor what's more, Andy Wilson's mare she never heared the like, and she just made the wan lep and landed in the strame' fornenst William; then James he tuk a howlt o' William, and "Bap yersel'," says he; and with that he coped him off his gran' white horse, and he drooked him in the watter.

'Then there was the fine play, and the best diversion ever ye seen. Some they were for William, and some they were for James, and every wan he up with his fut or his fist, or onny other weepon that come convenient, and the boys they were all bloodin' other and murder and all sorts.'

'I thought you were all friends at Scarva?'

'And so we were – just friends fightin' through other.'

ELEANOR ALEXANDER, *Lady Anne's Walk*, 1903

B Y THIS TIME THE SHAM FIGHT between King James II, the loyal institutions' hate figure, and their hero, King William III, was in train. It is a bizarre and rather touching event, given an emotional context because there is an oak tree in the grounds under which William is supposed to have camped on his way to the Boyne ... When I actually walked the route more or less backwards about twenty yards in front of the parade, I was highly diverted that the leading marshals were a King James and a King William in vaguely period uniform, in green and red respectively, adorned with tricorne hats with appropriate cockades. It rather takes away from the mystique when the two great enemies are engaged in moving bystanders out of harm's way, but then, except for a little ritual in Orange lodges, mystique is not much prized in that part of the world ...

That year I couldn't see a thing. The following year I got the hang of it when I was allowed on the platform. But what I did have was access to the Scarva joke, for I was marooned for quite some time outside the house where Molyneaux was eating with a Black marshal who was very fond of it. It runs: 'Who won?' (or, as he pronounced it, 'Hee wan?'), a question he addressed to me and about half-a-dozen different people over the next twenty minutes amid his chortles of delighted laughter. I learned that the accepted response is something along the lines of, 'I don't know. I'll have to ask.'

RUTH DUDLEY EDWARDS, *The Faithful Tribe*, 1999

A S FACTION-FIGHTING DIED OUT ELSEWHERE, it acquired a new and more sinister significance in the northern province. I do not minimise the gravity of the conflicts, but I do protest against the reasoning that assumes that every stone flung at an Orange procession, or every head broken on Lady Day when Nationalists hold their parades, is evidence of a hatred too fierce to be extinguished by any measure of statesmanship. As a matter of fact the actual belligerents take these encounters much more philosophically and in a much better spirit than their respective leaders. The majority hugely enjoy their skirmishes, and their attitude to their opponents is admirably summed up in the expressive Ulster phrase, 'friends fighting through other'. A proof of this is the fact that the deepest wrath of both sides is reserved for the unfortunate constabulary whose task it is to prevent the combatants from settling their differences in their own way.

JAMES WINDER GOOD, *Ulster and Ireland*, 1919

FOR FIVE MILES THE ORANGEMEN had stumbled back to the city through the fading heat, tired, their great banners weaving unevenly under the strain of keeping up the heavy poles, scarcely a man now finding the energy to cut the steps of a jig to the music, the only thing still brash and noisy and apparently as fresh as ever.

The starched white collars had soiled; the gay banners had ruffled and creased; the orange sashes, placed so carefully over the shoulder that morning had somehow twisted round; boots had whitened with the dust; faces had grown stubbled and tender with the sun.

An upsurge of perversity among their leaders made them, before they reached the city centre, swerve from their route and change direction towards Cromac Street, a Catholic quarter. Bravely they went marching down this cramped, ugly street. They were at the bottom before the Catholic mob attacked them from the slum openings leading off it.

The forefront of the procession, which had already cleared Cromac Street and emerged into the bright square, got the worst of it.

The Catholics had gathered in strength at the far side of Cromac Square, facing across the hard, white concrete surface. They had supplied themselves with enough ammunition; they had dug up the square sets from nearby streets being repaired.

The head of the procession spread and blunted and scrambled back upon those following as a jagged cloud of stones rained down upon them. For a moment, there was enormous confusion with everybody shouting.

Then some of the Orangemen, recovering from their surprise, ran forward, braving the stones, and engaged their tormentors in hand to hand scuffles. In a while, the Catholics fell back, having run out of missiles.

But before the Orangemen could gather the strength and purpose for a violent counter-raid into the district, battalions of police had appeared and, with drawn batons, had set about clearing the streets and square. The Catholic mob, left with only their futile fists, quickly lost courage and were easily put to rout.

The Orangemen continued to mill about, dangerously uncertain and hesitant, while police officers marched up and down pleading with them to reform their ranks. Eventually they did so. But it was an angry, incensed army of men who marched off, their drums and music thumping louder than ever, their flags and banners held higher yet.

They were still in this vengeful mood as they rippled down Donegall Place, cutting through the heart of the city, streams of rowdy followers funnelling along the pavements beside them, shouting and singing.

M.F. CAULFIELD, The Black City, 1952

THE CONSTABLE'S COMPLAINT
after 'A Policeman's Lot' by Gilbert and Sullivan

When an Orangeman's pursuing his enjoyment,
his enjoyment,
A-marching to his flute or bagpipe bands,
bagpipe bands,
He will tell you it's an innocent employment
'cent employment
Of time that would weigh heavy on his hands,
on his hands.
Oh, I like to see his banners all a-flutter
all a-flutter
And hear his flutes a-whistling very high,
oh so high,
But friend, my brains are not made out of butter
out of butter
And I don't like being in a fairground shy.

Oh,
When an Orangeman must march some other way,
other way,
He's as bad to policemen as the IRA,
IRA.

When an Orangeman's impressing Mrs Thatcher
Mrs Thatcher
And proving her Agreement cannot stick,
cannot stick,
He will chuck whatever missile that might catch her
that might catch her
Attention, from a bomb to half a brick,
half a brick.
He can't very well go blowing up Westminster,
up Westminster —
It would look bad, and Guy Fawkes was an RC,
an RC —

And he can't go shooting British Cabinet Ministers,
> *Cabinet Ministers,*

So the only target is the RUC.

Oh,
When the British say he has to mend his ways,
> *mend his ways,*

The Orangeman acts like the IRA,
> *IRA.*

When loyalists appeal to their tradition
> *their tradition*

And claim their critics sold out to the Pope,
> *to the Pope,*

You can bet appeals to reason have no mission,
> *not a mission,*

For their principles are permanent as soap,
> *just like soap.*

They didn't mind our bullets made of plastic
> *made of plastic*

When killing Catholic girls of ten or twelve,
> *ten or twelve,*

But now their shock and outrage are fantastic
> *quite fantastic*

When they find those bullets coming at themselves.

Oh,
When loyalists want policing to be fair,
> *to be fair,*

They want the Micks to get the Orange share,
> *Orange share.*

ROBERT JOHNSTONE, *Eden to Edenderry*, 1989

'FUCK THE POPE!' the voice beneath the window repeated. The man below the window had been drinking. Since the trip on Lough Erne I had been in Enniskillen for some time now, drinking in Blake's, swimming in the public baths, and exerting myself as little as possible. I hadn't walked an inch, let alone a mile. Soon I would start walking again, but not yet, O Lord, not yet. Now I was in bed wondering if the man below the window had any idea that up above him in adjoining rooms were two Papists, Tony O'Shea from Kerry and me from Wexford. Eventually, having made his point, he went home. The following morning there were signs up everywhere advertising Meat and Plain

Teas. Outside the bus station a brigade from the Salvation Army were trying to save men's souls. Members of the RUC were wandering about, joking with the residents of Ballinamallard, whose big day it was. The bands would march from a field on the Enniskillen side of the town to the other side, march back, and then return to their buses and go home. When they got home, they would march up and down the main street of their town, as they had done this morning, before dispersing.

Each band had a beautiful banner, with the name of its place of origin clearly marked and a scene from the pageantry of Unionism and Orangeism painted on to the cloth. They came from the places with Gaelic names: Clabby, Meenagleragh, Mullaghboy, Cornafanog, Glasmullagh, Augharegh; from places with English names: Florencecourt, Castlearchdale, Scotshouse, Brookeborough, Maguiresbridge, Church Hill. Some of the men carried swords, some wore bowler hats, most wore sashes, they played pipes, they beat drums, they played whistles and flutes, they beat more drums, they played accordians. I stood beside an RUC man, who was called Harry. I learned this, because one or two men out of every group knew him and shouted their greetings over to him ...

It was time for speeches. There was a special welcome for the Grand Masters who had come to Ballinamallard from the adjoining counties, the counties of the Orange diaspora: Cavan, Monaghan, Leitrim, Donegal, in the Republic of Ireland, which no longer had Twelfth of July parades. Then there was a moment of silence for an RUC man, a member of the Orange Order in Fermanagh, who had been killed recently by the IRA. He was the fourth member of his lodge to be shot dead, and this year the lodge had decided to stay away from the parade. Everybody stood in silence. 'God Our Strength in Ages Past' was sung.

COLM TÓIBÍN, *Walking Along the Border*, 1987

THOSE GLORIOUS TWELFTHS

At ten I saw exclamatory blood
On Earlswood Road, a cagecar and a beak-
Capped constable with crowblack gun. We went
To Portrush in July, the great event
Abstracted to indifferent gull and rock.

At twenty, reading law, I glimpsed a gun
Glint in the smile of D.I., former Tan,
War-hero who'd won fancy ribboned stuff
For gutting Germans. Dead Huns not enough,
He grilled halfbaked dissenting Irishmen.

At thirty, pigmy family nudging knee,
Wedged in a village dazed by roaring drums
That drowned my destination; trapped by tied
Tiers of faces blinding stonedeaf road:
Inactive, voiceless, I chewed famine crumbs

Like those who willed another hopeless day
Eyeing the shrivelled root and the stopped hand.
Now forty, knowing men in government,
And collared curs that bark down argument
And foul what they must fail to understand:

I hurry children from the bloodsmeared drums,
Myself from the Inspector. If I rein
My family back into integrity,
Into a lane that's lamed by a quick tree,
I'll turn a leaf will dock the nettle's pain.

But let me give them one clear argument
Aloof from cheers and flags, like faceless rain:
One unembarrassed guilty monument,
Skirting the queen outside the City Hall,
To smuggle flowers to graves it can't disown.

ROY MCFADDEN, The Garryowen, 1971

JUST BEFORE I SHUT THE DOOR behind me, I heard her exclaim, 'God, but I'd rather have the Pope of Rome living next door to me than that wicked oul' blert!'

Her choice of neighbours puzzled me.

MARJORY ALYN, The Sound of Anthems, 1983

THE SQUARE WAS A GREAT PLACE for parades, marches, exhibitions. Four days in the year had special significance and were observed with banners flying: two for Protestants, two for Catholics. The first was St Patrick's Day, March 17, and pipe-and-flute bands, as many as twenty from Catholic villages and towns throughout the North, came to Warrenpoint and marched around the town, the banners in gold and green. Then, on July 12, the famous 'Twalfth', Protestants arrived in similar numbers and gallantry, with banners commemorating the great and glorious victory of King William over the wretched James at the Battle of the Boyne in 1690. The banners showed the King crossing the river, victory in his crest. Protestants, mostly Orangemen, turned out for the march in black suits and hard black hats. The Catholics turned out again on August 15, Feast of the Assumption of Our Blessed Lady. Protestants answered back on the last Saturday in August, Black Preceptory Saturday, as it was called for no reason that I know. Someone told me that it had to do with the Freemasons or the Knights Templar.

These processions were indeed rival occasions, but they were not occasions of violence. Catholics watched the Protestant processions from the sidewalks but did not interfere with them or make any audible noise. Similarly with Protestants on the Catholic days. In any strict sense, the 'Twalfth', as we mimicked the Protestants in calling it, was the most aggressive of those days, the only one that specifically celebrated the historic victory of a Protestant King over a Catholic Pretender. The other Catholic days were days of religious celebration, but even St Patrick's Day didn't mark a victory of Catholic over Protestant; and the Assumption of the Blessed Virgin was entirely a matter of Catholic belief and practice; it had nothing to do with Protestants.

DENIS DONOGHUE, *Warrenpoint*, 1991

The Famous City
of Derry ... and
Ecclesiastical Armagh

DERRY

By day a place of wheels and looms
That struggle in a narrow space,
A shout of children in the slums
And girls with labour-stainéd face.

By night a queen with victory crowned,
For all her years of loud turmoil.
She spreads her beauty all around,
Reflects her glory in the Foyle.

FRANCIS LEDWIDGE

There are a number of flourishing towns in County
Armagh – Lurgan, with its splendid broad main street, the
birthplace of George Russell, the Ulster poet and visionary;
Portadown, famed for its roses and fine linen, the
birthplace of Sir Robert Hart, the famous Inspector-
General of the Chinese Customs; Tanderagee; Markethill.
But the city of Armagh historically dominates the county.
When you look at the map, all roads in the county seem to
lead to the city of Armagh.

HUGH SHEARMAN

I LANDED IN DERRY ... in the pitchy darkness of a coal-hole black-out, which was unfortunate; for the journey up the river is a very pleasant one, and Derry is, to my mind, the loveliest of all Northern cities, and in normal times looks lovely at night from the fortifications, with all the little lights of the valley below you to the west, and shining across the river below you to the east. As, for Connaught, I would willingly live only in Ballina, for the North I would willingly live only in Londonderry. Its river is noble. The town has antiquity and dignity. It has some very fine houses – such as the Deanery. Its main shopping district is bright and busy. Its size is about right, fifty thousand people – a little on the small side, perhaps, for a city but perfect for a large town.

I think that what makes me so fond of Derry is that it reproduces the pictorial effect of Cork – river, quays, hills, deep valley, and it has behind it the hinterland of the lovely Inishowen peninsula and all Donegal, just as Cork has the mountains to its west. If one took Cork, and bent it up in the middle, like the fallen-in cone of a volcano, or a great sombrero, that would be Derry. And when I got up in the morning and strolled around the ramparts, the Walls as they call them, wide enough to let forty men march abreast, and looked down over Bogside, towards the Clay Pits of Templemore and to the cathedral at Brooke Park, and saw all the little threads of morning smoke rising from the thousands and thousands of little houses far below, it was just like being up on Patrick's Hill, in Cork, and seeing the smoke rising from the little homes of Blackpool and Barrack Street. The Walls are hemmed in by houses and streets, so that one could drop a pebble from the gravel at one's feet down a Bogside chimney, and see into the top-floor windows.

SEAN O'FAOLAIN, *An Irish Journey*, 1940

TO THE MAJORITY OF ULSTER PEOPLE Derry is in its own way a kind of Holy City, a remembrancer, a rallying-place, a symbol, and anything but a place of bricks and mortar. For, as Donn Byrne said: 'The Walls of Derry will make your heart beat faster, for no gallantry in Froissart rivals that of the Thirteen Apprentice Boys who locked the Gates against James of the Fleeing, and held the City for eight long months, not only against James but against pestilence and famine.' And indeed the heart needs must beat faster at the sight of those Walls and the relics associated with them, symbolical of such steadfastness and courage and grim Ulster determination; and even those whose Faith and historical background might beget a different set of emotions could never find it in their hearts to grudge the grand old town its well-earned and most glorious fame. Derry of Calgach, Derry of Columcille, Derry of the Siege, Derry the Maiden City. In these names there is fame enough and to spare; the fame of battles nobly won; of a great siege gallantly withstood to mould the future history of Europe and perhaps of the world; of piety and Christian works. No need here to borrow a spurious fame of the name of a great and fair city on the English Thames.

> Were the tribute of all Alba mine
> From the centre to the border,
> I would rather the site of one house
> And it in the midst of Derry.

Thus the noble Columcille, Dove of the Church, away in Iona off the coast of Alba, or Scotland as we now call that place, whither he had gone after he had been censured by a Synod of the Celtic Church.

RICHARD HAYWARD, *In Praise of Ulster*, 1938

FROM LIFFORD TO DERRY, about twelve miles, is as beautiful a drive as can be conceived on the edge of that fine river which widens all the way and at Derry is as broad as the Thames at Lambeth. And the other side of the river fine meadows and gentlemen's houses with good plantations; the cabins very good and thick set, and spinning and looms or some other branch of the linen manufacture going on at every house. And on the left hand the high mountains of Donegal continue at five or six miles distance. The city of Londonderry is a very pretty large town, somewhat like Warwick in having four principal streets which meet at the market house. It is rather inconvenient for coaches for the streets are rather too steep to go up or down with safety. It is about twenty miles from the main sea but vessels of a large burthen come up to the town. The river widens below Derry and forms a large lough which empties itself into the sea. The situation being high and exposed there is a constant draught of air in the streets and in winter time is extremely cold. There is no land between them and the North Pole, so that it is a proverb at Derry, when the winds blow strong at north that you may hear the North Pole turning round its axis.

EDWARD WILLES, *from* 'Letters to the Earl of Warwick', *c.* 1759

AND THEN WE ARE ON THE WALLS thirty feet high that defended the original little town. These must have been the latest built city walls in Europe; I imagine that it was very soon after they were built that rampart-breaking artillery came into use. They are uncrumbled, and they make a promenade for visitors now. Looking from the walls I see the road which I had come along: high, green banks well planted with trees are along the Foyle. These green slopes with cattle grazing on them make a scene that is pastoral enough to recall the Doire, the old Oak Grove.

We walk along the Foyle towards its mouth. On one side are the bleak hills of Donegal; on the other, the cultivated fields of Derry County.

PADRAIC COLUM, Cross Roads in Ireland, 1930

PARTITION STRUCK DERRY A DEADLY BLOW; for it throve in modern times as the virtual capital of Donegal – that large, lovely, populous, richly-varied county which is almost a nation in itself, but now is severed from Derry by the irrational Border. On the trade of Donegal, and on the linen industry, modern Derry grew. It is fair to see, among cities. Walk the wide walls, by the old Georgian-porticoed houses, or go forth beside the broad Foyle waters with their pleasant banks of hills and tree-embowered mansions; admire the Gothic guildhall, the field-girt suburbs, the green-and-golden residential districts beside the now-idle shipyards – and, above all, visit St Columb's College. The college, on high ground without the walls, is housed in long, low, magnificent buildings which were erected by the fantastic Earl of Bristol, Protestant Bishop ...

The dancing hall that the Earl of Bristol built is a College chapel now, and his chambers house a wealth of sacred learning. Behold, beside the tomes of Aquinas, four immense manuscript volumes – the Annals of the Four Masters, copied by Eugene O'Curry for his own use, a miracle of penmanship and devotion. ...

Within the grounds, we may see the base of a tower and a stone oratory that date from the times of St Colmcille's own monastery. You are treading where he trod thirteen hundred years ago.

AODH DE BLÁCAM, The Black North, 1938

HE FOUND HIMSELF ON THE ROAD that runs out along the river towards the border. The city was behind him. The high warehouses were behind him and the bombed-out shops, 'business as usual', scrawled bravely on the doors. He passed the bus depot and the army barracks and the neat houses with their front gardens rimmed with raked flower beds. The wind blew aimless seagulls across the sky and the river moved, silver, towards the lough. Nothing could stop that. Then it was country, and high trees leant in winter loneliness against the tumbling walls of the big houses. Cattle searched in the fields for grass. The bare hills came closer with every step he took.

JENNIFER JOHNSTON, Shadows on our Skin, 1977

DERRY MORNING

The mist clears and the cavities
Glow black in the rubbled city's
Broken mouth. An early crone,
Muse of a fitful revolution
Wasted by the fray, she sees
Her aisling falter in the breeze,
Her oak-grove vision hesitate
By empty wharf and city gate.

Here it began, and here at last
It fades into the finite past
Or seems to: clattering shadows whop
Mechanically over pub and shop.
A strangely pastoral silence rules
The shining roofs and murmuring schools;
For this is how the centuries work –
Two steps forward, one step back.

Hard to believe this tranquil place,
Its desolation almost peace,
Was recently a boom-town wild
With expectation, each unscheduled
Incident a measurable
Tremor on the Richter Scale
Of world events, each vibrant scene
Translated to the drizzling screen.

What of the change envisioned here,
The quantum leap from fear to fire?
Smoke from a thousand chimneys strains
One way beneath the returning rains
That shroud the bomb-sites, while the fog
Of time receives the ideologue.
A Russian freighter bound for home
Mourns to the city in its gloom.

DEREK MAHON, *Courtyards in Delft*, 1981

ANNUALLY, TWO ANNIVERSARIES are celebrated: on December 18th, the Closing of the Gates; and on August 12th, the Raising of the Siege. At the December festival it is usual to burn in effigy the treacherous governor Lundy: and both are attended with processions of the most aggressively Protestant character. At least half of the population is Roman Catholic and Nationalist, so that these occasions are a fruitful source of street riots. Law has interfered and prohibited repeatedly all that might give offence to religious or political susceptibilities; but the anniversaries are still celebrated, and even those who are least in love with Orangeism would scarcely desire to see the historic commemoration of so valiant a feat of arms omitted. The police, I believe, still regularly exercise their faculties to discover beforehand the vile body of Lundy, stuffed with squibs and crackers; but at the critical moment he seldom fails to swing out of the window of the Prentice Boys' Hall. One of these triumphs was celebrated by a member of a very distinguished family in a poem beginning:

> A was the ardour with which we burnt Lundy,
> In spite of the magistrates noses' on Monday.
> B was the Bandroom of Prentice boys bold,
> Where Lundy was burnt and the Bobbies were sold.

It was on that occasion that the figure of Lundy was popularly supposed to have been concealed under a bed in the Palace; but this detail is mythical.

STEPHEN GWYNN, *Highways and Byways in Donegal and Antrim*, 1899

A T THE TIME OF THE AFTERNOON when we were accustomed to return from our walk, Mary O'Connell took us out. She turned down the little side street past the grocery shop, which had an uncle who was a monsignor, and instead of going through Bishop's Gate we went directly upon the City Walls, at their widest place, where the monument was. It was twilight and the cold air was sharpened for frost. There was a great crowd packed around the monument railings. Mary O'Connell put me upon one of the obsolete cannon which always kept their noses out of the gaps, waiting, as black as boars, to snort at the invader. Major [a dog] got upon the cannon too, behind James who kept telling Mary O'Connell that he wanted to see. Major and I had no desire to see. It got worse and worse, darker and darker, and there was something in the atmosphere that filled you with terror. It was an hour of gloom and doom. When it was almost dark enough for the moon to come out, the people crushed in together and let out an awful roar. They wanted Lundy – the way another crowd had wanted Barabbas. It was so dark that you could hardly see when one person ended and another began. And then, high up in space where the poor stuffed man swung on his gibbet, a star appeared. It stayed poised, waiting for the wind to swing Lundy towards it. As soon as his feet touched it it went off like a meteor and the blaze began. The traitor hung in the heavens like a lantern. He burned from his feet upwards. All his joints went off with cracks and explosions, and rags and tatters fell down in awful, ghostly wisps upon our faces. The more he burned, the more he exploded. It was pure terror to hear and wonder what part of him it was. Everybody cheered, except Major and I. Everybody seemed delighted, but we were delighted when it was all over, when the sparkle stopped and the night was as black as pitch. It was a relief when we got off the Walls, down into the streets where lamps were lit and all was in its customary position.

James pestered Mary to tell him more and more about Lundy. All that she would say was that: 'Lundy had opened the gates and that he was actually a hero.' He was certainly a hero when he was upon the gibbet. You forgot all about Mr Walker who had the monument. Father wished to take us up the monument by the spiral staircase which wound and wound inside it. Mother forbade him to do it. I told him quite politely that I had no wish at all to go up so far to see the view over the city. It was quite enough to peep over the noses of the cannon or, at the worst, over Waterloo Gate or down over Shipquay Gate where you saw the Guildhall and the river and the Ferry Landing. The gate I liked best was Ferryquay Gate where you could see right down into the pastry cook's where Mother bought buns and chocolates.

KATHLEEN COYLE, *The Magical Realm*, 1943

DERRY, I THINK, IS IN THE TRANSITION OR CHRYSALIS STAGE, and you will see the butterfly flutter forth ere long. It is a wonder that so beautiful, so desirable a city should be so lacking in literary fame so long. As you walk the Derry walls, or look along the broad Foyle waters with their pleasant banks of hills and tree-embowered mansions, you wonder that Derry has not teemed with poets and story-tellers. It is a clean, prosperous, and yet austere-looking city, with but little of slum disfigurements. It has no vast regions of decay like Dublin, and it is not a wilderness of little tight-packed brick-houses like Belfast. Its architecture is not decayed like the capital's, nor shoddy like that of Thompsonopolis (though its Guildhall has something of vulgar gaudiness in its overdone red-stone Gothic). Its streets, both the new ones running into field-girt suburbs, and its older and historic ones, are freshened by well-kept trees, and on a summer's afternoon you walk through Derry as cheerfully as you would through a country lane.

There are many romantic views, too. There is a glimpse of the silver river through green trees down a hill to be caught from the Northland Road, with the boat-club's pagoda and a wheen of masts, that sets you thinking with the imagination of a Stevenson. There is a shipyard building great iron armadas for France, where brown-dungareed workers pour forth at evening into a green and golden residential district – high modern industry set amid calm and lovely surroundings instead of in the heart of smoky bricks as in Belfast. The yard is not there long, yet a large body of Derry and Donegal youths are already become highly skilled industrial workers and show themselves capable of surpassing the men of other nations in technical skill. Long, snaky, red-bodied motor buses with glittering glassy sides are swarmed into by these workers, and bore their sinuous way through the traffic at lightning speed.

The people are a delightful surprise. They combine the business efficiency of Belfast with the grace and courtesy of Dublin, and they do not try to 'do' you. You are not obliged to ask the price of every article and every service in advance, nor need you take it for granted that promises are made to be broken. When work is over the Derry folk are well-dressed and smart, and you feel you are moving through some tasteful Continental city instead of a commercial and industrial centre. They are a handsome folk, with honest looks.

AODH DE BLÁCAM, *From a Gaelic Outpost*, 1921

*D*ERRY. THE LEAFY BOWER OF ST COLUMBA. The surroundings of this city are most attractive, with fine country houses standing in wooded demesnes on the banks of the Foyle, and Donegal at the doorstep, but the city itself would do better to remember that a lot of water has flowed down the river since the *Mountjoy* rammed the boom. At present it has the air of one of those rather blousy old ladies whom one meets at tea-parties in Irish country houses – all past, and quite unable to remember that the mere act of continuing to exist entails its obligations. I, for my part, remember the city as a place where I once served as a subaltern of infantry in Ebrington barracks; that and the memory of certain sunsets witnessed from the barrack square, when the spires and pinnacles across the water went climbing up into a blood-red sky, for at the hour of sunset, and seen from the Waterside, Derry has all the romance and drama of a medieval city – at any rate the romance and drama traditionally associated with medieval cities, since if the truth were known we inhabitants of the twentieth century would probably have been bored to death with them in a month, if we hadn't first been sickened by their stench. Nevertheless, Derry remains a city of dramatic contrasts, a border fortress set over against the Gael, as I discovered for myself one winter's night when walking round the walls. A murmur of voices from a lighted window attracted me, and looking over the parapet I saw through a chink in the curtains a room crowded with men whose faces bore an expression of passionate enthusiasm and conviction. They were all looking towards the curtained window, and soon a single voice proceeding from someone who stood with his back to me, facing his audience, took up the tale. The speech was in Gaelic, but from the expressions on the faces of the audience and the impassioned conviction of the speaker, I knew at once that I was witnessing a gathering of Irish patriots – the first mutterings of the storm that was to break two years later in O'Connell Street, Dublin; and as one who both understood and failed to understand, I thought it best to turn up the collar of my British greatcoat and disappear in the darkness.

DENIS IRELAND, *From the Irish Shore*, 1936

TODAY DERRY HAS OVERFLOWED its old walls, and even jumped the River Foyle, to grow into the suburb known as the Waterside, which is almost another town on its own. But from the cathedral tower, or from the Diamond, as the large central square is called, the formation of the old city within the walls may be clearly seen, and it will be obvious that this was developed from a military settlement. The City of York in England attracts thousands of visitors by the fame of its walls, and in lesser degree Chester and Canterbury do the same, but in none of these places are the walls anything like complete. The Walls of Derry remain intact to this day, and you may walk entirely round the city without ever leaving them for an instant. For this is the only city in the British Isles with a complete encirclement of walls and fortifications, which must look much the same today as they did in the stirring times of the Great Siege. The circumference of the walls is roughly a mile, and the defences consist of nine bastions and two half bastions, now pleasantly kept with grass and planted with flowers. You should certainly walk this mile round the old walls and note the various points of interest during your progress. In the bastions were mounted 'eight sakers and twelve demi-culverins', and during the siege these bastions were named, in order, the Double Bastion, where a gallows was erected for the threatened hanging of any prisoners; the Royal Bastion, 'from the advancing of red flagges upon it, in defiance of the enemie'; the Hangman's Bastion, where stood another gallows; the Gunners' Bastion; the Cowards' Bastion, 'it lyeing most out of danger, it's said it never wanted of company goode store'; the Water Bastion; the New Gate Bastion; the Ferry Bastion; and the Church Bastion. Many of these bastions are still in existence and have name-tablets affixed to them, and about them stand some of the old guns presented by the various London Companies. Others of these bastions have disappeared in the course of time, a fate which has also befallen the dry ditch which originally ran round the outside of the walls. The Gates now number seven, having been increased to that number in 1627 by the Irish Society. Originally there were four gates, one at the end of each main street, and if you will stand at Bishop's Gate and look straight down the hill, through the Diamond, to Shipquay Gate, you will observe the ancient plan in detail. Or similarly you may stand at Butchers' Gate and look up the old thoroughfare to Ferryquay Gate. The names of the seven gates are Bishop's Gate, Shipquay Gate, Butcher's Gate, Ferryquay Gate, the New Gate, the Castle Gate and the Northern Gate, the last-named being the most recent addition, and the four first-named being the original gates of the old fortification scheme.

RICHARD HAYWARD, In Praise of Ulster, 1938

MANY WRITERS WHO VISITED DERRY in the early nineteenth century commented on the new fast spreading suburb on its north side called Edenballymore and on the fine streets which had been established there. It was a suburb of contrasts. Bounded at one end by the Bogside and on the other by Great James Street and Queen Street, it contained both the best and worst in the town's housing. The southern end was much the poorer half, but as one went north towards William Street the quality improved until one reached the upper-class quarters in Sackville, Great James and Queen streets.

These latter streets, built off the Strand Road, formed a substantial part of the suburb. It was a new development. Simpson wrote in 1847:

> The extension of the town without the walls on the north and north-west has been in great measure limited to the last forty years. In our recollection all the districts now covered by Great James Street, William Street, Little James Street, Rossville Street, Abbey Street, Eden Place and the numerous lanes in that vicinity were occupied as meadow ground without a house: and that portion which is now covered with the respectable houses of Sackville Street and Waterloo Place was partially slob and the receptacle of filth – at that time only one cottage was on the Strand Road leading to the Pennyburn.

By 1850 this area was well developed as a residential district. The reasons for the development are seen in the types of houses built – mainly merchant houses of three or four stories. As an advertisement in 1835 put it: 'To be let. Two new houses in the new street leading from the Strand, well furnished and fit for the reception of genteel families'. This building development ... followed from the extension of business premises within the walls, displacing city residents who moved out to their new homes in the respectable suburbs. As this movement got under way, the *Ordnance Survey Memoir* (1837) noted that it involved 'the cessation of the ancient prejudice that to live beyond the hill was not respectable.' The hill referred to was Derry inside the walls.

JOHN HUME, Derry Beyond the Walls, 2002

THE HOUSE HUNG OVER THE VALLEY but our immediate view as children was blocked by our beeches. Some perfectly mad being, according to Mother, had had the idea of cutting down part of these trees to hedge the lawn. They were espaliered against space. They had their own beauty – the artificial beauty of branches twined on the margin of a missal. As trees they were deformed. The land on the other side sloped steeply down into the Trench Road. When you stood plainly in this field you could see the fertile valley, ribboned with a river and populated with woods. These were plantation lands. They had been ploughed in the deadliest antagonisms. They were at peace now, the feud only rising occasionally. You could see the estates, garrisoned with trees. The names of the people were Scottish. The place names were Irish. Picts and Scots. The age-old division. Stevensons and Maxwells and Thompsons and Beresfords and Cunninghams. Ardmore and Glendermott and our own townland, Altnagalvin.

KATHLEEN COYLE, *The Magical Realm*, 1943

RETURN

The train shot through the dark.
Hedges leapt across the window-pane.
Trees belled in foliage were stranded,
Inarticulate with rain.
A blur of lighted farm implied
The evacuated countryside.

I am appalled by its emptiness.
Every valley glows with pain
As we run like a current through;
Then the memories darken again.
In this Irish past I dwell
Like sound implicit in a bell.

The train curves round a river,
And how tenderly its gouts of steam
Contemplate the nodding moon
The waters from the clouds redeem.
Two hours from Belfast
I am snared in my past.

Crusts of light lie pulsing
Diamanté with the rain

At the track's end. Amazing!
I am in Derry once again.
Once more I turn to greet
Ground that flees from my feet.

SEAMUS DEANE, Gradual Wars, 1972

THE WHOLE WORLD SWUNG BENEATH THEM. The fortress city was below them, its grey walls and climbing houses quite plain to be seen, in the crook of the curling river which broadened then into the lough, beyond which the cliff of Benevenagh rose like a wall. Across Inishowen shadows moved constantly over the surface of Lough Swilly making it look as if it were alive with the creatures of different colours and shapes. Away beyond, divided from each other by brown hills Mulroy Bay and Sheephaven glittered and the great mountains of Errigal and Muckish rose above the rest, rising blue from the treeless boglands and rimming them along the Atlantic ocean, a silver line between the earth and sky. Storm clouds were banking up in the west, grey and white and sun-shot as if the sea was boiling up into the sky. Then back from the loughs and the sea the mountains subsided into hills again, and the bog became tilled winter fields neatly patterning the land, and trees waited and smoke blew bravely from the cottage chimneys, and the river Foyle again wound its way along its valley from Strabane to protect its own city. It was as if he owned the world.

'Oh', was all he could say, but he needn't have bothered as the wind pushed the exclamation back down his throat again.

So he walked around the walls in silence, and again and again, pushing his way against the wind, clutching from time to time protectively at his hair. The clouds gathered round Errigal, and as he watched, the distant mountain was quite hidden, as if it had never existed.

JENNIFER JOHNSTON, Shadows on our Skin, 1977

WHILE THE BOGSIDE BULGED WITH PEOPLE, iron law decreed that insufficient houses be built and prevented those which were built being allocated fairly. Ours was a teeming, crumbling area of ugly, tiny, terrace houses, mean streets where men stood in sullen groups at the corner while their wives went out to work and children skipped to songs of cheerful hatred:

Oh, St Patrick's Day will be jolly and gay,
And we will kick all the Protestants out of the way.

If that won't do
We'll cut them in two
And send them to hell with their
Red, white and blue.

There was no revolutionary ferment arising from it all. Expectations were little higher than the reality. As long as the state existed there would be discrimination, and as long as there was discrimination we would suffer unemployment and slum housing. Everyone knew that. Demands were made, of course, that discrimination be stopped, but more for the record than in real hope of result. Mr McAteer would get up in Stormont and allege that Catholics were being treated very badly. A Unionist minister would reply that this was a lie; it never happened; and even if it did it was no more than Catholics deserved since they were all disloyal subversives; and, what was more, if the situation was reversed Catholics would do the same thing to Protestants. The matter would rest. The fact that the resultant miseries could be looked on as a price to be paid for remaining true to the national ideal made them more easily acceptable. Any concentration on economic reform as opposed to pursuit of a united Ireland, appeared, in the light of that, to be near to national apostasy ... 'We don't want their jobs and houses,' shouted, a perorating Nationalist businessman to a cheering audience of Bogsiders at one of Mr McAteer's eve-of-the-poll rallies. 'We-want-our-Freedom!'

Nationalist feeling in the area achieved one of its periodic climaxes in 1951, when Mr de Valera came from Dublin to declare open a week of Gaelic games and cultural activities. The kerbstones were painted green, white and orange, and flags and bunting hung everywhere. When he came up Rossville Street in an open car the crowds surged forward and almost swamped him, waving their arms, delirious, cheering, laughing, and jumping up on one another's shoulders to be sure to see him. Women craned precariously out of upstairs windows waving hand-kerchiefs, frantic, screaming 'Dev, Dev, Dev!' He who had fought in 1916, the last living leader of the single most glorious episode in all our history, was come here among us, and for a day at least all care was quite forgotten. Everybody said afterwards that it was the greatest day there had ever been in Derry. That was the measure of our Bogside innocence, that the old Fagin of the political pickpockets could, by his mere presence, excite such uncensorious fervour.

EAMONN McCANN, *War and an Irish Town*, 1974

FRIEL'S TERRACE WAS A ROW of nine houses in the middle of Nailor's Row, known locally as 'The Back of the Walls' because it ran parallel to, and facing, the exterior western side of Derry's Walls from Butcher's

Gate to Long Tower Street at the Double Bastion. Just past the lower end of Friel's Terrace, and facing Paddy 'Peggy' Strain's house at number twenty-three, was the Royal Bastion with Governor George Walker's Pillar. The bastion pushed out the lower middle of Nailor's Row, causing the road to veer right at the top of Primrose Lane, an old cobbled track that curved down the banking. The lane emerged between two houses – McVicker's at the bottom of Fahan Street and a tenement house at the beginning of St Columb's Wells. The banking is the steep grassy slope that runs down from the Walls to St Columb's Wells, just on the edge of the Bogside, which derived its name from a marshy stretch of land once known as the cow bog.

Number two Friel's Terrace was my home from my birth in 1937. It was a two-storey house with two bedrooms upstairs and a front sitting room-cum-bedroom and a back living room downstairs where the cooking, washing and all the general household chores were done daily. There was no sink or indoor running water, the toilet and water tap being in the back yard. In winter, the tap would sometimes freeze up and my father would have to thaw it out using a burning, rolled-up newspaper.

At one time, there were eighteen people living in the house: my father and mother; three brothers, four sisters and myself; three half-brothers and one half-sister; and an uncle and an aunt on my mother's side who were both unmarried. Two cousins also lived with us and all were loved and cared for as one big family.

PHILIP CUNNINGHAM, *Derry Down the Days*, 2002

TEEMING TENEMENTS AND SLUMS, built directly beneath the city walls, attracted and frightened us. Hordes of people went in and out the same front door. The hallways were dark. There were low, deep arches leading into crammed courtyards. These people, we knew, were poorer than us. Beggar women walked about, wrapped in shawls. Men stood in the street, cap in hand, and sang, hoping for coins. Other men sold bundles of sticks, kites and newspapers. Smoke poured from chimneys. The children of these houses were skinnier than us, and had more sores about their mouths, and bigger snotters running down their faces.

I did not know then that my father's people grew up in the worst of these slums. His mother was a shirt-factory worker from Walker's Place; his father a tailor from Wapping Lane. They married in 1887, and prospered to the extent that they set up a second-hand clothes shop in Waterloo Street, the main Catholic shopping thoroughfare outside the Walls. The hilly top of Waterloo Street, which merged with the hilly top of Fahan Street, formed the apex of a triangle that led directly through Butcher's Gate into the walled city. This was the gate that the Protestant Apprentice Boys closed in 1690, to keep out the Catholic King James of

England, who had made his camp in the Bogside. My father's people travelled out of the Bogside to Scotland for the clothing, going over by ship on the Scotch boat, bringing it back to the Bogside and tailoring it, if necessary, for resale. My father's mother, Mary McCafferty, was known for the beautiful quilts she made from rags. She died before I was born, as did all my grandparents. My father's sister Kathleen took over the shop, and her daughter Mona opened a second outlet across the street, while her other daughter Dola married a watchmaker and they set up a jeweller's shop next door to Aunt Kathleen. Having three rich relatives in Waterloo Street was handy for an escape should Joe and I feel threatened in Fahan Street. If my father's people were rich compared to us, my mother would quip, her side of the family was the shabby genteel, being related to police and Protestants. All the same, it was magic to enter my Aunt Kathleen's sitting room one Saturday afternoon to watch England play football on a black-and-white television, one of the few sets in Derry in the 1950s. We sat on the floor at my father's feet, entranced. She remained in the front downstairs room, which served as her shop. 'If there's a penny to be made in Waterloo Street, I'll make it,' she used to say.

NELL McCAFFERTY, *Nell*, 2004

THE OPENING OF THE NINETEENTH CENTURY found Derry little more than a market town with a small port attached. But for the shirt and collar trade, Derry would hardly be more than a good-sized country town. The linen manufacture in the neighbourhood appears to have reached its peak about 1822 when four and a half million yards were exported from Derry annually. The decline of linen in Derry was rapid, and by 1889 only 214 persons in the whole county were employed in the linen manufacture. To the cottage spinners who were unemployed, shirt-making must have come as a great boon in the hard and difficult times popularly known as 'the hungry Forties'.

Furthermore, it was not only a means of rescue of unemployed linen-workers, but it was also a refuge for the remains of a once great Ulster industry, the cotton manufacture. The new shirt business was from the outset a mixed linen and cotton industry, and there can be little doubt that in its early days it gave employment not only to the unemployed hand spinners of flax, but also to the cotton workers, who had been displaced by the keen competition of Lancashire. The shirt manufacture is now almost entirely concerned with the making-up of cotton stuffs. Thus it is curious to notice that whereas Belfast was formerly a great cotton-working city, thought likely to rival Manchester, yet lost its cotton manufacture completely, nevertheless the cotton industry was not lost to the province of Ulster. It changed its locality and its methods, moving from Belfast to Derry, and converting itself from a spinning and weaving to a making-up business.

D.A. CHART, A History of Northern Ireland, 1927

TRADITIONALLY [DERRY] IS A CITY of masterful women. For generations the main local industry was shirt making and while wives went out to earn, husbands stayed at home with the children.

One can still clearly see the results of this in many families where women vigorously insist on their menfolk either supporting or not supporting the Provos. As the Troubles have progressed, from the first fine careless rapture of necessary self-defence to the founding of an efficiently run underworld, more and more women, even in strongly Republican families, have tried to restrain their sons from 'joining the lads'.

DERVLA MURPHY, A Place Apart, 1978

SO THERE IT WAS, our territory, with the old fort of Grianan on one hill overlooking Lough Foyle, the feud farmhouse on another hill, gazing on Lough Swilly, the thick neck of the Inishowen peninsula between, Derry gauzed in smoke at the end of Lough Foyle, the border writhing behind it. We would walk out there into Donegal in the late morning and be back in the city by six o'clock, in time to see the women and girls streaming home from the shirt factories, arms linked, so much more brightly dressed, so much more talkative than the men, most of whom stood at the street corners. We would call to them, but they would dismiss us as youngsters.

'Wheel that fella home in his pram. His mother'll be lookin' for him.'

'You and your wee red cheeks. Teethin' again!'

We'd retreat in disarray. Sometimes, the older boys would jump on to the back of a lorry or hang on to the luggage ladder on a bus and fly past them, whistling, shouting the names of girls and the boys who fancied them. When the women disappeared into the houses there was always a blank space, a stillness of air disrobed, gaiety lost. Smoke from the chimneys stood up in the sky, even in summer, and when one went on fire, the sheaf of flame was a delight to see.

SEAMUS DEANE, Reading in the Dark, 1996

NARRATOR:

    In the year of our Lord, 445, Patrick chose to build a church on this hill, and to make it the hub of all churches in Ireland. Climb up! And look, below you lies the city of the Cathedral – Armagh, with its hub-hubble of smokes and its hatchet roofs splitting the sunlight. From this hill the roads run out in to a rolling country, roads so often filled by war and emptied by peace. For this hill was also a fort. And men died bloodily here, loving the old ways and hating the new.

It's a lush land you see beyond, of orchard and lilac and beech, and patchwork fields with wild hedges, and bees hunting in the laburnum. And the air's cushioned like plush, and pin-pointed by the cuckoo and corncrake. And the stones of this place – look at that carved cathedral stone built into the cottage wall – the stones of this place are fat with history, slow and fat as the cattle scattered on a thousand hills.

CHILDREN (sing-song):
See-saw, Margery Daw,
    Sold her bed, and ...

MAN (angrily):
Get aff that boord or ye'll brak it, ye brats.

VENDOR:
Ardglass herrins! Ardglass herrins! Tuppence a piece, missus.

WOMAN:
Away out o' that wi' ye! Is it the basket ye're sellin'?

CHILD:
Hi, Ma! Luk at the German prisoners in the lorry!

CATTLE-DEALER:
Come on, now! Howl out your han' like a dacent man!

BALLAD SINGER:
At a fair or a wake I could twist my shillelagh,
Or trip through a jig with my brogues bound with straw,
And all the fair maids in the village or valley
Loved the bound Phelim Brady, the Bard of Armagh.

WOMAN:
Och, ay! Sure she's niver twice the wan way.
Always choppin' and changin' ...

W.R. RODGERS, 'Armagh: The City Set on a Hill', 1945

WHERE THE FREE STATE IMPINGES on Northern Ireland, the City of Londonderry occupies a commanding position on a hill round the base of which the tidal Foyle sweeps in a broad curve. Its name has always been associated with the Oak *(dair)*; its ancient designation was *Daire Calgaith*: then it became *Daire Columchille* (St Columba's oakwood); and it obtained its present title when the Irish Society of London received grants of land in the time of James I. A deep valley on the inland side of the city, only slightly above tide-level, completes the magic circle of its virginity. With its defiant walls still intact, decorated with 'Roaring Meg' and other ancient pieces of ordnance, its Protestant Cathedral set high on the hill-top, with soaring spire and chapter-house full of keys and cannon-balls and letters of Schomberg, the city seems to typify its history: the very street names – Artillery Street, Magazine Street, Lundy's Lane, Mountjoy Street, are redolent of 1688; while Cowards' Bastion and Hangman's Bastion are full of grim suggestion. There is a grimness, too, about, the squatting skeleton on the city's coat of arms; but that commemorates a much earlier episode. As is characteristic of Ireland, the dead past is not allowed to bury its dead: and Derry's Prentice Boys and Closing of the Gates and drumming and marching seem natural there. But the memory of the siege and of the gallant resistance of its burghers appears to satisfy it: Derry shows none of the desire to perpetuate political and religious warfare or intolerance to the extent of outrage and murder such as has so frequently in Belfast aroused the reprobation of all right-thinking people. In the working-class areas, which now spread across the valley and far up the opposite slope, the distribution of the emblematic signs placed on the doors at the time of the Eucharistic Congress in Dublin shows that an intimate mixing of creeds and politics need not of necessity constitute an explosive compound. At the same time, the establishment of a 'frontier' a couple of miles out, where the Free State begins, is wholly deplored, for it causes heavy loss equally to the city traders and to the Donegal farmers to whom Derry is an essential market. The city lies on the Donegal side of the Foyle, it should be noted; but the 'Liberties of Londonderry', some twenty-five square miles of land surrounding the town, push back the Free State border.

ROBERT LLOYD PRAEGER, *The Way That I Went*, 1937

TO UNDERSTAND THE APPEARANCE of the town, you must imagine a spacious square very nearly in the centre, the middle of which is occupied by the town-hall, formerly the guard-house whence the Boys snatched the keys on the memorable 7th of December; from this draw four perfectly straight lines forming a cross, and you have to the north-east Shipquay Street, terminating in the gate of the same name: to the south-west Bishop's Street, with Bishop's Gate at the end: to the south-east Ferryquay Street, ending at the famous gate which was first shut in the face of Lord Antrim's regiment, and to the north-west Butcher's Street, with its gate, where the Protestants, driven by De Rosen, lay perishing for three days in the sight of the famished garrison. All these are wide handsome streets, with excellent shops and private dwellings.

CHARLOTTE ELIZABETH, *Letters from Ireland*, 1838

M Y FATHER WAS BORN AND RAISED in Derry. His older brother never left there, taking over their father's business and, in turn, handing it over to his son (who will soon hand it over to his own). We visited regularly. We had walked around the city's great walls, still unbroken and complete, eighteen feet thick and never breached (thus Derry's nickname, 'The Maiden City'). They encircled the old city with a mile or so of imposing fortification. We had run our hands along the cold metal of 'Roaring Meg' and the other nameless death-dealing cannons that still line the battlements, nosing their heavy muzzles over the ramparts, long cooled from armament into attraction, the backdrop to countless family photographs. The fact that people had died *here*, with terrible want and violence, in our line of sight, the fact that in the Diamond (the city's original central square) people had once been under fear of genocide and ethnic cleansing, the fact that Shipquay Street, Butcher's Street, Bishop's Gate, and so on, all the names we knew, appeared in Walker's account draped in so different a livery from that of the ordinary day-today bustle of the place – all this acted to splice horrendous happenings onto known places with deadly effect. Together they acted like barbed head and shaft in an arrow that could get through that sense of distance which is proof against so many of the dark rain of missiles that fall on our awareness bearing news of atrocity and disaster. For all its antiquity, the book's story could not easily be exiled to some foreign place far removed from us and of only distant, marginal concern. These things had happened *here*, in a place for which, and to people with whom, we felt a close connection, the intervening centuries not-withstanding. And little did we guess, in those childhood visits to its walls, that the Maiden City's reputation would soon be besmirched with violence again. That the aunt we stayed with there would be blown off her feet by the blast from a terrorist bomb one afternoon when she was shopping; that the graveyard where my father's parents were buried would become unsafe to visit, that the monument erected in memory of the *Diary's* author, George Walker, would be blown up, as another turbulent chapter in the city's history was written.

CHRIS ARTHUR, *from* 'Under Siege', *Irish Nocturnes*, 1999

HOMECOMINGS

I stared with brown eyes
Down to the Foyle waters,
Held out a hand with sugar
To a breadcart horse.
Et ego in Arcadia ...
Among Derry oaks St Colum

'numbered the stars of heaven
        this teacher of all things
this Dove, this Colum Cille.'

City of Walls
City of Siege
Jewel of the north
Maiden of the west
Undone by drums and cymbals
Fat rats! Fat rats!
Fed on the Irish dead
Fat rats!
One for a shillin'.

A stranger among strangers
I look for my house of birth.
Pulled down years ago
I show the paper: 'I certify ...'
Ich bin ein Derryman
A stranger grips my hand.

I dawdle at the Guildhall,
Buy postcards, a newspaper,
Watch armoured cars
Patrolling history.
Over a Chinese sweet-and-sour
I chat to a local.
He files the claws
Of tribal words
For walls have ears.

The March wind
Body-searches the daffodils
I sip tea in a cafe
Read the despatches
Of bombing, kidnap –
'Teach us to care
and not to care.'

Donemana in Tyrone –
Grandmother's parish
Of Smyths and sheep.
Dour stone walls
Divide, eavesdrop
In a scrubbed landscape.

Home at last
To wet and winds.

ROBERT GREACEN, *Collected Poems*, 1995

A RMAGH IS ONE OF THE MOST lovable cathedral cities in the world, fair in its site, its sacred buildings and homes of learning, its air of quietude, culture and ease. The place where St Patrick founded his church and set up his crozier is on a central height. In concentric circles round that steep hill are streets of noble buildings – a library and Georgian houses, ivy-clad – and then of fine shops and modest dwellings. These circles go back to the very days of the national apostle; for they stand where, in ancient times, the ramparts of a vast double or triple rath were dug. Radiating streets are Irish Street, Scotch Street, English Street, marking the quarters assigned to the nations, a thousand years ago, when a university at Armagh gave hospitality like that of medieval Paris, to all who sought holy learning.

AODH DE BLÁCAM, *The Black North*, 1938

O NE OF THE GREATEST ATTEMPTS at town improvement took place at Armagh during the latter part of the Georgian period. In 1767, Dr Richard Robinson was promoted to the See and he at once set about the task of converting the place into a town fit to be the ecclesiastical capital of Ireland. Dr Robinson found the architecture of Armagh unimposing; he left it one of the most beautiful towns in the British Isles. In 1765, practically all the houses in the town were of mud, with roofs of thatch, while the Cathedral was roofed with shingles.

The new Primate caused many public buildings to be erected, some at his own expense and some by public subscription. He repaired the Cathedral and roofed the building with slates, he founded the Library and Observatory, he promoted the erection of a hospital and a college, while a military barracks and a gaol were erected under his auspices; in addition to these public buildings he built a number of private houses at his own expense. These buildings, all in local stone, are among the finest in the Province.

His Grace employed Thomas Cooley as his architect in the design of the buildings which were erected during the first part of his Primacy and Cooley was responsible for the design of the Royal School, the Primate's Palace and the Library, amongst other buildings in the town. On Cooley's death in 1784 Francis Johnston became architect to his Grace. Johnston was one of Armagh's most distinguished sons and founder of the Royal Hibernian Academy. He was responsible for the design of the

Observatory and, after the death of his patron, the County Courthouse, the Museum and two houses now occupied by Banking Companies.

GILBERT CAMBLIN, *The Town in Ulster*, 1951

IT IS IMPOSSIBLE TO STAND in the City of Armagh and not sense in the air all around you ghostly spiritual whisperings of the tremendous influence which this ancient and venerable city has had upon the history of Ireland, not only through the long centuries of the Christian era but for many centuries before that time. Armagh is one of that select company of the towns or cities of Ireland which assail one with an indefinable but subtly personal atmosphere all their own. In this company one thinks of Dublin or Cashel or Derry, and very much of Galway, the most Irish of all towns for all its proud Spanish air, but one thinks pre-eminently of Armagh; for there is atmosphere in every stone of this place, something springing from the generations that have passed, generations of great people and of lowly people, of secular princes and princes of the church, all of whom have made their homes here and through the fleeting centuries transmitted to the very bricks and mortar some ineffable quality of their own humanity. Speaking for myself I could never enter Armagh with the thought that this might just as well be Portadown or Lurgan or Ballymena, although I might easily enter one of these three places and find nothing to differentiate the one from the others, excellent as they all are. Armagh is Armagh and could never be anything else. It is one of the essentially individual cities of Ireland, and in this gracious place too the regrettable but inevitable division of the Irish people into two opposing schools of thought seems to find some kind of agreement. For this is the Ecclesiastical Metropolis of the whole of Ireland today as it was on that day when St Patrick first set up his initial Bishopric here and declared it to be the Primacy. And here the two chief Irish cathedrals of the two main persuasions of the Christian Faith stand in friendly proximity, and seem to whisper to each other that all this difference between the people who go to the one place and the people who go to the other is but another piece of poor human folly, for what is there in it after all but to worship God in whatever way seems right and fitting to you.

St Patrick loved this place and you cannot wonder at it. It is the very cry of his heart that we hear in the *Book of Armagh*: 'It is Armagh that I love, my dear thorp, my dear hill', and I often wonder whether he ever thought, when he chose this Holy City of his, how much it resembled in situation and character that other Holy City of Rome. For Armagh lay close to the seat of royal power in Ulster, and St Patrick sought and obtained the co-operation of those Kings of Ulster, just as in Rome when the Emperors became Christian the Popes sought and obtained their Imperial support. And as well as this, Armagh, like Rome, stands partly upon a number of small hills and partly in a valley between them, and indeed the Seven Hills of Armagh are often pointed out to visitors to this very day. But all this comparison of Armagh with Rome must not make us forget that the ancient Celtic Church founded by St Patrick was very much an Irish Church and not at all a Romish one.

RICHARD HAYWARD, *In Praise of Ulster*, 1938

ARMAGH (*ARD MACHA*, MACHA'S HEIGHT) is a fine county, its fertility increased by the presence of limestone in the north, where also the Eocene clays of Lough Neagh cover the portion of the area which approaches that sheet of water. Much of the surface resembles Down, save that lakelets are almost absent. For all purposes the most interesting centre is the ancient city of Armagh. It was founded by St Patrick about the year 444, but the great earthwork now called Navan Fort, the ancient Emania, carries its history back at least eight hundred years further. Emania was the seat of Ulster sovereignty during six centuries, ending in AD 332, when Fergus Fogha was defeated, and Emania burnt and pillaged. As in the case of Tara, little but uninspiring earthworks remain to tell of former greatness. Armagh is a small and pleasant town, a place of importance ever since its foundation, for it is the seat of government of both the Roman Catholic and the Protestant Episcopal churches in Ireland. It boasts two cathedrals and other buildings of note, such as the Public Library, which houses many valuable- old books and early records, and the fine Archbishop's palace. The handsome red marble with which the city is paved is obtained locally from a limited area of Carboniferous beds which intervene between the New Red and the Silurian rocks. One wishes that many other towns in Ireland were so well kept, and presented an appearance of equal prosperity and general well-being.

ROBERT LLOYD PRAEGER, *The Way That I Went*, 1937

THE FAIR CITY OF ARMAGH is an interesting one. It was here the great hall of 'Craob Ruadh' was built, where the order of knighthood was established. The Knights of the Red Branch were the finest body of men who ever lived in Ireland. King Alfred the Great wrote a poem in 683, which can be seen in the British Museum. He was educated in the school at Newry, and visited Armagh before returning to England. He mentions the beauty of the great church built by St Patrick. This is one of the verses, as it is translated by O'Donovan:

> I found in Armagh the splendid
> Meekness, wisdom, circumspection,

Fasting in obedience to the Son of God,
Noble and prosperous sages.

Town life, it is said, was alien to Irish civilisation till the Normans came.
Certainly the Gaels were mainly a rural race, like all the northern people,
till the founding of towns began in the tenth and eleventh centuries.
Nevertheless, they had towns from the age of St Patrick onward. In
Armagh there were seven churches; and the city was divided into the
Rath, the Great Third, the Third of Massay, and the Third of the Saxons
(Trian Saxan), the quarter formerly frequented by English students.
Around these sacred places, and protected by their walls, dwelt lay traders
and hereditary craftsmen, who busied themselves with the gold and silver
work which they carried to so high a level. King James II, in his progress
through the north to and from the siege of Derry, rested for a few days
at Armagh, which he described as having been pillaged by the enemy, and
very inconvenient both for himself and his suite. In 1690 Duke
Schomberg took possession of it, and formed a depot of provisions here.

THE REVEREND CANON FORDE, *Sketches of Olden Days in Northern Ireland*, 1926

M Y PROGRESS THROUGH THE SCHOOL was not marked by any
particular circumstance. I was reasonably diligent, tolerably clever
and was never punished for my lessons, and only once subjected to
birchen discipline, for bathing in the river Callan contrary to rule. I had
my share of boxing, but was neither quarrelsome nor scientific. The
sorest battle I fought was on Easter Monday, 1813, with my chum Joe
Radcliffe. Easter Monday was celebrated at the school by luxurious
breakfasts which the boys provided extra for themselves, laying in stores
of tea, muffins, baps (a kind of muffin) and especially numerous eggs, hen,
duck, turkey and if possible goose. The peasantry and lower townsmen
devoted Easter Monday to cockfighting. On this morning I was walking
with my breakfast 'crony', cronnying as it was called, discussing how long
eggs should be boiled in the earthen pipkin, provided for the occasion,
when some big boys, who having fags to do their breakfast work, had an
idle time and were on a look out for a cockfight.

They spied us by ill luck and as we were the two fattest boys in the
school we were a nice match – the two fatties should fight. They ordered
us to take off our coats. We did not dare to refuse but were gentle in our
attack, whereupon our attackers gave us a sound lick or two with rod or
fist. I do not recollect how, or exactly when my blood got up, but in half
an hour we were parted matches as the phrase was, both having our eyes
blackened, noses bloody and I remember my hands were so bruised with
hammering my friend's countenance, I could not shoot a marble for a
fortnight. However, as there is no use crying after spilt milk, so little did

we think there might be crying after spilt blood, and were as good friends as ever over our tea and eggs.

I remained at Armagh School till Christmas 1815 having been there in all five and a half years.

JOHN HAMILTON, Sixty Years Experience as an Irish Landlord, 1894

A HUMAN SMILE
for Finn

In trim blazers, beneath the shadow
of the new Cathedral, we paraded
in a slow crocodile, down Armagh town

Through Irish, English, Scotch Street,
nametags of our Northern metropolis;
the old Cathedral glooming over us.

Two by two, bright boots and shoes,
arms swinging, eyes fixed before,
small soldiers of the religious wars

We marched primly past Protestant boys
sauntering down from the Royal School.
Then – a tactical error – one day we crossed

A more unnerving race. All the girls
streaming down from the convent, uniforms
as well, but sporting pert looks, curls

That threatened to disrupt our column.
The Prefects had to give a signal.
One (a future bishop) raised his cap.

Sheepishly, we followed that gracious sign.
For one split second, grim habit's crocodile
blinked, risked a human smile.

JOHN MONTAGUE, Time in Armagh, 1993

ARMAGH JAIL LIES LOW AND QUIET and pale-grey across the wide southern end of one of the most pleasing county town streets or esplanades to be found anywhere, and I loved my morning walk there, taking my ease though the day was cold, from the Court House end, under great, bare trees. A gentle traffic – though nowhere ever again shall we be free of parking buses, or monster Cadillacs – flowed on the two wide roads, but I walked in the gravelled centre, where at this hour only a few perambulators, dogs and elderly people as respectable as myself enjoyed the bright peace. I admired the residential terraces of the late seventeenth and early eighteenth century which on the east side of The Mall testify almost princelily to the past of Armagh, but I liked too the less well preserved west side, into which Victorianism had thrust some ruddy expressions of piety and public service. And at last I was at the end, and there – very gentle and wide-eyed and William-and-Maryish – was the Jail.

KATE O'BRIEN, *My Ireland*, 1962

THE GAOL WAS BUILT IN 1780, but it was not until almost thirty years later that the County Courthouse was erected at the opposite end of the Common, now known as The Mall. A few years earlier a low wall had been built around The Mall, and in due course a street was constructed on the outer side of this wall. The former horse-course now became a public walk and trees were planted on either side, so that a pleasant public park of considerable size was formed. The outer frontage of the new street was made available for building and houses began to be erected soon after the building of the Courthouse in 1809. These houses were of the very finest character, and like the other new buildings in the town they were of local stone, the beautiful Charlemont Place being in dressed ashlar work. This terrace was of a standard equal to metropolitan architecture, and it is today one of the finest examples of Georgian architecture in Ireland.

The re-building of the City of Armagh marked the climax of the movement which had been manifested in the towns of Ulster for more than a century. The influence of the Georgian planners continued to be felt even after the end of the period, but from the second decade of the nineteenth century other influences were also felt, influences which were not conducive to good town-building and which in the end very largely resulted in the undoing of the work of improving and beautifying the towns of the Province which had been carried out during the eighteenth and early nineteenth centuries. Nevertheless, lasting traces remain, especially in the smaller towns of the Province, 'many of which still preserve the character and charm of the eighteenth century with its mastery of urban planning and building'.

GILBERT CAMBLIN, *The Town in Ulster*, 1951

ARMAGH IS ... JUSTLY SELF-CONSCIOUS of its architectural beauty as a city, not only in its individual buildings but in the town as a whole.

Armagh is a most striking city on several points. Firstly, it rejoices in several hills, not steep as Basel's hills are steep, but nevertheless steep enough to allow that variation of level, that changing viewpoint which makes, for instance, Bath a more interesting city than Cheltenham though both consist of fine Georgian buildings. And then, curiously, Armagh retained a medieval kind of street pattern, so that surprises occur at every corner, surprises which include some exquisite Georgian houses.

Francis Johnston was born here in 1760, a man of unusual sensibility who became one of Ireland's great architects in a period when much fine work appeared. Although Johnston spent most of his life in Dublin designing some of its finest public buildings, he left his native city with examples too. The most notable perhaps was the row of silver-stone houses in Charlemont Place which overlooks the green and its trees. He also designed the courthouse whose pedimented Doric portico looks sedately down the long stretch of grass. The courthouse was built with the same kind of pearly, light-catching stone as his houses, a stone which is peculiar to Armagh. Another house, now used by the Bank of Ireland, of extremely graceful proportions, also by Johnston, hides away in one of the narrow streets.

But apart from its Georgian ware, Armagh possesses one of Ireland's most splendid Victorian buildings. On a hill, twin towers and spires needle the sky in a paean of ... well, those who cannot stomach Victorian Gothic would call the Roman Catholic cathedral a pain in the neck. Certainly a pain in the neck was what I got from standing at the top of the long imposing steps which lead up to the west front, in order to gaze at those skyscraper spires of the beautiful light grey stone radiant in the sun.

Well I remember those towers being described to me in childhood as the Devil's horns! The Devil, I am sure, would be pleased to sport a pair of horns as fine as those, in the same way as the archbishop must be pleased to have such splendour in which to exercise his office.

ROBIN BRYANS, *Ulster: A Journey Through the Six Counties*, 1964

THERE WAS A HORSE-FAIR at the other end of the green and along the narrow hilly streets behind it, the rain shining on the patient flanks, and the smell of porter, bogwater and dung at every step. Indeed, the fair dominated everything. The cold and stately houses on The Mall seemed to have withdrawn fastidiously into themselves. Country folk had taken possession of the shops. The railway was taken over by horse-dealers. The town was relapsed into that aspect of it which, with modest houses, smoking chimneys, a few thatch roofs, clammy-looking pubs and small huckster shops, clutters about the two hills on which the cathedrals stand above the battle, with their appendages and outposts of episcopal palace, theological seminary, sedate library, presbytery, deanery, homes of church-warden and sacristan. I felt that I was getting a better smell of Armagh that morning than I would have got on a more tidy day. In spite of its many sedate and dignified retreats, such as the Green and the Mall and the cathedral close, it is the least typically Northern, the most Southern town I met in Ulster, so that it seemed in keeping that the streets should be untidy, and the crowds garrulous, and I would have not been surprised if the approach to the city had been lined by mud–cabins and cock-crowing farmyards as, so one resident told me, it was up to twenty-five years ago.

SEAN O'FAOLAIN, An Irish Journey, 1940

ARMAGH

There is a through–otherness about Armagh
Of tower and steeple,
Up on the hill are the arguing graves of the kings,
And below are the people.

Through-other as the rooks that swoop and swop
Over the sober hill
Go the people gallivanting from shop to shop
Guffawing their fill.

And the little houses run through the market-town
Slap up against the great,
Like the farmers all clabber and muck walking arm by arm
With the men of estate.

Raised at a time when Reason was all the rage,
Of grey and equal stone,
This bland face of Armagh covers an age
Of clay and feather and bone.

Through-other is its history, of Celt and Dane,
Norman and Saxon,
Who ruled the place and sounded the gamut of fame
From cow-horn to klaxon.

There is a through–otherness about Armagh
Delightful to me,
Up on the hill are the graves of the garrulous kings
Who at last can agree.

W.R. RODGERS, Europa and the Bull, 1952

Backroads

It was a summer evening, and, mellowing and still,
Glenwhirry to the setting sun lay bare from hill to hill;
For all that valley pastoral held neither house nor tree,
But spread abroad and open all, a full fair sight to see,
From Slemish foot to Collon top lay one unbroken green,
Save where in many a silver coil the river glanced between.

SIR SAMUEL FERGUSON, *from* 'The Ballad of Willie Gilliland'

TO PRESBYTERIANS, GLENWHIRRY – the home of my ancestors by my mother's side – is classic ground. It is easy of access from Argyllshire and the West of Scotland, as it is only a few miles distant from the port of Larne. Until about a century ago it had no road passing through it; and embosomed among mountains, it was in a manner secluded from observation. During the dark days of Scottish suffering in the reigns of Charles II and James II it was a place of refuge for the oppressed Covenanters. To it the celebrated Rev. Alexander Peden fled for shelter when driven out of the land of his fathers by pitiless persecutors. He here found an asylum, and his name is not yet forgotten.

W.D. KILLEN, *Reminiscences of a Long Life*, 1901

SAMUEL FERGUSON OF STANDING STONE, in the county of Antrim, the paternal grandfather of Sir Samuel Ferguson, had by his wife, Hessy Owens, a daughter and six sons, amongst whom he left a good estate, around and including the little town of Parkgate, County Antrim. The Ferguson property was situated in and about the valley of the Six-Mile Water, which empties itself into Lough Neagh near the town of Antrim. Here stands one of the earliest of the Irish round towers, and not

far distant may be traced the remains of the royal fort of Rathmore –
Moy-Linny. The region is dominated by the moat of Donegore. This
fine earthwork is a conspicuous object in the landscape. It commands an
extensive view over a rich and undulating country to Lough Neagh, with
its expanse of waters and boundary of distant mountains. To the north
rise the Connor Hills and the wedge-like mountain of Slemish. At the
base of the moat, or rath, stands the pretty church of Donegore. Here, on
its lower slopes included in the churchyard, is the burying-place of the
Ferguson family, and in this plot of ground repose the mortal remains of
the Poet and Antiquary ... He lies amid scenes endeared to him from
childhood, and often described by his pen. He sleeps among kindred dust
on an Irish green hillside.

LADY FERGUSON, *Sir Samuel Ferguson and the Ireland of His Day*, 1896

BACKROADS

No one was ever lost on backroads.
Their intrigues end in signposts, farmhouse doors,
The cottages their tributary lanes
Prompt to discover. These bent miles, the closest
Trails they go, are not more subtle
Than the minds that planned, the hands that laid them.

Still at their meetings creeping fields infringe,
An inch more than last year. Briar and branch
Conspire over the tar, the shears' edge,
The scythe's last swing forgotten. Another
Lane meanders to a square the weeds have taken,
Stone ribs in the undergrowth where lives were.

FRANK ORMSBY, *A Store of Candles*, 1977

A FEW MINUTES LATER Mick and Patsy and Fly came into the drawing-
room to ask Aunt Charlotte if she would like to go for a walk. They
were going down to the sea, they said.

Aunt Charlotte said she would be glad to go. She put on her hat and
gloves, and they started out.

On each side of the road there was a wall of loose stones bound
together by moss and brambles. In the distance at their right rose the
mountains; a turn of the road about a mile from the house brought them
within sight of the sea. They passed through the village – a long row of
whitewashed cottages with here and there a fuchsia bush by a door, a line

of bright nasturtiums under a window, or a potato patch dotted with kale by the side of a house.

Farther down the street the church stood back from the road in a graveyard full of tombstones and weeds. Aunt Charlotte said she was interested in churches, so they stopped to look at it. Coming back through the graveyard Mick showed her the tombstones of the rebels, with skull and crossbones on the top, and the grave of a great-uncle of theirs who had been hanged at the time of the rebellion.

'Serve him right, the old traitor!' said Patsy.

Aunt Charlotte was shocked.

'If he was your great-uncle, you should think of him with respect,' she said.

'And him an informer!' said Mick; ''deed I would have killed him myself. Andy Graham says he would have jabbed the brains out of him.'

'Lull says she would have rapped him on the head with a blackthorn stick,' said Fly; 'but whisht! − I do believe the old ruffian is lying in his grave listening to us.'

Aunt Charlotte shivered.

As they were going down the churchyard steps Patsy stopped.

'Look at those two old rats sitting on the wall like wee old men. They're just saying which of us will be brought there first.'

Aunt Charlotte, gave a little scream, and hurried out on to the road.

'You children have morbid minds, you have made me quite nervous.'

KATHLEEN FITZPATRICK, *The Weans at Rowallan*, 1905

IT DIDN'T ALWAYS RAIN: just enough to keep the grass tender and green, and make the flowers bloom in spring and the little streams run over the pebbles. One of the streams which I never saw was celebrated in a song:

> I remember my young days for younger I've been.
> I remember my young days by the Muttonburn stream.
> It's not marked on a map, it's nowhere to be seen,
> A wee river in Ulster, the Muttonburn stream.
>
> Sure the ducks they swim in it, the white and the green,
> They muddy the water but they make theirselves clean,
> And the ladies from Kerry the finest e'er seen
> Come to dunk off their clothes in the Muttonburn stream.
>
> Sure 'twill cure all diseases though chronic they've been
> Just to bathe in the waters of the Muttonburn stream.

Tra la la la la la la, tra la la la la leam,
A wee river in Ulster, the Muttonburn stream.

(The ladies didn't come all the way from Kerry as I supposed, but from
Carry: Carrickfergus.)

ALICE KANE, *Songs and Sayings of an Ulster Childhood*, 1983

THE VILLAGE IS CALLED FORKHILL. No matter from what direction you approach it, you see it against a background of encompassing hills. The western hill is twin-peaked, its eastern side strewn with an avalanche of loose, slate-purple boulders, quarried by time. A river-cleft gap to the south makes a rise of land. East across the river towers a cone hill, skirted by cool trees; rock which turns russet in the sunsets here and there pierces the sheen of velvety heather and the vivid green of growing bracken. The northern skyline is marked by the rock-serrated ridges of the hills beyond Mullabawn; and eastwards again, across tilled land and white houses snug and close to the earth, lies Slieve Gullion, with cabins tucked precariously on its slopes.

The houses are built on each side of the river; and from one part of the village, one can look down on the roofs of the others, some amid trees. You feel the smooth, calm peace of the delightful place. Then maybe the village anvil rings clear as the smith works; or maybe you hear the chugging grind of the mills where the waterwheels spin sweetly, despite their cumbersome size. Trout leap in the river, where old, drooping branches of riverside trees remind one of tired old fishermen who have quietly fallen asleep.

Happily enough, a huge tree shades the centre of the village street. From here, on both sides, uneven and varying rows of white houses ascend, like the gliding wings of a seagull. Little old roads dip and twist over ivy-quaint bridges. Perched on the rise are scattered cabins and lonesome, gale-gaunt trees. And though the touch of colour from a thatched roof is missing, [an] old-world atmosphere lingers about the village.

MICHAEL J. MURPHY, *At Slieve Gullion's Foot*, 1941

HISTORICALLY THE REGION [i.e. Slieve Gullion] is important, for these hills form the ancient as well as the present frontier of Ulster, and at the Moyry Pass (*Maigh Tréa*, Trea's Plain) south of Slieve Gullion (*Sliabh cuillinn*, holly mountain), many a battle was fought between English and Irish, and no doubt by others long before the English came. From Dundalk, road and railway climb for four hundred feet in order to win through to County Down. The hills slope southward to Dundalk Bay, and more level ground extends thence to Dublin. Several small square castles remain, visible from the railway and main road as one passes under the shadow of Slieve Gullion, to tell of troubled times: but more interesting and imposing are the earthworks, dating, it is believed, from the second or third century of our era, which tell of much more ancient fortification of the boundary of Ulster. On the western spurs of Slieve Gullion stand the remains of 'The Dorsey' (*Dorus*, a door or pass), an immense fortified camp of peculiar shape – an irregular oblong a mile and a quarter long by six hundred yards wide. The enclosure is encircled by a great earthen rampart, with a fosse on either side still about 23 feet deep, 12 feet or more wide at bottom: and external to these fosses are lesser ramparts. This great fortress was presumably associated with the imposing ditches known in different portions of their length as 'The Black Pig's Dyke', 'The Dane's Cast' and 'The Worm Ditch', of which fragments exist in many counties on either side of the boundary of Ulster, belonging apparently to three contemporary or more likely successive lines of defence. The most northern of them runs from Bundoran on the Atlantic by way of Lough Allen to the neighbourhood of Newry: it is upon this line that 'The Dorsey' is seated. The most southern stretches from Athlone on the Shannon to Drogheda. The intermediate ditch, more fragmentary and difficult to understand, lies roughly between the two. W.F. de V. Kane spent much time in tracing and mapping what is left of these ancient fortifications, but historically very little is known about them. The fact that no tradition remains among the people concerning them, and that supernatural agencies embodied in fantastic stories are brought in to account for them, points to an early date of construction.

ROBERT LLOYD PRAEGER, The Way That I Went, 1937

THE PLACE CALLED ARDBOE is the most remote region of a remote county – Tyrone – a large rambling shrub- and bush-covered county that stretches across the interior of the political state of Northern Ireland, often called Ulster – a misnomer, since Ulster, one of the four provinces of Ireland, far outreaches the latter-day political boundaries of Northern Ireland. Ardboe is a parish of small townlands, many of whose names are Gaelic. The parish is divided into Upper and Lower Ardboe, the one separated from the other by the enormous wedge of an aerodrome built in the middle of the Second World War, and which landed, all unbeknownst, in the lap of the parish like a monstrous cuckoo.

Lower Ardboe lies along the shores of Lough Neagh, the biggest lake in the United Kingdom, twenty-five miles long by eight miles wide, in effect an inland tideless freshwater sea, an extravagant expanse of water which laps the small fields of our farm, within sight and sound of our house. Its soughing music forms the aural background to each day of our lives.

We are almost an island, connected to the outside world by only one tiny road which dribbles its slack and twisting way into our hidden desmesnes, and which swerves and slings around the perimeter of the aerodrome like a girdle. To anyone coming towards us for the first time from the small market town of Cookstown ten miles away, following the road as it meanders towards the lough, it must appear to expire in a flaxhole and a tangle of bramble below the Moor Hill. But in fact, at that point, called the Cross Roads (although it is not strictly that), it turns at a right-angle, narrows and plunges towards Biddy's Brae, past our house and thence to the Old Cross of Ardboe, where it ends in the graveyard surrounding the cross. Another smaller spur road called the Car Road branches off alongside the lough shore towards the flat long beauty of Golloman's Point, and parallel to that old turf road is a new white concrete road leading to the pump house built for a water-supply to the aerodrome. Both these roads are hidden from view on the road to the cross.

POLLY DEVLIN, *All Of Us There*, 1983

I FOUND A POET IN A MANSE, a manse by the roadside in the County Tyrone. The poet was Alice Milligan. When she had given me tea she took me without to show me all that was to be seen from a height near where she lived. As I went with her I thought how little she had changed in the years since I had seen her. She wore a brown waterproof now, and I believed that she had worn a brown waterproof on the last occasion I had been with her. The sandy red was still in her hair and a wisp of it fell over her shoulder. And still she spoke casually of what she did herself and earnestly about what her friends were doing. I had never seen her without something in her hands that was intended for some practical purpose. Now she had a telescope, a long brass telescope such as sea-captains walk about with in their retirement. She could show me, she told me, the stronghold of the Ulster kings from this – Aileach.

PADRAIC COLUM, *Cross Roads in Ireland*, 1930

NEWTOWNARDS (NOVEMBER 7, 1796).
I had an opportunity of seeing this morning a large body of potato diggers – it was a pretty sight; a great number of young men marching along with smart girls leaning on their arms – they were going towards Comber to dig Maxwell's potatoes. I rode some distance with them and had a good deal of funny conversation; you may easily conceive I neither scolded nor attempted to argue them out of their intentions. We had a great number of jokes and nothing could be more good-humoured than

they were to me. I went over to enquire after some arms that were stolen last night from the soldiers ...

CASTLEREAGH, quoted in H. MONTGOMERY HYDE, *The Rise of Castlereagh*, 1933

WITH A BOAT AND A TENT one can have wonderful water trips from Enniskillen right up to Lough Oughter, but the bolder scenery and more open views which obtain on the Lower lake make it the more attractive. If you row down from Enniskillen, where boats are more numerous, better and cheaper than anywhere else I know, you pass the hill on which stands Portora House, a handsome eighteenth-century building erected to accommodate the Royal School founded in 1626 by Charles I. Below it on the water's edge is all that remains of Oldcastle, once a fortress, later a bishop's palace. Thence the river begins to expand, throwing out lake-like arms to right and left. Soon the large island of Devenish comes into view, with its round tower standing up grey behind the green grassy curve of its skyline. This is one of the most interesting of the round towers of Ireland, on account of the superior style of the masonry (grey limestone), and the very unusual feature of a cornice of rich Romanesque scroll-work just below the conical apex. Immediately below are four windows, above each of which is a well-sculptured human head. Around are the ruins of the Abbey, of the 'Great Church', of the House of St Molaise, and in the graveyard some ornate early crosses, all of which possess features of interest to the archaeologist.

ROBERT LLOYD PRAEGER, *The Way That I Went*, 1937

HOW WILL WE APPROACH FERMANAGH? If from the north, by the road from Omagh, we will ride over high swelling bogland, by a height from which we can look back over the vast pale-tinted northland away to the Sperrins, till we cross the watershed and begin to plunge through leafy lanes towards gleaming water far below.

A more often frequented approach is from County Monaghan, which we leave at Clones, the hill town in the vast market square of which an ancient Celtic cross stands to recall our land's former sanctity. Here we are at the Border again. It runs through water at some places, and I could tell you of a man who got big offers for a swimming cow – an animal which was not afraid of water, and would lead a smuggled herd. Here we find ourselves on a pleasant road that winds as much as the Erne itself, as it corkscrews its way towards the sunset. This eastern end of the county is all gravel hills, little domes – drumlins is the native name which has passed into geological language. In and out the level road swings, to the right round this hill, to the left round that, making S after S; and all the while we admire the neat fields on these little hills, every drumlin yielding land enough for three or four good farms and a stand for shining white homesteads with little, mathematically shaped, orchards. The land close to the road, however, is full of rushes and salleys, for it is barely recovered from the waters.

AODH DE BLÁCAM, The Black North, 1938

IN COUNTY FERMANAGH

From the lake the hill climbs up
With fields and hedges to the top,
And all that crazy patchwork quilt
Looks back and sees its pattern spilt
Where moorhens dabble in the reeds
And cattle wade and no one heeds.

Green rushes and the pheasant-brown
Deep bog where even a ghost would drown,
Black pyramids of turf whose jet
Is furred with dusky violet –
Colours that glow the more because
Light filters through the rain that was.

Under small hills lake water flows
Through inland archipelagoes,
Tideless unless their tide should be
Some motion of tranquillity,
Where the cold light is isled upon
The scattering brilliance of the swan.

This is that country which the mind
Ransacks without a thought to find:
A landscape exile lovelier makes,
Setting new islands in new lakes,
And every isle a stepping stone
Love itself would stumble on.

ROBIN WILSON, Raghley, O Raghley and Other Poems, 1955

L OUGH NEAGH IS ATTRACTIVE at every season of the year, not least in autumn and winter. When the leaves spread a brown carpet in the woods and the robin redbreast mourns in their otherwise silent halls, wings are whistling in strident clamour over the northern seas. From the chilling tundras of Spitzbergen and Greenland barnacle and brent geese, ranged in echelon, speed southwards. The barnacles fly down the wild western coast past the immense red bastion of Slieve League in Donegal and the cliffs of Mayo, where the Atlantic surf embroiders lace fringes round the crags beneath them, and alight to graze on the green winter turf by many a lough and estuary. The brent geese pass along the east coast, leaving the magpie cliffs of Rathlin behind until they see shining ahead the sea-loughs where the slitch grass grows on the black tidal mud. A gaggle may alight on Lough Neagh but they will soon pass on to more abundant pasturage. The swans, too, Bewick and whooper, in white queenly grandeur come with singing pinions out of the north; and the hosts of the duck tribe, fearing the clutching fingers of the frost and the howling Polar wind-devils, flying faster than express trains, drop from the tumultuous sky to Lough Neagh and her salt sister-loughs. In squadrons and battalions they come in — the dainty golden-eye, the red-headed pochard, the wild, shy, beautiful pintail, wigeon and teal and scaup and scoter; a few goosander to the sea-loughs and an occasional smew or long-tailed duck.

The Irish winters are milder than they used to be and the ducks are never frozen out of their feeding grounds — or rather, waters. There was a great frost in 1739–40 when the whole lake was frozen over, and again in 1815 when a bullock was roasted on the ice. In 1854 it was possible to skate to Ram's Island and in 1878–9 there was for weeks a dead calm while the thermometer stood far below freezing point. Thousands of birds died a lingering death and starvation made the larks so tame that they came into the streets of Antrim. Again in January 1881 the lough was frozen. There was severe weather also in 1894 and January 1940. It is not recorded whether, like the wild swans of the Scottish islands, the aquatic birds tried to keep the waters around them open by constant deliberate paddling.

EDWARD ALLWORTHY ARMSTRONG, *Birds of the Grey Wind*, 1940

WRITTEN IN WINTER

The green warl's awa, but the white ane can charm them
   Wha skait on the burn, or wi' settin' dogs rin:
The hind's dinlin' han's, numb't we snaw-baws, to warm them,
   He claps on his hard sides, whase doublets are thin.
How dark the hail show'r mak's yon vale, aince sae pleasin'!
   How laigh stoops the bush that's owre-burden't wi' drift!
The icicles dreep at the half-thow't house-easin',
   Whan blunt the sun beams frae the verge o' the lift.

The hedge-hauntin' blackbird, on ae fit whyles restin',
   Wad fain heat the tither in storm-rufflet wing;
The silly sweel't sheep, ay the stifflin' storm breastin',
   Are glad o' green piles at the side o' the spring.

JAMES ORR, *Poems on Various Subjects*, 1804

IN HIS SEARCH FOR THE HOMELY he taught me to see other things ...
But for him I should never have known the beauty of the ordinary
vegetables that we destine to the pot. 'Drills,' he used to say. 'Just
ordinary drills of cabbages – what can be better?' And he was right. Often
he recalled my eyes from the horizon just to look through a hole in a
hedge, to see nothing more than a farmyard in its mid-morning solitude,
and perhaps a grey cat squeezing its way under a barn door, or a bent old
woman with a wrinkled, motherly face coming back with an empty
bucket from the pigsty. But best of all we liked it when the Homely and
the unhomely met in sharp juxtaposition; if a little kitchen garden ran
steeply up a narrowing *enclave* of fertile ground: surrounded by outcroppings and furze, or some shivering quarry pool under a moonrise
could be seen on our left, and on our right the smoking chimney and
lamplit window of a cottage that was just settling down for the night.

C.S. LEWIS, *Surprised By Joy*, 1955

CLOSE OUTSIDE [BELFAST] IS SOME BEAUTIFUL COUNTRY, which has
ghosts also. The exquisite valley of the Lagan disentangles itself with
a sigh, and losing its slimy foreshores winds among solemn beech trees,
beside parks, and between round green hills. The river is crossed by small
bridges, and is flanked by backwaters overshadowed by alders; here and
there a house, inexpressibly sad even in sunshine, looks down a slope or
across a meadow, and seems the home of some mysterious secret which
will awake when the intruder has passed, and stealing forth without lifting
a bolt will seek the grey surface of the water or the disk of the moon.
Should one indulge in such a fancy, local legends are prompt to confirm
it; stories about fairies, told with every degree of affectation, can be
collected in the vicinity – fairy rings, fairy thorns, fairies ninety miles high
– proving, if nothing else, that the Irish mind turns easily to the
supernatural when it feels hospitable or tired. The charm of the valley –
that needs no proof. And as with the Lagan, so with other places in the
district; the Glens of Antrim, the cliffs near Ballycastle, the dark Mourne
Mountains to the south – all, despite the variety of their scenery, have the
sadness and the sense of unreality that we associate with an indwelling
power. It is only the ordinary Celtic atmosphere which may be breathed

more fully elsewhere, but it gains a peculiar quality when near to a great city and to such a city as Belfast.

E.M. FORSTER, *Abinger Harvest*, 1936

from TOWNLAND OF PEACE

Once in a showery summer, sick of war,
I strode the roads that slanted to Kilmore,
that church-topped mound where half the tombstones wear
my people's name; some notion drew me there,
illogical, but not to be ignored,
some need of roots saluted, some sought word
that might give strength and sense to my slack rein,
by this directed, not to lose again
the line and compass so my head and heart
no longer plunge and tug to drag apart.

Thus walking dry or sheltered under trees,
I stepped clean out of Europe into peace,
for every man I met was relevant
to the harsh clamour of my eager want,
gathering fruit, or leading horse uphill,
sawing his timber, measuring his well.
The crooked apple trees beside the gate
that almost touched the roadside with the weight
of their clenched fruit, the dappled calves that browsed
free in the netted sunlight and unhoused
the white hens slouching round the tar-bright sheds,
the neat-leafed damsons with the smoky beads,
the farm unseen but loud with bucket and dog
and voices moving in a leafy fog,
gave neither hint nor prophecy of change,
save the slow seasons in their circled range;
part of a world of natural diligence
that has forgotten its old turbulence,
save when the spade rasps on a rusted sword
or a child in a schoolbook finds a savage word.

Old John, my father's father, ran these roads
a hundred years ago with other lads
up the steep brae to school, or over the stile

to the far house for milk, or dragging the long mile
to see his mother buried. Every stride
with gable, gatepost, hedge on either side,
companioned so brought nearer my desire
to stretch my legs beside a poet's fire
in the next parish. As the road went by
with meadow and orchard, under a close sky,
and stook-lined field, and thatched and slated house,
and apples heavy on the crouching boughs,
I moved beside him. Change was strange and far
where a daft world gone shabby choked with war
among the crumpled streets or in the plains
spiked with black fire-crisped rafters and buckled lines,
from Warsaw to the Yangtze, where the slow-
phrased people learn such thought that scourge and blow
may school them into strength to find the skill
for new societies of earth and steel,
but here's the age they've lost.
                    The boys I met
munching their windfalls, drifting homeward late,
are like that boy a hundred years ago,
the same bare kibes, the heirloom rags they show;
but they must take another road in time.
Across the sea his fortune summoned him
to the brave heyday of the roaring mills
where progress beckoned with a million wheels.

The bearded man who jolted in his cart
on full sack nodding, waking with a start,
giving his friendly answer to my call,
uncertain of the right road after all,
might have been he, if luck had let him stay
where no shrill hooters break across the day,
and time had checked its ticking. Had I passed
a woman by a gate, I should have paused
to crack about the year the Lough was hard
and safe as frozen bucket in the yard.
and fit to bear the revel and the feast
when merry crowds devoured the roasted beast
beneath the bright stars of a colder year
than any living man remembers here,
to ask if she had lost her mother too
from famine-fever, or if it were true
she bore my family name. There's scarce a doubt
she would have, or, at worst, have pointed out

a house whose folk did, for it's common there
as berries on the hedges anywhere.

JOHN HEWITT, *Freehold and Other Poems*, 1986

MONAGHAN IS A PLEASANT COUNTY with little outstanding scenery.
It has a fringe of mountains to the north, which leaves it more a
geographical unity with Leinster than with Northern Ireland. To the
south its land is at times rich and hillocky like County Down. It is
sheltered, with large estates harbouring great Elizabethan mansions
among age-old beeches. Such houses as Rossmore Castle near Monaghan
town, Lough Fay at Carrickmacross, the Manor of Castleblaney, and the
mansion of the Pratts at Cabra are in the same denomination as the
chateau country of France. Very handsome these old houses can
look across their parkland of bluebells, punctuated with silver-trunked
beeches ...

Monaghan is a land of small lakes. Every bend of the road seems to have
its own special one. They are sedgy and many are preparing to return to
mere bog holes before drying up altogether. They are the homes of some
of the finest dragonflies, as well as some of the most relentless mosquitoes.

I said Monaghan is not outstandingly beautiful, but sometimes standing
on a high knoll watching the patchwork of grazing and tillage land
stretching before me, I have had to modify this statement. I put it higher
up the Irish list perhaps than would a casual observer, for I have known
its stately Georgian houses whose windows framed the lakes and the
stalwart trees. It is a country that I have seen decorated for Christmas,
each hedgerow and copse of trees resplendent in their tinsel of icicles –
'the land of the Snow Queen'.

DENIS O'D. HANNA, *The Face of Ulster*, 1952

MONAGHAN HAS BEEN A SORT OF CULTURAL WATERSHED. When I
was visiting Carrickmacross some years ago, a disgruntled person
staying there told me that southerners looked on Carrickmacross as the
black north and northerners looked on it as the dirty south, and that they
were both right. I must say, however, that I did not personally encounter
anything to confirm this adverse account of the place, and it seemed a
pleasant enough little town.

The county has only the quieter and more subdued kind of scenery, for
there are no really high hills; but there are many of the little hills and
rolling country which have been left by the retreating ice cap right across
the south of Ulster. Set among these little hills there are many lakes in
Monaghan. It is not a wild county with high hills and distant views, but

a place of trim hedges and cultivated land, and its beauty is that of near or middle distance.

HUGH SHEARMAN, *Ulster*, 1949

from MONAGHAN

Monaghan, mother of a thousand
Little moulded hills,
Set about with little rivers
Chained to little mills.

Rich and many pastured Monaghan,
Mild thy meadows lie,
Melting to the distant mountains
On the mirrored sky.

SHANE LESLIE, *Songs of Oriel*, 1908

I AM IN MONAGHAN; with Cavan and Donegal, it is an Ulster county in the Free State. Like Cavan, Monaghan is a county of little lakes. It is more fertile than Cavan and is better tilled; I think the fields here have a more shining greenness. I pass through a little town that has a name in a rhyme that is recalled to me:

Castleblaney besoms –
Better never grew.
Castleblaney besoms –
A penny buys the two!

A market-cry, I suppose, that was taken into a children's game. I wondered where they pulled the heather that made the besoms – on what hillside or in what bog hereabouts – and what reason the makers had for feeling so superior about their two-a-penny besoms which, piled upon the backs of asses, they brought into Cavan: two shillings' worth would make a load.

PADRAIC COLUM, *Cross Roads in Ireland*, 1930

SUNDAY IN COUNTY MONAGHAN, 1935

Dewy rose-bud in buttonhole
Hair slicked, violet-scented.
The minister prays for farmers' weather.
The harmonium swells in reedy praise.
I daydream beside still waters.
Outside the crumbling church they gather,
A dwindling clan, greying:
Adairs, Gillespies, Wilsons, Smyths –
King's men without a King.
Chat of government and crops.
Taxes, swine fever, price of land,
Sons prospering 'across the water'.
A drive back over powdery roads
And up the hunchback lane to chicken,
Uncle George's talk of Armageddon
And why the Kaiser lost the war.
A stroll across the townland.
Brontë pages skimmed under the elm,
Tea in Belleek china, ginger snaps,
'Throw Out the Lifeline' baritoned
On the wind-up gramophone.
A spin on the gleaming sports bike
A burnt-out house, thatched cottages,
'Up Dev!' chalked on a wall.
'Brave day,' cries Pat O'Byrne,
Jetting an arc of tobacco juice.
The twilit fields with cousin Jane,
A collie bark from Kelly's yard.

ROBERT GREACEN, *Carnival at the River*, 1990

MUINEACHAN, COUNTRY OF THE LITTLE HILLS, bundle upon bundle of odd-shaped fields, mounds, forts and keeps, topped by circles of ash and thorn, glacier-carved humps and hollows creating hundreds of natural amphitheatres and hidden townlands, the whole furnished with lakes and rivers, boglands and bottomlands, hedges of magical blackthorn, deep-dug ditches and some wonderful stands of planter hardwood, all of it accessible by more roads, lanes, tracks, by-roads, canal walks, farm passes, overgrown coachways and obsolete railway sidings than any other area in Western Europe, or so we claim. Lest this seem braggartly, it must be said that the mile of no man's land border road to Drumard (our farm) must be one of the most badger-riddled and bockedy in Western Europe!

The last three decades have brought steel-roofed barns, cemented yards, concrete-block farm buildings, silo and slurry pits, gleaming chicken and turkey broiler houses, and the long black plastic tunnels of a booming mushroom business, and a more expansionist outlook than Cavan, Sligo, Leitrim, Longford and Donegal put together (according to 1983 EEC figures) and a consequent spin-off in bungalows which seem less unnatural here in the green drumlins than in the stark beauty of Connemara.

EUGENE McCABE, *from* 'Co. Monaghan', *32 Counties*, 1989

GLENCULL WATERSIDE
Glen chuil: The Glen of the Hazels

From the quarry behind the school
the crustacean claws of the excavator
rummage to withdraw a payload,
a giant's bite ...

Tis pleasant for to take a stroll by Glencull Waterside
On a lovely evening in spring (in nature's early pride);
You pass by many a flowery bank and many a shady dell,
Like walking through enchanted land where fairies used to dwell

Tuberous tentacles
of oak, hawthorn, buried pignut,
the topsoil of a living shape
of earth lifts like a scalp
to lay open

The trout are rising to the fly; the lambkins sport and play;
The pretty feathered warblers are singing by the way;
The black birds' and the thrushes' notes, by the echoes multiplied,
Do fill the vale with melody by Glencull waterside.

slipping sand
shale, compressed veins of rock,
old foundations, a soft chaos
to be swallowed wholesale,
masticated, regurgitated
by the mixer.

Give not to me the rugged scenes of which some love to write –
The beetling cliffs, o'erhanging crags and the eagle in full flight
But give to me the fertile fields (the farmer's joy and pride)
The homestead and the orchards fine by Glencull waterside.

> Secret places
> birds' nests, animal paths,
> ghosts of children hunkering
> down snail glistering slopes
> spin through iron cylinders to
> resume new life as a pliant stream
> of building material.

These scenes bring recollections back to comrades scattered wide
Who used with me to walk these banks in youthful manly pride;
They've left their boyhood's happy homes and crossed o'er oceans wide
Now but in dreamland may they walk by Glencull waterside.

> A brown stain
> seeps away from where the machine
> rocks and groans to itself, dis-
> colouring the grass, thickening
> the current of the trout stream
> which flows between broken banks
> – the Waterside a smear of mud –
> towards the reinforced bridge
> of the new road.

JOHN MONTAGUE, *The Rough Field*, 1972

THE ROAD WANDERED by means of stone causeways in and out among the islands on the western shore of the lough. The blue cone of Donard wavered on the horizon, set sometimes in a gap between green hills, at others floating like an apparition above the water of a wooded bay; one moment invisible, the next dominating the landscape. Rain clouds were sweeping up from the Mournes, leaving intervals of bright, clear sunlight. In the cloudy intervals the lough, with the tide out, looked grey and heavy as lead, the woods about Mount Stewart on the farther shore black and threatening. I crossed the causeway from the mainland to Islandreagh, past a whitewashed cottage by the water's edge, a stone pier where an occasional brig unloaded coal for the neighbouring farmhouses, a fringe of fir trees fronting a wrack-strewn bay. The tide had begun to flow again, filling creek and channel, so that out here on the islands I had a feeling of being at sea; everywhere I looked I was surrounded by water.

At the next causeway a ruined castle commanded the crossing; I was on the last of the islands, a refuge famous in ecclesiastical history, where the apostles of St Patrick built the monastery of Nendrum, in green isolation with a view south-westwards to the blue barrier of the Mournes. Dangerous tide-rips cut them off from the mainland, but ruin often threatened from the lough itself and the long ships of the Danes. Now at weekends a procession of motor cars files across the causeway; teas are served near the ruins of the monastery in a whitewashed farmhouse converted into a golf clubhouse; and green-flags wave over the sheep-nibbled grass where the monks once walked and looked out across the sound, probably then as now alive with bevies of wild swans straining past on creaking pinions, to the woods of a neighbouring island.

DENIS IRELAND, *Statues Round the City Hall*, 1939

from STATION ISLAND

I was parked on a high road, listening
to peewits and wind blowing round the car
when something came to life in the driving mirror,

someone walking fast in an overcoat
and boots, bareheaded, big, determined
in his sure haste along the crown of the road

so that I felt myself the challenged one.
The car door slammed. I was suddenly out
face to face with an aggravated man

raving on about nights spent listening for
gun butts to come cracking on the door,
yeomen on the rampage, and his neighbour

among them, hammering home the shape of things.
'Round about here you overtook the women,'
I said, as the thing came clear. 'Your *Lough Derg Pilgrim*

haunts me every time I cross this mountain –
as if I am being followed, or following.
I'm on my road there now to do the station.'

'O holy Jesus Christ, does nothing change?'
His head jerked sharply side to side and up
like a diver surfacing,

then with a look that said, *who is this cub
anyhow*, he took cognizance again
of where he was: the road, the mountain top,

and the air, softened by a shower of rain,
worked on his anger visibly until:
'It is a road you travel on your own.

I who learned to read in the reek of flax
and smelled hanged bodies rotting on their gibbets
and saw their looped slime gleaming from the sacks –

hard-mouthed Ribbonmen and Orange bigots
made me into the old fork-tongued turncoat
who mucked the byre of their politics.

If times were hard, I could be hard too.
I made the traitor in me sink the knife.
And maybe there's a lesson there for you,

whoever you are, wherever you come out of,
for though there's something natural in your smile
there's something in it strikes me as defensive.'

'I have no mettle for the angry role,'
I said. 'I come from County Derry,
born in earshot of an Hibernian hall

where a band of Ribbonmen played hymns to Mary.
By then the brotherhood was a frail procession
staggering home drunk on Patrick's Day

in collarettes and sashes fringed with green.
Obedient strains like theirs tuned me first
and not that harp of unforgiving iron

the Fenians strung. A lot of what you wrote
I heard and did: this Lough Derg station,
flax-pullings, dances, summer crossroads chat

and the shaky local voice of education.
All that. And always, Orange drums.
And neighbours on the roads at night with guns.'

'I know, I know, I know, I know,' he said,
'but you have to try to make sense of what comes.
Remember everything and keep your head.'

'The alders in the hedge,' I said, 'mushrooms,
dark-clumped grass where cows or horses dunged,
the cluck when pith-lined chestnut shells split open

in your hand, the melt of shells corrupting,
old jampots in a drain clogged up with mud –'
But now Carleton was interrupting:

'All this is like a trout kept in a spring
or maggots sown in wounds –
another life that cleans our element.

We are earthworms of the earth, and all that
has gone through us is what will be our trace.'
He turned on his heel when he was saying this

and headed up the road at the same hard pace.

SEAMUS HEANEY, 1984

T HE SPERRIN MOUNTAINS ARE A PART OF ULSTER that is little visited either by visitors or by Ulster people themselves. My own visits to them have been brief but exhilarating. Under the somewhat capricious guidance of a little girl cousin, I have explored several lonely little roads running into the mountains and found them yet another of those lovely places where life can pause and be wise and detached, even during the very troubled period of history in which I went there. And I remember strolling among the great trees at Learmount Castle, a place since taken over by the Ministry of Agriculture as a forestry estate, and encountering some of the ninety little schoolgirls evacuated to that place and receiving ecstatic signals from some of them from an upper window when they thought that the eye of authority was not upon them.

HUGH SHEARMAN, Ulster, 1949

A RDARA IS THE CENTRE of the hand-weaving industry which has always existed in western Donegal, but has been recently developed by the Congested Districts Board and the Irish Industries Association, founded by Lady Aberdeen. Many efforts have been made to popularise

406

in England their stuffs and also the hand-knitted things of which Glenties is a great market. But they will probably continue to be produced chiefly for local use, and long may they continue; as it is, you will see everywhere poor men wearing stuff admirable in colour and pattern, which costs them no more than the cheap and nasty products of Manchester factories. The industry, for local purposes, is an old one; from time immemorial Donegal women have spun the wool of their own sheep, and Donegal weavers have woven. But up till quite recent times, the wool was left in its natural colour and the product was a grey frieze, which you may still see occasionally, especially in Inishowen. I can well remember old Lord George Hill's picturesque figure, which was never clad in anything else. Some twenty years back, however, Mrs Ernest Hart started at Derrybeg near Gweedore an institution for teaching the peasants to use dyes ready to their hand; heather, lichen and the rest. Since then skilled supervision has improved the spinning and weaving; better looms have been introduced, and a standard set to the workmen: and the few – or many – who choose to dress themselves in Donegal homespuns will find them very pleasant to look at, and comfortable and serviceable to wear. They are to be seen in the shops in any of these western towns and in the hotels at Carrick and Gweedore.

STEPHEN GWYNN, *Highways and Byways in Donegal and Antrim*, 1899

HOME GROUND

I

for S.H.

This was your home ground, comings and goings
When the sand martins collected in flight
Feathers and straw for untidy chambers
Or swooped up to kiss each tiny darkness,
Five white eggs changing to five white chins:

Childhood, and your townland poor enough
For gentians, fairy-flax, wild strawberries
And the anxious lapwing that settled there,
Its vocal chords a grass blade stretched
Between your thumbs and blown to tatters.

for P.M.

When they landed the first man on the moon
You were picking strawberries in a field,
Straggly fuses, lamps that stained the ground
And lips and fingers with reflected light,
For you were living then from hand to mouth.

Re-entering that atmosphere, you take
The dangerous bend outside the graveyard
Where your mother falls like a meteor
From clouds of may and damson blossom:
There the moon-rocks ripen in your hand.

MICHAEL LONGLEY, *The Echo Gate*, 1979

A ND NOW WE APPROACH the Dunore rivulet, a limpid stream that comes galloping from higher ground to be absorbed by the lake which is close at hand. We stop for a moment on the little bridge that spans it to behold its clear shallows, when, from beneath the archway, darts a thing of gorgeous beauty, like a swift-winged arrow tipped with blue and gold. The sun glints athwart its plumes and renders it a truly brilliant object. It is a kingfisher, a bird of shy and solitary habits. Well it is for the charming creature, we are not simply collectors of specimens, armed with deadly weapons. How men, when a rare living object is seen, can become intensely excited, and remain so until they have deprived it of life and made it their own, and profess at the same time to be lovers of animated nature, I cannot understand. Instead of destroying rare and beautiful creatures like the kingfisher, I would encourage, foster, and protect them, that the eye might more frequently feast upon their loveliness.

W.S. SMITH, *Historical Gleanings in Antrim and Neighbourhood*, 1888

O NE OF MY MOST VIVID MEMORIES of the lough is the sight of a gaggle of geese flying past in the light of the setting sun. I was standing on the crest of an island when the geese came speeding by, not seventy yards distant, grunting and croaking. The light shone full upon them as they passed in powerful flight – black outstretched necks adorned with little collars, grey, vermiculated backs contrasting with silver bellies, the dark wings of the phalanx beating a common measure but not in time. It is this mingled regularity and irregularity which is the secret, I suspect, of the satisfying artistic pattern which they present. So they passed against a background of watery blue sky and fields as green as only Irish fields can be in winter.

Considering how precarious is the future for wild geese as our shores and waterways become more frequented it is a matter of surprise and concern to those who enjoy just looking at such grand birds that often those who write most enthusiastically of them find greatest relish in killing them.

EDWARD ALLWORTHY ARMSTRONG, *Birds of the Grey Wind*, 1940

AS TO THE SCENES OF CARLETON'S stories we can easily identify them – so exactly and faithfully has he described them. We can visit the Red Well at the foot of the beautiful gorge called Lumford's Glen where Owen McCarthy had his pleasant home until ruin drove him and his family forth on the world. The ancient churchyard of Errigal Truagh (Carndhu) was the scene of the old emigrant's pathetic farewell to his dead wife on the eve of his departure for America (*Emigrants of Ahadarra*); we can follow the mountain road along which the lonely traveller made his way in the moonlight – the Drumfurrar Road, still haunted by the pedlar's ghost. Findermore, where the famous schoolmaster Mat Kavanagh reigned and was sentenced to be hanged, is near Clogher; and within a short distance is the Mullin Burn into which fair Rose Galh fell and was gallantly rescued by her lover, only to meet, later on, with a more terrible fate than drowning; St Patrick's rock-hewn chair and well before which Shan Fadh and Mary plighted their troth; and the hazel glen below Susan's house where Denis O'Shaughnessy, tenderly taking leave of her before going to college, was startled by her father's voice behind him shouting 'Me sowl to glory ye larned vagabone! Is that the way ye're preparing for Maynooth?' – the words enforced by blows from a stout cudgel in the hands of the angry old man.

Carleton is at his best when describing scenes of gloom and terror, such as the ordeal by touching the corpse which took place among the snowy wastes of the Slieve Beagh mountains ('The Midnight Mass') and the fearful fight between Orangemen and Ribbonmen in the ancient town of Clogher ('Party Fight and Funeral').

ROSE SHAW, *Carleton's Country*, 1930

from SLIEVE DENARD

Amongst the mountain's purple heath,
    On summer's sunny day,
The youngsters clamber from beneath
    To pluck the berries blae.

But Denard's brow of sullen gloom,
  With grim, terrific frown,
Looks down, as boding fatal doom
  Upon Newcastle town ...

And near the ocean's surgy shore,
  Lies, wide extended there,
Lord Roden's park of Tullamore,
  As blooming Eden fair ...

Far northward lies, extending wide,
  The beautiful Loch Neagh,
On which the buoyant vessels glide, –
  A wide and saltless sea.

The dim and distant Ennishowen
  Is wash'd by ocean's wave;
And over Belfast harbour prone,
  Hangs Antrim's mountain cave.

And westward Ecbatana's fane,
  Of ancient fame, is seen;
Majestic, with its lofty vane,
  And venerable mien.

And far remote full many a mile,
  We dimly can discern
Blue Molyash's mountain pile,
  Crown'd with an ancient *cairn*.

And as the circle's arch we sweep,
  Approaching to the south,
We see Slieve Guellian's rugged steep,
  And Cooly Mount, in Louth ...

From Denard's summit, high in air,
  In precincts of the sky;
So vast a prospect, and so fair,
  Has seldom met the eye.

JOHN WILLIAMSON, *Poems on Various Subjects*, 1839

IT IS DIFFICULT FOR US TO REALISE how much the introduction of the bus revolutionised the set ways of country life. Until its arrival the women of the farm were accustomed to walking long distances to market their butter and eggs. It must be said, however, that it was often in search of a better price rather than lack of transport that drove them on these weary journeys. The women of the Bailieboro' district in County Cavan were known to walk the twelve miles to Cootehill or Kells because they could get a penny a pound more for their butter at these markets than they could at Bailieboro' market. Whether the utopian fares charged by the owners of the early 'private' buses would have made the twelve-mile run along the Cavan roads worth while, I cannot say, but I know that in those parts of County Down remote from railway stations the market-day bus-ride became a social event.

SAM HANNA BELL, *Erin's Orange Lily*, 1956

ON A COUNTRY BUS FORTY YEARS AGO

The bus is crammed with laden passengers
not pledged to journey far, who drift away
down wet lanes in the waning winter day
over high stiles, up avenues of firs.
The bus grows stuffy; every window blurs;
we judge hills traversed by our lurch and sway
till at each stop chill flakes gust in and play
round a diminished crew of travellers.

Then, at some village, swarming farm-boys board,
well warmed with liquor, laughing, talkative;
our isolation shed, we strain to give
what skew attention our cramped seats afford
to the loud round of jests their coarse wits keep,
while two behind speak low of snow and sheep.

JOHN HEWITT, *Mosaic*, 1981

A BRIEF WORD ABOUT THE JOURNEY from Crosskennan to Dunadry. The last thing that a first-year apprentice (rushing for a bus four miles away) would be thinking about, would relate to the history unfolding as his bicycle careered sometimes on its wheels and at times on its side along that route. A mile from where I lived I passed a draw-well in the town-land of Hungary Hall. A few hundred yards and I passed the lane leading to the former home of William Orr, the United Irishman who was hanged at Carrickfergus in 1797. This was the townland of Farranshane and a few hundred yards further I would pass Rathmore, close to the seat of power of the Kings of Dalriada. The old Rathmore Hall was passed close to the home of Sam Orr, a man of advanced years. He played the fiddle. On an occasion in the nearby hall, Sam was playing his fiddle when the local rustics annoyed him with some interruptions or other. His ultimatum became a much quoted saying afterwards: 'Yine mair hough and a'll put the fiddle in the baag'.

I never knew if the threat was carried out. Further on, one passed 'Posy Row', a row of neat whitewashed cottages, and then the Rathmore Road ended at Dunadry village – now the site of Dunadry Inn.

BOBBY CAMERON, *Before That Generation Passes: The Story of a Shorts Apprentice*, 2000

D ONEGAL (*Dún na nGall*, fort of the foreigners) owes its topography to very ancient happenings. In times so remote that scarcely any portion of the present Ireland was in existence, the rocks of this area were crumpled together and thrown into ridges and hollows running north-east and south-west; the features thus impressed upon the region millions of years ago still persist. Look at a geological map and at a map showing elevation, and you will see how intimately related are the rocks with the modelling of the county; compare these with a general map, and you will note how human movement within the area, as demonstrated by the trend of roads and railways, obeys the ancient disposition. Communication is easy along the lines of folding, but railways and highways achieve a north-west direction with difficulty, and to the accompaniment of much clambering and twisting. Londonderry and Strabane, the natural centres of distribution, transmit their merchandise – human or otherwise – to the Atlantic coast only by devious meanderings among mountain ridges.

ROBERT LLOYD PRAEGER, *The Way That I Went*, 1937

THE LAST SHEAF

We meet that evening in The Last Sheaf
Which has gained mocking notoriety
Since the boss began to diminish
His own stock. A distempered house
At a crossroads, we mount guard
On neighbours cycling heavily past
As we jostle at the deal bar
In a brackish stour of stout,
Paraffin, stale bread.

After hours
All hands shift to the kitchen,
Snap down the blinds!
Our light is a grease fattened candle, but
In our gloomy midnight cave
No one minds, we have reached
The singing stage. 'The Orange Flute',
'The Mountains of Pomeroy', the songs
That survive in this sparse soil
Are quavered out, until someone
Remembers to call on Packy Farrel
To say a song.
       With the almost
Professional shyness of the folk-singer
He keeps us waiting, until he rises,
Head forced back, eyeballs blind.
an Bunnán Buidhe. As the Gaelic
Rises and recedes, swirling deep
To fall back, all are silent,

Tentacles of race seeking to sound
That rough sadness. At the climax
He grips the chair before him
Until the knuckles whiten —
Sits down abruptly as he rose.
Man looks at man, the current
Of community revived to a near-
ly perfect round ...
       Soon broken
As talk expands, in drunken detail.
'I said to him': 'He swore to me.'
With smart-alec roughness, Henry
Rakes up our family history:
'Was it patriotism, or bankruptcy?'
Austin Donnelly remembers our fight
Over a swallow's nest, a caning
For peering under the Girls' Lavatory.
An owl-sad child, shaken from sleep.
Watches us, in a tatty night-shirt
'A crying shame,' sighs one, but his
Publican father is so far gone, he
No longer bothers to trek to the bar
But strikes bottles on the flange
Of the Raeburn, until the floor
Is littered with green splinters

Of glass, tintops.
         It is the usual
Grotesque, half animal evening so
Common in Ireland, with much glum
Contrariness, much disappearing
Into the darkness, before we group
Outside, trying to mutter *Goodnight*.
My companions now feel the need
To continue. Fit as fiddles.
Fresh as daisies, we plan the next move;
The moon on the road is a river
Of light, leading to new adventure ...

JOHN MONTAGUE, *The Rough Field*, 1972

W E FARE INTO THE DARK, cavernous regions around Muckish, on the extreme bleak peak of which there is still a glow from the now invisible sun. Then suddenly we emerge from the rocky passes, and see below us sloping miles of moor, with the mighty ocean beyond, and Tory Island in the distance with its sharp headland facing the waters like the prow of a gigantic ship. Little white houses are sprinkled everywhere like snowflakes. The exquisite turf scent is in the air. In the car we whirl from the windy uplands into the calm village-clasping valleys, and fáilte, fáilte is the tune.

And now we are treading soil that the sandal of Colmcille often pressed: the place teems with memories of him, and the people have the old-world graces, the dignity of movement and gentleness of speech, the very features, the very accents, that were here in his times. I think he'd be more at home here than in Doire Colmcille, though I have great hopes for the latter: it's a fine city when you get used to it.

The Gaeltacht has changed greatly in the past two years: that is the first impression. There's a new air about it, and this would be yet more noticeable if the 'flu' had not worked such havoc, for the epidemic laid a tragically heavy hand on these glens and braes. Many is the house where they answer your inquiries as to how the world is using them, with a sad shake of the head and 'Tháinig an bás orrainn' – 'Death has visited us'. In one house, all but a baby were slain. The young men were the chief victims. From Scotland, several corpses used to arrive home daily: a sad harvesters' home-coming. As you hear the terrible stories you think you are back in the black '48: such desolation was only equalled then.

Of late there is a feeling in the Gaeltacht that new days are coming. Two years ago, the people were still disheartened. They would talk of 'Gaelig amaideach' – 'foolish Irish' – but you don't hear that talk now. There's a club with Irish speeches and lectures, and with the beginnings of a Gaelic library, where the young men are putting their hand to a great work. The old men are glad to talk in Irish instead of seizing every opportunity to show you that they can talk English. They have a feeling that the tide has at last turned in the fortunes of the Gael – that an Ghaelig is at last coming back into respect, into priority. The big men in politics nowadays talk Irish. That means to the inhabitants of these glens that the students and propagandists who come here learning the language stand for something real. Politics is not my concern, but I would vote for Sir Edward Carson himself if his party had achieved all this. This is reality: beside this parliaments and statute books are but dust and shadows.

AODH DE BLÁCAM, *From a Gaelic Outpost*, 1921

ONE FINE MORNING LAST AUGUST I found myself in the quaint old town of Maghera. My first visit was to the post office, where I bought some picture-cards, and inquired my way to Killelagh Church, the Cromlech, and the Sweat-house, as it is called, where formerly people indulged in a vapour-bath to cure rheumatism and other complaints. I was told to follow the main street. This I did, and when I came to the outskirts of the town I tried to get a guide, and spoke to a boy at one of the cottages. He, however, knew very little, but fortunately saw an elderly man coming down the road, who consented to show me the way, and proved an excellent guide. His name is Daniel McKenna, a coach-builder by trade. His father, who was teacher in Maghera National School for thirty-five years, knew Irish well, and I understand gave Dr Joyce information in regard to some of the place names in County Derry. Taking a road which led in a north-westerly direction, we came to the Cromlech, and a few yards farther on saw the old church of Killelagh.

My guide pointed out that the doorstep was much worn, doubtless by the feet of those who during many centuries had passed over it; he showed me, too, the strong walls, and said the mortar had been cemented with the blood of bullocks. This probably recalls an ancient custom, when an animal – in still earlier times it might be a human being – was slain to propitiate or drive away the evil spirits and secure the stability of the building. A similar tradition exists in regard to Roughan Castle, the stronghold of Phelim O'Neill, in County Tyrone.

ELIZABETH ANDREWS, *Ulster Folklore*, 1913

THE PRIVATE STILLS IN THE PARISH of Pettigo being at that time innumerable, made the whiskey cheap and plenty, which caused the people to be addicted to drunkenness, a vice among others prevalent there. The Catholics, who were most numerous, were chiefly remarkable for this; though the Protestants, as they called themselves, were but little better. At burials in particular, to which they flocked from all quarters, they drank most shamefully. It was the custom then with them, as soon as the corpse was buried, to meet all in a field adjacent to the churchyard, and pour whiskey, like cold water, down their throats. Twenty gallons of strong spirits of whiskey have been often drunk at such a meeting. When their blood was sufficiently heated by the spirits, they then, as it was natural, fell-boxing with one another, probably the near relations of the deceased, and thus cut and bruised each other most terribly. Many have been killed at such riotous meetings, either by quarrelling or whiskey.

THE REVEREND SAMUEL BURDY, *The Life of Philip Skelton*, 1792

THE PEOPLE OF CLOGHANEELY at that time called anywhere eastwards, from Muckish Mountain to County Antrim, the 'Lagan'. That part of the country hadn't got a very good reputation in our neighbourhood. When anyone referred to the 'Lagan', it meant slavery, struggle, extortion and work from morning till night. All the stories I had heard about it were wheeling around in my mind as the horse was trotting up the street of Letterkenny. My heart gave a jump when I saw the driver turning the horse towards the left hand. He drove on and it wasn't long until we were on the old back road to Errigal between Termon and Gweedore.

The Irish speaker – I found out that he was an O'Donnell – was a great companion. There wasn't a story about this historic district that he didn't relate to me: Doon Well, where everyone that passed by, did the station; Doon Rock above it, where the princes of the O'Donnells were crowned; Gartan, where Columbkille was born and where his traces were still to be found in church and stone – I heard the whole history on this journey.

MÍCHEÁL MacGOWAN, translated by VALENTIN IREMONGER, *The Hard Road to Klondike*, 1962

AN BUNNÁN BUIDHE

A Bhunnáin bhuidhe, 'sé mo léan do luighe,
Is do chnámha sínte tar eis do ghrinn;
Is chan easbhaidh bidh acht díoghbháil dighe
A d'fág in do luighe thu ar chúl do chinn;
Is measa liom fhéin na sgrios na Traoi
Tú bheith 'do luighe ar leachaibh lom',
'S nach dtearn tú díth, no dolaidh san tír,
'S nár bhfearr leat fíon no uisge poll.

Unquestionably Cathal's [i.e. Cathal Bui MacGiolla Gunna] best known poem and song is *An Bunnán Buí*. This song is known throughout the nine counties of Ulster and indeed also in the province of Connacht. It is an exquisite song of self-mockery and was absorbed into the mainstream of traditional Gaelic song. Anonymous verses were added from time in various Gaeltacht areas. Here is my own translation of it.

> 'Twas break of day but no bittern's horn
> Filled the waking morn with its hollow boom,
> For I found him prone on a bare flag blown
> By the loughshore lone where he met his doom,
> His legs were sunk in the slime and slunk
> A hostage held in the fangs of frost
> O men of knowledge lament his going
> For want of liquor his life was lost.
>
> O yellow bird, 'tis my bitter grief
> I'd as lee or lief that my race was run!
> No hunger's tooth but a parching drouth
> That has sapped your youth after all your fun.
> Far worse to me than the Sack of Troy
> That my darling boy with the frost was slain
> No want or woe did his wings bestow
> As he drank the flow of a brown bog drain.
>
> Degrading vile was the way you died
> My bittern beauteous of glowing sheen.
> 'Twas at dawn each day that your pipe you'd play
> As content you lay on a hillock green.
> O my great fatigue and my sorrow sore
> That your tail is higher than heart or head
> And the tipplers say as they pass this way
> Had he drunk his fill he would not be dead.
>
> O bittern bright 'tis my thousand woes
> That the rooks and crows are all pleasure bound
> With the rats and mice as they cross the ice
> To indulge in vice at your funeral mound.
> Had word reached me of your woeful plight
> On the ice I'd smite and the water free
> You'd have all that lake for the thirst to slake
> And we'd hold no wake for the Bunnán Buí.
>
> 'Tis not the blackbird that I'm bewailing
> Or thrush assailing the blossomed braes

But my bittern yellow, that hearty fellow
Who has got my hue and my wilful ways
By the loughshore bank he forever drank
And his sorrow sank in the rolling wave
Come sun or rain every drop I'll drain
For the cellar's empty beyond the grave.

PADDY TUNNEY, The Stone Fiddle, 1979

I WAS AWOKEN EARLY by the lowing of cattle. Dawn had barely broken. Leaping from bed to the window I saw herds and herds of cattle passing slowly like a roan stream into the town. Along the surface of meaty backs was a rippling of muscle, and occasionally, like a leaf floating on a stream, a head and horns would be tossed up, and a wild eye roll despairingly. Traps and spring-carts edged their way through the crush, and driving on the right side of the road was impossible. For hours already the cattle, horses, droves of donkeys and jennets down from the mountains, and orange-painted carts full of piglets, had poured over the lake bridges. It was the fair – unforgettable day!

I dressed and flew out like a shot. The roads were green and golden with manure and cow-claps, filling the air with a sour-sweet stench. Excited and confused animals broke ranks and ran amok in gardens, and later when the pubs opened, even crashed into the bars and courtyards. Cows jumped each other, and farmers' sticks broke over runaways' backs. The morning mêlée exhilarated and bewildered me. Lads ran up and down with horses for inspection, and prospective buyers passed capable, experienced hands over the horses' legs and forced open their mouths to find teeth with tell-tale defects. Farmers were stopped in the street, their cows patted by the dealers who settled on their haunches and tested for a blind teat there and then, leaving squirts of milk behind on the pavement. No bargain concluded without a 'luck penny', a pound note or so, which went on rounds of drinks in the pub. But before any deal was made, horny, knotted hands clasped, and the buyer spat on his palm and brought it down with a smack on the seller's for another assurance of luck.

ROBERT HARBINSON, Song of Erne, 1960

THE BALLAD

I named a ballad round a sparking fire,
the children squatting on the hobs, the mother
busy with cans; the husband turned his knife
in the pipe-ash and said: 'I knew the man

that wrote it years ago. He was a tramp
and beat about the roads here. Then he spoke,
a stanza from it in the singsong way
that things are learnt by heart and not by head.

I queried further. Aye, the names were right.
There was a smiddy once, and yon's the place
they saw the Yeos come riding from, and ran
to warn the blacksmith. Then the mother told
how once the tramp begged shelter in the house,
and how her mother sat with him all night
beside the warm fire singing song for song.

The father nodded, knowing the tale well;
the clustered children listened with bright eyes,
and so the ballad and its poet started
on five new journeys through the mounting years:
and I whose care is set on riming words
felt a sharp jag of envy and of pride.

JOHN HEWITT, *The Day of the Corncrake: Poems of the Nine Glens*, 1969

O N AN ISOLATED SWELLING HILL half-way between Londonderry and
Lough Swilly stands the most imposing monument of prehistoric
times found in the Inishowen region – the great cashel or stone fort
known as the Grianan of Aileach. *Grianán* means sunny place, and *Aileach*
a stone house; the exact significance of the name seems uncertain. Here
a sub-circular enclosure about seventy-seven feet across is surrounded by
a formidable dry-built wall seventeen feet in height, nearly vertical on the
outer face, stepped on the inner, so that two platforms intervene between
ground-level and the flat top; flights of steps lead from one level to the
next. In structure it approximates closely to Staigue Fort in Kerry, the
great cliff forts of the Aran Islands, and the cashel in Doon Lough near
Narin: and one may safely postulate the same race of builders and similar
date for all of them. The Grianan was surrounded by three concentric
rings of earth and stone, now but faintly marked: and in the wall of each
side of the doorway – a passage with slightly sloping jambs and heavy
lintels through the thirteen-foot rampart – though not connected with it,
there is a creep-passage down the centre of the base of the wall, as in the
Narin cashel. Its builders are unknown, but it was a residence of the
O'Neills, kings of Ulster, until demolished by Murkertagh O'Brien, king
of Munster, in 1101, and remained in a completely ruined condition till
restored by Dr Bernard of Londonderry in 1874–78. The restoration was
carefully carried out, and a line of tar on the masonry separates the

original wall from the replaced stonework. The monument is most impressive, and from its walls a very lovely prospect of Lough Swilly, the Donegal mountains and the Foyle valley is obtained.

ROBERT LLOYD PRAEGER, *The Way That I Went*, 1937

LYCHEES

You wonder at that Georgian terrace
Miles out of town where the motorway begins:
My great-grandfather was a coachman,
And knew how far away he was in the dark
By mysteries of the Rosary. My grandmother said
You could tell a good husband
By the thumbed leaves of his prayer-book.

A dead loss, my mother counts you.
Setting my teeth on edge at all hours,
Getting me to break the lychee's skin –
She underestimates the taste of sacrifice,
The irrelevance of distances,
Cat's-eyes, the cleanness of hands.

MEDBH McGUCKIAN, *The Flower Master*, 1982

WE KNOW FROM FINDS MADE in turf-cutting that it was the practice in former times to bury butter in containers in the bogs. The object appears to have been to preserve it, for it was made without salt, but the large number of deposits which have been found suggests that not all were buried with the intention of their recovery, and that some were placed in the bogs as offerings. In prehistoric times many such offerings, of gold and bronze, were made in bogs and lakes, and the bulk of Ireland's famous collections of prehistoric gold objects has been recovered from such sites.

From the account given by Harris we know that in the eighteenth century the cattle-herders also cut turf during their stay in the mountains. And it is probable that the women folk engaged in spinning wool from the sheep, though this is not mentioned by Harris. The cutting of turf, though by no means given up, has declined for various reasons, including the availability of coal in this sea-girt peninsula and the closing of the bogs in the High Mournes by the Water Commissioners. Several bogs, including the Castle Bog – named after Pierce's Castle – are almost cut out, leaving a waste of granite sand and bleached boulders. We may first describe a method of securing turf which has died out in the Mournes. Mud turf, as it is termed, was formerly made in the valley of the Leitrim River south of Hilltown. The scraw (sod) was first pared off an area about 12 feet long and 6 wide, and the turf was dug over to the depth of a spit with an ordinary broad-mouthed digging spade, and chopped up fine. Then water was poured in the hole and the turf worked into a sticky paste with a graip (fork). This was thrown out with a long-handled shovel and spread in a thick layer to dry in the sun. The process was repeated to a depth of four or five spits. When partly dry the layer of mud turf was baked (marked out) with the edge of the hand into oblong bricks. Severed with a spade, the turves were spread out to complete the drying, a long process involving much further handling and turning, footing, turn-footing, castling, clamping, and finally, hauling home and stacking.

Turf is cut either by breasting or under-footing, that is, by cutting out the turves either horizontally or vertically. Both methods may be seen in the Mournes, but under-footing is the usual mode. The practice may differ from one bog to the next, depending on the nature of the turf and its depth, for breast-cutting is not possible in a shallow bog. Much depends also on the grain of the turf and the degree to which its fibres have decayed. The Castle Bog is perhaps the only place where one may still see breast turf being cut, though the old style winged spade is now replaced by a broad-mouthed spade fitted with a short handle. Under-foot turf is cut in several places, especially in the Black or New Bog in the valley of the Rowan Tree River, and on Finlieve.

E. ESTYN EVANS, *Mourne Country*, 1951

FOOTING TURF

Footing turf on high Barard, the hip
of that long mountain, Trostan, it was cold
and wet, and every hair on sleeve or wrist
was globed with water, and the tangled grass
shod each chill foot with moisture. The whole world
was narrowed to a little dripping cave
walled by the weather and the bleat of sheep,
but when a gust of wind blew off the roof
the sky was clear and bright, and miles away,
down the landslope towards the quiet sea,
the day-long sun shone on the haymakers.

JOHN HEWITT, *The Day of the Corncrake: Poems of the Nine Glens*, 1969

B Y NOW THE MARVELS of Shanes Castle were beginning to impress themselves upon me. It was then and still is, despite all the scars of war-time military occupation, the most beautiful place in the world. After the accidental fire in 1816 there was never a beautiful house with beautiful views, but it had the most wonderful and enormous park of two thousand acres. Until 1932 this included a deer park of 500 acres, but unfortunately today this is a thriving forest of fir trees run by the Northern Ireland Ministry of Agriculture. It is along the northern shores of Lough Neagh that this beautiful park is situated, while the river Maine, having meandered down through County Antrim, flows majestically through the woods of the park under two bridges before it emerges into this vast inland sea.

The main drive from Antrim to Randalstown is five and a half miles long and even when I was a boy some twelve miles of private road was maintained. In my father's day there must have been twice that amount. As one stood on Nash's terrace at the old castle on a summer evening, gazing across the lough to the mountains above Belfast, it was impossible to imagine that, as the crow flies, one was only fifteen miles from the Falls Road and the Shankill, names unfortunately not unknown outside Belfast today.

TERENCE O'NEILL, *Autobiography*, 1972

T HE COUNTRY! THE VERY WORD was like a bell in my boyhood. 'Going down to the country' where my uncle permanently rented a cottage, was dying and going to heaven. We caught the green bus of the old Ulster Transport Authority (all country buses should be green) outside Lemon's Fruit Shop on the Albertbridge Road, and on its forehead were the words that transported us before we put our foot on the bus: Millisle via Moss Road or, if we didn't mind a walk at the other end, Millisle via Six Road Ends.

Six Road Ends! Lord Dunsany could not have done better. And the Moss Road spelled peace and joy. And indeed in the neighbourhood of my uncle's cottage (a few fields away from the cottages where my parents and other relatives sat out the war, my father commuting – travelling was the word then – every day to his job in the Sirocco Engineering Works) was a Wee Moss and a Big Moss. They weren't bogs but gorse–covered hillocks which my father and uncles shot. Farther afield was a flat acreage they called, evocatively, The Punjab. All this in Gransha, not far from Newtownards, within easy commuting distance from Belfast now, a pilgrimmage then.

JOHN WILSON FOSTER, 'A Country Boyhood in Belfast',
Irish Literary Supplement, Autumn 1989

THE BEECH TREES OF BROUGHSHANE
(A Song)

for Bob Johnston

The backroads of mid Antrim
have always brought me joy,
the long roads rising from the sea
to Buckna and Armoy.
They slip my mind for years
and then I come on them again,
standing along the road to Clough
the beech trees of Broughshane.

They rise up on the right-hand side
made shiny by the rain,
planted by some aristocrat
to mark his great demesne,
trunk after silver trunk along
this ordinary lane.
How could I have forgotten them,
the beech trees of Broughshane?

Though beauty thronged about our car,
today it thronged in vain,
for we were both hung over
and distracted by the pain
of aching heads, and bloodshot eyes.
We sucked Magnesia pills
and drove ahead uncertainly
towards Clough and then Cloughmills.

We should have stopped and walked
and laid our foreheads on the bark,
beneath umbrellas breathed fresh air
till the approach of dark.
Beauty and quiet remedy
our worldliness and pain.
The sun might have burst out and blessed
the beech trees of Broughshane.

JAMES SIMMONS, *The Company of Children*, 1999

T HE SMALL COUNTRY ROAD is one of the joys of the rural landscape. Many have existed for centuries along the lines of medieval and pre-medieval pathways. Others were built in the late eighteenth and early nineteenth centuries during the period of rapid population growth, both in countryside and towns. They were generally handcrafted, using only pick and shovel and wheelbarrow, respecting the natural lie of the land as they wound their way around the countryside, uphill and down dale. As a result they have fitted into the quilt-work pattern of fields, farmhouse buildings, rivers and other elements of the countryside and are an intrinsic and important visual, aesthetic and historical aspect of the rural landscape.

They are bordered by old hedgerows, often as old as the roads themselves, with a variety of indigenous plants and trees such as ash, sycamore, beech, hawthorn, honeysuckle, wild rose, fuchsia. The hedgerows also provide a habitat for a variety of wildlife, including birds, bees, badgers, and foxes. They change with the seasons: spare, sparse and quiet during winter, but intensely beautiful with a coating of frost or snow; alive and cheerful in spring with birds' song and new fresh and green growth; voluptuous and blowsy with their skirts of cabbage parsley during the summer; full of fruits and colours during the autumn.

Apart from providing an essential means of communication, the country road had a social significance. For generations, in many rural areas, work on the roads, whether with the county council or a local contractor, was a major source of male employment, because they required continuous maintenance.

The country road was also an important setting for social events. People walked or cycled on them to their work, to church or to the local village; children walked to school and often dillied and dallied along them on the way home, exchanging stories, picking wild fruits, playing games. Certain locations, through custom or habit, were social meeting grounds for exchanging news, playing games or just passing the time of day in the company of friends.

In recent years small country roads have been eroded by indiscriminate and ill-considered road-widening and new building developments, fuelled by a widespread indifference at both public and private level to their aesthetic, historic and ecological importance.

PATRICK SHAFFREY, *Irish Times*, August 2005

A FTER THAT FIRST SPRING DAY, when the hail shower cleared away and we saw Glenwherry in the sunlight, we made it our habit, whenever possible, to go exploring ... into the glens and hills of Antrim. We have penetrated into the glens from Ballyclare at the south side of them, from Larne or Cushendall on the east, from Ballycastle on the north, sometimes on foot, sometimes by car. And we found something worth having as the result of our explorations in most districts of those five-hundred-square-miles of wild country, something that remains a permanent possession in memories of the hills, the white clouds, the beech hedges, the black peat bogs, and the scent of heather and peat smoke, the sight and sound of the Atlantic or the North Channel, the sting of driving sleet, empty roads on wet, dark nights, spring and autumn colours, winter twilight.

HUGH SHEARMAN, *Ulster*, 1949

Towns of
Tolerable Magnitude

Irish parliaments had been infrequent since the passing of Poyning's Act. There had been five in the first half of Elizabeth's reign; but since that of 1587, called by Perrot to pass the attainder of Desmond, there had been none. That called twenty-six years later was also largely for the purpose of passing attainders. It was to differ from its predecessors in that not only were all the shires of Ulster to send knights, as even the least remote had done only for the first time in Perrot's Parliament, but Ulster boroughs were to be represented in it by burgesses. For this purpose a number of corporate towns were created in the winter of 1612 and the first months of 1613, Enniskillen having the honour of heading the list, and being followed by Lifford, Donegal, Belturbet, Coleraine, Limavady, Killyleagh, Rathmullan, Strabane, Bangor, Newcastle, Clogher, Newtownards, Augher, and Charlemont.

CYRIL FALLS, *The Birth of Ulster*

EXCEPT FOR THE VERY GREAT, the local tailor was considered sufficient, and that is a thing to be borne in mind about all these little towns of the time, that in most ways they were self-supporting and self-contained in all the commoner avocations. The more skilled trades were usually supplied by travelling tradesmen, who with their horse and saddlebags rode round the country staying here and there as custom offered. The making of stays ranked among the rarer arts ...

I have never been able to make up my mind whether life in general in these little towns was happier in the days of my grandmother's grandfather than it was in the days of my grandmother or in my own. The great difference of course was the absence of communication with the outside world as we understand communication, but that meant not only that less flowed into them, it also meant that less flowed out of them. They had to be more self-reliant and more self-supporting. Each had its tannery and brewery, made its own boots, spun its own wool, and wove its own cloth and made its own clothes; which is the same as saying that there was more general employment. At times I am inclined to think there was more comfort, ruder and perhaps coarser, than there is in the same places now when better communications and the manufactures of the large towns have sucked the life-blood out of all the little places. Then one is brought up against facts of a totally different kind in the pages of Dubourdieu and Skelton, where starvation walks abroad, and Skelton again and again had to beg and sell and borrow to save his wretched people from dying in the famines that fell upon the country every few years.

L.R. CRESCENT, *In Old Belfast (1740–1760)*, 1924

Bold Antrim! well befall thy rock-bound shore;
Peace to thy hills and vales, green-mantled Down!
May Freedom, Plenty, and each favouring Power,
Crown your fair fields as Love and Beauty crown.
Hail, Holywood! meet haunt of health and lore:
Hail, Carrickfergus! independent town;
Hail all your worthies, never hail'd before,

And hail your Castle of remote renown!

ANONYMOUS, *The Northern Athens*, 1826

WE CAME BETWEEN THREE ISLANDS and a town called Donahadee, which is a market town, and seems a good pretty one. We left it at our right and Copplen Islands at our left. (It should be the very contrary.) We saw after that at our left the village call'd Bangar, which is but a small one, but very fit for vessels to come to the very sides of it; both sides are very rocky. That small village is famous for Duke Schomberg landing there, with the forces under his command. Upon your right you see the castle of Carrickfergus, which is a strong place; we took it last year and lost no great quantity of men. We landed at the white house (five days after the landing of King William), where we saw on our arrival a great number of poor people. We went that night to Belfast, which is a large and pretty town; and all along the road you see an arm of the sea on your left, and on the right great high rocky mountains, whose tops are often hidden by the clouds, and at the bottom a very pleasant wood, very full of simples of all sorts.

GIDEON BONNIVERT, 1690

ENNISKILLEN IS A PRETTY LITTLE CITY – the prettiest in Ireland, I should say. It is a centre for Fermanagh, Cavan, and the southern part of Donegal – a little capital, in fact. It is within the administration of the Northern Government, and so certain superficial things make themselves noted – the red postal-boxes with the monogram of King George instead of the green boxes with the S.A. initials; Constabulary instead of Civic Guards; recruiting posters for the British Army. Enniskillen has always been a military headquarters – its modern history begins as a frontier post – and it has many mementoes recalling British military achievement. These mementoes do not seem out of place here as they would be likely to in other towns in Ireland. With this military achievement is interwoven the names and the honours of the land-owning families hereabouts. There has always been an entente between the town and the land-owning families; this, I feel, is what really makes the place different from towns in other parts of Ireland. The land-owning families felt an interest in the town, fostered its growth, brought some amenities into it; the townspeople were really proud of these families, rejoiced in whatever honours they were given, and put up monuments to them with a good heart. This, which would be a natural relation in England and Scotland and most places in Europe, is worthy of being noted in Ireland. Enniskillen shows the marks of this fostering ... I am at the railway station; a carriage with horses is waiting there; Lord —— arrives. There is a ripple of interest, of allegiance. The coachman drives off. The house he drives to is still a centre of influence.

PADRAIC COLUM, Cross Roads in Ireland, 1930

AMONG THIS MAZE OF ISLANDS where time stood still, I found the perfect contrast to my city life, led with the clashing cymbal accompaniment of trams and traffic. I wondered why nobody lived in those Elysian Fields. Later I learnt that the ambience of the islands' peace had fostered the building of abbeys and hermitages in the early years of Christianity – St Molaisse to the Island of the Oxen, St Ninny to the Island of the Plain of Sorrel.

Although not native to Fermanagh, Mr Morsett had soaked himself in its legends and history, and knew its geography, as his wife used to say, 'backwards'. On Sunday evenings we often took long walks over the drumlins, and as we roamed farther away from the house, Mr Morsett's shyness slid from him as he grew excited over some tale of the locality. Of course, I already knew about Enniskillen for it enjoyed a place in the Protestant heritage almost as great as besieged Derry itself. Five thousand Jacobite soldiers had stormed the town, and nobody had expected Enniskillen's two thousand to survive. But of the Catholic Royalists two thousand were slain, half a thousand taken prisoner, and all this for only twenty dead Protestants. This was resounding victory for William of Orange, our beloved King Billy, and ignominy for the Jacobite cause.

This success pleased King Billy so much that at the battle of Boyne Water he said to the Enniskilleners, 'Gentlemen, you shall be my guards this day, I have heard much of you. Let me see something of you.' Ever since, those words had echoed in Enniskillen's ears, and the little town wedged between the lakes had followed the success of its Dragoons and Fusiliers in their battles, in every part of the world. Never would the memory of glorious names fade from the streets of soft-grey architecture – Namur, the Netherlands, the Seven Years' War, American Independence, Waterloo, Balaclava, Sevastopol, South Africa, the Peninsular War, India and the Great War. I was twelve years old and thought it all wonderful.

ROBERT HARBINSON, *Song of Erne*, 1960

IN ENNISKILLEN WE ARE DEFINITELY in the west. The province may still be Ulster, but it is western Ulster, estranged by an invisible frontier from the factory chimneys of the Lagan valley. In the blue dusk of early spring we cross the invisible border and arrive by bridges over invisible rivers in the little island city where lights are twinkling in domes and pinnacles – at least so it seems in the twilight; in the morning we shall know the provincial reality, but tonight Enniskillen is a city of dreams, eternal, with an enchanting roofline that climbs like an illustration from a fairy tale up from the river towards the blue of the night sky ... The sound of water falling over a weir reverberates in narrow streets of whitewashed houses; the wheezy music of an accordion emerges muffled from behind a yellow blind; mysterious figures lounge in the shadow of gables; a whiff of turf smoke lingers in the air, for ever on the verge of banishing yet for ever present when you stop to sniff for it, an eternal reminder that this is western Ireland as well as Ulster, and that the Gael has stolen back again across the bridges from the Donegal and Sligo shore.

DENIS IRELAND, *Statues Round the City Hall*, 1939

THE LITTLE OLD TOWN WHERE I WAS BORN [i.e. Ballyshannon] has a voice of its own, low, solemn, persistent, humming through the air day and night, summer and winter. Whenever I think of that town I seem to hear the voice. The river which makes it rolls over rocky ledges into the tide. Before spreads a great ocean in sunshine or storm; behind stretches a many-islanded lake. On the south runs a wavy line of blue mountains and on the north, over green, rocky hills, rise peaks of a more distant range. The trees hide in glens or cluster near the river; grey rocks and boulders lie scattered about the windy pastures. The sky arches wide over all, giving room to multitudes of stars by night and long processions of clouds blown from the sea, but also, in the childish memory where these pictures live, to deeps of celestial blue in the endless days of summer. An odd, out-of-the-way little town ours, on the extreme western verge of Europe; our next neighbours, sunset way, being citizens of the great new republic, which indeed to our imagination seemed little, if at all, farther off than England in the opposite direction.

WILLIAM ALLINGHAM, 1869

LARNE CONSISTS OF AN OLD AND NEW TOWN; the latter chiefly of one long street, well built of stone, the houses of which have a great air of neatness; in the old town the houses are mostly decent, but the streets and lanes are narrow, crooked, and badly paved, which gives it an indifferent appearance ...

Larne is a place of some trade, and the residence of a collector; the duties amounted to £14,000 last year, and, though there are other importations, the principal is rock salt, as this is manufactured very extensively; there is also a sail-cloth manufacture, some rope-making, and tanning of hides. But the principal is weaving cotton. In the town are two book clubs; the gentlemen's club is extensive and well chosen, the other also contains same valuable works.

Markets are held on the first Monday of each month for linen, yarn etc., and fairs on the 31st of July, and 1st of December; a very great flour-mill was sometime ago erected close to the town. The places of worship are an established church, three dissenting meeting-houses, one Catholic and one Methodist chapel.

THE REVEREND JOHN DUBOURDIEU, *Statistical Survey of the County of Antrim*, 1812

GLENO

Stranger, in Ireland! if your mind
   The bless'd green isle with rapture fills;
As wand'ring o'er her plains, you find
   Grand groves, green lawns, and glassy rills
Descend these bleak and barren hills;
   And soothing contrast, see below,
A village, free from all the ills
   Of Art and Nature – sweet GLENO.

The breezy mount, whose laurels grace
   The winding walk, in flow'rs array'd;
Th' enchanting glen, the sweetest place,
   That Peace and Silence ever stray'd –
The golden glebe, the smooth green mead,
   O'er look'd by lime-cliffs, white as snow –
And gardens fine, that fragrance spread,
   Will charm your heart, that hails GLENO. ...

Sweet village! till thy stable shield
   The everlasting mountains bend;
May Husbandry, completely skill'd
   And Manufacture, thee befriend!
While from yon steep the streams descend,
   That turn thy mills, whose bleachfields glow;
May ample Recompence attend
   On honest Toil, in thee, GLENO.

JAMES ORR, *Poems on Various Subjects*, 1804

A T THE END OF THE STREET is the square, also tree-lined and clearly
intended as a focal point, with the Protestant school, the church, the
rectory, and two small terraces of two- and three-storey houses whose
height sets them apart from the rest of the village.

Castle Street slopes gently from its pinnacle at Duggan's corner, where
it joins Chapel Lane and Quay Lane and a nameless street leading over
the river. The slope, so slight as to be unnoticeable to the motorist, is a
stiff gradient when prams and handcarts and go-carts are being pushed up
against it and a fast downward track for skates, four-wheelers, gliders,
tricycles and freewheeling bikes. The slope tapers off at Hunter's store
and the street is flat and level, past the forge and Teague's shop until it
reaches the square.

This is the formal part of the village [i.e. Killough]. The magic is in the back ways: the Ropewalk, stretching from the quay along the shoreline and along the back-garden walls of the Castle Street houses, past a little crumbling jetty and a minute patch of sand, facing the expanse of the mud flats and the back shore of Coney Island, along the wall of the priest's lawn, through Nelsons' farmyard to the back of the Protestant school, the church and the square, with all possible progress along the shore blocked off by a graveyard full of headstones. Halfway down the Ropewalk, on the left, is the Nanny Sound, a wilderness of heath and overgrown grass and shrubs around the ruined stumps of old walls – in imagination and memory vast in extent, an ideal hiding place, but one from which wild beasts, ogres and giants could rush out to frighten little boys, but in fact, not much more than half an acre of waste ground.

MAURICE HAYES, *Sweet Killough, Let Go Your Anchor*, 1994

EXACTLY 135 YEARS AGO THERE were in Lisburn 800 houses, with a population of about 4,800. And of the 800 houses of that day 163 of them were occupied by weavers, Linenhall Street and Piper Hill being almost entirely given over to them. Next came shoemakers, who numbered 44, and of the 18 butchers then in the town 6 of them were named Dickey. There were 28 public houses and 2 inns, The Hertford Arms, in Market Square, kept by John McComb, and The King's Arms, also in Market Square, kept by George Moore. The linen merchants numbered 7, as did also the haberdashers. There were 6 hosiers in the town and only 1 hatter. Of apothecaries there were 3, and Doctor Samuel Musgrave lived at Market Square, as did Dr William Stewart at Castle Street. There were 3 tanners, but, strange to tell, none of them lived in Tan Yard Lane. There were 7 tailors and 7 schoolmasters in the town, and 4 magistrates, Nicholas Delacherois, William Hawkshaw, Thomas Johnston Smith, and Pointz Stewart, all lived in Castle Street.

And by Castle Street, crowded and all aglow with the bright March sunshine, we took our way to Castle Gardens, where, much to our regret, the year being all too young, we were denied a glimpse of the wide-swung, red-brown glory of the gardens' copper beeches. The terraced lawns, however, were green as an emerald ...

[A] description is given by an English traveller who came to Lisburn in 1635. Of the town he writes:

Linsley Garvin, about seven miles from Belfast, is well seated, but neither the town nor the country thereabouts well planted (inhabited), being almost all woods and moorish, until you come to Dromore. The town belongs to Lord Conway, who hath a good handsome house there.

The 'good handsome house', of which there is not now a stone upon a stone, stood in these same Castle Gardens, and all remains of its former grandeur is a part of the garden wall and the old red sandstone entrance gate with 1677, the date of its erection, carved above it. In the year 1641, Lis-na-Garvey was burned to the ground, and immediately after the catastrophe the name of the town was changed to Lisburn.

In the year 1700 many French refugees settled in the town, and one amongst them, Louis Crommelin, became a well-known linen manufacturer. He sought and obtained a patent for this purpose, and agreed to establish a centre in Kilkenny if his patent were extended, but that was another matter entirely. The English authorities set their faces against the patent, but agreed, under the influence of Ormond, to grant the extension, provided that the Southern manufacture would be limited to 'linen of the coarsest kind'.

CATHAL O'BYRNE, *As I Roved Out*, 1946

THE LITTLE TOWN OF DROMORE appeared to me to be situated in a valley; yet it derives its name from *Druim*, a back, and *Mor*, great; the great back of a hill. It was about ten in the morning when I approached it. The town was in shade, as was the lower part of the green hill beyond it. The upper part was cheerily illuminated by a radiant sun, and looked most gay and verdant. Dromore is a very ancient town, and bears all the marks of its antiquity. I clambered over a parcel of pigsties to have a look at an old castle, of which nothing remains, but two roofless walls, and a court overrun with nettles. The cathedral is very small, it is neither in form of a cross like others, nor has it any revenues for supporting cathedral service. I was looking through one of the windows at the inside, when a woman who had observed me, came running with the key. This was disinterested civility, for she would accept of no recompence; it was useless civility likewise, for there was nothing to see beyond the usual ornaments of a parish church.

JOHN GAMBLE, *A View of Society and Manners in the North of Ireland*, 1813

THE HOME-PLACE OF GREAT-GRANDFATHER Patterson was called the 'big' house in Greyabbey, where it remains still one of the best appointed in the locality. In addition to a farm, his people had a general store, selling everything from the proverbial needle to an anchor. In this home the Rev. James Porter, their minister, was an almost daily visitor. The sad fate that overtook their teacher in the Lord cast a shadow over all their lives and thinking. They themselves ... were never members of any secret society, orange or green. They diagnosed the troubles of their day as clearly as those who were, but they sought by constitutional means, and these alone, to bring about desired and necessary changes.

Soon after 1798, John Patterson left Greyabbey and came to reside in High Street (then a residential area), Newtownards. On the 4th April, 1810, we find him granted a lease by the Marquis of Londonderry for the houses 2 and 3 Castle Street. On the 1st September, 1830, he took out another lease for a plot of ground in Frances Street, then being opened up. On this he built for himself the house where I was born and about twenty-four of the one-storied type of houses then common in country towns. Some were for weavers and had what were termed two-loomed and four-loomed apartments. The chapter thus opened was only recently closed, after more than a hundred years.

THOMAS M. JOHNSTONE, *The Vintage of Memory*, 1942

THERE WAS NO REGULAR BOOKSELLER'S SHOP in Monaghan, but a couple of printers sold school books; and at a weekly market there was always a pedlar who supplied, at a few pence, cheap books printed at Belfast, of which the most popular were the *Battle of Aughrim* and *Billy Bluff*. The drama of the battle was in the hands of every intelligent schoolboy in Ulster, who strode an imaginary stage as Sarsfield or Ginkle, according to his sympathies. I can recall a device employed by a book-hawker at that time to stimulate the interest of his customers, which may perhaps have been borrowed from precautions invented in the penal times. 'I won't sell my book,' he cried, 'and I darn't sell my book, for the law forbids me to sell my book, but I'll sell my straw (producing a stalk of wheaten straw), and whoever buys my straw for a penny shall have my book for nothing.'

CHARLES GAVAN DUFFY, *My Life in Two Hemispheres*, 1898

BALLYCLARE ... IS WELL KNOWN for its horse fairs and monthly market for linens. It contains about 102 houses, supposed to be inhabited by more than 600 persons.

In the barony of Toome is Randalstown, on the Main water, about two miles to the north of Lough Neagh. The situation is good, and the view from the bridge remarkably fine, whether up the river towards Mr Dickey's, or downwards to the woods that hang over the river and form part of the scenery of Shane's Castle park. In 1800 this town contained fifty-one houses, and was a borough before the union. It has a good monthly market for linens on the first Wednesday, a church, and meeting-house.

Not far from thence, on the Main water, were formerly iron-works,

which of late years have not been worked; whether from want of ore or
of fuel, it is not said.

THE REVEREND JOHN DUBOURDIEU, *Statistical Survey of the County of Antrim*, 1812

A T THE TIME OF WHICH WE WRITE, the place [i.e. Ballyclare] was
neither more nor less than a quiet and comparatively secluded
country village. Railway trains were only heard from afar – the shriek of
the whistle coming to us over miles of quiet country. As children we
were sometimes awakened from sleep during the night by the sound of
this lonely, weird whistle, as the engine was engaged in shunting
operations at the distant station, and we were wont to imagine that it
betokened distress.

Railway travelling was not popular with our villagers. We preferred
making the journey to and from the city by Johnny Glenn's post-car,
which covered the distance three times each week – the horse, a veteran
of long experience, being turned out to graze on the sides of the roads
during the off days.

The farmers, when not requiring to take their horses on market days,
were accustomed to walk the distance (24 miles) there and back, carrying large baskets of butter and eggs, returning in same fashion with
their purchases. When not convenient for the head of the household to
attend market, the duty would be cheerfully undertaken by his wife or
daughter ...

On rare occasions the carrier would make the journey to Dublin and
back, joining in with a dozen others of the same calling from different
parts of the county, when they would travel together in jovial company,
stop at the same inns, completing the double journey in a fortnight. On
his return home the neighbours would come from far and near, anxious
to hear the latest news from the capital, and any remarkable experiences
encountered on the road. The carrier was the 'lion' of the place for many
days to come ...

People discussed the news, congregated in little groups about the
pump, or seated on the low wall of the Brig.

In summer nobody ever wore a coat except on Sabbaths or market
days. A straw hat generally lasted a man ten years or more, at which time
he would present it to his eldest son, or perhaps some farm labourer, who
would make it last for ten years longer.

There was a style of soft felt hat which was very common amongst us.
It could be doubled up and put in the pocket at church or public
meetings. If the sun shone brightly we turned down the rim in front; if
rain came on we turned it down all round.

ARCHIBALD McILROY, *When Lint Was in the Bell*, 1897

AFTER THE REBELLION of 1641, Ardglass rapidly declined, until now it is a veritable sleepy hollow, and its fishing industry is almost all that is left of its former greatness.

The railway may – let us hope – prove a benefit to the town, and also the golf links. Ardglass has all the natural advantages that go to make a prosperous watering-place. It has most lovely surroundings, fine air, and a wide open sea front with a stretch of view unsurpassed. It only requires to be better known, for, to a great many people, Ardglass is only a name.

MARY LOWRY, *The Story of Belfast and its Surroundings*, 1912

ARDGLASS

Ardglass is on a sloping hill,
    Which fronts the rising source of day;
And the full moon, at twilight, still
    Reflects her image on the bay. …

Upon the harbour's eastern shore,
    Wash'd by the ocean's surgy wave;
The curious traveller may explore
    An ancient grotto and a cave.

And on the west the Ward's *green hill*,
    Of conic form, and cloth'd with grass,
From which is trac'd, in Celtic still,
    The derivation of Ardglass. …

King's Castle, with its turrets four,
    Erects its huge and massy piles;
A beacon on the wish'd for shore,
    For seamen distant many miles.

Of old it was a fortress strong,
    Of much import and ample size;
But having sunk in ruins long,
    Its rebuilt towers majestic rise.

When Mountjoy and his warlike band,
    In arms contended with Tyrone,
Then Jordan's Castle did withstand
    A three years' lengthen'd siege alone.

And still it rears its lofty head,
  From which a stone has seldom fell;
And the historian well has said,
  It must have been the citadel.

And Margaret's Castle still remains,
  And also ivy-mantled Choud,
Which long have brav'd the rushing rains,
  And stormy tempests, fierce and loud.

Upon the ocean's shelvy shore,
  The range of Gothic halls are there,
Where dwelt the feudal lords of yore, –
  The powerful chieftains of Kildare.

Those halls are said to have been rais'd
  By the renowned Shane O'Neill,
Who by his warlike prowess seiz'd
  The fertile district of Lecale.

Of late, from Scotia, shrewd and wise,
  There dwelt renowned Ogilvie;
Who bade new halls like magic rise,
  And curb'd the wild and stormy sea.

To Leinster's Duchess he was bound,
  In strict accord with Hymen's will,
For sovereign beauty once renown'd,
  As the 'sweet lass of Richmond hill'.

He caus'd this ancient town to rise,
  By building streets, erecting piers;
Likewise the church wherein he lies
  Entomb'd, mature and full of years.

JOHN WILLIAMSON, *Poems on Various Subjects*, 1839

CARLINGFORD LOUGH (a true *fjord*, if you see it in winter, with the Lough and Down mountains rising from ice-blue water) widens out to Rostrevor, the little town where the roses flower on the yellow houses even at Christmas. A quaint and magical little town is this, one of the suntraps of Ireland, being held by mountains towards the light. The roads which strike from it up the glens lead to the Deer's Meadow, and to mountain plantations of larch and fir, where glittering streams sing. I think that almost the most beautiful view in all Ireland is that which you get as you return to Rostrevor from a tramp into those wooded heights.

AODH DE BLÁCAM, *The Black North*, 1938

NEWRY, THE CAPITAL OF THE COUNTY DOWN, is picturesquely situated in the 'gap of the North'. Lying in a valley on the Leinster frontier, the breezes from the Mourne and Carlingford mountains sweep over it. Carlingford Lough flows almost to its quays, and the dialects of three counties may be heard in its streets. It is essentially a border town. The little river Glanrye, flowing through it into Carlingford Lough, marks the boundary between Down and Armagh, the Lough itself the boundary between Down and Louth.

R. BARRY O'BRIEN, *The Life of Lord Russell of Killowen*, 1901

NEWRY IN 1922 WAS A TOWN with a hangover. The atmosphere was sour and full of hostility, the people divided denominationally and politically, each side resentful of things past and suspicious of the other side's every move, apprehensive about the future. The 'A' Specials in ill-fitting uniforms, formidably armed, were there in large numbers; on duty in the streets, racing through the countryside in a variety of vehicles, standing guard over important installations, watching and searching and sharply observing the townspeople.

PATRICK SHEA, *Voices and the Sound of Drums*, 1981

THE MAIN ROAD FROM ARMAGH to Newry is still known as the Coach Road. On it the stage from Armagh to Dublin would travel. A changing or post house now part of a farmyard exists on the above road about one and a half miles south of Markethill. It is in the townland of Magheravery, it is the first house on the left-hand-side when you pass under the railway bridge coming from Markethill. The brackets for the large lanterns were on the wall up to recent times.

(J.I.M., Co. Armagh)

Ulster Folklife, vol. 5, 1959

TODAY IS MARKET DAY IN PORTADOWN, and the streets are lively with people. A broad waterway connects the town with an industrial country back to Newry and on to Lough Neagh and Belfast.

Transportation is cheap and easy; industries are established; people are employed; Portadown looks a business-like place.

Portadown has its legend – the legend that makes it the ultra-Orange town of Northern Ireland. When a ballad-maker wanted to give a recognisable background to his character he placed him by writing:

> I am a loyal Orangeman
> From Portadown upon the Bann.

Mothers are said to keep their children out of forbidden places with the warning, 'There are wee Popes in it.' History joins with legend in giving Portadown this particular eminence: the conspicuous monument of the town is the statue of the champion of Northern Protestantism and the leader of the opposition to Home Rule in the 1890s, Colonel Saunderson.

PADRAIC COLUM, Cross Roads in Ireland, 1930

from BALLYCARRY FAIR
to the tune 'Green Grow the Rashes, O'

Sin' sunrise drudgin' i' the moss,
  I've dearly bought a shillin', O;
An' ho' to me a weighty loss,
  To spen it I'm fu' willin' O:
Sae I'se refit and want my rest,
  Tho' I'm baith wat an' weary, O;
For now the fair is at the best
  In sportsome Ballycarry, O.

> *CHORUS*
> *Hartsome is the claughin, O,*
> *Hartsome is the claughin, O,*
> *Where ev'ry hour I hae to spare*
> *Is past in mirth and laughin', O.*

The ginge-bread wife, that's now as drunk's
  An owl; the herds new whistle, O; –
The bumpkin beau, wi' pouther't funks,
  Like Downs upon a thristle, O –
Then men o' strength wha bullets play,
  Or putt in ilka alley, O;
An' circles warpin' to and frae,
  Mak' a' the spirits rally, O.

Hartsome is, etc.

The winsome wean, wi' heart fu' light,
   Smiles up, an' seeks a fairin, O;
The armless beggar craves a mite
   Whare'er he gains a hearin', O,
What tho' they'll waste whate'er we gie
   On *sweeties*, an' a *drappie*, O!
We'se gie them something; ae babee
   Apiece, wad mak them happy, O.
                    Hartsome is, etc.

What clusters pauvice roun' the stalls
   Whare pedlars streek their conscience, O!
An' whare the ballad-singer bawls
   A string o' noisy nonsense, O!
But sunset's come, an' aged ban's
   Step hameward at their leisure, O;
While younger folk mak' Herdman's han's
   Unlock the springs o' pleasure, O.
                    Hartsome is, etc.

Now earth revolvin' turns up night,
   The lanely streets' forsaken, O,
An' wine, an' love, an' frien'ship bright,
   Mak' hearts, aince cauldrife, waken, O:
Now bargains, courtships, toasts, huzzas,
   Combine in blythe disorder, O;
While *pairs* play pranks in Archy's wa's
   That I'll be nae recorder o'
                    Hartsome is, etc. ...

O village fam't for scenes like thir!
   Sae shelter'd, an sae healthy, O;
Thy sons are firm, thy daughters fair,
   In them, at least, thou'rt wealthy, O:
Till *Isle'magee* surround *Loughmorne*,
   Or yill spring frae the quarry, O,
May plenty, pleasure, peace, adorn
   Carrousin' Ballycarry, O!
                    Hartsome is, etc.

JAMES ORR, *Poems on Various Subjects*, 1802

IN A COUNTRY WHERE THE POPULATION is so great, and where, from its manufactures, there must naturally be such an exchange of different articles, fairs and markets must be much frequented; consequently fairs are held in all the towns at stated times, and in many places, where there are no towns, a few houses alone affording refreshment to those who resort to them; and in some cases tents are erected for this purpose ...

To the fairs come numbers of people for amusement from the vicinity, whose dress and appearance strongly indicate the prosperity of the country; and the increased civilization of it is shown by the absence of those riotous tumults, which formerly disgraced them.

The markets are either weekly or monthly; in these the disposal of linen and yarn are the principal objects, but many other things are also disposed of; and in all the towns of tolerable magnitude butcher's meat, fowl, eggs, etc. are sold, besides oatmeal and potatoes. Butter markets have been lately established in Ballymoney, Ballymena and Broughshane, where it is disposed of in casks for exportation to buyers, who attend, and who take it to Belfast, there to sell it on their own account.

THE REVEREND JOHN DUBOURDIEU, *Statistical Survey of the County of Antrim*, 1812

TO MAN THEM [I.E. THE TEXTILE MILLS] people poured in from the Ulster countryside, many being driven in by the famines of the 1840s. They came by rail and road, and once again it is necessary to gauge the importance of adequate communications in the growth of Belfast. By the 1830s there were regular coach services between Belfast and all the major towns of Antrim and Down; with Coleraine and Londonderry, with Enniskillen, Cookstown and Newry, as well as with Dublin ...

But the immigrants came mainly by rail, which, unlike the early railways in England and Wales, seems to have been used more for passengers than for freight in the earlier years. The first line in Ulster was that between Belfast and Lisburn which was opened in 1839, and it was soon extended to Lurgan (1841), Portadown (1842) and Armagh (1848), the link with Dublin being completed in 1853. In 1848 the County Down railway was opened, making Belfast easily accessible to the northern part of that county; and in the same year a line was opened which linked Belfast with Ballymena and Carrickfergus. This was later extended to Cookstown and Londonderry, thus tapping the human resources of counties Antrim, Tyrone and Londonderry.

The three railway termini were built on the edge of the early nineteenth-century town, and gathered around them mills and streets of mean houses which were filled with people driven in by poverty.

EMRYS JONES, *A Social Geography of Belfast*, 1960

THERE IS SHEER ROMANCE all along to the point of this fresh blade of land: tangible freshness, green knolls, a beach where sheldrake strut, a castle that may be a first-rate fake for all I know or care raising its romantic head from a wood; a sudden peep of the Mournes, that blue inscription of running mountains to be read from so many and such distant parts of Ireland. Thus we go by good, serious farms to the altogether captivating town of Portaferry.

Portaferry is unspoilt (that term *is* spoilt but there is no help for it unless one invents a new term for the same thing): a slumbering square, a grave castle, gulls crying over an age-mouldy harbour, a charming water-front hotel where one can meditatively watch the shimmer and sparkle of Strangford Lough while dining and, best of all things in this mad, new world, no through traffic. Portaferry is, metaphorically speaking, the last of old Ireland: a place that has not come up all ugly grins announcing that it is abreast with the times and going rapidly ahead of them; a place where the reconstruction of history is not a painful mental contortion. Before the Norsemen came, the simple Irish named the lake Lough Cuan (the 'harbour lake'), but the foreigners took a more realistic view and renamed the narrow-necked lough where the sea rushes in so fiercely, *Strang Fjord*, the 'violent inlet'. The name serves, in fact any name serves, but why, I wonder, did God give us such a geographical white elephant? Strangford Lough is just a bottle of agitated sea water, a service to none and fun only to hardy sportsmen and a few doughty owners of pleasure ships. Its many islets (here as elsewhere I need scarcely say that there are 365 of them, one for every day in the year) are the haunts of terns, oyster-catchers and mergansers. The gentle art of tearing oneself away is difficult in Portaferry. I stand by the mouldy harbour and watch a man preparing a meal on a boat called *Family Friend*; I hear the gulls crying and see Strangford across the water, quivering somewhat in the wind, its castle barely visible. But one has to leave Portaferry some time.

STEPHEN RYNNE, *All Ireland*, 1956

BANBRIDGE WAS A COUNTRY TOWN which had sprung up in the eighteenth century around a stone bridge which had been then thrown across the river Bann on what became the main coach road between Dublin and Belfast. It had later developed into a considerable centre of the linen industry and boasted, at the time I write of, of some half dozen weaving factories, a large spinning mill a little way out of the town, and several other works in connection with the trade. The Church of Ireland population, which was then numerically the largest, consisted mainly of artisans, weavers and mill hands, and in the country districts of small farmers and labourers, the manufacturers and shopkeepers belonging mainly to other denominations. I had had no wish to come to work in the North, which was largely associated in my mind with Orangeism and Presbyterianism, with neither of which I felt greatly in sympathy, and it was only in response to what I felt to be an irresistible call that I nevertheless decided to come. It was a decision I never had cause to regret. It was not long before I found that the people of Ulster, when you got to know them, and they you, were as kindly, true and staunchly loyal to their clergy and their church according to their lights as any clergyman could wish to work among; that the working-class Orangemen (though I never joined the order) – of course with exceptions – were commonly the backbone of all church work; and that Presbyterians were by no means necessarily the dour and 'black-mouthed' people as sometimes supposed in the South!

E.D. ATKINSON, *Recollections of an Ulster Archdeacon*, 1934

WHAT HE LOST IN POLITICAL INFLUENCE in Newtownards, Alexander Stewart made up in the social improvements which he effected as a resident landlord. The town, which lies on the northern shores of Strangford Lough, was founded by Sir Hugh Montgomery, and had been incorporated by James I with the other plantation colonies. Unfortunately its early prosperity declined along with the fortunes of its founder's descendants. Gone were the days when claret flowed 'from the spouts of the market cross, catched in hats and bowls by who cou'd or wou'd ... and good fellows [were] increasing their mirth and joy by good liquor.' During the early years of the eighteenth century when penal legislation depressed dissenters and Catholics alike, its condition grew so bad that when the new landlord arrived in the year 1745 there were not more than three good slate houses in it. Alexander Stewart therefore erected a large market house, and laid out an extensive square in front for a new market place, building also neat rows of houses in the adjacent streets. Although the style of architecture which he favoured may fall short of modern aesthetic standards, these houses of one and two storeys were the reverse of jerry-built, and served a fitter purpose than the miserable cottages in which his tenants had hitherto dwelt. The house which he constructed for himself was so strong that in the following century it was used as a factory. In less than twenty years two hundred new houses sprang up under his auspices, while the income from the two estates had doubled.

H. MONTGOMERY HYDE, *The Rise of Castlereagh*, 1933

NORTH WIND PORTRUSH

I shall never forget the wind
On this benighted coast.
It works itself into the mind
Like the high keen of a lost
Lear-spirit in agony
Condemned for eternity

To wander cliff and cove
Without comfort, without love.
It whistles off the stars
And the existential, stark
Face of the cosmic dark.
We crouch to roaring fires.

Yet there are mornings when,
Even in midwinter, sunlight
Flares, and a rare stillness
Lies upon roof and garden –
Each object eldritch-bright,
The sea scarred but at peace.

Then, from the ship we say
Is the lit town where we live
(Our whiskey-and-forecast
     world),
A smaller ship that sheltered
All night in the restless bay
Will weigh anchor and leave.

What did they think of us
During their brief sojourn?
A string of lights on the prom
Dancing mad in the storm –
Who lives in such a place?
And will they ever return?

But the shops open at nine
As they have always done,
The wrapped-up bourgeoisie
Hardened by wind and sea.
The newspapers are late
But the milk shines in its crate.

Everything swept so clean
By tempest, wind and rain!
Elated, you might believe
That this was the first day –
A false sense of reprieve,
For the climate is here to stay.

So best prepare for the worst
That chaos and old night
Can do to us; were we not
Raised on such expectations,
Our hearts starred with frost
Through countless generations?

Elsewhere the olive grove,
Naked lunch in the grass,
Poppies and parasols,
Blue skies and mythic love.
Here only the stricken souls
No springtime can release.

Prospero and his people never
Came to these stormy parts;
Few do who have the choice.
Yet, blasting the subtler arts,
That weird, plaintive voice
Sings now and for ever.

DEREK MAHON, *Courtyards in Delft*, 1981

A FEW GLIMPSES, AGAIN FOR THE MOST PART of the Londoners' lands, reveal some of the growing pains common to all new settlements. There is constant agitation for schools, churches, and bridges; there are many complaints of excessive customs duties and minor administrative abuses. In December 1618 we find the good folk of Draperstown grumbling about the conduct of the agent of the Drapers' Company, Robert Russell. The townsmen, evidently sober Puritans and perhaps rather smug, alleged that he was turning Draperstown into a saturnalia. The enterprising agent desired to create a 'Merry Ulster' to his own profit. He had built a brewery, and was converting the town's meagre water supply into beer. He was buying up houses to turn them into drinking-dens, and actually paying his own workmen partly in beer; with the result that the Sabbath was profaned, drunkenness was rampant, and there were distressing brawls in the streets. Evidently this complaint caused Mr Russell and his remarkable powers of organisation to be transferred from a scene where they were not appreciated by the more powerful citizens, who knew what was good for the others. A couple of years later we find the people of Draperstown better pleased with a new agent. They still had matter for complaint, however. The water supply was not yet adequate; there was no market; the streets were so foul that they had to don high boots when they walked from one house to another; and – eternal trouble, especially in that wild country of Glenconkeine, Tyrone's last refuge in 1603 – the wood-kerne was abroad and at his thieving.

CYRIL FALLS, The Birth of Ulster, 1936

IN THE MORNING SUNLIGHT, from a hill in the public park, with a shaft commemorating a veteran of the Peninsular wars soaring above us, we see the town with its spires and pinnacles clustered at its crossing-place over the water-barrier of the lakes. Northwards begins the many-folded line of the Donegal hills, while due west rises the steep blue mass of Benbulbin, above Sligo town, where through Grania's treachery and Finn's witchcraft Diarmuid was slain by the enchanted boar. But from all the widespread landscape, from green plain, silver lake water, and far blue hills, my gaze keeps returning to the roof-line of Enniskillen, tumbling down to the gap where the river flows through the town.

> Fare thee well, Enniskillen,
> Fare thee well for a while,
> With all thy fair waters
> And many a green isle.

A single campanile pricks above the roof-tops. Perhaps it was an accident of genius, but merely to have placed it there, in its exact relationship to sky and plain and clustering roof-tree, was an achievement that deserves a tablet all to itself. Behind it high-banked white clouds are massing over the Donegal hills.

DENIS IRELAND, Statues Round the City Hall, 1939

IT WAS MY GRANDFATHER'S MOVE to Belfast in 1887 that brought my father's contact with Ballymena to an end. The whole family connection with Ballymena ended only a few years later, in 1889, with an episode which is still remembered there. My great-grandfather was about to retire from his post as bank manager when he was murdered one evening by his own cashier. The cashier had put himself out of his proper mind with drink. Carrying a double-barrelled gun, he followed my great-grandfather along the Galgorm Road, where the old gentleman was placidly taking his regular evening stroll. There he killed the old man with one barrel of his gun and committed suicide himself with the other.

It is hard to compare [that] Ballymena ... with Ballymena as it is today. The town was, of course, smaller then than it is now, but the main streets were not very different from their present appearance. The footpaths were cobbled, however, except a piece of pavement outside the bank house, where all the little boys came to spin their tops.

But in the character of its inhabitants there has been little change. Ballymena is still surely a place where a man can be himself without having to care too much what his neighbours think about it. It is a very fine thing to have been born in Ballymena. My father certainly thinks so, and I myself never hesitate to claim a certain inherited virtue on account of the fact that I am the son of a Ballymena man.

HUGH SHEARMAN, *Ulster*, 1949

BALLYMENA, ONE OF THE TOWNS where quarter-sessions are held, is in the same barony on the Braid river. It is a most thriving place, containing 2,500 inhabitants, having a weekly market on Saturday for horses, cows, etc. There is also a regular sale of butter for exportation. The linen, of which there is a considerable quantity sold, is three-quarter's wide, and excellent in quality. There are a few old houses in the town built after a different fashion from the rest, having their gable ends to the front. In one direction an entire new street has been lately built. From whatever cause it proceeds, this is one of the most prosperous places in the county, though so far inland; and, as the markets are much frequented, there are two very comfortable inns. Wherever the linen-drapers regularly attend, decent accommodation at least may be expected. About the centre of the town is the market house, with a steeple sixty feet high, and near it a remarkable mount, called the moat.

THE REVEREND JOHN DUBOURDIEU, *Statistical Survey of the County of Antrim*, 1812

SOME TOWNS IN IRELAND REGISTER as little on the memory as a bump on the road. Towns to be remembered must either have good architecture or some unusual quality of their own. Strictly speaking, Ballymena has neither, and yet it is not a town that one passes over lightly. I can only think that it depends for recognition upon the character of its people. Ballymena seems to me to have fewer nonentities among its citizens than almost any town I know. It is industrialised, but not unpleasantly so, and it is never smothered by the smoke of factory chimneys. It is a town in which music and the arts, along with all pleasures of the mind, receive a kindly reception. It is linked by many sons to Oxford, Cambridge, Trinity College, Dublin, and the Scottish universities, for it is a proud boast of Ballymena that no town in the British Isles has got a higher proportion of educated men.

DENIS O'D. HANNA, *The Face of Ulster*, 1952

BALLYMENA WAS ... an important market centre which attracted many farming people from the surrounding districts. These people used to arrive on their carts, wearing clothes of a very antique fashion and often carrying huge umbrellas, with ribs made of cane and large brass joints, the sort of contraptions that came into use when umbrellas were first introduced to the British Isles. There was a tradesman in Ballymena who used to mend these umbrellas for the country people, and he referred to such umbrellas very contemptuously as 'ould Prasbytairians', for he himself was a sturdy upholder of Episcopacy, whereas the owners of the umbrellas were mostly Presbyterians.

HUGH SHEARMAN, *Ulster*, 1949

THERE WERE ... guards at Hillsborough, for it was the residence of Northern Ireland's governor, but these guards were khaki ones on routine sentry duty. The castle they guarded was a modest Georgian stone manor rather less interesting than the forecourt's splendid iron gates. The gates were only brought to Hillsborough in 1936 and had formerly stood at the entrance to Richhill Castle in County Armagh, and were almost certainly the work of the two Thornberry brothers from Falmouth who settled in Armagh early in the eighteenth century.

Like Armagh, Hillsborough stood partly on a hill and the town's main square was at the top of it with the famous gates closing one side of it. From this elevated place there were views out to the surrounding countryside. Elegant Georgian houses surrounded the town and gave it perhaps a stronger English flavour than could be found in other Plantation towns. Islanded in the square was the court house, a small but nevertheless fine building – the best I had seen since leaving Armagh. It was painted in pink and grey and white and besides its turret also had urns against the skyline.

Samuel Brown's pub opposite was an excellent vantage point from which to admire this little architectural opus of 1780. A farmer beside the pub door bolted out to capture a sow which somehow escaped from the trailer behind his car. The beast was caught before any damage was done to the sedate, Royalty-planted trees on the lawns of Government House.

One frightened sow can make quite a noise, but it was only a tiny squeak compared with the din that filled Hillsborough on its former fair days. The jostling farmers and moaning cattle and bleating sheep, the cries of country women with honey and butter for sale made dissonant music a thousand times over. But it was not dissonant for a Hillsborough boy who years afterwards recalled the joy and excitement in the scherzo of his 'Irish Symphony'.

Walking about Hillsborough breathing the sweet airs of County Down I thought of how often that boy, who afterwards became the great Sir Hamilton Harty, must have longed to return to his native town. The renowned musician did try to visit Hillsborough at least once a year. But music in the form of the Hallé Orchestra kept him prisoner in Manchester, a place he hated. On retiring from his post as the Hallé's permanent conductor he said, 'When well-intentioned people ask me how I left Manchester I reply "With pleasure".'

Harty was known for his wit, which no doubt developed early in repartee with Hillsborough's farmers and perhaps also with the good people of the parish church where his father played John Snetzler's eighteenth-century organ.

ROBIN BRYANS, *Ulster: A Journey Through the Six Counties*, 1964

JACK PENROSE AND PAMELA GREY lived in the little town of Hillsborough in the county of Down, that county which forms the south-eastern corner of Northern Ireland. It is scarcely a town as the word is understood in England, being little more than a collection of grey slate-covered houses fronting both sides of a single steeply falling street, with the church in the middle and the castle at the top. But though small, it is a town of honour in the province, for in the castle lives no less a personage than the governor – or lived, till a recent fire necessitated his removal. Its street moreover is no mere village street; it is part of the main highway from Belfast to Dublin, and though the unhappy division of the country has reduced the flow of traffic between the two cities, Hillsborough still rumbles by day and night with cars and buses and great lorries grinding their way north or south.

Hillsborough is some dozen miles from Belfast, to which city Jack and Pam were now bound. The road is good, comparatively straight and level, broad and with an excellent surface ... It was early in September and had been a day of gorgeous sunshine: if anything too hot. Now as they drove swiftly along Pam subconsciously feasted her eyes on the colours of the great trees beneath which they passed, dark with the full maturity of summer, but not yet beginning to turn to the reds and browns of autumn.

FREEMAN WILLS CROFTS, *Man Overboard*, 1936

WE GOT INTO OMAGH about seven o'clock. The coach stops at a house of which I have forgot the sign. I preferred the Abercorn Arms directly opposite, which, for cleanliness and civility, I found equal to almost any house I have ever been in. The landlord's name is Jenkins; he is a civil, obliging little fellow: he showed me every thing that was curious in the town and neighbourhood; and performed the part of cicerone with great success, considering it was his first appearance in that character. He assured me I was the only traveller who ever thought it worth his while to ask him a single question about Omagh, during the five years he had lived in it.

The approach to this town is pretty; it is situated on a rising ground. The country round is highly cultivated, intersected with hedges, and tolerably well planted. The church spire, and a small cupola erected on the sessions-house, give it a gay and somewhat of theatric appearance. The interior of the town, however, destroys the delusion. The streets are dirty and irregular, and though there are some good houses, they are by no means so numerous as those of an opposite description; yet I saw none of those hovels, which are described by travellers as forming the entrance to an Irish country town. In general the cabins were tolerably decent; what I allude to is the external state of the habitations of many, who no doubt belonged to the better order of inhabitants, and which indicated negligence and indolence, more than poverty and want. A number of the houses were thatched: being repaired at different periods, as necessity required, the roofs often presented a grotesque appearance, and were decked in all the colours of the year; the fresh straw of autumn on the part lately done, and the green verdure of spring in the plentiful crop of weeds which grew on the more ancient. At a distance, one might have taken it for the city of Babylon, with its gardens and green fields on the tops of the houses.

JOHN GAMBLE, *Sketches of Dublin and the North of Ireland in 1810*, 1812

I WAS RELIEVED FROM THE TRIBULATION of the mail coach at Strabane, a large ugly town, apparently a place of some trade and business, with a fine river running down to Derry. At four o'clock in the evening I hired a jaunting-car to carry me into the highlands of Donegal, a distance of about twenty-two miles, and late at night I arrived at my friend's house, after travelling along roads almost impassable, over hills almost inaccessible, every ligature and joint of my poor body nearly jaunted into dislocation. However, cordial hospitality, a soft bed, and a day's quiet, repaired and restored me so far as to enable us to begin our excursion and mountain rambles. My friend's glebe-house lies in a fine valley in the north-western district of Donegal, called the Barony of Kilmacrenan, and the whole district is the estate of Trinity College. This valley is watered by two beautiful rivers, which having worked their way and escaped from the mountains, here join and expand into a broad lake interspersed with islands, and surrounded by hills of the most abrupt and varied forms.

CAESAR OTWAY, *Sketches in Ireland*, 1827

DUNGANNON IS SITUATED about three miles from the south shore of Lough Neagh, and is a spacious, handsome, and well-built town. It consists of a square, and four principal and several smaller streets. The situation of the town, on a lofty hill of limestone, renders it both a healthy and pleasant place of residence. The Royal School was founded by letters patent of James I. It is situated on a gentle eminence on the east side of the town, on grounds comprising nine acres, purchased by Primate Robinson and given to the school.

THE REVEREND CANON FORDE, *Sketches of Olden Days in Northern Ireland*, 1926

THE DATE IS THE 13TH OF SEPTEMBER in the year of grace 1934. The scene is Cushendun, the Foot of the Brown River, in the county of Antrim, and God-made in the harvest time, and for our special delectation, it would seem, one glorious day.

The sea is a blue wonder, where the white mists lift and go trailing. Above the little lime-white town the hills are a dream in the golden air. Higher up Lurigeaden raises his royal head into the clouds, above the yellow radiance, keeping watch and ward about the little White Dún at the foot of the river, covering with his mighty shadow, as with a blue awning, the little singing streams and wooded glens, and trailing down through the blue of the air the lilac and purple of his regal robes across half the world.

CATHAL O'BYRNE, *As I Roved Out*, 1946

STRANGFORD, SLEEPY IN THE AFTERNOON SUNLIGHT, looks across the narrow sound to Portaferry perched over the reflection of its own coloured houses and green hill. The tide is on the turn, the sound like a millpond … rooks homing from the Ards peninsula with an occasional satisfied cawing. Then on again past Kilclief and the ruins of Norman castles, with the angry roar of Strangford bar rising to a crescendo on the left, past Ballyhornan to Ardglass and Killough with its tree-shaded main street, its leisurely general stores, and its deserted harbour that once cherished ambitions to become a terminal port for English mail steamers but is now given over to a few derelict rowing boats and small boys fishing from the pier. Killough, sunk in its backwater, seems content, the tragedy of my father and his red-brick warehouse in the smoky city of Belfast merely a tale told in the chimney corner. Time and tide heal all, says the rustle of the sea wind in Killough's shade trees. As if to prove it, the tide floods back into the harbour that once cherished ambitions, the rowing boats swing lazily and contentedly at anchor ... Then on again in the amber evening light, past St John's Point, with its black-and-white striped lighthouse, to the wide stretch of Dundrum Bay, with beyond it, sharp-edged in the spring sunset, the grape-blue barrier of the Mournes.

I sit amongst the tussocky grass of the sand hills, staring out across the brimming bay, watching the tangle of the mountains darken from deep blue to purple. The land of youth.

DENIS IRELAND, Statues Round the City Hall, 1939

DOWNPATRICK

1

The houses in Irish Street
Cling like clegs
And English Street
Steeples up to three
Saints on the cathedral;
But Scotch Street slopes
Away from the river
The swans and the island:
The Welsh I suppose
Given Saint Patrick
Declined to reside
By river or steeple.

2

My father was born there
In a brisk town, then the Quoile
Familiar with barges before
The railway came, and Belfast
Killed crafts – Quail furniture –
(Lynn Doyle on the wireless: Irish Chippendale).
But the swans remained on the river
Icebergs or islands
A wish of water away
From the steam, the steel and the hammer.

3
The swans I remember and
The cathedral footed
And fêted with April daffodils
Glimpsed from the fretting train then,
When exhausted with refugees
From German bombs, it stumbled forward
To a future of Irish bombs uniting
The grief of a girl
With one eye and an arm.

ROY McFADDEN, *Verifications*, 1977

DOWNPATRICK ... APPEALED TO ME perhaps because its streets were not flat and the town was arranged about a crossroads, an unusual feature of town layouts in Northern Ireland. The cathedral approach was by a gentle slope, planted with trees and bordered by buildings, any one of which would grace any town. The Blue Coat School was easily the best of these, a small-scale, stone-dressed building rather in the manner of William Kent, finished with a neat, central cupola. Immediately opposite the school was a pair of elegantly urban houses with Ionic pilasters about their doors and a view beside them, straight through to the meadows beyond.

ROBIN BRYANS, *Ulster: A Journey Through the Six Counties*, 1964

DOWNPATRICK ... IS AN ANCIENT TOWN which announces itself before you enter its old-world untidy streets. You have the same feeling as when you know you are about to meet an aged gracious lady who in her youth was beautiful. You are on your best behaviour. Somehow Downpatrick 'expects'. Perhaps the feeling came from a peep at the cathedral spire over the rolling hills of Down and the shining waterway of the Quoile. Perhaps you knew that the twelfth-century ruins of the abbey of Inch are hiding among the autumn-tinted woods. The bridge over the Quoile confirms your suspicions too that the place has tradition. Maybe it is just that you happen to know that here St Patrick preached. Up this very river came the Viking ships to sack the city. Here was born Dun Scotus, one of the early founders of Oxford (so tradition says), and this chocolate-brown earth under your feet was the stage on which the first scene of the Christian drama in Ireland was enacted. It is difficult to explain this feeling unless you accept the possibility that departed spirits still visit this earth, and that we can be half aware of their presence.

In Downpatrick there is a coaching inn. It could easily have more character than it has, but some of the eighteenth-century atmosphere is still left. The Parish Church is said to incorporate the walls of the Norman dining-hall of John de Courcy. Today it is little more than a pleasant old stone barn with a Renaissance east window ...

In English Street ... you go from the centre of the town up to the cathedral in an uninterrupted atmosphere of Dickens. There is the charming old Blue Coat School of red brick and stone dressings, founded in 1733 by the Southwell family. There are several very attractive houses of good Georgian proportion, with fanlighted doors. There is also a house, once attached to the barracks, with a bow front of Regency period, now, alas! in bad repair. It is a lovely street, and more lovely when one realises that it leads to one of Britain's most ancient cathedrals; but the Carnegie Library, situated in a strategic place to ambush the eye, is as discordant as a dog fight in a concert of chamber music.

DENIS O'D. HANNA, The Face of Ulster, 1952

A GIFT FROM DOWNPATRICK

I

From Killough and Ardglass two roads take aim
at a cathedral raised in Patrick's name,
down the Gallows Hill and over the Dam,
picking up speed for a millennium,
in from the coast, along the Old Course,
in past the Mental and the Flying Horse,
past the holy wells at Struell and the Priory
of St Thomas the Martyr, where the Spring of Glorie
still heals the sick at the Hospital of Downe,
then up John Street to the heart of the town,
the Gullion, on by Lynn Doyle Place
down Irish Street to the dead clock face
that turns to Saul and Kilclief up the hills
a timeless gaze, that yet never fails
to watch for three saints and their daffodils.

II

This is my town with all of us there:
the town of the Man from God Knows Where,
the Shambles Fight, the Purple and Black
on parade down Market Street and back
and shame on the man who won't stir a peg

for the great William Johnston of Ballykilbeg
or the old Archdeacon, who returned from Stormont
with whatever concession that Fenian would want.
The whole town's a shambles. For better or worse,
there's more than one rider on this old horse.

III

Fresh from the siege and Defence of Crossgar,
from the hospitals, banks and the Arkle Bar,
from Páirc Tomás Ruiseál and the Orange Hall,
from English Street, Irish, from Scotch and Saul,
inclusive and generous, eager to please,
there is a town you can live in with ease,
like Leslie Montgomery (aka *Lynn C. Doyle*),
in lovely Downpatrick on the banks of the Quoile.

DAMIAN SMYTH, *Downpatrick Races*, 2000

A FEW WORDS ABOUT THE MAIL COACHES by which we used to get, by
day or night, in about twelve hours from Belfast to Dublin or Derry.
In fine weather an outside seat on top of the Royal Mail was an
exceedingly agreeable mode of travelling. We saw the country to much
more advantage than from the railway, and, instead of skirting the dismal
suburbs of the towns on the way, we dashed up the best streets to the
chief hotel, where horses were changed, and a little crowd always
collected to admire. The inside, however, was always stuffy and often
crowded, and the outside dangerous and uncomfortable in cold and wet
weather. Besides, it was necessary to bespeak a place beforehand. I have
driven ten miles to Dromore for three successive mornings before I could
get a seat in the Dublin coach. The red-coated coachman and guards
were fine, manly fellows, and very friendly with the passengers, who, to
be sure, always tipped them. The caravans, machines, and long cars that
started from public houses in Cromac Street, or in Ann Street at the
Highlandman, to take us to Ballynahinch or Newtownards, were poor
affairs. The Derry coach started from the Donegall Arms, Castle Place
(Robb's), and the Dublin coach from 10 Castle Street. The Carrickfergus
and Larne coaches stopped in Donegall Street and North Street.

THE REVEREND NARCISSUS BATT, 'Belfast Sixty Years Ago:
Recollections of a Septuagenarian', *Ulster Journal of Archaeology*, vol. 2, 1896

THE TOWN WE LIVED IN [i.e. Monaghan] was an eminently historic one. It was founded by monks in the sixth century, and is heard of throughout all the contests with England. During the Elizabethan wars it was frequently besieged, and was occupied alternately by Irish and English soldiers down to the time of Cromwell, when Owen Roe was succeeded in command of the national army by a Monaghan man, Heber MacMahon, chief of the MacMahons of Oriel, and at the same time Bishop of Clogher. In 1798 the first martyrs for Irish liberty were three of the Monaghan Militia, who were shot for being 'Croppies'. But of this history we knew little except what concerned the affairs of '98. Survivors of that era were still plentiful in the north, and one old servant entertained me constantly in my boyhood with its legends and traditions. She even dazzled me with the hope of some day being shown where the Croppies hid their arms when the troubles were over if I were a good boy and minded my books; but I suppose my conduct did not answer her expectations, for I never was shown the buried treasures.

CHARLES GAVAN DUFFY, My Life in Two Hemispheres, 1898

WE CAME TO THE CHARMING LITTLE VILLAGE of Moy – or rather *The* Moy as it is always called. Lord Charlemont originally laid out The Moy in 1754 after he had been to Italy and seen Marengo there grouped around a piazza. The Moy certainly had an Italianate feeling. Its trees stood in circular, walled beds whose stones were whitewashed, a piece of grooming unusual for Ireland's free and shaggy trees. Until recently these trees and the piazza had been the scene of The Moy's celebrated horse fair. People came from all over Europe to buy horses and the little town made its fortune by supplying chargers to the armies of a score of nations.

Besides an Italian square and a name for horse-dealing, The Moy also had a band marching that evening to perform at the football field beside the Catholic church, even though it was late. But it was summer, and in that Scandinavian way, the light lingered in the western sky for hours after sunset. The Rev. P. Moore came out of his presbytery and asked the accordion band to play for us before it went into the football field. And so there was music in the air, the wistful, nostalgic wail of accordions which is one of the most melancholy sounds in the world.

ROBIN BRYANS, Ulster: A Journey Through the Six Counties, 1964

CARRICKFERGUS

I was born in Belfast between the mountain and the gantries
  To the hooting of lost sirens and the clang of trams:
Thence to Smoky Carrick in County Antrim
  Where the bottle-neck harbour collects the mud which jams

The little boats beneath the Norman castle,
  The pier shining with lumps of crystal salt;
The Scotch Quarter was a line of residential houses
  But the Irish Quarter was a slum for the blind and halt.

The brook ran yellow from the factory stinking of chlorine,
  The yarn-mill called its funeral cry at noon;
Our lights looked over the lough to the lights of Bangor
  Under the peacock aura of a drowning moon.

The Norman walled this town against the country
  To stop his ears to the yelping of his slave
And built a church in the form of a cross but denoting
  The list of Christ on the cross in the angle of the nave.

I was the rector's son, born to the anglican order,
  Banned for ever from the candles of the Irish poor;
The Chichesters knelt in marble at the end of a transept
  With ruffs about their necks, their portion sure.

The war came and a huge camp of soldiers
  Grew from the ground in sight of our house with long
Dummies hanging from gibbets for bayonet practice
  And the sentry's challenge echoing all day long;

A Yorkshire terrier ran in and out by the gate-lodge
  Barred to civilians, yapping as if taking affront:
Marching at ease and singing 'Who Killed Cock Robin?'
  The troops went out by the lodge and off to the Front.

The steamer was camouflaged that took me to England –
  Sweat and khaki in the Carlisle train;
I thought that the war would last for ever and sugar
  Be always rationed and that never again

Would the weekly papers not have photos of sandbags
  And my governess not make bandages from moss
And people not have maps above the fireplace
  With flags on pins moving across and across –

Across the hawthorn hedge the noise of bugles,
  Flares across the night,
Somewhere on the lough was a prison ship for Germans,
  A cage across their sight.

I went to school in Dorset, the world of parents
  Contracted into a puppet world of sons
Far from the mill girls, the smell of porter, the salt-mines
  And the soldiers with their guns.

LOUIS MacNEICE, *Poems 1925–1948*, 1949

THE SCOTTISH PLANTATION never reached Belfast, which was English,
but stopped with the high ridge of hills between that city and
Newtownards and struck down by Holywood, which was on its extreme
western boundary. In the seventeenth century the Holywood hills were
wooded, and transport across them very primitive, so that towns like
Newtownards and Belfast must have been separated in those days by
several hours of travel. Be this as it may, the Scottish influence round
Comber, Newtownards, and the northern end of Strangford Lough did
not penetrate into the English Plantation of the Lagan Valley.

DENIS O'D. HANNA, *from* 'Architecture in Ulster', *The Arts in Ulster*, 1951

THE SOCIAL LIFE OF CLONES was lively and when the people of the
town were set upon entertaining themselves, political loyalties were
overlooked. The regimental band played in the Diamond every Sunday
and there were dances and concerts and sporting events. The Regiment
had a team in the Summer Football League, a Black and Tan played for
the town team and the league championship was won by the Cavan
Police team, all of its members Black and Tans, who travelled to matches
in their armoured lorries. The division between Catholics and Protestants
had none of the tight-lipped sharpness we had experienced in
Rathfriland. Politically the alignment was more or less the same, but they
all enjoyed themselves together. When the Orangemen marched on the
Twelfth of July it was a day out for the whole town.

Attendance at a Protestant school was in harmony with my political
thinking. My fellow pupils were the sons and daughters of Unionists, our

458

history books were about British history, we were not taught Irish, the allegiance of our teachers was unshakably to the British Constitution. I was secure in my belief that the British Government of Ireland was in the best interests of all concerned, including the Sinn Féiners.

Tim and Tommy [i.e his brothers] went to the National School where the principal, a frail, querulous man and a fervent Republican, adopted an attitude of non-intervention when they were molested by boys who felt obliged to inflict punishment on the two young representatives of British oppression. One afternoon I went into the school yard as the boys came out and in the presence of the protesting principal and his pupils I horsewhipped the chief aggressor with the leather-thonged whip which I had learned to handle with more than average skill. In the unaccountable way that the affairs of boys are regulated, my victim and I were later to become good friends.

PATRICK SHEA, *Voices and the Sound of Drums*, 1981

THE OLD CROSS AT CLONES

The Old Cross stands so dead and dumb
Above the market-place of Clones:
But none, who pass, take bearings from
The wisest of the stones.

For compass-like it throws a stub
Way south to Ballybay:
Another northward from its hub
To hills of faraway.

The summit points to Heaven-home
Where Holy Patrick dwells:
And deep its blind root in the loam
Explores the road that's Hell's.

But none look up of market-folks,
Of all the chicken-laden crones:
'Mid crush of barrows and of yokes
Around the Cross of Clones.

SHANE LESLIE, *Poems and Ballads*, 1933

Darkest
Ulster

We have had enough of the rigid clichés of stubborn politicians, the profit-focused intensity of men of business, the dogmatic arrogance of the churches, the intolerance of sectarians, the lack of human sympathy of doctrinaire ideologues, of all those whose ready instinct is for violence in word and act.

JOHN HEWITT, 'No Rootless Colonist'

I was born in Ulster and never have been sufficiently grateful to Providence for the mercy shown to me removing me from Ulster: though I like the people, I cannot breathe the political and religious atmosphere of the North-East Corner of Ireland.

GEORGE RUSSELL (AE)

Hapless nation – hapless land,
Heap of uncementing sand;
Crumbled by a foreign weight;
And by worse, domestic hate.

WILLIAM DRENNAN, *from* 'The Wake of William Orr'

T HE TRAGEDY OF ULSTER is the conservatism which has kept [the] basic quarrel unresolved through nearly fifty years of turbulent history. The Catholic minority have held aloof from the state, both in sentiment and in practice; the Protestant majority have not in their hearts accepted Catholics as equal partners. The raw edges of antagonism have worn down over the years, but the underlying loyalties have not changed. It is idle to argue who is to blame, whether the chicken or the egg came first. The quarrel nowadays has a certain air of ludicrous anachronism. Do the sub-editors on Irish Nationalist papers, I wonder, still struggle to get 'Six Counties Prime Minister' into a narrow headline to avoid the forbidden use of 'Ulster' or 'N.I.'? Do obituaries in Unionist papers still describe the Unionist as 'staunch', but the Nationalist as 'convinced', thus carrying the value judgements of their politics beyond the grave?

JOHN COLE, Introduction to *Ulster at the Crossroads*, 1969

[M Y] HOPE, AS FAR AS IT RELATED to Catholic Emancipation, was soon checked by an artful manoeuvre. This was the holding up a prospect of concession, not 'total and immediate', but 'gradual and progressive'. The reasons assigned for this delusive measure were the profound ignorance of the Catholics, and consequent incapacity, not only of enjoying but *bearing* liberty. These reasons, or rather *shameless pretexts*, though equally *unfounded*, *insulting*, and *blasphemous*, imposed on a few, and gave others an excuse for opposing the public will, and public wish.

To my astonishment, this delusion operated on a small party in the enlightened and liberal town of Belfast; and displayed itself on the 14th of July, after a public review. In a discussion, before the great Volunteer body there assembled, gradual emancipation was introduced, and pleaded for, on the ground of Catholic ignorance and incapacity; and the language, in which the impolicy, danger, and folly of total and immediate enfranchisement was expressed, excited disgust and indignation in the minds of the people. Several gentlemen ably rejected, and warmly reprobated, the assertions made, and sentiments expressed.

WM. STEELE DICKSON,
A Narrative of the Confinement and Exile of Wm. Steele Dickson, 1812

'B UT LORD CHARLEMONT AND THE DUKE OF LEINSTER and a wheen more gallant gentlemen seen what a dangersome thing it wur to leave the countryside unprotected with them characters about, and all the soldiers away in Amerikay fighting under Lord Cornwallis — and poor enough work they made of it by the same token; so they riz up the famous volunteers and they drilled them and they giv' them arms, and then says they to the Parlyament, "Now, me brave boys, we want Catholic Emancipation, and we're wanting no more o' them tithes, and none o' yer embargoes and yer tests and yer disabilities and yer Poyningses laws; and what's more, bedad, we won't have them" – and that's the way to regulate them Parlyaments. Well then come on the Peep-o-Day boys and the Ribbon-men, and the Right boys and the White boys, and the Black-foots and the White-foots, and them they called the Patriots, and the Hearts o' Oak and the Hearts o' Steel, and there's tarrible work on many and many a darksome night. Whisht till I tell ye what the boys done in a lone house on the bog o' — ...

'The outcome of it all was that we got wer Act o' Repeal, and we're making the laws for wer selves, so we are, in Dublin town, the way we've no call to keep them; and Mr Grattan he's at the head o' the Parlyament and as good as the King his sel' any day.'

As the children grew older, the high hopes of Grattan's Parliament were dispelled. Discontent, outrage, and bitter animosity made the country miserable.

ELEANOR ALEXANDER, *Lady Anne's Walk,* 1903

DURING THE PERIOD OF WHICH I NOW WRITE, the country was in a state sufficient, in the mind of every liberal and thinking man, to fling back disgrace and infamy upon the successive administrations which permitted it. This was the period of Protestant, or rather of Orange ascendancy. There were at that time regular corps of yeomen, who were drilled and exercised on the usual stated occasions. There were also corps of cavalry who were subjected to the same discipline. Now all this was right and proper, and I remember when a review day was looked forward to as we used to look for Christmas or Easter. On those occasions there were thousands of spectators, and it would have been well if matters had ended there. Every yeoman with his red coat on was an Orangeman. Every cavalryman mounted upon his own horse and dressed in blue was an Orangeman; and to do both foot and cavalry justice, I do not think that a finer body of men could be found in Europe. Roman Catholics were not admitted into either service. I think I may say that I knew almost every yeoman in the parish, but I never knew of a Roman Catholic to be admitted into either force, with one exception – his name was William Kelly, a cousin of my own.

Merciful God! In what a frightful condition was the country at that time. I speak now of the north of Ireland. It was then, indeed, the seat of Orange ascendancy and irresponsible power. To find a justice of the peace *not* an Orangeman would have been an impossibility. The grand jury room was little less than an Orange lodge. There was then no law *against* an Orangeman, and no law *for* a Papist. I am now writing not only that which is well known to be historical truth, but that which I have witnessed with my own eyes.

WILLIAM CARLETON (1867), Autobiography, 1896

W E, THE RUSHLIGHT, having a sane mind in a sound body, – being strong in purpose, but weak in pocket; – having within us no principle of death, but perishing for want of the outward things of this world – do hereby make, constitute and appoint this our last will and testament, in manner and form following: ...

Item: Inasmuch as so many public men are struggling which shall enable himself to *sell* this kingdom of Ireland, with the live stock thereupon – we do hereby, to save them any further anxiety, freely bequeath and give away the said land (our mother, our nurse, our cradle, and our grave) to the established clergy, the absentee landlords (with their middlemen) and the close borough and pot-walloping corporations, to be among them divided, upon the equitable and ancient principle of *rug and rive*, established by the practice of venerable antiquity; they paying interest to the inhabitants at the rate of about 5 per cent per annum, to be by them the said inhabitants levied in house-burning, assassination, party feuds, and other the like commodities; until the said inhabitants come to years of discretion, when of course they will take their own affairs into their own hands.

Item: We leave the state of the country to embellish whig orations; to point the speeches of Catholic lawyers; to advance the fortunes of pretended patriots; to be belied by bookmaking tourists; and to be concealed in the bosoms of the wretched peasantry, until the progress of education shall enable the said peasantry to vindicate themselves – to make legal robbery as fatal as that which is illegal, – to repel the slander of libellers – and to paralyse the sinews of political oppression.

We leave and bequeath the spirit of religious animosity to be divided among the clergy of every denomination, share and share alike, to be by them applied to the purpose of strengthening popular prejudice, and weakening Christian charity; provided that every clergyman be deprived of his share of the above bequest, three fourths of whose sermons do not consist of a repetition of the doctrines of his *own* 'creed and confession', or an abuse of some other.

Item: We leave our countrymen to be gulled by religious pretenders, and starved by legal exactions; to be the victims of commercial and manufacturing monopolists, who are to prosecute them for counter-combination; to be lawfully oppressed, and peeled by acts of parliament; to be charitably fed out of soup-shops by rack rent landlords ...

Our approaching dissolution prevents us from being more particular in the distribution of our bequests; but relying on the known assiduity of the following, in promoting the interests of their minor relations and connections, – we leave 'the powers that be', to usurp the dominion of right, and the prejudices that exist, to darken the influence of religion, until the general dissemination of knowledge, and the consequent progress of truth and Virtue, shall have enabled men to see more clearly the dignity of their relative situation in the scale of existence, and to act in consistency with it, by bursting through every link of the trammels attempted, to be imposed on the free march of mind, by the ignorance or the errors of any portion of their fellow mortals.

LUKE MULLAN HOPE, *from* 'The Last Will & Testament' of *The Rushlight*, 1825

IN THE YOUNG IRELAND MOVEMENT of the forties, a few Protestant intellectuals, notably Thomas Davis and John Mitchel (an Ulster Unitarian), continued the 1798 tradition. Their writings, especially the stirring martial verses of Davis, kindled national pride, among Catholics, in that and later generations. They evoked little or no response in Ulster. There, the radical Presbyterian tradition of the late eighteenth century gave way everywhere to a kind of seventeenth-century revival, militantly anti–Catholic in character. The great controversies of the period, within the Presbyterian Church, were theological in form, but political and social as well as theological in content. Henry Montgomery, taking his stand upon the Bible alone, lost to Henry Cooke, insisting on a test – the Westminster Confession – which identified the Pope with Antichrist. Cooke, encouraged by the nobility and gentry, led Presbyterians in their thousands into the Orange Order. The radical Presbyterian tradition did not entirely disappear with the defeat of Montgomery: it continued as the intellectual heritage of a few families. Most Presbyterians however became, and remain, more conservative and anti-Catholic – more *verkrampte*, in South African terms – than members of other Protestant denominations.

CONOR CRUISE O'BRIEN, *States of Ireland*, 1972

THE FAMINE AFFECTED ALL PARTS of Ireland, but it was much more severe in the west, including western Ulster. In Ulster too the population dropped, and continued declining, but the decline was less steep than elsewhere in the country. A good deal of the migration consequent on the famine was not overseas but into the remarkably rapidly growing industrial town of Belfast – from Donegal, Leitrim, Cavan, Tyrone, Derry, Fermanagh, Monaghan, Antrim and Down. A great deal of this immigration into Belfast was Catholic; the people were in a low and wretched state; they crowded into segregated areas, about half of the Catholics in the post-famine period being in one district of the city. The situation and apprehensions of Ulster Protestants were such that Catholic strength and Catholic weakness were by now equally seen as a threat by the Protestant lower orders. To the Protestant majority of wage-slaves in Belfast the half-starved Catholics crowding in were enemies who would work for starvation wages. The first serious sectarian riots began in the decade after the famine, and the Orange order drew many recruits at this time from workers who listened to the sermons of preachers like Cooke and Hanna but whose devotion to the 'glorious, pious and immortal memory' of William III was inspired by their hope of obtaining protection against the economic competition of hungry Catholics. The city was no longer the handsome Georgian town of the late eighteenth century. Physically as well as in its intellectual character it was a different place: now dirty, overcrowded, and beginning to assume the industrial-revolution ugliness which distinguished it until recent years. The streets of little cottages, new in the 1850s, on the borders of the Protestant and Catholic areas were to be the battle-ground for riots which flared up at intervals throughout the second half of the nineteenth century. In 1857 many were killed and injured in riots which continued for a week, with much use of firearms, after the annual Orange celebrations in July. In 1864 again there were serious sectarian riots which continued for days, until 1,000 policemen and 1,300 troops with artillery had been employed to quell them. Again there were deaths and many injuries from gunshot wounds. There were numbers of dead and injured again in the week's rioting known as the 'battle of the brickfields' in 1872, and there were further serious riots in 1876 and 1878. By this date Orangeism was beginning to revive from the decline it had suffered from the measures taken against it by Drummond in the 1830s. These measures had to a large extent forced it back to its original condition of being a working-class movement of somewhat limited significance, but now it was becoming once again a political force as a result of the patronage of members of the upper and middle-classes, among whom the manufacturers and merchants of the now industrialised north-east were an important group.

LIAM DE PAOR, *Divided Ulster*, 1970

To the outsider Belfast is still a great citadel of orthodoxy, where the church-going habit is probably stronger than in Glasgow or Aberdeen. But those who know it intimately are well aware that the jeremiads of its pastors over the decay of enthusiasm are not mere scaremongering. Relatively to other centres it may hold its own; as compared with its record of a generation ago there has been a sad falling away from grace. Even as late as the nineties it was the pleasant habit of the youths in Unionist quarters to bombard Sunday trains with volleys of stones on the assumption they were bound to hit a Nationalist since no good Protestant would break the Sabbath in this fashion. Nowadays it is Protestants who do most of the travelling, and parsons themselves patronise Sunday trams, against which in my young days they hurled anathemas that would not have been too strong had the target been the Car of Juggernaut itself.

To be a Sabbath breaker was not so long ago only one degree worse than to be a theatre-goer. Cooke, though he swayed his congregations by his mastery of the actor's art, held the stage in abhorrence; and a contemporary has given a vivid impression of one of his famous addresses on 'the sin of theatricals'. 'The doctor,' we are told, 'entered, dressed in his Geneva gown and bands, and ascended to the pulpit with all the dignity of a monarch mounting the steps of a throne, and all the stern gravity of a judge about to pronounce sentence of death; and the people, for lack of room, crept quietly up the stairs after the preacher till they gained the summit, and outside the pulpit door stood on a level with himself.' According to the narrator, 'the burning flood of fiery declamation was as irresistible as a cataract from the hills', and 'theatricals in Belfast received a shock that evening from which they have not yet recovered'. The boycott of the theatre still remains in force, but official Ulster Presbyterianism, if it jibs at Shaw and Synge, has taken the kinema to its heart, and on Saturday nights turns its Church House into a picture palace, where cowboy dramas and sentimental 'scenas' are cheered by larger audiences than attend the sederunts of the General Assembly.

JAMES WINDER GOOD, *Ulster and Ireland*, 1919

WITHIN MY OWN MEMORY, there was nothing in existence for the Catholics for the worship of God except the mere altar, covered with a little open roof to protect the priest from rain, which it was incapable of doing. The altar was about two feet in depth, and the open shed which covered it not more than three, so that when the wind or rain or snow blew from a particular direction the officiating clergyman had nothing to cover him or to protect him from the elements. In my early life, three such 'altars' were the only substitutes for chapels in my native parish, which is one of the largest in the diocese. There was always a little plot of green sward allowed to be annexed to the altar, on which the congregation could kneel; and as these plots and little altars were always on the roadside, they presented something very strange and enigmatical to such as did not understand their meaning, for the following reason. During the winter months and wet weather in general, those of both sexes who attended worship were obliged to bring with them small trusses of either hay or straw on which to kneel, as neither man nor woman could kneel on a wet sward, through which the moist yellow clay was oozing, without soiling or disfiguring their dress, or catching cold from the damp. Indeed, I must say that during the winter months the worship of God was in one sense a very trying ceremony. These small trusses were always left on the place of worship, lying within a foot of each other, and as I said, presented an unintelligible sight to any person ignorant of the custom.

WILLIAM CARLETON (1867), *Autobiography*, 1896

DURING THE PREVIOUS WEEK there had been serious disturbances in Belfast requiring the intervention of the police. Every day, as the long debate on the so-called Government of Ireland Bill proceeded, the excitement of the populace increased. The first riots in 1864 had begun between the shipwrights and the navvies in the employment of Messrs Harland and Wolff on the Queen's Island. At this time again [i.e. 1886], two navvies, a Protestant and a Catholic, engaged in digging a dock, had a quarrel. The Catholic was reported to have said, 'When we get Home Rule you will not have bread to eat.' It was stated, truly or falsely, that the Protestant had been beaten. The next day a large body of shipwrights, iron and not wooden shipwrights, as for the most part they had now become, marched down on the Catholic navvies, put them to flight, and even drove some of them into the water. One young man was drowned. A serious collision began, and more or less continued until the Home Rule Bill had been defeated. The following day, in the large and populous district north of the town called the Shankill Road, there were great rejoicings over the rejection of the measure. Bonfires were lighted and a torchlight procession was organised. It was thought by some impartial observers that had the police allowed the bonfires to burn out in what was exclusively a Protestant quarter, the excitement might have quieted down. But they set to work to vigorously stamp them out, and therefore became the object of a series of the most determined attacks on the part of the enraged mobs.

These riots continued with little interruption for several weeks, and were more than once renewed. They had this remarkable feature at first, as distinguished from their predecessors: they were not so much attacks of a Protestant populace on the Catholic, or of a Catholic on the Protestant, as collisions of the Protestants with the police, who had become to them most obnoxious. The Catholics, evidently under the advice of their leaders, withdrew from the turbulent scenes and kept themselves quiet. But between the police and the lower-classes of the Protestants on the Shankill Road, in York Street, and on Bower's Hill, all more or less Protestant, there was very serious warfare. The police to protect themselves used their rifles with deadly effect, and, as is usual in such circumstances, innocent people were shot down. Certain Catholic taverns in Protestant districts were gutted, and the liquor was distributed among the rioters or poured into the streets.

THOMAS MacKNIGHT, *Ulster As It Is*, 1896

from AUTUMN JOURNAL

And the North, where I was a boy,
　Is still the North, veneered with the grime of Glasgow,
Thousands of men whom nobody will employ
　Standing at the corners, coughing.
And the street-children play on the wet
　Pavement — hopscotch or marbles;
And each rich family boasts a sagging tennis-net
　On a spongy lawn beside a dripping shrubbery.
The smoking chimneys hint
　At prosperity round the corner
But they make their Ulster linen from foreign lint
　And the money that comes in goes out to make more money.
A city built upon mud;
　A culture built upon profit;

Free speech nipped in the bud,
　The minority always guilty.
Why should I want to go back
　To you, Ireland, my Ireland?
The blots on the page are so black
　That they cannot be covered with shamrock.
I hate your grandiose airs,
　Your sob-stuff, your laugh and your swagger,
Your assumption that everyone cares
　Who is the king of your castle.
Castles are out of date,
　The tide flows round the children's sandy fancy;
Put up what flag you like, it is too late
　To save your soul with bunting.

LOUIS MacNEICE, *Poems 1925–1948*, 1949

NONO REMEMBERED ONE DAY on Royal Avenue as she came from a shop when she had seen a young boy in dungarees race past, his breath coming in painful gusts, his face a ghastly mask of terror; straight ahead he ran, looking neither right nor left; his eyes wide in an unblinking stare as if he neither saw nor knew where he was going and his muscles were merely obeying the only message they received from his brain – 'Run–run–run.' Not far behind him ran about fifty men, dressed like him in dungarees. They did not call or shout. Just ran after the boy.

Beside Nono stood an elderly man, who looked after them with a calm, curiously disinterested gaze.

'What is it?' Nono asked him.

'Islandmen chasin' a Papish.'

'Oh!' cried Nono, aghast. 'What will they do when they catch him?'

'Whut'll the' do?' He turned and looked at Nono with that look of bewildered exasperation which she had found so often on the faces of these Belfast folk when she asked a question.

'Whut'll the' do?' he repeated. And Nono felt she was indeed a fool to have asked.

NORA CONNOLLY O'BRIEN, *Portrait of a Rebel Father*, 1935

HERE IN IRELAND THE PROPOSAL of the Government to consent to the partition of Ireland – the exclusion of certain counties in Ulster – is causing a new line of cleavage. No one of the supporters of Home Rule accepts this proposal with anything like equanimity, but rather we are already hearing in north-east Ulster rumours of a determination to resist it by all means. It is felt that the proposal to leave the Home Rule minority at the mercy of an ignorant majority with the evil record of the Orange party is a proposal that should never have been made, and that the establishment of such a scheme should be resisted with armed force if necessary.

Personally I entirely agree with those who think so; Belfast is bad enough as it is; what it would be under such rule the wildest imagination cannot conceive. Filled with the belief that they were after defeating the Imperial Government and the Nationalists combined, the Orangemen would have scant regards for the rights of the minority left at their mercy.

Such a scheme would destroy the Labour movement by disrupting it. It would perpetuate in a form aggravated in evil the discords now prevalent, and help the Home Rule and Orange capitalists and clerics to keep their rallying cries before the public as the political watchwords of the day. In short, it would make division more intense and confusion of ideas and parties more confounded.

JAMES CONNOLLY (1914), *Socialism and Nationalism:*
A Selection from the Writing of James Connolly, 1948

HOW COMES IT THAT A CITY so splendidly set beneath a mountain carved by the ages in the likeness of a Sleeper's Head – a city so rich in genius and character, in romance, in goodness; a city which to know rightly is to love beyond all other cities – is one in which the ugliest passions of the human heart break forth, again and again, in words of incitement, in flaming homes, in fratricide? How comes it that Belfast, once the spear-head of Irish freedom, latterly was a spear pointed at the heart of Ireland's hopes?

AODH DE BLÁCAM, The Black North, 1938

I HAVE ALWAYS HAD WHAT may well be a proper dislike and disapproval of the North of Ireland, but largely, as I find on analysis, for improper – i.e. subjective – reasons. A harassed and dubious childhood under the hand of a well-meaning but barbarous mother's help from County Armagh led me to think of the north of Ireland as prison and the South as a land of escape. Many nightmares, boxes on the ears, a rasping voice of disapproval, a monotonous daily walk to a crossroads called Mile Bush, sodden haycocks, fear of hell-fire, my father's indigestion – these things, with on the other side my father's Home Rule sympathies and the music of his brogue, bred in me an almost fanatical hatred for Ulster. When I went to bed as a child I was told: 'You don't know where you'll wake up.' When I ran in the garden I was told that running was bad for the heart. Everything had its sinister aspect – milk shrinks the stomach, lemon thins the blood. Against my will I was always given sugar in my tea. The North was tyranny.

LOUIS MacNEICE, Zoo, 1938

THE LITTLE TOWN [I.E. PORTADOWN] gave me my first experience of what might be called Greater Belfast. It is a town of great prosperity, or that form of prosperity which is represented by large mills working at full time and giving constant employment to thousands of 'hands', male and female, all of them housed in comfortable dwellings of the ugliest possible form. The broad River Bann flows through the town and is spanned by a bridge, the appearance of which suggests a prosperity that is founded on proper principles. The large church that 'stands in its own grounds' in the middle of the principal street, the substantial houses on each side easing off, so to speak, to make room for the church property, suggests domination on proper principles to all comers.

'Well, what you say may be true,' said an Orangeman of an undemonstrative type to a stranger whom he met aboard the Liverpool steamer, and who had been assuring him that the Pope was really a great statesman as well as a worthy man personally. 'What you say may be true; but he has a very bad name in Portadown.'

F. FRANKFORT MOORE, *The Truth About Ulster*, 1914

THE STREETS HAVE BEEN REASONABLY quiet now for the best part of ten years; the 1935 outbreak being the culmination of a period of rioting that began when the bad times that followed the economic slump in 1929 seemed to be making towards a union of Protestant and Catholic in one common fight for the right to a livelihood. The Troubles in Belfast have never been without their economic implications and it is especially interesting to consider what was happening there in 1930 and 1931, then to consider in that light some of the reasons given for the outbreak of rioting. For the streets of Belfast that had seen so many processions saw, under the shadow of the great misery that came on the world's industrial cities in the early 1930s, Catholic and Protestant workers march together, carrying not the banners of the Boyne but less colourful banners inscribed with the words: 'We Want Bread' ...

That was in 1932. Within three years the union of the poor, the hungry, the unemployed, was broken; the Orange processions were again drumming along the streets; guns and bombs had taken the place of the old nineteenth-century rivets and cobblestones. Through those same streets a gun-carriage went with the coffin that held the remains of Lord Carson of Duncairn, watched with no great interest by men and women whose relatives had died like cattle at the Somme in 1916. But the men who had succeeded Carson could watch the pomp of his passing with a certain amount of shamefaced triumph, for they had made their protest against the alliance of the Catholic and Protestant poor that had three years before threatened their own political stability.

The protest was made in the usual manner, developed in the traditional way from the traditional beginnings, was inspired by the same inciting speeches that identified rebels with Papists, and Protestants with loyalists, that did not trouble to define the term loyalist or to say what exactly the rebels were supposed to be rebelling against.

BENEDICT KIELY, *Counties of Contention*, 1945

AN ULSTERMAN IN ENGLAND REMEMBERS

Here at a distance, rocked by hopes and fears
with each convulsion of that fevered state,
the chafing thoughts attract, in sudden spate,
neglected shadows from my boyhood years:

the Crossley tenders caged and roofed with wire,
the crouching Black and Tans, the Lewis gun,
the dead lad in the entry; one by one
the Catholic public houses set on fire;
the anxious curfew of the summer night,
the thoroughfares deserted, at a door
three figures standing, till the tender's roar,
approaching closer, drives them out of sight;
and on the broad roof of the County Gaol
the singing prisoners brief freedom take
to keep an angry neighbourhood awake
with rattled plate and pot and metal pail;
below my bedroom window, bullet-spark
along the kerb, the beat of rapid feet
of the lone sniper, clipping up the street,
soon lost, the gas lamps shattered, in the dark;
and on the paved edge of our cinder-field,
intent till dusk upon the game, I ran
against a briskly striding, tall young man,
and glimpsed the rifle he thought well concealed.
At Auschwitz, Dallas, I felt no surprise
when violence, across the world's wide screen,
declared the age imperilled: I had seen
the future in that frightened gunman's eyes.

JOHN HEWITT, An Ulster Recknoning, 1971

SEPTEMBER 1920 WAS JUST ABOUT THE START of the Troubles, and in those [years] I was to see sights that I have never been able to forget. Even today I cannot drive along the Newtownards Road without seeing in my mind the high wooden barricade that stood at the end of Seaforde Street to cut off a field of fire. Beside it a police cage-car, a square armoured-Crossley covered with a triangle of thick wire netting. Inside the men of the RIC hunched by their rifles. Farther along, charred and looted shops; the Roman Catholic chapel at Bryson Street with bullet holes in its windows. It was there that I ran into my first riot. The tram was city-bound in the usual rush of traffic; I was, I suppose, no more awake than any schoolboy is at 8.30 in the morning; and a bullet gives no warning. Looking down from the top deck, I saw a carter suddenly double up and fall limply to the ground. Then the sharp crack of the firing, the splintering of glass, and the shout from the conductor: 'Lie down, lie down.' And lay we did in the dust and cigarette butts on the rough, ribbed floor, squinting through the slit at the bottom and waiting, ears cocked for the shooting to stop. Thinking back, I cannot say that I was afraid; but that incident brought to a tight, nervous pitch the tension that people lived in in those days. School to me is a happy memory, but it is against a background of disorder, nights when the Belfast sky was red with scattered fires, Lewis guns rattled in the distance, and even in the quiet suburbs the loud 'Who goes there?' of the police patrol challenged anyone incautious enough to break the curfew. And my father being a journalist, the telephone would waken us night after night, and we would creep down stairs from bed to ask, a bit fearfully: 'What's happened?'

JACK SAYERS, radio broadcast, Northen Ireland Home Service, December 1960

DERRY

As a child in Derry I heard the shots
And the crackle of burning timber
That signalled the ancient quarrel
Of Prod and Papist, that ritual feud
Lingering on in a lost province
Where memories of long-ago battles
Are as fresh as today's headlines.
Memories of Siege and horror, of Lundy,
The Apprentice Boys and the Boom and Walker
And God-knows what fag-ends of history
Make a stirring tale for children
But light the fuse in the bitter heart.
Tales of blood and sectarian thunder
Lead to a coarse and brutal logic
Where my side is whiter than white
And yours black as a crow's wing.
Once more the thick urgent cries,
The pool of blood in the doorway,
The searing blaze of hate.

Yet I who have gone away
To safe and easy exile
Cannot just write them off
As simply ignorant thugs.

I, too, am involved in their crimes.

ROBERT GREACEN, *Young Mr Gibbon*, 1979

'CAN WE NOT DO SOMETHING against this demand for partition?' asked Nono of a group of Young Republicans who were gathered in the Freedom Club discussing the political situation. 'It's awful to feel so helpless and so useless. The Ulster Volunteers have a fearful weapon in that demand. No true Nationalist can submit to it, and Johnny Redmond's so in love with his Home Rule Bill I'm afraid he'll agree to it rather than lose Home Rule. Think, apart from everything else, what it will mean! The Catholics and Nationalists in the North-East corner will be absolutely at the mercy of the Orangemen.'

'Think what it'll mean,' repeated one of the boys. 'We don't have to think. We know. You have no idea what it'll mean. You haven't lived here long enough. I'll tell you some of the things it has meant without partition.'

And Nono heard tales they had heard from their mothers, their fathers, uncles and brothers; of unmerciful beatings; of battles with cobblestones; of men driven from work in fear of their lives merely because they were Papish; and on the Island, at the shipyards, where there were never more than three thousand Catholics and always more than twenty thousand Orangemen, and where Catholics, even though they were working, worked in danger of their lives; tales of weights falling, and pails of paint and red hot rivets dropped on Papishes ...

'Aw, what's the use of talkin'? You've got to live through it to understand.'

NORA CONNOLLY O'BRIEN, Portrait of a Rebel Father, 1935

THE UNIONIST GOVERNMENT had survived the boundary crisis with their territory intact, and even with the goodwill of the Free State administration. But their very success brought problems, for they now had to contend with a minority of one-third of the population who had been beaten and terrorised into submission and were deeply suspicious and resentful.

It was a crucial moment. Whatever policy the Belfast government adopted now would determine the minority's attitude to the state and the future history of the state itself. The obvious policy would have been to exert every effort to rule fairly and impartially in order to win the confidence of the minority and reconcile them to the new six-county state. But the Unionist leaders were not free agents: they had mobilised the Protestant masses to resist Home Rule and inclusion in the Free State, through the policy of discrimination and the ideology of Protestant supremacy. Now their followers were seeking their reward. If a lasting loyalty to the new state was to develop among the Protestant masses, they had to be given a privileged position within it. Moreover a government of industrialists and businessmen was no doubt not unmindful of the fact that a policy of discrimination and Protestant privilege would effectively prevent the emergence of any working-class solidarity.

So the Unionists set about constructing an Orange and Protestant state with almost all political power and patronage in their own hands – right down to the humblest rural council – and operated an elaborate and comprehensive system of discrimination in housing and jobs which kept the minority in a position of permanent and hopeless inferiority.

MICHAEL FARRELL, *The Orange State*, 1976

NORTHERN IRELAND 'SPECIALS' began raids and skirmishes on the Free State side of the border, and on 11th February [1922] the first shots in the Irish Civil War were fired at Clones in County Monaghan. Pogroms occured in Belfast, where, for example, a bomb was thrown among Catholic children playing in the street, killing three of them.

> Now don't play ball in Belfast Town
> For a big bomb will blow you to Kingdom Come.
> Think of the chislers, one, two, three,
> Down comes a big bomb, that's the end of me!

PATRICK GALVIN, *Irish Songs of Resistance*, 1956

KINDERTOTENLIEDER

There can be no songs for dead children
Near the crazy circle of explosions,
The splintering tangent of the ricochet,

No songs for the children who have become
My unrestricted tenants, fingerprints
Everywhere, teeth marks on this and that.

MICHAEL LONGLEY, *An Exploded View*, 1973

THE CHILDREN'S FACES WERE ... RED and tear-stained as they made their way with their equally terrified teachers towards where their parents were anxiously waiting at the Ardoyne shops.

'Niamh was in tears and shaking,' remembers Liz. 'She was always a jolly wee kind of person but that day she sobbed her heart out. She held my hand so tight. She didn't have a clue what was happening and just kept asking what she had done wrong.'

Another parent, Tanya Carmichael, mother of Emer and Emma (four and eight respectively) was amongst the group escorting children out through the back door and through the grounds of St Gabriel's. She says she pretended there was a fire drill to explain their hasty exit.

'As what had really happened filtered through, the older ones panicked. They knew they were being attacked and they were frightened. It was awful. There were kids running about screaming and crying. There were children literally wetting themselves.' ...

Tanya says, 'The Loyalists were behaving just like a pack of wild animals, I couldn't believe it. They were saying, "You Fenian scum, you'll never walk our road again" and "We'll burn your school down" and what they were going to do to ourselves and our children. The venom and anger and hatred in their faces was unbelievable. Our people were angry also because we didn't know where our kids were. We were telling the cops that we had to get our kids out, but they just pushed us back. The Loyalists were not locals, they had come from everywhere. I had never seen that many people in Glenbryn in my life. The police were very aggressive towards us and were constantly pushing us back. The Loyalists were shouting the whole time, "This is our road and you will not be back", and "Provo bastards", "No more Provie Fenian bastards are using our road".'

ANNE CADWALLADER, Holy Cross: The Untold Story, 2004

PETER:

    I have been the victim of a whispering campaign, Davy, that has gone the length and breadth of the shipyard, and I accuse that man sitting there of being the instigator of it.

ARCHIE:

    You're a Fenian liar.

DAVY:

    No interruptions, Brother Kerr. You'll get your opportunity to speak later.

ARCHIE:

    By Christ, I intend to.

RABBIE:

    Order, Brother Kerr, order.

PETER:

    That man has scandalised me around the shipyard as a Republican and a member of an illegal organisation. He has stirred up resentment against me because I'm a Catholic and a member of the district committee.

DAVY:

Now be careful, Peter. You aren't the only Catholic holding office in this union. Are the others complaining?

PETER:

This matter, Mr Chairman, only concerns me. I'm speaking for myself.

DAVY:

Very well then, proceed.

PETER:

That man has accused me of undermining the Union with Republicanism.

ARCHIE:

Aye, it's the truth Davy, and the truth hits hard.

DAVY:

Now just a minute, brothers. We're going to get nowhere if both of you begin shouting at each other.

ARCHIE:

I've said nothing about him that I wouldn't say to his face. Because you don't let him ram Republicanism down your throat, he thinks he's a martyr.

PETER:

That's a damned lie. I was one of the members who helped build this union up to what it is.

ARCHIE:

I done my share in building up the Union too.

RABBIE:

Now it seems both of you are intent on breaking it down again.

ARCHIE:

You're out of order with that remark, Brother White.

PETER:

You've no room to talk about anybody being out of order. Sure you're always bringing the Orange Order into branch business.

ARCHIE:

I resent that remark Davy, especially from a Taig.

PETER:

It's true and you know it. Sure Davy had to pull you up several times for addressing him in the branch room as the Worshipful Master.

ARCHIE [*pointing at* PETER]:

This man's a troublemaker. He's out to wreck the Union.

RABBIE:

The both of you ought to be bloody well ashamed of yourselves. Man, when I think back twenty years ago to the time we had a dispute on a boat about working conditions. Only four men had the courage of their convictions to walk off that boat in protest, and who were those four men? The both of you sitting there and Davy and myself … Now the pair of you are at each other's throats about religion and we're acting as peacemakers. Is that all you have learnt in twenty years?

PETER [*drawing himself up*]:

I'll let no man drag my religion into the gutter.

ARCHIE [*likewise*]:

Nor will I.

DAVY:

Order, brothers, order!

PETER [*shaking his fist*]:

I'll fight religious discrimination in this union.

ARCHIE:

And I'll fight republican domination of it.

[*They both jump to their feet, glaring fiercely at each other.* RABBIE *jumps up between them.*]

RABBIE:

If either of you make a move like that again, so help me I'll crown both of you with this box. Sit down and behave yourselves.

PETER:

Nobody'll call me out of my name. No wonder they call that ould waster Archie Boyne Water, for he's living in 1690.

ARCHIE:

Maybe I'm not as ancient as some of your sort. If they had their way, they'd take the buses off the Falls Road and put on Irish jaunting cars.

DAVY:

Order! Order! This is getting us nowhere.

SAM THOMPSON, Over the Bridge, 1960

DAISYMOUNT TERRACE

1
From the school in the Church Quarter
Lately laden with books and tasks
My brother whooped downhill,
Fighting allcomers, back
To paraffin lamps and griddle bread.
The Moat and the Church overhead,
And the Reverend Cottar poised
Pruning his sermon, but
The stream behind the houses stole
Pebbling his sleep:

For Daisymount Terrace
Was beyond the tramlines
And the festering city's war,
And himself with his popgun lost
Between the opposing armies –
But the stream had no name
Peopling his sleep serene
Among humpedup fields

And the cottages.
Gape Row limewashed, the gardens
Hunching up to the Moat:
And old bent kitchen spoons
Digging for giants' bones;
Dundonald a breath between
Beechfield Street eviction –
GET OUT OR BE BURNED OUT –
And later the house with the garden
Welcomed and planted and groomed
By certain familiar hands
Of our father creating our world.

2
Gardening I look at my hands
Veined like his the stream
Still stumbling unnamed,
And myself also aghast
Bewtween the opposing armies –
Slow to pluck weeds –
For Daisymount Terrace now
Lacks fields for a daisychain
For a mayor in a frightened town.

The stream stumbles unnamed
And a tithe
Of the Church Quarter
Enfolds the school, while I
Stumble downhill lacking
A shout from my brother
His keeper and sleeper
His brother grown in his place
With a father's hands and stance
In forgotten remembered ground.

3

With nettles in my hands
In an innocent afternoon
My brother running back
With whose guilt in my hands,
The stream a gutter now
Silenced by traffic ground
To a redhanded stop
A rumour of bombs –
I listen hand at ear
For a mercy of water and
My brother's confident shout
In an innocent afternoon.

ROY McFADDEN, *Verifications*, 1977

As 1964 DREW TO A CLOSE details of Professor Tom Wilson's economic plan began to emerge and the *Belfast News Letter* wrote a glowing leader on the subject entitled 'Face Lift to Meet the New World'. The final sentence read, 'For him [myself] and for Ulster, history may yet record 1964 as a turning point, as a year of greatness.' The future of Ulster was wrecked, not by Treasury meanness, not by lack of forward looking, thinking and planning, but by outdated bigotry. We had all the benefits of belonging to a large economy, which were denied to the Republic of Ireland, but we threw it all away in trying to maintain an impossible position of Protestant ascendancy at any price.

TERENCE O'NEILL, *Autobiography*, 1972

THE SIGHTSEERS

My father and mother, my brother and sister
and I, with uncle Pat, our dour best-loved uncle,
had set out that Sunday afternoon in July
in his broken-down Ford

not to visit some graveyard – one died of shingles,
one of fever, another's knees turned to jelly –
but the brand-new roundabout at Ballygawley,
the first in mid-Ulster.

Uncle Pat was telling us how the B-Specials
had stopped him one night somewhere near Ballygawley
and smashed his bicycle

and made him sing the Sash and curse the Pope of Rome.
They held a pistol so hard against his forehead
there was still the mark of an O when he got home.

PAUL MULDOON, Quoof, 1983

NORTHERN IRELAND INDUCES contradictory moods. For a while I'm
elated and hopeful because of the sheer likeableness and good sense
of the people I meet; then it seems possible that they will be able to sort
out their problems sooner rather than later. Yet within an hour I can be
cast into deep gloom by conversations that reveal the hard unchanging
core of those problems. I have now been four days with this family and
it is impossible to think of them as stereotyped bigots. The evening I
arrived we sat by an unnecessary fire (lit to underline how welcome I
was) and Betty assured me, 'There's no ill-feeling around here and never
has been. We'd all go to the end of the earth for each other. I respect
anyone who lives up to their beliefs and our Catholic friends feel the
same.' Did the lady protest too much? I don't think so. I have seen for
myself how good relations are in all sorts of little ways – ways which seem
to reflect a genuine wish on both sides to live in civilised harmony.

Yet the very fact that I automatically used that word 'sides' is ominous.
Nowadays Sam and his friends can be told at their Loyal Orange Lodge
meeting not to sell to papists for security reasons. But even if there were
no such convenient 'instant rationalisation' available, they would still have
been reminded not to sell to papists, period. He and Betty and their friends
aspire to tolerance, yet no ordinary individual can escape from the wheel
of intolerance to which their community has been bound for centuries.
And if someone did escape – what then? If Sam insisted on selling land to
a papist, what would happen to him? The Orange Lodges do not
encourage violence – we are told. They don't really have to; thousands of
Orangemen are well-armed and worship the sort of Old Testament God
who is always gratified by the elimination of his enemies. And of course
the Troubles have made it much easier to disguise bigotry as patriotism.

DERVLA MURPHY, A Place Apart, 1978

THEY WALKED BY THE WATER'S EDGE while they waited for Uncle
Peter to come and collect them. They were right down by the shore
of Lough Neagh, and from this part you could see the huge expanse of

water more clearly than from where they lived; you could see the shores in the distance. They looked out across at the Sperrins and Slieve Gallion, and they thought of their father, off at the march in Derry. Helen still wished that she had been allowed to go with him.

But when they got back to the house, they heard that the march hadn't gone off peacefully. There had been riots, and when their father and Brian didn't come home at the time they were expected, the children could see how worried their mother was, although she tried to hide it. The police had blocked the march and baton-charged the marchers. On television, they watched black-and-white pictures of crowds running, of people with blood on their faces and shirts; of men being pulled along the ground by the hair, or being beaten where they lay. They saw a man, one of the organisers, pleading for calm and reason, and before he could finish what he was saying, he was struck in the stomach with a baton. After that, Emily wasn't able to pretend any longer that she wasn't anxious. When at last they heard a car pull up outside, they all rushed out to meet him.

'There was no sense in what happened today,' he said, angry and shaken. 'They just hammered the living daylights out of people.' He said they were late home because Brian had been badly cut on the face, and they'd decided to take him to the hospital in case the wound needed stitches. They'd had to wait for a long time there because so many people had been brought in wounded, and then it had taken them a long time to get back to where the car was parked. He was glad that it had been on the television. 'I suppose it would have suited them better for all this to have been kept quiet.'

There were more civil rights marches organised in Belfast later that year, some organised by the students at the university, and although Charlie and Brian didn't go to them, all the talk at home now was about civil rights, and how things would have to change. The children couldn't understand all of what was being said. One phrase they heard people using over and over was, 'Live, oul' horse, and you'll get grass.'

DEIRDRE MADDEN, *One by One in the Darkness*, 1996

ABOUT EIGHTY PEOPLE, Queen's students and half a dozen supporters from Derry, set off from Belfast City Hall at nine in the morning of January 1st. Dr Paisley's right-hand man, Major Ronald Bunting, came with a Union Jack and a group of supporters to give it a barracking send-off. The march was a horrific seventy-three-mile trek which dredged to the surface all the accumulated political filth of fifty Unionist years. Every few miles groups of Unionist extremists blocked the route. Invariably the police diverted the march rather than open the road, so that much of the time it wound a circuitous way through country lanes from stopping place to stopping place. It was frequently stoned from the fields and attacked by groups of men with clubs. There was no police protection. Senior RUC officers consorted openly with leaders of the opposing groups. On the final day of the march, at Burntollet Bridge a few miles outside Derry, a force of some hundreds, marshalled by members of the B Specials and watched passively by our 'escort' of more than a hundred police, attacked with nailed clubs, stones and bicycle chains. Of the eighty who had set out fewer than thirty arrived in Derry uninjured. But they had gathered hundreds of supporters behind them on the way and were met in Guildhall Square by angry thousands who were in no mood for talk of truce. Emotion swelled as bloodstained marchers mounted a platform and described their experiences. Rioting broke out and continued for some hours.

EAMONN McCANN, *War and an Irish Town*, 1974

I VERY NOW AN' AGAIN we passed by housin' estates an' the people come out to look at us. At some estates they would be shoutin' encouragement an' givin' us cups of tay an' mince pies an' pieces of Christmas cake, but at others they would be hurlin' abuse at us an' callin' us effin popish scum. When we walked along chantin', wan man, wan vote, they jeered back at us, wan man, wan woman, because wan of our members was reputed te have a slightly unorthodox sex life. We just waved an' shouted, Seasons Greetin's an' Happy New Year back te them, but they spit at us as we went by ...

Up in the field above the road it wasn't just the Paisleyites that had gathered te greet us, because ivery wheen of feet, these big high heaps of heavy rock, that had come from a quarry down the road, were sittin' stacked up waitin' for us too. The marchers weren't prepared for anythin' like this size of an attack so a lot of panic broke out when they seen what they were faced way.

Some of them run away back in the direction we had come from, some of them jumped over the ditch on the left han' side that sloped away down te the river, an' some mad mortals like mesel' who really did believe that we could not be moved, stood our groun' on the road for a while an' kept on singin' our song:

> We're on our way to Derry,
> We shall not be moved.

As soon as the rocks started te bounce aff us, we collectively come te the hasty conclusion that maybe Derry wasn't the place we were headin' for at all, so some of us started te rise te the occasion by up-datin' the words we were singin':

We're on our way to heaven.
We shall not be moved.
We're on our way to heaven,
We shall not be moved.
Just like a tree that's
Standin' by the water's side,
We shall not be moved.

Wheniver the Paisleyites heard this song they made it known te us that Derry wasn't the only place where they intended we shouldn't go.

A have always been of the opinion that a body has te die sometime, so when a was hit on the back for the fifth time way a rock that winded me, a fell te the groun' an' lay there way me arms wrapped tight roun' me head, thinkin' that me number was up. A suppose a should of been sayin' me prayers te save me soul from iverlastin' hell, but the only thing a could do at the time was think of me poor ma an' all the trouble she musta went te havin' me, an' hope wile hard that she would be able te get over me tragic death, an' that the memory of it wouldn't blight the whole rest of hir life on hir.

As a was lyin' there thinkin', somebody that called me a fuckin' Fenian bastard started te kick me an' rain blows down on tap of me way some heavy implement that a could feel but didn't risk lookin' up at, despite me curiosity. Then somebody musta come te save me from me attacker, for a heard another voice, just as the blows stapped, sayin', are ye tryin' te murder hir, ye cowardly bastard ye, can't ye see that she's only a wain?

FRANCES MOLLOY, *No Mate for the Magpie*, 1985

AN ULSTER LANDOWNER'S SONG

I'm Major This or Captain That,
MC and DSO.
This Orange Lily in my hat
I sometimes wear for show,

so long as I can walk my dogs
around the old estate,
and keep the Fenians in their bogs,
the peasants at the gate.

I meet my tenants, decent men,
in Lodge, on market day,
and all seems safe till, now and then,
they start a small affray.

They stirred up an unwelcome noise,
it set my nerves on edge,
that day they beat those girls and boys
across Burntollet Bridge,

with journalists and cameras there
to send in their reports.
The world no longer seems to care
for healthy country sports.

JOHN HEWITT, An Ulster Reckoning, 1971

THE SIX-COUNTY STATE WAS NOT an arbitrary creation of British imperialism to enable it to keep a foothold in the most industrialised part of Ireland, however. The state had local roots: in the development of industries geared to serve the imperial market, and in the parallel development of a Unionist movement determined to stay part of the British economy. The Northern state was thus the product of a partnership between British imperialism on the one hand, and on the other the Ulster industrialists, businessmen and landowners united together in the Unionist party.

But the Unionist businessmen won their mass support through the Orange Order and by fostering and exploiting differences between Protestant and Catholic in the North. They consolidated that support by discrimination against Catholics in the industries and local councils which they controlled. Once in power in the new state, they had ample opportunity to step up discrimination and strengthen their position by gerrymandering and wholesale political repression. Britain did not interfere so long as the North remained stable and gave no trouble. And Britain allowed an elaborate sectarian police state to be built up without protest, permitting it to be backed in the last resort by British forces.

MICHAEL FARRELL, The Orange State, 1976

STILL CENTURY

The hard captains of industry
Held the province in a firm control.

Judges, your pious tyranny
Is baked bone-dry in the old

Bricks of a hundred linen mills,
The shadows of black tabernacles.

A crowd moves along the Shankill,
And lamps shine in the dull

Streets where a fierce religion
Prays to the names of power:

Ewart and Bryson, Craig and Carson.
On every wall, texts or a thick char.

Stacked in the corners of factory-yards,
The wicker carboys of green acid

Hold out their bitter promise of whiteness
To the bleachgreens above the city.

The orange smoke at sunset, the gruff
Accents of a thousand foremen, speak

To the chosen, saying they are the stuff
That visions, cutlery and Belleek

China are laid on. They are tied
To the shade of a bearded god,

Their dream of happiness is his smile
And his skilful way with the hardest rod.

TOM PAULIN, *The Strange Museum*, 1980

A WELL-SCRUBBED SORT OF A DAY with the country roads bone-hard. I thought of the town spread out in the drying air, tight and close around the junction of the Dargan river and the main Belfast–Derry road and then loosening and shaking itself out like bright confetti into the green fields. The railway skirts the energetic centre of population and separates also Protestants from Catholics. Out on their side on the Dublin Road (the name lingers from the time when that city was the navel of this whole island) is their chapel, black and manifest and, close to it, St Brigid's, our counterpart. Its architecture, like all Catholic schools, has that certain grey stone solidity, verging on the monastic, that emphasises the bond between their education and their religion. Our schools on the other hand have no fixed character. Annagh Primary is simply a flat, low E-shaped structure of glass, brick and speckled-green felt; it could easily have come out an outsize filling-station and no one would have been any the wiser.

I began to think about Catholics, not about Catholics I know because I don't really know any, but about them in general. Anything I found out about them has been second-hand, because, living in a community like this, one where the proportions are seventy-five for us, twenty-five for *them* (an inflammable mixture) division starts early – separate housing estates, then separate schools, separate jobs, separate dances, separate pubs … a people with a past and no interest in the present, because they have been frog-marched back to that past so often that they have long ago given up any claims to right now. A musical, entertaining people (like the Jews) with no neurosis about cleanliness or material wealth … I envy them their calm, inner knowledge of what they are, who they are and where they come from, but not their degrading, daily struggle to keep dignity in a country dedicated to keeping *them* 'in their place'.

MAURICE LEITCH, *The Liberty Lad*, 1965

WHEN WE BEGAN TO THINK of Fermanagh as an entity, one piece of the thirty-two-part jigsaw that was the map of Ireland; it seemed a peculiarly isolated place, one of those limbo-like, half-lost border counties, like Monaghan and Cavan, roughly equidistant from the centres of power. There were villages like Belleek, Pettigo and Belcoo, that seemed to straddle the border, and houses in the border sector which seemed to belong to neither Northern Ireland nor the Republic. To travel from one end of the county to the other was to hear people's accents take on a Donegal or Cavan or Monaghan twang. Yet, in spite of these shades and gradations, the political boundary was there, denied by the landscape and the dialects on either side of it, but visible as customs posts, road-blocks, the place names in both English and Irish on the signposts in the Republic, and as palpable in our minds and imaginations as if it had been a broad white band painted across roads and farms. It was palpable too in the tension and division that permeated almost every aspect of life in Fermanagh. Among the lakes, drumlins and housing estates of that deceptively placid, postcard county, a defensive Unionist minority, who controlled local government, and a Catholic majority, resentful of discrimination against them in housing and employment, squared up to each other perennially, loathed each other's festivals and sometimes shed blood.

FRANK ORMSBY, *from* 'Co. Fermanagh', *32 Counties*, 1989

ON 24 APRIL [1964], just over a year after I had become Prime Minister, I took my first step in the direction of improving community relations. I visited a Catholic school in Ballymoney, County Antrim. And what was more, it emerged quite naturally as a result of my known wishes and attitudes. I was making one of my 'meet the people' tours and this visit was included in the schedule. Of course it stole the headlines. The chairman of the Board of Governors, Canon Clenaghan, had been padre to the Connaught Rangers in the First World War. He gave me a particularly warm welcome, and this was reflected throughout the school. The only thing which I could see which differentiated it from a state school, attended by Protestant children, was a crucifix in the hall, and thereby hangs a tale. A Belfast paper told one of its photographers to try and get a 'shocking' picture of me during this first ever visit by a Prime Minister of Northern Ireland to a Catholic school. The photographer waited outside the front door and when, an hour later, I emerged, with the aid of his telescopic lens, he made it look as if the crucifix was over my head. I was later shown how Paisley was able to make use of this picture in his own paper. Years later the photographer told me that when he arrived he was horrified to find that there were no nuns or other equally 'shocking' people to greet me and then he suddenly saw the crucifix and realised that his finest hour had arrived. In such ways was co-operation made almost impossible. In such ways reconciliation was bound to fail. It did. As in so much else in Northern Ireland, this story can hardly be comprehensible in England.

TERENCE O'NEILL, *Autobiography*, 1972

IAN PAISLEY WAS BASICALLY A JOKE that became less funny each time you heard it. In fact he was so unfunny now it was starting to hurt, very badly. Whether he was dropped on his head when he was a baby or what, his eyes saw catastrophe at every turn; catastrophe for Ulster that is, or more particularly, catastrophe for the Protestant people of Ulster. The Papist hordes were closing in. Our Prime Minister, Terence O'Neill, who had once visited a Catholic school and spoke meekly of reform, was the arch-traitor. Paisley marched around the country trying to convince the Protestant people of Ulster that they were in need of his salvation (a statue of Nelson was blown up in Dublin on the fiftieth anniversary of the Easter Rising, which helped him no end) and, while most ignored him, not a few of them came along every Sunday to the church he had built for himself to be scared more. Others joined his Ulster Constitution Defence Committee and the Ulster Protestant Volunteers and marched around the country behind him. A handful formed a volunteer force of their own. The previous May a letter was sent to the papers declaring war on the IRA and its splinter groups. It was news to most people that there was enough of an IRA to splinter. The letter was signed Captain William Johnston, Adjutant, First Battalion, Belfast UVF. Late one night in June, this handful, sorry, *battalion* had ambushed four Catholic men coming out of a bar on Malvern Street off the Shankill Road, shooting one dead and badly wounding another two.

Among those arrested for the murder was a Hugh Arnold McClean who, according to the police, said in answer to the charge: 'I am sorry I ever heard tell of that man Paisley.'

GLENN PATTERSON, The International, 1999

WE WERE A CATHOLIC FAMILY. That meant that we bought our groceries at Catholic shops — Curran's, mostly, and the butcher, Fitzpatrick — and were on speaking terms only with Catholics. My mother was an exception: she was friends with Mrs Harper, wife of one of the policemen, a Protestant. They lived in Slieve Foy Place.

Many years later, I took part in a television programme, William F. Buckley Jr's *Firing Line*, debating the question of Northern Ireland with Captain Terence O'Neill, who had been Prime Minister of that dismal province. I shocked him by recalling that when I was growing up in Warrenpoint, I could spot a Protestant at a hundred yards. He claimed that this gave a most misleading impression of life in the North. Had he not invited to tea the Prime Minister of Ireland, Sean Lemass, and was not Mr Lemass a Catholic, and were they not the best of friends? Captain O'Neill didn't challenge me to say how I would spot a Protestant. What could I have said? I can spot a Protestant in the North of Ireland but not in the South? In the North a Protestant walks with an air of possession and authority, regardless of his social class. He walks as if he owned the place, which indeed he does. A Catholic walks as if he were there on sufferance. O'Neill is a Catholic name. How it settled upon Captain Terence or his father or grandfather, I have no idea. But if I saw him walking along Royal Avenue in Belfast and didn't know him from Adam, I would know that he was a Protestant.

The population of Warrenpoint was about two thousand in my time: a thousand Catholics, a thousand Protestants. There was no enmity between them; it was necessary only to keep your distance. My father, not given to phrase-making, told me once that my dealings with other people should be 'civil, but strange'. Power, such as it was, was in the hands of the Protestants: that was all a Catholic needed to know. My father, a splendid policeman, could not be promoted: he was not a Protestant, therefore he was not a Unionist, therefore he was not a member of the Loyal Order of Orangemen, therefore ...

DENIS DONOGHUE, Warrenpoint, 1991

THE IDEA THAT '*You can always tell them by their faces*' has no foundation in what can, in fact, be seen. It's entirely rooted in bigotry, not observation. It's a device to further reinforce divisions rather than an empirically demonstrable fact that helps us understand the world. But it can often *appear* as if people have the gift (if, indeed, it would be a gift) of reading faces in this way. Northern Ireland fosters sectarian semioticians of remarkable accomplishment, alert to the religious and political nuances of a host of little signs. Seeing them operate, it's almost as if they can detect the tiniest shift in humidity or air pressure, that their senses are attuned to another alphabet beyond the ordinary range of sight and sound. Outsiders are left dumbfounded by the speed with which the hidden sub-text is read, and they're amazed that anyone should be so interested in what it says. Names, schools, addresses, sporting interests, choice of newspaper or whiskey, these and a host of other apparently innocent signifiers are freighted with little cargoes of Protestant or Catholic associations. So, to take an easy example, from a first alphabet book of sectarianism, something any five-year-old Belfast child could decode, someone called Seamus O'Malley who'd attended St Joseph's College, lived on the Falls Road, read the *Irish News* and drank Power's whiskey would, without any doubt at all, be Catholic. And Billy White, from Sandy Row, who'd gone to Orangefield Academy, worked in Harland and Wolff Shipyard, read the *News Letter*, and drank Bushmill's would, with equal certainty, be Protestant. Everyone learns such signs – and many more subtle ones – as they grow up, so that someone of my uncle's age had a whole lifetime of semiotic practice to draw on. In conversation with him, someone would have to be very fleet of foot to evade or obfuscate their religious (or perhaps it's really more their tribal) origin. So many always noticed signs proclaim their background. Ulster folk are adept at a kind of instant religious triangulation, as they locate a newcomer on the map of friend or foe. Catholic or Protestant are pinpointed not by asking anything direct or remotely theological, but instead by inquiring about family, school, and where you live and work.

CHRIS ARTHUR, *Irish Willow*, 2002

THE STRONG SECTARIAN SPIRIT then [i.e. during the 1860s] pervading the population showed itself in various ways. The lower-classes among the Protestant populace delighted in publicly cursing the Pope; the lower-classes among the Catholics were equally ready to loudly anathematise King William III, the Deliverer, of Pious and Immortal Memory. Such utterances in the streets, as may be easily understood, were not conducive to the peace of the town [of Belfast] nor of the neighbouring counties.

THOMAS MACKNIGHT, *Ulster As It Is*, 1896

I REMEMBER DISCUSSING THE POSITION of the Ulster Party with a Northern Unionist just after the introduction of the last Home Rule Bill. He deplored the stupidity – the word was his, not mine – of his friends. 'If such a one' – he named a leading Ulster Unionist – 'were to die tomorrow and to be buried, the whole brains of Ulster Unionism would lie in that grave.' The statement was an exaggeration, though not a very grave one. Later on, in 1913, when the Ulster Volunteer movement had caught public attention, I listened one day to a discussion. 'Is Ulster in earnest,' some one asked, 'or is it putting up a great bluff?' A very able man, much experienced in political affairs and international diplomacy, closed the discussion with a definite pronouncement, 'Ulster must be in earnest. She is too stupid to bluff.' This, too, was an exaggeration. But it remains indisputably true that north-east Ulster has not displayed striking political ability or the faculty for manipulating events to her own advantage. Yet north-east Ulster has prevailed. The blank 'We'll not have it' of Belfast has torn through the spider webs of politicians and rendered the voting powers of majorities impotent.

GEORGE A. BIRMINGHAM, *An Irishman Looks at His World*, 1919

EDEN SAYS NO
(graffito in Eden village, County Antrim)

As a people favoured by the Almighty,
we discovered writing for ourselves
(we've got our own historians, and poets –
some have dubbed us handy with a phrase).
Hence that slogan daubed on the Garden wall.

A reptilian representative
from a firm of nurserymen
(not one of us, if you catch my meaning)
tried to induce us to turn commercial
with free samples of edible fruit
and all types of honeyed talk.

But we know what we've got in Eden
and we aren't about to throw it away.
The slogan reminds us, as much as them,
that our soil must stay pure and unsullied.
Within these walls fruit shall never grow
because Eden will always say No.

ROBERT JOHNSTONE, *Eden to Edenderry*, 1989

M ANY LOYALISTS HAVE SPOKEN of their sense that they were hoodwinked by the Unionist Party into voting for people who had little interest in their material welfare. Glenn Barr has said, 'They could have sent a donkey down the Shankill with a Union Flag wrapped round it and we would have voted for it.'

I think Catholics should acknowledge where they were hoodwinked too. While kids in English schools at our age were being told that their education was a right won for them through working-class struggle, we were being assured that it was a privilege bestowed on us by the Catholic Church, to which we would always be indebted. The fact is that the Catholic Church colonised the provision of education for the perpetuation of the faith, and in some sections of it, for the perpetuation of nationalism. We weren't given the option of free education that left you free to make up your own mind about your place in the world. We were conned. Education for us was not a liberation but an enslavement.

MALACHI O'DOHERTY, *The Trouble with Guns*, 1998

W E LEARNED LITTLE OF LOCAL or national history at school and had no sense of history as we passed through streets as historic as any in Ireland.

From the school at Barrack Street we passed by the Farset, which one teacher by name of 'Dirty Dick' Dynan told us could be seen from behind the houses in Durham Street. The houses are now gone, replaced by a car park, but the Farset can be seen still the same. We regularly dandered up Pound Street, knowing nothing of its history or even the old barracks which gives Barrack Street its name.

There were three RUC barracks in our day: one at Hastings Street, one at Springfield Road and another at Roden Street, flanking the area on its three sides. A fourth, at Cullingtree Road, had only recently been replaced. Not that we were worried or even interested in such places. Nowadays, of course, with heavily fortified British Army and RUC barracks and forts dotted strategically throughout West Belfast it is difficult to remain disinterested or neutral about their existence. It is especially so, in wet, wintry times, when the Falls Road, washed grey by drizzling rain and suffering from the ravages of war and redevelopment, appears bleak and shabby, with the omnipresent foot patrols of British soldiers treading carefully through back streets a threatening intrusion into an area hostile to their presence.

Not that British soldiers are a new feature of the scenery in West Belfast. Since its days as a country lane raids and harassment have been occupational hazards suffered by residents of the Falls Road.

GERRY ADAMS, *Falls Memories*, 1982

THE TOOME ROAD

One morning early I met armoured cars
In convoy, warbling along on powerful tyres,
All camouflaged with broken alder branches,
And headphoned soldiers standing up in turrets.
How long were they approaching down my roads
As if they owned them? The whole country was sleeping.
I had rights-of-way, fields, cattle in my keeping,
Tractors hitched to buckrakes in open sheds,
Silos, chill gates, wet slates, the greens and reds
Of outhouse roofs. Whom should I run to tell
Among all of those with their back doors on the latch
For the bringer of bad news, that small-hours visitant
Who, by being expected, might be kept distant?
Sowers of seed, erectors of headstones ...
O charioteers, above your dormant guns,
It stands here still, stands vibrant as you pass,
The invisible, untoppled omphalos.

SEAMUS HEANEY, *Field Work*, 1979

ARMAGH IS IN MANY RESPECTS a county of very different character from Antrim. It is predominantly an inland county, constrained between Lough Neagh to the north, the River Bann to the east, and the River Blackwater to the west: and with a wavering boundary to the south, running from Carlingford Lough to the high ground of the Fews. (The erratic course of this southern boundary through the town of Newry is particularly confusing.)

The county can be divided into three very distinct areas. To the north, the flat expanse bordering Lough Neagh, with its peatland, drains, reeds and birch trees, has been rendered only marginally prosperous by successive lowerings of the level of the lough. South of this there is a wide extent of rich, rolling, agricultural countryside, attractively wooded and orcharded, which over the years has produced fecund crops of corn, flax, apples, and (today's crop) mushrooms. This is the heartland of the seventeenth-century English plantation. South of this again, the land begins to rise; the rocky hills of the Fews lead to the very beautiful, volcanic mini-mountains of the Ring of Gullion; in this comparatively barren countryside took refuge those who had been evicted by the planters.

Here, the uneasy relationship between the Planter and the Gael reaches its climax: Armagh is the historic heartland of the political and religious troubles of Ulster. Drumcree in the north, Crossmaglen in the south, symbolise the two extremes of passionately held beliefs and convictions.

[I write] not about politics, but about buildings. I have for the most part sought to exclude buildings with strong political associations, be they Orange halls or the British army's watch-towers or the numerous IRA memorials of south Armagh. (I could not resist, though, including Colonel Saunderson wearing his sash on the Twelfth of July, a statue come to life like the Commendatore in Don Giovanni.) But buildings are very much affected by politics: not just by bunting, graffiti, and wall-paintings, but by bombs and bullets. Every town and village in the county has suffered their ravages: the most important buildings have, for the most part, been laboriously restored; but the lesser shops, pubs and homes that line so many main streets have mostly lost the details that gave them their character.

C.E.B. BRETT, *Buildings of County Armagh*, 1999

RED BRANCH
(*A blessing*)

Sing a song for the broken
towns of old Tyrone:
Omagh, Dungannon, Strabane,
jagged walls and windows,
slowly falling down.

Sing a song for the homes
or owners that were here today
and tomorrow are gone;
Irish Street in Dungannon,
my friend, Jim Devlin.

Sing a song for the people,
so grimly holding on,
Protestant and Catholic, fingered
at teabreak, shot inside their home:
the iron circle of retaliation.

Sing a song for the creaking branch
they find themselves upon,
hollow from top to bottom,
the stricken limb of Ulster,
slowly blown down.

Sing an end to sectarianism,
Fenian and Free Presbyterian,

the punishment slowly grown
more monstrous than the crime,
an enormous seeping bloodstain.

Sing our forlorn hope then –
the great Cross of Verdun,
Belfast's Tower on the Somme –
signs raised over bloody ground
that two crazed peoples make an end.

JOHN MONTAGUE, *The Dead Kingdom*, 1984

DESERTMARTIN IS AN ANGLICISED VERSION of Gaelic words that mean 'Martin's hermitage', implying a history of religious devotion. Today, the village announces its religious preferences with a great flutter of Union Jacks and by painting its kerbstones red, white and blue, as in Randalstown. Many years ago, before his health began to fail, my father and my brother Colm drove there to try to unearth some family history. They went into a pub somewhere in the area of Desertmartin and ordered Power's whiskey, my father's favourite tipple, distilled in the Irish Republic, but usually available in Northern Ireland. The pub's customers ceased talking. Faces stiffened.

'What?' the barman said.

'Two glasses of Power's, no ice, just water,' my father said. The barman glanced at his other customers, most of whom were looking on sullenly. He turned back to the new arrivals and rapped the bar with a forefinger, as though banging a drum.

'Ye'll get no such whiskey in this house,' he said. 'Thon's a republican whiskey ye're askin' me for. We don't sell that sort of whiskey. And I'll tell ye somethin' more into the bargain. We don't serve them who's askin' for it.'

CAL McCRYSTAL, *Reflections on a Quiet Rebel*, 1997

DESERTMARTIN

At noon, in the dead centre of a faith,
Between Draperstown and Magherafelt,
This bitter village shows the flag
In a baked absolute September light.
Here the Word has withered to a few
Parched certainties, and the charred stubble
Tightens like a black belt, a crop of Bibles.

Because this is the territory of the Law
I drive across it with a powerless knowledge –
The owl of Minerva in a hired car.
A Jock squaddy glances down the street
And grins, happy and expendable,
Like a brass cartridge. He is a useful thing,
Almost at home, and yet not quite, not quite.

It's a limed nest, this place. I see a plain
Presbyterian grace sour, then harden,
As a free strenuous spirit changes
To a servile defiance that whines and shrieks
For the bondage of the letter: it shouts
For the Big Man to lead his wee people
To a clean white prison, their scorched tomorrow.

Masculine Islam, the rule of the Just,
Egyptian sand dunes and geometry,
A theology of rifle-butts and executions:
These are the places where the spirit dies.
And now, in Desertmartin's sandy light,
I see a culture of twigs and bird–shit
Waving a gaudy flag it loves and curses.

TOM PAULIN, *Liberty Tree*, 1983

I HAVE FALLEN IN LOVE WITH FERMANAGH – especially the rough border stretches, all mountains and moors and wide silent lakes. In places one can still imagine how it must have seemed to the English in 1606, when the touring King's Deputy and his retinue had to sleep in their tents because throughout the whole county there was not even an attempt at a town. The assizes had to be held in a ruined monastery, the only building big enough. Fertile ground here for Orange myth-making! The good land going to waste, populated only by savage Gaels living mainly on curdled milk in cramped wattle huts without chimneys – a people ignorant of and indifferent to the fast-changing world of Renaissance Europe. So what a good thing that along came the industrious planters to develop this wilderness, just as their relations were in due course to develop the US, Canada, Australia, New Zealand, large areas of Africa – all places populated by other savages who were mostly easier to cope with than the Gaels, possibly because they weren't the same colour.

It helps to remember that the Protestants have been in Northern Ireland longer than the Whites have been in the US. It *is* now their country as much as the Catholics'; they have no other. Had the Gaels been 'subdued' as effectively as the Red Indians and the Aboriginals there would be no disputing that point in the 1970s. But apart from anything else Gaelic labour was needed, just as convict labour was needed to develop Australia. Then religion (can't get away from it) frustrated widespread miscegenation; and was reinforced by the settlers' feelings of racial superiority — something linked to yet other than the religious difference. Not to mention the blood-pride of the Gael — a strong and silent pride, far removed from sentimental word-spinning in Celtic twilights. Something old as the bogs and tough as the oak in them. I can see it still on the lean dark faces of the hill-farmers here. And feel it still, too, occasionally, stirring in my own mongrel blood of the Pale. So there could be no merger of races; and recurring rebellion throughout the rest of Ireland kept the pot of sedition and suspicion simmering in Ulster — and sometimes boiling. And here we are ...

DERVLA MURPHY, *A Place Apart*, 1978

W HEN WE LOOK BACK UPON 1966, while it has not lacked achievement, we cannot ignore incidents which inhibited our progress and disfigured our reputation throughout the English-speaking world, and indeed beyond. From one side came the extreme Republicans, who sought to flaunt before our people the emblems of a cause which a majority of us abhor, and who once again refused to renounce violence as a political weapon. From the other side came those self-appointed and self-styled 'loyalists' who see moderation as treason, and decency as weakness. Let us learn the lesson of these events and apply our energies, not to a rehearsal of the enmities of the past, but to an examination of the problems of the present and a realisation of the opportunities of the future.

TERENCE O'NEILL, House of Commons, 13 December 1966

T HE MASS OF CATHOLICS sank into resignation and inwardness. Protestant state for Protestant people, so Catholic schools for Catholics — doctors, lawyers, shopkeepers who 'were your own': what had been custom before partition became dogma. The reinforced segregation of the Troubles, as documented in recent statistics, is no more than the most recent manifestation of a historic pattern, as in Dungannon's Scotch Street and Irish Street, Carrickfergus's Irish Quarter West and Scotch Quarter West. Even in those areas where they lived side by side, it was possible for Catholics to lead most of their lives — as Protestants did — through their own institutions. There are towns throughout Northern Ireland where the main street has a 'Protestant' side and a 'Catholic' one: Protestant-owned businesses down one side, Catholic on the other; and there are many who make considerable effort to transact as much business as possible inside their own community.

FIONNUALA O CONNOR, *In Search of a State: Catholics in Northern Ireland*, 1993

ALTHOUGH I AM CONVINCED that the Catholic grievances did not amount to oppression, and certainly did not justify the recourse to force that followed the early peaceful demonstrations of the civil rights movement, I stand firmly by the statement that, in a great number of ways, the Catholic minority received less than fair treatment from the Protestant majority. I think the Unionists could, without the slightest risk to their entrenched positions of power, have met these Catholic grievances with a spirit of fairness and generosity. Had they done so, I do not believe that any of the Troubles of the years since 1969 need have occurred. But perhaps saddest of all, though understandable enough, the Catholic sense of bitterness and oppression has survived and grown, even though the intervention of Britain has produced reforms that, in my view, have met all the legitimate complaints from which the Troubles sprang in the first place.

C.E.B. BRETT, *Long Shadows Cast Before*, 1978

THE RUMBLINGS OF DISCONTENT that were to be heard all over the world and in all communities and strata of society during the uneasy sixties eventually reached Northern Ireland, which awoke from its ancient slumber with an abruptness that alarmed everybody concerned. Civil rights groups sprang up overnight, and eventually, as was inevitable, violence ensued. Barriers were built across ancient Londonderry streets and from each side bricks, paving-stones and other missiles were flung, while groups marched and counter-marched. Some marched for votes and other rights for Catholics; others, particularly an extremist Protestant sect led by the Rev. Ian Paisley (later elected to the Northern Ireland Parliament and later still to the one at Westminster), to stop the Pope setting up stakes in every market-place at which to burn heretics, a practice which Mr Paisley and his followers devoutly believed the Pope was still given to.

The inevitable charges of police brutality followed, some of them being fully justified, and eventually the Prime Minister of Northern Ireland, Captain Terence O'Neill, was faced with the uninviting prospect of doing something to satisfy the demands of the minority without actually upsetting the feelings, and still less the power, of the majority. Matters were not made any easier for him by the fact that a number of members of his Cabinet, including the Deputy Prime Minister, Mr Brian Faulkner, had not for some time seemed eager to show their enthusiasm for Captain O'Neill; in the sudden flood of passion undammed by the Civil Rights campaign and the bigotry of Mr Paisley there was found an excellent opportunity to displace him. Eventually they succeeded in doing so.

BERNARD LEVIN, *The Pendulum Years*, 1970

T HE NORTHERN IRELAND PROBLEM repeatedly provokes such ghastliness that it has come to be seen from outside almost as a morality play featuring allegorical figures impossible to think of as people like us; the figures of Anger, Pride, Greed, Revenge – or (rather less conspicuously) Temperance, Humility, Forgiveness. After eight years of terror and horror the mental gulf separating the North from the rest of the British Isles is immense. Even before 1969 it was wide enough because of Northern Ireland's chronic introversion. For historical reasons the region has always been inward-looking and during its half century of self-government it 'got lost', as far as the rest of the world was concerned, and simmered unhealthily in its own mythological juices. Then it was found again, but in circumstances that emphasised its isolation by making it seem – to the uninformed outsider – physically unapproachable, economically unreliable, morally undesirable and generally not nice to know. (Or at best, to the more charitable, an object of exasperated pity.) If this disdain is not tinged with guilt it should be. The Republic is guilty for having until quite recently encouraged Northern Catholics to adhere to the Green myth; and Britain is guilty for having ignored the dire influences of the Orange myth on the administration of one area of the UK.

DERVLA MURPHY, *A Place Apart*, 1978

T HE PRACTICAL PRIORITISATIONS I am thinking of ostensibly operate on the assumption that it may be important to emphasise difference not for its own sake, but for the sake of reconciliation. Here the rationale seems to be that only communities strong enough in their own sense of themselves can embark upon a path of reconciliation without fearing the consequences. This rationale appears to have gained significant support within community organisations and funding bodies. It underpins growth of the media through which a single identity consciousness is developed and represented, as local communities strive to acquire more self-assured and inventive appropriations of their traditions. Particularly striking examples are on display during the annual West Belfast Festival, where we see increasingly vibrant and self-confident expressions of an Irish republican identity that are out of kilter with the self-understandings and mores of unionist parts of the city. If nationalists and republicans have stolen a march in capitalising on the funding available for creative plans to enhance a single identity consciousness, unionists and loyalists have begun to play catch up. Funding aside, Protestant East Belfast now seems to be treated to annual summer painting sprees undertaken by loyalists anxious to mark out their territory in ways designed to engender self-pride in their Protestant/British identity. Or so we are told.

Now, there is no doubting that many community relations workers regard single identity projects as fitting into the bigger picture of reconciliation between the two traditional communities; and there is no doubt too that the political parties most closely associated with community developments in West and East Belfast – Sinn Féin and the Progressive Unionist Party (PUP) respectively – claim to be keenly interested in reconciliation. But, without querying anyone's sincerity, two main worries remain. First, it is not obvious why, having lived together for three to four hundred years, we still need coaching with our own before engaging properly with the so-called other. It is tempting to retort that when considering how, when, where or if we should dabble in cross-community exercises, there is no better advice than that offered by the Nike advertisement – 'just do it'.

Second, it is not clear that affirmations of our separate identities are making the business of reconciliation easier to conduct; rather, they appear to exaggerate our differences in sometimes unhelpful ways. Decorating East Belfast with red, white and blue paint, loyalist graffiti and symbols, and seeing their equivalents replicated in West Belfast may make (some) people in those areas feel better about themselves, but it does not necessarily make them feel better about each other. Or, more to the point, the better republicans feel about themselves, the worse they are regarded by unionists/loyalists, who are decidedly unnerved by shows of republican self-confidence (and perhaps vice versa). At any rate, not too many Protestants/unionists are keen to participate in the West Belfast Festival, even when invited. And republicans need not even expect to be invited to comparable events in East Belfast.

NORMAN PORTER, *The Elusive Quest*, 2003

IT IS NOT THE FAULT OF ANY living person that the system of government in Northern Ireland is unjust. The forces that drove the Protestants of Ulster in the 1910s to demand their own separate state and threaten civil war if they failed were too deeply ingrained in their history, psyche and politics. Nor is it any individual's fault that Protestants founded and maintained a Protestant state based on religious hatred and the politics of exclusion; everything in their history taught them that to compromise, to surrender, to accommodate the native Irish enemy, was destruction. When the natives again rebelled in 1969 the security forces of the state and its Protestant mobs could only react the way they had always reacted, with brutality, in a furious attempt to beat back down the rebel enemies who sought to overwhelm their citadel.

But equally it is not the rebels' fault that the Protestants of Ulster refused and still refuse to learn the simple lesson of history: that all colonisers will one day be overthrown by those natives they hold in bondage. For there to be peace in Ireland the Protestants must make the great historical accommodation that another Protestant people, the Afrikaners, made with their historic enemy.

KEVIN TOOLIS, Rebel Hearts, 1995

from WHATEVER YOU SAY, SAY NOTHING

Men die at hand. In blasted street and home
The gelignite's a common sound effect:
As the man said when Celtic won, 'The Pope of Rome
's a happy man this night.' His flock suspect

In their deepest heart of hearts the heretic
Has come at last to heel and to the stake.
We tremble near the flames but want no truck
With the actual firing. We're on the make

As ever. Long sucking the hind tit
Cold as a witch's and as hard to swallow
Still leaves us fork-tongued on the border bit:
The liberal papist note sounds hollow

When amplified and mixed in with the bangs
That shake all hearts and windows day and night.
(It's tempting here to rhyme on 'labour pangs'
And diagnose a rebirth in our plight

But that would be to ignore other symptoms.
Last night you didn't need a stethoscope
To hear the eructation of Orange drums
Allergic equally to Pearse and Pope.)

On all sides 'little platoons' are mustering –
The phrase is Cruise O'Brien's via that great
Blacklash, Burke – while I sit here with a pestering
Drouth for words at once both gaff and bait

501

To lure the tribal shoals to epigram
And order. I believe any of us
Could draw the line through bigotry and sham
Given the right line, *aere perennius*.

III

'Religion's never mentioned here,' of course.
'You know them by their eyes,' and hold your tongue.
'One side's as bad as the other,' never worse.
Christ, it's near time that some small leak was sprung

In the great dykes the Dutchman made
To dam the dangerous tide that followed Seamus.
Yet for all this art and sedentary trade
I am incapable. The famous

Northern reticence, the tight gag of place
And times: yes, yes. Of the 'wee six' I sing
Where to be saved you only must save face
And whatever you say, you say nothing.

Smoke-signals are loud-mouthed compared with us:
Manoeuvrings to find out name and school,
Subtle discrimination by addresses
With hardly an exception to the rule

That Norman, Ken and Sidney signalled Prod
And Searaus (call me Sean) was sure-fire Pape.
O land of password, handgrip, wink and nod,
Of open minds as open as a trap,

Where tongues lie coiled, as under flames lie wicks,
Where half of us, as in a wooden horse
Were cabin'd and confined like wily Greeks,
Besieged within the siege, whispering morse.

SEAMUS HEANEY, *North*, 1975

Poverty
Mountain

Standin' out on the mountainside with the sheep and it
rainin' heaven's hard, and you without another coat to
your back. And out at the fishin' at night with the cold
wind and the frozen lines, and your trousers clammed to
your knees. Your boots squelchin' in the shughs after divils
of cows, and maybe not a bite of shop's meat from one year
to another. In water and out of water, in shughs and out of
shughs ...

MICHAEL McLAVERTY, *from* 'The Prophet'

W HEN HUNGER BECAME ACUTE, and it often did, my mother
would tell us fairy stories, stories of miraculous supply by the
leprechaun. The stories were convincing, but my own last
resort was to stand with my bare feet on the baker's cellar grating, or in
the doorway of the bakery, and inhale the fumes of new-made bread ...

At 'the bottom of the world', as my mother called our alley, we had as
close neighbours the chimney sweeps, the local ragman, a process server,
and a lot of widows and orphans and wastrels and derelicts who were
uncataloguable. How they all managed to eke out existence has always
been a mystery to me. One soft-headed little woman next door gave birth
to a child nearly every year for a long time. This growing family became
a drain on the neighbours. When advised by my mother to bring some
of these barnyard fathers to a sense of responsibility, she excused them all
by the statement, 'Shure, th' poor craythers couldn't help it.' ...

The word 'poverty' inadequately describes the condition of life in that
alley. It was stark destitution. We were all chronically, hopelessly hungry
and utterly unconscious that there was anything unusual about it. We

never complained. We never connected our condition with economic systems or governments good or bad. As a child I had an idea – dim and hazy, it is true – that things in the world were just about as God ordered them. 'The Man above only knows,' my father would say to some of our questionings, 'and He won't let on.'

Despite the rags and dirt and hunger and cold, despite the limitations, economic, physical and mental, we were, on the whole, a happy lot.

ALEXANDER IRVINE, *A Fighting Parson*, 1930

THE BRACKEN

The forests of the bracken
  Come up thin lipped and white,
Through the deep spoor of the bullocks
  Pushing into light.

Great fronds put out their branches
  And canopy the plain,
Till the hooves of the cattle find them,
  Or the frost has them slain.

In autumn the poor people
  Take scythes and sharpening stones,
And gather the rusted mattress
  To put under their bones.

JOHN LYLE DONAGHY, *The Flute Over the Valley: Antrim Song*, 1931

I HAVE NOW FINISHED MY CIRCUIT [in Downpatrick], and in my return home must carry you twenty-three miles to Newry where we come into our old road to Dundalk through a different country than any we have travelled over. Though but twenty-three miles it is a hard day's journey being over the Alps and Apennines of Ireland: they are called the mountains of Mourne and the mountains of Newry. Within these twenty years it was an absolute uncivilised country, and any one who ventured to go among them did it at his peril, it being almost the inaccessible retreat of Tories and Raparees and outlaws. But a good road being made through the country, and some gentlemen who had land there being determined to improve it, it is much civilised to what it was. But it is the wildest and most mountainous country I have seen, except one part which Lord Annesley is improving, where he has built a very pretty town (Castlewellan), and is now building a magnificent seat for himself. The cabins one sees on the sides of the hills are the most miserable huts I ever saw, built with sods and turf, no chimney, the door made of a hurdle, the smoke goes all out of the door, the cocks and hens, pigs, goats and if perchance they have a cow, inhabit the same dwelling. They seem much upon a rank with the American savages, excepting that they have some notion of making the sign of the cross and stand much in awe of their priests. And yet there must be times when the master and mistress of the family are merry and jolly, for one sees the cabin doors crowded with little naked boys and girls. In one part of these mountains is a place of public resort for people of fashion who come to drink goats' whey, which in Ireland is esteemed preferable to asses' milk, and a great purifier of the blood, and the herbs that grow on these mountains are thought to be the most medicinal of any.

Newry when we came to it made amends for the rest. It is a large town and there is the best inn I ever was at in Ireland. From thence we went the next day to Drogheda and the next morning to Dublin.

EDWARD WILLES, 'Letters to the Earl of Warwick', c. 1759

IN PETTIGO THE GREATER NUMBER OF THE INHABITANTS were poor Catholics living in wretched hovels among barren rocks and heath; of whom there were many real objects of charity, that required the assistance of the humane. In such a place the benevolent disposition of Mr Skelton found full room for exercise; and I may safely say, that no human breast ever had more genuine charity than his. His wonderful acts of goodness will be remembered for ages in that remote corner of the North, and be transmitted from father to son for successive generations ....

He also practised physic at Pettigo as at Monaghan, and bestowed on his people medicines that he had procured for the purpose. His medicines and advice must have been indispensibly requisite in a country so uncivilized, where such assistance could not be easily obtained. Yet in dangerous cases he would not depend on his own skill, but sent fourteen miles off to Enniskillen for his intimate friend Dr Scott, to whom, for his trouble in attending his parishioners, he allowed, I am assured, rent-free, the whole glebe of the parish of Pettigo ... which is now set for forty pounds a year.

THE REVEREND SAMUEL BURDY, The Life of Philip Skelton, 1792

THE FAMINE YEARS WERE LESS CATASTROPHIC in County Down than in the south and west of Ireland, but conditions were bad nonetheless, especially in the Ards peninsula; anyone who knows that countryside will know how many ruins of roofless and abandoned cottages are still to be found there. There are several references to the Famine in letters to Wills Brett from his aunt Elizabeth Corne: 'If you had seen the number of miserable looking creatures that went down this avenue yesterday, your heart would have been grieved – not less than 700 who were going to Crossgar for tickets to work on the road – their wages a shilling a day.' And: 'You are all going to do a noble act by setting up a Public Bakery and all the other helps you are getting for the poor.'

C.E.B. BRETT, Long Shadows Cast Before, 1978

WHEN THE COUNTRY HUNGERS the city starves, and 1756 stood out in the recollection of my grandmother's grandfather as the year of the hunger riots in Belfast, when the mob plundered stores and put the fear of death into the hearts of respectable merchants, who had neither soldiers nor police to protect them, and, who knows, made the innocent suffer with the guilty.

'Who was right and who was wrong,' said my grandmother's grandfather, 'I do not know, but you see what the mob thought of it.' Anyhow there was a very great riot, much robbery and destruction, and many of the rioters thought it prudent afterwards to take to absence or hiding. There were, of course, two parties – those who cried for the blood of the insolent rascals, and those who cried for the blood of the regrators. It was the first time, the old gentleman told my grandmother, that he had ever heard the word or the word fore-staller either. A 'regrator', he told her, was a person who buys up goods, especially victuals, in order to sell again at a profit in the same or another market, and a 'fore-staller' one who buys up goods before they reach the market, the implication being that they made thereby swollen profits out of the needs of their hungry neighbours. But as well as these two violent and warring factions there was a moderate party:

> We whose names are hereunto subscribed, the principal linen weavers and other working tradesmen of the town of Belfast take this method of publicly declaring our abhorrence of some of the proceedings of the late rising and mob; and that we will when called upon use our endeavours to suppress and as far as in us lies prevent the like for the future.
>
> But at the same time that we dislike and disapprove of the conduct of some of the persons concerned in the said mob, yet we can't help complaining of the distress to which many of the poor were reduced by the cruelty and oppression of the hucksters, regrators, and fore-stallers of the markets. We have had the best of opportunities of knowing the condition of the poor, which we can truly say was really miserable and their misery was greatly

heightened if not solely occasioned by the avarice and extortion of the hucksters and fore-stallers, and this plainly appear'd to us by their refusing to sell meal at the market price, chusing to conceal quantities thereof under ground and suffering it to rot rather than sell it at the current price, hoping it would still rise higher (altho' it then bore a very high price) and in that case they expected it would sell be it ever so damaged and rotten.

And from our personal knowledge of many of the persons concerned in said mob we take upon us to say it was on account of these kind of oppressions and the want of bread to support their families that induced many of them to be concerned therein, and not out of any idle, loose, or disorderly way of living or thinking ...

L.R. CRESCENT, *In Old Belfast (1740–1760)*, 1924

THE GREAT FAMINE, and the many less spectacular famines that recurred through the nineteenth century, led to a general deterioration of the arts of cooking and the standards of living, and they have not recovered. Today the diet of the poorer rural families is monotonous in the extreme, and now that sugar and tea, bread and jam are bought from the grocer's van the resources of mountain and seashore are sought no more. They are regarded as in some way degrading, presumably because, though once a wise supplement to the diet, they had become grim necessities during lean years. Some of the 'austerity' foods, champ and potato bread, have kept their hold, but sweet stewed tea – kept ready like more nourishing stews for the men returning from the fields or the shepherd from the hills – has taken the place of the old drinks – crowdy, posset and skink – made with water, sweet milk, buttermilk and oatmeal. Along the shore the blocken are no longer salted and placed on the thatch to dry before hanging in readiness on the kitchen baulks. Even the herring, fresh, salted or kippered, now goes overseas and finds little sale in Mourne. Mackerel are despised and the sand-eels and razor-fish lie safe on the shore. The house, too, has lost much of its former importance as a social centre where neighbours gathered for their *ceilidhe*. Bus and bicycle take the young folk of Mourne to the town cinemas, while young townsfolk flock to the hostels to escape into the hills.

E. ESTYN EVANS, *Mourne Country*, 1951

LIKE DOLMENS ROUND MY CHILDHOOD,
THE OLD PEOPLE

Like dolmens round my childhood, the old people.

Jamie MacCrystal sang to himself
A broken song, without tune, without words;
He tipped me a penny every pension day.
Fed kindly crusts to winter birds.
When he died his cottage was robbed.
Mattress and money box torn and searched.
Only the corpse they didn't disturb.

Maggie Owens was surrounded by animals.
A mongrel bitch and shivering pups.
Even in her bedroom a she-goat cried,
She was a well of gossip defiled.
Fanged chronicler of a whole countryside:
Reputed a witch, all I could find
Was her lonely need to deride.

The Nialls lived along a mountain lane
Where heather bells bloomed, clumps of foxglove.
All were blind, with Blind Pension and Wireless.
Dead eyes serpent-flickered as one entered
To shelter from a downpour of mountain rain.
Crickets chirped under the rocking hearthstone
Until the muddy sun shone out again.

Mary Moore lived in a crumbling gatehouse
Famous as Pisa for its leaning gable.
Bag-apron and boots, she tramped the fields
Driving lean cattle from a miry stable.
A by-word for fierceness, she fell asleep
Over love stories, Red Star and Red Circle,
Dreamed of gypsy love rites, by firelight sealed.

Wild Billy Harbinson married a Catholic servant girl
When all his loyal family passed on:
We danced round him shouting 'To hell with King Billy'
And dodged from the arc of his flailing blackthorn.
Forsaken by both creeds, he showed little concern
Until the Orange drums banged past in the summer
And bowler and sash aggressively shone.

Curate and doctor trudged to attend them.
Through knee-deep snow, through summer heat.
From main road to lane to broken path,
Gulping the mountain air with painful breath.
Sometimes they were found by neighbours,
Silent keepers of a smokeless hearth.
Suddenly cast in the mould of death.

Ancient Ireland, indeed! I was reared by her bedside,
The rune and the chant, evil eye and averted head,
Fomorian fierceness of family and local feud.
Gaunt figures of fear and of friendliness,
For years they trespassed on my dreams,
Until once, in a standing circle of stones,
I felt their shadows pass

Into that dark permanence of ancient forms.

JOHN MONTAGUE, *The Rough Field*, 1972

KILDARGAN ISN'T ANY DIFFERENT from any of the other mill villages which you see in this part of the North. They were all built about a hundred or so years ago and their sites chosen for hard-headed, money-making reasons when the linen bubble was at its fattest and most iridescent. For a start, they were placed as close to a river as possible; our row have their privies on stilts out over the water, which is a good idea when there's a flood on but not so good in a July and August heatwave. All the houses suffer from damp and there's a cold river mist which wraps itself lovingly around you as soon as you open the back door.

The Dargan slides along fast and rounded and the same colour as a gun-barrel too, in the straight, dangerous stretch behind the houses. Young Tommy Scullion from number seven was drowned there in the school summer holidays last year. Four miles further on the spate of water spearheads a way out into the big lough, then loses thrust, merges into the buff, turgid waters and dies. It is twenty-eight miles in length, and there are derelict basalt-built mills on its banks and on the banks of its tributaries for most of that length. The black walls merely get blacker with age but the softer, less durable insides have rotted long ago. Each mill has its row or rows or square of houses and these are still occupied, although any life centred around the mill has long lost any meaning. They are ugly, depressing places to live in. There are about three mills left which are still in operation. Kildargan is one of them.

MAURICE LEITCH, *The Liberty Lad*, 1965

WHEN I CAME BACK WITH THE TWO BUCKETS the wee ones were just ready to start a bit of codding, but I had to make them learn their lessons for the next day. Every night that week Bertie was away out to swing in an old tyre tied to a rope on Barney's tree, but he could not do that now even if he was back, for the cottage had people in it and they would not like it, forbye he would be looking in their windows and cheering and yelling. He is mad about aeroplanes and pretends he is flying one and shooting down Germans. Daddy was through the war and he says he never saw a German, only Italians. He says they ran as if they were reared on senna pods when they heard General Montgomery was coming with the deserts rats. He was a desert rat and he is proud of it.

Mammy came back, shivering and rubbing her arms. Her jersey has short sleeves now because it had big holes in the elbows so she cut off the sleeves just above the holes to make it look civilised.

'Is it dark?' asked George. He is like a wee old man. I do not think he knows what dark is.

'It's dark all right,' said Mammy. 'Dear but this is cosy now we have a bit of fire. I think it's freezing. The moon's all crined in wee, and you can hardly hear the river. It's very like a night you would have snow. Where the devil is your da and why isn't he home? I declare this is scandalous.'

'Is Bertie all right to come back by himself?' said I. 'Sure if he misses the Stick Bridge he'll be in the river before he knows.'

'Not him,' said Mammy, 'I tied my apron to the far end of the handrail. He's to gather it up and bring it with him when he's coming back. Take off that kettle, it's boiling. Where are the dishes, or did you do them when you got my back turned?'

'I did them,' said Agnes, 'I did the dishes and she did not.'

'Well she was not idle,' said my mammy to her, for she knew it was me did the nappies and fetched water and kept the fire up and started the wee ones at their lessons. 'Go on, ye boys ye!' she said to the wee ones. 'See who is finished first and I'll hear you your tables.'

'I haven't any tables,' said Mervyn.

'Never mind,' she said, 'I will teach you some and then you will be able for them when you do get them. It pays to be smart.'

It was time Agnes and I started our tables because we are learning hard ones. Agnes is at parts of a pound and I am at per cents. I would rather do per cents than parts of a pound for I have done them twice and I don't know yet what one eighth is, a twelfth, or a sixteenth.

E.L. KENNEDY, *Twelve in Arcady*, 1986

ONE WILD STORMY NIGHT I went with two speakers to a village on the coast near Dungloe. We were greeted by men and women along the roadside holding flaming torches at the doors; the blackness of the winding road was dotted by the leaping flames of light as the car moved on. An old man spoke in Irish, a rush of words, soft, sibilant, vibrant; all I could catch was an occasional 'is', I listened in a glow to the inflections of his voice, interrupted by cries of 'maith thú' from the crowd.

Again I visited the companies from Ardara where homespun is made to enrich retailers far away, to the Rosses, the Irish-speaking district. Bare, boulder strewn land backed by purplish heather and misty mountains. The people lived close to the soil pushing back the soft bog and making it give food; a barren troubled existence. Yet this country grips their body and soul; it haunts the imagination in its cruelty, strength and beauty and the bleak coast with its wild angry sea, changing skies, crashed rocks, as if old gods had sported with pieces of granite mountain, can be recalled when sleek fat land is forgotten. There is a hunger for the soil, an elemental feeling that even the stranger or foreigner can sense. There was little tillage, very little grass save under the lee of the rocks where it was sweet. There was no wood for firing; in places no turf. The coarse top scraws were dried in the sun. The sea had smashed the Rosses into islands, slashed out bays from the land and spattered it with lakes.

Seagulls with despairing cries flew in before storms, wind roared inland, seas crashed in awful desolation and the air was misty with spendrift. Steel grey mornings came with daffodil skies, days of brilliant hard sunshine and sunsets of pale rose and mauve. White fronted geese in wedges flew overhead, their sharp penetrating cries came down the wind or their foolish laugh, and gannets with ruddy throats cruised slowly or dropped suddenly for fish. There were nights as if I was on a fishing boat at sea; house lights dipping through the washing of rain and wind blowing salty in the throat.

'An stranger' I was spoken of in their houses. It would be easy for information to be brought to the police, but though the people talked much amongst themselves, as if making up for lost time when they met, yet there were walls between them and the outside world. Tales of the Spanish Armada, ships that had been wrecked off Aranmore, stories of the O'Donnells and Fionn ... Ghost stories with the by-ways of elaboration so that with a wrench 'to make a long story short' they came back to the subject ... Spirits, good and bad left at cockcrow ... The dead walked around, there was an acceptance of their presence, no horror and little dread, the wall was thin between their living and their dead. The fairies; accounts of their shape and the clothes worn; their fear of iron, and the prayer when they see a sudden unexpected swirl of dust for 'they're surely in it'.

They were hardy. The boggy land and faulty drainage predisposed them to tuberculosis. Never the poor mouth, always an attempt to have an egg for my breakfast, which with many a sleight of hand I induced the children to help me eat. I preferred the Rosses and the North where I founded companies and felt at home. It was a pleasure to see a clump of trees; but, if they were in any quantity it meant good land which had been planted by English or Scotch settlers.

ERNIE O'MALLEY, *On Another Man's Wound*, 1936

A T THE FOOT OF CROCKNANEEVE is the townland of Derryconor and the far portion of it lies by the sea and is called Pollanaranny. It is there, in a little thatched cottage that still stands, I came into the world on the 22nd November, 1865. My father was Thomas MacGowan and my mother Bridget Cannon. Twelve children all told were in our household of which I was the eldest, a position that left me open to enough anguish all throughout my life.

It's not easy for this generation to understand the circumstances of life as they were when I was young. Often now, as I think back over life as it was then, I feel as if I'm dreaming. Life was untroubled enough in the manner of the times and the people were content even if they didn't think so then. Neither turmoil nor tumult, on sea or on land, existed to disturb them. Neither books nor papers were available to them; they were unlearnt and untaught and they were never troubled by any convulsions in the great world outside ...

But there was another side to the story. The people of this area – including my own people – were as poor as could be. They had no land worth talking about and it was hard to make any kind of a living out of the little bits of soil between the rocks. But there was one gift the people had: there was friendship and charity among them; they helped one another in work and in trouble, in adversity and in pain and it was that neighbourliness which, with the grace of God, was the solid stanchion of their lives.

There was no work to be had by the men of my parish in the district when I was young – apart from the bit they'd do on their own parcel of land and, God knows, that wouldn't keep food in their mouths for long. Mostly they survived on potatoes and they worked hard to raise that particular crop. Spades were used in our area all the time. There was an odd wooden plough here and there but there were so many rocks and stones around the place that even that could hardly be used. There was no talk then about artificial fertilisers and, as every family had only one cow, that left natural manure in short supply. People had to go down to the seashore to watch the tides early and late, collecting seaweed and wrack to put on the land. Even this needed permission from the landlord and then something, small or large, would be added to the rent for this privilege. Anyone who couldn't pay this would have to spend so many days working on the landlord's estate at Ballyconnell. In a good year, the crop would be fine but in a bad year, when it failed, both beast and human would go hungry.

When I was young, there were households that ate potatoes four times a day – on two occasions they were boiled, and on the other two they were in the form of potato-cakes. They lay heavy on the stomach but, in those days, fresh fish were as plentiful as grass – and as cheap. Fresh ling and cod from Tory sold at two-pence apiece. They had these and other good food as well: limpets, periwinkles, cockles, dulse, laver, mussels. Many is the time when there would be real hardship that they would have to make do with that food alone. I often heard the old people say it was this food saved the people in the 'Bad Year' (1847) and in another poor year when I was a child.

MÍCHEÁL MacGOWAN, translated by VALENTIN IREMONGER,
The Hard Road to Klondike, 1962

SOUTH OF THE BOLD PROMONTORY of the Bloody Foreland stretches an indented coast with many outlying islands, of which Gola and Owey are specially attractive. One can stay at Middleton or Bunbeg or Burton Port, and have fine sailing hereabouts, and exploring among the bays and peninsulas. The rock is a handsome red granite, contrasting finely with yellow sand and green pastures and bright sea: and I know of no place that is more inspiriting when the wind is coming in from the ocean and the sun is shining – and it should be noted that rainfall, which is high in the mountainous parts of Donegal, is less on these flatter coastal grounds. Here we are in the extensive low hummocky region called The Rosses (*Ros*, a promontory), a land of innumerable lakelets, a windswept heathery region, with small peaty fields grudgingly yielding difficult crops of potatoes and oats and turnips, and roads meandering through granite hillocks.

ROBERT LLOYD PRAEGER, *The Way That I Went*, 1937

EXAGGERATION AND DISTORTION are probably the most characteristic features of the writing from beginning to end of this book [i.e. Flann O'Brien's *The Poor Mouth*]. The very setting of the novel is a distortion, although a delightful one. From his house, reeking of pigs, the baby Bónapart can see Donegal, Galway and Kerry – a spectacle hardly available to any other house in Ireland. The food is dreadful. The weather is worse. It's hard to tell which of the two is dirtier – the people or the pigs. It is a world of unrelieved stupidity, filth, superstition and congestion. Fate is totally malignant and every circumstance is moronically accepted as part of God's will. And at the back of it all lies the origin and product of *an béal bocht* – poverty. At bottom, Myles na gCopaleen is showing us the sad, ravaging mental attitudes that result from severe physical poverty – materialism, opportunism, suspicion, the closed mind, incestuous stupidity, the lack of definite identity (everybody in the area is called Jams O'Donnell), the prevalence of brutality and thievery, and the strange, predominant sense of evil and oppression. Listening to that list, you might think this is a gloomy book, a modern anatomy of melancholy and malaise. It is, on the contrary, packed with laughter, full of its own special gaiety. ...

BRENDAN KENNELLY, The Pleasures of Gaelic Literature, 1977

T HE COTTAGE AND THE LITTLE FARM belonged to my grandfather, but my father and mother lived there also, and it was they who did the work. Our name was Emmet, and my father was called David and my mother Rebecca. My name was Wolfe.

It was when my father married that my grandfather bought the farm and added the extra rooms to the cottage, but he did not come to live there himself till I was ten years old. Before that he had lived in the school at the village, for he had been a schoolmaster all his life.

He had chosen the cottage because it was very lonely, and he could look out over the sea. Yet my father and mother often complained that the land was bare and unfruitful and brought poor return for their labour. There were only a few fields, and in many places the hard, grey rock jutted through the soil. Whins grew here and there, and in the marshy places were rushes and bog-cotton. Nearly all round us was the sea, for we were close to the headland, and on the other side of the hill were the Far Bay and the open Atlantic.

STEPHEN GILBERT, The Landslide, 1943

from THE ISLANDERS

Homely cares have the women – the food-providers –
Spreading the daily board and milking and churning,
Baking the fragrant farls on the hanging griddle.
Ready they are with help for the one that is troubled,
Care for the sick, or a hearty word for the children,
And in their houses a guest is welcomed with honour.
They too can work with their men, can shoulder the turf-creel;
Grey-haired women there are who can handle the tiller,
Watching with eyes alert for the shoal or the sandbank,
Judging the currents and making the difficult harbour,
When with red-kerchiefed heads they come to the mainland,
In to the shop at Bunbeg for their tea or their oatmeal,
Or it may be for the wonderful posting of letters.

That is the place for talk, when they meet on the quay-side:
Thus it will go – 'An' who's for the fair on Monday
Over in Derrybeg?' – 'There's Molly from Gola,
She has a couple of calves she'll be selling a bargain' –
And 'Joe has sheep on the Foreland, he'll drive them on Sunday' –
And 'Owen, God help him, is sick and lying this long time' –
So ring the busy tongues at the shop through the archway,
Or on the old grey quay, where the boats are huddled.

ELIZABETH SHANE, *By Bog and Sea in Donegal*, 1923

HUGHIE AND HIS FIELDS had parted company. He couldn't fit into a drain in the centre of his crop and feel at ease with it all. The constant rain was doing its work; all rain and no strength in his arms weakened the crops. Hughie now walked in his own fields with a grudge in his heart against them. Heather was popping up in most unexpected places.

A good crop might have won Hughie back to his fields; a good strong sun crusting the soil and draining the meanness out of the bog would have put heart in crops, fields and Hughie. But only rain, and dull skies, and a glug of water under foot.

The harvest that he gathered in that year was the poorest ever. His old wound grew worse; there was a running sore. Brigid wanted to sell some of the potatoes and let Hughie go to the doctor. They quarrelled over that and Brigid cried; it was the first time that there had been such a scene between them. In the end Hughie promised that if it wasn't all right in a week he would do what Brigid asked.

'I have no heart for them fields,' he said to Brigid one day …

Hughie's sense of irritation against his fields increased. He could scarcely send his spade to the ears without touching bog. He tried to deepen drains but he was flooded out. He cursed the mountain about him that day with its bellyful of water. He was in that mood when Tom Pheggy came along.

'It's not easy drainin' here,' Tom said.

'I'm just bein' drowned,' Hughie said; 'just bein' drowned,' he added.

'The mountain is movin' down agin us,' Tom said. 'It's worst up here. It's bad with everybody.'

'God knows, but I feel like a wet sod,' Hughie said; 'I feel as little meanin' in meself as that.'

PEADAR O'DONNELL, *Adrigoole*, 1929

THERE ARE MANY … REASONS why spoken Irish was abandoned in a relatively short period of time and within living memory in southeast

Ulster, not least the effects of the Great Famine (1845–7), leaving entire communities with only a vague memory of the language and traditions of their grandparents, and causing a breakdown of communication between generations, often between parent and child, and with it a significant loss of ancestral memory. Mary Harvessy from Clonalig, the last great singer in County Armagh and inheritor of the songs of Art Mac Cumhaigh, did not speak Irish to her own daughter Mary. Cití Sheáin Dobbin, another distinguished singer, from Omeath, did not speak Irish to her daughter Anna O'Hanlon. Indeed, many older people only spoke Irish to avoid their children or grandchildren understanding their conversation. There was a uniform unwillingness to inflict the stigma of shame associated with the speaking of Irish on another generation: 'the many causes of anglicisation in Omeath included the growth of tourism and clerical opposition to the Irish language ... there was much opposition to the speaking of Gaelic as it grew to be considered the language of poverty, want and backwardness. For this reason the people of the hills, who retained the language longest, were despised by the English-speaking shore-dwellers'. From the early seventeenth century, spoken Irish had no public function. English was the language of law and order, of commerce and education and of all the churches, including the Catholic Church – except for the use of Latin in the liturgy. Throughout the southeast Ulster region, as in most other places in Ireland, gravestones from the eighteenth to the twentieth centuries record in English the deaths of countless men and women whose only language was Irish. English was the language of progress and material advancement while Irish was associated with poverty, punishment, hardship and fear.

PÁDRAIGÍN NÍ UALLACHÁIN, *A Hidden Ulster:*
People, Songs and Traditions of Oriel, 2003

THERE WAS ALWAYS A GREAT DEAL of singing, and in the evening when we brought out a mug of tea from the house to the pub, a hundred yards away, we would hear old men singing songs or reciting verses. We knew them all, the singers and the songs, but we thought of them as the embarrassing outbursts of men stocious with drink. Only when we grew up and left home and looked back were we able to appreciate, at an irrecoverable remove, the secret life that subsisted in that deep countryside – the music of a hidden Ireland with its complex harmonies and quavering grace-notes, the passionate concealed underground life of another country whose difference was deceptive, because the common language seemed the same.

If the men in the pub were asked to sing these songs when they were sober they would become what they called 'bashful'. 'They're only auld come-all-yees,' they'd say, 'rubbidgy old songs. Yous don't want to hear them.' Such attitudes obtained all over Ireland. When music producers from Radio Éireann, the Irish radio station, went around the country in the 1950s in the vanguard of the folk-boom to record the fiddlers, the tin whistlers, the pipers, the singers of the countryside, they found an enormous reservoir of talent. But the people were often reluctant to reveal themselves as traditional musicians, because such music was despised; and some fiddle-players went to join fellow musicians with their fiddles hidden under their coats because they were ashamed to be seen.

POLLY DEVLIN, *All Of Us There*, 1983

MY FATHER TOLD ME HIS MOTHER came a bride to this place the year before the Famine. It was 1845. There were then fourteen houses in the townland of Gortaree – today there is only one but you can still see the remains of a few of them, just dry-built limestone walls with not even a bit of plaster inside or out. Even in my father's memory there were here and there a few of them inhabited. They might count the cattle for the summer months when they strayed far up the heather and they would dig out old turf or heather banks for to burn in the cabin. Some of them took a creel on their back and went round the farmers' houses begging. They got potatoes and would often carry a full creel home. One old man would dig out the hard white sand and take it all round the countryside to the farmers' wives and to some of the land-owners' wives for scouring the churns and for that he would get a copper or two, but these landless poor people have all disappeared this sixty years or more but you can still see where the turf was so crudely dug out and still see on an odd green spot of land the track of where the little field was tilled and let out to grass again in ridge and fur.

(G.S., Co. Fermanagh)

Ulster Folklife, vol. 5, 1959

FOR THE LABOURERS, THE SCHOOLCHILDREN, the beggars, the mill-workers, the hawkers, the poor housewives, for indeed the majority of the people, it was walk here, walk there, walk anywhere that was necessary. For many, it stretched beyond healthy exercise into the realm of hardship, especially if boots were thin or even non-existent, and more especially when icy frost or bitter rain made outings unpleasant even for the well-clad. But Mary's people were a hardy race, and if old age and hunger had not destroyed their resilience, they plodded their weary miles optimistically, holding on until St Patrick should turn up the warm side of the stone again, and spring be here.

FLORENCE MARY McDOWELL, *Other Days Around Me*, 1966

GOING WITHOUT SHOES was a mark of poverty in the culture outside the mill and factory. One of the early objectives of many female wage earners was to provide themselves with proper footwear to be worn in public, and it was not long before this item served as one of the measures of social acceptability of a job in the industry, tied in as it was with dry, clean working conditions. The weaver worked in shoes, although she might change at the factory into an old pair or into slippers. She also went to and from work properly shod, partly to maintain her image, one might assume. The mill girls, by which term was usually meant the wet-spinners, suffered by comparison on both counts. Not only were they forced to work in their bare feet, but, whether through habit, greater poverty or simple preference, many continued to travel to their jobs barefooted.

The shawl also came to symbolise poverty and low status. Once both weavers and spinners, along with other female members of the working-class, had gone about wrapped in that useful article. But the factory girls, either to differentiate themselves from those they considered to be inferior or because they acquired sooner the means to imitate the dress of the 'gentry', adopted the coat much earlier for everyday wear. The spinners, on the other hand, may have had a coat to wear to town but used the shawl for work. By the mid-thirties even they had put aside the shawl almost completely, to the dismay of Conor, who had painted them so often in the garb. Until that time, however, the coat was one of the significant status symbols of the female linen workers:

In the factory, they always went with their coat on them.
Well, the other went with their shawl on them. And that's
why one thought they were higher than the other.

BETTY MESSENGER, *Picking Up the Linen Threads*, 1975

BY THE END OF THE NINETEENTH CENTURY, there emerges a serious overcrowding problem in the area. No doubt the influx of people from rural parts seeking work and the proximity of Carrick Hill to the city's industrial heart contributed to the vast growth in numbers resident there. The newer residents were predominately poor, desperate for work and provided the human fodder which fed the burgeoning industrial city of Belfast. The conditions they lived in were squalid, basic and unsanitary. Squeezed into tiny courtyards and alleys, scores of families used the same water and toilet facilities.

Waste disposal was almost non-existent and, consequently, disease and contagion flourished in such circumstances. The area around Carrick Hill received further documentation by various social reformers in the late nineteenth century when the instances of cholera, scarlet fever and typhoid were gauged among the highest in Ireland, particularly around the slums of Pepper Hill Steps. Major slum clearance policies in the last decade of the 1800s removed some of the worst eyesores but the causes of such poverty remained – high unemployment and the discrimination against the largely poor Catholic populace meant that there was little in the way of stable income for those whose home was Carrick Hill.

By 1900 a mixture of small houses and whitewashed cottages, small courts of houses, each containing several families, rubbed shoulders with firms like Baird's Telegraph Office, the Foundry, Marsh's Biscuit Factory, Stewarts Neat Foot Oil and M. O'Connor who made clay pipes in Stephen Street. Rag stores and McCurdy's Irish Linen Stores were just some of the variety of businesses conducted on Library Street. That side of the Hill had a smell all of its own with the large stables needed for the horse-drawn vehicles belonging to the 'Tele' and Marsh's factory coupled with the piggeries belonging to Tommy Foots in Kent Street, and James McKinney. The odour was less than rosy when the droppings were brushed down an open grate into one large inadequate sewage system.

CARRICK HILL RESIDENTS' ASSOCIATION, *Green Peas an' Barley-O: A People's History of Carrick Hill*, 1989

I TURNED RIGHT INTO BEECHMOUNT. Beechmount looked like Beechmount always looked – small, unprosperous. Little terraced houses with little terraced people standing on the doorsteps. Some kids ran about the pavement as they always did and some broken glass lay around as was habitual. The walls were painted with a variety of crude scenes depicting how much nicer Catholics were than Protestants and a series of inventive tableaux in which large numbers of British soldiers were maimed and killed.

These were the Belfast mean streets, the internationally famous and dreaded West Side jungle. It was no big deal. The scorbutic children and big mamas were stock stuff. You could see worse in any city. Even as nearby as Dublin and London you could find more dramatic poverty, more profound deracination. You mightn't come across the same quality of Armalites but everything else would look much the same.

There was a species of suffering here that was supposed to be different. A crucial disenfranchisement, a particular oppression. These people, we were told, weren't living in the country they wanted to be living in. I'd been in lots of poor places and I'd never found anyone there who thought that that was the place for them.

ROBERT McLIAM WILSON, *Eureka Street*, 1996

A WISP OF PAPER CAUGHT in a wind eddy soared to roof height and, watching from Cosgrave Street below, I took flight with it. Up, up and over the moss-tinted slate acres to the clear sky beyond, in the favourite flight-dream that bubbled its way more often than any other to the top of my mind, rising through the tumble of wonderings and fancies that were there.

The laugh of the childless woman at the door brought me back, startled.

'You were miles away. Away up in the sky. Weren't you?'

Arms folded, she looked at me with a fond intensity. I turned away and ran off up the narrow street, past Newington Church. Here the bumpy cobblestones changed to sound-absorbent tarmac so that the horses' iron shoes and the heavy cartwheels would not shut out the voice of God from the Presbyterian women, with their iron stays, who worshipped in the church.

I turned the corner to the left, still running and skipping, then veered hard right into Collyer Street, stopping at number seventy-one. By a faint shade the people in this street seemed poorer than those in my own. The houses seemed even more tightly pressed together. They were not brightened up by the teams of out-of-work shipyard tradesmen who passed by regularly, offering to paint window-frames and sill for sixpence.

The people who lived in Collyer Street could not even afford the single pennies that bought music from the mandolin and banjo players with blacking on their faces – patternmakers and riveters in disguise.

In this street Uncle Thomas was the top earner, with an income of fifteen shillings to a pound a day from the docks. With only himself to keep he was the richest man in the street.

SAM McAUGHTRY, *The Sinking of the Kenbane Head*, 1977

BALLYMURPHY WAS A PLACE APART, a unique place to grow up in. As a new housing estate it lacked the roots that characterised the Falls, where people had lived in the same streets all their lives and everybody knew everybody else, where there were networks of families, cousins living in adjacent streets or down the same street. Neither did it possess the security of its own school, church, library and shops. It was badly built, badly planned and badly lacking in facilities, but it nonetheless possessed a wonderful sense of openness, there on the slopes of the mountain.

We were poor, but it didn't matter, at least not to us children. We didn't know any different, and we were too busy to notice. Besides, everyone else we knew was poor as well. The streets and the surrounding fields, the river, the brickyard and the mountain – especially the mountain – were our playground. All the families in Divismore Park had clutches of young children and we quickly made friends, girls and boys in separate peer groups, and throughout the summer months in particular our lives were lived outdoors. Everyone played skips and hopscotch and rally-oh and marleys (marbles) out in the street. Paddy and I were great ones for playing marleys out by the green box, as we called the electricity generator at the end of the street; we said it was our green box and tried to fight other kids off it.

GERRY ADAMS, *Before the Dawn*, 1996

HUGH WENT OUT BY THE BACK DOOR. The greyhound sniffed at him timidly, and then realising who it was, licked his hands and barked joyously. The roof of the goat's shed was littered with stones which children had flung on top of it. Everything about the waste ground seemed strange to him, as if his mind were dazed. The round roof of the brick yard gleamed with fresh tar, and towards the archways of the kilns men with rolled-up sleeves and red dust on their trousers were wheeling barrows of clay brick, while others came to the edge of the river and tumbled barrows of ash down the shelving side, the dust rising in a cloud, thinning out and merging into the air. The wheels cut tracks in the soft mud and now and again one of the men would sit on the shaft and gaze into the flooding river. To the right of the brick yard, children were rooting amongst the piles of paper, tins, and bottles that sheered to the water's edge. Hugh saw Frankie squatting on his hunkers and putting sticks and cinders into his bucket, but he didn't call to him. He remembered himself as a boy collecting empty bottles and the day he found university examination papers and was astounded to read that it took three hours for one paper.

He hitched a stone over the bank and when the dog scrambled after it he ran off laughing to escape from him. He came out on to the street that led to Eileen Curran's. The pavements were wet, drab-looking, and even the look on the people's faces seemed subdued and inert. The air was frosty, and over the roofs of the houses the dusk was falling and gathering into doorways and entries. A few little girls rope-swinging from a lamp-post spoke to him: 'Mister, would you tie the rope further up till we get a better swing?' The word 'Mister' pleased him. He had grown stout during his term in prison; his cheeks were still pale though no longer hollow, his black hair clipped close, his shoulders broader.

The lamplighter with his yellow pole over his shoulder passed him and Hugh turned round to see the children scrambling to pull down the rope. He had knotted it too tightly. The children ran, and from the seclusion of an entry they jeered at the lamplighter as he cut the rope and stuffed it into his pocket. He lit the lamp and a halo of weak light spread itself into the air.

MICHAEL McLAVERTY, *Lost Fields*, 1942

SHANCODUFF

My black hills have never seen the sun rising,
Eternally they look north towards Armagh.
Lot's wife would not be salt if she had been
Incurious as my black hills that are happy
When dawn whitens Glassdrummond chapel.

My hills hoard the bright shillings of March
While the sun searches in every pocket.
They are my Alps and I have climbed the Matterhorn
With a sheaf of hay for three perishing calves
In the field under the Big Forth of Rocksavage.

The sleety winds fondle the rushy beards of Shancoduff
While the cattle-drovers sheltering in the Featherna Bush
Look up and say: 'Who owns them hungry hills
That the water-hen and snipe must have forsaken?
A poet? Then by heavens he must be poor.'
I hear and is my heart not badly shaken?

PATRICK KAVANAGH, Collected Poems, 1964

THE FOLLOWING MAY IT WAS DECIDED to send me to the Lagan, and in case you don't know I'd better explain that we call 'the Lagan' all that land lying between Letterkenny and Omagh in County Tyrone. The majority of the people of that place are Protestants. Most of them are fairly well off and they hire people from the Gaeltacht. That was how the tables had turned. They would have been hired by us 'but alas, Aughrim and the Boyne were lost'.

There were four hiring fairs a year in Strabane but the May Fair was the big one. When I was a boy most of the young people of the Rosses went to the Lagan around May time. They would stay out there for the summer half of the year and come home at Hallowe'en to spend the winter half at home. When a young lad had spent a few seasons hired out in the Lagan he was ready to go to Scotland.

The May Fair was fast approaching this year and we were preparing to set off. I got a complete moleskin suit, trousers, frockcoat and waistcoat. I was very proud of the waistcoat. It was the first one I ever had. It made me look like a youth.

The Sunday before the market 'the young people of the Lagan' assembled on the white strand of An Bháinseach. They spent the time giggling and joking away, but most of them had a forlorn look – the ones who had been out before knew what was in store for them. They are homesick today as they look at the white strand and dunes of An Bháinseach and Na Maola Fionna. It would be hard to assemble them next Sunday. They will be scattered throughout County Tyrone. County Tyrone! That was the name 'the young people of the Lagan' called the land of the Protestants. There was no mention of Eoghan's Land. They were not familiar with Eoghan's Land, they only knew County Tyrone. Hundreds of them knew that Tammy Herston was in Eadaí Mór and George Ewring in Láib an Dois. But only the odd person knew that pure flowering branches of Niall Frasach were once at Tulach Óg. They had all heard of the Fair Day at Strabane, bur few had heard of 'that renowned day of the Yellow Ford'.

At any rate, the eve of fair day arrived and I got ready to leave. My father was going with me to arrange my hiring.

My mother put whatever little bits of ragged old clothes I possessed into a flour bag. She didn't say a word but her two eyes were welling up. If she had spoken she would have burst into tears; she was trying to hold them back as long as she could. My father went outdoors and looked at the tide.

'It's time we were leaving,' he said as he came back indoors. 'It is nearly eight o'clock and it will take us an hour to walk to Crolly.'

SÉAMUS Ó GRIANNA (1942),
translated by A.J. HUGHES, *When I Was Young*, 2001

O N THE ROAD SEVERAL BOYS AND GIRLS, all bound for the hiring market of Strabane, joined me. When we were all together there was none amongst us over fourteen years of age. The girls carried their boots in their hands. They were so used to running barefooted on the moors that they found themselves more comfortable walking along the gritty road in that manner. While journeying to the station they sang out bravely, all except one girl, who was crying, but no one paid very much heed to her. A boy of fourteen who was one of the party had been away before. His shoulders were very broad, his legs were twisted and his body was all awry. Some said that he was born in a frost and that he got slewed in a thaw. He smoked a short clay pipe which he drew from his mouth when the girls started singing.

'Sing away now, ye will!' he cried. 'Ye'll not sing much afore ye're long away.' For all that he was singing louder than any three of the party himself before we arrived at the railway station.

The platform was crowded. I saw youngsters who had come a distance of twelve miles and who had been travelling all night. They looked worn out and sleepy. With some of the children fathers and mothers came.

'We are goin' to drive a hard bargain with the masters,' some of the parents said.

'Some of them won't bring in a good penny because they're played out on the long tramp to the station,' said others.

They meant no disrespect for their children, but their words put me in mind of the manner of speaking of drovers who sell bullocks at the harvest-fair of Greenanore.

PATRICK MacGILL, *Children of the Dead End*, 1914

A LL THE BOYS FROM THE VILLAGES were making for Letterkenny for the hiring fair – one of four similar fairs that were held there each year. In those days, the people from the Lagan were looking for boys that would herd and give a bit of service around the house and for bigger boys that would help in the agricultural work.

I hadn't even reached my ninth year by then. I had hardly got into trousers and I don't suppose I would have been in them even then but that my mother had already resolved to send me off. All boys at that time wore petticoats until they were grown, sturdy lads. But a few nights before the fair, my aunt came over from Dunlewy with a new homespun suit for me and that was the first suit I wore and the last one I wore until I was able to buy one for myself. The day before the fair, my mother bound my little bit of baggage up in a kerchief of the kind that women wore then and, when she had done a bit of tidying around the house, herself and myself set off for Letterkenny …

There were crowds there – old and young, men, women and children. Others of my own age were there just like – though not comparing them – sheep at a fair. The big men from the Lagan were there walking about amongst us and sometimes one of them would come over to us and strike one of us between the shoulder-blades and say something to his companions about us. I remember to this day what one of them said about myself. He came over to me, caught me by the two shoulders and shook me well. 'He's a sturdy wee fellow,' he said to the man with him. At the time, I didn't know what the words meant but I remembered them and it wasn't long until I found out.

The end of the story was that two men came over to my mother and started to make a bargain with her. One of them had plenty of Irish and I think the other man had brought him with him to translate. They offered a wage of a pound for me from then until November. They went into a long story about the care that would be taken of me, about the food I would get, that I would be looked after just like one of themselves, and I don't know what else they said. My mother wasn't satisfied to let me go with them for a pound but the end of the story is that the bargain was made for thirty shillings from then until November. My new master then told me where to wait until he would be ready to collect me. Between times, my mother and myself went to an eating-house and we both had something to eat.

Up to then, I hadn't felt at all sad. But shortly now, my mother and I would be separated from each other. Up to then, everything was fresh and wonderful. The big houses and the shops and the crowds of people had taken my mind off what was before me but now a great wave of grief enveloped me. I had no further interest in anything. I was sitting on the chair in the eating-house as if my breath was choking me.

MÍCHEÁL MacGOWAN, translated by VALENTIN IREMONGER,
The Hard Road to Klondike, 1962

IN MY EARLY DAYS PEOPLE that hadn't work at home, that hadn't a big farm or something to work at, they hired with some other gentleman for six months. In every small town in the country there was a hiring fair – they had a certain day for it. There'd be an ordinary fair day and a hiring day and there was some places that had a hiring fair just on its own. They had that in the town of Clones. The hiring fair was always held in May, it would be the first or second Thursday in May in Clones, and the same in November when their six months would be up. It could happen on a fair day, or it could happen on a middle-market day, but it was Thursday always. It's well back now, over thirty-five years since I remember a hiring fair. It was the day for everyone changing places that were working. A man working for the last six months, we'll say with some man, he would be changing or maybe staying on. If he was staying on there'd be no call for him going to the hiring fair. The man would give him maybe the same wages, or maybe more, to stay for another six months with him. But the men or women that was leaving the place that they wrought for the last six months, they went to this hiring fair and hired with some different man.

JOHN MAGUIRE, Come Day, Go Day, God Send Sunday, 1973

DURING ONE LUNCH PERIOD I walked along North Street, a tumbledown part of old Newry, to the Butter Market and found myself in the midst of a hiring fair; a fair in which the merchandise was human beings. Those doing business were standing about in small groups, talking quietly; a sturdy man holding out for what he thought he was worth as a ploughman, a rosy-cheeked servant girl listening and nodding as the conditions of the offered engagement were explained to her by a farmer and his wife, a mother handing over her fourteen-year-old son on the understanding that in return for his apprentice labour on a farm he would be kept and given three meals a day and after six months she would be paid perhaps five or six pounds.

Hiring fairs were peculiar to the northern part of Ireland. Happily they are held no more.

PATRICK SHEA, *Voices and the Sound of Drums*, 1981

IN THE DAYS OF MY YOUTH capacity or desire for either political analysis or social criticism was unthinkable.

Loyalty to the *status quo* used to be a fetish with us, submission to authority was our eleventh commandment and discontent was treason or worse. A new spirit, the spirit of the times, is making itself felt, and great changes are imminent. It is largely because of that that I am going back to the period I know best to make a few more footnotes to the history of my people.

Poor as we were in those mid–Victorian days, we considered ourselves amongst the elect. Yet I well remember how nimbly and instinctively I hopped out of a policeman's line of vision as a sparrow hops out of the way of a motorcar in the crowded city streets.

Policemen, gamekeepers, and watchmen were our natural enemies. We had a right on public highways, but were only half convinced of that. The moment we stepped off the street or the highway we were trespassers.

In my childish heart there grew a hatred – an implacable hatred against the high stone walls that hid from our view the lake and the woods. I saw it a few weeks ago, and I hated it with a fiercer hatred than I did when a boy. I am told it was built during the Great Famine in order to provide work. Better a thousand times that a thousand men should die of starvation than that their children and children's children should be starved of that view which belongs to them!

A wise man once described poverty as 'the sepulchre of brave designs'. But we had no designs. We did have occasional longings for something larger and better but they flickered out before they got any hold upon us. We had subservient minds and gave without grudge whatever respect was demanded of us. 'Our betters' was no mere empty phrase. It had the sanction of religion, and was to us a religious duty. It never occurred to us that respect might have a reciprocal relation. We expected nothing, and getting it, were not disappointed.

ALEXANDER IRVINE, *The Souls of Poor Folk*, 1921

ON THE OUTSKIRTS OF ANTRIM there were already houses where Union Jacks and Ulster flags were hanging out for the Twelfth of July, even though it was only mid June. Red, white and blue bunting hung across the streets. 'I thought we might as well go this way, through town,' Helen said, 'take the scenic route, rather than go by the motorway. We're in no great hurry.' On the far side of Antrim Cate noticed small pieces of wood with messages on them nailed to the trees and telegraph poles. 'WHERE IS YOUR BIBLE?' they said, 'ETERNITY WHERE?' and 'REPENT!'.

Between Antrim and Randalstown was a stone wall which in the past had run unbroken the whole four miles, enclosing the estate around Shane's Castle. Like the other estates she knew of, it had fascinated Cate when she was a child, a fascination she knew instinctively to keep well hidden, especially from Uncle Brian. Life in there must be so different, she thought. She even half-persuaded herself that the trees themselves, which she could see on the other side of the wall, were not at all like the trees that grew around her father's farm. It would be like something out of a book, she thought. She imagined rooms full of beautiful things, and gilt-framed oil paintings of women with long pale faces; she thought of people riding through the estate on wonderful grey ponies, or doing embroidery by the fire and when they wanted tea, they would ring a bell and a maid would bring them in a tray with china cups and a silver teapot. She smiled now to remember all this. Uncle Brian used to talk about the wall and the poor local people who had built it. 'Tuppence a day and a pound of oatmeal, that's the pittance they got for their labours,' he said.

DEIRDRE MADDEN, *One By One in the Darkness*, 1996

THE BEST FLAX FIELD IN OUR DISTRICT was at the Moor Hill, where a fairy tree grew, near Rosy Campbell's house. We always had an uneasy feeling passing this house which we attributed, if we tried to reason it out at all, to the presence of the fairy tree and its omens. Certainly the atmosphere of unease there had to do with powerful superstition – but not wholly. There was a rational explanation, although as children we did not know it and breathed in the air of unease and insecurity as a natural part of things. The land bailiff had lived in that house; for even such an obscure and poverty-stricken parish as Ardboe had been part of a great estate given to an English family – the Alexanders – who lived in a great house some thirty miles distant, and who collected rents and dues until the land was ceded back to the descendants of the earlier dispossessed. If there had been a bad season, or a remittance payment from an emigrant son or daughter did not come through and the rent was defaulted on, a farmer might lose his cow, or his crop, or worst of all be evicted in lieu of payment. Though those days had gone when we hurried past the Campbell house, the insecurity and threat still lingered around it.

POLLY DEVLIN, *All of Us There*, 1983

STONY GREY SOIL

O stony grey soil of Monaghan
The laugh from my love you thieved;
You took the gay child of my passion
And gave me your clod-conceived.

You clogged the feet of my boyhood
And I believed that my stumble
Had the poise and stride of Apollo
And his voice my thick-tongued mumble.

You told me the plough was immortal!
O green-life-conquering plough!
Your mandril strained, your coulter blunted
In the smooth lea-field of my brow.

You sang on steaming dunghills
A song of cowards' brood,
You perfumed my clothes with weasel itch,
You fed me on swinish food.

You flung a ditch on my vision
Of beauty, love and truth.
O stony grey soil of Monaghan
You burgled my bank of youth!

Lost the long hours of pleasure
All the women that love young men.
O can I still stroke the monster's back
Or write with unpoisoned pen

His name in these lonely verses
Or mention the dark fields where
The first gay flight of my lyric
Got caught in a peasant's prayer.

Mullahinsha, Drummeril, Black Shanco –
Wherever I turn I see
In the stony grey soil of Monaghan
Dead loves that were born for me.

PATRICK KAVANAGH, *Collected Poems*, 1964

I WAS STANDING UP ON THE GRASS VERGE of the High Road looking down ... The flat valley-bottom's narrow at that point – just enough room for the mill buildings and the houses and not much else. The High Road is built on the first shelf above the river, and on the opposite shelf runs the railway and the main Belfast to Derry road. They converge on Annagh.

Away on the furthest, highest side of the valley rim facing me, Knockaddy Mountain, covered almost to its knob with regular afforestation, rose above the lesser, bluer Antrim hills.

Up there the roofs of the cottages are of bleeding, corrugated tin, and the people who live under them – large families packed into two–three, small, low, thick-walled, dark rooms – are as hard as the stones that break through the soil every time you strip off a sod. They haven't changed since their ancestors first arrived from Ayrshire and the other depressed Scottish shires three centuries ago, not to better themselves, as it turned out, but to mark time, strugglingly. Hill folk. The same as the other side of the valley too, behind me. In the valley, living *on* the valley, people of the same stock, but not so elemental – farmers with Land Rovers and a new bright red or blue Fordson Major every other year. And then *us*, neither one or the other – the industrials.

MAURICE LEITCH, *The Liberty Lad*, 1965

'YOU MIGHT AS WELL GO to River Side works for a job,' he says. 'It's better than working for the farmers.'

'He'll not stick it,' Ma says biting her knuckles. 'He'll do something mad and get caught in a machine or get drowned with all that water around.'

River Side was a textile factory built across a river. It was a very unhealthy place to work. Most of the young boys around the countryside got a job in there. They all said that it was until they got something better, but some of them spent all their life there.

'I know Bob Wright,' Da says. 'I'll ask him what the chances are for you to get in. He's well in there you know, in fact he might be getting promotion.'

'Okay Da,' I says. 'If he says there's a job to be done there I'll go and see about it.'

Da was an Orangeman like Bob Wright and what Orangemen would do for each other was no man's business. They could recognise each other by the way they shook each other's hand, but even if you couldn't tell by that you could tell by their names. Da's family and Ma's family too were well up in the Orange Order, we all knew that, although it's a big secret and there's no telling what you have to do to become an Orangeman. Da wouldn't even tell Ma and she could get most secrets out of most people. It had something to do with the Bible and not liking Catholics – that's all I know.

Da went to see Bob Wright over the weekend – he must have given him the right handshake because he said there was plenty of work to be done, and if I could go and see Jim Smith on Monday morning he was sure I would get a job.

IAN COCHRANE, A Streak of Madness, 1973

THE SHRINKING RURAL POPULATION is farming less and less of the area of the province. While statistics show a greater area under the plough in 1943 than any year since 1918, there is unmistakable evidence in the field that this ploughed area occupies a smaller part of the surface. The abandoned fields on hill slopes, the traces of former ridges in rough grassland and steeply sloping fields, and everywhere the mute evidence of ruined houses all point to a concentration of the remaining population in the more fertile or more accessible lands. The samples from County Fermanagh showed numbers of abandoned farms; the maps of the island there illustrated a tendency for population to flow away from the backward regions. The forsaken clachans in mid-Antrim, the large farms of north Antrim, the hill slopes of the Mournes, all showed this population drift to more accessible regions.

JOHN M. MOGEY, Rural Life in Northern Ireland, 1947

EVERY DAY WHEN THE SUN SHONE and when the children had come from school Hugh could see the old woman taking them up to the sloping fields above the brickyard. There she had discovered a sheltered hollow overtopped by a thorn bush, reminding her of a hedgy stone in the country where she used to rest with her basket on a summer's day. She always carried pieces of bread for the children and a bottle of water, which she pushed into the shade at the foot of the bush. She would spread a newspaper on the grass and take out her knitting from a green canvas work-bag which Mary had made for her. The little girls would peel off their stockings and run barefooted in the cool grass, resting now and then to make daisy chains or to hold buttercups under each others' chins.

While they played she sometimes rested her knitting on her lap and gazed down at the city – plunged in a haze of smoke, its throbbing noise muffled in the summer heat. She could see the sluggish river, the waste ground with white clothes swaying on the lines, and Johnny's fence with a yellow tin advertisement showing clearly. A longing for the country would infect her mind, and it was Lena coming back for a drink of water that would notice the tears in her eyes.

'Granny, you were crying?' she would say taking the cork from the bottle of water.

'I wasn't child – the grass makes me sneeze. Run on now and play,' and she would watch the shining bubbles racing from the mouth of the bottle.

In the evening the sun would wheel round, the bush lean its shadow in the hollow, and shreds of sunlight flicker upon her lap. Stiffly and reluctantly she would rise, lift the newspaper with the two middle fingers of one hand, and call the children. Carrying bunches of buttercups they would run to her and sit on the crushed grass to put on their shoes. Above their heads the sun shone, revealing on the bush a red piece of rotting rag. One evening the old woman saw it and a vision of Church Island on the Bann came to her – the water jabbling on the black stones of the shore, the gulls' feathers on the short grass, and on the tree that sheltered St Patrick's stone pilgrims' rags drooping from the branches. She walked home in silence. Lena took her arm, Ann carried the work-bag, and Rita the empty bottle. They kept up a senseless chatter, and pointed to Hugh who was wheeling his barrow towards the drying shed. But her mind was on another world.

MICHAEL McLAVERTY, *Lost Fields*, 1942

*J*ULY 1952. *Sounds of Orange bands playing 'The Sash My Father Wore'. The GRANDMOTHER, MAISIE and BETH as a child of eleven come dancing into the GRANDMOTHER's house, singing and giggling. They all fall laughing on to the sofa. SARAH comes in from the other side of the stage carrying a tray of tea in china cups.*

SARAH:
Beth, look at the state of you, your face is black.
GRANDMOTHER:
Ach, leave the child alone, you can't expect her to be neat and tidy all the time.
SARAH:
She looks like one of them wee street urchins from the Catholic quarter.
MAISIE *spits on a handkerchief and cleans* BETH's *face.* BETH *finds this unpleasant and struggles.*
GRANDMOTHER:
Is Sammy still sleepin'?
SARAH:
He is, he must be sickenin' for somethin'. His face is awful hot.
MAISIE (*to* BETH):
Keep still, child ... there now, that's a bit more Protestant-lookin'.

BETH:

Are all the Catholic children dirty?

MAISIE:

I never seen a clean one yet.

BETH:

Why are they dirty?

GRANDMOTHER:

It's just the way they are. They're not like us.

MAISIE:

They never scrub their front steps nor black-lead their fires nor nothin'. They're clarty and poor.

BETH:

Are we not poor?

GRANDMOTHER:

There's poor and poor. We keep our houses nice, always dress clean and respectable. There's no shame in a neat darn or a patch as long as a body is well washed.

MAISIE:

And we don't go about cryin' poverty and puttin' a poor mouth on ourselves the way they do neither. Did you hear thon oul nationalist politician on the wireless the other day? Tellin' the world about goin' to school bare-fut in his da's cut-down trousers? I would cut my tongue out before I'd demean my family like that.

BETH:

Mammy made this dress out of one of her old skirts.

SARAH:

Don't you ever go sayin' that to strangers.

BETH:

Why?

SARAH:

Because you just don't, that's why. I don't know where I got her at all. She hasn't the sense she was born with.

CHRISTINA REID, *Tea in a China Cup*, 1983

JOE'S FAMILY HAILED FROM A MARKET TOWN in County Tyrone. He and his two sisters and one brother had grown up in a three-bedroom house his parents shared with his mother's own father and mother and their son, Joe's uncle, also called Joe. His parents had had their name on a council waiting list since they were married and each time a child was born they called at the council offices to see were they any closer to the top of the list, but always it seemed there were people whose need was more urgent. It wasn't that there were no council houses to be had, there were, just not in Joe's parents' part of town. And it wasn't that Joe's parents cared particularly which part of town they lived in, they didn't care about anything beyond getting a house of their own; but the council cared, the council cared very much. The council had ward boundaries to think of, majorities to return where no majority existed. It was a hard old job, people didn't know the half of it.

Ingrid was not stupid, though you didn't need to be especially clever to see that more than one local government in Northern Ireland could not have stood without the aid of substantial rigging, even so she was staggered by the cold calculation that crammed two families – three generations, four children and five adults – into the one house.

'It could have been worse,' Joe said. 'The toilet could have been inside taking up room.'

GLENN PATTERSON, The International, 1999

TOBACCO HOLE

The rubbing boats mark the twin churches,
The priest's ravine, the rector's gentle bushes,
Donal's lamp in line with Isaac's-on-the-Hill,
Green Harbour dodging Kibby's Mill.

The women bait the thorns with half-blood knots.
Their carts assemble in the driftweed moon
Near Lady Annesley's fish-traps, where the heron
Is shot in the low tide.

The lifter herds are summering on poverty mountain.
The black bog from the meadow of the deer
To the wood of wild garlic, the vanishing lake,
Is white as the bride's show.

There's no skin from the wooden plough.
On the washed-up ladder farms; the foals' tails
Shine with the pulp of the whin, like the coastguard
In the tarted-up houses, widows' row.

MEDBH McGUCKIAN, Single Ladies, 1980

I WAS BORN IN 1911, and that was a time when Ireland was beginning to experience not only a revolution in its form of government, but an upheaval that led to a rebellion. And in 1920, when the Government of Ireland Act gave Ulster the Home Rule it never wanted, I was nine. Old enough to go daily by myself from Knock to the Methodist College on the Malone Road; old enough to see, through childish but impressionable eyes, the near-anarchy in which Northern Ireland was born.

So it is as a boy and as a man that I have grown up with the province; seen it establish itself and its security, and develop in a way that has proved, and quite remarkably, the effectiveness of a system of administration for which, at the start, few were prepared to predict success.

For me a symbol of 1920 was the tram, clanking over the square setts of the Newtownards Road and across the Queen's Bridge. We must have been a hardy race in those days, for the ends of the tram, top and bottom, were open to the wind and the rain. The drivers, winding at their brass handles, had no protection at all: in winter they were wrapped up like Sam Weller's father on the coach-boxes of seventy years before. But those things were not questioned, any more than I questioned many of the sounds and scenes of Ballymacarrett – the women in their head-shawls hurrying into the ropeworks like mourners to a wake; the scent of poverty and dirt that came from the tram's lower compartment with its shiny lengthwise cane seats. When the black, tasselled shawl was everyday wear, it was common to see mothers suckling their babies as the tram swayed along. Whatever would we think of such naturalism today? The Newtownards Road was lined with its public houses, spirit grocers and pawnshops. The three brass balls over windows that displayed the most intimate and pitiable of private possessions – blankets, boots, even the medals of the war that ended such a short time before – were the heraldry of hard times. But if I cannot say that at the age of nine I was conscious of such social conditions, there were other things to tell me that Belfast was a distressed and distressing city.

JACK SAYERS, radio broadcast, Northern Ireland Home Service, December 1960

THE WELSH MATCH

The red trams, open-ended at the top,
　　Hirpled and clanged and rang;
2d, they said, would get you anywhere.
Street-lamps, knocked up at dusk, coughed, said ahem;
　　Later, crooned lullabies.

In those days we played Wales at Ravenhill.
　　Saturday-morning's streets
Made way for scarves and favours, red and white
Insignia; gesticulating trams
　　Stormed, swaggered to the ground.

The games themselves were rarely memorable;
 The chant alone remains.
But I recall small children frenziedly
Scrambling for pennies tossed down from the trams
 On threadbare thoroughfares.

ROY McFADDEN, *Last Poems*, 2002

Bright With
Ancestral Delph

Like Hardcastle in the play, I love everything that is old —
old customs, old religions, old constitutions, and old
governments.

JOHN GAMBLE, *A View of Society and Manners in the North of Ireland*

from DREAMER IN THE GLEN

With divil a sock to our foot,
And divil the hair we cared,
We roamed the green glen then
And the little we had we shared.

Divil a barefoot child
The length of the long glen now.
The worst of the want is gone
And that's good, anyhow.

But something else is gone,
Something that grew by itself
In kitchens flagged with stone
And bright with ancestral delph.

SIOBHÁN NÍ LUAIN, *The Sally Patch*

RITE, LUBITAVISH, GLENAAN

Above my door the rushy cross,
the turf upon my hearth,
for I am of the Irishry
by nurture and by birth.

So let no patriot decry
or Kelt dispute my claim,
for I have found the faith was here
before Saint Patrick came.

The healing well by Rachray's cliff
that answers to the tide,
the blessing of the gentle bush
deep in my pulse abide.

Before men swung the crooked scythe,
I flung my hook with care,
and from the stook-lined harvest field
bore off the platted hare.

And yesterday as I came down
where Oisin's gravestones stand,
the holly branch with berries hung
thrust upright in my hand.

JOHN HEWITT, *Collected Poems 1932–67*, 1968

ALL THROUGH THE PROVINCE there are remnants of seventeenth and eighteenth-century rural industry, such as corn-mills with water-wheels, probably orange against a white wall, the whole fabric now being slowly devoured by greedy ivy and the death-watch beetle; but they still stand making a bold show beside a vivid blue cupful of water fringed with sedges, their tangled gables and sagging slates like the backcloth of a rural ballet. The scene is still enlivened by the quack, grunt, and gaggle of the farmyard, the heritage one thousand years of husbandry has bequeathed to us. Something dreadful will happen to the soul of the nation when, on the sites of such mills and barns, corrugated iron finally rises triumphant.

DENIS O'D. HANNA, *from* 'Architecture in Ulster', *The Arts in Ulster*, 1951

NOT FOR THE FIRST TIME, I wonder about the coupling of 'folk' and 'transport', and am reminded that here, 'folk' is mostly 'material culture' — cottages, a spade mill, stone walls, a schoolhouse, handlooms, churches, and a water-mill. Of particular interest is a bleach-green look-out post built like a birdwatcher's granite sangar, from which the unseen sentry could observe the linen-rustlers, then step out and boldly sound the early-warning system of his pawl-and-ratchet, whirligig-type rattle. It reminds us that Ulster culture resides more in what you do than what you say or sing or play: O linen-weavers, builders of barns, rope-winders, intricate masons! It is but a short step to the vehicle: O makers of motor-bikes and tractors! Builders of the *Belfast* and *Titanic*! Constructors of the Harlandic diesel electric locomotive commissioned by the Buenos Aires Great Southern Railway Company! Perfectors of the four-cylinder, triple-expansion, steam-reciprocating engine!

CIARAN CARSON, Last Night's Fun, 1996

CULTRA MANOR: THE ULSTER FOLK MUSEUM
for Renee and John

After looking at the enlarged photographs
of obsolete rural crafts, the bearded man
winnowing, the women in long skirts
at their embroidery,
the objects on open display, the churn,
the snuff-mill, the dogskin float,
in the Manor House galleries,
we walked among the trees to the half-dozen
re-erected workshops and cottages
transported from the edge of our region,
tidy and white in the mild April sun.

Passing between the archetypal round pillars
with the open five-barred gate,
my friend John said:
'What they need now, somewhere about here,
is a field for the faction fights.'

JOHN HEWITT, Out of My Time, 1974

IN ANTRIM, AS IN DOWN and many other parts of Ulster, one sees those great, round, fat gateposts of solid masonry, generally whitewashed. Where these have been built they tend to set up a standard for gates, for one cannot have such fine gateposts without feeling some urge to see that the gate is worthy of them. And those gateposts, plump, white and prosperous looking, give quite a character to a piece of Ulster countryside where they are common.

HUGH SHEARMAN, *Ulster*, 1949

GATEPOSTS

A man will keep a horse for prestige,
But a woman ripens best underground.
He settles where the wind
Brings his whirling hat to rest,
And the wind decides which door is to be used.

Under the hip–roofed thatch,
The bed–wing is warmed by the chimney breast;
On either side the keeping–holes
For his belongings, hers.

He says it's unlucky to widen the house,
And leaves the gateposts holding up the fairies.
He lays his lazy–beds and burns the river,
He builds turf–castles,
And sprigs the corn with apple–mint.

She spreads heather on the floor
And sifts the oatmeal ark for thin–bread farls:
All through the blue month
She tosses stones in basins to the sun,
And watches for the trout in the holy well.

The poem makes reference to ancient Irish fertility customs, 'burns the river': alters its course by setting fire to parts of the bank.

MEDBH McGUCKIAN, *Single Ladies*, 1980

ONE OF THE NOTABLE FEATURES of [Ulster] country life has always been the *ceilidhe*, the nightly gathering of neighbours in a farmhouse to talk and argue, and sing, and tell stories till 'the small hours' of morning. For if the Ulsterman has few works of fine art yet he *has* a wealth of folk-story and folk-song unsurpassed in Western Europe, and he is a natural actor. The industrial avalanche that buried so many rural peoples of Europe has only touched the hem of his life. So that all over the Ulster countryside you may still find peasants who make their own lively poems and songs as easily as they make their unique potato-bread.

Ulster retains many customs and beliefs that have vanished from the face of other European countries. Even the commonest things of daily life have here this link with the past. You may find that the peat fire which glows in the farm kitchen you visit has not been allowed to go out for two or three hundred years: every night the ashes are heaped over the embers to keep them alive. For they believe that when the fire goes out in the heart of the house, the life goes out of the people of the house. They will not tell you this, of course; you must find it out for yourself.

And those huge, twin, whitewashed pillars which are a unique feature of the Ulster countryside, and which guard and gatepost the entrance to every farmhouse and field – what are they but the old monoliths in which dwelt the ancestral spirits, guarding the exits and entrances of life?

Indeed, the whole pattern of Ulster life is one that has been worked over and perfected by countless generations of people. It is not built round the individual but round the community: and it embraces not only the living but the dead, the past as well as the present. And, because it has its feet deep in the past, you will find that the pace of life here is slower and more stable than that of the rootless industrial countries.

W.R. RODGERS, *The Ulstermen and Their Country*, 1952

LULL

I've heard it argued in some quarters
That in Armagh they mow the hay
With only a week to go to Christmas,
That no one's in a hurry

To save it, or their own sweet selves.
Tomorrow is another day,
As your man said on the Mount of Olives.
The same is held of County Derry.

Here and there up and down the country
There are still houses where the fire
Hasn't gone out in a century.

I know that eternal interim;
I think I know what they're waiting for
In Tyrone, Fermanagh, Down and Antrim.

PAUL MULDOON, Why Brownlee Left, 1980

IN THE LONG WINTER EVENINGS the oats may be threshed with flails on the hard earthen floor of the house, or perhaps some of the neighbours may 'happen in' on their 'kailyee' (*ceilidh*, a visit), and there will be fiddling and dancing and old songs and stories. All Hallow E'en and Old Christmas Day (Twelfth Night) are specially festive occasions. All Souls' Eve is sacred to the memory of the departed. After the floor has been swept and a good fire put down on the hearth, the family retires early, leaving the door unlatched and a bowl of spring water on the table, so that any relative who has died may find a place prepared for him at his own fireside. On that one night in the year the souls of the dead are loosed and have liberty to visit their former homes.

On branches overhanging the Holy Well in the glen are festoons of fluttering rags, put there by sufferers who hope that in this way they may leave their ailments behind them.

ROSE SHAW, Carleton's Country, 1930

from A WINTER NIGHT IN THE NORTH OF IRELAND

> When surly winter 'gins to blaw,
> An robe himself wi' frost and snaw;
> See roun' the ingle, in a raw,
>   The rural folks
> Sit down and pass the time awa,
>   In cracks and jokes.
>
> The grey haired couple cozey sit,
> Weel pleased to hear the youngsters' wit;
> The guidman maks and coals the split,
>   And mends the fire,
> And snuffs and smokes as he thinks fit,
>   Like ony squire.

The bleezin fire o' sod and peet,
Gars some sit back, and ithers sweat,
And thaws the amaist frozen feet
    O' rustic Will,
Wha' scoured the muirs, through snaw and sleet,
    His e'e to fill ...

The rustic smokes, and talks o' lear,
Or how folk may mak muckle mair,
By risin early, takin care,
    An spendin nane;
Nor fails to please the runkled pair,
    Into the bane.

They talk o' houses, lan' and kye,
When this ane calves, an that ane's dry,
And how folk's hurried, that maun buy
    Baith milk an' butter;
For plash o' tea, it's waur than whye, –
    It's but het water.

Neist tales o' ghaists an magic spell –
O' witches lowin out o' hell,
And tricks o' Nickie-ben himsel',
    Gae roun and roun,
Till ilka youngster thinks, pell mell
    He's comin down.

But time, that flies though we sit still,
Brings roun' the hour, that sorry Will
Maun cross the eerie glen, or rill
    O' murmurin lay:
The auld son puts him owre the hill,
    And points the way.

JOHN McKINLEY, *Poetic Sketches*, 1819

CONALL WAS THE FINEST OF COMPANY at a céilidh. I well remember
one night when he was in our house, when I was only a small boy
– I'll never forget it if I live for a hundred thousand years – for he spent
the night telling of wraiths and phantom funerals and of the fairy host. I
can still picture the bright one thousand-windowed castle which he saw
at the bottom of Na Reannacha Liatha one autumn night when he was
out lifting nets. One fine still night at the end of autumn just before the

dawn. The castle was brightly lit up and music was being played that would restore the dead to life. A boat was approaching gradually until she was within a couple of hundred yards from the bottom of the cliffs. The crew was then lulled off to sleep. When they awoke, day had half-dawned and they could see only the grey promontories of the Rosses and could hear only the melancholy moaning of the waves at the edge of the strand.

SÉAMUS Ó GRIANNA (1942),

translated by A.J. HUGHES, *When I Was Young*, 2001

JOSEPH CAMPBELL, HERBERT HUGHES and Padraic Colum were members of a literary circle that frequented the Kilmacrennan district during the early years of Irish literary revival in the borrowed tongue. Near Doon Rock, the spot where An Dálach, The O'Donnell, was crowned clan chief in the days before any Saxon bodach attempted to rule in Royal Donegal, tradition says these earnest young men held their courts of poetry.

It was there Hughes collected that beautiful air, 'The Belfast Maid', where it had survived in wordless isolation for the Lord knows how long. Collaborating with him, Campbell wrote the words of 'My Lagan Love' and together they gave us an art song that is so akin to the idiom of the people that it is frequently mistaken for a traditional song. No greater tribute could be paid to the Kilmacrennan collaborators.

It matters not an iota that down in Ballinasloe in County Galway they sing a particularly grizzly murder ballad to the same air or, shall we say, a setting of it. Hughes and Campbell were first in the field with the tune and, indeed, the song, so to them the credits must go.

PADDY TUNNEY, *The Stone Fiddle*, 1979

THE CROSS–COMMUNITY INVOLVEMENT in the first Glens Feis, an affirmation of Gaelic culture in north Antrim, resonated throughout Ireland at the time [i.e. 1904]. The event was widely reported in the Unionist press as a worthy cultural event that transcended class, creed and politics in the north of Ireland. Much was made of the fact that the last Gaelic poet of the Glens was John McCambridge, a Protestant and the author of the beautiful lament, 'Áird a' Chuain'. McCambridge was an uncle of Sir Daniel Dixon, Unionist MP for North Belfast in the early 1900s and a former Lord Mayor of Belfast ...

There are countless examples of northern Protestants actively involved in the language revival in the late nineteenth century. These included Bishop William Reeves of Down and Connor, the antiquarian and a former headmaster of Ballymena Diocesan School, Sir Samuel Ferguson, the poet and lawyer, and James McKnight, the journalist and land reformer. A native of Rathfriland, County Down, McKnight was the son of a Presbyterian native Irish speaker. A lover of the language, he was a firm Unionist in politics.

The Gaelic League, founded in 1893 by Douglas Hyde and Eoin MacNeill, attracted significant Ulster Protestant support in its early years. The Belfast branch, founded in 1895, grew out of the Belfast Naturalists' Field Club. Its first president was Dr St Clair Boyd, senior surgeon in the Samaritan Hospital and a firm Unionist who lamented the decline of 'such a beautiful and noble language'. A vice-president of the League was the Rev. R.R. Kane, the leading Unionist and Orangeman.

EAMON PHOENIX, Introduction to *Feis na nGleann*, 2005

TALKING OF THE GAELTACHT IN THE WINTER, why should it not be visited even for holidays only, as at Christmas and the New Year? This suggestion may surprise many. 'What,' they will say, 'leave our cosy frequented haunts for the bleak mountains and the wild Atlantic's verge? And what sort of a time would we have there, anyway?'

But the cityman's notion of the West in winter is erroneous. Your cities are damp and draughty, and colds are very easily got as you run from the hot theatre to the tram. Beside the Atlantic, the winter is wild and blustrous, but it is not excessively hard; there is, in fact, a mildness in the air that you don't get in the east. The rain dries away quickly under the bracing, exhilarating winds, and when there is frost, and the sun climbs through crystal air over the sharp cut distant mountains, the hard roads and the mellow slopes beckon you out for long, delightful, stimulating walks. In the relaxing summertime you see but a quarter of the beauties of the Gael's homeland.

And in winter alone can you make acquaintance with the Gaeltacht's social life. The men are now home from Scotland, and the nights are long. Now is the seanchaidhe's hour, when the turf-fire glows and the neighbours come ceilidhing. Now, too, the country dances are in swing, the fiddles and the pipes are busy. If you would get to know Irish-Ireland, the winter is your time. A little stream of initiates realising this, visits the Gaeltacht every Christmas, but winter sessions should be a feature of the Irish colleges; social sessions, if the term is permissible. Far more effective use would be made of the Gaeltacht by mixing in its social life in winter than in flooding it with English speakers (who keep to themselves all the time) in the summer. Perhaps it would be well, indeed, if lightning winter visits were not centralised at the Irish colleges, but spread over the whole Irish-speaking territories. Much would be done to save the Gaeltacht if enthusiasts penetrated into every corner of it. In Donegal, for example, the untouched Gaeldom of Fanad, Inishowen, Gweedore, Glencolumcille, etc., should be visited by little groups instead of making a mass invasion of one parish.

AODH DE BLÁCAM, From a Gaelic Outpost, 1921

WINTER NIGHTS
for Seosamh Watson

Oícheanta geimhridh agus muid ag cuartaíocht
i dtigh Neddie Eoin i mbarr na Míne Buí
bhíodh seanchiteal súicheach ag portaíocht
ar an chrochadh os cionn na tineadh
ag coinneáil ceoil le seit na mbladhairí
a dhamsaigh thart i dteallach na cisteanadh ...

Winter nights when we rambled
to Neddie Eoin's at the top of *Mín Bhuí*
A sooty old kettle lilted
on the hook above the fire
keeping time with the flames
as they danced a set on the hearth.

Hill winds clattered on the threshold
– blackguards who weren't let in –
while we composed ourselves, mugs of tea steaming in our hands,
as we sat before the storyteller,
the red sparks of his words spluttering
to life in our imaginations.

While he crackled with stories there in his corner
we'd explore the fire-place of his mind
stirring the embers of his memory
with the vexed questions of our curiosity,
as he'd hold us with yarns of the Lagan
and about the farms of East Lothian in Scotland.

His voice was warm as a bogwood fire
hissing and soughing as he
rattled off one of Burns' poems from start to finish –

'Tam O' Shanter' or maybe 'Kellyburn Braes'
and as soon as he struck up 'Scots Wha Hae'
you'd see the flames flashing in his eyes.

Smoke syllables rose from his clay pipe
when he drew down the mad horseman of *Aileach*
who'll resurrect some morning at daybreak
to defend Ireland in the War of the Two Kings
while we rode the old yellowstool
galloping to meet them in Muckish Gap.

And we hunted food with the Fianna
from *Oirthear Dhumhaigh* to the top of *Beithí*
played hurling with the heroes of *Eamhain*
on the grassy dunes of *Machaire Rabhartaigh*,
and saw the Otherworld on hallowe'en night
sporting on the road to *Fana Bhuí*.

Oh how I'd love to ramble again
these Winter nights to Neddie Eoin's,
to warm myself in the spell of his talk,
blushing in his praise –
each word a red hot coal firing
me from the hearty glow of his story.

His fire is out these twenty years
or more at the top of *Mín Bhuí*
but here in the banked hearth of my memory
a live coal or two from that fire sparkles,
and those sparks will dissolve the gloom
I feel in my heart tonight.

CATHAL Ó SEARCAIGH, translated by GABRIEL FITZMAURICE,
An Bealach 'na Bhaile/Homecoming: Selected Poems, 1993

THE OLDER SOCIAL LIFE, with the townland or a neighbourhood unit of a few townlands as its spatial extent, has virtually ceased to exist. In the Mournes and to the south of Lough Erne in Fermanagh, traces of these older ways of life persist. Everywhere there are memories of the local *ceilidhe* houses, but in almost all areas families have become isolated one from another. The base of the older social life, the system of mutual aid between neighbours, has now ceased to be essential with the introduction of improved implements and greater wealth. In our opinion, once the necessity to work together has disappeared or is disappearing, the customs of the age also vanish. There is therefore no point in pleading for a revival of the old friendliness of the countryside in the old forms. Friendliness and good relations between neighbours still exist. The aim for the future must be to build upon what is good in rural society and to erect a social framework suited to the modern needs.

JOHN M. MOGEY, *Rural Life in Northern Ireland*, 1947

THERE ARE PRIVATE STILLS in other arts than brewing: and when John the Bard said to the man who wrote these poems that he was one of the only two poets in Tyrone who had 'the right rhyme', he was admitting him to a fraternity as old as the heather-stills: it is a different technique, but both the right rhyme and the whiskey are distilled from the same heather. It is the kind of verse that comes into a man's head to keep his heart up when he has

> Fothered all the cattle, an' there's nothin' afther that
> But clockin' roun' the ashes wi' an ould Tom cat.
> An' the place is like a graveyard, bar the mare wud
>   give a stamp.

Or on a spring night in Bernish Glen when it is only

> Across the Gap
> There's light to see
> A lone crow flap
> To Athenree.

It is not folk song, and it is not pure ballad, and there is even a ghostly sophistication of the eighteenth century about it; just as John the Bard is the equivalent of Thomas the Rhymer. But it rhymes and it sings. You cannot follow the drums to *vers libre*, nor keep time to it with your fists on the table and your feet on the floor, nor dance to it in a loft. This poetry has memories of no paved streets or tiled houses unless when it boasts that

> When Derry was a village and Belfast a little town,
> We learned the holy Latin in Dungannon.

It is the kind of verse that goes to the tunes you pick up from a fiddler at fairs, or tagging with short legs behind the drums on the Twelfth.

HELEN WADDELL, Introduction to *Ballads and Verses from Tyrone*, 1929

THE HOUSE, IF OLD, IS LONG, low, thatched, and comfortable-looking. The kitchen, flagged by rough slabs from a neighbouring quarry, has little furniture beyond a large table and a bench, on which the servants sit at meals, a dresser, a rack for tin-ware, and a few chairs and stools. The front and back doors, unporched, are opposite each other. The fire is of peat, built on the hearth; a huge swinging crane over it carries the pots continuously filled with potatoes for man and beast. The best room, ill-lit by a solitary window, is boarded but uncarpeted, has a comfortless sofa and comfortless chairs stuffed in black hair-cloth. There is a chest of drawers and on it a few old books; in it, the farmer's black cloth Sunday suit, the one of his life, and the mistress's black silk dress. On the walls a sampler or two, and a few framed lithographic prints with the titles in German and English. The bedrooms have earthen floors, windows which do not open, and, if the family is large, are divided by wooden partitions into compartments, some of which have no direct light.

JOHN STEVENSON, *A Boy in the Country*, 1912

IN THE SEPIA LIGHT OF THE KITCHEN George wet strong tea from the black range. They faced each other across the blue checkered oil-cloth; on the wall smoky portraits of the Queen, Carson and Paisley, a row of faded sashes, a large drum sitting beside a disused dash-churn in one corner, alongside it a thick pile of *Protestant Telegraphs*. As a child the sound of the drum frightened Eric so much that he crept to his mother's bed at night.

'It's only Uncle George with his drum,' she whispered, 'nothin' to be afeered of.'

EUGENE McCABE, *Heaven Lies About Us*, 2005

ALL THE HOUSES IN THE AREA were thatched. Most of them had three rooms: a kitchen and two bedrooms. Usually the kitchen was in the middle with a room on either side. Our house was like that. The byres used to be against the house at that time also and, indeed, I remember seeing cows tied in some of the kitchens. Reeds were used to thatch our house and the other houses in the area. They were plentiful down by the sand-banks at Magheraroarty and everyone's land had a strip by the sea both there and at Derryconor. They have such to this day. The bogs and their limits are the same now as they were hundreds of years ago. This is the way the limits are fixed: as the reeds are cut, those along the edge are left uncut so that the owner can come along and tie what remains into knots. This is done year after year and in this way everyone knows his own. When the men were cutting reeds as I was young they had a kind of toothed sickle – a sickle with an edge something like a saw. The reeds had to be cut under the sand and they would go about the cutting on soft days when there would be nothing much doing on the land. They would often be wet to the skin at this work. Then they would sell a load of reeds for a couple of shillings and well might it be said that this was money earned the hard way.

MÍCHEÁL MacGOWAN, translated by VALENTIN IREMONGER,
The Hard Road to Klondike, 1962

WHILE WE WERE RESTING I asked about rush crosses, which are put up in many cottages at Maghera, and, gathering some rushes, Daniel McKenna showed me how they were made. He told me that on St Bridget's Eve, January 31, children are sent out to pull rushes, which must not be cut with a knife. When these rushes are brought in, the family gather round the fire and make the crosses, which are sprinkled with holy water. The wife or eldest daughter prepares tea and pancakes, and the plate of pancakes is laid on the top of the rush cross. Prayers are said, and the family partake of St Bridget's supper. The crosses are hung up over doors and beds to bring good luck. In former times sowans or flummery was eaten instead of pancakes. I have heard of similar customs in other places. At Tobermore those who bring in the rushes ask at the door, 'May St Bridget come in?' 'Yes, she may,' is the answer. The rushes are put on a rail under the table while the family partake of tea. Afterwards the crosses are made, and, as at Maghera, hung up over doors and beds.

ELIZABETH ANDREWS, *Ulster Folklore*, 1913

THERE IS NO END TO THE LORE of the lone thorn-bush. I recently asked a strong Protestant farmer in Mourne why he troubled to plough round and did not remove a thorn tree growing near a rath on his land. He expressed scorn for all superstitions, but clearly was taking no risks, for as I was leaving he called me back and, in a whisper, offered me £5 if I would get rid of the tree for him.

Then there is the hungry grass, a mountain grass of no known species which, if the unwary shepherd or hunter treads on it, brings on hunger and overpowering weakness, even if he has recently eaten: indeed 'they say it's worse on you if you're full'. The remedy is to take a bite of oaten bread, and the moral is a useful one – always carry some concentrated food when you take to the mountains, for mishaps may occur, even if you escape the hungry grass. The virtues of oaten bread, sweet milk, butter and salt, and old iron, run through many of the tales of Mourne.

Strange animals, too, may be encountered in the hills: the hare that turns to human shape, ragweeds converted by the fairies into horses, the monstrous worm that lives in the Eel Hole at the head of the pass between Hilltown and Rostrevor, and the black water-horse of Cleomack Mountain that rolls on the banks of Lough Garran on sunny days and then disappears into the water. Around Cleomack some families on May Eve still put a piece of rowantree in the shape of a cross over each door of the farm, 'even down to the door of the duck-house', to keep away ill-luck. More widely distributed is the custom of gathering May flowers and placing them, before sundown on May Eve, on the roof above the door of the house and at the well. The thatch just above the door had special virtues, for instance straws taken from this part of the house of a cow-blinker were used in the cure of a cow that had been 'blinked' by him, whose milk, that is, would not yield butter.

E. ESTYN EVANS, *Mourne Country*, 1951

THE QUERN-STONE

Lucky man
Puts his hand
On 'Cloch-Bhrón',
The Quern-Stone!

As I gaed up the Gowden Knowe
Tae fetch a stane tae mak' a quern
I spied an antick little body
Hiding i' the rankèd fern.

His face was like a tanner's thumb,
His eye a well o' wicked glee;
The cock upo' his coggie-cap
Cam' only tae my knee.

Says he, 'And what are you speiring for?'
Says he, 'And why dae you come your lane?'
'My gudewife packed me out,' says I
'Tae pick a wee white stane!'

He girned at me like a bag o' nails,
He tumbled on his peary head,
And whiles I turned tae rub my eyes
He sput on his heel, and fled!

I clambered up the Gowden Knowe,
I picked atween the rankèd fern,
And straightaway as I stooped tae pick
I found a fairy quern.

It was a fairy quern, indeed,
Wi' spots o' red and blae and green,
And rings and crosses cut on it
Most antick tae been seen.

I hoised it up and ya'en it hame,
And gave it tae my leman dear,
And she has ground her corn in it
These five-and-forty year.

And a' the dealing-folk that come
Tae barter i' the wee grey toun
Would fain buy it an I would sell –
Were't for a silver pound!

But I'll not swap an I can help,
But save it like a pinchpenny,
For it has made a lusty man
O' my ald wife and me!

JOSEPH CAMPBELL, *The Rushlight*, 1906

MY NATIVE PLACE WAS A SPOT RIFE with old legends, tales, traditions, customs and superstitions; so that in my early youth, even beyond the walls of my own humble roof, they met me in every direction. It was at home, however, and from my father's lips in particular, that they were perpetually sounding in my ears. In fact, his memory was a perfect storehouse, and a rich one, of all that the social antiquary, the man of letters, the poet or the musician would consider valuable. As a narrator of old tales, legends, and historical anecdotes he was unrivalled, and his stock of them inexhaustible. He spoke the Irish and English languages with equal fluency. With all kinds of charms, old ranns or poems, old prophecies, religious superstitions, tales of pilgrims, miracles and pilgrimages, anecdotes of blessed priests and friars, revelations from ghosts and fairies, he was thoroughly acquainted. And so strongly were all these impressed upon my mind by frequent repetition on his part, that I have hardly ever since heard, during a tolerably enlarged intercourse with Irish society, both educated and uneducated – with the antiquary, the scholar, or the humble *seanachie* – any single tradition, legend, or usage, that, so far as I can at present recollect, was perfectly new to me or unheard before in some similar or cognate dress. This is certainly saying much, but I believe I may assert with confidence that I could produce, in attestation of its truth, the names of Petrie, Sir William Betham, Ferguson and O'Donovan, the most distinguished antiquaries, both of social usages and otherwise, that ever Ireland produced. What rendered this, however, of such peculiar advantage to me as a literary man was, that I heard them as often, if not oftener, in the Irish language as in the English; a circumstance which enabled me in my writings to transfer the genius, the idiomatic peculiarity and conversational spirit of the one language into the other, precisely as the people themselves do in their dialogues, whenever the heart or imagination happens to be moved by the darker or better passions.

WILLIAM CARLETON (1867), Autobiography, 1896

from AUTUMN SEQUENCE

... Halloween.

This was the night that specially we went down,
When we were small, to the kitchen where the cook,
A Catholic farmer's daughter from Fivemiletown,

Poked up the fire in the open range and took
Her apron off and dropped her crochet work
And dropped the apples in the tub and shook

The lamplight with her laughter; quiz and quirk,
Riddle and slapstick, kept the dark at bay
Though ghosts and goblins, we well knew, must lurk

No further off than the scullery and today
The bogs, the black domain of the Will o' the Wisp,
Had closed in round our house from miles away.

No matter; apples were sharp and nuts were crisp,
She practised divination with cups of tea
And we responded in a childish lisp

To what our future brides or grooms should be,
And cracking nut on nut were unaware
Of the god that grinned at us from the hazel tree.

An ancient Celtic world had filled the air,
The cropped black sow was lurking at the gate
To seize the hindmost, and the empty chair

That creaked was creaking from the unseen weight
Of some dead man who thought this New Year's Eve,
The Celtic world having known a different date.

The white ash dropped; the night kept up its sleeve
The Queen of Apples, the Ace of Fires, the Jack
Of Coffins, and one joker. Soon we should have to leave

The lamplight and the firelight and climb back
Into our small cold beds with a small cold
Wind that made the blind in the window clack

And soot fall down the chimney on to the six months' old
Newspaper frill in the fireplace. Climbing asleep in the snow
Of the sheets I remembered again what I had been often told:

'Aye, you are here now – but you never know
Where you will be when you wake up.' I lay
Fearing the night through till the cock should crow

To tell me that my fears were swept away
And tomorrow had come again.

LOUIS MacNEICE, 1954

NEWLY BAKED SODA BREAD was pure heaven, split while still warm, buttered and spread with strawberry jam, or even blackberry or damson. This was the everyday snack of Ulster children and they asked as they came through the door: 'Give us a piece, Mammy.' One child I knew thought that the Lord's Prayer contained a request for the perpetual provision of this piece. Wheaten bread (a version of soda bread made with wholewheat flour) was also cooked at home on the griddle or sometimes in the oven, and fadge or potato bread was a griddle delicacy also ...

Bakers' bread, the kind we called fancy bread, was delivered fresh every day by the Ormeau Bakery (which still exists and sells to Canada). The baker's man was called by us children 'Billy-a-Bun' and we loved a ride on his cart.

Besides 'fancy bread' Billy-a-Bun brought us such dainties as fruit loaf and the very special fruit loaf of Hallowe'en, known as barm brack. It was welcome not only for its raisins and spice but for the treats hidden away inside in little twists of paper. Hallowe'en was a great fortune-telling time in Ulster and these miniatures had a significance for the grown-up that we did not understand. To us children a little thimble or a silvery button was just as welcome as a ring or a three-penny bit. Oh, yes, and Billy brought baps, those wonderful chewy buns brushed with sugar of which all Ulster children sang:

> My Aunt Jane she called me in,
> She gave me tea outa her wee tin.
> Half a bap with sugar on the tap,
> And three black lumps outa her wee shop.

ALICE KANE, *Songs and Sayings of an Ulster Childhood*, 1983

THIS IS LOUGH CUAN OF THE OLD Irish chronicles, the Harbour Lake; but the Northmen, when they came in their raven-crested galleys, renamed it *Strang Fiord* after the fierce current with which the tide rushes in and out at the lough's narrow neck. These warriors have left many other traces of their language in the present dialect of this countryside. When, as a boy, I said: 'He did it ram stam', I was using Old Norse *ramm-strong* meaning 'in a headstrong way', and when I spoke of a 'greip', the usual term for a garden fork, I was unwittingly employing a derivation of the Old Danish *mogreve* – a dung fork. 'Blather' comes from Old Norse *bladr* – to speak inaccurately, and 'full', meaning drunk is derived from *fullr* with the same meaning. When they say in County Down: 'He's gleg at the uptak!' you may not realise that it means: 'He is quick to understand,' but to a Viking it would be quite clear, for he would know that *glögg* means 'clever or clear-sighted' and *upptaka* 'understanding'.

The vernacular resembles in many respects the idiom of Burns, for in the days of the Plantations numerous families from Scotland settled in 'the Ards' as this district is called. The hills are 'braes', the brooks 'burns', the curlews 'whaups', and the cormorants 'skarts', and you will hear 'gey' and 'bonny' and many another homely word; and some of these, too, such as 'skart' and 'brae' have come from the old Viking speech. There is a steep hill at Killinchy descending to the churchyard called 'Lang-hame Brae': In Old Norse *lang* is 'long', *heim* is 'home', and *brae* 'hill'; so we have: 'The Hill leading to the Long Home' – the grave. If you are not familiar with the dialect you may, at first, find it difficult to understand what the friendly folk say, and even those accustomed to it may come across baffling words and expressions. Once I met a boy who spoke of finding 'gurkin' on the lough shore. Perhaps he meant a kind of edible seaweed, but to this day I have never been able to find out. 'It tastes like hens' feet, only more weasly', was his description of the delicacy. They are a sturdy, independent people in the County Down – 'As fine folk as ever put hats on their heads', as a Southerner once said to me. You have only to see their farms, groups of small fields enclosed with stone walls, often with the rock cropping out in the meadow, to admire their patient, indefatigable industry. The housewives seem to be always baking. How pleasant it is to come home tired and hungry when you know that the fragrance of potato-cake and soda farls will welcome you as you approach the half-door. Ancient traditional customs still survive, for I have seen in cottages above the fireplace the 'churn' plaited from the last wisp of straw after the harvest.

EDWARD ALLWORTHY ARMSTRONG, Birds of the Grey Wind, 1940

EVERYWHERE IN IRELAND there are to be found survivals of the speech introduced by Englishmen in the old days and forgotten or disused among Englishmen today. In Ulster, however, especially outside the industrialised and Scotticized north-east and the larger towns, there are more than anywhere else, and they are of the language of the first colonists, the language of Shakespeare, of the Jacobean Privy Council, of Chichester, and of Davies. When James wrote of a 'civil Plantation' he used the adjective as it is still used in Ulster; 'civil' is orderly, and 'civility' means orderly behaviour more often than courtesy. Chichester's description of Audley as 'near to himself' stands for any close-fisted fellow. Davies's 'prosperably' is a common version of prosperously – and how much handsomer! His hope that the Ulster Irish would learn 'to love neighbourhood' – to live in communities in neighbourly fashion – also embodies a current phrase. A 'cross man' is, not a man in a temper, but a cross-grained man. A schoolboy does not crib but 'cogs', a word which implies foul throwing of dice. A girl who has 'great resort' is one very fond of (male) company – a fast minx. If you ask your way in hill country you may be told that your road later becomes 'dangersome' for a car. If you visit a lonely farm at night the owner will offer you a wee drop from 'the bottle in the press'. He may then volunteer to 'convoy' you as far as the main highway. And if it is not raining – perhaps, indeed, if there is only a little rain – he will speed you on your way by observing that it is 'a brave night'.

Sometimes the Elizabethan or Jacobean form is one that is still current English but has ceased in England to be the usage of the people. 'He'll rue the day he crossed me'; 'I'd as lief go without', are anyone's phrases in Ulster. Sometimes a word has disappeared, like the Shakespearean 'renage', for, back out of an undertaking, change one's coat: 'I thought he was to be trusted, but he renaged on me.'

CYRIL FALLS, The Birth of Ulster, 1936

I N THE DISTRICT AROUND LURGAN and Portadown, where hand–loom weaving is an industry largely in evidence, many words and phrases are current that would be quite unintelligible to a native of Carrickmacross or Cootehill. To take a still more concrete example, the speech of the Ards is entirely different from that of the kingdom of Mourne, while that in its town differs from the language used in that portion of the Bann valley lying between Ballyroney and Lawrencetown, although all three districts are in the same county. With a greater intervening space, the strongly marked Lowland Scotch accent and phraseology of County Antrim is widely different from the Gaelic intonation of 'dark Donegal'.

This will serve to indicate the extent and variety of districts into which Ulster may be divided, for the purpose of recording its dialect, in the forming of which the two predominating factors seem to have been the native Gaelic, which even a century ago was largely spoken in many districts where it is now unknown, and the Lowland Scottish speech of so many of the Plantation colonists.

Ulster speech differs from that of the other three provinces in being more abrupt and decisive, taking its tone from the character of the people – a character that to strangers seems somewhat harsh and discourteous, contrasted with the suavity of the South. That this is not the downright boorishness some would have us believe, but the earnestness that, in looking at the realities of life, is somewhat prone to neglect the courtesies and amenities of society, is evidenced by the Ulster saying – 'Too sweet to be wholesome'. This sincerity of character has its effect in directness of speech, and a tendency to clip letters or syllables, where possible, off words. In Ulster the words 'old' and 'cold', for instance, are generally called *owl* and *cowl*, softened as we proceed southwards in *owld* and *cowld*; while the Antrim 'caddié', in Mid–Ulster counties, is softened into *caddie*, pronounced soft like Clady, in the ballad –

> This is the banks of Clady, fair maid, whereon you stan'.
> Do not depend on Johnnie, for he's a false young man.

This illustrates the shortening process, where stand is made *stan'* to rhyme with man. Another instance of this directness and use of words in their shortest possible form is the Ulsterman's treatment of the terminal letter 'g', which he seems to regard as altogether unnecessary and superfluous, and to be omitted whenever possible from his 'comin' into the world till his dyin' day'.

JOHN J. MARSHALL, 'The Dialect of Ulster', *Ulster Journal of Archaeology*, vol. 10, 1904

T HIS REGION OF SOUTH TYRONE, Fermanagh and Monaghan is rich in folklore and ancient ways. The customs of May Eve are still alive and it was hereabouts that I stumbled on the current belief in the Fairy Spade. 'Of course I believe in it,' said a south Tyrone farmer, 'and why wouldn't I, for who is going to say what is the right way of it at all. I wouldn't start to the building of any house before I'd plant a new spade on the standing of it. And I'd be watching that same spade all night to see would the geltne people move it. And if they didn't do that I'd know the house would be lucky on me.' It's in this countryside too you'll see the mountainy cottages with their *corrags*, or 'ould men', standing at the door to keep away the blasts of wind, and a *corrag* nothing but a bundle of heather tied with a bit of an old rope. And the men of this region still light their pipes with a *griosach*, a live ember from the turf fire which they often miscall a *greesh* now that the Irish language is no longer spoken here, and offer that same pipe round the company for 'a wee pull' in friendship – the Irish pipe of peace.

You'll hear the grandest talk in the world round the turf fires of the Slieve Beagh country, as I know from experience, and many a turn of expression will take you straight back to the days of the first Elizabeth. A 'boon' is a company hereabouts, 'gentle' means haunted or fey, to 'join' is to begin, to 'convoy' is to accompany, 'diet' is the word for food, and you 'cut' the sign of the cross instead of making it. In one of my notebooks I have this sentence, gathered long ago in these parts: 'If you have a fatigued suit of clothes you would bestow on a body I would redd your bit of a garden for you and bring my own diet.' And I have this too: 'She took out a trinnell of bread and buttered me a whang of it, and she gave me a noggin of bunya-rowar to kitchen it.' 'Kitchen' is the common Irish word for anything supplementary to the main meal, so that you might have a meal of boiled potatoes with a herring for 'kitchen', and 'bunya-rowar' is almost perfect Irish for thickened milk. As I have remarked, the Irish language is no longer spoken here, but it lingered late and the English dialect of the region is sprinkled with a multitude of both Gaelic and Tudor-English survivals.

I have a lively remembrance of a conversation between two farmers of this district. They were discussing some commodity or article that was very scarce, and one said to the other: 'Are they all that scarce?' 'Scarce!' replied the one who was questioned, 'listen man: even if you worked in a saw-mill you could still count them on the fingers of the one hand!'

RICHARD HAYWARD, *Border Foray*, 1957

from OVERTURE FOR AN ULSTER LITERATURE

Our speech is a narrow speech, the rags and remnants
of Tudor blades and stiff Scots covenanters,
curt soldierly despatches and puritan sermons,

with a jap or two of glaar from the scroggy sheugh,
the crossroads solo and the fair-day ballad.

But even this bare tongue will serve our purpose
if we're obedient to the shape of the land,
to the shifty weather with its crazy habit,
cold and dry in the spring, wet in the summer,
dry again at the heels of the Lammas floods.

We can make something of it, something hard
and clean and honest as the basalt cliffs,
patchy with colour like the coast in July,
bold as Slieve Bernagh and the bald Mourne peaks,
flat and reflecting as a Lough Neagh sunset,
as nourishing as potatoes out of the mould,
maybe not more shapely than the potato.

JOHN HEWITT (*c.* 1955), *Collected Poems*, 1991

THE OLD CLOCK TICKS AND STRIKES as strongly and timely as ever after 143 years. It tick-tocked through the rebellion of 1798, the big wind of 1839, the famine years of 1845–6, the religious revival of 1859, the land agitation of 1871–80, the Home Rule crisis of the opening decade of the twentieth century, the great war of 1914–1918, and the greater war of 1939– . It looked down on scenes both grave and gay, on births and deaths, hopes and fears, successes and failures. It sounded at dawn the hour for the toiler to turn out to his task, at even-tide for little ones to say their prayers and get to bed. Now it is mine, and, like Hugh Miller in the matter of his grandmother's wedding ring, 'I would hesitate to exchange it for the Holy Coat of Treves, or for wagon-loads of the (so-called) wood of the Cross.'

Many things were in that 'good' room ... On the walls were three framed pictures or portraits – Queen Victoria, dressed in deep mourning, visiting a Highland cottage; the Rev. Dr Henry Cooke, celebrated Ulster divine, who came often to pay rent for a relative in one of grandfather's houses, and William Ewart Gladstone. These three pictures symbolised the dear and durable things for which the home stood – loyalty to the Throne, the Presbyterian religion, and Liberalism.

THOMAS M. JOHNSTONE, *The Vintage of Memory*, 1942

MY FATHER WAS BORN IN THE PARISH of Carnmoney, near Belfast, about 1768. He was brought up on a farm occupied by his father on the face of the Cave Hill, not far from what is now known as Greencastle. I have heard him tell how, one day in 1778, when on the brow of the hill along with some other boys, he witnessed the sea fight between the celebrated Paul Jones in the *Ranger* and a British war vessel on the lough below. My father belonged to an old Irish family long settled at Lecale in County Down, where residents of his own name may still be found. His mother's maiden name was Blanche Brice, who was lineally descended from the Rev. Edward Brice, minister of Broadisland or Ballycarry. Edward Brice settled there early in the seventeenth century, and was the first Presbyterian minister who came to Ireland from Scotland about the period of the Ulster Plantation. In the course of time some of his descendants removed from Kilroot, near Carrickfergus, their original home in Ireland, to the neighbourhood of the Cave Hill, and a number of them have since been elders in the congregation of Carnmoney.

W.D. KILLEN, *Reminiscences of a Long Life*, 1901

IT IS NOT SO EASY, EVEN WITH the help of grandmother's grandfather, to visualise the clothing worn by the commonalty. They must, of course, have been dressed very much after the manner of young William Filluna, who had run away from the widow Morrison:

On Sunday, 28th of this instant July, 1750, a little boy named William Filluna, about 14 or 15 years of age, a servant belonging to Widow Morrison, nigh Clady, near Templepatrick, being sent with some money to pay a cow his mistress had bought from a man nigh Connor, did not go, but went off and carried the money with him. The boy has short red hair, and had on when he went away a coarse linen coat and waistcoat, much worn, a pair of old leather breeches and black-yarn stockings, and a pair of new broags and a coarse shirt and an old hat. Whoever takes up the said boy and confines him in any gaol and sends word to the said Widow Morrison or to Samuel Birney, at Clady, in the county of Antrim, nigh Templepatrick, shall have half a guinea reward paid by said Widow Morrison or Samuel Birney. N.B. The said boy had been guilty of stealing money and a watch from a master he once lived with before, for which he was try'd for his life in either Dublin or Armagh.

Then there was a William Wilson who robbed the widow Creighton of Ballymena of a hickory stick varnish'd yellow and sevenpence in cash; he wore a brown rateen coat, strip'd vest, brown leather breeches, light blue stockings, and a brown wig. A William Rea ran away from Downpatrick and feloniously carried with him a parcel of wearing cloathes, the property of Richard Mulloy, of Downe, baker, to wit, a light-coloured surtout coat with a velvet cape, a feather shagg red-coloured waistcoat, and a scarlet pair of breeches. A deserter, William Miller, of Clough, had on when he ran away a grey rateen coat with a white velvet cape, a scarlet waistcoat with white buttons, a white wig. and short black hair; and a Thomas Egan, who ran away from his master, James Donaldson, of Castle Dillon, County Armagh, wore a black coat, strip'd waistcoat, leather breeches, sharp-toed boots strapt behind, and a black wig.

All these things, except perhaps the leather breeches, suggest that the poor were dressed in the cast-off clothes of the wealthy. Apart from the beautiful things worn by lords and ladies, there were many materials, said my grandmother's grandfather, which people have forgotten. There was, for instance, to be sold by James Hood, of Ballymena, a good sortment of English and Irish broadcloths, Forrest cloths, German serges, sarge denims, worsted and hair shaggs, cotton thick-setts, jeans, fustians, cloth sarge, linings, rateen, beaver druggets, lastings, velvets, sattings, persians, riggs, poplins, crapes, chamblets, stuffs, callamancoes, damasks, sattiniscoes, padaway serge.

L.R. CRESCENT, *In Old Belfast (1740–1760)*, 1924

T HE MAKING OF FLANNEL I MUST write about! The yarn was spun by my mother. The wool was mixed, so much black and say twice as much white, and the thread spun as fine as possible and rolled into hanks. Those hanks had to be converted into flannel. There was only one weaver and he lived ten miles away. The loom was old and the cloth was woven by hand, very loosely. I can remember the weaver throwing the shuttle from side to side, and twenty yards of flannel was put together. It looked like a mottled tweed. The pony or donkey was used for carrying it home. Then came the task of thickening it.

It seems to me now a strange procedure. All those yards of flannel were arranged on a big board on the barn floor. The men rolled up their trousers and they so arranged themselves that their bare feet would meet the flannel. My mother or a helper would pour warm soapy water over it and the men would move the flannel vigorously with their feet – left, right, and so on until it was the desired thickness. Next day it was washed free from soap and put out to dry on the hedges. Some of the flannel was coloured, a reddish brown. The moss for colouring was picked from stones in the rocks. I think that was the only colour. The flannel was made into shirts, waistcoats, and perhaps underpants and petticoats for the old people. I think the first pants the boys wore were made from this grey flannel. It was great wearing and lasted for years.

I have what I am sure is the only handmade bedspread in this country. The reddish flannel was tacked to a frame and lined, and the women stitched it back and forth and cross-ways, until it was finished. Later on I saw bedspreads made, but they were sewn on a tailor's sewing machine. My mother managed to make a few petticoats for some of the old people who were so very poor.

This whole thing was the only sort of life – comings and goings – and still the people had plenty of enjoyments, like weddings and a ceili. After the old people died, or the young left, they were there in their sorrow to help. Now, years afterwards, the houses are empty; no one to take care of anything; the old have died and the young emigrated. Eventually the houses were only ruins; the children had finished their schooling and left.

KATHLEEN SHEEHAN, Ulster Folklife, vol. 31, 1985

THE QUILTING

I hold the quilt in my hands.
The blue and white squares fall
Over my feet and out and over the floor.
The blue is twilight now and the white is white no more.

Fifty years ago,
Six girls came into the kitchen,
Light-frocked, laughing and happily bundled together,
Over the cool worn tiles, and out of the hot June weather.
Not quite out of the sun
That followed them into the kitchen;
Sun on the scrubbed deal dresser; sun on the coloured delph
Shadow on open hearth, on hanging brown book-shelf.

There was the quilting frame
With the quilt set in awaiting
Flurry of silver needle, white thread and golden thimble;
Wise fingers, golden helmed, for the helm is Minerva's symbol.

Sweet silence! All brows bent
On the work that lay before them.
From opposite sides of the frame went the fingers fleeting,
Till they laughed again at the golden thimbles meeting.

What do their likes do now
In the glen where I was born?
Are there young girls there at all?
Are they gone across the water
Taking on alien roads their small skills and their laughter?

I left the glen long ago
And I never once went back.
I don't know what became of the heads of brown and gold
Their quilt is faded now, but their quilting stitches hold.

SIOBHÁN NÍ LUAIN, The Sally Patch, 1971

PUSHING OPEN THE HALF-DOOR, we are welcomed, given the seat of honour at the fire, and offered a drink of sweet milk. 'I wish you well of your cattle,' should be the reply, but you must not praise the children – call them rather 'rogues, rascals and tories' – lest the fairies should take them. Here in the kitchen everything has its proper place, and there are right and wrong things to say, lucky and unlucky things to do. Stones and trees and birds around the house, too, may be lucky or unlucky. The general layout of the kitchen in the old-style house is much the same everywhere, though details vary from one part of our region to another. Along the shore, for instance, light was procured from fish oil burning with a rush wick in a cruisie which, to allow the smells to escape up the chimney, stood on a wooden ledge in the wall-hole on the right side of the fire. On the back side the long 'resin slut', in a wrought iron holder, gave better illumination for the hemmers. When paraffin came in it was first brought with other goods from Belfast to Annalong in the returning stone-coasters.

Near the fire, against the back wall of the house, is the settle-bed, a bench by day and a bed by night; and on the opposite side a small window which gives light to the hearth. A small table lies against the wall between the window and the door, leaving the centre of the room free for passage to the hearth. The dresser, with its rows of shining delph, its bowls, platters and a noggin or two, lies opposite the fire at the end of the room. A creepie and some straw-seated chairs complete the furniture, apart from the churn, baking board, an ark for oatmeal and a crock for water drawn from the well.

The fire on the hearth is the sacred flame around which the life of the family revolves, and many are the beliefs and superstitions attaching to it. The iron crane with its many fittings, which replaced the crook-stick and chain when the stone chimney breast took the place of the wattled chimney brace, is often an elaborate piece of machinery ... The crane, like the farm gates, should swing 'with the sun' for luck. Some cranes were fitted with a windlass enabling the largest iron pot, taking a hundredweight of potatoes at a boiling, to be lifted on and off the fire. Here were suspended, over the open turf fire, the pots and griddle and other cooking appliances. Oatcakes, butter, porridge and eggs were sup-plemented, and in poorer homes replaced, by the potato: a stone a day, and very little else, was eaten by farm labourers. In difficult times, resort was had to boiled charlock (pressiagh) and the haws of the may-tree (skeehony), to seaweeds and shell-fish.

E. ESTYN EVANS, *Mourne Country*, 1951

PALIMPSEST

I pace these lanes where progress and decay
scribble wry palimpsest across the scene;
the raw byre gable shoulders concrete-clean
where once a reeking midden seeped away;
the tractor treads have sliced into the clay
but left a middle track still clover green;
once homesteads, now those wallsteads bulge and lean,
and nettles flower where children used to play.

And all those old men gone, those slow old men,
whose thumbs were thick with skills I could not share,
at loanen-end or gate, shall not again
foregather, nor at church door or the fair,
the shepherd, scythesman, blacksmith, carpenter,
as life drains surely down the tree-dark glen.

JOHN HEWITT, *Loose Ends*, 1983

IT WAS A SMALL KITCHEN, contriving to hold an enormous quantity of dissimilar things. Diagonally opposite the outer door was a staircase almost like a ladder ascending into the ceiling. Under the one window with its geranium stood a table set out with American oil-cloth, an oil lamp, sundry cups and saucers, a heap of home-baked bread, a basin of chicken food, a pair of boots, a hammer and a tabby cat. Under the table was an array of saucepans, tin bath-pans and a stock-pot, all dirty from use during the day. Between the table and the staircase, the remaining space was taken up by an open fireplace, black with soot, and heaped with cinders that had been accumulating at the back of the fire for years. A kettle, as black as everything around it, rattled its lid unheeded, and a cauldron of mash smoked at the side. The eternal teapot simmered on the hob. Beside the fire was a high-backed oak chair, old and sooty-looking too, with a cushioned seat of torn patchwork, its legs and arms heavily dented. A coarse cloth that had once been a hearth-rug lay before the fender. At the foot of the staircase was a dresser, very upright, groaning beneath the weight of crockery, tin basins, teapots, glassware, fishing-tackle and ropes that encumbered it. Across the wall farthest from the fire and almost hindering the opening of the outer door was a long wooden settle, also cushioned in torn patchwork, while between it and the dresser was a corner filled with everything that can possibly be found in a Rathnaheena kitchen inhabited by four people. Two great buckets of spring water stood beside a bunch of six-foot 'sheafing' rods, and oilskins and heavy waders hung from hooks, along with dead hens and a field-lantern.

OLGA FIELDEN, Island Story, 1933

THE SETTLE BED

Willed down, waited for, in place at last and for good.
Trunk-hasped, cart-heavy, painted an ignorant brown.
And pew-strait, bin-deep, standing four-square as an ark.

If I lie in it, I am cribbed in seasoned deal
Dry as the unkindled boards of a funeral ship.
My measure has been taken, my ear shuttered up.

Yet I hear an old sombre tide awash in the headboard:
Unpathetic *och ochs* and *och hohs*, the long bedtime
Anthems of Ulster, unwilling, unbeaten,

Protestant, Catholic, the Bible, the beads,
Long talks at gables by moonlight, boots on the hearth,
The small hours chimed sweetly away so next thing it was

The cock on the ridge-tiles.
        And now this is 'an inheritance' –
Upright, rudimentary, unshiftably planked
In the long ago, yet willable forward

Again and again and again, cargoed with
Its own dumb, tongue-and-groove worthiness
And un-get-roundable weight. But to conquer that weight,

Imagine a dower of settle beds tumbled from heaven
Like some nonsensical vengeance come on the people,
Then learn from that harmless barrage that whatever is given

Can always be reimagined, however four-square,
Plank-thick, hull-stupid and out of its time
It happens to be. You are free as the lookout,

That far-seeing joker posted high over the fog,
Who declared by the time that he had got himself down
The actual ship had been stolen away from beneath him.

SEAMUS HEANEY, *Seeing Things*, 1991

THE SETTLE BED DROPPED DOWN on hinges when used as a bed, and
served as a table when folded up. It was the same in everybody's
house then, always kept in the kitchen. I knew an old cottar who lived
in a wee house with just one bay, it served as a kitchen, bedroom and
parlour. A neighbour went to his house one time to get him to work.
After knocking at the door he couldn't get in for he was in bed and had
sure to wait till he dressed and buckled up the settlebed. He was quite
happy for he said 'Och' says he 'I'm not afraid of thieves getting in for
when I let down the settlebed it bars the door.' Really I have seen people
in these old houses sitting on stones, hadn't even a chair in the house, but
they were the poorer class. Others had roped chairs, the first of these sort
of chairs were roped with oat straw twisted fine and braced round the
wooden frame of the chair. Then later these were roped with manilla, it
made a finer job and easier to sit on.

One thing much appreciated was the salt-box. It was made of wood
with a slanting lid on hinges. When closed it looked like a house with a
high wall on one side slanting down to a lower one and roofed over. I
know a house this shape and its called the salt-box still. These boxes held
about a stone weight of salt. The old woman of the house was very
careful about salt.

(W. McM., Co. Down)

Ulster Folklife, vol. 5, 1959

from THE STORM

Old Annie Millar of Kildonan farm
Sits by her hearth, determined to get warm.
Happed on her creepy, like a roosting hen,
She plies the bellows with the zeal of ten,
While at her feet the collie and the cat
Make one furred tangle on the patchwork mat,
And faint, premonitory, murmurs tell
That water soon will boil, and all be well;
For Annie, in her four score years and three,
Has found no friend unchangeable as tea.

So now, as comfort creeps along her veins
She eyes, with unconcern, the streaming panes,
And pictures, smiling to herself, out bye
Beltie, securely grunting in his stye;
And how, full fed, the very ducks forsake
The haggard, now a chill, unsavoury lake
To nest, where wadded in their plumage white,
The Leghorns squat, mistaking day for night.
Then, to increase content, she turns to see
The little room, her life's epitome:
The food appointed for her mid-day spread,
Butter, and eggs, and jam, and soda bread:
Her father's clock: the text in red and blue
Worked by her mother when her days were new;
And plenitude of Christmas nick-nacks sent
By unknown grandchildren: the colours blent
Of tartan rugs; and on the window sill
Where one geranium flouts the winter's chill,
The Bible and the *Life of Henry Cooke*,
'Old Moore', 'Bell's Standard' and the knitting book.
The pots and pans, the washtub: all the gear
That serves her busy hands from year to year;
The hearth, the dresser furnished out with delft;
The black-nosed spaniels on the mantle shelf:
The painted scene, where, through Cerulean tides,
Brave, on his pawing steed, King William rides.

NESCA ROBB, Ards Eclogues, c. 1974

IN BALLYCLARE THERE WAS ONE of the most wonderful shops in all the world – Fanny Cannon's. It was on the left as one proceeded down the Main Street, a toy shop joined to its house in which Fanny lived. From her front room as she sat crocheting, Fanny, a tall, iron grey woman, could see into her shop through a glazed door. To serve, she merely had to lay down her work, push her spectacles to the top of her head and step into the shop. On Christmas Eve, 1904, Mary and Little Sister clasped one another's hands as they jostled and shoved their way through the crowds of Christmas shoppers on the pavement of Main Street. Light and dark were intermittent in the early evening, as one moved from shop window to shop window. It was said that the new Urban Council, only two months old, was going to provide street lighting with oil lamps just as good as in any great city. In the meantime, light was fitful from the lamp of one gay window to the next.

Moving candlelights on the muddy street showed the dark moving shapes of horse-traps and pony-traps, the sidecars and the huge black swaying boxes of the bakers' vans. Swinging hurricane lamps hung from the trambs of stiff carts. The girls had to be on the look-out for cars and carts left on the pavement edge, shafts in the air, their horses gone to the livery stables and their owners to the shops. An occasional brilliant white light piercing the darkness came from the still rare bicycle. No light at all illumined the infrequent horseman.

FLORENCE MARY McDOWELL, *Roses and Rainbows*, 1972

Most of the towns in this county [i.e. Derry] still show fragments of the original Plantation defences. The bawn or defended manor-house at Bellaghy is a case in point, where one of the great corner towers is still intact, as well as much bawn wall. The adjoining farm buildings incorporate a considerable amount of original work. Some fresh whitewash and light green paint would enhance a building which has much merit. Somehow, I know not why, in the bawn of Bellaghy, Ireland has gone momentarily French, though it is difficult to say why a district so essentially English should look French.

There is nearly always a Planters' Gothic church, either in use or in ruins in the Derry towns. Why so many new churches were built about seventy years ago, when there stood the makings of a charming old parish church, crying out for renovation, I do not know. In Ulster we do not prize our traditions sufficiently, and we would do well to remember that the nation with the greatest future is the one who can best appreciate her past.

DENIS O'D HANNA, *The Face of Ulster*, 1952

CUSHENDUN

Fuchsia and ragweed and the distant hills
Made as it were out of clouds and sea:
All night the bay is plashing and the moon
    Marks the break of the waves.

Limestone and basalt and a whitewashed house
With passages of great stone flags
And a walled garden with plums on the wall
    And a bird piping in the night.

Forgetfulness: brass lamps and copper jugs
And home-made bread and the smell of turf or flax

And the air a glove and the water lathering easy
And convolvulus in the hedge.

Only in the dark green room beside the fire
With the curtains drawn against the winds and waves
There is a little box with a well-bred voice:
What a place to talk of War.

LOUIS MacNEICE, Poems 1925–1948, 1949

IN MY CHILDHOOD I WAS FORTUNATE enough to live for several years in the household of a small farmer, Alexander Gaw. Alexander was about seventy at the time, heavily bearded and his shoulders bowed by hard work. He divided his time between his five acres of land (or four, really, for one of his fields was marred by a whin knowe), and his harness-making business which he carried on in a lean-to at the gable of the house. His daughter 'took in flowering', that is to say, she acted as an agent for several of the linen firms in the city of Belfast, and distributed embroidery work to the needle-women of the district. These activities of the Gaws made their hearth a meeting place for their neighbours. In the evenings, when their day's work was done, the young men came with broken harness and wrenched buckles for Alexander's attention. The farm women, with their skirts kilted against the wet grass of the fields, would bring their finished embroidery. There was talk around the hearth of crops and markets, births and deaths, and if someone had brought a paper Alexander read it aloud, down to the (*Government Cheers*) and (*Opposition uproar*).

No one outstayed his welcome. When all the transactions had been settled the company rose to go. Several of the young men and women found that their homeward road lay over the same paths, and where they had arrived singly, or in twos, now a little cluster of lamps moved over the dark fields.

When the last neighbour had gone, supper was set on the table. Alexander usually had hot buttermilk, the rest of the family, tea. When the meal was finished Alexander took down the family Bible and read a few verses. It was now evident why the evening meal was delayed until the neighbours had gone. This hour was reserved for the dignity and privacy of the family. When the reading was finished the family knelt at their chairs and Alexander prayed. Experience had taught the younger members of the household to rise from their knees reluctantly, as it were, and to stifle any sigh of relief. Alexander could withdraw hand and eye from heavenly contemplation with devastating speed.

SAM HANNA BELL, Erin's Orange Lily, 1956

I HAVE IN MY MEMORY A RICH STORE of sights and sounds and smells that I laid up in William's forge; the dazzling, quivering glow of incandescent metal as it was drawn from the fire; the intense white radiance of the fire itself when the bellows were in full blast, and the blue flame that played over it when the bellows were at rest – which was not often when I was in the shop; the flat sheets of sparks that flew beneath each stroke of the great sledges; the clank and wheeze of the bellows and the roar of the fierce flame; the upthrown head and clattering hoofs of a startled horse; the restless pawing of an impatient one; the alternate thud and ringing clink as William struck the softened metal and his anvil time about, for some occult reason known to blacksmiths only, though I was always careful to follow his practice myself when he allowed me to spoil a shoe now and then; the short, sharp hiss as he plunged a finished shoe into the cooling-trough; the inky water in the trough, from which, for some odd reason, I first formed a visual image of the River Styx; the light fragments of iron leaf that floated thereon, and the thin steam that wandered over its surface; the smell of burnt hoof and singed apron; the thick smoke that hung above our heads and stole away little by little through the open door.

LYNN DOYLE, An Ulster Childhood, 1921

THE PEOPLE

The children come out on the moorlands
  With wide-eyed solemn air;
They have bright dresses and the wind
  Stirs in their brown hair.

The women are afoot from dawn
  About their ancient rights;
They fodder the shilty and the cow;
  They make red tea at nights.

The hillmen go after their sheep
  And at evening return
To the white walls and the settled reek
  From the peat-clods they burn.

JOHN LYLE DONAGHY, The Flute Over the Valley: Antrim Song, 1931

THE COLLECTING OF TALES AND LEGENDS – as well as of other items of folklore – required, and, requires, a studied and sensitive approach.

The storyteller could be shy: could be hesitant to trust a memory which hadn't heard or 'rehearsed' the tales for years because of the decay of the traditon. Furthermore, the quest itself and the occupation of folklore collecting were strange, and suspicions had to be allayed: people tended to suspect the collector of all kinds of secret missions – a government agent keeping an eye on valid and invalid subsidies of one kind or another, a clerk who had absconded with the till, a schoolmaster hounded from his school, even a revolutionary on the run!

My background of country living in south Armagh aided me immensely. Before I took on folklore collecting as a job, and not the hobby it had been most of my life, I was a farm labourer and freelance writer; I understood the work and crafts of the countryside, its manners and its vernacular.

I knew that a favourite starting point could be the blacksmith's forge. Most of these have now vanished; but the men often had to wait hours at the forge and there was an opportunity to talk and gossip. The smith, sometimes a storyteller himself, could verify and supplement one's assessment about this or that man who appeared to have the aptitude for folk storytelling. Or he could direct one to someone in the area known to have folklore and tales. He could also name houses where neighbours gathered at night to talk or 'crack' and tell tales; ordinary dwelling houses which we know in Ulster as 'céilí-houses'. Once the smith was assured of my good faith, I was recommended to use his name as an introduction.

As well as the blacksmith's forge, the cobbler's shop was another good source; these too have vanished from the countryside. I've also collected folklore and folktales in hospitals and in homes for the old people. Today, unless one has some prior contact in a fresh area, the pub is the usual starting point. The storyteller however is happier and more at ease when seated by his own or a neighbour's fireside where the mood is right. And it must be added that no storyteller was ever paid for his tales nor was payment expected.

I've met storytellers whose art was unknown in a locality and often unsuspected: so one keeps asking and making talk with any man or woman met on a road.

The storytellers were country people with normal occupations in the land or related crafts. Most of them were men, but I did find a few women storytellers. Among these was a representative of another vanished class known traditonally and romantically as 'The Travelling Woman'. She was a spinster or widow without a home or family ties; and while never designated as being a beggar-woman, roamed the countryside for miles and was welcomed warmly in the houses where she received food and shelter for the night on a makeshift bed in a corner of the kitchen close to the hearth.

MICHAEL J. MURPHY, Introduction to Now You're Talking:
Folk Tales from the North of Ireland, 1975

T HE DECLINE OF IRISH AS THE VERNACULAR of the people of southeast Ulster, and with it the Gaelic song tradition, is a story of division and alienation attributed, mainly, to the machinations of church and state. Its cultivation and tenuous survival, however, is a story which connects all strands of community – all classes and creeds – bringing together the learned and the illiterate, scribes and scholars, singers and storytellers, priests and ministers, poets and harpers, their patrons and the poor. The varied names with equally varied backgrounds of Dobbin, Young, O'Hanlon, Murphy, McCrink, Morris, Ó Muiri, Hollywood, Mac Cumhaigh, Quinn, Ó Doirnín, Donnellan, Tierney, McKevitt, Lloyd, O hUallacháin, Campbell, Donaldson, Bunting, McKeown, Harvessy, Nelson, Courtney, Graham, Balmer, Ó Dubhda, Devlin, McGahon, Ennis, Humphreys, Ó Baoill and Hannon are testament to a shared inheritance and awareness, and include but a small number of those whose story this is.

My aim ... is to tell the story and, as a singer, to make these songs accessible again so that they will find a voice once more in a wider community. They tell us a wealth about the human heart, about the people who made them, the times in which they lived and the traditions of their communities. The themes of many of the songs reflect dimensions of the human experience which we all share. Though they are no longer heard in the context of local community life, as they once were, I have attempted to place them in a social context and to give stories and lore associated with the songs, where possible. My aim is also to enliven the memory of the men and women who lived here the day before yesterday; who carried the songs orally for centuries and who, despite many deprivations and hardship, held fast to their individual and collective voice through song, for as long as was possible. And, not least, I am compelled to honour the many collectors, both local and from farther afield, who trudged the hills and valleys of southeast Ulster avidly gathering what they knew then to be the last living remnants of an ancient and once vital tradition. They worked with what was described as 'a desperate zeal' and with an unsettling sense of urgency. Their work reveals an extraordinary commitment. Whatever might have motivated them in the context of their own times, their surviving manuscripts manifest a high regard for language, tradition, people and place. This story also reveals the thread of connection and circumstance which has kept the southeast Ulster song tradition alive in a fragile, but nonetheless continuous, unbroken, oral tradition.

PÁDRAIGÍN NÍ UALLACHÁIN, *A Hidden Ulster: People, Songs and Traditions of Oriel*, 2003

T HE COUNTRY FROM LISBURN TO BELFAST is pleasantly English in home-county style, but not outstandingly beautiful after the coastal

Antrim ... though if you want to spend time by the towpaths of the Lagan you will find them rewarding, especially in the season of autumn tints. Surely there must still be cargoes that do not mind if they are transported by the romantic and leisurely method of the barge. Must everything now be hustled to us by rail or road at sixty miles per hour because we forget to order it in time? Something will have gone from our life and landscape when in the placid canals of the Lagan Valley the bargee, leaning on his rudder, is no longer dragged by the drowsy horse into the disc of the setting sun.

DENIS O'D. HANNA, The Face of Ulster, 1952

'WAY UP, GIRL,' HE SHOUTED TO THE MARE, ''way up, Maggie!' and his veins swelled on his arms as he leant on the handles. The breeze blowing up from the sea, the cold smell of the broken clay, and the soft hissing noise of the plough, all soothed his mind and stirred him to new life.

As the day advanced the sun rose higher, but there was little heat from it, and frosty vapours still lingered about the rockheads and about the sparse hills. But slowly over the little field horse and plough still moved, moved like timeless creatures of the earth, while alongside, their shadows followed on the clay. Overhead and behind swarmed the gulls, screeching and darting for the worms, their flitting shadows falling coolly on Paddy's neck and on the back of the mare. At the end of the ridge he stopped to take a rest, surveying with pleasure the number of turned furrows, and wondering if his sisters were proud of him now. He looked up at the house: it was low and whitewashed, one end thatched and the other corrugated. There seemed to be no life about it except the smoke from the chimney and a crow plucking at the thatch. Soon it flew off with a few straws hanging from its bill.

MICHAEL McLAVERTY, *from* 'The White Mare', *The Game Cock and Other Stories*, 1949

I WILL GO WITH MY FATHER A-PLOUGHING

I will go with my father a-ploughing
To the green field by the sea,
And the rooks and the crows and the seagulls
Will come flocking after me.
I will sing to the patient horses,
With the lark in the white of the air,
And my father will sing the plough-song
That blesses the cleaving share.

I will go with my father a–sowing
To the red field by the sea,
And the rooks and the gulls and the starlings
Will come flocking after me.
I will sing to the striding sowers,
With the finch on the greening sloe,
And my father will sing the seed–song
That only the wise men know.

I will go with my father a–reaping
To the brown field by the sea,
And the geese and the crows and the children
Will come flocking after me.
I will sing to the tan-faced reapers,
With the wren in the heat of the sun,
And my father will sing the scythe–song
That joys for the harvest done.

JOSEPH CAMPBELL, The Rushlight, 1906

A T DAWN THE FARMER IS UP AND OUT. He ploughs, harrows, carts, spreads lime or manure, cuts hay, does everything, indeed, that his men do, and in all weathers. Inside, his wife bakes griddle-bread for household and servants, makes butter, helps a woman servant to milk, and to prepare food for fowls and pigs. The pair eat hurried, comfortless meals of tea and bread or bacon and potatoes, in the comfortless best room; the children, if any, are compelled by school conditions to take their meals at different hours, and they take them in the kitchen.

All through the day the kitchen is cumbered by great potfuls of food for beast or for the servants, whose last meal in the evening is, in summer, of potatoes and buttermilk. A huge potful of potatoes is emptied directly on the table, little heaps of salt are placed, also on the wood, beside tins of buttermilk; the men sit round and peel and eat their potatoes without knife or fork.

JOHN STEVENSON, A Boy in the Country, 1912

I WAS CLOSE BESIDE HIM NOW and I walked on thinking, with one hand holding his stirrup and the other clutching the pocket where I still had the lizard. At last I remembered a sermon of Father Binyon's: 'Father Binyon says that Man is lord over the animals.'

'That's true, I dare say, but lords aren't everything. Just think what animals do for Man, and how Man repays them.'

I thought about it for a while. 'Dogs,' I said presently.

'Dogs don't count. They're overlords too, and practically men.'

So I couldn't say anything at all, because I knew too well how animals were treated. I thought of cows who provided milk for us, year after year; and as a reward we took away their sons and killed them and ate them. And as soon as they themselves could no longer provide milk, we killed *them* and ate them also. And when a horse who had served us for years grew old, we killed him too, rather than continue to feed him. And when we had killed him, we didn't even leave him his skin to lie in, but took that because we could use it.

'And rabbits,' said Gran'papa, who must have been watching me. 'Man is the same in everything – there is practically no creature whom he does not kill.'

STEPHEN GILBERT, *The Landslide*, 1943

THE ARDS CIRCUIT

When Kaye-Don Kershaw ran the horse and cart
Delivering things, a bed, a chest of drawers,
The dog ran underneath short of the heels
Pacing the wheels with acquiescent paws.

When Kaye-Don stiff as candle in the hearse
Was pulled by two black horses to his grave,
Underneath in spite of spit and curse
The dog persisted, pacing destined wheels.

ROY McFADDEN, *Verifications*, 1977

OUR KITCHEN WAS BIG AND BARE, with whitewashed walls, and a floor of grey stone slabs. The hearth was so wide and open that you could walk into it and look up the chimney at the stars. That was when the fire was small. But it was unlucky to let the fire go out completely, and this only happened once that I know of. Now there was a huge turf fire which lighted the room as well as heated it, and round the fire were figures, seeming vague after the darkness without. The floor, because of its unevenness and the flickering of the flames, was covered with rippling shadows like a pool of water. If I looked up I saw neither ceiling nor roof, only a vague darkness, with a suggestion of something there, but when, from time to time, there was the flare of a brighter flame, I could see the black oak of the rafters and catch a glimpse of an old spade or a fishing rod, or the barrel of an antique gun. But beyond the rafters, and the lumber that lay stretched across them, there was thicker darkness still, heavy and impenetrable. Up there, where the bats slept in the daytime, was our ghost, watching over us. I saw the wink of his eye, from the blackness, and looked away again fearfully.

I heard Gran'papa's clock which repeated again and again, as it slowly swung its pendulum, 'Tock, tock'. I couldn't see it because it was a dark old clock, and always stood in the duskiest corner of the kitchen, but I could see the white scrubbed wood of the table and the chairs.

STEPHEN GILBERT, *The Landslide*, 1943

THE LAST SATURDAY IN ULSTER

Behind her radiator
the leather purse is caring
for the old denominations:
liverspots of giant pennies,
fifty pences thick as lenses.

A Pentecostal home outside Armagh:
antimacassars, oxygen masks,
Martha glancing towards the screen
as if checking delay and departure.

An Orange march in Antrim
will see me late arriving:
and standing out at Aldergrove
an English girl might well believe
that time is how you spend your love.

Undriven cattle graze the long acre.
Pheasants fidget and flit between townlands.
The coins were warm as new eggs
in the nest of her priestly-cool hands.

NICK LAIRD, *To a Fault*, 2005

I KNOW THAT THE McDOWELLS AND CRAIGS came over from Scotland about 300 years ago and a story is told that three Craig brothers came and were given their choice of land. One chose Carneal (above Gleno). They were still there a few years ago when the house was burnt down and the last Craigs of Carneal died shortly afterwards. Many interesting stories are told about the Craigs of Carneal. Theirs was intelligence above the average and their interest in books is still remembered. A niece of these last Craigs described 'The Library' which her grandfather organised at Carneal House, how the neighbouring farm-folk subscribed to it, and how they used to bring the books to change, when there would be hospitality and 'good crack'. She also described how they had a 'Library Soirée' in the barn, with forms round the walls (and cloth fastened to the walls to keep the girls' dresses clean) and where fiddlers played for the dancing.

(—, Larne, Co. Antrim)

Ulster Folklife, vol. 5, 1959

ALL SOULS' EVE

I have decked my fireside with the haws glinting red,
Left the half-door open, set the table spread
With brown bread of my baking, and cups of gold and blue;
We two will sit together as once we used to do.

I have said three prayers for you since dayli' gone;
That the moon be your lantern, and the stars glimmer on
The dark ways you wander, and no cold mists there
Draw their clinging fingers through your yellow hair.

I will hear your footsteps seven miles away,
Feet the mould has fettered in a house of clay;
I would walk on your road, but you'll travel mine,
To see the red haws gleaming and the candles shine.

I have made the place gay with brown leaves and red,
Here the turf is flaring; here the board is spread.
God, Who took you from me, show you to my sight!
Lest I turn away from you, you who walk tonight.

FLORENCE M. WILSON, *The Coming of the Earls*, 1918

KICK-THE-TIN, A HYBRID OF TIG and hide-and-seek, employed an empty tin can as a release-mechanism, which, if kicked away from its central location, allowed players time to find new hiding-places while 'it' retrieved the can and replaced it on its spot. Thus the can was a kind of clock with differential radii, depending on the angle and length of the kick: it recalls the vatic tin-can ghost of the Lower Falls, which was heard tripping down the gutter, but never seen, any time there might be trouble in the offing. It was first heard in the twenties, when a policeman was shot dead outside the National Bank on the corner of Balaclava Street; since its habitat has been demolished, it has not been heard, but its memory lives on, even within the minds of those who'd never heard it, since it had acquired the status of a story.

Now, when I lie awake on a windy night and hear the vacillating roulette trickle of a tin can, I feel a shiver of impending doom, as Glandore blurs into Balaclava, the can resounding off the street in fits and starts — melismatic, rallentando phrases, broken by lulls and false denouements — till at last it ticks to a stop, or I fall asleep. Then I am prompted to step out of my body, to glide at second-storey level through the dark streets in a Wee Willie Winkie nightgown, making sure that everyone is safe in bed —

> *Rapping at the windows, crying through the lock,*
> *Are the children in their beds? Now it's eight o'clock —*

which reminds me, that in my father's and mother's time, men were hired to walk the streets with long poles in the dawn to knock on bedroom windows, like antonyms of lamplighters, waking people up for work, before the advent of alarm-clocks.

CIARAN CARSON, *The Star Factory*, 1997

from A NORTHERN HOARD
NO SANCTUARY

It's Hallowe'en. The turnip-man's lopped head
Blazes at us through split bottle glass
And fumes and swims up like a wrecker's lantern.

Death mask of harvest, mocker at All Souls
With scorching smells, red dog's eyes in the night —
We ring and stare into unhallowed light.

SEAMUS HEANEY, *Wintering Out*, 1972

Some Generic,
Gull-Pierced
Seaside Town

IN SUMMER TIME

Oh, some go to the Rosses,
And some go to Gweedore,
And others go to Port-na-Blagh
To paddle on the shore.
But we will go to Burtonport
And sail to Arranmore.

JOHN IRVINE, *By Winding Roads*

… To Bangor and to Ballyholme,
By early trains to thee I come.

JULIUS McCULLOUGH LECKEY CRAIG

TO THE SHORE

My childhood went by in a green Antrim glen;
The world and its ways were far from us then;
But we had a pony with wings to her heels,
And a little round trap with red shining wheels

To bring us to chapel, to town or to tea
With faraway cousins, or down to the sea.
Dad would say: 'Look here, children!' – in June it would be –
'If next Sunday's fine, we might go to the sea.'

Away we would scamper and pull out the trap,
And fill up our cans from the big water-tap,
And wash it all over, with 'We're for the shore!'
And shine the red wheels till they couldn't shine more.

We'd dust the brown cushions, shake out the blue wrap,
And polish the harness, each buckle and strap,
And brush Fanny's coat till it deepened and shone,
And plait her long mane and tie bright ribbons on.

Then we'd pray very hard that next Sunday'd be fine,
And fine it would be, nine times out of nine.
After first Mass on Sunday the fuss there would be
Fitting us in the trap. 'Michael, sit here with me!'

'Mummy, please, beside Dad! He promised I'd drive
For a piece of the way!' ... 'Well, then, mind little Saive.
Now, Anne dear, move over!' ... The little trap rocks
With the wriggling and squirming and crushing of frocks.

Then Dad would say: 'Look, we'll be here for the day!
Huph! Fanny Girl, huph!' ... We're off! We're away!
Down through the long village, across the bog road,
And no pony carried a merrier load,

All squooged-up together, all sticky and hot,
With happiness reigning where comfort was not,
And all our small pulses in time with the beat
Of the pony's clip-clopping, small, silver-shod feet.

Round the old Crooked Bridge, and the glen fell away
As we stood up to catch the first glimpse of Red Bay.
A mile or two more, then the long golden strand!
Shoes and socks are flung off and we rush down the sand,

And wait for the kiss of the waves cool and sweet
On little bare ankles and little bare feet
We'd splash and we'd frolic and swim our small boats
Build tall golden castles with trenches and moats,

Buy dulse from old Jenny – 'Rale creagan,' she'd say
''Twas cut in Ardclinis beyont in the bay,'
Or from Tommy who'd say, with the grin of an elf
'It's as clean as a penny, I cut it myself.'

At the red Wishing Arch we'd explore the dark caves
And play tip and run with the big shining waves
And we gathered the shells when the sands had grown grey,
And the lights of the sunset were over the bay.

I have one of them yet, over there on the sill
And, times, in the twilight, when everything's still
I put my ear down and I hear the sea plain
And the little red trap wheels are rolling again.

SIOBHÁN NÍ LUAIN, The Sally Patch, 1971

'LOOK BACK,' SAID A LADY whose taste is as pure as her mind is accomplished – 'Look back towards Glenarm, and up the valley to the left, when you come to Red Bay.' We did her bidding; we can imagine nothing to surpass the beauty of the scene. The sun was shining upon the wide expanse of sand, and the day was so clear, the atmosphere and water both so transparent, that every rock, and promontory and huge stone was reflected. How an artist would have luxuriated here, enlivening the foreground with the whispering ripple of the light wave that imparted a deeper tone of colour to the shining sand, and especially in the picturesque groups that were collecting seaweed to make 'kelp' – the bright tartan shawl, the red kirtle or golden neckerchief of the women, and scarlet vest of the men – 'freshening' the picture; the children dotting the beach, as they turned over and over the stones looking for flints; the lazy boats drawn up on the sands, and the white sails of such as remained in the water hanging inertly from the masts; then the baskets, creels, ropes, cables – all were grouped in the most pictorial manner; and a huge dog kept running in and out of the ocean, amusing a parcel of boys, who appeared to have no earthly care except shouting to the kind animal that contributed to their enjoyment.

MR and MRS S.C. HALL, Ireland, Its Scenery, Character, etc., 1842

TO STRETCH THEIR LEGS and get rid of their travel weariness, the elderly aunt and her two gauche nieces walked smartly from the station along Portrush's Main Street. Without a halt, they walked till they were at the furthest possible extremity of Ramore Head. There the everlasting breezes of the Atlantic blew away the last school cobweb from the brains of Mary and her little sister. Aunt Laetitia stood for a long time on the head, gazing along the coast in the direction of Castlerock on the other side of the River Bann. All of this north coast was her territory, and she loved it with the intensity of attachment to a piece of mother earth that is possible only to the Irishman and the Israelite.

Having adored her Lares and Penates, Aunt Laetitia turned with softer face than usual to the girls.

'Come,' she said. 'Let's look at the shops in Main Street.'

A happy hour's dawdling down one side of Portrush Main Street and up the other brought to view not only some lovely clothes, jewellery, silver, cakes and boots, but the more exotic and specifically watering-place offerings – souvenirs. Mary and Little Sister exclaimed over the pleasures and prettinesses of them all. Although they did not hope to buy, they got a deal of pleasure from just looking. 'Window shopping,' Aunt Laetitia called it. There were seaweed frames, shell boxes, a multiplicity of fine chinaware for what-nots, often emblazoned with the arms of the town and the legend 'A Present from Portrush', so that one could prove one had been there. It was fatiguing work, this window shopping, and Little Sister was not slow to announce this, especially with a prompt from Mary. Aunt Laetitia was in a softened mood, induced by breathing the air she loved. She agreed immediately and they all betook themselves to the Strand, walking just far enough to be by themselves.

The smooth stones and the humpy stones, lying here and there in the huge stretch of sand, were warm to the touch. With a little searching, they found suitable seats among them. Aunt Laetitia produced her fine laundered handkerchief and ordered the others to do the same. They spread out their upholstery thus and seated themselves. From under the half-lid of her basket, Aunt Laetitia produced a clean tea towel, three thick tumblers and a bottle of lemonade. Opening the other half-lid, she handed Mary a packet of sandwiches in a damp cloth and a similar packet to Little Sister. Mary's were lettuce and cress from the garden, Little Sister's hardboiled egg. All this food they could produce themselves and it was no novelty, but somehow partook of a novel quality in these surroundings. They handed and swapped the sandwiches back and forth, swilling them down with lemonade. All three were hungry now that food was in sight. Mary, the 'far lands filled', leaned back happily on her warm rock and gazed dreamily at the Skerries. Here it was, she thought, that the emigrant ships of a hundred and fifty years before had lain at anchor. In the shelter of these rocks had rested the Ulster Scots setting out to create the true America.

FLORENCE MARY McDOWELL, *Roses and Rainbows*, 1972

WE WERE TIRED FROM RUNNING about in the heather and, already growing hungry, we felt the nearness of supper, and bed, with that calm faith which belongs only to children and saints devoted to the love of God and sure of the delights of communing with him. In that faith, that certainty of coming joys, we existed in a contentment so profound that it was like a lazy kind of drunkenness. I can't count how many times I enjoyed that sense, riding in a sidecar, whose swaying motion would have put me to sleep if I had not been obliged to hold on; so that while my body and head and legs were all swinging together in a half dream, my hand tightly clutched some other child's body; and the memory of bathing, shouting, tea, the blue smoke of picnic fires, was mixed with the dark evening clouds shaped like flying geese, the tall water stretching up to the top of the world, the mountains sinking into darkness like whales into the ocean and over all a sky so deep that the stars, faint green sparks, seemed lost in it and the very sense of it made the heart light and proud, like a bird.

JOYCE CARY, *A House of Children*, 1941

THACKERAY, DURING HIS IRISH VISIT in 1842, visited Portstewart, and gives an account of his visit in his *Irish Sketch Book*. It appeared to him that the whole place had an air of comfort and neatness which was seldom seen in Ireland.

It was intended that the Ballymena and Portrush Railway, which was opened in 1858, should go through Portstewart, but, owing to the opposition of Mr Cromie, who feared that the method of travelling would lead to Sunday desecration, the line was diverted to within a mile and a half of the town. The townspeople deeply regret Mr Cromie's obstinacy on this point, and he himself was wont to admit that he had made a mistake in opposing the original intention of the promoters. Little now remains of old Portstewart but the two thatched cottages at the base of the castle wall − the last of the Bone Row, so called because the inhabitants fastened the thatch with the bones of fish instead of wooden pegs − and a few thatched houses on the Coleraine Road. Its bathing facilities, water supply, electric light, and its two interesting golf courses would reflect credit on many a richer and larger community − all uniting not only to make Portstewart one of the most desirable watering-places, but also an ideal spot for permanent residence.

THE REVEREND CANON FORDE, *Sketches of Olden Days in Northern Ireland*, 1926

THE ARCHAEOLOGIST

Portrush. Walking dead streets in the dark.
Winter. A cold wind off the Atlantic
rattling metal in the amusement park.

Rain. The ornate dancehall, empty on the rocks,
bright paint worn thin, posters half torn away,
sweet-stalls, boarded up and locked with padlocks.

Returned to the scene, at once I see again
myself, when ten years younger, and a girl,
preserved in an almost perfect state by the brain.

That is her window, high on the side wall.
Beneath it figures, projected by the mind,
are moving. I am about to call.

I give her name and wait. She is called down.
Without taking thought I know what I want to do.
Love, like electric current, lights the town.

Nothing is tawdry, all our jokes are funny,
the pin-table is brighter than Shakespeare's works,
my handful of warm coins is sufficient money.

Imaginative reconstruction shed
some light upon a vanished way of life.
I cannot live like them, and they are dead.

The cold makes me simpler and breaks the spell:
I don't mind crying, but I hate to shiver,
and walk quickly back to my hotel.

JAMES SIMMONS, Ballad of a Marriage, 1966

TOWARDS THE END OF THAT SUMMER when the holidays were nearly
over Colm, Jamesy and Clare went with their mother on the last
excursion of the season to Bangor. It, too, was on a Sunday. Crowds of
people waved the boat off as she swung out from the wooden pier, and
sailed down the lough. Behind, the boat left a suddy path in the water;
gulls' shadows skimmed across the deck; and far away now, tiny trams
were sliding over Queen's Bridge.

The city lay spread out in a loop, Cave Hill and the Divis range at one
side, and the field-patterned Castlereagh Hills at the other; and because it
was Sunday there was little smoke from the tall factory chimneys, but
below in a blue haze stretched parallel rows of red-bricked houses
choking each other for space. High up on the slope of the Black
Mountain Colm pointed out to Jamesy where Toneroy lay; and then as
the boat passed the shipyards with the skeletons of ships seen through a

net of scaffolding, they began to play hide-and-go-seek with Clare ...

Then as they drew near Bangor the boom of a Salvation Army Band came to them over the quiet water. All the people crowded to one side, tilting the boat, and nearly putting the heart out of Clare and her mother, Colm and Jamesy laughed at them and they both leaned over the rails in an attempt to cant the boat a little more.

Out at Ballyhome they paddled in the water and screamed with joy. Colm would cover Clare's legs with sand, the cold taking her breath away, and she would call out, 'Look, Mammie, look! I've no legs!'

The mother bought them Bangor rock and Clare chewed hers quickly, fascinated by the name that never disappeared however much she ate.

And the mother sitting with her umbrella beside her smiled happily, looking at the sun-winking waves breaking on the sand. And she'd smile again and shrug her shoulders as she'd hear the happy screams of her children: 'Aw, but it's a grand day, thank God,' and she'd join her hands on her lap, looking at a gull making a nest of rings for itself in the water.

Near them a few girls went in for a bathe and when Colm saw them he thought of Uncle Robert and Aunt Maggie and he repeated their remarks: 'Look at them bold heelers and not as much clothes on them as'd dust a flute.' His mother lifted her umbrella and made a clout at him.

MICHAEL McLAVERTY, *Call My Brother Back*, 1939

A LMOST EVERY GENERAL SHOP shows festoons of sand shoes, cascades of little buckets and bunches of wooden spades to delight the heart of the young Belfastians. The small builders design some wondrous architecture on the sandy beach, while the older generation disport themselves in the blue waters of the bay.

Long may Bangor flourish as a health-giving outlet for the city of Belfast.

MARY LOWRY, *The Story of Belfast and its Surroundings*, 1912

A WAY WENT THAT TRAIN DOWN to Banger West, County Down, the loveliest, fastest train ever, for I was going off on my very first holiday. It seemed as if slow, agonizing years passed from the time when we initially heard about it, until the actual day arrived. Holiday, the word of magic! But anything could go wrong; even at the last minute, some twist of fate could snatch away the holiday. But nothing did. My mother and sisters and I scrambled out of the train, and made our way to the summer home for poor people, trailing our luggage which was parcels of brown paper and newspaper.

We had to share a room with two other families; a young widow like my mother and her son, and an elderly woman and her granddaughter. The old woman never failed to amaze me, when every night and morning she struggled in or out of her combinations, standing on thin legs like a stork at the edge of a pool. The other boy had some pet mice, and one night he let them run across the room, as the spindly apparition struggled out of its woollens in the semi-darkness. Poor old girl, she thought the mice were in her coms, in the bed, and she shrieked so much that an attendant came and moved her, granddaughter and all, to another room.

Our relatives in Canada, so my mother reckoned, would be pleased to have photographs of the holiday, and accordingly she borrowed a box camera for the snaps. We 'borrowed' a raft from the yachting club up the beach, and my sisters, the boy from our room and I, sat on it, while my mother tried her hand at the complications of a camera. It was a novelty, and as she was finding out how to work it, a strong current took hold of the raft. The tide was going out, and within minutes we were swept far beyond reach. Luckily for us, the boating club people, who had probably disapproved of their raft being taken, saw the danger and rescued us in a motorboat, thereby adding another thrill to our day.

On most afternoons, weather permitting, we bundled off to Bangor proper. Here were sandy beaches to play on, clean and left in ridges by a receding tide, waiting naked like an artist's canvas. But even here we could not play as we liked, could not cover that canvas with, our own inventions of sandcastles and moats. Yet another evangelical movement waited for us. Bribing us with prizes, it cajoled us into making wide circles of sand pies. In the centre of these, scriptural texts must be written, and the whole decorated with rich ornaments of shells and various seaweeds. Like a rash of ringworm the Bangor sands bore these circular sermons for long stretches. As if a prehistorical race was building defensive forts, young souls laboured to beautify the many versions of 'God is Love', 'Jesus Saves' or 'Trust in the Lord'. All the skill and ingenuity was lavished on them that bakers devote to sugar icing on birthday cakes. Whether we lacked faith or art nobody could guess, but certainly no prizes for such righteous work, on which we spent many hours, ever came my family's way.

ROBERT HARBINSON, *No Surrender*, 1960

THE ROAD RUNNING DOWN the scythe blade of the Ards hardly ever leaves the coast. The hummocky land is well farmed; the tillage fields are as dry as shot and the silvery sands by the sea look as if they would slip through some colossal hour-glass at the rate of a ton a second; the air has a tonic quality. Ballywalter and Ballyhalbert have little harbours with coloured houses and benches set outside them; men in caps and dungarees working on boats (sienna yellow of masts, odd dashes of vermilion), their minds occupied with herrings; the sea *legato* rather than *fortissimo*. 'No tourists, no trees, no flies,' summarises my companion. The Ards seems a fine place for a lazy holiday.

STEPHEN RYNNE, All Ireland, 1956

IN THE EARLY SPRING ... the Art Master planned an excursion for the class to Newcastle to sketch in the Mournes. They went by bus, through country crowded with small farms, all astir in the spring sunshine. The newly ploughed land was purple-brown, the larch trees' film of green threaded over the woods, the whins were ablaze.

The bus stopped in the main street, and they all spilled out, laden with sketching kit and overcoats. The seaside town was empty of visitors – they would come in their thousands from June to September – but it looked as if every landlady in the town had chosen this day to start her spring-cleaning. Blankets billowed on scores of clothes lines, eiderdowns lay across windowsills, and there was a rhythmic beating of carpets from every house that had a garden large enough to beat them in. The class separated, some to climb up into the bowl between Donard and Commedagh, some into the woods on Drinahilly, some to the harbour.

Laura hesitated which group to join. She had made no friends among the girls in the class, and Tom was the only man she had ever spoken to. Coming down in the bus she had been sitting beside a girl with a large heavy face who seemed as friendless and silent as herself. Now Tom came and took her elbow. 'Come on, we'll try the shore,' he said, and together they went onto the wide stretch of pale sands. The tide was halfway up the beach and was coming in, a lazy tide, hardly troubled by waves. Each wave was just a bar of darker grey that resolved itself slowly as it neared the beach, and then hung suspended for an infinite sunlit moment before it came down in foam and was sucked back again. The hills too were tranquil, rising one above the other into the sunlight. Between hills and sea the busy seaside town laboured, and the smoke rose white from a hundred chimneys.

JANET MCNEILL, Tea at Four O'Clock, 1956

A SEASIDE TOWN

We went where we had often been when young,
to test for happiness: the promenade's
Victorian bay windows parched for paint;
the unfrequented station's padlocked gates;

the whitewashed lighthouse basking on its cliff.
Rimmed by black rocks, on scanty fans of sand,
a few shrill children waded, bucketed,
and wagtails flickered in beached bladderwrack.

But still that magic spring; below high tide
sweet water issued unobtrusively,
and a woman clambered down to fill her pail,
its permanence accepted; here before
the lighthouse winked its warning, and family men
owned season tickets for those summer trains.

JOHN HEWITT, *Time Enough*, 1976

I FANCY THAT THE ONLY STATIONS I could ever really love were small
stations – not these roofed-in affairs smelling of some strange and
unpleasant drug, but little stations open to the sun and rain – wayside
stations or termini that look like wayside stations. I certainly felt a twinge
of sorrow when the old Portrush Station was destroyed to make room for
a roofed building like any other important terminus. When I knew it first,
it was bathed in sea air, with the sea excitingly visible from the platform.
The engine and the engine driver, as one walked down the platform,
were a part of nature. Now everything is mechanical, hidden from the
eye of day. Nor was Portrush Station in those days the only beautiful
station on the line. Every station at which we stopped was beautiful. How
enviable the people who got out at Cullybackey seemed! How enviable
the country people on the platform! It is one of the curiosities of railways
that if you are in the train, the people on the platform seem to be leading
extraordinarily interesting lives, and, if you are on the platform, the
people in the train seem to be leading extraordinarily interesting lives.

ROBERT LYND, *from* 'Railway Stations I Have Loved', *In Defence of Pink*, 1937

THE LITTLE PORTS OF ANTRIM AND DOWN and the coast towns and
villages are ... contributors to and sharers in the general prosperity.
There is not one of them that I do not know intimately, and there is not
one that is not as picturesque as any of the coast villages of Cornwall,
Devon or Dorset. It is unnecessary to mention Larne or Portrush; all the
world crosses to Ireland from Stranraer and goes to see the wonder of the
Giant's Causeway, and those visitors who have a day to spare go on to
Derry and stand on those carefully tended walls that withstood the shock
of the cannons of the Irish Army for one hundred and five days, during
the most memorable siege in the history of Great Britain. But Lough

Foyle is not nearly so beautiful a landlocked bay as many others further south. The lovely wooded windings of Strangford Lough, with its many green islands and brown strands, will never be forgotten by anyone who has sailed through its placid waters – by no means placid at the entrance when the tide is running at six knots. In her home at Old Court lived for many years Lady de Ros, the daughter of the Duchess of Richmond who gave the famous Waterloo Ball at Brussels, at which, as a girl, Lady de Ros had danced; and not far away, at Killyleagh Castle, the girlhood was spent of the present Dowager Marchioness of Dufferin and Ava.

F. FRANKFORT MOORE, The Truth About Ulster, 1914

A T CARRICKFERGUS YOU ARE ALREADY well advanced on the prettiest road in all Ireland – that which skirts the northern shore of Belfast Lough, then, crossing the neck of Island Magee peninsula, carries you past Larne's inland water, and from Larne follows the cliffy shoreline up to where Fair Head marks the northern limit of Antrim's eastward-looking coast. Then, cutting in behind the head, it emerges on the pleasant town of Ballycastle, sheltered in its bay, and so follows the coast again past the castles of Dunseverick and Dunluce, famous ruins, and past the Giant's Causeway, that still more famous piece of an older and more majestic architecture. Portrush ends your journey if you be a golfer; but dearer to me than the links at Portrush are the sandhills beyond Portstewart and the long strand at the entrance to Lough Foyle – ten miles of a stretch, but the Bann's outflow divides it. No other beach that I have known is rich in such a variety of shells; on no other sandhills do the little delicate sandflowers, ladies'-slipper, thyme, ladies'-bedstraw, and the rest, grow so charmingly.

STEPHEN GWYNN, Ulster, 1911

B ELFAST IS THE STARTING-POINT of the county's second scenic region. The way to the Ards peninsula is along Belfast Lough, a cheerful route through lively towns and villages with the sight of ships on the sea. Ireland comes alive in the North. In a country where most of the bays are deserted and neglected, the lough is an ever-open gateway to the world, where vessels entering and departing is normal instead of extraordinary. This coast is well developed and for a time the villages are in almost English plenty: Holywood with its Maypole, an exotic 'plant' in Ireland; Crawfordsburn with its white inn and its tree-framed views of the bordering lough. Then comes the large and still-growing town of Bangor where half the world and all Scotland arrive for summer holidays. But Bangor is accustomed to crowds. The first began here fourteen hundred years ago when Saint Comgall founded his monastic school, which was a name to conjure with for many centuries. Saint Columbanus of Bobbio carried Bangor's fame to Europe. Sacked by the Danes, the abbey endowments passed into the hands of laymen and the buildings fell into ruin. But Bangor had a second spring in the twelfth century when Saint Malachy became its abbot. He helped to restore the ruins with his own hands and his example was enthusiastically followed by a crowd of disciples. Today there is not a trace of the monastic school. Instead there are promenades, gardens, parks, bathing-pools and hotels beyond counting. A fine sample of rough sea flings itself into two small bays; the sea walls are capped with rosy red stones; the sea front has that old faded look that the heart hungers for as the second half of this century goes on its brash, concrete-block way.

STEPHEN RYNNE, *All Ireland*, 1956

IN AUGUST [LORD DUFFERIN] CROSSED to Ireland. He travelled via Dublin and Belfast and from there took the little train that runs along the lough. The familiar stations passed him one by one – Holywood, Cultra, Craigavad. The smell of the seaweed puffed into his carriage and across the water lay Carrickfergus and the line of the Antrim coast. The train stopped at Clandeboye station, which he had rechristened Helen's Bay. He was home again after five years.

The station at Helen's Bay was in those days (and indeed until the advent of the motor-car eliminated the train journey from Belfast) one of the most fantastic in the United Kingdom. Just before entering the station the train crossed a high bridge which spanned the two-and-a-half-mile avenue between Clandeboye and the sea. The station itself did not, at first sight, differ from the other stations of the Belfast and County Down Railway. There were the same long low buildings, the same weather-boarding painted a faint pink, the same 'approach' where the jaunting cars waited for possible passengers, their drivers standing up upon the footboard waving expectant whips. Yet the last door on the left opened upon a little corridor which in its turn led to Lord Dufferin's private waiting-room ...

Having rested in the waiting-room, the visitor was then conducted back into the corridor and down a flight of steep stone steps which led to the level of the avenue. On reaching the bottom he was startled to find himself in a large pentagonal forecourt. The walls of this propylaea were constructed of black granite irregularly morticed together with thick cement. There were a large number of turrets, pinnacles, barbicans, embrasures, machicoulis, ramparts, merlons, battlements, and arrow-slits. The avenue passed through this outer ward at right angles to the railway line. To the right there was a high portcullised gateway which led down to the sea. To the left an even more imposing feudal arch disguised the railway bridge. Each of these two arches was decorated with a large coat of arms – dexter, a lion with a tressure flory counterflory, or sinister, a heraldic tiger ermine.

Today, the avenue, the forecourt, the waiting-room, and indeed the railway station, are seldom used. The tressure of the lion has become more counterflory than ever; some of the balls have dropped from the coronets; and the arrow-slits are hidden in ivy. But on that August morning of 1889 the whole outer ward glistened in welcome. The carriages were waiting at the door of the staircase; the agent and the tenants formed a mounted escort; Lord Dufferin, accompanied by Ronald Munro Ferguson, his impending son-in-law, drove in happy triumph to his home.

HAROLD NICOLSON, *Helen's Tower*, 1937

FAHAN WAS A WONDER. It was where the seaside really began, where the waves came in. The tiny seaside houses were perched aslant the mountain so perilously that they were only held from slipping, it appeared, by the strokes of their white fences or low white walls crusted with shells. The hedges were thick with fuchsias and honeysuckle and the field marguerites had become so tame and civilised that you could see they were the sunflowers' white daughters. They had the same eyes. There was one place on the narrow ledge of road where tea roses caught in your hair as you passed. You had to drive close to the hedge because of the danger on the other side where you might go over into the ravine. Far down below the black crawling train puffed into Fahan Station. People buzzed from it like flies, one stream going up the stairs and coming over the bridge to the mountainside, and the other stream trickling out through the railings to catch the toy steamer at the end of the toy pier.

From Fahan we went down again into the safer road, past the golf links, where Mother drove fast because of the madman. We never saw him but we always saw his collie. Then we came to the road where the O'Dohertys began. Every O'Doherty house had an orchard. People came out to see us go by. We could hardly wait to get out of the governess cart so as to pick everything up again and belong to it.

The shore was the last miracle. The rocks stood up, dripping with sea wrack, the sea breaking against them in fountains; then it lowered its steps and slippered in upon the white, pure sands. There was a high ridge of shells banked against the spiny sea grass.

KATHLEEN COYLE, *The Magical Realm*, 1943

M Y ARRIVAL IN NEWCASTLE was inauspicious. It was still raining and I was still wet ... Newcastle, like Bangor, was full of holiday-makers, and it took me half-an-hour to find a room in seafront boarding-house. As far as possible I dried myself but felt disinclined to stay in with nothing more provided by the house in the way of entertainment than the one solitary book, *Handbook for Mental Nurses*.

I shared the shelter of some shop awnings with visitors wrapped in plastic macs and got my bearings. Even the rain could not disguise the wonder of Newcastle's setting, though I had already seen enough to tell me that architecturally the little resort had nothing commendable. But its wide sands stretched for miles in a bay whose sea edge was lost in the distance by the salt spray hanging over the waves. The scene was like the shore landscapes beloved by Bonington and Boudin. It was a most ideal place for children.

As if this were not enough, beyond the town the giant forms of the Mourne mountains, smooth and vast, reared into the sky, sweeping, in the manner made famous in the song, down to the sea with huge headlands. And as I looked in wonder at these mountains, a rift appeared in the clouds. The high profile of hills, obscured a moment before by trails of rain, suddenly became bold and clear and rich with greens and purples and rusty browns in the late afternoon sunshine. The lower slopes were planted with fir, but the upper reaches, culminating in Slieve Donard's peak almost three thousand feet above the sea, were bare except for heather.

The clouds continued to be driven out of sight inland and soon the sun was striking warm again. My own joy at the sun was nothing compared with the children's. I thought I had never been in a place with so many children. They swarmed everywhere, looking Scandinavian with their spun gold hair and blue eyes and butter-golden skin. Newcastle was a place for the young, mooning lovelorn teenagers and young married couples, some of whom were still teenagers themselves. So far as all these people were concerned the rain had not drowned their happiness and something of their enjoyment infected the air. The myriad children were part of this for they were not excluded from any family activity. Wide-eyed without a hint of sleep about them, they sat up to ten o'clock or more with the grown-ups in the cafés drinking fizzy drinks and eating enormous platefuls of fish and chips.

Partly because of the afternoon's rain and partly because it was the inviolable high tea time the sands were not fully occupied. I walked along them feeling that soft-hard, mysterious quality of sea-sand underfoot which fascinates me now as much as it did in childhood. The tide was right out, so that the sea had withdrawn to the distance. The few figures of bathers looked remote and might easily have been merboys and mergirls sporting at the water's edge.

ROBIN BRYANS, *Ulster: A Journey Through the Six Counties*, 1964

THAT COUNTRY IS TOURIST-HAUNTED NOW. Even Ballintoy, surely most perilous of all boat havens, has its tea-room, which would be a dreadful desecration if it were not housed in a cottage which was there before the tea, and run by two ladies who have been tuned into harmony by the spirit of the place. I am told that the crossing of the rope bridge at Carrick-a-Rede is now counted as a little thing. But when I was a boy there was a real risk in crossing, for the bridge swung free, far above jagged rocks and breaking waves, without even a handrail. The white rocks at the end of Portrush Strand are, alas! tourist-haunted now, like so much that once was solitary. But they were lonely places when I was young, the scene of adventurous scramblings at the lowest ebb of spring tides. We used to make expeditions to the Skerry Islands, sailing out there in the powerful fishing-boats which were used on that rough coast. These boats were rigged with two dipping lugs, a form of sail unsuitable for beating to windward. I can remember the business of putting about, at the end of a tack. It was a moment of great excitement to me. As the boat hung head to wind the great sails were lowered and the yards hauled round to the other side of the masts. The change was effected with great quickness while the boat lay head to wind, plunging heavily into the seas. There was a wild confusion of wet canvas, writhing ropes and heavy yard-arms in the boat. We who were passengers were advised to crouch on the floorboards until the change was complete. In the evenings we used to go lithe-fishing. I have never heard this fish, which is common all round the coast, called by this name anywhere else except off the Antrim coast ...

They say that wild animals try to get back to their familiar dens when the time comes for them to die. I should like, when my time comes, to creep back to that storm-swept, treeless coast, and see again before the end the black cliffs and long wave-trampled strands, and hear the half-Scottish, half-Irish speech of Neil Weir's descendants.

GEORGE A. BIRMINGHAM, *Pleasant Places*, 1934

ROCK MUSIC

The ocean glittered quietly in the moonlight
While heavy metal rocked the discotheques;
Space-age Hondas gurgled half the night,
Fired by the prospect of fortuitous sex,
I sat late at the window, blind with rage,
And listened to the tumult down below,
Trying to concentrate on the printed page
As if such obsolete bumph could save us now.

(Frank Ifield, Clodagh Rodgers, where are you now?
Every night by the window here I sit.
Sandie and Bobby, I still remember you –
As for the Arcadia, though I remember it,
It no longer remembers the uncouth Coke-heads
Who trembled here in nineteen fifty-six
In ice-cream parlours and amusement arcades;
Oddities all, we knew none of the tricks.

Cinema organ, easy listening, swing, doowop, bebop,
Sedate me with your subliminal sublime
And give me that old trashy '50s pop,
Suburban burblings of an earlier time;
The boogie bins bouncing in rotary light,
Give me my toxic shame, mean woman blues,
That old self-pity where, lonesome tonight,
I sit here snarling in my blue suede shoes.)

Next morning, wandering on the strand, I heard
Left-over echoes of the night before
Dwindle to echoes, and a single bird
Drown with a whistle that residual roar.
Rock music started up on every side –
Whisper of algae, click of stone on stone,
A thousand limpets left by the ebb-tide
Unanimous in their silent inquisition.

DEREK MAHON, *The Hunt by Night*, 1982

MEMORIES OF DONEGAL CROWD in my mind: rocking along on the little motor-railways through flax fields; the weird hoots; buxom women discussing the wicked price they were charged for yellow meal in Letterkenny; passengers left off at places suspiciously unlike official halts. The sea beside the road to Moville jerks the thoughtless, contented traveller into a sudden awareness of it – to think that those frightening depths were all around us all the time! When the weather is fine, as it is off and on, the population comes out-of-doors and goes on show. I remember passing through Buncrana on a sunny afternoon: every man, woman and child seemed to be in the streets, arrayed in glad rags; licking ice-creams; playing accordions; gales of laughter and outbursts of skitting. There is a fête whenever the sun shines in Donegal. It does not have to be organised, being merely a matter of high spirits.

STEPHEN RYNNE, *All Ireland*, 1956

A WHITE LINEN TABLECLOTH already spread with food from opened wicker baskets, unbreakable picnic teacups and saucers laid out in a row, ready for tea and, fussing, pulling a piston in and out on a primus stove, Dr Fadden, kneeling, an old-fashioned elegant holidaymaker in white Panama hat, the brim pulled rakishly down all around, brass-buttoned navy blazer, cream woollen flannels, white buck golf shoes with red-brick rubber soles, a cream tennis shirt with a striped silk foulard. And in a temper. 'Damn stove! Damn petrol's flooded the wick!'

... the wicker hampers stood, their lids open, the white linen cloth, weighted at its corners by stones, the fruitcake, strawberries and cream, anchovy paste, macaroons, tongue slices, cream puffs, watercress sandwiches, egg salad, jam roll, ham sandwiches, all ready for the eating. He wanted to be there, to go back to those birthday picnics where, after everyone had swum, or paddled in the sea, or walked on the sands, or hunted in rock pools, there would be this summer feast, and afterward the birthday cake would be cut up and tasted, and he would be given his birthday presents to open, there on the strand, the envy of his brothers and sisters, the birthday boy, unscoldable, to whom, on that one day of the year, all would be allowed.

But this was not day, it was night; it was not Portstewart strand in Ireland, but Zuma Beach in southern California.

BRIAN MOORE, *Fergus*, 1971

M OTHER LOWERED THE WINDOW and the salt wild smell of the sea caught us. It was the strong Atlantic coming in with waves that were curled like iron, inky black with wrack. This sea belonged to the granite landscape. The first station we came to was Castlerock. Mother stood up when the train stopped. 'I think,' she said, looking at me as though she expected argument, 'we could get out here instead of going on to Portrush. What do you think?' What could I think? The sea was there. I was exalted by it, entranced by its strength and splendour. Its music filled me like an orchestra. It drew me like a magnet and I was unable to say let us wait until we come to Portrush. Castlerock was just as good to me. Miss Elliot had said that the Giant's Causeway was one of the Seven Wonders of the World. Aunt Ahn had told my mother who had told me that the Giant's Causeway was the Earl of Bristol's hobby. He went all over the world examining basaltic formations that rivalled it. What were the Seven Wonders or a bishop's hobby when compared with the salty flowing sea which was only a hand's throw from our train? I said yes. So we got out of the train again and another porter took the bags.

We walked through the deserted seaside streets full of wind and sunshine. Mother found what she was looking for immediately: a little cottage perched high on the cliffs with white railings and a green porch and the red twines of fuchsias and snow-white pebbles bordering the paths. She settled for it there and then with a woman in a white apron that blew like a banner. The woman gave us tea in a kitchen with a flagged, sanded floor. We had boiled eggs and a plate stacked with buttered fadge. We walked by the sea with our hats in our hands. We found shells that had piled up through the winter, and lay crusted as flowers against the spiny, grey sea grasses.

KATHLEEN COYLE, *The Magical Realm*, 1943

IT WAS THE DAY OF THE LAMMAS FAIR at Ballycastle, and it was a fair day, cloudy and sultry, but with little sun. The wide expanse of the Diamond was occupied, every yard of it, with booths, stalls, stands and tents for the sale of clothing, new and secondhand, confectionery, hardware, delph, fruit, vegetables and articles for household use of every colour, make and kind.

In holiday mood, and in their thousands, the country people for many miles around thronged into the great square. Men and women, boys and girls, greeted friends and acquaintances gaily, as they elbowed their way through the narrow lanes between the booths and stalls with much laughter and in great good humour. All were not given to thoughtless gaiety, however. Here a sonsy country woman bought 'bargains' in delph, blue-rimmed bowls and cups and jugs. Beside her shy young girls cheapened trumpery at a cheap-jack's barrow. A wild-eyed man, with quivering nostrils, thumped a Bible cheek by jowl with a burly, dark-browed Rabelaisian rascal who, while he dispensed his wares, kept his audience in roars of laughter with his quips and stories. On the edge of the great throng a few Salvation lasses sang, amid the din, a 'hymn' to the tune of 'Drink to Me Only With Thine Eyes', while the heedless crowds passed on laughing and jostling their way through all the fun of the fair. A tall and extraordinarily handsome policeman regulated the traffic where it converged in the square from all the roads that led to Ballycastle on its great fair day. And his job was not an easy one.

Making our way through the surging light-hearted throngs we took the road that led down to the sea, and there on a green mound above the yellow strand we rested through long hours of the sultry afternoon. A white mist was on the brow of Fair Head, and on the green heights of Rachrai Island, where it lay beyond in the bay. But a bright glittering light was spread over the waters between, and in the distance the lime-white cliffs of the island seemed to be piled up on the blue horizon like wreaths of drifted snow.

CATHAL O'BYRNE, *As I Roved Out*, 1946

IT WAS ONLY A TWO-STOREYED FARMHOUSE, with an orchard at the side, and a long green garden that was splashed with daffodils and snowdrops in springtime. A drive led to it from the private bridge over the river, and it lay in the best part of the glen, just above a large trout pool, yet only a mile from the sea, where endless games might be played. Or, if it seemed better to play more dangerous games by a rougher tide, the Peyton children went out of the back gate, cut over the lift of moorland that belonged to Ardree House, and so reached the wild cliffs of the north Antrim coast. Here old Jamesey Toole lived in his three-roomed cottage, and he was always ready to take them to the Giant's Pillar Cave, except when he was too busy with the summer visitors ...

There was always so much to do: if it was no day for the sea, they could follow up the river, through the upper glen where the wild raspberries grew, and explore the moors which stretched for miles in a confusion of turf cuttings and heather and bogland. Even when it was too wet for sea or moors, Tullynagardy [i.e. Ballycastle] could be reached in five minutes on their bicycles, and it had shops where 'Peggy's Leg' rock and toffee apples could be bought. In August a fair was held there which crammed the main street with farmers and fishermen, while their wives and children swung giddily on the humming roundabouts on the fair-green, or patronised the big swings which swooped out over the sea's edge near the harbour.

META MAYNE REID, *All Because of Dawks*, 1955

THEY [I.E. THE MOURNES] RISE GREY AND BLUE only to sweep green and furze-gold into the sparkling spread of the sea far below. The beauty of these mountains is their close grouping; they cover an area of no more than fourteen miles by seven. County Down's box of granite peaks is one of the most precious scenic possessions of the whole country, affording ideal scope for the climber and the walker (bless them for their energy) and comfortable exploring for the humble motorist. A whole series of roads turn off the coast road to penetrate the Mourne mountain fastness. It is an arrangement resembling a system of field drainage depicted in an agricultural textbook ...

The 'run' of the Mourne mountains behind the village [i.e. Annalong] is notched and varied; parts of the mountain lap are still spotlit by the sun as the village grows dark. Annalong is lovely. It does not want us, you and me. I got talking to a fat man about the whiting trade, but he distrusted me and soon moved off. Clearly he thought I was a queer fish. Annalong has its own affairs to attend to and, ever perversely, we love it the more for that reason. Those small hotel-less, icecream-less seaside places in Ireland make one ache to stay in them and grow familiar with their moods.

STEPHEN RYNNE, *All Ireland*, 1956

NEWCASTLE AND ROSTREVOR, with their old castles and planters' demesnes, offered just the right setting for the elegant visitors of the eighteenth century. The castles around which the little towns grew had been placed there for the same reason that attracted the health-seekers: the conjunction of mountain and sea. Rostrevor, in particular, had a 'mild and salubrious climate', facing its sheltered lough and protected from the blasting cast winds. Its reputation was enhanced by the fact that it was the only town in Ulster which escaped the fever epidemic following the famine of 1816. By this time, as the *Picturesque Guide* bluntly puts it, 'the romantic retreat of Rostrevor, highly fashionable for the gentry of Ulster, had become a place of retirement for the merchants, lawyers and others of the wealthy classes who tread on the heels of the aristocracy.' There was also the attraction of the Carlingford oysters, and luxury foods were imported by sea. Newcastle, too, was 'neatly fitted up for the accommodation of bathers' and was 'advancing very rapidly in public favour. The old castle served as a Custom House until about 1830, when it was replaced by an hotel, signifying the trend of the times.'

The improvements in travel by horse-drawn 'long car' and later by train leads on to the days of the motorcar and coach, the cyclist and holidays with pay. The golf courses and other attractions of Newcastle have given it the lead: Kilkeel and many other places by the sea are becoming favourite summer resorts for those who seek peace and quiet. Credit for pioneering the modern phase of mountain exploration goes to the Belfast field naturalists, Templeton, Thompson, Stewart, and above all, Dr Lloyd Praeger, and the many young naturalists he inspired, who opened up the mountains and revealed the interest and exhilaration they hold for the ordinary rambler. The booley builders, the blaeberry gatherers and the pilgrims toiling up Slieve Donard are no more, but the high mountains still bring enjoyment and health to their spiritual successors whose summer camps are the youth hostels.

E. ESTYN EVANS, *Mourne Country*, 1951

PADDLING AND SWIMMING, sand-castling and jumping on bladder-wrack to make the gas vesicles go pop were only a few glories of the great dream a mere twelve miles away along the coast of County Down.

Even in the cold winds of March we street boys stole rides on the backs of lorries going along the coast so that we could snatch a glimpse of the rolling open sea and turn in the waves breaking on the sands of Ballyholme. History, however, would confirm that our Spartan be-haviour was nothing new. As far back as the sixth century the young men of Bangor were moonlight bathers. The difference was that they were monks, who, under St Comgall, first abbot of Bangor, were obliged to sit in the cold water in order to subdue the passions of the flesh, reciting the while the whole of the Psalter. It was small wonder that so many died. The survivors of this rigorous brand of holiness spread the knowledge of salvation abroad, earning for Ireland the title 'The Isle of Saints and Scholars' from other European nations.

Ulster people do love to be beside the seaside and particularly at Bangor, which is a kind of Irish Southend. It is small, with most of the town near enough to the sea to fill its boarding houses. Behind the purple bloom of veronica hedges the bay windows look across the bay, themselves crammed with crowded high tea tables, where, in the centre of each one stands a kind of monstrance used in this daily five o'clock ritual – the three-tier cake-stand.

Every boarding house window showed itself not to be inferior to its neighbours in possession of the cake-stand. And indeed, the three-tiers were vital for the tables were loaded, as are all tables in Northern Ireland, with such a variety of different kinds of bread and cake and pastry that one tier alone would not have sufficed. Only in Denmark have I ever found a similar versatility on the baker's part.

ROBIN BRYANS, *Ulster: A Journey Through the Six Counties*, 1964

IT WAS A LONG, SINGLE-DECKED, OPEN CHARABANC with, I think, solid rubber tyres. I, aged five, stood up on the back seat beside Aunt Minnie and waved goodbye to my parents, Father scowling and shaking a last admonitory fist at his sister as we chugged away up the street of mill terraces, the doffers cheering wildly and singing 'Oh I do like to be beside the seaside ...'

... En route to the briny Aunt Minnie distributed stout to the girls and lemonade to me. She yelled for the driver to stop a mile beyond the Belfast tram terminus and threatened to turf out two mean sisters unless they paid the final instalment of their fare – which they did. She led the singing (not, I might add, the doleful work songs that I've since heard attributed to mill girls by academic folk singers but plaintive old melodies such as 'Fuck the Pope an' no surrender / Bash he's balls agin' the fender ...' to the tune of 'Dixie'). She stood up on the seat beside me, peroxide perm shattering in the wind, her great bolster of a chest rolling up and down beneath her jumper, and scored a bull's-eye on the driver's neck with a hard bread bap from the hamper. She was twenty-seven then, a fine looking targe of a woman posed in the middle of a snap taken on Tyrella beach that day, skirt tucked up in the legs of her drawers and me perched on her shoulders, surrounded by her gang of tipsy doffers.

JOHN MORROW, *Northern Myths*, 1979

from NIGHT THOUGHTS

Night thoughts are best, the ones that visit us
where we lie smoking between three and four
before the first bird and the first tour bus.
Once you would wake up shaking at this hour
but now, this morning, you are a child once more
wide-eyed in an attic room behind the shore
at some generic, gull-pierced seaside town
in war-time County Antrim or County Down –
navies aglow off Bangor and Whitehead,
dark sea, Glenn Miller's 'Moonlight Serenade',
huge transport planes thundering overhead.
Each white shoe you can remember, each stair-rod,
each streaming window on the Shore Road,
a seaside golf-links on a summer night,
'pale sand-dunes stretching away in the moonlight'.

DEREK MAHON, *The Yellow Book*, 1997

THE RESORT REMAINS A SOURCE OF JOY. The only tears it ever squeezed from me came not from grief or disappointment, but from the blinding whiteness of its sunny promenade. As I walked down it once more, blinking wetly in the afternoon sun, I saw well enough that the town was very much as I remembered it, its inhabitants just as agreeable. I stayed at a guest house not far from the derelict station – an agreeable change from those earlier accommodations, which had been cramped, rumpled from their weekly turnover: night shelters. Urgency did not drive me from the place, as it once drove me from the lodgings of my youth when guests from Lancashire sang hymns after high tea, sending me fleeing to the devil in the amusement arcade. A two-mile strand curved gently westward from a golf club to the Bann mouth, its swirling waters so treacherous that we were forbidden to swim there. The beach itself is safe and, thanks to the National Trust, stays spotless, the dunes preserved, and the tide, in its big surfing surges, cleaner than almost anywhere in the British Isles. The dunes are so extensive that it was easy for me, as a boy, to imagine I was crossing a desert, on my sunburnt way to a far-off *kasbah* where languorous girls in diaphanous garments reposed upon silken sofas.

There was little else on our minds then. No bombs exploded, no bullets flew, no threat of revolution rushed to engulf us like the wild, white surf. My father (probably under my stepmother's influence) had gone a bit 'arty', abandoning waistcoats and taking to dark-brown and bottle-green rayon shirts. Yet even lovely, loosely knit Portstewart gave off little whiffs of sectarian preference which the sharp, saline breezes could never quite obscure. Although my brothers and I were happy to ignore the occasional lines of demarcation, we were well aware that some hotels, like some guest houses, were staunchly Protestant and others traditionally Catholic and that, for a time at least, the Herring Pond was a Protestant bathing place, while Port-na-Happel was a place for Catholics. Nevertheless, the resort always seemed more than capable of alleviating stress, accommodating the diverse and minimizing trouble ...

On the promenade, Christians still gather with brass and sheet music to praise the Lord. The summer pulse hasn't really changed in four decades. Portstewart fairly swarms with visitors: well-off farmers from mid-Ulster, professionals from Belfast, Scottish excursionists. The faces I observed, on hobbling pensioners and on their tugging grandchildren, might have been sketched from my youth. Conversation remained full of the bland warmth in which Ulster folk wrap themselves for fear of unwanted controversy or causing offence to visitors. Going back was a transcendent exercise, at times dependent neither on memory nor on fresh perception. It was the kind of pilgrimage which can replace nostalgic clarity with sudden confusions. The diapason sometimes may hurt the ear. But one continues to hear the rhapsody.

CAL McCRYSTAL, *Reflections on a Quiet Rebel*, 1997

PORTRUSH. NO RUINS HERE, but a clean, windswept town, full of bright tea shops, dance halls, cinemas, and solid middle-class boarding-houses. A heavy sea is breaking along the green chain of the Skerries that forms a natural breakwater to the bay, and an incredibly healthy looking old gentleman explains to me that at one time an Atlantic terminal harbour was planned in the lee of the islands. The name of the town is, he tells me, derived from the Gaelic *Port ruis*, which, translated, means 'the harbour of the promontory'. Certainly whichever way one looks, down the vista of a street, or from the window of a tea shop, one sees what a modern Irish poet has labelled 'the gaudily striped Atlantic', for the town is almost an island, connected with the mainland only by the strip of land along which run the railway and the coast road. Today the streets are crowded; there is an air of bright, cheerful prosperity; even without its famous golf links Portrush would still be attractive on account of something exotic, something oddly continental in its atmosphere.

It is a last paradoxical outpost of the Anglo-Irish, and at night the lighthouse on Inishowen Head beyond the entrance waters of Lough Foyle has the effect of flashing in a foreign land.

DENIS IRELAND, *Statues Round the City Hall*, 1939

TERENCE DOZED OFF and when he awoke he was in Ballycastle. There was the smell of turf and the air heavy with heat. Down past a siding they walked where wooden sleepers were sticky with oil and smelt sharply of tar.

They stopped at a shop and Terence bought ice-cream, a wooden spade, and a red bucket with black letters: A Present from Ballycastle.

They took the long road to the sea. Men with twisted towels round their necks passed them. Blinds were pulled down in the big houses and on the lawns old ladies sat on deckchairs under the shade of red umbrellas. Terence shook a pebble from his sandal, and Mr Devlin walked on, fanning himself with his hat. The big chestnut trees that lined the road were stiff with heat, but under the leaves flakes of shadow quivered. The tarred road crackled as a motor raced by, then a drove of cattle came up, their hooves sticking in the tar, their dung-caked sides as dry as the bark of a tree.

'If we get weather like this, Terence, we'll not know ourselves on the way back.'

While Mr Devlin went to inquire about the boat Terence leaned over a sun-warmed wall and saw below him boys and girls playing tennis. Boys hung blazers on the net-posts, hitched up their belts, and through the sun-sifted air came the cord-rattle of tennis balls hitting the net and nearby a lazy plunge of waves falling on a curve of sand. Idly he picked moss out of the crevices in the wall, and then a finger flicked his ear and he turned to see his father smiling down at him: 'We'll go over to the quay now; the boat's going to the island shortly.'

Alongside the quay lay a boat, a brown sail wrapped round the mast and old motor tyres hanging over the sides. The outgoing tide had left pools of water on the quay, and strands of seaweed had entangled themselves under the mooring rings. At the end of the quay three boys were fishing for fry and behind them sat glass jam-jars filled with shining water and green moss. Terence yearned to take off his sandals and dabble his scorched feet in the pools, but already his father was handing the suitcase to a man in the boat and he joined him to see the cargo being taken aboard: two bags of flour, a tea-chest filled with loaves and covered with sacking, a coil of barbed wire and two panes of glass.

MICHAEL McLAVERTY, *from* 'The Schooner', *Collected Short Stories*, 2002

WARRENPOINT WAS A SEASIDE RESORT, if you please. I don't recall that the local Urban District Council displayed coloured pictures advertising the charm of the town; nothing like 'Come to Sunny Prestatyn' in Philip Larkin's poem, with a laughing girl in a swimsuit and, behind her, hotels with palm trees expanding from her thighs and arms. Nothing as grand as that. As a resort, Warrenpoint relied not upon laughing girls or golden weather but upon three more reliable considerations. One: you could get to the place easily from any part of the North by train, since it was the terminus of the Great Northern Railway's branch line from Newry. No longer; the train is gone. Two: Warrenpoint has the largest square in Ireland, a great place for amusements, circuses, swings and roundabouts, ice-cream carts, parades, celebrations. The square was promiscuous in the wiles of display. Three: the licensing laws for the sale of alcohol are stricter in the North than in the South, mainly because Presbyterians keep the Sabbath more severely than Catholics do. If you came to Warrenpoint for a Sunday trip, you would find the public houses shut, but you could go by ferryboat across to Omeath, an open town on the Sabbath, for drink and noise. Meanwhile, children and their mothers passed the Sunday on a rough pebble beach in Warrenpoint and watched the yachts and rowing boats in the lough. If the pleasure of watching other people enjoying themselves wore off, the mothers could walk to the town park and see their betters playing tennis. Or walk along the coast road to Rostrevor, a smaller and prettier town than Warrenpoint and socially several cuts above it. Warrenpoint had tea shops, but Rostrevor had the Great Northern Hotel, a place of emphasised elegance. Not now: it was decisively bombed some years ago by the IRA, and the remains of it have been removed.

DENIS DONOGHUE, Warrenpoint, 1991

W HO THAT WAS LUCKY ENOUGH to be born in the golden age – when dates cost a halfpenny for a quarter of a pound and many people could not afford the halfpenny – can ever recall his childhood at its most golden except as a spade-and-bucket childhood? To arrive at Portrush, to be led by the hand along Main Street ... to the toy shop with its cornucopia of little sailing boats, shrimp nets, fishing rods, pencils looking through the end of which you could see a picture of Dunluce Castle, mugs bearing an inscription in gold letters: 'A Present from Portrush' or 'A Present for a Good Boy', dolls, photographs, penknives, and everything that the soul of man in the tadpole stage could desire – above all, spades and buckets, iron spades and wooden spades, blue buckets, red buckets, and green. In Mr Priestley's play They Came to a City, some of the visitors to the ideal city are disappointed and repelled. No child was ever disappointed in Portrush as he received his first spade and bucket from the hands of the man in the toy shop. He knew – even if only subconsciously – that he was in heaven. With a shrimp net and a sailing boat (price 4d.) added, he knew that he was in the seventh heaven.

How charming, then, was the descent to the sands. There are three stretches of sand in Portrush – the White Strand, the Black Strand, and the Ladies' Strand. As Mr Shaw's Androcles would have done, I frequented in those days the Ladies' Strand. There ladies, waterlogged in extraordinary heavy blue costumes that seemed more suitable for keeping an Arctic explorer warm than for enabling a lady to enjoy a swim, bobbed up and down a few feet out during the best part of the day, as clamorous as seagulls. We paid little attention to them, however. We were intent on our own pleasures. To fill a bucket slowly with sand, to turn the bucket upside down and, removing it, to see a castle built, as it were, with one's own hands – it was to feel for the first time the joy of artistic creation.

ROBERT LYND, *from* 'Spade and Bucket', *Things One Hears*, 1945

It Goes as
Follies

I'm livin' in Drumlister,
   An' I'm gettin' very oul',
I have to wear an Indian bag
   To save me from the coul'.
The deil a man in this townlan'
   Wos claner raired nor me,
But I'm livin' in Drumslister
   In clabber to the knee.

W.F. MARSHALL, from 'Me an' me Da'

Heard ye no' tell of the Stumpie's Brae?
   Sit down, sit down, young friend,
I'll make your flesh to creep today,
   And your hair to stan' on end.

CECIL FRANCES ALEXANDER, from 'The Legend of Stumpie's Brae'

from THE ROUGHFORT FAIR
A Rustic Parody on Gray's Elegy

The day, at length, to evening's edge is come,
   And cools his axle in the western sea;
The mellow farmers drive their heifers home,
   And leave the fair to *social mirth* and me.

The glimmering candles light each festive room,
  And rural transport flies from nook to nook,
Save where the drunk man tumbles o'er the loom,
  And stagg'ring seeks some private place to puke.

Save that from yonder cobweb-mantled bed,
  The drunk-down jockey's sullen snores resound,
Who wishful turns, but turns in vain the head,
  For that repose which cannot there be found.

In farthest bed, with humble checquer hung,
  Heaving the rug, two social fellows rest,
Who gay till six o'clock, carrous'd and sung,
  But forc'd, alas! to give it up at last ...

In vain for them the blazing hearth may burn;
  Their wives in vain the supper may prepare;
In vain the children wish their sire's return,
  Expecting sweets and play-things from the fair.

Poor wives! how often are ye but deceiv'd
  With husband's promise when they go away;
For thus they tell you, and are still believ'd,
  'Upon my word, indeed, we will not stay'.

Howe'er, let not the shrew, with brazen face,
  In search of husband to the alehouse roam;
It plays the devil, and it brings disgrace;
  Far better stay and nurse their wrath at home.

Yet there are some, to all decorum dead,
  Like fiends will after to the ale-house fly;
Who boast the breaking of their husband's head,
  And how they can the social scene destroy! ...

Perhaps in this gay festive place may lie
  The frothy schoolmaster, ere break of day;
Dull as a musket ball each turn'd up eye,
  That beam'd on truants the despotic ray.

But Knowledge to his eyes her ample page,
  Rich with the spoils of Time, did ne'er unroll
Nature withheld from him the *noble rage*,
  And froze the current of his stupid soul.

Full many a blockhead, impudent, and fool,
  The few intelligent are doom'd to bear;
Full many a worthless scoundrel keeps a school,
  And poisons intellects both far and near.

The stiff-neck formalist, with bigot breast
  That vain new-light men ever keen controuls;
The subtle deist, held Religion's pest,
  Here fall together, all as drunk as owls.

Th' applause of sober people to command,
  The '*merry roar*' and bottle to despise
Nay, on their feet like men to go or stand,
  Or e'en when fallen, up again to rise.

Their state forbids; but holds them here *incog.*
  In friendly Robin's hospitable shed;
Forbids to wade, all fours, thro' ditch and bog,
  Or tumble, zig zag, home to wife and bed.

The struggling pangs of vomiting to hide,
  And paley face from other's eyes to keep,
Some stragglers slip out to the garden side,
  Puke, yawn, and tumble over sound asleep.

Beyond the reach a while of grog and din,
  They sleep, and dream perhaps of wife and care
Till waken'd sober, they again come in,
  And help their fellows to conclude the fair.

SAMUEL THOMSON, *Poems on Different Subjects*, 1793

FORKHILL WAS THE SCENE of an annual and animated fair. This was held every Michaelmas Day. On the Fair Green – now rather built over – tents and dancing-decks were erected; and to use the words of my old informant: 'With the best of aytin' an' drinkin', an' dancin' an' sport, it was a great set day.'

To this fair in Forkhill gathered all the fiddlers and musicians of both town and country, each vying with the other to receive the highest award. Collections were made in a hat for the musicians, but they genuinely sought for praise, too.

Young and old went to the fair. Every courting man was disgraced if he failed to take his intended to the festival.

MICHAEL J. MURPHY, *At Slieve Gullion's Foot*, 1941

from CREESLOUGH FAIR

If you have never been to a Creeslough Fair,
Nor had a look at the doings there,
In the olden time – Lammas or May –
You have missed a rousing holiday.
'Tis a pleasant task once more to recall
The buying and selling by Hasting's Wall;
Where to cheer the heart and banish care,
Crowds gathered from far to the Creeslough Fair.

They came from Fanad, Glen and Castle Doe;
From Cloughaneely and around Myroe;
From Ramelton and all along the Lennon,
Letterkenny, Milford, and Kilmacrenan;
On horse, on foot, on loaded cart,
From Dunfanaghy, Fougher, Derryart;
By the side of Muckish, past Crinesmair; –
They travelled in groups to the Creeslough Fair.

Sturdy farmers, children from school;
Housewives bringing spun lint and wool;
Young men and the girls they most did prize,
With a wealth of hair and dangerous eyes –
Black, blue, or brown – there was always peril
In going to a fair with a Donegal girl,
For full many a match came unaware
And two hearts made one at a Creeslough Fair.

There were donkeys, horses, foals and mares,
Cows, heifers and calves, bullocks in pairs;
Sharp drovers, tinkers, and keen farmer boys
Buying and selling with hand–clap and noise; –
The seller extolling the best that he could
The beast that the buyer pronounced no good,
As he looked in its mouth with a nonchalant air,
But at last closed the deal at the Creeslough Fair.

There was the man who auctioned goods down,
Who began at a guinea and dropped to a crown;
Then seeing the buyers to bid were unwilling,
Let the bargain go at last for a shilling.
There were hawkers with much that a housewife
   needs –

Cutlery, spools, pins, needles, and beads;
Some spent all the money they had to spare,
Buying odds and ends at the Creeslough Fair ...

When the buying and selling were over
   and done,
The time then arrived for the frolic and fun;
In the inns for refreshment luck-money was paid,
Old friendships renewed and new ones were
   made;
Near the jugglers were sparrers entering the lists,
Harlequins, puppets, and ventriloquists;
Irish pipers a-playing, trained dogs, dancing bears,
And proud, peerless 'peelers' parading the fairs.

JAMES NICOLL JOHNSTON, Donegal Memories and Other Poems, 1910

NEXT MORNING AFTER BREAKFAST they sat in the sun on the bench before the hotel smoking their pipes. An old woman hobbled by.

'*Maidin breagh*!' she cried in a hearty voice, a smile wrinkling all over her face.

'*Ana bhreagh*,' replied Eugene and McGurk together.

'What was that?' asked Willoughby.

'Fine day,' said Eugene.

A labourer going down the hill to his work shouted the same salutation, and three or four others who passed in succession did likewise.

'They seem mighty interested in the weather in this locality,' observed O'Flaherty.

'No wonder,' said McGurk. 'It's not often they get the chance to say "*lá breagh*" up here. "*Lá bog*" is the usual complaint.'

'Say, boys,' said O'Flaherty a little later, 'Willoughby's just itching to have a near view of the natives. What about a tour of inspection?'

All were agreed and they set out at once. They stopped at a small but crowded shop in the village to buy cigarettes, and Willoughby for the first time realised that he was in a foreign country. Nothing was to be heard anywhere but this strange Irish language of whose existence he had been ignorant until quite recently. Dublin, save for some minor local peculiarities, had seemed but a part of his own country, where putting his watch back twenty-five minutes was the greatest wrench in the scheme of things. Now he suddenly felt himself a stranger isolated in a distant land.

On Bernard also this first continuous rush of the language that should have been his own had a strange effect, but a different one. The sound had a baffling enchantment for him and he felt an extraordinary desire to join in the conversation, half-expecting that his native language would

come bubbling from his lips by some miracle of atmosphere and
willpower ... He registered an instantaneous resolve to learn the language
at once.

EIMAR O'DUFFY, *The Wasted Island*, 1923

THE GRAVEYARD OF CREGGAN CHURCH
Art MacCooey

An File:

    Ag úirchill a' Chreagáin sea chodail mé aréir faoi bhrón,
    Is le héirí na maidne tháinig ainnir fá mo dhéin le póig,
    Bhí gríosghruaidh ghartha aici agus loinnir ina céibh mar ór,
    'S gurbh é íocshláinte an domhain a bheith ag amharc ar a'
        ríon óig ...

Poet:

    By the graveyard of Creggan I slept last night in grief;
    At daybreak a fair maid came towards me with a kiss;
    Her rosy cheeks were glowing and her hair a golden sheen;
    A healing balm for everyone to gaze on this young queen.

Fairywoman:

    Kind nobleman do not languish here in clouds of grief forlorn
    But rise up quickly and come with me, west along the road,
    To the sweet land of honey where the stranger has no hold,
    And in the halls you will delight, being enticed by strains of song.

Poet:

    My sweet queen, are you Helen for whom many were destroyed,
    Or are you one of Parnassus' nine fair maids, once in human form;
    Where in the world, unblemished star, have you been reared
    That you should want the likes of me, whispering with you
        on the road?

Fairywoman:

    Do not ask me questions, for I sleep not this side of the Boyne,
    I'm a little fairychild reared by the side of Gráinne Óg;
    In the rightful court of poets I openly inspire song,
    At nightime I'm in Tara, in the heart of Tyrone by dawn.

Poet:
It's my great woe that from us the Gaels of Tyrone have gone,
And the heirs of the Fews, in sorrow, under slabs beyond,
The pure branch of Niall Frasach that never abandoned song,
But at Christmas would clothe the poets who would so
    honour them.

Fairywoman:
Alas the tribes in Aughrim and the Boyne were ruined,
And the heirs of royal Ír who would shelter every druid,
Wouldn't you be better by my side each noon, in fairyforts,
Than the arrows of the Williamites ever piercing your heart?

Poet:
I would not refuse your bidding for all the gold of kings
But I hesitate to leave my friends who are still living here,
The spouse whom I enticed once, with promises, when young,
If I forsake her now, I know that she would surely mourn.

Fairywoman:
I do not think your kindred here are indeed your friends,
You're penniless and poor, distressed and undone,
Far better to go with the fair maid of the smooth-fingered hands,
Than all about here mocking each burst of song you sang.

Poet:
My beloved one, if destiny has fated me to be your own;
Guarantee and promise me before I take the road at dawn;
Should I die in Egypt, by the Shannon, or Manaan's Isle,
That with the Gaels of Creggan you will bury me in soil.

PÁDRAIGÍN NÍ UALLACHÁIN, *A Hidden Ulster: People, Songs and Traditions of Oriel*, 2003

THIS WAS ART MacCOOEY'S MOST POPULAR SONG. It might be called the national anthem of south Ulster. Everyone in the counties Louth, Armagh, and Monaghan who could sing any Irish could sing 'Úirchill a' Chreagáin'. Mothers sang it as they spun, and at the end wiped away a tear as they recollected how their own mothers used to sing it when they themselves skipped about light-hearted children. It is a beautiful song, but its beauty will not altogether account for its popularity; much of the latter was due to the fact that it harmonised so fully with the national feelings of the fallen Gael, smarting under the oppression of the 'Clann Bhullaigh'; it offered them a medium by which they could vocalise their own sorrow, and its suggestion of a land of promise, where the Gall held no sway, was dear to a people who seemed to live through an endless night.

Local tradition says it was composed by MacCooey while hiding in the O'Neill vault in Creggan churchyard, with the minions of local tyranny on his track. So that the opening line, stating that he slept last night in Creggan churchyard, is literally true. We can picture the feelings of such a man lying awake through the long, long night, in the presence of the dead whom he loved, yet who filled him with an awesome feeling. With the first rays of daylight a little robin came to the door of the vault, and this sign of life broke the spell of death, comforted him, and made him glad. He envied the little bird its freedom, and all this acting on his strained imagination suggested the idea of the fairy maiden coming to him with a call to a land of freedom and happiness.

The song is rarely heard now, and will soon be forgotten, though in my boyhood's days there was hardly any gathering in Farney or in south Armagh where, if called for, one or more persons would not be found able to sing it.

ÉNRÍ Ó MUIRGHEASA, *Art MacCubhthaigh's and Other Songs*, 1926

NINE HOSTAGES

I cut my hand off at the wrist and threw it at the shore.
The goblin spilled a bag of red gold in my lap.
He wore emerald boots and a bloody fine cap.
Let Erin remember the days of yore.

I'd been riding the piebald mushroom for some time,
Following the Admiral's vermilion cruise.
He wore a blue cocked hat and tattered tartan trews.
We were both implicated in the crime of rhyme.

Up in the deep blue like a red balloon I flew,
Following the sickle grin of Old Man Moon.
Gun-metal gunships sailed in through the foggy dew.

In Creggan churchyard last night I fell into a dream
Confronted by a red dragoon, a green gossoon.
The red hand played the harp with oars of quinquereme.

CIARAN CARSON, *The Twelfth of Never*, 1998

'FJB' WAS STEADFAST IN HIS LOVE FOR IRELAND, its people, its history, its monuments and its folk-customs. In common with many other

Protestant landed and professional figures in the 1890s and early 1900s, he became a firm supporter of the movement to preserve and revive the Irish language – then still spoken in the less accessible parts of Ulster such as the Glens of Antrim. In April 1894 he delivered a paper on 'Local Gaelic Placenames' to the Celtic class of the Naturalists' Field Club, and he was a constant attendant at the Irish language classes conducted in Belfast by P.J. O'Shea. He became a member of the Coiste Gnótha of the Gaelic League – founded in 1893 by Dr Douglas Hyde, the son of a Church of Ireland rector in County Roscommon, and Eoin MacNeill, a historian and native of Glenarm – and president of its Belfast Council. As a lecturer on Irish archaeology at the Irish School (Coláiste Comhaill) in Bank Street, he was brought into close contact with the leading Gaelic scholars of the time such as Hyde and MacNeill. In June 1904, he was involved with a number of prominent individuals in north Antrim, including Miss Margaret Dobbs of Portnagolan, Miss Ada McNeill of Cushendun, Miss Rose Young of Galgorm Castle, John Clarke (the writer 'Benmore') and Andrew Dooey of Dunloy in the founding of the Glens Feis – a colourful festival of Irish language, culture, crafts and games.

EAMON PHOENIX, *from* 'Francis Joseph Bigger', *Feis na nGleann*, 2005

THE FAIRY THORN

'Get up, our Anna dear, from the weary spinning-wheel;
For your father's on the hill, and your mother is asleep;
Come up above the crags, and we'll dance a Highland reel
Around the Fairy Thorn on the steep.'

At Anna Grace's door 'twas thus the maidens cried,
Three merry maidens fair in kirtles of the green;
And Anna laid the rock and the weary wheel aside,
The fairest of the four, I ween.

They're glancing through the glimmer of the quiet eve,
Away in milky wavings of neck and ankle bare;
The heavy-sliding stream in its sleepy song they leave,
And the crags in the ghostly air.

And linking hand-in-hand, and singing as they go,
The maids along the hillside have ta'en their fearless way,
Till they come to where the rowan trees in lonely beauty grow
Beside the Fairy Hawthorn grey.

The Hawthorn stands between the ashes tall and slim,
Like matron with her twin grand-daughters at her knee;
The rowan berries cluster o'er her low head grey and dim
In ruddy kisses sweet to see.

The merry maidens four have ranged them in a row,
Between each lovely couple a stately rowan stem,
And away in mazes wavy, like skimming birds they go,
Oh, never carolled bird like them!

But solemn is the silence on the silvery haze
That drinks away their voices in echoless repose,
And dreamily the evening has stilled the haunted braes,
And dreamier the gloaming grows.

And sinking one by one, like lark-notes from the sky,
When the falcon's shadow saileth across the open shaw,
Are hushed the maidens' voices, as cowering down they lie
In the flutter of their sudden awe.

For, from the air above and the grassy mound beneath,
And from the mountain-ashes and the old white-thorn between,
A power of faint enchantment doth through their beings breathe,
And they sink down together on the green.

They sink together silent, and stealing side to side,
They fling their lovely arms o'er their drooping necks so fair,
Then vainly strive again their naked arms to hide,
For their shrinking necks again are bare.

Thus clasped and prostrate all, with their heads together bowed,
Soft o'er their bosoms beating – the only human sound –
They hear the silky footsteps of the silent fairy crowd,
Like a river in the air gliding round.

Nor scream can any raise, nor prayer can any say,
But wild, wild the terror of the speechless three –
For they feel fair Anna Grace drawn silently away,
By whom they dare not look to see.

They feel their tresses twine with her parting locks of gold,
And the curls elastic falling, as her head withdraws.
They feel her sliding arms from their tranced arms unfold,
But they dare not look to see the cause.

For heavy on their senses the faint enchantment lies
Through all that night of anguish and perilous amaze
And neither fear nor wonder can ope their quivering eyes,
Or their limbs from the cold ground raise.

Till out of night the earth has rolled her dewy side,
With every haunted mountain and streamy vale below:
When, as the mist dissolves in the yellow morning-tide,
The maidens' trance dissolveth so.

Then fly the ghastly three as swiftly as they may,
And tell their tale of sorrow to anxious friends in vain –
They pined away and died within the year and day,
And ne'er was Anna Grace seen again.

SIR SAMUEL FERGUSON, 1834

IT WAS SUNDAY NIGHT AT THE HUTS, and the members of the Fianna were discussing the coming procession on 'the Twal'th'. The Twelfth of July was sacred to the Orangemen. All places of business were closed; the streets were given over to the processionists; the big drum and drumming parties were heard all over the city and nearby districts; members of the Loyal Orange Order paraded decked in their orange sashes and carrying banners ending up at a big field outside the city, where with their families they ate their lunches and listened to speakers, who in one breath proclaimed their loyalty to the British Crown and hatred of the Pope and 'the papishers'.

It was felt by the Fianna that something should be done to show that the Nationalists and Catholics were not cowed by this greatest of all Orange demonstrations, but consciousness of their youth and their small number made it difficult to decide what to do. A bright idea struck one of them. 'Nono,' he asked, 'is your father home tonight?'

'He is,' answered Nono. 'He's writing.'

'Let's go up and ask him. He'll be able to suggest something.'

The suggestion was acclaimed, and about a dozen started up the road to the house.

'Daddy,' said Nono, when they arrived, 'we want your advice.' They all took turns in explaining their difficulty.

'H'm,' said Daddy, as he looked from one to the other with twinkling eyes. 'Let me see.' They all waited expectantly.

'How would this do?' he asked, taking a piece of paper from the table and commencing to write. 'Wait a minute. I must get it exact.' He took a book from the case. 'Here it is.' He wrote rapidly for a few minutes and then copied something from the book.

'What I suggest is that we get thousands of leaflets printed with this on them, and on gummed paper. On the night before the procession you send parties out to stick them all along the route; plaster them thickly; every tram and lamp-standard should have one; every corner, every hoarding, every shutter. Make such a job of it that it will be too big a job to tear them all down. What do you think of that?'

They all crowded round the table to see what he had written. It told the Orangemen that in celebrating King Billy's victory at the Battle of the Boyne they were celebrating a Popish victory; that King Billy was in league with the Pope and sent word of his victory to the Vatican; and that when the Pope heard the news he ordered a thanks-giving service; that Te Deums were sung, and the whole Vatican lighted up in celebration. Most of it was a quotation from a Protestant historian.

There was great glee when it was read.

'Is that true, Mr Connolly?' one boy asked, with dancing eyes. 'Think of King Billy and the Pope houl'in' han's!'

Gurgles of laughter greeted this. 'We'll do it,' they cried. 'There won't be a lamp-standard empty on the Twal'th.'

'I'll help pay for the printing,' said Daddy.

'Man, dear, we wouldn't doubt you,' and back to the huts they tramped triumphantly.

It was the night before the Twelfth and the Fianna boys and girls were mobilised. It was a triumphant, gleeful party that waited to be assigned districts and receive the leaflets.

'Man, dear!' said one, when he had read it. 'Do you know what? I'd love to go to the field tomorrow when all the Orangemen are gathered round waiting for the speeches. I'd like to have a big voice you could hear for half a mile. I'd like to go on the platform and in a big roar say: "Orangemen of Belfast and surrounding districts. In the name of the downtrodden papishes of Belfast, I want to thank you for the wonderful way in which you have celebrated this great victory of the Pope."' He broke off to say, with a world of longing in his voice, 'I'd only last a minute, but, man dear, it would be worth it.'

Amid cheers and laughter the leaflets were gathered up and the parties departed.

NORA CONNOLLY O'BRIEN, *Portrait of a Rebel Father*, 1935

AFTER BREAKFAST, KITTY SORTED OUT two sprigs of shamrock, and pinned them to their jackets.

'There you are,' she said. 'Away you go, and don't roll in the muck in them good suits.'

As they walked up the Row, Neilly said, 'Come on over and see if Pachy's up.'

The boys had heard their father and mother talking about him and Kelly during breakfast.

'I suppose they're sitting over there without a bite,' Kitty had said. 'Well, if they are, that's their look out! They'll not get me running over after them this morning.'

The boys crossed over, and peered through the tears in the old curtain over the window. There was no one in the kitchen; they could see the heel of a loaf, and a tin of condensed milk on the bare table.

Neilly put his lips to the keyhole and called softly. Next moment, as though in direct answer, the patter of stockinged feet sounded faintly from up the stairs and Pachy's voice shouted, 'Who's there?' The feet descended, the key rattled in the lock, and Pachy looked out. The hair was standing on him, and his face was dark with beard stubble.

'Oh, it's you!' he smiled. 'Where in the name of God are you going to at this hour? What time is it?'

'We're going to chapel. It's about half-past nine.'

'Oh, yes; St Patrick's Day. Holiday of Obligation!'

'Where's Johnny Kelly?' Neilly asked. 'Is he in?'

'Kelly? Kelly's lying up the stairs, dead. Are you coming in to say a prayer for him?'

The boys drew back, shocked.

'Johnny Kelly, dead?'

'Aye, dead asleep.'

They smiled. 'Ah, you're only funning!'

Pachy said, 'Where's Kate? Is she in?'

'She says that if you're sitting over here without a bite it's your own look out,' Shemie told him seriously. 'She says she's not coming over again.'

Pachy broke into a laugh.

'Did she? Well, what d'you know? Never mind, a drop of black tay'll do us rightly. It's a bad thing to be ateing all the time.'

A voice cried from upstairs: 'Who's that, Pachy?'

'God help us,' said Pachy, 'the dead has riz.'

'Ah, it's only the boys,' he called up. 'Go back to sleep again.' He nodded out towards the street. 'Who's that? Is that young Devine waiting on you over there?'

The boys turned and nodded. Neilly shouted, 'Wait there, Jackie.'

They said so long to Pachy. Pachy saluted them and closed the door again. The boys crossed over to where the other lad was standing, and they strolled up to the Corner.

They stood against the Dining Room, emitting now and then a series of short, piercing whistles and, one by one, other boys came running up from their houses. They stood together for a little while making remarks, complimentary and otherwise, about each other's shamrock. When there were about eight of them, they moved away, and trotted up the road, laughing and jingling their money. They were in great spirits, for it was a lovely morning, clear and warm, with the sun already shining, and the birds singing. Halfway up the Asylum Hill they unpinned their shamrocks and 'drownded' them by dipping the sprigs into the little drain running beneath the hedge. They held them under for a good while, to make sure they were well and truly 'drownded', and then, with a great deal of lip twisting and screwing down of the eyes, they repinned their sprigs and continued on their way.

They walked about the town, after Mass was over, admiring the decorations. The place was brilliantly decked out for the great occasion. All the shops were closed, and arches and banners gaily coloured and bearing numerous inscriptions, stretched across the street. Flags hung from the windows drooping in the warm, breezeless air. The Mass crowds dandered about slowly, in their Sunday finery. Despite the crowds, the streets were comparatively quiet, but in the soft murmur of the people's voices there could be sensed an air of tense excitement and expectancy. The boys took a walk up towards Scotch Street, at the far end of the town but, just as they expected, this street was bare, colourless, and empty. One or two of the boys, in a fit of bravado, shook their fists.

'You Prodesans better stay in your houses the day,' they jeered.

The sunny, lifeless street offered no taunt in return, so the boys drew back into their own domain, and hurried down towards the station to meet the bands coming off.

JOHN O'CONNOR, *Come Day – Go Day*, 1948

I WAS VERY BUSY JUST THEN [i.e in the summer of 1927] on a book about the wood engravings of the sixties, and in the thick of my labours received an invitation from George Buchanan to spend a week with him at his father's house, Kilwaughter Rectory, which is about a mile inland from Larne. It seemed to me a capital plan; we should have the rectory to ourselves; and I could do as much writing as I liked because George himself, I gathered, was putting in from eight to ten hours a day on a novel. Therefore down to Larne I went.

It was perfect weather and we worked out of doors in the grounds of Kilwaughter Castle, usually by the side of a lake. Every morning after breakfast we went there, I with my notes and manuscript, George with some writing paper and a bathing suit. We sat on the shore of the lake and George thought of his novel, while I, having undertaken to deliver my manuscript by a certain date, was obliged to adopt more active methods. Kilwaughter Castle, I believe, has attracted the attention of the

Society for Psychical Research but I knew nothing of this, nor did I ever cross its doors; it was in the archery green beside it that I became conscious of something unusual. What that consciousness was I can best, though still unsatisfactorily, describe as a sense of the past – of the past veiled by, yet imminent in, the present. It was no more than that, yet very definite, and doubtless, working on my imagination, it was this that created a flickering, unsubstantial, and always transparent vision of a small stone building at the farther end of the green, where certainly no building now was. Again I must call it no more than an atmosphere, but again it was confined to this one spot, and when I moved on I left it behind me, exactly as one might some low continuous sound like the droning of bees.

On the other hand, at the rectory itself I slept in what George told me was the haunted room, and remained completely insensitive. The only hauntings reaching me there were those of the rectory hens, who gathered outside my window in the first glimmering light to discuss the surprising advent of a new day.

FORREST REID, Private Road, 1940

DOWN BY THE LAKE, encircled by swelling green parkland and the purple of the winter woods, the shooting brakes and victorias, even the humble jaunting-cars, were parked as near the ice as they could get. Footmen in top boots, white breeches, long coats with brass buttons, and top hats adorned with cockades carried rugs and hampers. In the background bunched the jarveys, inclined, like most Belfast jarveys, to be sardonic, but slightly subdued by the 'quality', not to mention the footmen.

Hampers were opened, bottles produced, bonfires lit: all that was missing was a brass band playing the 'Skaters' Waltz', or a Hungarian string orchestra in blue hussar uniforms. Nevertheless, the inevitable couple who disrupt such occasions by skating better than everybody else were already whirling on the ice. *He* wore riding breeches and had skates that turned the rest of us green with envy by curving back over his toecaps; *she* caused a lot of adverse comment and staring through lorgnettes by showing at least two inches of leg below the hem of her long, gracefully billowing skirt. The general verdict among the lorgnette users in the victorias and landaus was that she was a foreigner – which, of course, explained everything, including the two inches of leg and the fact that she could do the outside-edge backwards.

The rest of us just clattered and stumbled round the ice, getting in the real skaters' way. The instruments (hardly to be classed as skates) on which I clattered were made of wood, with long straight blades inserted underneath. To put them on involved contortions with a gimlet (with which you bored holes in the heels of your boots) and struggles, reminiscent of the infant Hercules strangling the snakes, with complicated ligatures of straps. The snag was that you nearly always forgot the gimlet.

The woods were turning deeper purple in the frosty dusk, the red of bonfires already reflected in the ice, when we turned for home on the hired jaunting-car. There was talk of skating by torchlight, of midnight suppers on the island in the frozen lake. Uproar, no doubt due to bottles in hampers, was already rising from the lake and its surroundings; the whole affair was taking on the abandonment of a crowd scene in a Russian opera; and the young woman showing two inches of leg, now whirling with other partners beside the one in the riding breeches, was enjoying what would have been described in a Paris theatre as a *succès fou*. No place for us, my mother decided; with the addendum for the weaker vessels like myself that, unlike the nobility and gentry, not to mention the raffish elements now appearing unbidden over the demesne wall, we had work, stern Presbyterian work, to do the morning after.

So home, *clip-clop*, down dark tree-shadowed country roads, through the purple of the frosty twilight, to the twinkling gas-lamps of south Belfast and a monumental high tea in a red-brick terrace house – a high tea at which, with bulging silver muffin dishes and silver kettles steaming over flames of methylated spirit as on some kind of Presbyterian altar, the un-Presbyterian motto might have been *Et in Arcadia nos*.

DENIS IRELAND, *From the Jungle of Belfast*, 1973

WHEN WE WERE CHILDREN I remember Lough Neagh freezing for miles. Papa took us walking on the ice from the Sand Gates entrance to the lough, across to Antrim about half a mile away. It was our first walk on ice, and we fell many times on the journey. The ice was so clear we could see the bottom in the shallows near the edge. When we got to Fir Field at Antrim crowds of people were skating. I cannot remember how we got home.

Again, in the year 1895, when I was grown up, there was a great frost everywhere. Lough Neagh was completely ice-bound for six weeks and was a scene of gaiety and amusement. A large refreshment tent was erected near the shore in the Fir Field on Lord Massareene's estate, and special trains ran from Belfast, Lisburn and Ballymena. After the first moon had passed, tar barrels were burnt at night at intervals along the shore, and later large Lucian lights were brought by the Northern Counties Railway Company, which also provided a rescue gang with ladders and ropes in case of accidents; but there were no serious mishaps. One day Sir Frank Benson and seven of his Company came from Belfast to skate and were a source of great interest as they were all dressed in skating costume and danced an Eightsome Reel on the ice. They were acting at the Belfast Theatre at the time, doing Shakespeare plays.

GRACE C. BONTHRONE, *from* 'Childhood Memories of County Antrim',
Ulster Folklife, vol. 6, 1960

IN JANUARY, 1881, THE LAKE was again frozen, but much more extensively than in January of 1879. Not for upwards of sixty years had there been so much ice. Skaters from Belfast and other places arrived in considerable numbers, many of whom penetrated to the outer border of the great ice-sheet, probably two-and-a-half miles from the Antrim shore. On making one's way out, the scenes beheld were truly novel. Group after group of skaters and sliders, picnicking parties and onlookers, who had, in consequence of the haze, been previously invisible, came into view, while those who had reached the outer extremity, and when not more than half a mile distant, appeared no bigger than nine-pins moving about on the horizon. The effect was very peculiar, the distance being magnified in a most remarkable manner. These had pushed on until they had discovered a skater's Eldorado – a belt of beautiful, glassy ice, on which not a single snowflake rested – while beyond appeared gurgling waters, mist, chaos. Some of the skaters had brought sails with them, and were being blown at a terrific speed to and fro like miniature railway trains. Others were gliding gracefully on 'the outside edge', while others again, the less skilful, were enjoying themselves in the best way they could.

W.S. SMITH, *Historical Gleanings in Antrim and Neighbourhood*, 1888

IFANCY THAT THAT REMARKABLE religious phenomenon known as the Great Revival of some fifty years ago was due in some measure to the fervency of the Methodists. No volume, however desultory, that purports to touch upon life in Ulster during the second half of the last century can ignore this extraordinary movement. Considering the stolidity of the people in the midst of whom it broke out, I think that it has never been paralleled in the history of Great Britain. There have, of course, been strange religious outbursts in various communities from time to time, but nearly all have been the direct result of the preaching of one man, and nearly all have taken place among a highly emotional people and at times of great national excitement. But the Ulster Revival started in an obscure village in County Antrim – I think it was either Broughshane or Cullybackey – and within a fortnight it had swept over three or four counties with the rapidity of an epidemic, until there was scarcely a town or a village that was not affected by it.

I think I am correct in saying that it started at a Methodist preaching; but it was soon far beyond the scope of any Methodism; and to anyone interested in the phenomena of panic, it afforded a unique opportunity for observing their operation and development and their eventual disappearance ... here was a small crowd of stolid Antrim folk – highly respectable and quite religious, probably never missing a service of their church or an attendance at Sunday-school – here were these people, old and young, flung about as with a form of epilepsy, shrieking out for salvation in an ecstasy of apprehension; and at the last becoming amenable to the decencies of civilised life by the delivery of a few phrases in a fervent but sympathetic tone by a man as unacquainted with theology as with the literature of hysteria!

This was something quite beyond ordinary experience.

F. FRANKFORT MOORE, *The Truth About Ulster*, 1914

THE EXCITEMENT SEEMED CATCHING and on the increase, and yet all seemed perfectly truthful. It was excitement certainly, such as one may suppose to exist if a theatre or assembly room was on fire, and it amounted almost to a panic; but it did not appear to be a fanciful excitement, such as people can sometimes work themselves into without any reasonable cause. The cause in this instance was manifest – the apprehension of going to hell if they died. This danger had previously been unperceived or disbelieved, and now it came upon them in all the vivid colours of a terrible reality. The way to escape was accordingly earnestly sought, as those only seek it before whose eyes a pit of horror is suddenly disclosed into which they believe they are liable at any time to fall. By degrees the excitement increased. The magnitude of the danger became to their minds more apparent and real, and the anxiety to escape more intense. Preachers of various denominations came forward to point out the way of escape, and were listened to with the most marked attention; whilst with one voice they declared the only way of safety, the only door of escape, the only path of light, to be an implicit trust and reliance upon the blood of Jesus Christ, applied to their souls through faith, as a sufficient atonement for sin, and as able to wash away their guilt.

The Roman Catholics looked on at all these proceedings in mute wonder and astonishment. They could not make out what it was all about. They had always considered their Protestant neighbours as prudent, sensible men, and, as a class, generally better educated, and quite as moral, as themselves, and the puzzle to know what new thing had seized upon their imagination was very sincere and perplexing.

WILLIAM STEUART TRENCH, *Realities of Irish Life*, 1869

Before the hysterical hymn had given place to a feverish prayer, there was certain to be another shriek for mercy – another and another – the barn resounded with shrieks – men, women, boys, and girls were grovelling and writhing on the floor, and the men who were pointing out a way to 'find peace' were even more noisy than the people who were affected. Wherever peace might be found, it certainly was not in the barn or the schoolhouse which was the scene of these manifestations.

F. FRANKFORT MOORE, *The Truth About Ulster*, 1914

Islandmagee, from its geographical situation, is not very accessible, and like other remote islands and peninsulas has been the scene of unhallowed deeds and the home of strange superstitions. Early in 1642 a band of Scotchmen, that is to say, Northern Presbyterians, descended on Islandmagee by night and murdered a number of Roman Catholic inhabitants, men, women, and children together. This action was probably a hideous form of revenge for the ill treatment of the Protestants by the rebels elsewhere. Slaughterford Bridge is said to receive its name from this massacre.

In 1711 eight women, two being from the Irish and Scotch quarter of Carrickfergus, one from Braidisland, one from Kilroot, and the remainder from Islandmagee, were tried at Carrickfergus for practising witchcraft in Islandmagee upon a young woman named Mary Dunbar. According to the prosecution the victim was affected by a strange sickness accompanied by fits and ravings. On recovering from these she said she was tormented by several women whose appearance she indicated. The country was scoured for women answering to the description. These when found were brought to the house, whereupon the suffering of the young woman was redoubled. On the other hand, it was deposed on behalf of the unfortunate defendants that they went to church, could repeat the Lord's Prayer, and some of them had lately received the Communion. Two judges tried the case, one was for acquittal, the other for condemnation, and the jury agreed with the latter. However, the extreme penalty was not inflicted, and the prisoners were sentenced to twelve months imprisonment and to stand four times in the pillory at Carrickfergus. The people were greatly incensed against them, and one is said to have lost an eye from the effect of the missiles hurled at her. Mary Dunbar's complaint was, in all probability, the combination of a nervous hysterical temperament with a frail body, and would now be treated in a sanatorium where little notice would be taken of her fancies on emerging from delirium.

D.A. CHART, *A History of Northern Ireland*, 1927

MARGARET MITCHELL

I shall go into a hare,
With sorrow and sigh
And mental torment.

Above the hill of the man of the yellow hair,
Birds skim like stones on an ocean of air;
Clouds are thick and coloured like a bruise.
And across the sloping hill-top field,
The wind runs a light green shimmer in the grass
To where he sits and shelters by the whin-bushes

... sits and broods upon the times
She'd huddled against him in that spot ...
Surely not ... Was she guilty of such crimes?
What secrets had she hid from him?
When did the stated sorcery begin?

Persuaded of the magic in her rhymes,
They have stood her in the Carrig stocks
And mocked her as a crazed young witch –
Hounded like the fabled lurker in the ditch.
Yet she only used the phrases that were heard

On lips around the townlands, and beyond,
And I would laugh and scorn, in my usual way,
And she would call me rude, and swear
That I could really madden her.

But there's madder than you, my love,
Though you be as mad as a March hare:
Many who will never trace
The scars of stones upon their neck
Or feel the smack of cabbage stalks
Against a reddened face.

A smurr of drifting rain
Rounded up the birds inland,
And he lifted up his hands, as if to pray,
But only breathed on them, to warm them,
Then started back for home across Drumgurland.

She lay silent in the castle hold,
As in a form, or souterrain –
Sequestered from the mind's intrigue,
The tongue's accusation,
The pishrogues of men.
Ye yarrow, yarrow, I pull thee –
And under my pillow I'll put thee
And the first young man that speaks to me
Will my own true love be.

ADRIAN RICE, The Mason's Tongue, 1999

I N THE YEAR 1849, IT CAME BEFORE MY NOTICE that eleven women, principally from the mountains, brought illicit whiskey into Bessbrook, concealed in baskets which were apparently filled with calicoes, tapes and ribbons. By placing a watch over this traffic, we succeeded in excluding all these peddlers except one. This widow was a very determined creature and used to disguise herself in a variety of ways. She became a sort of mythical personage and for twelve months evaded us; but at last, I traced her to her best customer's house and followed her, sitting down at the fire beside her, and chatting, while poking my stick into the basket to find the hidden treasure. But it was not there. After leaving the house, half an hour did not elapse until it was reported all over the place that she had hoodwinked Mr Richardson by taking out the gallon of whiskey and making a 'stool' of it for herself. This woman at last emigrated to America, and from that day, as far as we know, there has been no 'sinful stuff' sold at Bessbrook. Of course I soon became an abstainer myself to encourage our people.

JAMES N. RICHARDSON, c. 1894, quoted in
James Nicholson Richardson of Bessbrook, 1925

S HE WALKED ON TO MAKE GOOD HER EXIT ... When entering the archway, a hand was gently placed on her shoulder.

'I beg your pardon, Madam, for interrupting you, but I think it such an unusual incident seeing a young lady alone in this out-of-the-way nook of the departed that really, prompted by sheer curiosity, I thought to follow you and enquire whether or not you are interested in any remains sequestered within this region of sacred solemnity. If you are mourning the loss of some dear friend whose grave, perchance, you might wish to see, can I assist you to find the object of your sorrow? Pray, can I?'

His voice was low and pathetic, tinged with traits of suffering he seemed to suppress as he awaited her reply.

'Sir,' she said, 'I thank you heartily but I have no one here in this home of rest and hallowed dust whom I mourn presently.'

An ancient coating of darkest green ivy around them seemed densely congested with infant song. Nothing was heard but the continuous stream of sweetest melody which served to act as companion to Helen as she continued: 'True I am in sorrow for the nearest and dearest of relatives but they lie in a vault in the old churchyard at Kilmore.'

Swathed in silence, he waited for her to resume.

''Tis but one month ago my mother and brother were laid therein and three weeks after my father likewise shared their bleak home, so my sorrow is, indeed, great. Observing these tributes to the departed, I thought to come and have a look through and at the same time rest under the cooling shelter of these beautiful trees that protect one from getting too scorched by the hot rays of Sol.'

He kept pulling the ends of his moustache while she had thus addressed him.

'Alas, poor girl,' he said, 'how burthened with sorrow and you so young,' eyeing her kindly in a sweet plaintive tone of voice. 'May I ask where you live?'

'At Annadorn,' she answered.

'Ah me!' he exclaimed. 'Good God! Annadorn,' pressing his hand to his heart.

AMANDA MCKITTRICK ROS, *Helen Huddleson*, 1969

ABOUT FIVE MINUTES' WALK from the village they came to a lane that ran down to the sea – black mud underfoot and a stone wall on either side. The lane widened into a small farmyard. There was a low, whitewashed cottage with a sodden thatched roof, a stack of peat at one side, and a few hens picking about in the mud.

'What a squalid scene!' said Aunt Charlotte; 'is it possible that any human being can live there?'

The children did not answer, for to their disappointment the door was shut.

'She's out,' said Mick.

A few yards from the cottage the land ended on the seashore. The sand was covered with brown seaweed; a cart filled with it was propped up with stones. Bits of cork and wood were strewn about in every direction; and beyond the line of dry seaweed there were big round stones covered with golden brown seaweed still wet, for the tide was only halfway out.

Aunt Charlotte did not like the seashore. She said it was so untidy; not even the beautiful green crabs that Fly caught for her under the wet seaweed pleased her, so after a few minutes they turned back. They were sure Jane Dwyer would not be back yet; but just as they were passing her cottage Aunt Charlotte gripped Mick's arm.

'Who is that?' she said sharply, 'there – coming down the lane.'

Fly smothered an hysterical giggle.

A tall figure dressed in an old green coat tied in round the waist by a dirty apron was coming towards them; white hair fell about its white face, and its big bare feet splashed in the mud. As it came nearer it muttered and scowled and shook its fist.

'Who is it, I say?' said Aunt Charlotte.

'It is Jane Dwyer.'

She came swinging along muttering and cursing to herself, stopping here and there to pick up a stone till her apron was full. Then with a sudden leap in the air she aimed. The stone hit Fly on the shin, who gave a scream of pain and was over the wall in a second. The boys followed her, while a volley of stones and curses came from the lane.

Aunt Charlotte was left behind. They heard her scrambling over the wall, the loose stones rolling off as she scrambled; and as they ran they could hear her screaming, 'My God, my God, this is terrible!'

Two fields away the boys found Fly sitting on a bank nursing her sore leg.

'Did you hear her taking her Maker's name in vain?' said Patsy. He rolled over on the grass with laughter.

'I never saw old Jane in better fettle,' said Mick.

KATHLEEN FITZPATRICK, *The Weans at Rowallan*, 1905

THE NUMBER OF THEIR [I.E. THE COVENANTERS] congregations in this country is about twenty. They have now public worship pretty generally in houses – formerly it was almost universally performed in the open fields. Their ancestors were driven by persecution to wilds and glens, where only they could worship their Maker by stealth and in secrecy; and by a natural association, more pleasurable than otherwise, they retained the custom long after the original cause was removed. I recollect being at one of those meetings when I was a very little boy, it is present to my recollection as fresh as if it were only yesterday. I see it now as if it were before my eyes; the bright sun, and clear sky – the wild glen, and dark woods, and foaming torrent – the thin dapper figure – the sharp face, and keen visage of the preacher, as he projected his head from the little pulpit covered with canvas placed on the verge of the hill; the immense multitude of all ages and sexes, in scarlet and grey mantles, and blue and russet-coloured and heath-dyed coats – in hoods and bonnets, and mob caps, and old-fashioned hats, standing, sitting and lying, around.

JOHN GAMBLE, *A View of Society and Manners in the North of Ireland*, 1813

A LICE SAT VERY QUIETLY ABSORBED in her Sabbath-school lessons, and Jim also was supposed to be engaged in this same meritorious occupation. Eunice sat apart on the low window-seat of the wide front window that looked on the lawn. A neglected book lay on her knee as she watched the drip, drip, drip of the disappointing rain that had followed such a bright morning and looked wistfully down the avenue past the wet shrubs and late spring flowers to the public road beyond, which was out-of-bounds on the Sabbath Day.

Aunt Matilda dozed frankly in her low favourite chair over *The Life of the Reverend Henry Cooke, DD, LLD*. She was intensely interested in Dr Cooke, for she had known him and he had actually been a guest in that house in her father's time and had preached in Kildarragh. That was on his Homeric pursuit of the heterodox Reverend Henry Montgomery, DD, from meeting-house to meeting-house in order to vindicate orthodoxy and check the spread of heresy.

And what a great man he was! Her mind dwelt on that familiar theme again – so courtly, so eloquent. How strange it was that his own sons were said to be neglectful of Gospel Ordinances. She recalled a story told in connection with that serious shortcoming. Admonishing one of them for not attending public worship, his father said: 'Harry, there will be no sermons in hell,' to which Harry replied, 'Well, it won't be for the want of ministers.'

LYDIA M. FOSTER, *Elders' Daughters*, 1942

T HE NIGHT BEFORE THE TWELFTH OF JULY the Orange bonfires were lighted and from the brickyard Colm, Jamesy, and their friends saw the sky reddening over the city and the chimneys in many streets glow fiercely in the leaping flames. Then in the still summer air the songs were carried to them: 'Dolly's Brae', 'Derry's Walls', 'The Sash My Father Wore', 'The Boyne Water', and 'God Save the King'.

'The Pope will get a quare scutching the night,' said a woman who had brought her child up to see the flames.

'It won't be long, Missus,' said John Burns, ''till the Fifteenth of August and we'll show them how to make a bonfire.'

They were filled with a wild frenzy of impatience as they saw the fires grow bigger. And as they were going home they were all making plans for their bonfire: Jamesy was to collect old boxes from his shop, Croppy Caulfield was to ask his da to get old bicycle tyres, and John Burns was to lead a gang of boys over McCrae's palings to chop down trees.

The next day Colm got up early and went down town to see the Orangemen marching. It was like a Sunday. Shops were closed and they had the whole town to themselves. They marched in four deep, most of them in navy-blue suits, hard hats, and orange sashes. Glossy-painted banners, some of biblical subjects, led each section, followed by a band. There were bands of all kinds: flute bands, brass bands, pipers' bands, accordion bands, all playing at once with here and there men in their shirt-sleeves hammering the big drums. The air was alive with sound; the notes from the miscellany of instruments whirled in the air, interlaced, shrieked and descended to be sent sky-high again by the stone-crushing noise from the big drums. And all the time the men marched, strong and tough and gay. Small boys with sashes also marched, and once a man passed wheeled in his bathchair, his sash round his neck, and the colour of death on his face.

'God love him!' said a woman near Colm, and gave him a special cheer for himself, and the man who was pushing the chair, straightened up, and there was strength of steel in his face.

That day passed in peace, but the fire of the leaders' speeches smouldered for days in the minds of the common people, and towards the end of the month a mob of them, armed with sticks, invaded the shipyards and chased out the Catholic workers. Then riots began in the poorer parts of the city. Snipers hid on the roofs of houses and factories and swept the streets with bullets. The military were called out, and the lovely summer evenings were perforated by the rattle of rifles and machine guns.

At night the MacNeills prayed that the riots would cease, and thanked God that their street was quiet. But in the mornings they heard the newsboys shout: 'Twelve shot dead! Two hundred wounded.'

A paper was bought and Colm read out loud; how a brother was shot dead standing at a window in the monastery and of the shootings in Ballymacarret and York Street. And the mother wrung her hands and said, 'God protect us all! Why can't they live in peace!'

For two weeks the shootings and the lootings continued. In the early evenings the streets were deserted and lorry loads of steel-helmeted soldiers passed to and fro. But in the middle of August peace came to the city again, and Jamesy and the boys from the street went around collecting boxes for their bonfire. If the Orangemen celebrated the Twelfth of July, the Catholics celebrated the Feast of the Assumption, and the Ancient Order of Hibernians carved out A.O.H. on trees and byre doors, marched with green sashes, drank porter, talked about Home Rule for Ireland while the Sinn Féiners fought and died for a Republic. In Jamesy's street half of the people were Hibernians and half Sinn Féiners, but on a night like the Fifteenth of August they all joined together and contributed to the bonfire.

MICHAEL McLAVERTY, *Call My Brother Back*, 1939

Small country boys in big boots, knickerbockers, stiff celluloid collars that could be cleaned for Sunday by a rub of a wet cloth, and close-cropped heads with fringes like scalping locks above the foreheads, scattered before us to the hedges and the grass margins, then closed again like water divided and rejoining, and pursued us, cheering, for a hundred yards. One of them, frantic with enthusiasm, sent sailing after us a half-grown turnip, which bounced along the road for a bit, then sought rest in a roadside drain. Looking backwards I pulled my best or worst faces at the rustic throng of runners.

– In Tattysallagh, said my father, they were always an uncivilised crowd of gulpins.

He had three terms of contempt: Gulpin, Yob and, when things became very bad he became Swiftian, and described all offenders as Yahoos.

– Cavanacaw, he said, and that lovely trout stream, the Creevan Burn. It joins the big river at Blacksessiagh. That there's the road up to Pigeon Top Mountain and the mass rock at Corraduine, but we'll come back that way when we've circumnavigated Dooish and Cornavara.

We came to Clanabogan.

– Clanabogan planting, he said.

The tall trees came around us and sunlight and shadow flickered so that you could feel them across eyes and hands and face.

– Martin Murphy the postman, he said, who was in the survey with me in Virginia, County Cavan, by Lough Ramor, and in the Glen of Aherlow, worked for a while at the building of Clanabogan Church. One day the vicar said to him: 'What height do you think the steeple should be?' 'The height of nonsense like your sermons,' said Martin, and got the sack for his wit. In frosty weather he used to seal the cracks in his boots with butter and although he was an abrupt man he seldom used an impolite word. Once when he was aggravated by the bad play of his wife who was partnering him at whist he said: 'Maria, dearly as I love you there are yet moments when you'd incline a man to kick his own posterior.'

– There's the church, my father said, and the churchyard and the haunted gate and the crossroads.

We held our breath but, with honeyed summer all around us and bees in the tender limes, it was no day for ghosts, and in glory we sailed by.

BENEDICT KIELY, *A Journey to the Seven Streams*, 1963

A BALLAD OF MASTER McGRATH

*Lord Lurgan's great greyhound, which won the Waterloo Cup
in 1868, 1869, and again in 1871*

1868 being the state of the year,
Those Waterloo sportsmen did grandly appear,
To gain the great prizes and bear them awa' –
Never counting on Ireland and Master McGrath.

On the 12th of December, that day of renown,
McGrath and his trainer they left Lurgan town;
John Walsh was the trainer, and soon they got o'er,
For the very next day they touched great England's shore.

And when they arrived there in big London Town,
Those great English sportsmen they all gathered roun' –
And one of those gentlemen gave a 'Ha! Ha!'
With: 'Is that the great dog you call Master McGrath?'

And one of those gentlemen standing around
Says: 'I don't care a damn for your Irish greyhound';
And another he laughs with a great 'Ha! Ha! Ha!
We'll soon humble the pride of your Master McGrath.'

Then Lord Lurgan steps forward and says: 'Gentlemen,
If there's any amongst youse has money to spen' –
For youse nobles of England I don't give a straw –
Here's five thousand to one on my Master McGrath.'

And Rose stood uncovered, the great English pride,
Her master and keeper all close by her side;
They have let her away and the crowd cried: 'Hurrah!'
For the pride of all England – and Master McGrath.

McGrath he looked up and he wagged his ould tail,
And he winked at his lordship to know he'd not fail;
Then he jumped on the hare's back and held up his paw –
Give three cheers for ould Ireland and Master McGrath.

ANONYMOUS

AT MASTER McGRATH'S GRAVE

I

He had a long white streak
On his deep chest,
A small white patch
Over one of his shoulders,
And two white claws
On each of his forepaws.

Over his lean back
He was all ticked with white,
As if a shower of hail
Had fallen and never melted.

II

Should he not still smoulder,
Our shooting star,
That claimed the Waterloo Cup
In eighteen sixty-nine?

I'm standing at the edge
Of Lord Lurgan's demesne
Where the Master is stretched
Under his plinth,
A bucket of quicklime
Scattered all along his length.

III

The overhanging elm-trees
And the knee-high grass
Are freshly tinged
By this last sun-shower.

I'm not beside myself with grief,
Not even so taken by McGrath,

It's just the way these elm-trees
Do more and more impinge,
The knee-high grass
Has brought me to my knees.

PAUL MULDOON, *Mules*, 1977

THERE WAS ONE HOUSE I VISITED, though only one – Ballyhackamore House, belonging to the Montgomeries – where all my views about animals were shared. Mrs Montgomery was, I think, the gentlest and sweetest old lady I have ever met. Latterly she was an invalid and confined to one large room on the ground floor – the drawing-room really, though her bed had been brought down to it. And I have gone in to see her, and found a vigorous young rooster perched on the back of her chair, a polecat in her lap, a blind old dog slumbering at her feet, and a pony looking in at the window. Naturally this was a room I liked, and these visits had something of the quality of the golden age about them. Mrs Montgomery herself talked little, but that did not seem to matter. She produced upon me an impression of goodness, absolute goodness, that was strangely peaceful. There was no question here of religion, of conscientiousness, of duty; it was the real thing, pure, unmixed, a natural gift. I never heard her passing an unfavourable remark about anybody, and I cannot even imagine her doing so. It was with infinite reluctance, and because it was forced upon her, that she once reproached me with certain laxities of style – the use of 'and which', for instance, the ending of a sentence with a preposition – but it seemed more a caress than a criticism, and the trouble it caused her made me laugh.

In Ballyhackamore House even mice were sacred. No traps might be set, and if a mouse were discovered (naturally they had grown bold), he was conducted out at the back door, and who can blame him if he promptly returned by the front. This, I may say, actually did happen, unless the mouse who entered was a twin brother.

FORREST REID, *Private Road*, 1940

THEY WERE RATTLING PAST the asylum wall now. Through the darkening air the corner of the Row was in sight.

'Where're the donkeys, Pachy?' Shemie asked, straining his eyes. 'I can't see any.'

'Never mind, they're about somewhere. Ah, well, home, sweet home, and the fire out! Hold on tight, boys.'

They turned into the Row, Neilly and Shemie laughing wildly as the cart gave a great lurch, almost flinging them off. In excitement and wonder they looked down the Row. A sheet of water stretched from the low side halfway across the street, from the bottom almost up to the corner. All the lower windows on the flooded side were dark; the occupants having retreated upstairs from the flooded kitchens. Through the top windows, the yellow gaslight streamed down onto the cold, rain-freckled water. On the other side, most of the upstairs windows were lit as well as the bottom, as the people prepared for their evacuation also. Through the top windows children waved and made faces at each other, their high-pitched chatter echoing piercingly along the street. Here and there, on the side which the water had not yet reached, women craned over the half-doors seeing, in their imagination, the dark waters swirling and edging through their neighbours' houses, and judging fearfully every inch of its sinister and inexorable approach to their own.

The reflection of the gaslight rippled like silk as the cart cut through the edge of the flood; Pachy waved his hand in answer to the greetings that were shouted at them; Neilly and Shemie peering down between their legs, at the water wriggling round the wheel, and shouting out as, down at the bottom, they glimpsed the four donkeys huddled miserably in the corner.

Kitty, at the rattle of the cart, had rushed to the door. She stood peering out with angry impatience as they approached – a woman with a head of auburn hair, still rich and thick, though tinged here and there with grey, and a pale, sharp, rather pinched face which belied the wiry vigour of her slight, work-thinned body.

'My God, this holy day and hour!' she cried, as the cart stopped outside the door. 'A nice looking set of ornaments you are, I must say, sitting there like pilgrims in the night, and the water running out of you. Where did you leave that Eugene fellow?'

'Ah, the bold Kate, there,' Pachy greeted. 'How's the heart? I can't stay. I've got to see to my dearly beloved brethren down there at the dunkill. Where's Kelly? Have you seen him?'

'I'm sure you're uneasy about my heart. The same fellow, roaming mad through the country as if nobody owned you. Come in, come in, for God's sake, before the whole Row is out.'

She slapped the door behind them. 'You might have sent the childer home, Malachey, at least, standing under a railway bridge off a day like that, and the wind whistling through them.'

'Ah, now, don't start, for God's sake! Let's get into the house first. You'd think I was a weather expert to hear you.'

JOHN O'CONNOR, *Come Day – Go Day*, 1948

O UTSIDE, IT WAS VERY DARK. He found the car and sat in it. Were the German pilots already airborne, coming up through Holland and Belgium, their compasses set on Ulster? He mustn't fall asleep. He heard the car door open and turned to see Dr Dancey sitting beside him, the pipe now in his mouth.

The car had started. Its taped headlamps threw their tiny beam on the road ahead. They drove down a street he had known all his life, a street which once looked familiar, but now, like a broken set of teeth, revealed strange cavities. They passed the nurses' home, a blackened, windowless ruin. As the car turned left in the Antrim Road, going toward the

Cliftonville Road, The Swan, the pub he had passed last night, The Swan wasn't there. He wondered, idly, if there were whisky bottles in the rubble and broken barrels of porter oozing in the mud and dust. Or had Captain Lambert rescued the spirits? Beside him, Dr Dancey was saying something. He tried to concentrate.

'And York Street's worse. Levelled, completely levelled.'

'Oh.'

'Is your house all right?' Dr Dancey asked.

'I don't know.'

He looked back again, as the car went up the Cliftonville Road. There was a moon tonight, a bombers' moon. Every morning of his school life he had passed The Swan. He remembered hiding at the entrance to the family bar, playing hide-and-seek with other boys. Now, The Swan was gone.

'I'll let you off on the corner,' Dr Dancey said. The car came to a stop. 'Good luck. I hope everything's all right at your place.'

'Thank you.'

He stood alone in the avenue, remembering last night, walking along the pavement toward the house in which he had been born. In the moonlight, the roofs of the houses on either side of the avenue presented an even, unbroken facade. And then, coming closer, he saw that there was a gap. He stopped, caught in a moment's panic, but, no, it was not his house, it was the Miss Dempsters' house, four doors down. Like The Swan, it was no longer there. He began to run.

The iron railings in front of his parents' house had been removed last year to be melted down for guns. He remembered his father's angry complaints at the time. He jumped over the low stone plinth in which the railings had been embedded and ran up the narrow strip of grass which was the front garden. He saw that the front door was ajar, pushed it inward, and reached familiarly for the light switch. The light did not work. Striking a match, he went down the hall, finding the switch at the dining room entrance. Again, it did not work. He remembered that his mother kept candles in a cupboard over the kitchen door. He struck his second-to-last match, but the wind blew it out.

The house was very cold. Moonlight came in through the broken windows of the dining room, striking down on the dining room table, showing slivers of glass and dust on its surface. He turned back into the blackness of the hall, forgot the step down into the kitchen and stumbled when he met it. The kitchen was moonlit, and, looking out of the shattered window at the silent, empty backyard, he wondered if there were people in any of the other houses in the avenue. Had everyone gone away? Mr Hamilton, the dentist next door, was a staunch Churchill man, not likely to run. But still, there was a haunted, empty silence all around. He turned, found the cupboard and the candles, and carefully lit his last match.

He dripped hot wax from a candle end onto the kitchen table and anchored the candle in it. The candle flame cowered from the cold wind at the window. Lighting two fresh candles, he went out of the kitchen and began to climb the stairs. At the turn of the stairs, leading to the breakfast room, his father's favourite print, a framed engraving of the Parthenon, had fallen, face down, its glass shattered. Hot candle wax dripped on his fingers. He was reminded of books he had read: a boy alone, holding a candle in either hand, going upstairs in a haunted house. Yet this house was not haunted. Its dangers were real. The sirens had not sounded yet, but Lord Haw-Haw had spoken. Somewhere, above the clouds, the bombers roared over the continent, coming in for the kill.

BRIAN MOORE, *The Emperor of Ice-Cream*, 1966

THERE HAD BEEN ONE DEVELOPMENT so spectacular and charming that not even the considerable disillusion in which it ended could prevent it from becoming one of the most memorable and characteristic political episodes of the entire decade. This was the election to the Westminster Parliament, in a hard-fought by-election for an Ulster constituency which had previously returned Unionist members with comfortable majorities, of one of the leaders of the student wing of the Civil Rights movement, Miss Bernadette Devlin. Herself a student at the time of the election, Miss Devlin became overnight indistinguishable, in the minds of many, from Joan of Arc, and when she took her seat at Westminster just in time to contribute, against all Westminster tradition, a fiery and uncompromising maiden speech in a debate on the Northern Ireland situation, the effect on the House of Commons was astonishing to behold, many of its members writing her not just the customary polite note of congratulation, but multi-page letters. The House is not an exceptionally sophisticated place; but this could not alone account for Miss Devlin's reception, any more than her diminutive size (five feet and half an inch), her age (twenty-two) or her waif-like appearance. Nor could it have been her opinions, which were on the whole as silly as they were well-meaning. What enabled her to conquer the place was the fact that she was the first representative to be elected to Parliament, perhaps the first to the national legislature in any of the major democracies, of the younger generation's protest and revolt against conditions which they found materially adequate but spiritually impoverished. Most Members of Parliament had, quite literally, never met anybody like Miss Devlin before, nor heard, except filtered through the distorting trumpet of the newspapers and television and the clangorous echo-chamber of the young people's publicity-hunting leaders, any such voice, and when, a few months after her election, she entered the House wearing trousers, the place surrendered. Miss Devlin was soon reported to have had enough of politics and not to be seeking re-election, though if so she changed her mind and was triumphantly returned, going on almost at once to the traditional Irish martyrdom of imprisonment for the cause – an event which looked likely to precipitate something like civil war in the embattled province. But she had been the first to pass through a door that many had long clamoured to open, and the fact that the keepers of it hastened to fling it wide for her did not lessen the magnitude of her achievement.

BERNARD LEVIN, The Pendulum Years, 1970

A S SOON AS SHE OPENED THE MACHINE ROOM DOOR it wasn't just the din that hit me. In fact a hardly noticed the noise atall way the shock a got when a seen the cut of the place.

It could be said te have had a family atmosphere a suppose, dependin' that is on which particular family it was ye happened te belong te. A took a deep breath an' thanked almighty god for the first time in me life for givin' me the wee screwed up protestant face that so grieved me ma an' a smiled at them all as if a had just been given the most wonderful birthday surprise.

FUCK THE POPE. DEATH TO ALL PAPISTS. LONG LIVE PROTESTANT ULSTER. THE ONLY GOOD CATHOLIC IS A DEAD CATHOLIC. GOD SAVE THE QUEEN. ULSTER IS BRITISH. GOD SAVE KING BILLY. REMEMBER THE BOYNE. an' things like that were written on banners an' hung wan after the other for the full length of the factory. A allowed that if a knew what was good for me a would act the part of a real loyal protestant for the rest of that day.

Things went smoothly enough while a was sittin' at me machine that was nicely decked out in red white an' blue buntin' way two wee union jacks that were flutterin' happily away in the gentle breeze of an overhead fan. A thought te mesel' that if a was able te keep me terrible secret all the way through lunch break a just might be lucky enough te get mesel' outa the place in the evenin' in much the same shape as a went inte it in the mornin'.

As soon as the bell sounded for the start of the lunch hour all the girls come crowdin' over roun' my machine way big wide welcomin' smiles on their faces te take me aff te the canteen. They were all wile civil, an' wheniver they heard the news that a come from our town (that is, a ninety-five per cent catholic town) they were wile shockin' sympathetic te me allthegether an' said that they could see why a wanted te lave a hole like that. A agreed that it was indeed a terrible place, an' a toul them that a was wile, wile glad te see the back of it.

Te begin way, a had te be very careful not te say the wrong thing in case they twigged on that a was catholic, so a limited mesel' te repeatin' verbatim what the dreadful catholics from our town said about us protestants, an' only repeatin' some of the better known anti–catholic slogans, but as me confidence increased, a got te enjoy the part a was playin' so much, that a become more excessive an' outspoken than any of the others in me scathin' criticism an' condemnation of fuckin' popish scum. (God was a glad that me ma was outa ear-shot.)

The day passed aff so well that be the time a was finished work in the evenin' a had made arrangements te meet three of the girls at eight that night, at an address a remembered from lookin' up flats in the paper before a come te live in Belfast. They were plannin' te take me te a big do in an orange hall where some wile shockin' big important high-up man be the name of the Reverent Ian Paisley was comin' te make a speech. A toul them that a had niver had the pleasure of meetin' him before an' they assured me that a was in for a treat.

Nixt mornin' a didn't go te work. At ten a-clock a phoned up the manager te say that a wasn't comin' back. He asked me was a catholic be any chance. A toul him that a was. He said he could see how a job in that factory would be completely unsuitable for a catholic girl, but he'd thought that a was a protestant because a had applied or he would of warned me. He said he was an Englishman an' couldn't understand all this catholic–protestant carry-on.

FRANCES MOLLOY, *No Mate for the Magpie*, 1985

PROTESTANT COURTS CATHOLIC

Too tired, and too fastidious for lies,
he said, 'Let's make love when you're free.'
'Just like that?' 'Yes, just like that. No ties.'
She said, 'You wouldn't want to marry me.'

Although his devious honesty made him sick,
'You'll give yourself to someone. Who?' he said.
'The unknown husband. I'm a Catholic,'
she smiled. He said, 'Don't smile and shake your head.'

Intrigued, he argued, but she never budged.
She blamed the church. He said she was a sham.
'You have to judge in order to be judged.'
Her smile was roguish, false. 'That's how I am.'

'Look, I'm the serpent you have read about.
The law says no, I'd like it if you would.
You're free either to stretch your fingers out
or not. Choose, knowledge or servitude.'

Seducer turned to saviour on a whim,
he lavished hours of rhetoric on her.
Her faith protected her from men like him,
useless at home, dynamic in a bar.

To be the star, attended, made her tremble.
How seriously drunken poets play;
but Irish girls are brought up to dissemble,
to blush and listen and to get their way.

'In these cases we still have judgement here.
It's you who'll suffer, so it can't be right
to leave choice to the priests.' Swallowing beer,
smoking, he stood and argued half the night.

At closing time he left so solemnly
you might have thought he went to meet his death.
She had hysterics on her wedding day
when she smelt lager on her husband's breath.

JAMES SIMMONS, Energy to Burn, 1971

WHEN I WAS A TEENAGER [i.e. during the 1930s] the Glen Road on summer Sunday afternoons was teeming with young boys and girls, always out walking. Sometimes an accordion or a fiddle was brought to the crossroads at the top of Shaws Road and an open air dance would take place. Boys and girls were always talking in groups all along its length and many a date was made and many met their partners for life. It was a parading ground for young people for years but as time passed, this old custom faded away.

JIMMY WEBB, Raglan Street and Beyond, c. 1980

THE YOUNG PEOPLE OF BOTH SEXES are fond of dancing, and have frequent meetings in the village, or in the farmhouses, where, in imitation of their superiors, they keep up the revel from eight or nine in the evening till daybreak. Amongst their other amusements, the game of shinny, as it is called by some, and common by others, is worthy of note. Common is derived from a Celtic word *com*, which signified 'crooked', as it is played with a stick bent at its lower extremity somewhat like a reaping hook. The ball, which is struck to and fro, in which the whole amusement consists, is called nag, or in Irish *brig*. It resembles the game called golf in Edinburgh. Christmas is the season when it is most generally played. It prevails all through Ireland, and in the highlands of Scotland. Nor is it confined to any sect, as Dissenters and Romanists seem to be equally attached to it.

The trundling of eggs, as it is called, is another amusement, which is common at Easter. For this purpose the eggs are boiled hard, and dyed different colours, and when they are thus prepared, the sport consists in throwing or trundling them along the ground, especially down a declivity, and gathering up the broken fragments to eat them. Formerly it was usual with the women and children to collect in large bodies for this purpose, though nothing can be, to all appearance, more unmeaning than the amusement and they yet pursue it in the vicinity of Belfast. Here it is generally confined to the younger classes. It is a curious circumstance, that this sport is practised only by the presbyterians, though it is admitted that it is a very ancient usage, and was spread over the Russian Empire and Greek islands long before the Reformation.

WILLIAM SHAW MASON, *Staticstical Account, c.* 1800

T HE DAY WAS SATURDAY, and the month either June or July, when, having started for home from Glasslough, a distance of at least sixteen miles across the country, which to me was nothing, I had arrived at the townland next to Springtown, named Cargah, immediately above which was a very pretty smooth eminence ending in a flat greensward. On this table-land I found there was a dance, in which was engaged a number of young men and women, with nearly every one of whom I was acquainted. It was not, I soon found, an ordinary dance, but what they call in the north an *infare*, or the hailing home of a newly married bride to the house of her husband, of which she is to be the future mistress. At these *infares*, there was generally such a dance as I found on the table on Cargah Hill, animated to a greater sense of enjoyment by plenty of excellent poteen whisky. Here I danced with the bride, whom I looked upon for the first time, and several other girls with whom I was intimately acquainted. Even at this time I was celebrated as a dancer.

WILLIAM CARLETON (1867), *Autobiography*, 1896

THE GIRL'S LAMENTATION

With grief and mourning I sit to spin;
My Love passed by, and he didn't come in;
He passes by me, both day and night,
And carries off my poor heart's delight.

There is a tavern in yonder town,
My Love goes there and he spends a crown,
He takes a strange girl upon his knee,
And never more gives a thought to me.

Says he, 'We'll wed without loss of time,
And sure our love's but a little crime;' –
My apron-string now it's wearing short,
And my Love he seeks other girls to court.

O with him I'd go if I had my will,
I'd follow him barefoot o'er rock and hill;
I'd never once speak of all my grief
If he'd give me a smile for my heart's relief.

In our wee garden the rose unfolds,
With bachelor's-buttons and marigolds;
I'll tie no posies for dance or fair,
A willow-twig is for me to wear.

For a maid again I can never be,
Till the red rose blooms on the willow tree.
Of such a trouble I've heard them tell,
And now I know what it means full well.

As through the long lonesome night I lie,
I'd give the world if I might but cry;
But I mus'n't moan there or raise my voice,
And the tears run down without any noise.

And what, O what will my mother say?
She'll wish her daughter was in the clay.
My father will curse me to my face;
The neighbours will know of my black disgrace.

My sister's buried three years, come Lent;
But sure we made far too much lament.
Beside her grave they still say a prayer –
I wish to God 'twas myself was there!

The Candlemas crosses hang near my bed;
To look at them puts me much in dread,
They mark the good time that's gone and past:
It's like this year's one will prove the last.

The oldest cross it's a dusty brown,
But the winter winds didn't shake it down;
The newest cross keeps the colour bright;
When the straw was reaping my heart was light.

The reapers rose with the blink of morn,
And gaily stook'd up the yellow corn,
To call them home to the field I'd run,
Through the blowing breeze and the summer sun.

When the straw was weaving my heart was glad,
For neither sin nor shame I had,
In the barn where oat-chaff was flying round,
And the thumping flails made a pleasant sound.

Now summer or winter to me it's one;
But oh! for a day like the time that's gone.
I'd little care was it storm or shine,
If I had but peace in this heart of mine.

Oh! light and false is a young man's kiss,
And a foolish girl gives her soul for this.
Oh! light and short is the young man's blame,
And a helpless girl has the grief and shame.

To the river-bank once I thought to go,
And cast myself in the stream below;
I thought 'twould carry us far out to sea,
Where they'd never find my poor babe and me.

Sweet Lord, forgive me that wicked mind!
You know I used to be well-inclined.
Oh, take compassion upon my state,
Because my trouble is so very great.

My head turns round with the spinning-wheel,
And a heavy cloud on my eyes I feel.
But the worst of all is at my heart's core;
For my innocent days will come back no more.

WILLIAM ALLINGHAM, *Irish Songs and Poems*, 1887

I WELL REMEMBER ONE AFTERNOON he [i.e. the master] gave us a certain amount to learn off by heart at home that night. I spent the entire evening until bedtime wrestling with it, and a short while in the morning before school. I had learned it in a kind of way when I left home and I had my book open on the way to school, revising. I got up as far as Tom na hAiteannaighe murmuring to myself *Wisdom, understanding, counsel, fortitude, knowledge.* Up to Beanna na Lochlannach and Tobar an tSasanaigh fervently learning all the while.

As I came to the old road who should I meet but Donnchadh Mhicheáil Éamoinn.

'Have you learned your *catechism*?' I asked.

'Our class didn't get *catechism* last night, we got *poethry*,' he answered, 'and I haven't managed to learn even the half or the third of it. My mother and father were at a wake in Mín na Craoibhe last night, and we spent the night making wee boats and playing buttons. I thought I'd get a chance to learn my lesson this morning but I didn't. I'll be slaughtered!'

I can see those two boys as clearly today as if they were standing before me now. I see them going eastwards along the road each with two sods of turf under his oxter and an open book in the other hand mumbling earnestly and paying no heed to anyone who might salute them, or even noticing that they were there. Onwards they went until they reached Peadar Phaidí's house. Peadar was out at the door and addressed them, but that was all the conversation he got. He was replied to from the books:

'There's the fine fellows this morning.'
'*Wisdom, understanding, counsel, fortitude.*'
'I say, you are the right boys.'

> '*Such empty phantoms, I freely grant them,*
> *But there is an anthem more dear to me,*
> *'Tis the Bells of Shandon that sound so grand on*
> *The pleasant waters of the River Lee.*'

Liam Beag bumped into us at the eastern part of An Carracamán.
'What kind of early potatoes has your father sown?' he asked me.
'*Wisdom, understanding, counsel, fortitude.*'

> '*For memory dwelling on each proud swelling*
> *Made the belfry knelling its bold notes free.*'

Brighid Naois met us a little further to the east.
'Has your mother's clutch of chicks produced many pullets?' she asked one of us.
'*Wisdom, understanding, counsel, fortitude,*' I said.
'*Such empty phantoms, I freely grant them,*' added Donnchadh ...

When we reached the schoolhouse my own class was called out to the floor where the master was asking them their *catechism*. Donnchadh Néill Phaidí was there with his arms thrust under his oxters. Peadar Dhonnchaidh Bháin was there wincing with pain from ear to ear. Máire

Chonaill Shéarlais was sobbing. That was the scene that lay before me as I put my head round the door, and such was my trepidation that I instantly forgot everything I had learned from the previous night. *Wisdom, understanding, counsel, fortitude* deserted me. I could not recall a single word in English I had ever heard apart from the few lines of the poem that the boy who was with me on the road to school was learning.

It was not long before my turn came. The master asked me to say the *seven gifts* but he might just as well have asked me to recite an excerpt from Homer. It was as if a sing-song of disordered words filled my ears and I could not get rid of them until he asked me a second time and I blurted out whatever came into my mouth without knowing what I was saying. I was like a man who has fallen into the sea and who grasps at a straw or a piece of stick or a stalk of seaweed, as if it would save him from drowning.

'Say the seven gifts of the Holy Ghost,' ordered the master.

'Such empty phantom I freely grant them
But there is an anthem more dear to me,' I said.

The poor master thought that I had begun to mock him, for my people on both sides were renowned for their sarcasm. That may be so, but I did not take after them. They say that a bird flies off from every flock, and it may well be the case for a bitter or hurtful word has never passed my lips. For all that, the master flew into a rage and did not wait to ask me to hold out my hand, but gave a lash of the cane across the backs of my legs. '*Wisdom,*' he said with the first lash, '*understanding*', with the second and I felt the venom of *understanding* much more than that of *wisdom*.

SÉAMUS Ó GRIANNA (1942),
translated by A.J. HUGHES, *When I Was Young*, 2001

THE IRISH DISEASE

My copy is literally coming apart as I write; so common is this failing in paperbacks published in Ireland that I fear it may become known as the 'Irish disease'.

GERRY HEALEY, *Linenhall Review*, vol. 2, no. 3

'Be gentle, it's my first time,'
thinks his latest fancy,
cracking a catastrophic smile.
New acquaintance is always chancy.

'She went to pieces in my hands,
halfway through she fell apart,'
the young critic complains;
'If she didn't mean it, why start?

'One after one, promising much,
they open up like flowers,
but, however gentle my touch,
petals drop in showers.'

An eager reader, soon ankle-deep
among the fallen leaves,
he rummages to pick them up
and reconstruct his splintered loves.

He peruses the pages again,
searching the initial savour:
'A dirty word and three puns
(although he's from impeccable Faber)

'suggest a consciousness like Muldoon.
Is this the iconoclast Foley,
with bodily functions and spoof jargon?
And could this be Mathews, or is it Sweeney?

'This is in dialect – Marshall or Paulin?
This must be Simmons, because it's rude.
And this could only be Medbh McGuckian:
I don't understand it, but I think it's good.'

In libraries and bedsitters
grow the snowy paper-drifts.
Like old flames the Irish writers,
Oliver Goldsmith, Gulliver Swift,

Patrick Kavanagh, Louis MacNeice,
Oscar Wilde and J.M. Synge,
lie together, lie at peace.
To the memorials readers bring

Mahon's shed, the bog of Heaney;
Poems of the Dispossessed,
every one a pleasant memory,
in the bundle with all the rest.

So let philanderers learn philology:
no sweetheart banned from the big anthology!

ROBERT JOHNSTONE, *Eden to Edenderry*, 1989

I BECAME EXOTIC FOR MY IRISH-SPEAKING.

And yet. I also sang 'McCafferty' *à la* Ewan McColl, in an histrionic Cockney, and I'd heard it sung as a child by my grandma in her Falls Road accent, but somehow didn't connect the two. I sang it with my own guitar accompaniment in Salisbury Street before its downfall or demise, which had been initiated by the long-since defunct tabloid Belfast paper, *Cityweek*. Dutiful investigative reporters had abandoned their habitual gaberdines and slouch hats for duffel coats and woolly scarves, and had infiltrated the aforesaid premises. They had mingled freely with persons of both sexes, long before 'sex' would be replaced by 'gender'. They were offered cider at the door. They said, 'Cool'. The air was blue with dubious cigarette smoke. Girls appeared to have nothing on beneath their bum-length V-necked beatnik mohair sweaters. The outside lavatory was communal. In fact, the whole place was communal or free-thinking, and these reporters were astonished at the freedom which abounded on the premises and the opinions volunteered to them unasked. There was much promiscuous and uncalled-for singing. A so-called entertainer in a Pancho Villa moustache perched on a stool next to the Victorian fireplace and sang the words 'tea' and 'sugar' with a bluesy innuendo.

By now, the air was blue entirely: sapphire, turquoise, Cambridge-blue and Oxford-blue, hyacinth and bluebell-blue abounded on the premises of indigo and slate; various planes and dimensions were disturbed from Prussian regiments of azure and forget-me-nots, as the whole blue laminated archaeology was transformed by the smoke and gutturals of solitary singers into Lawrentian gentians of Pluto-blue. The duffelled-up reporters thought it just as well they'd worn dark glasses, for they did not want to be imbued with blue. And then they went upstairs into a further, bluer zone.

DOES YOUR CHILD GO TO THIS PLACE?
– A special *Cityweek* exposé –

the headlines proclaimed. I was eating a Saturday fry when the news broke. 'What was the name of that place,' said my mother, 'that you used to go and study folk-song in?'

'Oh,' I said, with some pretend aplomb, 'there's a lot of houses in Salisbury Street, they must have been somewhere else.' The matter was let drop.

Then, one Sunday afternoon, when John Moulden was conducting his folk soirée where we debutants of folk were playing our guitars and singing our socially aware folk-songs in workshop fashion and we were undergoing *education*, for God's sake, and I was singing someone's version of 'East Virginia' with a borrowed guitar and I'd come to the line:

All I want is your love darling,
Won't you take me back again?

and there was a knock at the door and someone politely opened it. There stood my mother and my father in their Sunday coats, and my mother took one look at this Bohemia and cried, 'Sacred Mother of God, come you out of there, Ciaran!' I had no option but to go. I did my duty as a true performer. Shamed before my peers, I went reluctantly, and afterwards, for years, I used to hear the cry of peers, going, 'Sacred Mother of God, come you out of there, Ciaran!'

Salisbury Street closed down soon afterwards. Not that it was ever open, in the way the Boom-Boom Rooms or The Plaza or The Orpheus were open, where you paid to drink warm Coca-Cola and shuffle on a crowded sweaty floor to uniforms of dance bands; and everybody went there. Salisbury Street was an insider's state of mind. And after its demise, the action moved elsewhere, to whatever places might accommodate that cast of mind. New roads opened up; peripatetically, we followed them, over many years.

CIARAN CARSON, Last Night's Fun, 1996

Sixty-Nine the
Nightmare Started

Sixty-nine the nightmare started,
Loyalist anger rose:
sweet shops, butcher shops and pubs
were burned down, forced to close.

JAMES SIMMONS, *from* 'The Ballad of Gerry Kelly: Newsagent'

By the Wednesday ... Amelia had counted thirteen houses
from the top of one side of her street and nine houses from
the top of the other that had been burnt in these Troubles
so far. Amelia's house was eighth up from the bottom so,
according to her sums and the laws of rationality, that
meant there were still six houses to go before the burners
got to hers. That night, before the rioting, she tried to tell
her mother this. She thought it might calm and reassure
her mother but strangely, it did not.

ANNA BURNS, *No Bones*

'We missed the worst of it. It went off further up the street.
Your father was so angry about it. "It's our kind doing this
to us". That's what he kept saying.'
  'The IRA?'
  'Who else?'
  'It's awful.'
  'It's a policy they have now. Blowing the hearts out of
all the wee towns.'

BERNARD MacLAVERTY, *Grace Notes*

I T IS STRANGE TO SIT IN A COMFORTABLE farm kitchen – with cattle lowing nearby, bright copper pans on the walls, a sheep-dog and two tabbies on the hearthrug, Queen Elizabeth II in coronation robes over the mantelpiece – and suddenly to realise that this is, and for fifty-five years has been, a society governed under the surface by guns. In past years the guns of the B Specials, the RUC and at intervals the IRA; more recently the guns of the UDR, British army, Provos, Stickies, UDA, UVF, UFF, and countless individual gangsters who have not found it hard to acquire weapons under prevailing conditions.

DERVLA MURPHY, *A Place Apart*, 1978

T HE KEY AREAS OF SECTARIAN UNREST in the Ulster capital began only a few hundred yards from the central street, Royal Avenue. Three streets branched out at right angles from Royal Avenue which disappeared into the hinterland of Catholic and Protestant slums. The first few yards of the streets were large shops and businesses, but gradually these trickled away into the pubs, tobacconists, shops and houses of the sectarian communities. The streets, although they had other names at either extremity, were generally known as the Falls Road, the Shankill Road and the Crumlin Road, running almost parallel out of the city. The Falls Road was the centre of the Catholic area. At the end nearest to the city centre stood Hastings Street police barracks, where for weeks the police had lived in a state of tacit siege, venturing out cautiously, and then usually in vehicles. Two hundred yards higher up stood a vast new Catholic housing block, Divis Flats – a tower facing on to the road, with three other buildings in the complex a little way back from the street, each with long concrete terraces on each level. Beyond that, the Falls was just a dirty, unprepossessing ramble of ageing buildings, interspersed occasionally with churches, factories, and one or two new buildings. On either side the whole of its length, side streets of exactly identical decaying terraced houses ran off, on one side leading to the Grosvenor Road, on the other to the perils of the Protestant Shankill, some four hundred yards away. At some almost precisely definable point along each street between the Falls and the Shankill, Catholic territory ended and Protestant ground began. In some unhappy places, spurs of Catholic territory – vulnerable salients – jutted out into Protestant country, where the Union Jacks and obscenely anti-Catholic slogans on the walls began. Catholic slogans advocated 'Join your local IRA' or, later, 'Long Live Free Belfast'. On the Protestant walls, however, it would be 'Fuck the Pope' or 'Craig for PM'. The overwhelming impression on both sides of the battlefield was of dull, unbroken, depressed gloom. The children crawling in the dirty streets, the silence, the few cars parked by the roadsides, and the air of pointless hate ate into one's spirit within an hour or two in the area.

MAX HASTINGS, *Ulster 1969*, 1970

from WREATHS

THE GREENGROCER

He ran a good shop, and he died
Serving even the death-dealers
Who found him busy as usual
Behind the counter, organised
With holly wreaths for Christmas,
Fir trees on the pavement outside.

Astrologers or three wise men
Who may shortly be setting out
For a small house up the Shankill
Or the Falls, should pause on their way
To buy gifts at Jim Gibson's shop,
Dates and chestnuts and tangerines.

MICHAEL LONGLEY, *The Echo Gate*, 1979

IF YOU STAND AT THE CHILDREN'S PLAYGROUND in north Belfast, high up on the Oldpark Road, Ardoyne stretches out beneath you, a tightly packed enclave of tiny houses with long, narrow gardens.

Holy Cross Church across the valley looks, physically and metaphorically, like a mother hen with her chicks gathered around her. Beyond the church's twin spires, the Belfast hills reach to the sky. It is a peaceful setting. From the same spot, however, you can also see the jagged 'peace-lines' encircling Ardoyne, impermeable twenty foot-high metal barriers severing the area from the surrounding Protestant housing estates. If your eye follows a straight line leading right from Holy Cross Monastery, you can also see the square block of concrete and glass that is Holy Cross Girls' primary school, just outside the main bulk of Catholic Ardoyne.

More than anywhere else in the North, apart from perhaps Derry's walls, you are seeing history writ into brick, stone and metal – outward signs of the political tensions that have riven this turbulent community for centuries. Going down into the streets of Ardoyne, teeming with small children, there are murals, social clubs, republican memorials, a Sinn Féin advice centre and projects to create much-needed work. Every yard of pavement has a story to tell, if only you could hear it. Gardens where gunfights ended in death and imprisonment. Streets where children learned how to make petrol bombs. Pavements where British soldiers and IRA men bled to death. In the last thirty-five years of the conflict, ninety-nine local Catholics have died, a disproportionately large number of its seven thousand inhabitants. Ardoyne's republicans have also inflicted much on their Protestant neighbours; the mutual hostility with the nearby staunchly loyalist Shankill Road is legendary.

ANNE CADWALLADER, *Holy Cross: The Untold Story*, 2004

THE FIRST SCHOOL I WENT TO had, at the centre of its crest ... a bloody, amputated hand. The striking dissonance of having so violent a symbol emblazoned onto the uniform of every pupil, particularly at what was a Quaker school, never dawned on me while I was there. It wasn't until years later that it struck me as peculiar. I suppose we were so used to this sign of Ulster that it no longer shocked us. There are various stories about the origin of Ulster's famous Red Hand. One of the most common versions (and the one that was current among us at school) tells of two clan chieftains sailing towards the shores of Ulster, each wanting to claim it as his territory. On the principle that the first one to touch the shore would be granted ownership, it looked as if the matter was settled, one ship having pulled ahead of the other. But then the chieftain in the lagging ship, seeing the prize about to be snatched from his grasp, took out his sword, cut off his hand and threw it ashore. The bloody hand reached the shore first and claimed the land by proxy. Depending on your allegiances and grasp of history, various interpretations of the story can be made. The sharply divisive (and historically ridiculous) one favoured by many of my peers had the two chieftains representing Catholic and Protestant, as if making the bloody hand a Protestant one somehow legitimated the claim of one half of the sectarian divide to ownership of Ulster.

Other readings associate the story with the voyage of the Milesians, an ancient Celtic people, from their native Spain to the Isle of Destiny (which turned out to be Ireland). Some specifically link the story of the Red Hand to one powerful family, identifying the chieftain who won ownership of Ulster as an O'Neill (and whatever the truth of this may be, a Red Hand has appeared on the O'Neill coat of arms for over five hundred years). It's also possible that the story of the Red Hand in fact refers to the gruesome practice of those Irish mercenaries who served in pharaonic Egypt and who, after battle, cut the hands off fallen enemies and brought them to the scribes so as the number killed could be accurately recorded and reward or censure given out. Others prefer a less literal reading, seeing in the hand a representation of kinship (the wrist is the king, the palm his male offspring, the fingers his grandsons).

However the legend of the Red Hand of Ulster is read, it seems to have a grim resonance with much of the country's modern history. The violence of a severed hand, the brutality of throwing it to land bloodily on the shore, the ruthless determination to claim territory against rivals, all this seems to accord with much that has happened in the place. That the national symbol is a hand drenched in its own blood, reddened with a self-inflicted wound, is surely very much in tune with the chiromancy of events from 1969 until the new-found peace took hold.

CHRIS ARTHUR, *from* 'Handscapes of the Mind', *Irish Willow*, 2002

TWO LORRIES

It's raining on black coal and warm wet ashes.
There are tyre-marks in the yard, Agnew's old lorry
Has all its cribs down and Agnew the coalman
With his Belfast accent's sweet-talking my mother.
Would she ever go to a film in Magherafelt?
But it's raining and he still has half the load

To deliver farther on. This time the lode
Our coal came from was silk-black, so the ashes
Will be the silkiest white. The Magherafelt
(Via Toomebridge) bus goes by. The half-stripped lorry
With its emptied, folded coal-bags moves my mother:
The tasty ways of a leather-aproned coalman!

And films no less! The conceit of a coalman ...
She goes back in and gets out the black lead
And emery paper, this nineteen-forties mother,
All business round her stove, half-wiping ashes
With a backhand from her cheek as the bolted lorry
Gets revved and turned and heads for Magherafelt

And the last delivery. Oh, Magherafelt!
Oh, dream of red plush and a city coalman
As time fastforwards and a different lorry
Groans into shot, up Broad Street, with a payload
That will blow the bus station to dust and ashes ...
After that happened, I'd a vision of my mother,

A revenant on the bench where I would meet her
In that cold-floored waiting-room in Magherafelt,

Her shopping bags full up with shovelled ashes.
Death walked out past her like a dust-faced coalman
Refolding body-bags, plying his load
Empty upon empty, in a flurry

Of motes and engine-revs, but which lorry
Was it now? Young Agnew's or that other,
Heavier, deadlier one, set to explode
In a time beyond her time in Magherafelt ...
So tally bags and sweet-talk darkness, coalman.
Listen to the rain spit in new ashes

As you heft a load of dust that was Magherafelt,
Then reappear from your lorry as my mother's
Dreamboat coalman filmed in silk-white ashes.

SEAMUS HEANEY, The Spirit Level, 1996

SHE HAD PASSED CATHOLIC UNITY FLATS, which stretched from the corner of the Protestant Shankill, and she was now heading up Clifton Street to the religious fork just above. From Carlisle Circus she could head left up the Crumlin but of course, given her persuasion, she would do no such thing at all. She was just thinking that she was wrong, that she hadn't seen anything fleeting up above her, when a shadow crossed over from the babyclothes shop thirty yards on. When the shadow came close, she saw who it was.

'Danny!' she shouted.

'Amelia!' he shouted back. Their voices echoed. They were standing just outside the derelict Protestant churches with all their broken windows and their half-missing walls. Nearby was the Orange Hall, fortified all round, with King Billy, holding his broken sword, sitting on his rearing horse, on top of it. Both Amelia and Danny were drunk.

'Where were you tonight?' said Amelia.

'Where were you?' said Danny.

'Where're ye goin'?' said Amelia.

Danny opened hazel eyes. 'Amelia,' he said. 'Kiss me.'

Amelia got annoyed and was about to say catch yourself on, when she changed her mind and moved closer and kissed him. She put her arms round his neck and he put his arms round her waist and they kissed and kissed, and kissed even more. It was a remarkable kiss Amelia was thinking, and she was just about to be very pleased with it when something occurred to her and she frowned and pushed Danny off.

'Hol' on a minute,' she said. 'Aren't you married now Danny? Didn't you marry somebody once?'

'Oh,' said Danny. He looked sad and hung his head. Then he lifted it. He was smiling. They kissed again. Then Amelia pushed him off for the second time. 'That's enough,' she said. 'Catch yourself on.' But more than that, she said goodbye. 'Goodbye Danny,' she said. 'Goodbye.' And off she went, into the Antrim Road, past the Clifton Street graveyard, up the Cliftonville, past the Home For The Blind, the poor Poor Clares, the row of billboards in front of the wasteground where the big old black house used to be, then into Rosapenna, past the milk lorry, through the Bone, up to the Bally streets, over the Brickfield then round to Ardoyne and her nice cosy bed.

Danny Megahey, happy, cheerful, in very, very good humour, turned away from Amelia and headed downtown. He was going the other way, down into Donegall Street, past St Patrick's Chapel, planning to be home in his house in the Markets in no time. But he wasn't. After hardly going any distance, a red car pulled up out of nowhere, and in an unexpected twist of events, Danny was taken, very much against his will, into the heart of the Shankill, where he met his protracted, grisly and truly awful end. His ordeal began at a quarter to four in the morning.

ANNA BURNS, *No Bones*, 2001

WOUNDS

Here are two pictures from my father's head –
I have kept them like secrets until now:
First, the Ulster Division at the Somme
Going over the top with 'Fuck the Pope!'
'No Surrender!': a boy about to die,
Screaming 'Give 'em one for the Shankill!'
'Wilder than Gurkhas' were my father's words
Of admiration and bewilderment.
Next comes the London–Scottish padre
Resettling kilts with his swagger-stick,
With a stylish backhand and a prayer.
Over a landscape of dead buttocks
My father followed him for fifty years.
At last, a belated casualty,
He said – lead traces flaring till they hurt –
'I am dying for King and Country, slowly.'
I touched his hand, his thin head I touched.

Now, with military honours of a kind,
With his badges, his medals like rainbows,
His spinning compass, I bury beside him

Three teenage soldiers, bellies full of
Bullets and Irish beer, their flies undone.
A packet of Woodbines I throw in,
A lucifer, the Sacred Heart of Jesus
Paralysed as heavy guns put out
The night-light in a nursery for ever;
Also a bus conductor's uniform –
He collapsed beside his carpet slippers
Without a murmur, shot through the head
By a shivering boy who wandered in
Before they could turn the television down
Or tidy away the supper dishes.
To the children, to a bewildered wife,
I think 'Sorry Missus' was what he said.

MICHAEL LONGLEY, *An Exploded View*, 1973

THE BOY TOLD HIM that there'd been a big bomb down the town and that forty people had been killed. Roche had sold the boy three cigarettes for fifty pence before they parted.

Aoirghe, Matt and Mamie, Mary, even drunken old Tick all found out about Fountain Street in their various ways at their various times and to their varying degrees of horror or pity. Suzy, Rachel and several of the other women with whom Jake had failed to sleep also heard, learnt and discovered. By the time darkness fell, the knowledge had spread through Belfast with the imperceptible but unstoppable velocity of the fading light itself.

The knowledge permeated the city like weather, like a very local depression. That night's nightlife was desultory, hushed. Some had found the news heart-stopping, some had found it dull but there were few who had not found it. Some parents held their children in a tighter embrace that night, some lovers spoke more gently, even some fighters didn't quite fight. The citizens were busy, they couldn't think about it all the time but they thought about it all the same, and there were few who would not have wished it away if they could.

The city and the citizens knew that this act had supposedly been committed on their behalf. A mandate was claimed. As the citizens fought, worked or idled their way through their evening, they almost all knew that no vote had been taken, no proposal put forward. Nearly every citizen thought privately, individually. No one asked me. It was a silent but complete unanimity. It was a silent but complete rejection.

The evening passed and the city grew darkly quiet once more. The southside shop-fronts, all the streetlit sidewalks became deserted. From up high, the city looked the same as it had looked the night before. There was one floodlit patch where you might spot rubble and searchers, but generally Belfast looked like it always looked.

The streets still glittered like jewels, like small strings of stars.

ROBERT McLIAM WILSON, Eureka Street, 1996

OUT OF TOWN, ROLLING HILLS crowned with neat white farmhouses. Farmyards with sheds of green and red corrugated iron. John Deere tractors parked in neat lines in neat lanes. Outside another village a placard hung from a lamppost, reading 'Ulster Says NO', while two Union Jacks fluttered over the Presbyterian church. Then more painted kerbstones; more bunting; and another banner, this one showing Queen Elizabeth surrounded by a circle of Sweet William and orange gladioli; also more shields on lampposts, these ones emblazoned 'UVF 1912–89' and 'Ulster' above a picture of the 'Red Hand', a hand (bloodstained by tradition) palm up and fingers outstretched (the classic 'no' or 'stop' position, as many commentators have observed), and a symbol of the Province which often features in Loyalist or Unionist material; then finally, on the village outskirts, lest there should be any misunderstanding as to whom the territory belonged, the simple message,

Taigs Beware

with a gallows underneath and a stick man hanging by his neck.

In between these showcases the housing estates of the 'other side' (especially as we came into Belfast): green, white and gold kerbstones (echoing the Irish tricolour) and freshly painted in readiness for their own marching season; gable-end paintings of Gaelic chieftains standing shoulder to shoulder with balaclava-clad 'freedom fighters' wielding Armalites (an obvious attempt to link the current situation to the mythical past); doves trapped in barbed wire; the Nationalists' riposte to the Protestants' 'No Surrender', 'Our Time Shall Come'; and this chilling line – as chilling as 'Taigs Beware' although wittier – which I saw on the wall in West Belfast:

Semtex kills more germs than Vortex

In my notebook I wrote, 'All very interesting, colourful and alarming – two cultures shouting through their emblems vociferously at one another and yet not having the slightest interest in communicating.' We got through Belfast and pointed ourselves towards our destination: Enniskillen.

CARLO GEBLER, The Glass Curtain, 1991

THE ERRIGAL ROAD

We match paces along the Hill Head Road,
the road to the old churchyard of Errigal Keerogue;
its early cross, a heavy stone hidden in grass.

As we climb, my old Protestant neighbour
signals landmarks along his well trodden path,
some hill or valley celebrated in local myth.

'Yonder's Whiskey Hollow,' he declares,
indicating a line of lunar birches.
We halt to imagine men plotting

against the wind, feeding the fire or
smothering the fumes of an old-fashioned worm
while the secret liquid bubbles & clears.

'And that's Foxhole Brae under there —'
pointing to the torn face of a quarry.
'It used to be crawling with them.'

(A red quarry slinks through the heather,
a movement swift as a bird's, melting as rain,
glimpsed behind a mound, disappears again.)

At Fairy Thorn Height the view fans out,
ruck and rise to where, swathed in mist
& rain, swells the mysterious saddle shape

of Knockmany Hill, its brooding tumulus
opening perspectives beyond our Christian myth.
'On a clear day you can see far into Monaghan,'

old Eagleson says, and we exchange sad notes
about the violence plaguing these parts;
last week, a gun battle outside Aughnacloy,

machine-gun fire splintering the wet thorns,
two men beaten up near dark Altamuskin,
an attempt to blow up Omagh Courthouse.

Helicopters overhead, hovering locusts.
Heavily booted soldiers probing vehicles, streets,
their strange antennae bristling, like insects.

At his lane's end, he turns to face me.
'Tell them down South that old neighbours
can still speak to each other around here'

& gives me his hand, but does not ask me in.
Rain misting my coat, I turn back towards
the main road, where cars whip smartly past

between small farms, fading back into forest.
Soon all our shared landscape will be effaced,
a quick stubble of pine recovering most.

JOHN MONTAGUE, A Slow Dance, 1975

WE ARE UNDOUBTEDLY FACED ... with antagonistic historical self-understandings, which strongly infer the incompatibility of the two traditions. Each relies on an exclusive narrative – of siege or of oppression – in which very different dates and events are celebrated. Just as 1690 and 1912 are important dates for unionists, so 1798 and 1916 are for nationalists and, more particularly, for republicans.

The meanings carried by the events these dates refer to nourish the dissimilar experiences and memories that reinforce cultural-political divisions in Northern Ireland. They screen out the claim and entitlements of the other tradition. So, if such meanings are constitutive of our traditional identities, how can we avoid conceding their incompatibility?

Possible answers lie in three considerations. First, traditional narratives, like any others, are partial. It is not inappropriate in principle, despite the acrimony any hint of revisionism attracts, to ask whether the meanings of celebrated events are not more complex than each tradition is comfortable admitting, and to probe what the implications of historical complexity might be for how unionist and nationalist identities are understood. Second, it is equally appropriate to raise questions about events omitted from traditional canons, which suggest that antagonism has not been an invariant feature of relations between our main traditions, and which prompt alternative narratives capable of narrowing the divide between unionists and nationalists. Third, it is not clear why we should assume that historical narratives, interpretations and identities that emphasise exclusiveness and antagonism must persist as inflexible fixtures, which cannot be adjusted to suit changing circumstances.

It is the cumulative effect of these three considerations that has the power to wear down the incompatibility argument. This is not to deny that various traditional expressions are incompatible, especially those anticipating the demise of the other. And it is not to say that traditional narratives of siege and oppression lack any credibility, or that there will not continue to be differences of opinion and emphasis between unionists and nationalists on account of their dissimilar historical experiences and memories. But it is to ask by what warrant differences between traditions have to be taken to imply irrecusably antagonistic divisions that must thwart any effort to occupy common ground.

NORMAN PORTER, The Elusive Quest, 2003

THE EXTERNAL REALITY AND INNER DYNAMIC of happenings in Northern Ireland between 1968 and 1974 were symptomatic of change, violent change admittedly, but change nevertheless, and for the minority living there, change had been long overdue. It should have come early, as the result of the ferment of protest on the streets in the late sixties, but that was not to be and the eggs of danger which were always incubating got hatched out very quickly. While the Christian moralist in oneself was impelled to deplore the atrocious nature of the IRA's campaign of bombings and killings, and the 'mere Irish' in oneself was appalled by the ruthlessness of the British Army on occasions like Bloody Sunday in Derry in 1972, the minority citizen in oneself, the one who had grown up conscious that his group was distrusted and discriminated against in all kinds of official and unofficial ways, this citizen's perception was at one with the poetic truth of the situation in recognising that if life in Northern Ireland were ever really to flourish, change had to take place. But that citizen's perception was also at one with the truth in recognising that the very brutality of the means by which the IRA was pursuing change was destructive of the trust upon which new possibilities would have to be based.

Nevertheless, until the British government caved in to the strong-arm tactics of the Ulster loyalist workers after the Sunningdale conference in 1974, a well-disposed mind could still hope to make sense of the circumstances, to balance what was promising with what was destructive and do what W.B. Yeats had tried to do half a century before, namely, 'to hold in a single thought reality and justice'. After 1974, however, for the twenty long years between then and the ceasefires of August 1994, such a hope proved impossible. The violence from below was productive of nothing but a retaliatory violence from above, the dream of justice became subsumed into the callousness of reality, and people settled in to a quarter century of life-waste and spirit-waste, of hardening attitudes and narrowing possibilities that were the natural result of political solidarity, traumatic suffering and sheer emotional self-protectiveness.

SEAMUS HEANEY, from 'Crediting Poetry', The Nobel Prizes, 1995

THE MEDIEVAL PARISH OF SHANKILL not only embraced the Falls as one of its native divisions, but was also directly linked to the monastery at Bangor. A church document of 1615 lists the chapel of Cromoge, located within the parish of Shankill, as one of six 'altarages', or parochial chapels, belonging to the monastery of Bangor, where oblations might be presented and dues paid.

Tragically, to many people the words 'Shankill' and 'Falls' are synonymous with a deep-rooted communal divison which some claim is unbridgeable. However, just as both districts were once embraced within one parish, it is my earnest hope that a proper exploration of our historical and cultural inheritance will reveal the full extent to which that inheritance has always been a *shared* one.

IAN ADAMSON, *Dalaradia: Kingdom of the Cruthin*, 1998

HE DRUMMED HIS FOREHEAD in frustration. 'And then there's MOPE.'
'MOPE?'

'An acronym of the "Most Oppressed People Ever" – a nickname for republicans which in this case applies to their cultural storm-troopers. I thought everyone knew it.'

'I pay as little attention to Irish politics as is humanly possible. If they're not bombing London, I forget about them.'

Amiss sighed. 'Great. It's exactly that attitude among our politicians that encourages MOPE's mates to bomb London if they're craving attention.' He leaned forward and poured himself some more wine.

'God, what a pain in the arse they are. It's bad enough that they're such a whingeing, aggressive bloody crew, but then on top of that you have to put up with their PC concerns about gender balance and parity of esteem with every other shagging delegation regardless of importance, size or consequence. I swear they'll probably measure the bedrooms to make sure no one's got a square foot more than them.'

'The whingeing seems to be contagious.'

'Stop being so unsympathetic. I haven't even told you about DUPE yet.'

'What?'

'It's what my new friend Simon Gibson – my Northern Ireland civil service go-between – calls MOPE's loyalist equivalents. You know, those fringe working-class Prods ...'

'Prods?'

'Local argot for Protestants. DUPEs are the ones with paramilitary mates – stands for "Downtrodden Unionists for Parity of Esteem". They're serious students of MOPE tactics and employ them to good effect in their own attention-seeking efforts.'

'It all sounds delightful.'

RUTH DUDLEY EDWARDS, *The Anglo-Irish Murders*, 2000

Come all you boys that vote for me, come gather all around,
A Catholic I was born an' reared an' so I'm duty bound
To proclaim my country's misery and express our Papish hope,
To embarrass all the Orangemen an' glorify the Pope.

Our allegiance is to Ireland, to her language and her games,
So we can't accept the border boys, as long as it remains,
Our reason is the Gaelic blood that's flowin' in our veins,
An' that is why our policy is never known to change.

ANONYMOUS

I REMEMBER AN ATTITUDE in my childhood that it was good to sing rebel songs like 'Kevin Barry', but that singing 'Sean South of Garryowen' had a different meaning. Kevin Barry was a legitimate hero of the war for independence, but South was a skitter and a criminal. Now he has the vintage that Barry had then, but would he have understood in his own day the modern Sinn Féin vocabulary of Mitchel McLaughlin, any more than Kevin Barry would have understood the republicanism of the 1950s?

'Sean Sabhat, like so many Irishmen and women before and since, decided to strike for Irish freedom in an attempt to force Britain to negotiate a withdrawal from the occupied Six-Counties,' said McLaughlin. But the notion that a British withdrawal should be a negotiated withdrawal is a creation of the 1990s.

The nobility and human decency of people who plant bombs in cities is perhaps overemphasised in republican tributes to counter the fact that it is so little noticed outside republican circles. It is a mythology that helps republicans to cope with their own experience of vilification, or 'demonisation', as they would call it. Anyone reading the writings of prisoners, particularly about the period of the hunger strikes, must be struck by the mix of affection and adulation that republicans had for the ones who died. What republican culture provides is a space within which people who have been appallingly violent will be remembered only for having been brave and good and true. Whatever doubts they might have had in their own lives about whether it was right to kill and destroy for politics, the continuity of the culture determines that there will always be people who will think well of them for what they did.

MALACHI O'DOHERTY, The Trouble With Guns, 1998

REMAINDERMEN

Because what I liked about them best
was their ability to thole,
that weathered silence and reluctance,
fornenst the whole damn lot.

They've lived alone for years of course,
and watched their cemeteries filling up
like car parks on a Saturday,
their young grow fat for export.

There are others who know what it is
to lose, to hold ideas of north
so singularly brutal that the world
might be ice-bound for good.

Someone has almost transcribed
the last fifty years of our speech,
and has not once had the chance
to employ the word *sorry*

or press the shift to make the mark
that indicates the putting of a question.
The arch was put up wrong this spring
outside my father's office.

When you enter it states
Safe Home Brethren,
and upon leaving the place
Welcome Here.

NICK LAIRD, To a Fault, 2005

I THOUGHT OF THE ULSTER PROTESTANTS ... A fear of Catholics bred into them from childhood until it became instinctive like a terror of spiders. Their lifelong drill of eccentric Ulster commandments. 'Never drink from the same glass that a Catholic has drunk from. Any such glass should be broken immediately.' And then their feeling of always being beleaguered, with the enemy pressing its full weight against the feeble ribbon of the border. Their suspicion that the enemy's prohibition on birth-control was a crafty long-term plan to out-breed them. Finally, their way of seeing the enemy – it's a very common way of seeing enemies – as dirty, lazy and cruel, plotting and promiscuous, and with one extra unforgivable vice – prone to dancing on a Sunday.

What happened? Everyone asks this as they look at the rubbled streets of Belfast and Londonderry on the television. The question never seems to be well answered, and only leads to more questions. If there had been no Catholics, would the Ulster Protestants have found it necessary to invent them? Certainly for years and years they provided the only spark of thrill and threat which could blast the monotony of the Ulster everyday. Month after month I remember listening to the same repeating rumours that the Catholics were marching up from Dublin – 'mustering' on the border – and infiltrating industry. Did all those interminable Ulster sermons seem less tedious when it was envisaged that iron-handed Papists might very soon try to put a stop to them? Did the polluted belch of Northern industry seem less hideous if it was felt that greedy Papal fingers were tentacling out to grasp the factories?

CAROLINE BLACKWOOD, 'Memories of Ulster', *For All That I Found There*, 1973

STREET NAMES

I hear the street names on the radio
and map reported bomb or barricade:
this was my childhood's precinct, and I know
how such streets look, down to the very shade
of brick, of paintwork on each door and sill,
what school or church nearby one might attend,
if there's a chance to glimpse familiar hill
between the chimneys where the grey slates end.

Yet I speak only of appearances,
a stage unpeopled, not the tragic play:
though actual faces of known families
flash back across the gap of fifty years;
can these be theirs, the children that today
rage in the fetters of their fathers' fears?

JOHN HEWITT, *An Ulster Reckoning*, 1971

I T IS NO LONGER EASY TO BE pedantic about terminology. The modern compulsion to reflect on identity has given many people difficulty – much as thinking about the spelling of a word makes the proper spelling begin to look not quite right. Terms of self-definition used automatically for years begin to spin and shift under scrutiny. For decades before the Troubles simply being a Catholic in Northern Ireland was identity enough: as one observer put it, 'Just being a Catholic is a political act.' The state was Protestant and Unionist. Being born into the minority defined you as nationalist, republican, disloyal in thought if not in deed. For some, there was a blacker realisation: that partition redefined Northern nationalists as unionists, that Northern Catholics had effectively ceased to exist as part of a political entity, had ceased to have a political identity that counted. *You* were Irish: Northern Ireland was British. People born and grown to adulthood before partition in a thirty-two-county Ireland still thought of Dublin as the capital and believed the new arrangements for the six counties could not last.

Children grew up to view the machinery of government, dimly and at a distance through the barricades of church, school and home, as alien and hostile. The level of hostility and the way it was expressed varied, from near-total withdrawal to violent protest. In every decade some attacked the state with bombs and bullets: blew up public buildings or tried to, shot policemen. For its part unionist Northern Ireland set out by exclusion, by harsh legislation, by electoral manipulation and by discrimination, to ensure that this disaffected and dangerous minority remained a minority, and a powerless one. Emigration by both Protestants and Catholics had always been high, but the Catholic rate settled at around 60 per cent of the total.

FIONNUALA O CONNOR, *In Search of a State: Catholics in Northern Ireland*, 1993

ULSTER SAYS YES

One Protestant Ulsterman
wants to confess this:
we frightened you Catholics, we gerrymandered,
we applied injustice.

However, we weren't Nazis or Yanks,
so measure your fuss
who never suffered like Jews or Blacks,
not here, not with us;

but, since we didn't reform ourselves,
since we had to be caught
red-handed, justice is something
we have to be taught.

JAMES SIMMONS, *Poems 1956–1986*, 1986

A 'BEATEN DOCKET' IS BELFAST PARLANCE for a betting-slip that has
passed its sell-by date; so it is appropriate that a public house not two
doors away from a bookmaker's (Crown Turf Accountants) should be so
called. The Beaten Docket is on a corner of Amelia Street and Great
Victoria Street, directly opposite the Crown Liquor Saloon on the other;
both face the allegedly most-bombed hotel in the world, the Europa,
which occupies the site of the former Great Northern Railway Station,
demolished in 1967, the first terminus of the Ulster Railway, whose train
service from Lisburn to Belfast opened in August 1839.

CIARAN CARSON, *The Star Factory*, 1997

from LETTER FROM IRELAND
for Vincent Buckley

Black sacks flapping on street corners, stiff
  Drummers walk to the Republican plot.
Behind them women in black parade with
  Flags dipped slightly. At the sacred spot
  A sheltered man proclaims a speech — *We will not
Stop struggling until the British leave.
There will be no ceasefire. We give no relief.*

Black sacks on hedges, black sacks on doors,
  Black plastic rustling as black hearses pass.
Fertiliser bags tied to electricity poles
  Signal an anger at the ultimate impasse.
  Refuse sacks, strung and stuffed, have heads to match
Thatcher or Paisley, and across a bridge some hand
Has painted in white: *Remember Bobby Sands.*

Black sacks in the doorway, black sacks in the field,
  Black rifles uncovered on a Donegal strand.
Black border on photographs, black dresses for grief,
  Black berets on coffins, black bowlers and bands,
  Black bullet holes in hallways, black words of command.

Black taxis, black jackets, black bruise and contusion.
Black crepe on a letter box, the Royal Black Institution.

Death stalks the farms of south Tyrone.
   Ruffles its cold clothes and changes
Direction for Armagh, stopping to take home
   A soldier ambushed at greeting's range.
   Nobody seems to think it strange
When Death makes some mistake and takes
As well a girl near a farmyard gate.

SEÁN DUNNE, *The Sheltered Nest*, 1992

A T FIRST I HEARD THE RUMBLE of the saracens up on the Glen Road, the high-pitched whirr of their engines. They came closer. They had turned into Carnan. Out in force. They would be coming for somebody. As they approached I heard for the first time the piercing of whistles in the distance, then closer and closer, then more and more whistles blown powerfully from houses and gardens all over the estate. The dogs joined in, barking, yelping, howling, disturbed by the din, and more so by the panic it induced. In no time women appeared on the street crying that the soldiers were coming. Dozens of men all over Andersonstown slipped out of their houses under cover of the dark and the bloody awful racket set up to warn them.

I had dressed quickly and joined my parents in the street where they stood with a group of neighbours.

'If they're coming for us at least they'll not find us lying down,' declared Mr Gilroy boldly. But then Mr Gilroy was a bus driver who had never so much as let his dog foul the pavement. It was unlikely that he would be a prime target of the security forces.

'Never you worry yourself, Mr Gilroy,' said Mrs French reassuringly, 'They'll have to take you over my dead body.'

The army continued its thunderous advance, making brief stops at street corners. I could chart their path by the sounds of alarm that preceeded them. But it still wasn't enough, this noisy cacophony of warning. It lacked the resonant threat of the Lambeg drum. It had no rhythm. Then someone somewhere had an inspiration. They banged a bin-lid on the concrete of a garden path. A full and satisfying metallic clatter erupted from the clash of concrete and steel. The sound carried, vibrating painfully on the ear, the rhythm battered out powerfully over the whistles and cries. A new instrument, had been added to the community repertoire, a struck instrument. Soon bin-lids appeared on every path, on the road, the pavements, against gable walls. The chorus of banging bin-lids drowned even the advance of the saracens. A powerful response to

665

the threat of re-invasion, a new tribal call that would rebound for years to come off shops and homes and eating houses, drinking establishments and other places of worship, betting offices and public amenities, schools and bus stations and unemployment offices. The great and wholly original tinny howl of the people.

The army came anyway, swooped into Bunbeg, blocked the roads and got out of their vehicles. The three officers commanding the operation were not intimidated by the noise and hostility of the thickening crowds. But they were too late. They broke into two houses in Macroom and found only smouldering hearths and empty beds. The next day another government instrument, the Northern Ireland Housing Trust, was obliged to send out teams of carpenters to repair the damage. The soldiers turned their attention to a row of flats and maisonettes.

MARY COSTELLO, *Titanic Town*, 1992

PARADISE FATIGUE

Above the falling blade of the Hatchet Field a cloud shrouds, a star
hums, a moon pendulums, a merlin scythes the air
with angled wings, a wind sings in the cat's cradle
of a transmission aerial.

Below Black Mountain a kneeling cherub with a fractured wing
swings from the jib of a crank and ratchet crane
in a monumental sculptor's yard strewn
with half-engraved memorials.

Under the sign of two beaten angels hanging by a brazen wing
at the place where six roads cross
a stolen zephyr brakes, spilling
strings of angel dust.

Elsewhere the wings of a broadsheet fold round the globe of
    a hazard
lamp alternating in circuits of blips and quarks
a quirk of light in the spaces
between the words.

EILISH MARTIN, *Slitting the Tongues of Jackdaws*, 1999

TODAY I LEFT CAVAN TOWN SOON after eight o'clock – a sunny morning with a strong cool wind and swift white clouds. In

Belturbet post office advice about cross-border routes was offered by a friendly clerk and a tall old farmer with a leathery face. They thought a cyclist might be able to get across, if the water was low, where the bridge used to be. 'It was blown up twice,' explained the clerk, 'so now they'll leave it that way.' When I asked who had blown it up, and why, they obviously thought I was 'leading them on' and changed the subject. But I genuinely wanted to know. I have a very limited understanding of these matters.

Beyond Belturbet the hilly third-class road passed a few poor little farms and presented two crossroads without signposts. Uncertain of the way, I approached a depressed-looking farm dwelling. As I crossed the untidy yard I called out 'Anybody at home?' – not realising (stupidly) the effect an unknown voice would have quarter of a mile from the border. As I stood at the open door the whole family faced me silently like figures in a tableau, eyes full of fear, everybody motionless. A thin bent granddad stood in the centre of the kitchen floor leaning on an ash-plant, his hat pushed back off his forehead. A woman of about my own age, with unkempt foxy hair and a torn pink jersey, had been making bread and stood with floury hands held over a basin. A young woman with impetigo, a ragged skirt and sandals not matching, was just inside the door holding an empty pail. A skinny, freckled little boy had been pulling a cardboard carton full of turf sods across the floor and he it was who broke the silence by beginning to cry. It is many years since I last saw that degree of slovenly poverty in my own part of rural Ireland. (Yet the inevitable television set stood in one corner.) But it was the fear, not the poverty, that shook me; that instant of pure terror before my harmlessness was recognised. Then everybody relaxed – except the child – and the women came out to the road to give me precise instructions. They didn't think the stepping-stones would be above water today – and they were right.

DERVLA MURPHY, *A Place Apart*, 1978

A POSTCARD FROM NORTH ANTRIM
in memory of Sean Armstrong

A lone figure is waving
From the thin line of a bridge
Of ropes and slats, slung
Dangerously out between
The cliff-top and the pillar rock.
A nineteenth-century wind.
Dulse-pickers. Sea campions.

A postcard for you, Sean,
And that's you, swinging alone.
Antic, half-afraid,
In your gallowglass's beard
And swallow-tail of serge:
The Carrick-a-Rede Rope Bridge
Ghost-written on sepia.

Or should it be your houseboat
Ethnically furnished,
Redolent of grass?
Should we discover you
Beside those warm-planked, democratic wharves
Among the twilights and guitars
Of Sausalito?

Drop-out on a come-back,
Prince of no-man's land
With your head in clouds or sand,
You were the clown
Social worker of the town
Until your candid forehead stopped
A pointblank teatime bullet.

Get up from your blood on the floor.
Here's another boat
In grass by the lough shore,
Turf smoke, a wired hen-run –
Your local, hoped for, unfound commune.
Now recite me *William Bloat*,
Sing of *the Calabar*

Or of Henry Joy McCracken
Who kissed his Mary Ann
On the gallows at Cornmarket.
Or Ballycastle Fair.
'Give us the raw bar!'
'Sing it by brute force
If you forget the air.'

Yet something in your voice
Stayed nearly shut.
Your voice was a harassed pulpit
Leading the melody

It kept at bay,
It was independent, rattling, non-transcendent
Ulster – old decency

And Old Bushmills,
Soda farls, strong tea,
New rope, rock salt, kale plants,
Potato-bread and Woodbine.
Wind through the concrete vents
Of a border check-point.
Cold zinc nailed for a peace line.

Fifteen years ago, come this October,
Crowded on your floor,
I got my arm round Marie's shoulder
For the first time.
'Oh, Sir Jasper, do not touch me,
You roared across at me,
Chorus-leading, splashing out the wine.

SEAMUS HEANEY, *Field Work*, 1979

THAT PART OF BELFAST where I grew up was integrated and civic-minded. The neighbourhood had streetscapes of working-class terraces, corner shops, entries and allotments, nestled in behind lower middle-class three-storied houses with little gardens, fronting the main roads, rising further out towards substantial upper middle-class villas, with grounds and gardens. Where picture-houses, churches, parks, bowling greens, family shops and the magical nooks and crannies fitted into some sense of a community living together.

What I saw on a recent return home was an ugly inversion of all that. Houses bricked-up; in one attractive triangle which I knew like the back of my hand, the once sturdy family homes converted willy-nilly into flats; front doors with steel girders; gardens full of crap. Houses which I recalled standing, if sombrely, in Sunday afternoon light, blinds drawn, the outside door opened to the vestibule, were now demolished, or dark and tawdry versions of their earlier selves.

Faceless Iceland hangars, the cheap made-over facades of Quik Fix shops, pound shops; big windy soulless petrol stations, derelict 1960s buildings patrolled by invisible security companies; even a spur of a motorway cutting its way right through what had once been a vibrant built-up district. Those who had lived in the inner reaches of the city had clearly fled to the suburbs or left the city for good. What I saw was the physical (psychic?) impact of political failure, a failure inscribed in the actual fabric of the place.

GERALD DAWE, *from* 'The Revenge of the Heart', *The Cities of Belfast*, 2003

THE WOMEN IN THE HOUSEHOLD apparently had their own ideas about these house-burnings and about this war. The boards were up, the women themselves had their sticks and their bricks and their knives and their pokers ready, water was in everything and the long hose was on the tap. Lizzie and Amelia, in their outdoor clothes, their Dexters and their shoes on, were put under the table with cushions and blankets and told to sleep there. Mick and Jat, who were twelve, were allowed to help the women. Lizzie, who was eight, was very annoyed, for she was not.

The dog was under the table with them. It was on a lead and it, too, was very annoyed. It knew something was wrong and that shortly, the yelling and the men's footsteps and all the noise outside would be starting again. It pulled on its lead, which was tied to the table leg. 'Don't let her go. She'll only get in our way,' said the women. Amelia talked to her. Lizzie held her by the scruff.

ANNA BURNS, *No Bones*, 2001

MARTIN MOVED OFF. It was a strange feeling to be in the world's eye. Things of note were happening in his place – it hardly mattered that they were *bad* things. The pride was in getting noticed. There were pictures of his town in every paper in the world, every TV in the world – the fact that it was pictures of his town being burned or blown to fuckin bits was neither here nor there.

The next lights were green. It was weird – it was rush hour and everything should have been much busier. In fact the nearer he got to the town centre, the less busy it was. Going at some speed he turned right on to the Boyne Bridge. The road was littered with stones and bricks. It was like a waste ground instead of a main road. What the fuck was going on? A van was blazing and the air was filled with the smell of burning rubber. He tried to steer between the debris but bounced heavily over a half-brick. A bottle smashed in front of him. Holy fuck – what was happening? He looked over his shoulder and there in the road opposite was a phalanx of police and Land Rovers. Guys were running up to the brow of the bridge and chucking stuff across the road and Martin was in the middle of the whole fucking war on his bicycle. He spun round and retreated, bumping up on to the pavement where there was less crap lying on the ground. He stood on the pedals and flew down the hill. Something hit him on the back. A half-brick or something – he didn't know what. But he didn't feel it. He sensed it, but it wasn't painful. He turned the corner out of the line of fire and headed towards the City Hall as fast as he could, still on the pavement. Why didn't the fuckers give you some warning? TAKE CARE. RIOT IN PROGRESS. Jesus Christ. He could have been shot, got a rubber bullet up his arse or anything. When he felt he was out of the firing line he applied the brakes. He joined the watching crowd.

'What's going on?'

'A bit a trouble.'

'What about?'

'How would you know? Somebody probably said something.'

There wasn't much happening now – the occasional splish of a glass bottle breaking on the street surface, shouting that was hard to make out, 'Yafuckinbastard' kind of yelling. The police just stood.

Martin looked at his watch. He'd need to be getting on. Now that Sandy Row was blocked he'd have to go the long way round ... He pedalled up Great Victoria Street slowly, approached Shaftesbury Square, where the Ulster Bank was with its two Elizabeth Frink statues halfway up the wall. Flying Figures or Falling Figures it was called. But locally they'd become known as Draft and Overdraft. Traffic was coming from all directions. Fuckers came out of junctions. Straight at you. He negotiated the Square, then stood on the pedals, panting up the incline to the university. Trees, green lawns, birdsong.

BERNARD MacLAVERTY, *The Anatomy School*, 2001

A S DAWN CAME IN THE EARLY HOURS of the morning, spasmodic firing was still breaking the silence, and plumes of black smoke drifted skywards from the fires. The police gradually withdrew, taking the Specials with them. Including those who died of wounds, six men had died in Belfast during the night, including one shot down as he crossed his own kitchen; 105 people had been injured by the official count, and many more lay having their wounds dressed at home, reluctant or afraid to appear at a hospital. Even the figure for the dead was uncertain. There was word of others whose bodies lay charred to cinders among the ashes of buildings in which they had been shot. More than one hundred homes had been destroyed, more than a dozen factories, while over three hundred houses had been damaged by petrol bombs. All these counts ignored the endless broken windows and charred shop fronts. The Falls Road looked the battlefield it had been.

As the day lightened, with every traffic light shattered, young Catholics stood directing traffic amidst the rubble. Many buildings were still blazing and the roadway was covered with the litter of rocks and glass.

The police had melted away: they stayed tightly shuttered in Hastings Street barracks and the other stations across the city, while between Catholic and Protestant areas the barricades were built up to huge proportions, and intermittent skirmishing continued throughout the daylight hours. Of the dead, only one was Protestant; of the houses burnt, all but a handful were Catholic. At the further end of the Falls Road the scene was incredible, with almost every tree and telegraph pole chopped off at its base to form a barricade. Sixty buses were commandeered by the Catholics on Thursday evening and during Friday, by the simple expedient of telling the drivers to get out or be pulled out. These too were forced across the streets along with bakery vans, upturned cars and trucks, scaffolding and vast numbers of paving stones to create mountainous barricades eight or even ten feet high, every one manned. The Protestants had their own barricades, and clustered behind them making occasional forays.

MAX HASTINGS, Ulster 1969, 1970

'A WOMAN CALLED TO ME from an upstairs window: "Get out of the mouth of the street." Something like that.

'I shouted: "But the people! The people in the houses!"

'A man ran out and dragged me into a doorway. "They're empty!" he said. "They got out last night!" Then we both ran down to the bottom of Balaclava Street and turned the corner into Raglan Street. If he hadn't been holding me by the arm then that was the moment when I would have run back up towards the fires.'

'Why did you want to do that? Why did you want to run back into Conway Street?'

'My grandmother lived there – near the top. He took me to Sultan Street refugee centre. "She's looking for her granny," he told a girl with a St John Ambulance armband on. She was a form below me at school. My grandmother wasn't there. The girl told me not to worry because everyone had got out of Conway Street. But I didn't believe her. An ambulance from the Royal arrived to take some of the wounded to hospital. She put me in the ambulance as well. It was the only transport on the road other than police vehicles. "Go to the hospital and ask for her there," she said.

'It was eight o'clock in the morning when I found her sleeping in a quiet room at the Royal. The nurse said she was tired, suffering from shock and a few cuts from flying glass. I stayed with her most of the day. I don't remember that she spoke to me. And then about six I had a cup of tea and wandered on to the road up towards the park. Jack McHenry was there, writing it all down: "It's all over," he said. "The Army are here." We both looked down the Falls; there were several mills that I could see burning: the Spinning Mill and the Great Northern, and the British Army were marching in formation down the Falls Road.'

ANNE DEVLIN, *from* 'Naming the Names', *The Way-Paver*, 1986

SOCIAL AND POLITICAL LIFE in Northern Ireland is in a sorry condition. Some say it always has been; few dispute that it has been since 1969. Its condition is sorry not only because many citizens experience serious social deprivation but also because Northern Ireland is a deeply divided society. Conflicting political aspirations lie at the heart of its divisions and sectarianism remains an ugly blight on the social and political landscape producing as it does practices of violence, discrimination and segregation. The reality of sectarianism makes trust among opposing political actors a scarce commodity and contributes to an impasse that characterises many aspects of political affairs. One result is a politics of constitutional standoff between unionists and nationalists which drains politics of much of its meaning for citizens. It also cramps political possibilities and inhibits progress beyond the current form of undemocratic government prevailing in Northern Ireland. All political parties express dissatisfaction with the present status quo, but it persists because agreement on its alternative is extremely hard to find.

NORMAN PORTER, *Rethinking Unionism*, 1996

OF ONE THING I AM CERTAIN: there is unlikely to be any amicable resolution of the Ulster problem in my lifetime; probably not in that of my children. The wounds of the last ten years are too deep. The children of those who have been murdered or maimed, the children of those who have murdered and maimed others, will not themselves forget, and will not allow others to forget, the terrible wrongs that have been suffered and inflicted in these Troubles.

But there is a pattern in history, and certainly a pattern in the history of Ulster. There will come a time when the fires of passion and grievance will burn lower, when once again an impatient generation will genuinely wish to put an end to the divisions of three centuries and more. Such a moment of equilibrium occurred in Ulster in the late 1780s; had the leaders of the United Irishmen been willing then to bring together Protestant and Catholic for peaceful purposes, not for an armed (and doomed) rebellion, much might have been achieved. Another such moment perhaps occurred during the 1830s, between the passing of Catholic Emancipation and the Famine, despite the unrest of that period. Yet another such period came in the late 1860s, the time of my great-grandfather's enthusiastic involvement in the politics of liberalism and reform. And, in my own lifetime, such an opportunity certainly existed in the middle 1960s. What a lost opportunity that was! For the first time in a century the Catholic community in Ulster expressed willingness to forget old scores and to play a constructive part in public affairs. Had the Protestant majority been ready to respond with even a modicum of generosity, the Troubles need never have happened. And it would, then, have taken little enough to satisfy legitimate Catholic complaints; had the Unionists then conceded voluntarily only a fraction of what they have since conceded under the duress of British and world opinion, they might have retained, with some honour, their constitution, their parliament, their government, and their leadership. But all of these, including honour, the Protestants of Ulster have needlessly thrown away.

I am being wise after the event. I tried my hardest to be wise before the event, but I was not wise enough.

C.E.B. BRETT, *Long Shadows Cast Before*, 1978

SIX LOUGHS

No bird sings on Belfast Lough.
On Carlingford, on Swilly, on Foyle
Silence has settled, like death in a house
Long prepared. Tall rushes, like mourners
Standing in rain, shadow the waters
Of the two Ernes.

After all the fraudulent mouthings
That for so long revised the truths
All our people saw and knew, this is rest.
She consorted with the other sort; his behaviour
Was anti-social; this one was an informer;
We will not tolerate

Criminal elements. In the meantime
On some bare headland there stands a grey-cloaked figure
Still, bell in hand, eying grey swans, waiting
For another Patrick. But we need a long silence
Now; and a good rain-shower to wash away this sense
That words may mean anything.

So, the place must lie fallow,
While wind-storm and rain-cloud curve
In round the Mournes and over the Sperrins,

From the West crossing the Bluestack mountains
To bleach skeletons, to achieve time's ends
On bodies buried with lies

And false justifications, spoken over them,
After the beatings and the hoodings and the shootings
By roadside and by lake and by mountain stream,
In fields of grass and grain stained twice:
Who now could celebrate the miller's loaves
Bequeathed to us.

On Slemish and in Armagh silence reigns.
A silence carried up from deep Newgrange inhabits
Antrim's glens. The very air is thick with it
And bird and beast wait for some ending of it,
For the breaking of it by some fresh word.

SAM BURNSIDE, *Walking the Marches*, 1990

Over my Special K I watched the wind-jostled camera bring another pair into view: John Hume, the leader of the Social Democratic and Labour Party, the party of constitutional nationalism, and Davey Adams, one of the leaders of a small loyalist party affiliated with the Ulster Defence Association, a paramilitary organisation responsible for the random killing of hundreds of Catholics. A few years earlier, months of meetings between them, let alone a meeting of minds, would have been political pie-in-the-sky. Yet that is precisely where these two Moderns – one preeminent, one improbable – had now ended up, this very moment, stepping out of the marathon of the final all-night negotiations. Who was to be more admired, the one who had not changed, or the one who had changed?

Hume, always alert to the language of occasion, edged forward and took pole position to speak. He has always seemed to me to be cut from the same cultural cloth as his fellow Derryman Seamus Heaney. Both belong to the Redmondite tradition of constitutional nationalism, but the affinity strikes me as deeper than mere politics or even the traditional Catholicism of the upbringing of each. It is more a matter of cultural poise; of being at home in equal proportion in their *provincia*, on the island, within the wider world.

What the two make of background navigates the Scylla and Charybdis of Ulster's culture wars: the laager mentality of the unionists, and its gangrenous doppelganger, the martyrological imperative of armed republicanism. In distinct but overlapping spheres, politician and poet have fashioned a discourse of the optative Ireland where 'hope and history rhyme,' and where the parish is comprehended – as the great Irish essayist Hubert Butler once put it – from the vantage of the cosmopolitan: '*The interpreters will be those who can see the national life as well as live it. To acquire this detachment, they will need to have access to other forms of society, so that they can see their own lives objectively and in totality from the threshold.*' And now, it seemed, was the crowning moment, when the optative had begun to transmute to the present continuous.

Visibly moved, Hume said simply, 'This a Good Friday gift to the people of Ireland,' before giving way to Adams, who made to speak. But all that issued was the strangled beginnings of an opening *Uh*. He was choked up, near tears. You felt the moment in yourself, the camera lulling for a second on the silent pair, before being magicked up to the anchorman in a Portacabin studio above the parking lot.

It was late afternoon when I drove home ... On the hills above west Belfast the whitethorn blossom of the hedgerows put me in mind of combers foaming down through the quilted fields. It was cloudy but lightsome, and the streets, emptying early before the long weekend, were spangled with showers. A pillar-box painted green caught a sudden shaft of declining sun. By the time I reached south Belfast, the west had cleared to a deepening hue of cobalt, a last late sunshine bathing the brick of an old terrace district. The scruffy kerbstones of Primrose and Gypsy Streets were awash in a sudden preternatural glow. About this time, I would notice later on the news, the final Stormont plenary had convened for the cameras; Senator Mitchell announced 'the new British-Irish Agreement'; and the eight delegations emerged successively onto the steps of Government Buildings to address the massed ranks of the global media – braving, over the next hour, and only a few miles away, a final meteorological fitfulness of gusts, drizzle, sunshowers and sleet.

Towards eight I walked out ... to see what was playing at the cinema a few blocks away. A last deep glaze of jade, darkling and translucent, lay on the horizon under a streak of stratus. The Moonrise had just lifted over the silhouette of the houses beyond the thoroughfare of the Ormeau Road. Among the innumerable images for its elemental presence, would I ever quite find the one that got the beauty, the minerality, the geometry of that bright alabaster disc, its Minerva's owl's-eye, light out of the dark, magnificence reflected in the void?

CHRIS AGEE, *from* 'Weather Report: Good Friday Week, 1998',
Irish Pages, Spring 2002

PROGRESS

They say that for years Belfast was backwards
and it's great now to see some progress.
So I guess we can look forward to taking boxes
from the earth. I guess that ambulances
will leave the dying back amidst the rubble
to be explosively healed. Given time,
one hundred thousand particles of glass
will create impassible patterns in the air
before coalescing into the clarity
of a window. Through which, a reassembled head
will look out and admire the shy young man
taking his bomb from the building and driving home.

ALAN GILLIS, Somebody, Somewhere, 2004

An Ulster Imagined

[The] northern part of Antrim ... has a wonderful atmosphere which makes it different from any other place that I have ever visited. One seems to run into that atmosphere as one enters the Glen country north of Ballymena. What is 'atmosphere'? How is it created? It seems to me to arise from something more than fresh air and associations, fine scenery and natural influences. It seems, indeed, to be something much more psychical than physical. A powerful, astringent presence seems to brood over a great area of north Antrim. It varies from place to place, but it seems to be fundamentally one great influence over the whole area. When I read that a certain individual, a bishop, claimed to have seen great angels in north Antrim, I did not feel at all inclined to question it.

HUGH SHEARMAN, *Ulster*

The whole point of the ideal Ulsterman is ... that he must carry within himself elements of both Scots and English with a strong charge of the basic Irish.

When I discovered, not long ago, that the old Planters' Gothic tower of Kilmore Church still encloses the stump of a round tower and that it was built on the site of a Culdee holy place, I felt a step nearer to that synthesis. It is the best symbol I have yet found for the strange textures of my response to this island of which I am a native. I may appear Planters' Gothic, but there is a round tower somewhere inside, and needled through every sentence I utter.

JOHN HEWITT, *from* 'Planter's Gothic'

O NCE OR TWICE AS I HAVE GONE about the circuit of Ireland I have noted down something like this: 'A setting for a novel'. Youghal was one, Clonmel another, and I would now add Derry, or Coleraine. What I meant by that, I think, was that something in the atmosphere of these places – indefinable, impalpale – blustered life into articulate and significant relationships. Perhaps it was the atmosphere of history; or that the people have adopted a certain kind of position, almost a pose, appropriate to the dramatic meaning of their own kind of life; and this had gone into the very stones of the town, all its ways and outer signs, as the face and body of a man reveals his inner nature. Why should it not be so? We say of a man that he has a strong personality. Why may we not say it of a town?

SEAN O'FAOLAIN, *An Irish Journey*, 1940

T HE FIRST SCHOOL ESSAY I remember writing was called 'How to Light a Fire'. It was in the days when all of Belfast burned coal and the factories were like convoys of destroyers, their tall smoke-stacks belching out in chorus as they wove their fat skeins of smog across the city ...

It is freezing cold: one of those February days when, perversely, the marble-shooting season would begin and your knuckles are skinned and raw, chapped blue and purple from squinting and shooting 'marlies' in their complicated planetary rituals and ricocheting paths. Or two of us are sent out into an opalescent fog to skid and skate across the black bottle-glass rink of the granite yard. We are the milk collectors. The galvanised-iron milk-crate burns frostily into our palms and fingers, it clinks and tingles as we teeter back, the pair of us, like out-of-synch zinc buckets, on a milkmaid's swaying yoke.

I step into the sudden fug of the classroom radiator-warmth. When we take the bottles out they're frozen solid halfway down their half-pint length. We rack and clunk them up like snowman soldiers on the regimental cast-iron pipes. Gradually, a sour-sweet thaw will blend its milk-aroma with the other fug ingredients: chalk-dust, pencil-shavings, plasticine, sweaty socks, damp raincoats, schoolbag leather, ink, lino, blotting paper, oak and varnish, the interiors of pencil boxes, the exhalation of our breath against the de La Salle Brothers' blackboard-black soutane. Snow, too, is in the air; it will soon snow down like algebra. After the preliminary joy of crowding to the window, we settle down to write: 'First, you take a bundle of sticks ...' No, 'First you get your coal. You go out to the coal shed.'

It was a bunker, really, brick-built against the yard wall, open to the freezing air, since no one thought of a lid. In snowy weather, black lumps sparkled craggily below the snowcap. The shovel grated wetly as it scraped into the aperture. The coal clunked into the scuttle with a bumpy, hollow sound: a tiny, momentary, melismatic avalanche, each daily rhythm different to the next, but in its special chunkiness of timbre, reminding you of yesterday. You tilted your shoulder and your arm ached at the elbow as you took the strain. Underfoot was slush. You picked and slipped your way across it to the kitchen door and worked the tick-tock of the latch.

Kneeling before the still-warm empty grate, you tore and crumpled up the *Irish News*. Or, the *Irish News and Belfast Morning News*, as it was more grandiosely known then. The sticks, bundled up in hairy coarse string, were purchased from a ragged man who wheeled his wares in a pram and called them out at intervals along the early-darkening street, until the gas-lamps came on one by one. Then he was gone into the fog. I felt he was a sleeping-partner of the coal-brick man, whose flat hand-cart bore a ziggurat of steaming coal-brick still hot from the press. His shouts of 'c-o-o-a-a-al b-r-r-e-e-e-k' lingered in the air long after he had passed.

CIARAN CARSON, *Last Night's Fun*, 1996

THE LANDSCAPE WAS SACRAMENTAL, instinct with signs, implying a system of reality beyond the visible realities. Only thirty years ago, and thirty miles from Belfast, I think I experienced this kind of world vestigially and as a result may have retained some vestigial sense of place as it was experienced in the older dispensation. As I walked to school, I saw Lough Beg from Mulholland's Brae, and the spire of Church Island rose out of the trees. On Church Island Sunday in September, there was a pilgrimage out to the island, because St Patrick was supposed to have prayed there, and prayed with such intensity that he branded the shape of his knee into a stone in the old churchyard. The rainwater that collected in that stone, of course, had healing powers, and the thorn bush beside it was pennanted with the rags used by those who rubbed their warts and sores in that water. Then on a clear day, out in the Antrim hills beyond Lough Beg, I could see the unmistakable hump of Slemish, the mountain where the youthful Patrick had tended sheep. That legend, and the ringing ascetic triumph of the lines in his *Confession* where he talks about rising in the frosts of winter to pray to his Christian God, all combined to give Slemish a nimbus of its own, and made it more potent in the mind's eye than Slieve Gallon, a bigger, closer mountain that we faced on the road home from school, and which took its aura from our song 'Slieve Gallon's Braes'. On Aughrim Hill, between the school and the lough, somebody had found an old sword, deemed to be a Viking sword, since we knew those almost legendary people had sailed the Bann a thousand years before; and on a shelf in the master's room there was a bit of wood that had been turned to stone by the action of the waters of Lough Neagh.

There, if you like, was the foundation for a marvellous or a magical view of the world, a foundation that sustained a diminished structure of lore and superstition and half-pagan, half-Christian thought and practice. Much of the flora of the place had a religious force, especially if we think of the root of the word in *religare*, to bind fast. The single thorn-tree bound us to a notion of the potent world of fairies, and when my father cut such a thorn, retribution was seen to follow inexorably when the horse bolted in harness, broke its leg and had to be destroyed. The green rushes bound us to the beneficent spirit of St Brigid: cut on Brigid's Eve, the first of February, they were worked into Brigid's crosses that would deck the rooms and outhouses for the rest of the year. Indeed, one of my most cherished and in some way mysterious memories is of an old neighbour of ours called Annie Devlin sitting in the middle of a floor strewn with green rushes, a kind of local sybil, plaiting the rushes and plaiting all of us into that ritualized way of life.

Then on May Eve, the buttercups and ladysmock appeared on the windowsills in obedience to some rite, and during the month of May the pagan goddess became the Virgin Mary and May flowers had to be gathered for her altar on the chest-of-drawers in the bedroom, so that the primroses and the celandines also wound us into the sacral and were wound into it in their turn. Late summer, and my father plaited harvest bows from the new corn and wore them in his lapel. Hallowe'en, and the turnip, that homely and densely factual root, became a root of some kind of evil as the candle blazed in it from a gatepost in the dark. At the fireside then, the talk of old times when cows were blinked and men met the devil in the shape of a goat or heard him as a tinkle of chains on the road after dark, or saw him, or powers of some sort, in lights dancing in spots where no lights should be. Such naming of examples is a pleasure to me, and that is, I believe, itself an earnest of the power of place.

SEAMUS HEANEY, *from* 'The Sense of Place', *Preoccupations: Selected Prose, 1968–78*, 1980

ELEGY IN A PRESBYTERIAN BURYING-GROUND

in memoriam: J.L.D.

I

The meeting-house is not what it used to be
Since the new church was built,
But the white-washed walls still make a pleasant setting
For the ash-trees at the gate,

And the round windows – though the red panes are gone –
Have dignity upon the simple wall,
And the door, level to the grass, without steps or porchway
Might open yet to all.

II

The white pavilions of gateposts, stained with damp
And with rusty iron (where the gate had hung)
Still point the way to the stable, where horse and pony could
    nuzzle,
Till the second sermon was done,
And the elders came out, to draw the shafts of the traps up,
And load their wives and children into the well
With their bibles and their black dresses and farmyard faces.
Farewell, farewell!

III

I could have buried a poet here under these hedges
And left him happy. Son of the manse he was,
And drew his integrity from these white-walled precincts,
His rhetoric from his father's pulpit phrase.
Though he himself had made his Covenant elsewhere,
An older, darker and more troubled one,
With the certainty of a leaf, of a stone, of a dewdrop,
He knew his Election.

IV

He would remember the nooks where the first primroses
Christened the moss, and the freckled thrush would come
Mating its melody with his own grave elegiacs
To turn a Scottish psalm.
And whenever the men stood up, with their backs to the pulpit,
Hiding their faces from Jehovah's glare,
He would be with them, though he prayed another
And more contentious prayer.

V

There are some townlands more in league with heather
And the dark mountain, than with fields where men
Have sowed and planted; and his rebel spirit
Still sought the farthest glen,
Whose Sabbath was a solitude, whose gossip
Was the wind's whisper. There he broke the bread
Of meaning, in a silence, that his verses
So well interpreted.

VI

Yet he would grieve with me for the dereliction
That has overtaken this place,
For he cared for it. And the burying-ground beside it
Held many of his race.
He would not be surprised to find it sadly neglected,
Who was himself so negligent of fame.
And I?
– I would be proud to be the stoneyard mason
Who had incised his name.

R.N.D. WILSON, 1949

DURING THE HOURS when I am not at work in the *Northern Whig* I am attending Gregory Smith's lectures and – what else? Sometimes I walk beyond Balmoral, where I see the misty mountains and grass flecked with raindrops; or I go to the poetry shelves of the Linen Hall Library, or take part in academic talk about the sonnet and the merit of writers. We belong to a community where it is possible for many people to be known to one another. As I catch the train on my way to Larne I may chance upon Professor Meredith at the station. At Kilwaughter Rectory familiar acquaintances and parishioners are coming and going. There are arguments, or somebody sings, and I sit on a sofa and gaze at the fire. One moment I am in the thick of things; another moment I am solitary. For example, I sit on a mossy boulder in the river valley near Kilwaughter, with a glimpse of blue sea in the distance. The water passes under the shadow of a low chestnut. Brian the red-setter paddles on the wet stones. Where is everyone? No train puffs up or down the valley. I lie in the grass, and a thrush or chaffinch strikes with a sharp note through the monotone of summer …

On my Saturdays and Sundays, thus, I step beyond the urban circumstance of Belfast and am among persons with different problems from those which generally appear in the newspapers. I see the difference between events reported in the press and slow steady events which will not make the headlines. I am in the unaccented non-topical present. Here are minutes of such times, caught from the atmosphere: going to certain houses; games of tennis; bathing in a bay with shining currents; being with groups of the young, dancing; reading poems before getting into bed; being much about in an area of which I am vividly conscious, noting its suburban and country objects – beech and chestnut trees, red and yellow broom, old men with lawn-mowers, ladies at tea among flowerbeds, tulips in a walled garden, the neck of water where the ferry crosses to Islandmagee, rain coming down when it is sunny – naming them to my diary in a grateful acknowledgement. These are what count and make the colour and pressure of subordinate, busy days. And people:

Forrest Reid, Professor Hugh Meredith, Lyle Donaghy, Alex Glendinning; the journalists, including a new one, Suffern: and strangers too — a beautiful face in the train.

GEORGE BUCHANAN, *Morning Papers*, 1965

from THE GLITTERING SOD

Mine is historic Ulster, battlefield
of Gael and Planter, certified and sealed
by blood, and what is stronger than the blood,
by images and folkways understood
but dimly by the wits, yet valid still
in word and gesture, name of house or hill,
and by the shapes of men whose texture was
determined by the nature of the place,
flogged by the strong wind, soothed by the soft rain,
flushed by the April sunshine's gay champagne,
shod by the heather, heeled by the yielding moss,
till, wayward and persistent as the grass,
they kept their roots, or when chance drove them off,
held earth about them close and strong enough
to feed their stature with new skies to fill,
from Alexander Irvine back to Colmcille ...

I claim the birthright which I must defend
against the guile of foe and sloth of friend,
for one would bind us supine in the thrall
of ancient error and its crumbling wall,
the other in his dullness cannot see
the future gay with possibility,
and howls dismay at change, though it must come,
crests to its flood and lips into a foam.
Yet we shall ride the waters in their spite,
who thrash and wallow to the left and right,
drop gurgling down into the Romish pit,
or on a melting iceberg scold at it.
We shall drive on, obedient to the tide,
yet tacking as the current winds provide
to the safe haven of an ordered state,
rock-based and fertile, generously great,
and scaled to offer, for individual growth,
the peace of age, the ecstasies of youth.

But who am I to speak so in this wise,
consigning this and this as loyalties?
And by what right? Were it not better done
for me to listen like a grateful son,
and step with you and go where you would go
than drag you on a path you do not know?
I urge but this. When you have stood awhile
and watched the shadows running mile on mile
over the heather and the wind-bleached grass
where heroes strode, where heroes still may pass;
when you have flung your pebbles in the sea
from the black cliff; when, stepping leisurely,
you've come upon a grey-walled meeting house
where lichened headstones tilt in dumb carouse,
and know your people lie there, clay in clay;
when you have heard the loud drum far away
throb through the stillness of a summer night,
you too have this illimitable right.

Just so with me. Against this weight of pride
for years I'd set my wits, instead I'd tried
to wring a simple meaning out of sense,
equipping my slow mind for swift response
to painted panel or to printed book;
yet every road I travelled brought me back,
back to the sunlight on the glittering sod,
back to my fathers and their silent God.

JOHN HEWITT, *Freehold and Other Poems*, 1986

O N OUR WAY TOWARDS MUCKER I remembered the Beeog's Lane
and I concentrated my memory on the wiry grass that grew on the
banks of the road, remembering how I had often sat there. And I saw a
hump of hill and on the top of that hump I was a young man of twenty
and it was a day in early April and we were sowing oats. And I felt the
sharp wind of April that was blowing hope and sadness. And I could be
again myself as I was looking over the hedge at the long white road that
stretched far away.

And beyond the railway level-crossing was the house I was born in.
Once it was home, now it meant almost nothing. Deserted and the spirit
departed. We drove past the gate over the top of which I had so often
leaned happy, unconscious, warm and comfortable at the heart the myth.
The worry of my fields was around me then ...

We passed many important landmarks of my childhood – the Gullet and the Big Bush and Woods' Gate and Cassidy's Whaal – what does 'Whaal' mean, by the way? It is a real Gaelic sound. And then we pulled up at John Lennon's house. Many's the day, as the fella said, meself and John wrought together and listened to his father telling stories of the great fist-fighters. Jim Corbett and Jack, the Nonpareil, Dempsey that he had seen in action in America.

The leading question was 'Do you remember ...?'

I wanted to remember my way and I was helped to remember my way back into the warm myth of my rural days.

'Do you remember the time we were cutting the corn in the Well Field,' said John, 'and you grabbed all the Champion spuds out of the basket when the dinner came out? You'd eat nothing but the Champion, they were very floury.'

None of this may sound very exciting but in the atmosphere this conversation lived. It was the story of private lives, the only story that is of any importance, the story with which the poet is always concerned.

PATRICK KAVANAGH, *The Bell*, 1954

from STATION ISLAND

A hurry of bell-notes
flew over morning hush
and water-blistered cornfields,
an escaped ringing
that stopped as quickly

as it started. *Sunday*,
the silence breathed
and could not settle back
for a man had appeared
at the side of the field

with a bow-saw, held
stiffly up like a lyre.
He moved and stopped to gaze
up into hazel bushes,
angled his saw in,

pulled back to gaze again
and move on to the next.
'I know you, Simon Sweeney,
for an old Sabbath-breaker
who has been dead for years.'

'Damn all you know,' he said,
his eye still on the hedge
and not turning his head.
'I was your mystery man
and am again this morning.

Through gaps in the bushes,
your First Communion face
would watch me cutting timber.
When cut or broken limbs
of trees went yellow, when

woodsmoke sharpened air
or ditches rustled
you sensed my trail there
as if it had been sprayed.
It left you half afraid.

When they bade you listen
in the bedroom dark
to wind and rain in the trees
and think of tinkers camped
under a heeled-up cart

you shut your eyes and saw
a wet axle and spokes
in moonlight, and me
streaming from the shower,
headed for your door.'

Sunlight broke in the hazels,
the quick bell-notes began
a second time. I turned
at another sound:
a crowd of shawled women

were wading the young corn,
their skirts brushing softly.
Their motion saddened morning.
It whispered to the silence,
'Pray for us, pray for us,'

it conjured through the air
until the field was full
of half-remembered faces,
a loosed congregation
that straggled past and on.

As I drew behind them
I was a fasted pilgrim,
light-headed, leaving home
to face into my station.
'Stay clear of all processions!'

Sweeney shouted at me
but the murmur of the crowd
and their feet slushing through
the tender, bladed growth
opened a drugged path

I was set upon.
I trailed those early-risers
who had fallen into step
before the smokes were up.
The quick bell rang again.

SEAMUS HEANEY, 1984

GLENDESHA, OR *GLEANN DÉISE* as the older people called it ... is where I now live. It is typical of many remote places in southeast Ulster where, until recent times, some of its last native Irish-speakers and singers lived. It is a narrow mountain road with a scattering of empty ruined houses bridging the townlands of Shanroe and Carrive and cutting through the Ring of Gullion hills. It leads towards the border dividing part of the north from the south of Ireland, where once it led to *Bealtaine, Gróbh na Craoibhe, Cnoc a' Damhsa* – and other nearby places that echo other days. This road meanders through a landscape of standing stones on high ground – relics of a secret past – and in lower overgrown places are the large slabs of mass rock and market stone once used for secret prayer and busy trade. It is lined with native trees of rowan, holly and fairy thorn and hazel groves where herds of wild goat now wander freely. Fields are small and stony and used for sheep and cattle grazing while idle meadows yield willingly to the invasive yellow-ochre ragwort. In late spring the thorny whins erupt in a blaze of golden blossom awakening the senses with a sweet and heady fragrance and mingling with the magical May flower of the hawthorn – the harbinger of summer – once a potent symbol of fertility at the heart of rural festivities. Later in the season the hedges and ditches edge along in filigree of wild hemlock, guarded by the purple-hooded foxglove or 'banshee', as it was known here. The hawk still hovers above Glendesha at *Sáil na Bróige*, swooping from the wooded hills on unsuspecting prey. Autumn glows with an abundance of hazelnut and edible berries – fraughan, sloe and black bramble and crops of wild mushroom to feed the remaining populace of squirrel, fox and pheasant. Winter draws in with a lonesome, hibernating stillness. It is a tranquil place, a place of memory – a silent Gaeltacht.

PÁDRAIGÍN NÍ UALLACHÁIN, *A Hidden Ulster: People, Songs and Traditions of Oriel*, 2003

HERE AT CAISEAL NA gCORR STATION
for Michael Davitt

Anseo ag Stáisiún Chaiseal na gCorr
d'aimsigh mise m'oileán rúin
mo thearmann is mo shanctóir …

Here at Caiseal na gCorr Station
I discovered my hidden island,
my refuge, my sanctuary.
Here I find myself in tune
with my fate and environment.
Here I feel permanence
as I look at the territory of my people
around the foot of Errigal
where they've settled
for more than three hundred years
on the grassy mountain pastures
from Mín 'a Leá to Mín na Craoibhe.
Here before me, open
like a book,
is this countryside now
from Doire Chonaire to Prochlais.
Above and below, I see the holdings
farmed from the mouth of wilderness.
This is the poem-book of my people,
the manuscript they toiled at
with the ink of their sweat.
Here every enclosed field is like a verse
in the great poem of land reclamation.
I now read this epic of diligence

in the green dialect of the holdings,
understand that I'm only fulfilling my duty
when I challenge the void
exactly as my people challenged the wilderness
with diligence and devotion
till they earned their prize.

Here I feel the worth of poetry.
I feel my *raison d'être* and importance as a person
as I become the pulse of my people's heart
and from this certainty comes peace of mind.
My desires are tamed, my thoughts mellow,
contradictions are cancelled on the spot.

CATHAL Ó SEARCAIGH, translated by GABRIEL FITZMAURICE,
An Bealach 'na Bhaile/Homecoming: Selected Poems, 1993

BUT THERE IS, AFTER ALL, a sociological parallel to the geological contrast as between Antrim and Donegal: for may we not compare life in that old land of the north-west, with its primitive rocks, its worn-down hills, its mild dreamy atmosphere, and its people of ancient race still harbouring old legends and traditions, with the newer erupted land of the basaltic area, its traces of ancient life all burnt and buried far beneath, and now crowded with a stalwart race largely projected into it in recent times by eruptions from Scotland and England, and vigorous in the bracing air of Antrim?

ROBERT LLOYD PRAEGER, *The Way That I Went*, 1937

THIS ANTRIM AIR IN SUMMER

This country's air is cleansing to the heart;
Atlantic-fresh, and washed with spray and rain,
it leaps off leaves and blusters down the lane;
in frolic gusto sometimes spins apart
to pluck at peat-reek, bearing in its stride
that friendly tang across a sheltered glen;
whips flax-dam's ripples to a thrusting tide,
or heads the drifting swan's-down back again;
shaped by the running lines of crag and hill,
combs tossed bog-cotton tufts, lifts flagging crow,
stripping cloud's corner, clears the bare blue sky,

or, drunk on hawthorn, hoards the heat until,
startled at sudden thunder stumping by,
it cuffs the thistle with a rocking blow.

JOHN HEWITT, *Loose Ends*, 1983

BEYOND BALLYCASTLE THE CHARACTER of the country changes. The last of the nine glens is left behind and with it the imprint of the Gael. No more green tangles of mountains, no more valleys ablaze with gorse and fuchsia. Ahead lies the stern, wind-swept country of the Route, aptly enough the scene in which George Birmingham set the opening chapters of his novel *The Northern Iron*, a country of castles, or the ruins of castles, perched high on cliffs confronting the Atlantic – Kenbaan, Dunluce, Dunseverick; and just what it means to confront the Atlantic on this coast is best realised by standing beside the ruins in a winter storm and watching the surf on the rocks below. Inland the scenery of the route may be level and uninteresting, at times positively dreary, but on the rock-bound coast the drama of the Atlantic and the cliffs is stupendous and the sea-wind would, in the vivid imagery of the district, blow life into a corpse.

DENIS IRELAND, *Statues Round the City Hall*, 1939

from IRELAND

Of the Mournes I remember most the mist,
The grey granite goosefleshed, the minute
And blazing parachutes of fuchsia, and us
Listening to the tiny clustered clinks
Of little chisels tinkling tirelessly
On stone, like a drip of birds' beaks picking
Rapidly at scattered grain. I think of those
Wet sodden days when we, for miles and miles,
Steadily padded the slow sponge of turf
That squealed and squelched cold between our bared toes;
Or on airy ridge, urgent and agile, ran,
A chain of jigging figures on the sky-line;
Or, skilfully in file, followed, tricking
The hoops of hairy bramble in our path,
Poking in undergrowth and picking
The bitter berries that prickle the springs
Of the dark mouth. There was Bloody River
Where the granite pickles bristled and blazed, and
Ebullient water bellied over

Boulders with the sweep of a bell's shoulders,
And pancaked out in pools: Drinihilla
Where the gales smoothed and glued back the eyelids:
The granite river that is called Kilkeel,
Whose beds were clean and gritty like oatmeal:
And Commedagh in whose high summer heat
Nothing stirred, only the shimmering bleat
Of sheep; and we, as we sat and chattered,
Marked the motionless shine of falls far-off
On Binyon, and nothing at all mattered:
And Legawherry so soft and grassy,
Where the white scuts lazily scattered,
And never in their remotest burrows
Did ferret-Fear come closely after them:
Slieve-na-brock and its long pig-tail trickles
That hung down the bald rocks, reaching to
The glossy backs of the bracken. And Donard
Where, high over all hanging, the strong hawk
Held in his eyes whole kingdoms, sources, seas,
And in his foot-hooks felt all things wriggling
Like the single string of river niggling
Among the enormous mountain bottoms.
Bearnagh and Lamigan and Chimney-Rock.
Spelga, Pulgarve, and Cove – all these names lie
Silently in my grass-grown memory,
Each one bright and steady as a frog's eye;
But touch it and it leaps, leaps like a bead
Of mercury that breaks and scatters
Suddenly in a thousand shining strings
And running spools and ever-dwindling rings
Round the mind's bowl, till at last all drop,
Lumped and leaden again, to one full stop.

W.R. RODGERS, *Awake! And Other Poems*, 1941

IT IS A MEMORABLE EXPERIENCE to peep over the embankment on the County Down shore of Belfast Lough on a winter afternoon as the sun is sinking below the purple Antrim hills, suffusing sky and sea with rosy splendour. There, not far from land, swim the silent swan-flotillas, a vast, scattered fleet. The wine-red dimples of the lazy wavelets form a perfect foil for the snowy birds as they placidly float or dip their necks to feed. Here and there a curve of the neck or breast or back, catching the sun's rays, gleams with a pink radiance such as the lucky traveller sees when an Alpine peak blushes in the sunset. Beyond, appearing only as dark lines on the ruffled sea, lie squadrons of ducks – wigeon, mallard, scaup, golden-eye or scoter. A belated heron flaps away into the glowing sky leaving loneliness in his wake. The gentle, chilly wind stirs the dry grasses, and the rank invigorating smell of sea-wrack pervades the air. There is hardly a sound; only the lapping of the water on the rocks and the occasional whistle of a redshank or curlew.

The sun sets, the purple hills turn black, the sea becomes grey and sinister. Yet, out on the lough, undismayed, in lonely majesty ride the white swans, until the moon rises to reveal the multitudinous congregation of silver birds on the dappled sea.

So they rest month by month, until with the larks winging above the slob-lands and the white blossom beginning to mantle the blackthorn, there stirs in them the call to seek calmer waters where each pair may rear a brood undisturbed by competitors of their own race. They fly off, two by two, peopling all the loughs and tarns of Ulster and bringing delight wherever they pass or linger. Happily, however, some remain, to redeem the dreariness of the mud-flats.

EDWARD ALLWORTHY ARMSTRONG, Birds of the Grey Wind, 1940

ART McCOOEY

I recover now the time I drove
Cart-loads of dung to an outlying farm –
My foreign possessions in Shancoduff –
With the enthusiasm of a man who sees life simply.

The steam rising from the load is still
Warm enough to thaw my frosty fingers.
In Donnybrook in Dublin ten years later
I see that empire now and the empire builder.

Sometimes meeting a neighbour
In country love-enchantment,
The old mare pulls over to the bank and leaves us
To fiddle folly where November dances.

We wove our disappointments and successes
To patterns of a town-bred logic:
'She might have been sick ... No, never before,
A mystery, Pat, and they all appear so modest.'

We exchanged our fool advices back and forth:
'It easily could be their cow was calving,

And sure the rain was desperate that night ...'
Somewhere in the mists a light was laughing.

We played with the frilly edges of reality
While we puffed our cigarettes;
And sometimes Owney Martin's splitting yell
Would knife the dreamer that the land begets.

'I'll see you after Second Mass on Sunday.'
'Righ-o, right-o.' The mare moves on again.
A wheel rides over a heap of gravel
And the mare goes skew-ways like a blinded hen.

Down the lane-way of the popular banshees
By Paddy Bradley's; mud to the ankles;
A hare is grazing in Mat Rooney's meadow;
Maggie Byrne is prowling for dead branches.

Ten loads before tea-time. Was that the laughter
Of the evening bursting school?
The sun sinks low and large behind the hills of Cavan,
A stormy-looking sunset. 'Brave and cool.'

Wash out the cart with a bucket of water and a wangel
Of wheaten straw. Jupiter looks down.
Unlearnedly and unreasonably poetry is shaped
Awkwardly but alive in the unmeasured womb.

PATRICK KAVANAGH, *Collected Poems*, 1964

WHEN GARDENING FAILED HIM [i.e. Art MacCooey] or when he lost
his job, he must needs seek employment in the coarser work of the
farm. On one such occasion he was employed by a farmer called Jones at
Layther Hill. It was springtime, and Art was engaged carting up manure
from the farmyard to the summit of the hill, and Layther Hill, like so
many others in County Armagh, is very steep. It was slow tedious work,
and MacCooey's heart was not in it. The birds were singing their love-
carols, all nature was astir under the rejuvenating influence of spring, and
MacCooey became possessed with the spirit of song. Having filled his cart
of manure he hummed his lines, ever seeking sweeter rhymes, as the
horse slowly travelled up the steep hill-slope. Having reached the field or
place where the manure should be deposited, the poet, now completely
lost in abstraction, so absorbed was he by his theme, turned the horse
around and marched down the hill again to the farmyard. Here

mechanically taking up the manure-fork to fill the cart, he found it full, and so marched up the hill again. And thus for four or five times MacCooey carted up and down the same load of manure, until at length his employer discovered him bringing down a cart full instead of an empty one, when a shout and a few rough words awoke him from his dreams, and brought him back from the Elysian fields of poetry to the hard facts of Layther Hill.

ÉNRÍ Ó MUIRGHEASA, Art MacCubhthaigh's and Other Songs, 1926

THE DISPLAY CASE

Last night Hibernia appeared to me in regal frame,
In Creggan churchyard where I lay near dead from drink.
'Take down these words,' she said, 'that all might know my claim.'
I opened up a vein and drew my blood for ink —

I'd no accoutrements of writing, save the knife;
The pen she gave me was a feather from her plumage,
And my arm the parchment where I'd sign away my life.
'You seem,' she says, 'to have a problem with the language,

Since you've abandoned it for lisping English,
Scribbling poems in it exclusively, or so I'm told.
Turncoat interpreter, you wonder why I languish?'

Her full speech is tattooed for all time on my mummied arm,
A relic some girl salvaged from the scaffold
Where they quartered me. *God keep the Irish from all harm!*

CIARAN CARSON, The Twelfth of Never, 1998

THERE WAS THE BEAUTY of an autumn afternoon in the Ormeau Park at dusk, when, with the dead leaves thick on the deserted paths, I had sat listening to a German band playing somewhere out of sight beyond the railings. Through the twilight, with its yellow twinkling of street lamps, the music floated. The tune was the old 'Lorelei', but into the plaintive twang of those instruments all the melancholy of the earth had passed. It was as if the very soul of the empty park had found a voice, and were sobbing out its complaint to the November sky ...

There was the beauty of the Lagan Valley, filled with the sound of hidden running water, where the sluggish river plunged down through foaming weirs. A beauty, in summer, when the dark soil had burst into a pagan riot of growth, rich and green and luxuriant; but in winter desolate enough, suggestive of broken, unhappy loves, of last walks together, while the grey light gradually faded from the marshlands beyond the towpath, and the trees stooped down over their own dark images ...

There was the beauty of the sea – an unearthly beauty, because it washed on the shores of my dream world. A strip of golden sand over which the dark blue water splashed in little creamy waves – thus it came back to me, forming always the same picture – a picture that more than any other was *my* picture. For, most of us, I suppose, have one picture that is somehow a part of our life, in which our life really takes place, and which is the last sight, perhaps, our dying eyes will see.

FORREST REID, Apostate, 1926

from HARVEST

And so she pictures how they'll come again
Home from the fields, bearing in triumph brief
The intricately plaited Granny sheaf,
And how the whiskey, tea, and talk will flow,
And tales be told of harvests long ago ...

Till as she watches by her apple tree
Through fruited boughs the shimmer of the sea,
Disquiet falls on her, as if she were
No more alone; as if the limpid air
Grew charged, impatient as the pause between
The lightning and the thunder, while the green
Life-long-familiar prospect looks agley,
A painted setting for an unknown play,
With unseen actors crowding in the wings
Waiting the curtain bell: but ere it rings
All's over and – the foolish fancy gone –
She's just in time to put the dinner on.

Fancy? Yet who can tell what signals dart
Along the storied blood, and bid the heart
Stir with occulted memories? For she
Is heir to all that vanished company
Who built the low barn church, the forge, the mill
The farm, white-clustered by the sheltering hill
With gateposts round as Nendrum's fallen tower;
Of all who laboured here through sun and shower;

Kept tryst with lovers; vigil by the dead;
Knew loneliness, and saw the evening's red

Fade behind Scrabo on a winter's day;
Or slopes of green, moist-bright on cloudy grey
In rainbow weather. All who knew the deep
Content of finished work and coming sleep;
The smith, the carpenter, the weaver bent
Above his clacking loom, the provident
Strong farmer, and the fisher tanned with brine;
Shipwright and mason, doctor and divine;
And unremembered women-folk, who bore
Children and taught them all the country lore;
Fed poultry, and drove in the cows at night,
And baked and spun and kept their linen white.
And, wearied, slept at length beneath the sod
Like one Jean Hay who 'went with joy to God
Where was her heart' – so the old headstone reads ...

Oh far beyond the grasp of thought, recedes
Man's ancient interfusion with the land,
The thorn-crowned barrow and the drifting sand
Epitomise the generations gone;
And old already was that standing stone,
When, on the rocks beyond the salt-bright blue
Of Strangford, Patrick landed, and there grew
From that first prayer by Quoyle's unhurrying flow
New sanctities; Columba's exiled woe;
Armagh; and Bangor's angel-haunted choir;
And all who brought the world-renewing fire
To Europe's darkness.
   Here with foam and din
The strong tides bore the Viking raiders in:
Here keeps and cloisters of the Pale had stood
Long roofless when, in threatened solitude,
The Planter made his home, and nurtured there
His last-born son, first born in Irish air,
Who, in old age, his final harvest done
Sat by this stream to feel the westering sun
And watch his barefoot grandchildren at play
Enact the Boyne, a fight of yesterday;
And thanked his God who gave the year's increase
And prayed for them a heritage of peace.

NESCA ROBB, *Ards Eclogues, c.* 1974

BUT OF COURSE IT WASN'T JUST THE OLD RELIGION that exhaled its fragrances in that place. The more recent sectarian varieties were also intimately bound up with different locales. The red, white and blue flagpost at the Hillhead, for example, was a totem that possessed all the force of a holy mountain, and the green chestnut tree that flourished at the entrance to the Gaelic Athletic Association grounds was more abundantly green from being the eminence where the tricolour was flown illicitly at Easter or on sports days. Even Annie Devlin's rich and overgrown garden, with its shooting leeks and roofings of rhubarb leaves, even that natural earth was tinctured with the worst aspects of our faiths, insofar as that lovely flower, Sweet William, became suspect in the imagination from its connection with William of Orange, the king we sent to hell regularly up the long ladder and down the short rope.

All this was actual, all of it was part of the ordinary round if only a part of it, but all of it has by now a familiar literary ring to it. And if it has, that is partly due to a new found pride in our own places that flourished suddenly in the late nineteenth century and resulted in a new literature, a revived interest in folklore, a movement to revive the Irish language, and in general a determination to found or re-found a native tradition.

SEAMUS HEANEY, *from* 'The Sense of Place', *Preoccupations:*
Selected Prose, 1968–78, 1980

CUTTINGS

Methodical dust shades the combs and pomade
while the wielded goodwill of the sunlight picks out
a patch of paisley wallpaper to expand leisurely on it.

The cape comes off with a matador's flourish
and the scalp's washed to get rid of the chaff.
This is the closeness casual once in the trenches

and is deft as remembering when not to mention
the troubles or women or prison.
They talk of the parking or calving or missing.

A beige lino, a red barber's chair, one ceramic brown sink
and a scenic wall-calendar of the glories of Ulster
sponsored by JB Crane Hire or some crowd flogging animal feed.

About, say, every second month or so
he will stroll and cross the widest street in Ireland
and step beneath the bandaged pole.

Eelmen, gunmen, the long dead, the police.
And my angry and beautiful father:
tilted, expectant and open as in a deckchair

outside on the drive, persuaded to wait
for a meteor shower, but with his eyes budded shut,
his head full of lather and unusual thoughts.

NICK LAIRD, To A Fault, 2005

Y OU SEE LEAFY STREETS and you see leafless streets. You can imagine leafy lives and leafless ones. In the plump suburbs and the concrete districts your eyes see some truths, some real difference. The scars and marks of violence reside in only one type of place. Many of the populace seem to live well. Many prosper while many suffer.

Belfast is a city that has lost its heart. A shipbuilding, rope-making, linen-weaving town. It builds no ships, makes no rope and weaves no linen. Those trades died. A city can't survive without something to do with itself.

But at night, in so many ways, complex and simple, the city is proof of a God. This place often feels like the belly of the universe. It is a place much filmed but little seen. Each street, Hope, Chapel, Chichester and Chief, is busy with the moving marks of the dead thousands who have stepped their lengths. They leave their vivid smell on the pavements, bricks, doorways and in the gardens. In this city, the natives live in a broken world – broken but beautiful.

ROBERT McLIAM WILSON, Eureka Street, 1996

from ARMAGEDDON, ARMAGEDDON

Not to worry. From where I lived
We might watch Long Bullets being played,
Follow the course of a pair of whippets,
Try to keep in time with a Lambeg Drum.

There'd be Derryscollop, and Cloveneden,
The parish where W.R. Rodgers held sway,
And where the First Orange Lodge was founded,
An orchard full of No Surrenders.

We could always go closer if you wanted,
To where Macha had challenged the charioteer

And Swift the Houyhnhnm,
The open field where her twins were whelped.
Then, the scene of the Armagh Rail Disaster.
Why not brave the Planetarium?

PAUL MULDOON, *Mules*, 1977

MALIN TOWN HAS WHITE HOUSES set round a triangular village green. I pass through the town like a somnambulist, listening to the cawing of the rooks in the fresh green branches overhead. The road runs by the edge of Trawbreaga Bay, with the water shining emerald green over the shallows and misty blue mountains lining the farther shore. Twenty years before, looking across the variegated carpet of the bay from those very mountains, I had told myself that some day I would visit this town that lay beyond the water to the north, its white houses shining in the sunlight and black specks of rooks clustering above its tree-tops ... and now, twenty years later, I am there; the whitewashed gables of Malin glitter in the spring sunlight and deafening clouds of rooks thresh and caw amongst the fresh green branches overhead. But for some reason I do not believe in the town any more: it is all an illusion; a painted backcloth without depth or solidity; the reality is the road that has brought me to it. A long, twisting road that leads backwards across continents and oceans to the glimmering square of the nursery window, the jamjar full of tadpoles that stood on the chest of drawers in front of it, the pond in the gardens with its almost mythical black and white swans, the silver birch that stood and shivered on the bank, the bell that rang at the park gates and the distant voices calling in the dusk of winter evenings *all out, all out, all out*. Then home to tea up the darkling Malone Road where the gas-lamps bloomed like daffodils and old Dr Walton Browne's hansom cab went jingling past in the darkness between the lamps, *clip-clop, clip-clop, clip-clop*, with its two yellow eyes shining and its mysterious figure inside sitting bolt upright in a frockcoat and top hat, with, according to rumour, a mysterious black bag reposing on the seat beside him, the shadow of the horse elongating and shortening, hastening and retarding in the space between the jewelled streetlamps.

DENIS IRELAND, *Statues Round the City Hall*, 1939

from EPILOGUE: DRIVING SOUTH

Driving South, we pass through Cavan,
lakeside orchards in first bloom,
hawthorn with a surplice whiteness,
binding the small holdings of Monaghan.

A changing rural pattern means clack
of tractor for horse, sentinel shape
of silo, hum of milking machine:
the same from Ulster to the Ukraine.

Only a sentimentalist would wish
to see such degradation again:
heavy tasks from spring to harvest:
the sack-cloth pilgrimages under rain

to repair the slabbery gaps of winter
with the labourer hibernating
in his cottage for half the year
to greet the indignity of the Hiring Fair.

Fewer hands, bigger markets, larger farms.
Yet something mourns. The iron-ribbed
lamp flitting through the yard at dark,
the hissing froth, and fodder scented warmth

of a wood stalled byre, or leather thong
of flail curling in a barn, were part
of a world where action had been wrung
through painstaking years to ritual.

Acknowledged when the priest blessed
the green tipped corn, or Protestant
lugged pale turnip, swollen marrow
to robe the kirk for Thanksgiving.

Palmer's softly lit Vale of Shoreham
commemorates it, or Chagall's lovers
floating above a childhood village
remote but friendly as Goldsmith's Auburn –

Our finally lost dream of man at home
in a rural setting! A giant hand
as we pass by, reaches down
to grasp the fields we gazed upon

Harsh landscape that haunts me,
well and stone, in the bleak moors of dream
with all my circling a failure to return
to what is already going.
                    going
                    GONE

JOHN MONTAGUE, *The Rough Field*, 1972

from SÉAMAS MAC MURFAIDH

Ar mhullach Shliabh gCuilinn bhí an choirm á réiteach,
'Gus Séamas Mac M(h)urfaidh 'na thaoiseach ar an fhéasta,
Cha dtabharfadh sé urraim do bhodaigh a' Bhéarla,
'Gus anois tá sé in Ard M(h)acha is gan fáil ar a réiteach.

On the summit of Slieve Gullion the gathering was prepared,
And Séamus MacMurphy, the chieftain of the feast,
Who never would submit to the English churls,
Now lies in Armagh with no hope of release.

A year from today we were at the Pattern of Killeavy,
And a year from tomorrow at the races in Dunleer,
Today I'm left in Armagh as hundreds were before me,
At the foot of this street my death will be decreed.

Alas that my leg or my arm was not broken
Before I drank the cup of whiskey on Sunday morning.
They stole my hat and plundered my pockets,
And I was struck with bad luck which did overcome me.

Alas I'm not a blaeberry on the side of the mountain,
Or as a bright primrose within the sun's rays,
Or as Séamus MacMurphy the finest in Ireland,
And Christmas in Creggan I'd spend, were I able

Alas that I'm not on Ardaghy or above on Fathom,
Drinking from quarts in your parlour, young maid.
I'd make a few poems, upon my word with pleasure,
O, white-breasted lady, it's you who left me dismayed.

If I were a blaeberry on the top of Fathom,
Or as a stem of fern in the beam of the sun,
I would go as a blackbird to the woods of Dunreavy
And round by Carnally, reared with honour when young.

What we know of Séamas Mac Murfaidh comes from the oral tradition
of lore and song in the locality. He was born in Carnally near
Crossmaglen in or about the year 1720. One version of the song suggests
that a Paddy and Rose McArdle reared him. He was a young man when
the 'Young Pretender' made his bid to capture the throne of his ancestors.
He was reputedly betrayed 'by his own people' and hanged in Armagh
between 1750 and 1760. There is no evidence that he was a poet though
this song is written in his voice.

PÁDRAIGÍN NÍ UALLACHÁIN, *The Hidden Ulster:*
People, Songs and Traditions of Oriel, 2003

I HAVE A TANGLED RECURRENT DREAM of the dense urban space of
Arthur Square and its confluence of five streets – Corn Market, Ann
Street, Castle Lane, William Street South and Arthur Street, each with its
tributaries of arcades, alleyways and entries. It is a precinct crammed with
shops, stores, offices, public houses, cafés, cinemas: here are Joseph
Braddell & Son, Gunmakers, Fishing Rod and Tackle Manufacturers;
Guest, Keen & Nettlefolds, Ltd, Iron & Steel, Bolt, Nut & Screw
Manufacturers; Wm Rodman & Co., Heraldic and General Stationers,
Fancy Goods Warehouse, Print Sellers, Gilders, Picture Frame Makers,
Photographic and Artists' Materials Depot; M'Gee and Co. Ltd, Military,
Naval and Ladies' Tailors, Inventors of the Ulster Coat and Slieve
Donard Coat; the X.L. Café and Restaurant; Gillis & M'Farlane, Mayfair
School of Dancing; W.J. Kidd & Sons, Boot Upper Manufacturers and
Leather Merchants; and The Ulster Cinematograph Theatres, Ltd,
(Imperial Picture House & Café) ...

Pleasurably lost, I wander through the palpable dream, touching its
surfaces of brick and granite, sniffing the soot-flecked air; usually, it is
night-time, but the shops are all lit up and open, forming bright inviting
porticos. Sometimes, with a *doppelgänger* jolt, I recognise this is the real
world, only slightly altered from when last I visited, or was invited, and
I acknowledge my shadow. Finding myself in the sleep department of a
vast emporium – I have just climbed its marble Versailles staircase – I

resist the urge to bury myself in a double bed, since this is a lucid device for escaping the dream, should one wish to; instructed by an exit sign, I am led down some steps, and emerge in the upper lounge of the Morning Star in Pottinger's Entry, inhaling its immediate smoky beery aura. The barman is none other than William Hartnell, who played the head barman in Carol Reed's 1947 film, *Odd Man Out*, which starred James Mason as a fugitive revolutionary, Johnny McQueen.

CIARAN CARSON, *The Star Factory*, 1997

FIELD OF VISION

I remember this woman who sat for years
In a wheelchair, looking straight ahead
Out the window at sycamore trees unleafing
And leafing at the far end of the lane.

Straight out past the TV in the corner,
The stunted, agitated hawthorn bush,
The same small calves with their backs to wind and rain,
The same acre of ragwort, the same mountain.

She was steadfast as the big window itself.
Her brow was clear as the chrome bits of the chair.
She never lamented once and she never
Carried a spare ounce of emotional weight.

Face to face with her was an education
Of the sort you got across a well-braced gate –
One of those lean, clean, iron, roadside ones
Between two whitewashed pillars, where you could see

Deeper into the country than you expected
And discovered that the field behind the hedge
Grew more distinctly strange as you kept standing
Focused and drawn in by what barred the way.

SEAMUS HEANEY, *Seeing Things*, 1991

Acknowledgements

The editor and publisher gratefully acknowledge permission to include the following copyright material:

ADAMS, GERRY, from *Before the Dawn* (Brandon, 1996); *Falls Memories* (Brandon, 1982), both by permission of Mount Eagle/Brandon Publications.

ADAMSON, IAN, from *Dalaradia: Kingdom of the Cruthin* (Pretani Press, 1998), by permission of the author.

AGEE, CHRIS, 'Weather Report: Good Friday Week, 1998' from *Irish Pages* (Inaugural Issue, Spring 2002), by permission of the author; 'Flag-Iris' and 'Occam's Rime' from *First Light* (The Dedalus Press, 2003), by permission of The Dedalus Press.

ALEXANDER, ELEANOR, from *Lady Anne's Walk* (Edward Arnold, 1903), copyright holder not traced.

ALYN, MARJORY, from *The Sound of Anthems* (Hodder & Stoughton, 1983), reproduced by permission of Hodder & Stoughton and St Martin's Press Ltd., London, copyright © 1983 by Marjory Alyn.

ANDREWS, ELIZABETH, from *Ulster Folklore* (Elliot Stock, 1913), copyright holder not traced.

ANONYMOUS, from 'The Committee's Collection', *Ulster Folklife* (Vol. 5, 1959).

ARMSTRONG, EDWARD ALLWORTHY, from *Birds of the Grey Wind* (Oxford University Press, 1940), by permission of Oxford University Press.

ARTHUR, CHRIS, 'A Paper Star for Brookfield', 'Going Home' and 'Under Siege' by Chris Arthur from *Irish Nocturnes*, ISBN 1-888570-49-0, published by The Davies Group, Publishers (1999), Aurora, Colorado, USA; 'Handscapes of the Mind', 'Train Sounds' and 'On the Face of It' by Chris Arthur from *Irish Willow*, ISBN 1-888570-46-6, published by The Davies Group, Publishers (2002); 'Water Glass' by Chris Arthur from *Irish Haiku*, ISBN 1-888570-78-4, published by The Davies Group, Publishers (2005).

BARDON, JONATHAN, from A *History of Ulster*, new updated edition, Blackstaff Press, 2001, reproduced by permission of Blackstaff Press.

BEHAN, BRENDAN, from *Brendan Behan's Island* (Hutchinson, 1962), by permission of the Tessa Sayle Literary Agency.

BELL, SAM HANNA, from *Erin's Orange Lily* (Dennis Dobson, 1956), by kind permission of Fergus Hanna Bell.

BIRMINGHAM, GEORGE A., from *An Irishman Looks at His World* (Hodder & Stoughton, 1919); *Pleasant Places* (Heinemann, 1934); *The Northern*

Iron (Newnes Ltd, 1907); *The Red Hand of Ulster* (Smith, Elder & Co., 1912), all reproduced by kind permission of Susan Harper.

DE BLÁCAM, AODH, from *From a Gaelic Outpost* (Catholic Truth Society, Dublin, 1921); *The Black North* (M.H. Gill & Son, 1938), by kind permission of the Estate of Aodh de Blácam.

BLACKWOOD, CAROLINE, from *For All That I Found There* (Duckworth, 1973), © 1973, Caroline Blackwood.

BONTHRONE, GRACE C., from 'Childhood Memories of County Antrim' from *Ulster Folklife* (Vol. 6, 1960), by permission of *Ulster Folklife*.

BOYD, JOHN, from *Out of My Class* (Blackstaff Press, 1985), reproduced by kind permission of Gavin and Angela Boyd.

BRETT, C.E.B., from *Buildings of Belfast* (Weidenfeld & Nicolson, 1967); *Buildings of County Antrim* (Ulster Architectural Heritage Society, 1996); *Buildings of County Armagh* (Ulster Architectural Heritage Society, 1999); *Long Shadows Cast Before* (John Bartholomew & Son Ltd, 1978), all reproduced by kind permission of Adam Brett.

BROWN, MALCOLM, from *Sir Samuel Ferguson* (Bucknell University Press, 1973), by permission of Bucknell University Press.

BRYANS, ROBIN, from *No Surrender: An Ulster Childhood* (Faber, 1960; Blackstaff Press, 1987); *Song of Erne* (Faber, 1960); *Ulster: A Journey Through The Six Counties* (Faber, 1964; Blackstaff Press, 1989), all reproduced by kind permission of George Balcolmbe.

BUCHANAN, GEORGE, from *Green Seacoast* (Gaberbocchus Press, 1959); *Morning Papers* (Gaberbocchus Press, 1965); *Rose Forbes* (Faber, 1950), all reproduced by kind permission of Sandra Buchanan.

BURNS, ANNA, from *No Bones* (Flamingo, 2001), reprinted by permission of HarperCollins Publishers Ltd, © Anna Burns, 2001.

BURNSIDE, SAM, 'Six Loughs' from *Walking the Marches* (Salmon Publishing, 1990), by permission of the author.

CADWALLADER, ANNE, from *Holy Cross: The Untold Story* (The Brehon Press, 2004), reproduced by kind permission of The Brehon Press.

CAMBLIN, GILBERT, from *The Town in Ulster* (William Mullan & Son, 1951), copyright holder not traced.

CAMERON, BOBBY, from *Before That Generation Passes: The Story of a Shorts Apprentice* (Escoumains Publications, 2001), by permission of the author.

CAMPBELL, FLANN, from *The Dissenting Voice* (Blackstaff Press, 1991), copyright holder not traced.

CAMPBELL, JOSEPH, 'I Will Go With My Father A-Ploughing', 'The Quern-Stone' and 'The Women at their Doors' from *The Rushlight* (Maunsel & Co., 1906); ''Tis Pretty Tae Be in Baile-Liosan' from *The Mountainy Singer* (Maunsel & Co., 1909), all by kind permission of Simon Campbell.

CARNDUFF, THOMAS, from *Life and Writings 1954–1994* (Lagan Press, 1994), published by kind permission of Sarah Ferris, executor of

Thomas Carnduff's Literary Estate. (Thomas Carnduff's papers are held by QUB Special Collections Library.)

CARRICK HILL RESIDENTS' ASSOCIATION, from *Green Peas An' Barley-O: A People's History of Carrick Hill* (Carrick Hill Residents' Association, 1989), by kind permission of Carrick Hill Residents' Association.

CARSON, CIARAN, 'Interior With Weaver' and 'Linen' from *The New Estate and Other Poems* (Blackstaff Press, 1976; Gallery Press, 1988); 'August 1969' and 'Slate Street School' from *The Irish For No* (Gallery Press, 1987); '1795', 'Nine Hostages', 'The Display Case', 'The Lily Rally', 'The Londonderry Air' and 'The Rising of the Moon' from *The Twelfth of Never* (Gallery Press, 1998), all by kind permission of the author and The Gallery Press, Loughcrew, Oldcastle, County Meath, Ireland and Wake Forest University Press; *Last Night's Fun* (Jonathan Cape, 1996), reprinted by permission of The Random House Group Ltd and Wake Forest University Press; *The Star Factory* (Granta Books, 1997); *Fishing for Amber* (Granta Books, 1999), all by permission of Granta Books; 'The Lament of Nuala O'Neill for Donegal in the Region of James I, King of Britain' (July 2005), by permission of the author.

CARSON, KERRY, 'Mourne' from *A Rage for Order: Poetry of the Northern Ireland Troubles*, edited by Frank Ormsby (Blackstaff Press, 1992), by kind permission of the author.

CARY, JOYCE, from *A House of Children* (Michael Joseph, 1941), reprinted by arrangement with the Trustees of the J.L.A. Cary Estate.

CASEY, DANIEL J., from 'Carleton and the Court', *Seanchas Ard Mhacha* (Vol. 8.1, 1975–76), by kind permission of the author.

CAULFIELD, M.F., from *The Black City* (Jonathan Cape, 1952), copyright holder not traced.

CAUSLEY, CHARLES, 'HMS *Glory*' from *Collected Poems* (Macmillan, 1992), by kind permission of David Higham Associates.

CLARK, WALLACE, from *Linen on the Green* (The Universities Press, 1982), by kind permission of the author.

COCHRANE, IAN, from *A Streak of Madness* (Allen Lane, 1973), copyright holder not traced.

COLE, JOHN, 'Introduction' to Terence O'Neill, *Ulster at the Crossroads* (Faber, 1969), by permission of Faber and Faber Ltd.

COLUM, PADRAIC, from *Cross Roads In Ireland* (Macmillan, 1930), copyright holder not traced.

COSTELLO, MARY, from *Titanic Town* (Methuen, 1992), by kind permission of Methuen Publishing.

COYLE, KATHLEEN, from *The Magical Realm* (Wolfhound Press, 1997), by permission of the trustees of the Estate of Kathleen Coyle.

CROFTS, FREEMAN WILLS, from *Man Overboard* (Collins Crime Club, 1936), by permission of The Society of Authors as the Literary Representative of the Estate of Freeman Wills Crofts.

CUNNINGHAM, PHILIP, from *Derry Down the Days* (Guildhall Press, 2002), by permission of Guildhall Press.

DAWE, GERALD, from *The Rest is History* (Abbey Press, 1998), by kind permission of the author; 'The Revenge of the Heart' from *The Cities of Belfast*, edited by Nicholas Allen & Aaron Kelly (Four Courts Press, 2003), by permission of Four Courts Press.

DEANE, SEAMUS, 'Return' from *Selected Poems* (Gallery Press, 1988), by kind permission of the author and The Gallery Press, Loughcrew, Oldcastle, County Meath, Ireland; *Reading in the Dark* (Jonathan Cape, 1996), by permission of The Random House Group Ltd. US copyright © 1996 by Seamus Deane, reprinted courtesy of Alfred A. Knopf, a division of Random House Inc., New York.

DEVLIN, ANNE, from *The Way-Paver* (Faber, 1986), by permission of Faber and Faber Ltd.

DEVLIN, POLLY, from *All of Us There* (Weidenfeld & Nicolson, 1983), by kind permission of the author and the Little, Brown Book Group.

DIXON, HUGH, from *An Introduction to Ulster Architecture* (Ulster Architectural Heritage Society, 1975), by kind permission of The Ulster Architectural Heritage Society.

DONAGHY, JOHN LYLE, 'The Bracken', 'The Flax Pulling', 'The Hill' and 'The People' from *The Flute Over the Valley: Antrim Song* (Inver Press, 1931), copyright holder not traced.

DONOGHUE, DENIS, from *Warrenpoint* by Denis Donoghue, published by Jonathan Cape. Reprinted by permission of The Random House Group Ltd. US copyright © 1991 by Denis Donoghue. Used by permission of Alfred A. Knopf, a division of Random House, Inc.

DOYLE, LYNN, from *An Ulster Childhood* (Maunsel & Roberts, 1921), copyright holder not traced.

DUNNE, SEÁN, 'A Letter from Ireland' from *Collected* (Gallery Press, 2005), by kind permission of the author's Estate and The Gallery Press, Loughcrew, Oldcastle, County Meath, Ireland.

EAGLETON, TERRY, 'Homage to Francis Hutcheson' from *Heathcliff and the Great Hunger* (Verso, 1995), by kind permission of Verso Books.

EDWARDS, RUTH DUDLEY, from *The Faithful Tribe* (HarperCollins, 1999). Reprinted by permission of HarperCollins Publishers Ltd and the Robinson Literary Agency Ltd. Copyright © Ruth Dudley Edwards 1999. From *The Anglo-Irish Murders* (HarperCollins, 2000), reproduced by permission of the Robinson Literary Agency Ltd.

ELLIOTT, MARIANNE, from *The Catholics of Ulster* (Allen Lane, 2000), by permission of the author; *Watchmen in Sion* (Field Day Pamphlet No. 8, 1985), by kind permission of Field Day Publications Ltd.

ERVINE, ST JOHN, from *The Wayward Man* (Collins, 1927), by permission of The Society of Authors as the Literary Representative of the Estate of St John Ervine.

EVANS, E. ESTYN, from *Mourne Country* (Dundalgan Press, 1951), by kind permission of Dundalgan Press.

FALLS, CYRIL, from *The Birth of Ulster* (Methuen, 1936), by kind permission of Julia Carlyon.

FARRELL, MICHAEL, from *The Orange State* (Pluto Press, 1976), by permission of Pluto Press.

FIELDEN, OLGA, from *Island Story* by Olga Fielden, published by Jonathan Cape (1933). Reprinted by permission of The Random House Group Ltd.

FORDE, REV. CANON, from *Sketches of Olden Days in Northern Ireland* (McCaw, Stevenson & Orr, 1926), copyright holder not traced.

FORSTER, E.M., from *Abinger Harvest* (Edward Arnold, 1936), by permission of the Provost and Scholars of King's College, Cambridge and The Society of Authors as the Literary Representatives of the Estate of E.M. Forster. US permission: excerpt from 'Forrest Reid' in *Abinger Harvest*, copyright 1936 and renewed 1964 by Edward M. Forster, reprinted by permission of Harcourt, Inc.

FOSTER, JOHN WILSON, 'A Country Boyhood in Belfast' from *Irish Literary Supplement* (Fall, 1989); *The Titanic Complex* (Belcouver Press, 1997), both by kind permission of the author.

FOSTER, LYDIA M., from *Elder's Daughters* (Quota Press, 1942); *Manse Larks* (Quota Press, 1936), copyright holder not traced.

FRIEL, BRIAN, from *Translations* (Faber, 1981), by permission of Faber and Faber Ltd and The Catholic University of America Press, Washington, DC.

GAILEY, ANDREW, from *Crying in the Wilderness: Jack Sayers, A Liberal Editor in Ulster, 1939–1969* (Institute of Irish Studies, QUB, 1995), by kind permission of the author.

GALVIN, PATRICK, from *Irish Songs of Resistance* (The Folklore Press, 1956), by kind permission of the author.

GATT, MARGARET, from *Unpublished Reminiscence* (2004), by kind permission of the author.

GEBLER, CARLO, from *The Glass Curtain* (Hamish Hamilton, 1991), by kind permission of the author and Antony Harwood Ltd.

GILBERT, STEPHEN, from *The Landslide* (Faber, 1943), by permission of Faber & Faber Ltd.

GILLIS, ALAN, 'Progress' and 'The Ulster Way' from *Somebody, Somewhere* (Gallery Press, 2004), by kind permission of the author and The Gallery Press, Loughcrew, Oldcastle, County Meath, Ireland.

GOGARTY, OLIVER ST JOHN, from *I Follow St Patrick* (Rich & Cowan, 1938), copyright holder not traced.

GOOD, JAMES WINDER, from *Ulster and Ireland* (1919), copyright holder not traced.

GREACEN, ROBERT, 'Derry' and 'One Day in August' from *Young Mr Gibbon* (Profile Poetry, 1979); 'Sunday in Co. Monaghan' from

Carnival at the River (Dedalus, 1990); 'Homecomings' from *Collected Poems* (Lagan Press, 1995); *The Sash My Father Wore* (Mainstream Publishing, 1997), all reprinted by kind permission of the Jonathan Williams Literary Agency.

GUINNESS, DESMOND and WILLIAM RYAN, from *Irish Houses and Castles*. Copyright © 1971 Thames & Hudson Ltd, London. Reproduced by kind permission of Thames & Hudson.

GWYNN, STEPHEN, from *Highways and Byways in Donegal and Antrim* (Macmillan & Co., 1899); *The Charm of Ireland* (Harrap, 1927); *Ulster* (Beautiful Ireland, 1911), copyright holder not traced.

HAMMOND, DAVID, from *Songs of Belfast* (Mercier Press, 1978), published by Ossian Publications © 2006 Novello & Company Ltd, part of the Music Sales Group.

HANNA, DENIS O'D., from 'Architecture in Ulster', in *The Arts in Ulster* (Harrap, 1951); *The Face of Ulster* (Batsford, 1952), copyright holder not traced.

HASTINGS, MAX, reproduced from *Ulster 1969* (Gollancz, 1970) by Max Hastings (Copyright © Max Hastings 1970), by permission of PFD (www.pfd.co.uk) on behalf of Sir Max Hastings.

HAYES, MAURICE, from *Sweet Killough, Let Go Your Anchor* (Blackstaff Press, 1994), by kind permission of the author.

HAYWARD, RICHARD, from *Belfast Through the Ages* (Dundalgan Press, 1952); *Border Foray* (Arthur Barker, 1957); *In Praise of Ulster* (Arthur Barker, 1938), copyright holder not traced.

HEANEY, SEAMUS, 'A New Song' and 'No Sanctuary' from *Wintering Out* (Faber, 1972); 'Whatever You Say, Say Nothing' from *North* (Faber, 1975); 'July' and 'Trial Runs' from *Stations* (Ulsterman Publications, 1975); 'A Postcard from North Antrim', 'The Singer's House' and 'The Toome Road' from *Field Work* (Faber, 1979); 'The Sense of Place' from *Preoccupations* (Faber, 1980); 'Station Island' from *Station Island* (Faber, 1984)); 'The Old Team' from *The Haw Lantern* (Faber, 1987); 'Field of Vision' and 'The Settle Bed' from *Seeing Things* (Faber, 1991); 'Crediting Poetry' from *The Nobel Lecture* (1995); 'A Sofa in the Forties' and 'Two Lorries' from *The Spirit Level* (Faber, 1996); 'At Toomebridge' from *Electric Light* (Faber, 2001), all by permission of Faber and Faber Ltd and Farrar, Straus and Giroux LLC.

HEWITT, JOHN, 'A House Demolished', 'A Seaside Town', 'An Ulster Landowner's Song', 'An Ulster Reckoning', 'An Ulsterman in England Remembers', 'Conacre', 'Cultra Manor: The Ulster Folk Museum', 'Footing Turf', 'On A Country Bus Forty Years Ago', 'Overture for an Ulster Literature', 'Palimpsest', 'Pro Tanto Quid Retribuamus', 'Rite, Lubitavish, Glenaan', 'Sonnet', 'Street Names', 'Sunset over Glenaan', 'The Ballad', 'The Booleys', 'The Christmas Rhymers, Ballynure, 1941', 'The Colony', 'The Dilemma', 'The Glittering Sod', 'The Mile-Long Street', 'This Antrim Air in Summer', 'Townland of

Peace', 'Ulster Names', 'Ulsterman', 'William Conor RHA, 1881–1968' from *Collected Poems of John Hewitt*, edited by Frank Ormsby (Blackstaff Press, 1991); 'No Rootless Colonist', 'Planter's Gothic', 'Regionalism: The Last Chance' from *Ancestral Voices: The Selected Prose of John Hewitt*, edited by Tom Clyde (Blackstaff Press, 1987), all reproduced by permission of Blackstaff Press on behalf of the Estate of John Hewitt.

HILL, MYRTLE and VIVIENNE POLLOCK, from *Image and Experience* (Blackstaff Press, 1993), by kind permission of the authors.

HOBSON, BULMER, from *Ireland Yesterday and Tomorrow* (Anvil Books, 1968), by kind permission of Anvil Books, Dublin.

HUME, JOHN, from *Derry Beyond the Walls* (Ulster Historical Foundation, 2002), by kind permission of the author.

HYDE, H. MONTGOMERY, from *The Rise of Castlereagh* (Macmillan, 1933), reproduced with permission of Curtis Brown Group Ltd, London on behalf of the Estate of H. Montgomery Hyde. Copyright © Estate of H. Montgomery Hyde.

IRELAND, DENIS, from *From the Irish Shore* (Rich & Cowan, 1936); *Statues Round the City Hall* (Cresset, 1939); 'Sketches from War-Time Belfast' from *From the Jungle of Belfast* (Blackstaff, 1973), all by permission of the Linen Hall Library, Belfast.

IRVINE, ALEXANDER, from *The Souls of Poor Folk* by Alexander Irvine (Appletree Press, 1981), © Appletree Press; *A Fighting Parson* (Williams and Norgate, 1930), copyright holder not traced.

IRVINE, JOHN, 'In Summer Time' and 'Townlands', from *By Winding Roads* (H.R. Carter Publications, 1950), copyright holder not traced.

JAMIESON, JOHN, from *The History of the Royal Belfast Academical Institution, 1810–1960* (William Mullan & Son, 1959), reprinted by kind permission of the Royal Belfast Academical Institution.

JOHNSTON, JENNIFER, from *Shadows on our Skin* (Hamish Hamilton, 1977). Copyright © Jennifer Johnston, 1977.

JOHNSTONE, ROBERT, 'Eden Says No', 'The Constable's Complaint', 'The Irish Disease' and 'The Liberal's Lament' from *Eden to Edenderry* (Blackstaff Press, 1989), by permission of the author.

JOHNSTONE, THOMAS M., from *The Vintage of Memory* (Quota Press, 1942), copyright holder not traced.

JONES, EMRYS, from *A Social Geography of Belfast* (Oxford University Press, 1960), by permission of Oxford University Press.

JOPE, E.M., from *Ancient Monuments in Northern Ireland* (HMSO, 1952), copyright holder not traced.

JORDAN, ALISON, from *Margaret Byers* (Institute of Irish Studies, 1992), copyright holder not traced.

KANE, ALICE, selections from *Songs and Sayings of an Ulster Childhood* (Wolfhound Press, 1983) by Alice Kane © 1983. Published by McClelland & Stewart Ltd. Used by permission of the publisher.

KAVANAGH, PATRICK, from *Tarry Flynn* (Penguin Classics, 2000);

'The Linen Industry' and 'The Greengrocer from "Wreaths"' from *Poems 1963–1983* by Michael Longley, published by Secker & Warburg. Reprinted by permission of The Random House Group Ltd. Copyright © Michael Longley 1979. US permission for 'Kindertotenlieder' and 'Wounds' from *Poems 1963–1980* (Wake Forest University Press, 1987), by permission of Wake Forest University Press. 'Trade Winds' from *Gorse Fires* (Secker & Warburg, 1991). Copyright © Michael Longley 1991.

LOWRY, MARY, from *The Story of Belfast and its Surroundings* (1912), copyright holder not traced.

LYND, ROBERT, from *Home Life in Ireland* (Mills & Boon, 1909); 'The Promenade' from *The Goldfish* (Methuen & Co., 1927); 'Railway Stations I Have Loved' from *In Defence of Pink* (J.M. Dent, 1937); 'Spade and Bucket' from *Things One Hears* (J.M. Dent, 1945), copyright holder not traced.

MACARDLE, DOROTHY, from *The Irish Republic* (Gollancz, 1937; Wolfhound Press, 2005), reproduced by permission of Wolfhound Press, Dublin.

McAUGHTRY, SAM, from *The Sinking of the Kenbane Head* (Blackstaff Press, 1997), by permission of Blackstaff Press.

McCABE, EUGENE, 'Co. Monaghan' from *32 Counties* (Secker & Warburg, 1989), by permission of A.P. Watt Ltd on behalf of Eugene McCabe; *Heaven Lies About Us* by Eugene McCabe, published by Jonathan Cape (2005). Reprinted by permission of The Random House Group Ltd and by permission of Bloomsbury, USA.

McCAFFERTY, NELL, from *Nell* (Penguin Books Ireland, 2004). Copyright © Nell McCafferty, 2004, reprinted by kind permission of Penguin Books and Abner Stein.

McCANN, EAMONN, from *War and an Irish Town* (Penguin Books, 1974), by kind permission of the author.

McCRYSTAL, CAL, from *Reflections on a Quiet Rebel* (Michael Joseph, 1997). Copyright © Cal McCrystal, 1997.

McDONALD, PETER, 'At Castlereagh Church' from *Pastorals* (Carcanet Press, 2004), by permission of Carcanet Press Ltd.

McDOWELL, FLORENCE MARY, from *Other Days Around Me* (Blackstaff Press, 1966) © Florence Mary McDowell 1966; *Roses and Rainbows* (1972) © Florence Mary McDowell 1972, both by kind permission of the Estate of Florence Mary McDowell.

McFADDEN, ROY, 'Those Glorious Twelfths' and 'Sheepdog Trials' from *The Garryowen* (Chatto & Windus, 1971); from *Threshold* (Vol. 26, Autumn 1975); 'Downpatrick', 'The Ards Circuit' and 'Daisymount Terrace' from *Verifications* (Blackstaff Press, 1977); 'The Innocent Eye' from *After Seymour's Funeral* (Blackstaff Press, 1990); 'The Welsh Match' and 'The Flowersellers at the City Hall' from *Last Poems* (Abbey Press, 2002), all by kind permission of Margaret McFadden.

MacGILL, PATRICK, from *Children of the Dead End: The Autobiography of a Navvy* (Birlinn Ltd, 2000), reproduced by permission of Birlinn Ltd.

MacGOWAN, MÍCHEÁL, from *The Hard Road to Klondike* (Routledge & Kegan Paul, 1962), by permission of Taylor & Francis Group.

McGUCKIAN, MEDBH, 'Gateposts', 'Lychees' and 'Tobacco Hole' from *The Flower Master and Other Poems* (Gallery Press, 1993). By kind permission of the author and The Gallery Press, Loughcrew, Oldcastle, County Meath, Ireland.

McGUINNESS, FRANK, from *Observe the Sons of Ulster Marching Towards the Somme* (Faber, 1986), by permission of Faber and Faber Ltd. Copyright © 1985 by Frank McGuinness. US rights reprinted by permission of Rosenstone/Wender.

MacLAVERTY, BERNARD, from *Grace Notes* by Bernard MacLaverty, published by Jonathan Cape (1997). Reprinted by permission of The Random House Group Ltd. Copyright © 1997 by Bernard MacLaverty. US permission granted by W.W. Norton & Company, Inc. From *The Anatomy School* by Bernard MacLaverty, published by Jonathan Cape (2001). Reprinted by permission of The Random House Group Ltd and copyright © 2001 by Bernard MacLaverty. US permission granted by W.W. Norton & Company, Inc.

McLAVERTY, MICHAEL, from *Call My Brother Back* (Longman, Green, 1939; Blackstaff Press, 2003); *Lost Fields* (Jonathan Cape, 1942; Blackstaff Press, 2004); 'The Poteen Maker', 'The Prophet', 'The Schooner', 'The White Mare' and 'The Wild Duck's Nest' from *The Collected Short Stories*, edited by Sophia Hillan (Blackstaff Press, 2002), © the Estate of Michael McLaverty, reproduced by kind permission of the Literary Executors.

MacNEICE, LOUIS, 'Northern Ireland and her People' from *Selected Prose* (Oxford University Press, 1941); 'Autumn Journal', 'Carrickfergus', 'Cushendun', 'Halloween', ' Valediction' and 'Train to Dublin' from *Collected Poems of Louis MacNeice* (Faber, 1979); from *Zoo* (Michael Joseph, 1938), all by permission of David Higham Associates.

McNEILL, JANET, from *Tea at Four O'Clock* (Hodder & Stroughton, 1956), by kind permission of David Bradbury Alexander.

McNEILL, MARY, from *Life and Times of Mary Ann McCracken* (Figgis, 1960), copyright holder not traced.

MAC PÓILIN, AODÁN, 'The Irish Language in Belfast Until 1900' from *The Cities of Belfast* edited by Nicholas Allen and Aaron Kelly (Four Courts Press, 2003), by kind permission of Four Courts Press.

MADDEN, DEIRDRE, from *One by One in the Darkness* (Faber, 1996), by permission of Faber & Faber Ltd and A.P. Watt Ltd on behalf of Deirdre Madden.

MAGUIRE, JOHN, from *Come Day, Go Day, God Send Sunday* (Routledge & Kegan Paul, 1973), copyright holder not traced.

MAHON, DEREK, 'Derry Morning', 'Northern Star', 'North Wind: Portrush' and 'Rock Music' from *Collected Poems* (Gallery Press, 1999); extract from 'Death in Bangor' and extract from 'Night Thoughts' from *The Yellow Book* (Gallery Press, 1997), all by kind permission of the author and The Gallery Press, Loughcrew, Oldcastle, County Meath, Ireland.

MARSHALL, JOHN J., from 'The Dialect of Ulster', in *Ulster Journal of Archaeology*, (Vol. 10, 1904), copyright holder not traced.

MARSHALL, W.F., 'Me An' Me Da' from *Livin' in Drumlister: The Collected Ballads and Verses of W.F. Marshall* (Blackstaff Press, 1983), by permission of Caroline Marshall.

MARTIN, EILISH, 'Paradise Fatigue' from *Slitting the Tongues of Jackdaws* (Summer Palace Press, 1999), by kind permission of Summer Palace Press.

MAYNE REID, META, from *All Because of Dawks* (Macmillan, 1955), copyright holder not traced.

MESSENGER, BETTY, from *Picking up the Linen Threads* (University of Texas Press, 1975; Blackstaff Press, 1980), by kind permission of the author.

MILLIGAN, ALICE, from *Dublin Evening Telegraph*; 'When I was a Little Girl' from *Hero Lays* (Gill & McMillan, 1954), copyright holder not traced.

MOGEY, JOHN M., from *Rural Life in Northern Ireland* (Oxford University Press, 1947), by permission of Oxford University Press.

MOLLOY, FRANCES, from *No Mate for the Magpie* (Virago, 1985), copyright holder not traced.

MONTAGUE, JOHN, 'Even English', 'Epilogue: Driving South we pass through Cavan...', 'Red Branch: A Blessing', 'Glencull Waterside', 'Like dolmens round my childhood...', 'The Last Sheaf', 'A Lost Tradition', 'The Black Pig' and 'The Errigal Road' from *Collected Poems* (Gallery Press, 1995); 'A Human Smile' and 'Retreat, 1941' from *Time in Armagh* (Gallery Press, 1993), all by kind permission of the author and The Gallery Press, Loughcrew, Oldcastle, County Meath, Ireland.

MOORE, BRIAN, from *The Lonely Passion of Judith Hearne*, Little, Brown & Co., © 1956 by Brian Moore; *The Feast of Lupercal*, Little, Brown & Co., © 1957 by Brian Moore; *The Emperor of Ice-cream*, Viking Press © 1965 by Brian Moore; *Fergus*, Holt, Rinehart & Winston, © 1970 by Brian Moore, all by permission of Curtis Brown, Ltd.

MORRISSEY, SINÉAD, 'In Belfast' from *Between Here and There* (Carcanet Press, 2002), by kind permission of Carcanet Press.

MORROW, JOHN, from *Northern Myths* (Blackstaff Press, 1979); from *Pruck* (Lagan Press, 1999), both by kind permission of the author.

MORTON, MAY, from *Spindle and Shuttle* (1951), copyright holder not traced.

MULDOON, PAUL, 'Clonfeacle' and 'Kate Whiskey' from *New Weather* (Faber, 1973); 'At Master McGrath's Grave' and 'Armageddon, Armageddon' from *Mules* (Faber, 1977); 'Early Warning' and 'Lull' from *Why Brownlee Left* (Faber, 1980); 'The Right Arm' from *Quoof* (Faber, 1983); 'Hard Drive' from *Moy Sand and Gravel* (Faber, 2002), all by permission of Faber and Faber Ltd and Farrar, Straus and Giroux LLC.

MURPHY, DERVLA, from *A Place Apart* (John Murray, 1978), reproduced by kind permission of John Murray (Publishers).

MURPHY, MICHAEL J., from *At Slieve Gullion's Foot* (Dundalgan Press, 1941), by kind permission of Dundalgan Press; 'Introduction' to *Now You're Talking* (Blackstaff, 1975), copyright holder not traced.

NÍ LUAIN, SIOBHÁN, 'The Narrow Gauge Line', 'The Quilting', 'The Thatcher', 'To the Shore' and 'Dreamer in the Glen' from *The Sally Patch News* (*Irish News*, 1971), by kind permission of the *Irish News*.

NÍ UALLACHÁIN, PÁDRAIGÍN, from *A Hidden Ulster* (Four Courts Press, 2003), by kind permission of Four Courts Press.

NICOLSON, HAROLD, from *Helen's Tower* (Constable, 1937), reproduced by permission of the Executors of Harold Nicolson's Literary Estate.

O CONNOR, FIONNUALA, from *In Search of a State: Catholics in Northern Ireland* (Blackstaff Press, 1993), by kind permission of the author.

Ó GRIANNA, SÉAMUS (MÁIRE), from *Nuair a Bhí Mé Óg, When I was Young*, translated by A.J. Hughes (Dublin, 2001), reproduced by permission of A. & A. Farmar.

Ó MUIRGHEASA, ÉNRÍ, from *Art Mac Cubhthaigh's and Other Songs* (Dundalk Press, 1926), by kind permission of the Dundalgan Press.

Ó SEARCAIGH, CATHAL, 'Here at Caiseal Na gCorr Station', 'Ruin of House in Min na Craoibhe', 'Winter Nights' and 'Sunrush' from *Homecoming – An Bealach 'na Bhaile* (Cló Iar Chonnachta, 1993), by kind permission of the author and Cló Iar Chonnachta.

O'BRIEN, CONOR CRUISE, from *States of Ireland* (Hutchinson, 1972), by kind permission of the author and Mulcahy & Viney Ltd.

O'BRIEN, KATE, from *My Ireland* (Batsford, 1962), by kind permission of the author and David Higham Associates.

O'BRIEN, NORA CONNOLLY, from *Portrait of a Rebel Father* (Rich & Cowan, 1935), copyright holder not traced.

O'BYRNE, CATHAL, from *As I Roved Out* (*Irish News*, 1946; Blackstaff Press, 1982) by kind permission of Roland Benner.

O'CONNOR, JOHN, from *Come Day – Go Day* (Golden Eagle Books, 1948), copyright holder not traced.

O'DOHERTY, MALACHI, from *The Trouble With Guns* (Blackstaff Press, 1998), by kind permission of the author.

O'DONNELL, PEADAR, from *Adrigoole* (Jonathan Cape, 1929), by kind permission of Ann O'Donnell.

O'FAOLAIN, SEAN, from *An Irish Journey* (Longman, Green, 1940).

RICE, ADRIAN, 'The Lovely Rebellion of William Drennan' from *The Poet's Place* (Institute of Irish Studies, QUB, 1991); 'Margaret Mitchell' from *The Mason's Tongue* (Abbey Press, 1999), all by kind permission of the author.

ROBB, NESCA, 'Harvest', 'July' and 'The Storm' from *Ards Eclogues* (1974), copyright holder not traced.

RODGERS, W.R., 'Armagh', 'Epilogue', 'Ireland' and 'Field Day' from *Poems* (Gallery Press, 1993), by kind permission of the author's Estate and The Gallery Press, Loughcrew, Oldcastle, County Meath, Ireland; from *The Ulstermen and their Country* (British Council Pamphlet – Longman, Green & Co., 1952), by kind permission of Lucy Rodgers Cohen.

ROS, AMANDA MCKITTRICK, from *Helen Huddleson* by Amanda McKittrick Ros, published by Chatto & Windus (1969). Reprinted by permission of The Random House Group Ltd.

ROWLEY, RICHARD, 'The Lagan' from *Workers* (Duckworth, 1923); 'Ardglass Town' from *Selected Poems* (Duckworth, 1931), copyright holder not traced.

RYNNE, STEPHEN, from *All Ireland* (Batsford, 1956), copyright holder not traced.

SHAFFREY, PATRICK, from *Irish Times* (20 August 2005), by kind permission of the author.

SHAW, ROSE, from *Carleton's Country* (Talbot Press, 1930), copyright holder not traced.

SHEA, PATRICK, from *Voices and the Sound of Drums* (Blackstaff Press, 1981), copyright holder not traced.

SHEARMAN, HUGH, from *Northern Ireland* (HMSO, 1948), copyright © Hugh Shearman, 1948; from *Ulster* (Robert Hale, 1949), copyright © Hugh Shearman, 1949.

SHEEHAN, KATHLEEN, from 'Life in Glangelvin, Co. Cavan, 1900–1920', in *Ulster Folklife* (Vol. 31, 1985), by kind permission of *Ulster Folklife*.

SIMMONS, JAMES, 'The Beech Trees of Broughshane' from *The Company of Children* (Salmon Poetry, 1999), by kind permission of the Estate of James Simmons; 'Ulster Says Yes', 'The Archaeologist', 'Protestant Courts Catholic' and 'The Ballad of Gerry Kelly: Newsagent' from *Poems, 1956–1986* (Gallery Press, 1986), by kind permission of the Estate of James Simmons and The Gallery Press, Loughcrew, Oldcastle, County Meath, Ireland.

SMITH, CHARLOTTE FELL, from *James Nicholson Richardson of Bessbrook* (Longman, Green, 1925), copyright holder not traced.

SMYTH, DAMIAN, 'A Gift from Downpatrick' from *Downpatrick Races* (Lagan Press, 2000), by kind permission of the author.

STEPHENS, JAMES CURL, from *The Londonderry Plantation, 1609–1914* (Phillimore, 1986), by kind permission of the publisher Phillimore &

Co. Ltd, Shopwyke Manor Barn, Chichester, West Sussex, England
(www.phillimore.co.uk).

STEWART, A.T.Q., from *The Ulster Crisis* (Faber, 1967); *The Summer Soldiers* (Blackstaff Press, 1995); *The Shape of Irish History* (Blackstaff Press, 2001), all © A.T.Q. Stewart.

THOMPSON, SAM, from *Over the Bridge* (Lagan Press, 1997), by kind permission of the Estate of Sam Thompson.

TÓIBÍN, COLM, from *Walking Along the Border* (Queen Anne Press, 1987), by kind permission of Macmillan, London, UK.

TOOLIS, KEVIN, from *Rebel Hearts* (Picador, 1995) copyright © 1997 by the author and reprinted by permission of St Martin's Griffin and by kind permission of Macmillan, London, UK.

TOPPING, WILLIAM, from *A Life in Linenopolis: The Memoirs of William Topping, Belfast Damask Weaver, 1903–1956* edited by Emmet O'Connor & Trevor Parkhill (Ulster Historical Foundation, 1992), by kind permission of the editors.

TUNNEY, PADDY, from *The Stone Fiddle* (Gilbert Dalton, 1979; Appletree Press, 1991), © Appletree Press.

VANCE, NORMAN, from *Irish Literature: A Social History* (Four Courts Press, 1999), by kind permission of Four Courts Press.

WADDELL, HELEN, from Introduction to *Ballads and Verses from Tyrone* (Talbot Press, 1929), by kind permission of the Estate of Helen Waddell.

WATSON, GEORGE J., from *The Yale Review* (1986), by kind permission of Blackwell Publishing.

WEBB, JIMMY, from *Raglan Street and Beyond* (December Publications, *Andersonstown News*, 1990), by kind permission of the Estate of Jimmy Webb and the *Andersonstown News* Group (www.irelandclick.com).

WEST, ANTHONY C., from *The Ferret Fancier* (MacGibbon & Kee, 1963), copyright holder not traced.

WILSON, FLORENCE M., 'All Souls' Eve' and 'The Man from God-Knows-Where' from *The Coming of the Earls* (The Candle Press, 1918), copyright holder not traced.

WILSON, ROBERT MCLIAM, from *Eureka Street* by Robert McLiam Wilson, published by Secker & Warburg (1996). Reprinted by permission of The Random House Group Ltd and copyright © 1996 Robert McLiam Wilson. US permission: reprinted from *Eureka Street* by Robert McLiam Wilson published by Arcade Publishing, New York, New York.

YOUNG, ROBERT M., *Belfast and the Province of Ulster in the Twentieth Century* (W.T. Pike, 1909), copyright holder not traced.

Every effort has been made to trace and contact copyright holders before publication. If notified, the publisher will rectify any errors or omissions at the earliest opportunity.

Index of Authors